MARJORIE'S WAR

Marjorie Secretan

MARJORIE'S WAR

Four families in the Great War

1914 - 1918

Reginald H. Fair

Charles S. Fair

MENIN HOUSE

Menin House an imprint of
Tommies Guides Military Booksellers & Publishers

Gemini House
136-140 Old Shoreham Road
Brighton
BN3 7BD

www.tommiesguides.co.uk

First published in Great Britain by Menin House Publishers 2012

Paperback edition ISBN: 978-1-908336-18-7
Hardback edition ISBN: 978-1-908336-19-4

Cover design by Tommies Guides

Printed and bound by CPI Group (UK) Ltd, Croydon, CR0 4YY

Contents

Acknowledgements

We should like to thank those who have encouraged us to put together this collection of letters in book form. Many members of the Western Front Association who attended our talks at some of their monthly meetings felt that the story needed to be recorded and brought to a wider audience.

Our gratitude is also due to the late Dick Champion and his sister Jill Woodhouse for supplying information relating to their father, Lieutenant Colonel Carl Champion DSO, and for the loan of his diaries and photographs.

We are particularly indebted to the late Guy Dodgson for searching out and lending us his father's and uncles' letters and his copy of Philip Pilditch's fascinating diary. Guy was particularly enthusiastic and supportive of the concept of a book recording the parts played by our respective families in the Great War. He himself had had experience of warfare in WWII, taking part in Major-General Orde Wingate's campaign in Burma. It saddens us that neither Guy nor Dick have lived to see this finished book.

We should like to thank another Chindit, the late Andrew Railton MC, for permission to reproduce the photograph of his father on p.197 and to quote from his father's letters which are held at the Imperial War Museum. In addition, we should like to thank James Dartford for permission to reproduce the photograph of his father on p.200. We are also indebted to Martin Timmis for information and photographs about George Fulton.

Reggie would like to thank Alastair Macpherson, Honorary Archivist at Haileybury College, for further information on the careers of Charles Fair and Carl Champion.

Charles would like to thank staff at The National Archives at Kew, the Department of Documents at the Imperial War Museum, the National Army Museum, the Royal Regiment of Fusiliers Museum at the Tower of London and the Green Howards Museum at Richmond in Yorkshire. Members of the St Pancras (19th London) Regiment Old Comrades Association have provided fine comradeship on various visits to the battlefields.

Charles is also grateful to members of the Great War Forum and British Commission for Military History for their comments on queries raised during the course of editing this book. Particular thanks are due to the late Bob Coulson for his expertise on officers of The Yorkshire Regiment (Green Howards), Dave Risley for information concerning the 11th Battalion South Lancashire Regiment (St Helens Pioneers), and Stuart Arrowsmith for information and photographs concerning the 7th (London) Brigade Royal Field Artillery.

Special thanks are owed to an Old Marlburian, Charles Messenger, for agreeing to write the foreword to this book without realising what he had taken on.

Finally, we owe a particular debt of gratitude to Reggie's wife Janet who has constantly urged us on and offered advice, while her computer skills have been particularly invaluable during the final few intensive months of editing before publication.

Reginald Fair
Charles Fair
March, 2011

The Great War: 1914-1918
Chronology of the Main Events on the Western Front

1914	4th Aug.	Declaration of war by Britain
	23rd Aug.	Battle of Mons. BEF begins retreat.
	7th – 10th Sept.	Battle of the Marne (followed by the 'Race to the Sea')
1915	9th May	Battle of Aubers Ridge
	15th – 27th May	Battle of Festubert
	25th Sept. – 18th Oct.	Battle of Loos
1916	21st Feb. – Nov.	Battle of Verdun (French sector)
	1st July – 18th Nov.	Battle of the Somme (capture of High Wood, 15th Sept.)
1917	Feb. – Mar.	German retirement to the Hindenburg Line
	9th April – 16th June	Battle of Arras (incl. capture of Vimy Ridge and the Battles for Bullecourt)
	7th -14th June	Battle of Messines
	31st July – 10th Nov.	Battle of Passchendaele (also called the 3rd Battle of Ypres)
	20th Nov. – 3rd Dec.	Battle of Cambrai (incl. German counter-attack at Bourlon Wood)
1918	21st March	German March Offensive (followed by other offensives ending in July)
	8th Aug– 11th Nov.	The Hundred Days (Allied advance)
	11th Nov.	The Armistice

List of Maps

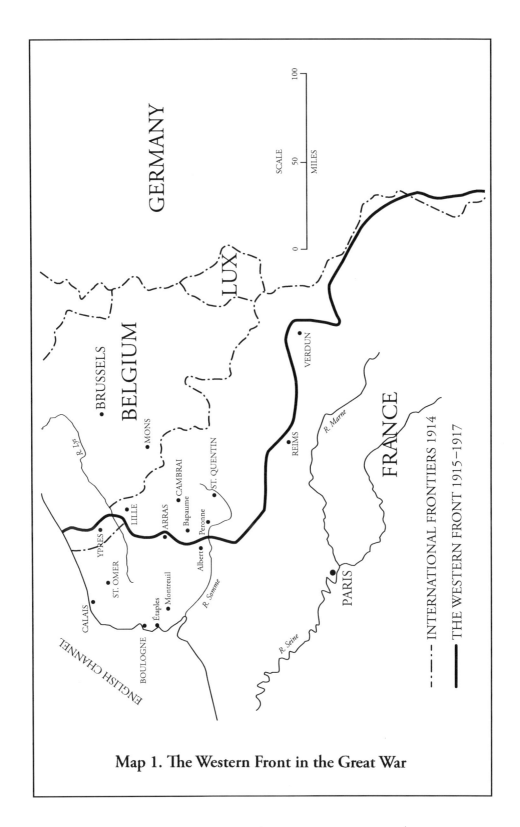

Map 1. The Western Front in the Great War

GERMANY

BELGIUM

LUX

FRANCE

BRUSSELS

MONS

VERDUN

REIMS

R. Marne

ST. QUENTIN

CAMBRAI

ARRAS

Bapaume

Peronne

Albert

LILLE

R. Lys

YPRES

ST. OMER

Montreuil

Etaples

R. Somme

CALAIS

BOULOGNE

ENGLISH CHANNEL

PARIS

R. Seine

SCALE

0   50   100

MILES

– · – · – INTERNATIONAL FRONTIERS 1914

———— THE WESTERN FRONT 1915–1917

Abbreviations

ADC	Aide-de-Camp	Lt	Lieutenant
Adjt	Adjutant	Lt Gen	Lieutenant General
ASC	Army Service Corps	2/Lt	Second Lieutenant
Bde	Brigade	Maj	Major
BEF	British Expeditionary Force	Maj Gen	Major General
BGRA	Brigadier General Royal Artillery	MC	Military Cross
Bn/Btn	Battalion	MGC	Machine Gun Corps
Brig Gen	Brigadier General	MM	Military Medal
Bty	Battery	MO	Medical Officer
Capt	Captain	MTASC	Motor Transport Army Service Corps
C in C	Commander-in-Chief	MVO	Member of the Royal Victorian Order
CCS	Casualty Clearing Station	NCO	Non-Commissioned Officer
CQMS	Company Quartermaster Sergeant	OTC	Officers' Training Corps
CO	Commanding Officer	OC	Officer Commanding
Col	Colonel	OCA	Old Comrades Association
Coy	Company	OH	Old Haileyburian
Cpl	Corporal	OM	Old Marlburian
CRA	Commander Royal Artillery	OP	Observation Post
CRE	Commander Royal Engineers	OTC	Officer Training Corps
CSM	Company Sergeant Major	PO	Post Office
CVO	Commander of the Royal Victorian Order	POW	Prisoner of War
		Pte	Private
CWGC	Commonwealth War Graves Commission	PUO	Pyrexia of Unknown Origin
		QM	Quartermaster
DAC	Divisional Ammunition Column	RAMC	Royal Army Medical Corps
DCM	Distinguished Conduct Medal	Regt	Regiment
DR	Dispatch Rider	RE	Royal Engineers
DRS	Divisional Rest Station	RFA	Royal Field Artillery
DSO	Distinguished Service Order	RFC	Royal Flying Corps
FOO	Forward Observation Officer	RMO	Regimental Medical Officer
Gen	General	RMSP	Royal Mail Steam Packet
GHQ	General Headquarters	RMSS	Royal Mail Steam Ship
GOC	General Officer Commanding	RSM	Regimental Sergeant Major
GRU	Graves Registration Unit	RTO	Railway Transport Officer
GSO	General Staff Officer	Sgt	Sergeant
HAC	Honourable Artillery Company	TF	Territorial Force
HE	High Explosive	TNA	The National Archives
[K]CB	[Knight] Commander of the Order of the Bath	VAD	Voluntary Aid Detachment
		VC	Victoria Cross
[K]CMG	[Knight] Commander of the Order of St. Michael and St. George	WAC	Women's Army Corps
		WO	War Office
LDV	Local Defence Volunteers	YMCA	Young Men's Christian Association
LOB	Left out of Battle		

Organisation of the BEF and Naming of Units

The BEF consisted of a hierarchy of organisations which have their own terminology and a corresponding rank structure. As these formations and ranks are referred to throughout the text a short explanation is helpful. The table below shows the typical organisation as it would have been experienced by the letter-writers in this book for much of the war from mid 1915 until early 1918.

Table 1: Outline Organisation of the British Army

Formation or unit	Commander	Composition	Approximate number of men
Army	General	Two or more corps	200,000 or more
Corps	Lieutenant General	Two or more divisions	60,000 – 100,000
Division	Major General	Three infantry brigades, plus a pioneer battalion	18,000
Infantry Brigade	Brigadier General	Four infantry battalions plus machine gun company and trench mortar battery	4,000
Battalion	Lieutenant Colonel	Four companies, battalion HQ and specialists	1,000
Company	Major or Captain	Four platoons and company HQ	200
Platoon	Lieutenant or 2/Lieutenant	Four sections	48
Section	Corporal or Lance Corporal	n/a	12

The BEF was commanded by the Commander-in-Chief (C-in-C), and from May 1916 onwards consisted of five armies totalling about two million men.

The number of men stated in Table 1 is that if the organisation was at full strength. However, casualties and a delay in the arrival of reinforcements meant that a unit could be considerably under strength. In practice – particularly in the latter stages of the war – a battalion might have as few as 600 men and a division 12,000 or less.

Armies, corps and divisions also included a wide variety of supporting arms and services. Those of particular importance were: artillery (RA), engineer field companies (RE), field ambulances (RAMC) and transportation (ASC).

Naming Conventions Used in *Marjorie's War*

Higher level formations are named in this work with the following convention: Fourth Army, IV Corps, 7th Division and 141st Infantry Brigade.

Naming of infantry battalions can be subject to confusion given that the parent regiment might have both a formal and informal name, and that an individual battalion might have its own semi-official name. In order to save space and to ensure consistency, infantry battalions are referred to using the short names shown in the table below.

Table 2: Infantry Battalions Featured in *Marjorie's War*

Full name	Short name	Infantry Division	Infantry Brigade	Character
2nd Battalion, The Queen's (Royal West Surrey) Regt	2nd Queen's	7th	91st	Humphrey Secretan
8th (Service) Battalion, Alexandra, Princess of Wales's Own (Yorkshire Regt) (Green Howards)	8th Yorkshires	23rd	69th	Francis Dodgson ("Toby")
11th (Service) Battalion, The South Lancashire Regt (St Helens Pioneers)	11th S Lancs (St Helens Pioneers)	30th	n/a	Carl Champion Alan Champion Eric Champion
10th (Service) Battalion, The Royal Fusiliers (City of London Regt) (Stockbrokers)	10th Royal Fusiliers	37th	111th	Humphrey Secretan
1/1st Battalion, The Hertfordshire Regt	1/1st Hertfordshires	39th	118th	Reggie Secretan Guy Dodgson
1/19th (County of London) Battalion, The London Regt (St Pancras)	1/19th Londons	47th	141st	Charles Fair

The table also shows the parent division and infantry brigade that each of these battalions belonged to when the relevant letter-writer joined that battalion. Battalions tended to stay within the same brigade and division. However, two of the battalions were transferred into new divisions and infantry brigades in 1918 and these reorganisations are referred to in the text.

Divisions were moved between corps every few weeks as they were rotated into and out of active sectors of the Western Front. Less frequently a division would be transferred from one army to another when it moved a longer distance e.g. from Second Army in the Ypres Salient to Fourth Army on the Somme.

As well as thirteen battalions of infantry, an infantry division in 1915 also included four brigades of Royal Field Artillery (RFA). Each RFA brigade was commanded by a Lt Col and consisted of three batteries of guns and an ammunition column comprising nearly 800 all ranks in total. Divisional artillery was subject to considerable reorganisation, particularly in 1916. The only letter-writer to feature in this work who is not listed in Table 2 is Philip Dodgson who served with the 7th London Brigade RFA which was part of the 47th (London) Division.

The four companies in an infantry battalion were usually named A, B, C and D. The sixteen platoons in a battalion were numbered sequentially from 1 to 16, thus '8 Platoon' would be in 'B Company.'

A 'section' could also refer to a small team of men performing special duties for a company or battalion (e.g. signals section or sanitary section).

The organisational structure of the Army evolved during the course of the war in response to tactical requirements and new weapons and equipment. The most significant restructuring occurred in early 1918. Changes to unit organisation as

Officers of an infantry battalion. The officers of the 2/19th Battalion, The London Regiment (St. Pancras) at White City, 1st Jan 1915. The Commanding Officer, Lt Col Christie is seated fifth from left in the middle row. On his left is the Second-in-Command, Major Hubback, and on his right is the Adjutant, Capt Hatherly. Also in this row are various Majors and Captains who commanded the rifle companies and the Medical Officer. Seated on the floor or standing are the most junior officers - almost all newly commissioned 2/Lieutenants - who commanded the 16 rifle platoons. Of the 29 officers in this picture, five were killed during the Great War. Charles Fair (see Chapter 5) is sixth from right in the back row and refers to a number of the other officers in his letters. These are: back row - 2/Lt J. J. Sheppard (extreme left) 2/Lt A. G. Gauld (second from left) and 2/Lt R. C. G Dartford (extreme right); middle row - Capt. J. G. Stokes (third from left) Capt. H. Fox (second from right); front row - 2/Lt G. W. Baker (extreme left).

they affect individuals and where commented upon in their letters are described in footnotes.

Taking a break from a route march. An infantry section of the 10th Royal Fusiliers (Stockbrokers), early 1915. The Section was the lowest level subunit in an infantry battalion and was commanded by a corporal or lance corporal. Corporal Humphrey Secretan is seated on the far left and wears two chevrons. This section of ten men has been joined by the platoon sergeant who wears three chevrons and is sitting on Humphrey's left. They are wearing 1908 pattern web equipment and are wearing packs. When fully laden with rations, ammunition and water the weight of their clothing, rifles and equipment would have been just over 60 lbs.

Foreword

Published diaries and letters from the Western Front 1914-18 are now legion, but this collection is different. Marjorie Secretan of the title became engaged to Toby Dodgson, who was killed on the Somme in 1916. She then married Charles Fair, but both men kept many of the letters she sent them and they have survived to this day. The result is that we not only get a feel of what was happening on the Home Front, but also a very intimate view of two romances divided by tragedy. This helps to give the book an almost unique character. There is, though, much else besides which will be of value to anyone with an interest in the Great War.

There is the social aspect. The families concerned are of the typical Edwardian middle class, the men public school and Oxbridge educated and mainly joining up in 1914 from jobs in the City or, as in the case of Charles Fair, school mastering. Their attitudes reflect the mores of the day, such as their strong sense of duty towards Britain and its Empire. All become officers, although some do see service in the ranks first. Charles Fair enlisted in the Honourable Artillery to learn about soldiering prior to being commissioned in the 19th Londons and then rising rapidly to become Second-in-Command of the 1st/19th and earning a DSO. Reggie Secretan, on the other hand, answered the August 1914 call for Royal Engineers motorcycle despatch riders, but was turned down on account of his eyesight and then joined the ASC (MT) and was the first of our young men to land in France, at the very end of 1914.

Those commissioned immediately, or almost so, had served in their school and/or university OTC and, apart from a four week course, had to learn how to be junior leaders on the job. In 1916, when Reggie Secretan was eventually commissioned, officer training became more formalised and he had to attend a four months' course at an Officer Cadet battalion. As for the regiments they all served with, one was with a Regular infantry battalion, three with Territorial battalions, and five with New Army battalions, including the three Champion brothers serving with the 11th South Lancashires, 30th Division's pioneer battalion. The only one who was not an infantryman was Philip Dodgson, who became a Territorial Field Gunner.

The letters cover the fighting on the Western Front from the beginning of 1915 until the moment the guns ceased firing and beyond. The correspondents took part in all the main battles and provide some fascinating accounts of them. But much of what the letters describe is the normal humdrum life in France and Flanders - the discomforts of trench warfare, rest and training. The social gulf between officers and men is very clear. The officers are sustained by numerous parcels of foodstuffs and clothing from home and can expect to have leave back in England every four months or so, while some of their men could go eighteen months and longer before their turn for leave came. This might seem outrageous to modern eyes, but we live in a very different world to that of one hundred years ago, when the class divide was so very much wider and generally accepted as such. Indeed for many in the middle classes the war provided the first opportunity they had to get to know those of the lower orders – what became known as 'the comradeship of the trenches'.

The front line soldier's attitude to the Staff is well brought out – its demands for trifling pieces of information in the midst of desperate fighting and the privileges that it enjoyed. It should, however, be pointed out that staff work improved radically as the war went on and by 1918 it was generally first class. This was all part of the BEF's 'learning curve', which is also reflected in the increased number of courses, designed to keep junior officers abreast of the latest developments in tactics and weaponry. One aspect which may surprise some is the frequency with which our young men came into contact with senior officers, from brigade commanders right up to Haig himself. This contradicts the popularly held belief that the 1914-18 generals were remote from their men.

Reginald and Charles Fair (son and grandson of the Charles Fair) are to be much congratulated on bringing this fascinating collection of letters to light and enabling them to be enjoyed by a wider audience. They are a fitting tribute to those who fought, and sometimes died, in what they hoped was the war to end all wars.

Charles Messenger
August 2011

Introduction

"Marjorie's War" is a narrative of the Great War based on previously unpublished letters written by several young men who fought on the Western Front. All came from relatively privileged backgrounds and were public school educated, representing the Edwardian middle class. None of them was a regular soldier: they were all volunteers who were related or in some way connected, Marjorie Secretan being the link between them. They all became infantry officers apart from one who served in the Royal Artillery and their service encompassed a range of Territorial Force, New Army and Regular Army units. Two spent some months on the Western Front as Other Ranks before they were commissioned. Although none of the letter-writers was posted to other fronts such as Gallipoli, Salonika or Palestine, at least one saw action in almost every major battle involving the British Expeditionary Force (BEF) on the Western Front after May 1915.

There are at least eight hundred Great War letters held in the archives of the Dodgson and Fair families. All three Dodgson brothers left letters, numbering several hundred, as did the two Secretans, though fewer of these remain. Over three hundred have survived of those written by Charles Fair, the father and grandfather of the authors of this book. Sadly there are none in existence written by the three Champion brothers, although the eldest, Carl, kept a personal diary which is quoted in this book. It is remarkable that any of Marjorie's letters going out to the Front survived, but a number of these have been quoted. Apart from her feelings for the men with whom she corresponded, her letters and diaries also give some idea of what life was like for the families back at home.

The photographic record is also good, with approximately four hundred contemporary photographs surviving in the archives of the Fair, Dodgson and Champion families. As a keen amateur photographer Carl Champion took nearly two hundred pictures whilst serving with his unit. He took many when training in England but none were taken on the Western Front during the period of fighting, as cameras, other than those officially sanctioned, were not permitted in fighting zones. However, Marjorie's brother Humphrey ignored that rule and did take a camera to the Western Front. Nearly a hundred of his photographs remain. A number of pictures were also taken by the survivors and their relatives on pilgrimages to the Western Front in the 1920s. Unfortunately space allows the inclusion of only the most significant photographs from this large collection.

By no means have all of the archive letters been included in the following chapters, and those that are quoted have been substantially abridged, by the omission of many endearments and references to matters unrelated to the war. The authors have made only minimal changes to the original scripts; for example occasional alterations to punctuation to clarify the sense of a passage. Likewise, the spelling of such words as "Boche" and "dugout" have been standardised to modern English.

Although those on active service were allowed to state their unit on letter-headings, they could not of course indicate their whereabouts for security reasons. In the following transcriptions, text which has been added by the authors, such as place names acquired from the relevant War Diaries, is shown in square brackets. Any added place name for an artillery battery is usually that of the relevant artillery brigade (i.e. Brigade HQ) and not necessarily that of the battery itself. Other explanatory information has been shown in footnotes. Belgian place names in the text and maps are those used in 1914-1918 and referred to in the letters. This means that the majority are in French rather than, as now, in Flemish: so "Ypres" rather than the modern "Ieper".

These young officers wrote, often vividly, about the appalling conditions of life in the trenches, particularly in the wet winter months, but they did not in general tell their families of the great dangers they faced, or else tended to understate them: a battle, or at least an active engagement with the enemy, would merely be referred to as 'a bit of a show'. However, their correspondence reveals the contrasting characters of the writers, which is particularly significant in those cases where they sacrificed their lives, so it is the authors' intention to let these letters speak for themselves.

However, we have aimed to put the letters in their context as far as possible, and this has meant the inclusion of explanatory linking text. While it is not intended to give a detailed description of every action in which the letter writers fought – that would require a book many times longer – we have given particular attention to those actions in which they were killed, wounded or decorated. For this reason Chapter 11, "The Somme" – in many respects the pivotal chapter of the book – required a more detailed focus. Footnotes have been used to give further commentary on the letters, for example to explain colloquialisms, events on the home and other fronts as well as give additional details from their units' war diaries. Biographical footnotes have been used to give thumbnail sketches of the men, officers and generals who are mentioned in the letters.

We have aimed to structure the book in order to tell several parallel stories at the same time, yet move them forward in such a way that the narrative is still coherent with the chronology of the Great War. This has occasionally meant that we have had to 'backtrack' in order to bring a character up to the same point as another where their stories intersect. The main instances of 'backtracking' are to introduce new characters. These are in Chapter 5 which introduces Charles Fair and Chapter 9 which introduces the three Champion brothers. Starting from Chapter 11, "The Somme", onwards, each major battle or campaign fought by the BEF on the Western Front has its own chapter, as in general several of the characters saw action in each. We hope that this arrangement does not cause any confusion.

Finally, we hope this book is sufficiently well researched and referenced to appeal to the serious student of the Great War as well as to those with little knowledge of the period who perhaps may wish to follow the broad narrative without reference to the more detailed footnotes. We have aimed to edit the letters and write the linking text in such a way as to give no prior indication of the eventual fates of the writers, as we believe this makes the narrative more compelling.

Chapter 1

Two Hertfordshire Families

Down the slopes of the northern parts of the Chiltern Hills flow two small streams, the Gade and the Bulbourne. They meet at Two Waters and then flow on in a south-easterly direction towards Watford and the River Thames. The Chilterns form a considerable barrier to movement between London and the Midlands, but these valleys, characteristically steep-sided, have provided important routeways for centuries. Their significance was enhanced by the construction of the Grand Union Canal in 1798, which encouraged the development of industry in the small market towns along its route. This engineering feat was followed in 1837 by a railway linking London with the Midlands and the North West. For the first time this allowed men to work considerably further from home. West Hertfordshire, in the Home Counties, had entered "the commuter age".

In 1912, on his retirement from working in the City of London at Lloyds, Herbert Secretan and his wife Mary moved their family from Surrey to Hertfordshire, where house prices were cheaper. They also hoped to escape from the noise and pollution that cars were creating in the popular residential areas of Surrey. They moved to Bennetts End near the small village of Leverstock Green, once a rural backwater but, since the Second World War, submerged in the "new town" of Hemel Hempstead. Their house "The Dells", so-called after the old gravel pits on the property, was by no means large but there was room for all the family and plenty enough garden space to include a tennis court and some additional fields. The property lay within a few miles of Boxmoor and Apsley stations which gave easy access to London.

Humphrey Secretan was twenty-four when the family moved. He had been educated at Marlborough College, boarding in "Littlefield", the house where his uncle Henry Richardson was the housemaster.[1] Humphrey enjoyed most aspects of school life, singing as a treble in the choir, being a member of the Gymnastics VIII and playing games. At the outbreak of war Humphrey was working in the City as an insurance clerk at Lloyds.

Humphrey's two sisters, Marjorie (23) and Esmé (20), had been educated at St Felix School, Southwold. The Secretans were rather ahead of their time in sending daughters to a boarding school. The girls loved their years on the Suffolk coast, in particular the games, drama and literature. The youngest member of the family

....

1 Richardson served on the staff of Marlborough College from 1870-1905 and was a housemaster from 1886.

was Reggie (17) still at school at Oundle in 1912. He did not follow Humphrey to Marlborough as he was thought to be less academic, but he showed an interest in all things mechanical – a talent which Oundle would nurture. It was not long before he acquired a motor-bike. He was an out-going, friendly lad who enjoyed life and, though the youngest and very much "the apple of his mother's eye", was by no means spoilt.

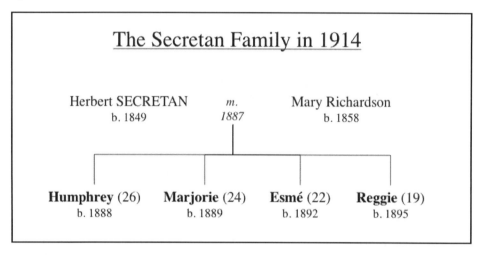

The Secretan Family in 1914

Herbert SECRETAN	*m.*	Mary Richardson
b. 1849	*1887*	b. 1858

Humphrey (26)	Marjorie (24)	Esmé (22)	Reggie (19)
b. 1888	b. 1889	b. 1892	b. 1895

Not long after the Secretans arrived in Hertfordshire they became friendly with the Dodgson family on the other side of the Gade valley. Henley[2] and Helen Dodgson lived at Bovingdon Green and had moved there from Hampstead a few years earlier. Their house, "Green Lodge", was a large building of unusual design, with many outbuildings and a substantial garden. Within reasonable access down the hill lay Boxmoor station, in a rural location yet with proximity to London.

"Green Lodge", Bovingdon, Hertfordshire

....

2   Henley was a distant relative of Charles Lutwidge Dodgson, who is best known by the pseudonym Lewis Carroll, author of the *Alice in Wonderland* books.

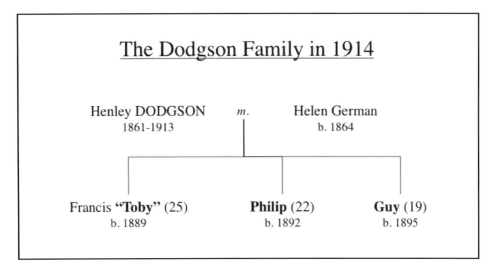

The Dodgson Family in 1914

Henley DODGSON   *m.*   Helen German
1861-1913   b. 1864

Francis **"Toby"** (25)   **Philip** (22)   **Guy** (19)
b. 1889   b. 1892   b. 1895

Henley and Helen had three children, all boys. The eldest, Francis, though usually known to his family and friends as "Toby", was born in 1889. He was educated at Marlborough College in Wiltshire where he enjoyed his years. Together with Humphrey Secretan, he was an accomplished member of the Gym VIII and played other games as well. A military career would have been his choice but, on leaving Marlborough in 1907, he was rejected by the Military Academy at Woolwich because his eyesight was below standard. Instead, in the following year, he entered Trinity College, Cambridge, to read Mechanical Sciences. His university life was a full one: he played tennis for his college and gained early military experience in the Cambridge University Officer Training Corps. After graduating in 1911, Toby went to work in the City as a clerk in the family stockbroking firm, Hope Dodgson.

The two younger Dodgsons, Philip born in 1892 and Guy three years his junior, were both educated at Winchester College. They were almost certainly cadets in the school OTC. Philip followed his elder brother to Trinity College at Cambridge, while Guy who did not leave school until 1913 ventured to Stuttgart in Germany to study music.

The Secretan and Dodgson families met at tennis parties, played golf on Berkhamsted Common and enjoyed socialising at parties and dances, while a particular friendship began to blossom between Marjorie Secretan and Toby Dodgson. But the happy, carefree life the younger generation lived was sadly shattered by Henley Dodgson taking his own life in 1913, reputedly because of financial troubles. Despite their loss, Helen and the boys were still able to live comfortably at "Green Lodge" and continue their association with the Secretans.

Chapter 2

Enlistment and Early Days

In the summer of 1914 following the assassination on 28th June of Archduke Franz Ferdinand of the Austro-Hungarian Empire, the young men of the Dodgson and Secretan families must have gradually come to realise that war was a possibility. War became inevitable once German forces had crossed the Belgian frontier on 4th August. The armed forces were mobilised and the Territorial Force was embodied with units taking up their war stations in the defence of the country. The Secretary of State for War, Lord Kitchener, realised that the war would not be short and that Britain would need a large army. On 7th August he appealed for men to join the Army.

Leverstock Green became a hive of activity with The Queen's Westminster Rifles (1/16th Battalion, The London Regiment) being billeted in the village on taking up their war station on 16th August. Battalion headquarters was established in the school and the companies were billeted in various farms. While at Leverstock Green the battalion underwent a thorough course of training, including 'a short musketry course'. Some of the officers were billeted with the Secretans. Captain J. O. Henriques, OC 'C' Company, was one of these and he wrote the following footnote in the regimental history:

> 'A miniature range was made in the garden of "The Dells", Bennett's End, which was placed at the disposal of the Battalion by Mr Secretan. This was suitable for use with service ammunition, and was particularly useful for training machine-gunners and for revolver practice.'[3]

No records exist as to whether the young Dodgsons and Secretans discussed their options with one another. Reggie Secretan and Guy Dodgson, both only 19 years old and with no determined career plans, perhaps saw enlistment as a temporary means of employment combined with a certain excitement. All five young friends had some acquaintance with military life, having had experience in the OTC at their schools and, in the case of the two elder Dodgsons, also at university.

On 22nd August **Humphrey Secretan** applied to enlist as a private in the 10th (Service) Battalion of the Royal Fusiliers. Interviews and a medical examination

....

3 Henriques J. O., *The War History of the 1st Battalion Queen's Westminster Rifles 1914-1918*, p. 7

followed over the next few days. The 10th Royal Fusiliers was one of the most unusual battalions raised as part of Kitchener's New Armies and was known as "The Stockbrokers' Battalion". On 19th August over lunch at the Travellers' Club in Pall Mall the Director of Recruiting, Sir Henry Rawlinson, suggested to Major the Honourable Robert White that he should raise a battalion of City men. White accepted and set to work, opening a recruiting office at his firm, Messrs. Govett, Sons

Humphrey Secretan as Corporal with 10th Battalion The Royal Fusiliers (Stockbrokers)

& Co., 6, Throgmorton Street, on 21st August.[4] By the 27th August 1,600 men had been enlisted, although the next day the War Office announced that they would take only 920 of the men recruited.[5]

Lord Roberts inspected the Battalion, 1,147 men, in Temple Gardens on 29th August. He made a 'most stirring' speech. Led by the band of the Grenadier Guards the Battalion then marched to the ditch by the Tower of London. Here, the Battalion was attested as a whole by the Lord Mayor of London, Sir W. Vansittart-Bower.[6] The men had no uniforms, so paraded 'in all varieties of clothing, from silk hats to caps etc'.[7] Humphrey completed his enlistment that day and was allocated the regimental number STK/822. The Battalion then marched back to Trafalgar Square 'where we gave three cheers for the King and were dismissed'.[8]

Humphrey's firm, Lloyds Insurance, paid his full salary of £300 a year while he was in the Army. The Battalion had a Guards' Sergeant for every platoon, and the RSM and CSMs were also guardsmen. In September he became a Lance-Corporal and by the end of the year he was promoted to full Corporal when the Battalion was stationed at Windmill Camp, Andover. The Battalion - part of 111th Infantry Brigade, 37th Division - did not arrive in France until 30th July 1915, by which time Humphrey had reached the rank of Sergeant.

....

4 'Bobby' White was a partner at Govett's. He had already had a colourful army career. As a young officer he had played a prominent role in the Jameson Raid which was an ill-judged attempt to trigger an uprising in the Transvaal. However, he was captured on New Year's Day 1896. He was sent home to be tried for making war on a State with which the British Empire was at peace. Disgraced, he was convicted and served seven months in Holloway Prison. He commanded the 10th Royal Fusiliers from Nov. 1914 to Sept. 1916.

5 White, Robert, *Extracts from the Diary of Brig Gen Hon Robert White CB, CMG, DSO*, pp. 3-4

6 White, op cit, p 4

7 10th (Service) Battalion, Royal Fusiliers, *Royal Fusiliers Chronicle*, Sept. 1920

8 White, op cit, p 4

Toby Dodgson was commissioned as a 2/Lt into the Yorkshire Regiment ("The Green Howards") on 12th September. He was posted to the 8th (Service) Battalion which was being formed at Richmond, Yorks. In this unit the majority of the men were "drawn from the industrial and mining districts around Middlesbrough and in the east of the county of Durham".[9] This Battalion was part of the 69th Infantry Brigade, 23rd Division, which consisted mainly of northern regiments, being part of Kitchener's Third New Army. The Division began assembling at Frensham in Surrey from 16th September 1914, under the command of Major General Sir James Melville Babington, KCB, KCMG. The history of The Green Howards records that, on the 28th September, Major E. G. Caffin arrived at Frensham with no other officers, but with a Sergeant Major, a CQMS and over a thousand other ranks. His task was to turn this body of untrained men into the 8th Battalion of The Green Howards.

Toby Dodgson

Toby Dodgson joined them a few days later and was posted to "C" Company. On 18th October he was promoted to Lieutenant.

Toby's brother Philip was not commissioned until 4th October when, as a 2/Lt, he joined the 7th London Brigade Royal Field Artillery, part of the divisional artillery of the 2nd London Division TF (later renumbered the 47th Division). The Brigade was headquartered at the drill hall on Fulham High Street and comprised three batteries of 15 pounder guns and the 7th London Brigade Ammunition Column.

Amongst the other junior officers in the Brigade was 2/Lt Philip Pilditch,[10] a school contemporary and friend of Philip Dodgson. Most of the officers came from well-known public schools and there was even one peer of the realm, Major Lord Gorell.[11] The divisional artillery, as TF units, had just completed their annual training on Salisbury Plain and had to be recalled to London. On 16th August these gunners

....

9 Wylly, H. C., *The Green Howards 1914-1919*, p 251

10 Pilditch was the eldest son of Sir Philip Pilditch, 1st Baronet, JP and was born 30th Oct. 1890. He was educated at Winchester College (1904 - 1909) and had a BA from Pembroke College, Cambridge. He was an architect and was commissioned into the 7th London Brigade RFA on 26th Aug. 1914.

11 The 2nd Baron Gorell, (Henry Gorell Barnes) was born on 21st Jan. 1882 and was the son of the Rt Hon Sir J. Gorell Barnes, late President of the Probate, Divorce and Admiralty Division of the High Court of Justice. Lord Gorell was educated at Winchester College (1895-1900) and at Trinity College, Oxford (BA 1903 and MA 1908). He also studied at Harvard College from 1903 to 1904. He was called to the Bar by the Inner Temple in 1906 and was secretary to his father who was raised to the peerage (becoming the 1st Baron Gorell) in 1909. On the outbreak of war he was a captain and acting OC of the 19th (County of London) Battery RFA. He was promoted to Major on 19th Aug. 1914.

moved from Fulham in West London to Hertfordshire. This journey was recorded in some detail by Philip Pilditch, who kept a diary[12] of his war years:

> "We were off by 6.30. I had to collect a water cart and two transport wagons from each of the three batteries and the ammunition column; making twelve in all. I soon found I had much more to look after than the mere wagons. Every battery left a rag, tag and bobtail of odd horses, sick men and other items too disreputable to march with the Battery. ... I soon found I had too much to do to worry much about our appearance! I saw it would take me all my time to get them all to Boxmoor.
>
> About midday when we were all tired and dusty, and very thirsty, the column halted at The Welsh Harp, Hendon, and the horses were watered at the ponds. It was a strange sight, hundreds of horses being ridden into the lake. Luckily there was plenty of room. ... After about an hour there, and a sandwich and drink, we harnessed up and started off again. I found I had almost doubled the lot I had started with. ... We went along past Edgware, Stanmore and Bushey. We created lots of interest everywhere. People ran to windows and garden gates. ... Later on in the afternoon it got baking hot and I had to put the men up on the horses and make them walk in turn. ... Near Watford people came out with beer, and water, cups of tea, apples, bread and butter and all sorts of things for the men. ... Some angels in human form had taken a restaurant and gave us all free tea.
>
> The dismounted men began to struggle and get into pubs and sit down. ... Some were so bad that I got them a lift in the Doctor's cart. ... We halted for twenty minutes until most of the men were up and started at about two miles an hour, me walking in front. ... They came along the last miles wonderfully well; poor devils, it was a stiff march for a start, all fresh and soft as they were. Thirty-four miles at least and on a baking day."

The Division was spread from St Albans, where the divisional HQ was comfortably ensconced in The Peahen Hotel, westwards to the Gade and Bulbourne valleys. The 7th London Brigade RFA was established with its guns and horses on the common at Boxmoor, little over two miles down the hill from the Dodgson home in Bovingdon Green. While the infantry of the Division could practise manoeuvres and even fire on ranges in the immediate area, the gunners had to travel to Salisbury Plain to use live ammunition. In September the Division was inspected by Lord Kitchener at Gorehambury Park close to St Albans. Christmas was celebrated with ample dinners and suitable social events. Preparation for the 7th London Brigade RFA's move to France was badly upset by an outbreak of mange among the horses. Philip Pilditch recorded this:

....

12 *"The War Diary of an Artillery Officer 1914-18"*, now housed in the Imperial War Museum. Philip Pilditch also presented a copy of the diary to his friend Philip Dodgson, who in due course left it to his son.

Artillery of the 2nd London Division at Hemel Hempstead, late 1914. The 15 pdr guns and their limbers can be seen closest to the hedgerows. (Photo courtesy of Stuart Arrowsmith)

"Affairs are still very black. The mange, caught I suppose from some of our ramshackle old stables, has taken firm root and can't be suppressed. A week ago our Brigade was put out of the Division and more or less disgraced. The Third London Brigade (out of a Home Service Division) has come down here to take our place and, I hear, is in an awful state of unreadiness; also having no foreign service stores or equipment, they will probably take over ours! They have already had a lot of our ammunition given over to them. The day that we give over our guns and wagons to them I think I shall die of shame. What we shall do then I can't think. We shall be back in pre-mobilisation state and probably be included in a backward or Home Service Division. Seven months of hard work and valuable time wasted. I hear Kitchener and the War Office are furious and I dare say they will make examples and scapegoats of some of us, though I am certain the mange was caught from places now known to have been infected with it long before the War."

Major General C. St L. Barter, the Divisional Commander, and Brigadier General J. C. Wray, the CRA, inspected the 7th London Brigade RFA which they found in no condition to go to France. The Brigade was hastily moved to Cassiobury Park at Watford to be thoroughly disinfected and eventually set out for France on 17th March, 1915.

* * * * *

Little is known about **Guy Dodgson**'s enlistment, but it is on record that by the autumn of 1914, aged 19, he was a junior officer in the Hertfordshire Regiment.

* * * * *

Reggie Secretan, also aged just 19, had left school at Oundle only a few days before the outbreak of war. Luckily for posterity his mother wrote an account of his efforts to enlist:

> "On the outbreak of War he dashed up to London on a motor cycle belonging to a friend who was abroad, and tried to enlist in the first lot of Dispatch Riders, but was rejected because his motor bicycle was too old, and also he was short-sighted. He tried eight or ten times to enlist, but was always rejected for eyesight, he was A1 in every other respect. ... A friend wrote, "Never shall I forget your boy in the first days of the War, dashing about the country on his motor bike entreating to be enlisted anywhere and in any regiment!" Influence was tried – quite useless – he used to see a possible chance in the paper and off he would go, and come home calling out, "Same old luck, won't have me!" During one of these excursions he met a man and made friends with him so that he let him drive his car to Hertford at night, almost the first time he had driven at all.
>
> At last he got into a private Motor Bicycle Machine Gun Corps at Wembley, much to his joy, but after a few weeks a good many of the men were disbanded.[13] Determined to enlist somehow, he and twenty others from the Corps went to Grove Park in December, and were at once accepted by the MTASC there.[14] He wrote home, "I am so bucked! I am a real soldier at last!" This was just before Christmas 1914. Orders had come that no one was to be sent overseas until they had been inoculated, so he felt pretty sure of being there for some time. He had expected to get Christmas leave, so I drove down to the station, three miles away, in the cart with his old friend the donkey to meet him at six o'clock on Christmas Eve; after waiting three hours in the fog I returned home to find a wire "On duty; no leave." On Christmas Day, feeling uneasy, I went to see him at Grove Park, and found to my joy, that he had got a few hours' unexpected leave, and had gone to spend it with some great friends in London: he hugely enjoyed the afternoon.
>
> On Monday there was a great storm, and all the telegraph wires were down – no news of the boy. Tuesday something seemed to tell

13   His service record (TNA WO 374/61195) shows this confusion. He joined the '1st London Machine Gun Regiment' at Wembley Hill on 4th Nov. 1914. This unit appears to have been unofficial and an example of a unit that was raised by private individuals during the *ad hoc* creation of Kitchener's Armies. However, on his record it is crossed out and replaced by the 'Motor Machine Gun Service' of the Royal Horse & Royal Field Artillery. Presumably the Royal Artillery had merely taken over the former unit. He is shown as being posted into the Motor Machine Gun Service on 6th Nov. 1914, and it is this date from which his service has been calculated.

14   He was transferred to the Motor Transport section of the ASC at Grove Park on 19th Dec. 1914.

Reggie Secretan on his motorbike at "The Dells", Bennett's End

me I must go to him again. I got to Grove Park Barracks at 6.00 p.m., the time when he would sometimes get out. The sentry sent for him, and there was the bright face saying, "Oh Mother, I am so glad you have come! I start for France in two hours and I did not know how to let you know, the wires are down!" The same presentiment had made me take his suitcase with his leather jacket, and many necessary things which he had left at Wembley. "Oh, how thoughtful you are!" he said, as he seized them.

I went to Waterloo, and presently saw him arrive with about eighteen other men and an officer. He had begged me to try and get his sisters to see him off; only one message got through, to his youngest sister [Esmé] working at a London hospital. She ran up just ten minutes before the train started. He was so delighted that we saw him off – "The only ones on the platform!" as he would say afterwards.

That was 28th December, 1914. When they all arrived in France no one seemed to want them, or to expect them! At last, Reggie and another man were given brooms, and told to sweep up the dockyards! They had all been accepted as skilled mechanics and motorbike riders, but many of them had to be helped on their bikes when they landed, which rather gave them away!"

Of the young men in this story Reggie was the first to disembark in France, despite having been the last to enlist. He began writing home to his parents shortly after arriving.

1st January, 1915

At last I have got a job. I am a DR attached to GHQ [at St Omer] in France: a jolly good job and I like it awfully. The sad part about it is that we are not together, but all my pals are stationed at the various parks round, so I see them nearly every day. I have had no letters yet: the posts are awful.

15th January, 1915

I arrived in last night about 11 o'clock covered with snow. As I plodded wearily upstairs a voice greeted me, "Lucky dog, five letters for you". By Jove, I did the rest of the stairs in record time. Letters are beginning to pour in now, so I am happy – just got five more!

I was out from 4.30 p.m. to 2.00 a.m. the other day. It was foggy and raining; the last part of the journey I had a companion. We both got hopelessly lost, not a house, or a soul in sight, just a bit of a road and a white wall of fog. We laughed until we could hardly steer our bikes, though it was rather serious, but we got home at last!

It was very exciting with the roar of the guns, but we must wait till K's men come out for the real exciting time. …

The other night I met all my old pals at a café, miles from anywhere. We drank *café au lait* till we could hardly stand, and ended up with a sing-song. I started for home at [midnight], with the big guns booming away. I had forty miles to go all by myself, but I enjoyed every mile of it, and the old bike was a treat, and landed me back in the best of spirits. I have a jolly nice room here, where the GHQ are. We have a stove to dry our things. We get good clothes served out to us. I was out in the rain from six to eleven yesterday and kept quite dry. …

27th January, 1915

I got the Burberry suit today, and it couldn't be better: the bags are the envy of the whole place. I am much happier now I have settled down a bit and made friends. I have always managed to make pals wherever I have been so far, and find taxi and bus drivers jolly good pals: one doesn't see the true side of their character in civil life.

29th January, 1915

Thanks awfully for the helmet, etc. … Yesterday early I had to go about fifty miles up into the hills. It was a lovely day, but terribly cold; everything frozen solid. I dashed round to the PO, seized your parcel, tore it open, clapped on my helmet, and was off in no time. Oh, how thankful I was for it and for the wind-proof bags! I had gloves on, but had to stop at cafés all along to thaw myself, because I could not manage the bike, my face ached with cold, and my eyes watered and froze, but the rest of me kept quite warm. I am sure I should have been a block of ice without those things! …

A few days later Reggie's family had a letter to say he had been sent down to the base, as he had been kicked by a horse.

February, 1915

I miss Neal and all my old pals; I was quite broken-hearted when I left them. Oh, this camp! [Audax Camp, Rouen] It is all canvas and a sea of mud, not a dry spot anywhere; the tents are very dirty, stale crumbs and litter about. One must expect these rough bits, and I don't mind a bit when it can't be helped, but this discomfort is due to neglect. ... We get up at 5.00 a.m. and work till 5.00 p.m. ...

[Wolfe Mill, Bapeaume, near Rouen]

4th February, 1915

I am writing this letter in the house of a little cobbler. I had a buckle sewn on my gaiter, and he insisted that I should come here of an evening to write and have a chat with him and his family; he invited me in and gave me supper. I can just get along with the French that I know; they can't speak a word of English, but have been awfully kind to me, having dried all my clothes and blankets. It is so nice to have somewhere to go in the evening to write and have a little peace! Now will you please write this saddler a nice letter telling them how I appreciate it all? ...

25th February, 1915

Still here, but I am marked down for duty up country. I have been through "it" once or twice and may have to do it again: if so can only do my best! I want boots and things before I go up, but I don't want you to spend any more money on me than is quite necessary. How I miss all my old pals: I was quite broken-hearted when I left them. I was fed-up, but I feel in a better temper now! How I long to get home just for a few days, but leave is out of the question. I must do my best and stick it.

Later: Pleasure does not come without pain! The Captain who was in charge of us during our unloading job has just asked me what I thought of Audax Camp, and I told him in pretty plain language what I thought of it.

He said, "Will you come into my office as a clerk?"

R. "No."

"Well, what do you want?"

"A dispatch riding job on a bike."

Capt. "I am afraid that is impossible, but I can give you a dispatch riding job in a car if you can drive one?"

R. "Oh yes, I have driven for years, and am at home with most makes of cars!!"

[He had driven a car about three times before he went out, and only once after dark.]

He took me outside and gave me a little two-seater Singer. She is a beauty! When a call comes I am to be the first to go.

I have just come back from a run with the Captain. He did not seem to think my driving was perfect! So now I am in new quarters with a roof, and close to a YMCA hut, and am quite happy. ... All the roads here are awfully narrow, bordered by a couple of yards of mud with a ditch each side. It is a question of one or the other for the ditch when one meets another car, I usually have to give way because my car is the smaller.

1st Army GHQ, RE Signals
[Aire]
23rd March, 1915

I am right up there now and expect to have some exciting times soon. ... I am attached to the REs, and have to drive an officer around to inspect all the little Signal Stations, and I can assure you we have had some rough roads, but thank Heaven they are dry now. ... I could hardly have wished for a better job. All the fellows at GHQ are horribly envious of me and my little car. I have got into a kind of mood that I always feel content wherever I am put, and wherever I have to sleep. It is no use grumbling out here. Last Sunday it was a glorious day. I started off to the hills at dawn; the country was simply beautiful with the sun on the hills. It seemed impossible to imagine that within a short ride there was a great battlefield up there where it is terrible, but a few miles back all is perfect peace except for the rumble of the guns. The inhabitants are carrying on just the same with their farming; I have seen a man ploughing his field where the shells had been dropping only a few moments ago, but he didn't care a bit!

[Guinchy]
15th April, 1915

... I take my officer up to the trenches every morning and call for him at night – he steps off the car right into the reserve line. I have to dash off with the car as there are lots of stray bullets whistling about – very few shells so far, but one village I pass is a mass of ruins – a very terrible sight. ... I got the shock of my life when I went to look at a church one day: the grave yard had been literally ploughed up with shells, shell holes full of water, coffins sticking out of the ground, grave stones, skulls and bones all over the place – it was terrible – and all as still as death. I played in a footer match for the Signals the other day, and scored a goal, great applause from pals! It was real funny, all the spectators were shouting out "go it 'Specks'!" ...

17th April, 1915

I hope to get a few days' leave soon, I would give anything just for a glimpse of home again and the family. ... The *pavé* roads out here are all right for big cars, but it shakes my little car to bits. It breaks one's heart to drive it over them.

[Merville]
4th May, 1915

Whilst I was out to-day the town was shelled, and I missed it all! Oh, I was sick! When I was on my way back the guns sounded quite close, and there was an aeroplane surrounded by bursting shrapnel. When the shells burst a cloud of smoke hangs in the sky. It was a very pretty sight: it looked like a little silver speck sparkling in a cloudless sky, except for a few little white puffs all around it.

[Hinges]
15th May, 1915

The lady where I am billeted is awfully nice: she only charges us three francs a week and that includes hot baths, and coffee at night and in the morning; so you see we are doing pretty well up here. They are awfully good to us – you see we are not far away from the Huns. I call her *"Ma mère pour la Guerre!"*

[near Hinges]
20th May, 1915

I am up here with the 1st Canadian Division, driving for Major Earl, whom I used to drive at the advanced place before; we are close up, about four miles behind. I sleep on a very grubby floor packed with Canadians.

The guns keep up a small bombardment all day, and we can see the shells whisking about quite clearly. Are we going to see another winter out here? I hope not. I'm sure the roads would vanish altogether! The *pavé* roads here have been the salvation of our transport: they are awfully rough but no other roads would have stood it.

[near Béthune]
2nd June, 1915

I had a very hot time of it up there. It was my first experience of being under shell fire, though I have often seen them burst before. I was more curious than nervous; one can't feel afraid with all the fellows around taking no notice of it a bit! ... I shall want a nice large hamper for my birthday, full of cakes and eatables to make a spread for the fellows here who have been awfully good to me. There are no billets here, so we established ourselves on the top of a high mound covered with trees. I sleep out in the open with the stars to watch over me. I often think of home and long for leave to see you all, but it is no use thinking about that when there is work to be done out here.

[Hinges]
12th June, 1915

We have just had a glorious day of sports, got up by the officers. We had all the horses up from the RE Camp, and there were stable and driving competitions. We entered for the five-legged race, and carried off five prizes! There are three DRs and myself here, so we had a practice the night before, and after some fearful falls on the road we mastered it, and were able to get along at a steady trot; a three-legged race is bad enough, but five is awful. ... The last event was really "it": we had to run to the edge of the swimming bath, undress, swim across round a pole, back again, dress and run back to where you started. I was first in the water and back again, straight into clothes dripping wet, then I stopped to do up braces and buttons as instructed, but some other fellows never did up a thing – awful swindle, as I could easily have been first. ... Is it not extraordinary that all this took place within five miles of the trenches which we can see quite easily with glasses?

[Hinges]
23rd June, 1915
[June 22nd was his birthday.]

Thanks awfully for all the parcels, they were glorious! ... I went out after dinner and did not get back till after tea, and there were nine parcels all stacked up against the walls! So I set to at once and we all began tea all over again! So I had an awfully nice birthday out here. ... A Jock coming back from the trenches the other day, threw me a German cartridge clip. The bullets were dum-dums. The beasts – it does make one boil to think of it!

[Hinges]
12th July, 1915

When I am driving my officer in the little car, I always assist him in his work, which consists in laying out the ground for telegraph lines across country, and also find out what is wrong. ... There is a farm where I keep my car and lots of animals. My favourite is a grey goat, which has made great friends with me, and follows me about like a dog, and whenever the mat of the car is put down he is on it like a shot, and has a good snooze! ...

[near Aire]
15th September, 1915

I am back again at GHQ. We are in a camp here and it is going strong, we have just rebuilt our hut, there are four of us in it, and we can stand upright! Two sleep each side, one above the other and it is "the goods" – quite the best here: floor covered with canvas and boarded ceiling. I have been terribly busy, out most of the night, and all spare time taken up in cleaning the car, but things are quieter now.

* * * * *

Humphrey Secretan, Reggie's elder brother, had been promoted to Sergeant on 24th July, 1915. His Battalion, the 10th Royal Fusiliers, now part of the 37th Division, landed in France on the 30th July. Between the 17th and 24th August it underwent a period of instruction in the trenches at Houplines, near Armentières. From the 3rd to 13th September the Battalion occupied trenches at Fonquevillers. On the 15th September the Battalion was relieved and marched to rest billets at St Amand, where the brigade became the divisional reserve.

The following letter, written to his younger sister Esmé, is the only one of Humphrey's that survives from this period and gives his impression of trench life.

[St Amand]
16th September, 1915

Dear Puss,

Thanks very much for your letters which I have not been able to answer before. The last dated 12th I got this morning, together with a letter and parcel from father. The apples are lovely. What a pity we are not at home. The tea, etc., I shall take to the trenches next time I go there. ...

I wrote home I am sure about the 6th or 8th September so mother need not worry. The trouble is, here you lose count of days absolutely. You will hear all right at once if anything happens. It isn't as if there was any fighting here. All casualties are stray shells and bullets.

... I haven't been able to write before because we have been up into the trenches for six days and we are so busy there that we hardly have time to turn round. ... They were only 800 yards or so away but it seems a long way up the winding communications trench. A great pity I think we have changed all the French names and called them by English names like Regent Street, Rotten Row, etc. which by the way the Pioneers spelt "Rotton."

The trench itself was not so bad, only there is a lot of work to be done. There were four dugouts, one for a section. I had rather bad luck as the Sgt Maj took mine which was a lovely one. Of course I could not say anything. The French do not have as many officers as we do, so the better class dugouts are not enough to go round. Well, we found them fairly comfortable though very sticky in wet weather. The dugouts are clean. I never had a bite, but rats and mice abound and bring down earth on you through the roof at night. ...

The programme is six days in village [Fonquevillers], six in trenches and twelve in village [Souastre] three miles back where we were before and arrived last night very tired. We are kept on the go continuously for the six days. We work in shifts, as on board ship, half at a time. ...

Our arrangements for killing Germans as far as the platoon is concerned are nil. The only shot we fired during the six days was one rifle which went off by mistake. There are special men as snipers. We do not have any time. No German shells came near our bit of trench, but our artillery sends a few over every day. I hear the battery behind our battalion is obliged to fire 47 shells a day. Why that exact number is beyond me. The German trenches are 400 yards away about and you can see them quite plainly at parts, but I have never managed to see a man yet. There is barbed wire in front of our trench of course, through which there are several ways out and we went out through them the other night just to find the way for certain. Our men are not allowed to fire a shot without permission of an NCO.

The other night I had a narrow escape. I was sitting on top of the parapet arranging some sandbags outside to strengthen it. It took quite a long time to conceal them and I had just finished and got back in the trench when one of the sentries on my right came along, in a great state of excitement, saying he had seen a man bobbing up and down quite close to him and he was going to challenge him. This sentry was an NCO and so could fire without permission. We crept along on tiptoe and then he got up on the fire-step and to my horror began pointing his rifle straight along our parapet instead of in front. Of course I said at once it must have been me but he wasn't satisfied until I went back and stood up where I was and then he saw it was me. The other sentry said he had quite a job to prevent him firing without coming and asking me.

One of our officers found a dead Frenchman the other night. He did not know what he was and caught hold of him by the head and it came off. We are now three miles or more back for rest and have a decent billet in a barn, but the other fellows left it very dirty – cheese and bacon under the straw. We have spent all day cleaning it out and there is great difficulty in getting disinfectant and we have no sprays. ...

Love to mother and father.

Your loving brother, Humphrey

Humphrey stayed with the Battalion in France only until late October 1915 when he returned to England. On 15th November he was commissioned and then spent a month at an OTC at Queens' College, Cambridge.[15] He asked to be commissioned into the Queen's Royal West Surrey Regiment because his family had recently moved from Surrey. He was posted to the 3rd Battalion, a Special Reserve (militia) battalion, based at Chatham. There are no details of his service here, but he probably had some responsibility for training.

* * * * *

Over the next few months Reggie continued to write to his parents:

[Aire]
18th November, 1915
There is a BEF canteen not far from here where everything is cheap. We have awfully good meals here. I generally leave at 6.30 p.m. with car and dispatch rider, do the round, and get back any time between midnight

Humphrey Secretan in officer's uniform at Bennett's End

and 3.00 a.m. Our billet is an old French military bake house, a huge room downstairs for the bikes, and a large room upstairs where we sleep, we all have beds and a large stove, and plenty of blankets. We have made cupboards out of old packing cases, so you can see that it is a second home to us. The Sergeant is my great friend (Sgt T. Walker, formerly the King's servant), an awfully nice chap, and all the other fellows are so nice. The weather is terrible, with very severe frosts in the night, the infantry are getting a terrible time of it. My new car has not arrived yet, so I am still running about with lorries. I never realized what cold is really like till I came out here, but I am well equipped for the winter.

....

15   Those officers commissioned in 1914, such as Toby Dodgson, were posted straight to their units and learnt 'on the job' with their only formal training being any received pre-war with an OTC. However, by 1915 officers were receiving some training on commissioning. Humphrey's service record reveals that he spent a month in Cambridge between mid-Nov. and mid-Dec. 1915. This was at a 'school of instruction', one of which existed in Cambridge. According to Hew Strachan the courses it provided 'lasted about a month' and 'three platoons from the school were quartered in various colleges.' (*History of the CUOTC*, p.145) The system of Officer Cadet Battalions was not set up until Feb. 1916.

Humphrey and Reggie Secretan with their parents at "The Dells", December 1915. Humphrey is wearing the uniform of a newly commissioned officer. Reggie is wearing a white over blue signallers' brassard.

Reggie Secretan in an MTASC vehicle depot, probably near First Army HQ, Aire-sur-la-Lys, 1915.

Chapter 3

Marjorie and Toby

October 1914 to August 1915

Marjorie Secretan and Toby Dodgson found they had much in common, with mutual interests in music and literature, and by 1913 they were corresponding regularly about books they enjoyed reading, games of golf and tennis and other events in their lives. Their wartime letters start from October 1914 while Marjorie kept a diary from January 1915. Her early letters to Toby give some good descriptions of the home front at that time, conveying something of the excitement of the early months of the war.

During the previous year Marjorie had been living in east Hertfordshire at Stanstead Abbotts helping her mother's brother Basil Richardson (nicknamed "Padie"), a widower, by keeping house for him.

"Hill House", Stanstead Abbotts, Hertfordshire

Marjorie to Toby

Hill House
Stanstead Abbotts
Ware
31st October, 1914

Frensham Common under canvas sounds rather cold and wet now the rain has come. I hope they have built those huts for you all. I know that part of the country pretty well as I have often stayed with an aunt who lives along the Hog's Back and I don't wonder you say it is beautiful, especially now the leaves are turning. You must have lovely views all round, if only you are not too chilly to appreciate them.

Soldiering must be a tremendous change of life after the usual quiet respectability of the 9.15 train and playing golf on Sundays. It is splendid that you find the men so keen. One hears that everywhere, and from all accounts they had a good deal to put up with at first. It is sickening to find that all the professional loafers, one could so well afford to spare, are not attempting to enlist. As a soldier said to me the other day: "Them's the sort of chaps we ought to put in front to use up the German bullets". However, Kitchener apparently means to have every available man before long, so that their time will come.

The Division quartered all round Leverstock Green and St Albans have orders for France: they expect to leave tomorrow; 20,000 of them.[16] I was over there yesterday and found them all fearfully excited, with things ready to pack, and very proud of their newly served out rifles. There are thousands going in a day or two. We are hoping it means the Germans are wavering and that French means to have heaps of fresh troops to turn their retreat ino a rout.[17]

How one hopes the whole ghastly affair will be over before many months are gone. When are we going to find another way of settling things? ...

It is very interesting meeting all these Belgians. One hears almost as much French as English spoken in London. They are curiously stoical and uncomplaining and very few convey any idea of tragedy. I have been up to these places where they are received and sorted out and they all sit in rows patiently waiting to be allotted somewhere to live. Those in the village here are very nice and so grateful for a peaceful home again. What a stupid lot English people are over foreign languages. I was helping dole out clothes in a big house in Warwick Square yesterday and had an awful time explaining things to them. German words kept coming into my head and getting all mixed up, but heaps of the other ladies would not say a word at all. ...

Esmé is reported to have killed two patients in the first week![18] Reggie has got into a motor cycle corps. They have armoured side cars with Maxim guns. Humphrey on the subject of army management is too lovely for words. He must

....

16   This was the 47th (2nd London) Division. 'At the end of October the Division was selected as one of the Territorial Divisions to be taken complete to France.' (Maude, *The 47th (London) Division*, p. 3) In fact, the Division did not actually go to France until Mar. 1915. However, two battalions of the London Regiment, the 1/13th (Kensington) stationed at Abbots Langley and the 1/16th (Queen's Westminster Rifles) stationed at Leverstock Green, were detached from the Division and sent to France arriving on 3rd/4th Nov. 1914 where they joined the 8th and 6th Divisions respectively.

17   This is a reference to the 'Race to the Sea', a period of mobile warfare on the Western Front. The German advance into France had stopped at the First Battle of the Marne, after which the two sides attempted to out-flank each other in a series of engagements in Northern France. The Race culminated in the First Battle of Ypres (19th Oct. – 22nd Nov.) and the Battle of the Yser (18th Oct. – 30th Nov.). The resulting stalemate led to the formation of a continuous line of trenches from the North Sea to the Swiss border.

18   Marjorie's sister Esmé was training to be a nurse at a London hospital.

be dreadfully unpopular with his sergeant and officers as he continually lodges complaints. He told me he knew some of the men were thieves, as someone had stolen two of his dish cloths and a scrubbing brush! I saw Guy in Hertford the other day with the Territorials. I hope he will come over here one day. ...

Hill House
29th November, 1914

I do hope you are all safely in barracks by now. It must have been awful under canvas in that bitter weather. I hear a question was asked about the soldiers on Frensham Common in the House, so I hope the authorities have been stirred to move in the matter.

... I saw Esmé in London last week. ... You are fortunate in being able to get off so often at weekends. Yes, I often 'find myself' in town and there is no reason why it should not be

Esmé Secretan in VAD uniform

Saturday afternoon. If you let me know when, I'd be very pleased to meet you for tea one day. It must be tiresome being such miles from anywhere; as you say, it's so stupid being cut off from everyone one knows.

But it sounds quaint you being so bored with uniforms, for in this quiet corner, the mere sound of a bugle brings us tearing out of the houses and going miles to see the soldiers pass. On Friday I took the car over to Leverstock Green as I heard it was being attacked by "the enemy" advancing from St Albans to Redbourne. The big guns were just outside our gate and what a noise they made. They were altogether too much for the advancing force which never got near us. ...

Toby to Marjorie   Ramillies Barracks
Aldershot
3rd December, 1914

Your letter arrived just before we left Frensham where we certainly did have rather a poor time of it during the last three weeks or so. The end was quite dramatic as the camp was partially wrecked by that gale last Sunday night. The hospital and PO tents being blown down and two of the large mess tents each seating about 1,000 men collapsed the next morning. As it pelted incessantly from Saturday till Tuesday morning you can imagine it wasn't very pleasant. We had to arrange to get the men fed somehow in their own tents. I never in all my life saw such a quantity of mud: it was a forlorn sight and looked very much as if the much talked of air raid had actually taken place! Thank goodness it was fine the day we moved in here where we are in the most comfortable quarters. I can't tell you how luxurious it seems to see a fire again and to be able to see what you are doing during the dark hours.

I am so glad you think you will be able to manage a Saturday.

Marjorie to Toby   Bennetts End
                                                                     Leverstock Green
                                                                     Hemel Hempstead
                                                                     6th December, 1914

... It would be great fun to go to some 'show' but I don't know what to choose. It's ages and ages since I have done anything so gay and I have not the faintest notion what you like. My tastes are cosmopolitan ...

How splendid that you are at last in barracks ... It must have needed a lot of patriotism to put up with it all. Here the whole family is assembled for the weekend and we are just off for a route march, Esmé and I a little nervous as to how far we are being taken. The village is appalled because a German lady has come to live here and is building a shed with a cement floor. Of course it is <u>called</u> a cow-shed but you never know!

Goodbye till Saturday.

Toby to Marjorie   Bovingdon
                                                                     4th January, 1915

It really is a pity that you had to go off this morning and I am not feeling at all philosophical about it. Although it is a horrid day and raining hard, there is a pleasing air of warmth and comfort in here in front of the fire and, being of a lazy disposition, I am enjoying it. But I am tired of reading and it is so dull having no one to talk to, especially as I am feeling loquacious and have thought of heaps of things that I want to cross-examine you about since yesterday.

... Yesterday was a ripping day and I enjoyed it all, except for the few moments when I thought I was going to be taken to church, particularly the walk. ... It is ages since I had such a good talk. I've had rather a rotten time of it this last year and the real me inside has been feeling horribly upside down ... I wanted you to know that the world seemed a cheerier place when you were here than it did before.

                                                                     Ramillies Barracks
                                                                     8th January, 1915

... I am feeling a trifle depressed at coming back here and had very much the same sensations as I used to at the end of the holidays when I was quite a kid. Certainly I am tired of being a soldier, but I expect we shall be out in France before we know where we are. ...

Marjorie, do you think there is any chance of another afternoon in Town? I should love it, if you think it could be managed ... Keep smiling ...

Marjorie to Toby   Hill House
                                                              10th January, 1915

... This week has flown away in a stupendous rush of the usual things that assail the harassed householder when she has been away and returns to a house full of guests: but across miles of correspondence, tea parties and cutting out pyjamas, there is a very pleasant remembrance of a week in the woods. ...

If you really want another afternoon in town one Saturday I will certainly come up. ... May I write again about it soon? London is a horrid place compared to the wilds of Bovingdon but soldiers can't be choosers – not in wartime. ...

You are a nice lad Toby – sometimes. What about Saturday 23rd? But I'm not certain yet. I'll write again. Thank you for Wagner.

Toby to Marjorie   Sandhurst
                                                                    Berkshire
                                                              12th January, 1915

As far as I can tell the 23rd will do admirably though I am not quite sure where we shall be then. ...

My feelings are that if by any chance it should be fine we might keep out of doors. Kew is quite an attractive place, do you know it? If the weather is beastly we can do a theatre, picture gallery or whatever we feel in the mood for. ...

I'm in a simply first rate billet here. Mr and Mrs Toye are frightfully nice. He was a housemaster at Wellington for many years and is really a dear old man. She is quite charming and busy making me feel quite at home at once so that I was pretty fed up at falling ill which I did after being here two days. ...

You seem to have had a dull time of it, those household duties would drive me crazy. ... I have finished "The Harrovians" (I liked it) and am now in the middle of "The Trumpet Major". I will talk to you about them when we meet. ...

Oh Marjorie, damn the war. I get more fed up with it every day: it is all so utterly futile and disgraceful. Life is much too precious and interesting to be wasted in such an absurd way. ...

Marjorie to Toby   Hill House
                                                              17th January, 1915

I am so sorry you have been ill. Hurry up and get well. ...

You are indeed lucky to be in such a nice billet. It sounds delightful. It's very pretty country too, isn't it? I remember very jolly walks in those pine woods at Sandhurst. ...

... If your leave for next Saturday continues to hold good, will you please write to me at Bennetts End? ... I go there Thursday and the posts there are so few I probably won't get your letter if you write here. I will be coming back here on Saturday so will be in London. In any case I've never been to Kew! Won't it be fun at lunch when I feel inspired for the British Museum (archaeological section) and you hanker after the Vauxhall Bridge Road cinematograph!

... Please excuse more. My head is fuddled between a cold and house accounts.
... I do hope you are all right again. It is indeed d--- the Germans, only that's much too good for them. They'll never see the absurdity of the whole thing: there's not an ounce of humour in the race.

Toby to Marjorie

Ramillies Barracks
20th January, 1915

I have got my leave all right though some departure from the truth was necessary in order to get it, as now we are not moving into billets till Saturday owing to the inspection by Kitchener and the French Minister of War which is to take place on the previous day. ...

... Pray for a fine day on Saturday. Till then, *au revoir.*

Hartfield House
Hartley Wintney, Hants
1st February, 1915

... Hasn't the weather been splendid? You ought to have been here yesterday. I went for a walk to Eversley across magnificent country, great stretches of breezy open flats and large pine woods. ... When are you coming down to the Hog's Back to shock your worthy aunt with your modern ideas and advanced notions?

... I will write properly next time and be more communicative. I am more and more bored with soldiering so write me a nice letter sometime and ask questions if you want to. I don't mind a bit from you – you can say just what you think about me without any politeness ... Of course lots of people scoff at the idea of these modern friendships: they will tell you that in nine cases out of ten one or the other (sometimes both) fall in love. Certainly it does happen so very often I think. What do you think about it? As to falling in love, it is an unfortunate thing to happen to anyone. Do you believe in LOVE? Note, I don't mean marriage which so many people seem to regard as the same thing! ...

Hartley Wintney
7th February, 1915

... I was myself very much amused by the series of conundrums at the end of my letter. They were quite unpremeditated and I could all of a sudden then have written ever so much, only I had to go to dinner so there was only time to fire off those questions at you. ... I believe you imagine me a sort of person who is always falling in love and treats the affair in a thoroughly light-hearted manner. But though there is much to be said for this method of ordering one's life, I have never been able to manage it. When you say that you can't make out just how seriously I take things, you hit the nail on the head. By nature I take everything seriously and everything is real to me ... and so to falling in love, well perhaps it is the best way, only when the falling out comes along you are likely to hurt each other more; but there, one always has to pay for any happiness in this world, so what does it matter? ...

"The green plains of pleasant Hertfordshire" sound very nice and I am sure the Colonel won't object ...

Monday: Plans are altered again this morning. Now we are to leave Aldershot next Sunday and march to Folkestone; they are arranging for us to do about fourteen miles a day, so that we shall not be idle, as there will be all the billeting to make each day. We are expected to get down there the following Sunday and if we have anything like decent weather it should be quite good fun and very instructive. ...

Dorking
February, 1915

It was a very depressed Toby that arrived back at Aldershot last Sunday night, but he was not allowed to remain in a contemplative mood for long as the morrow brought a host of things that had to be seen to and thought about, two days absence having accumulated them no end. We got away all right on the Tuesday which was an ideal day and reached Guildford without much bother, though our billeting was a business, the company being distributed in no less than a hundred small houses which I had to stay behind and pay for today.

I did so enjoy those days at Hill House but I can't write you a proper letter now midst all this turmoil and bustle – it must wait till we are safely by the seaside. We go to Edenbridge, about twenty-five miles, tomorrow then Tonbridge, Maidstone, Ashford, Folkestone (The Leas Hotel). The PO at any of those places will find me if you feel inclined to write and cheer on the weary plodder! I believe Kitchener or the King is to inspect us at Tonbridge which is a darned nuisance. ...

Good night, Marjorie dear, and write sometime.

The Leas Hotel
Folkestone
2nd March, 1915

It was very nice to find your letter waiting for me here ... It feels quite strange to be settled down again in one place after all that tramping which seems rather like a dream. ... I thought Dorking a ripping spot. ... That twenty-five miles to Edenbridge was the most strenuous day we had, but oh! such glorious weather. ... The fourteen miles to Tonbridge was the best of all, including as it did Chiddingfold and Penfold, both ideal little villages ... I enjoyed it immensely right up to the end, though I tremble to think what it might have been like if the weather had been wet and beastly, instead of frosty and sunny. We only had half-an-hour's drizzle the whole way down except at Folkestone when we were greeted by a regular Arctic blizzard, with thick snow for about an hour or so just as we were marching in. I think we ought to have rather a good time here. It's a nice healthy place anyhow and I love the sea even when it is spoilt by promenades and all the atrocities that go to make up these so-called resorts. Still, considering what they are, the Leas are quite inoffensive and at night, now that they are not allowed any vulgar lamps, etc., quite attractive. ...

... You know you really are the limit to have been such a good girl for such a long time. I don't call it at all fair - just look at the responsibility it puts on me! ... Did ever two people pursue such diametrically opposite courses and yet, at the advanced age of twenty-five, we collide in this delightful manner, quite in the dark. ...

... That day we walked through the woods in the rain was the first time I felt in the very least like my old self inside and you little guessed how kind you were being when you let my hand touch yours. You literally breathed new life into me!

The Leas Hotel
Folkestone
18th March, 1915

I was much entertained by your "mad" letter which caught me in rather a similar mood, engendered no doubt by the sea air and general levity of this place, which is something quite extraordinary. For example, I went to two dances and a "*thé dansant*" last week, all full of most cheery people, from which you will infer quite rightly that I have developed quite a keenness for dancing again. ... Why on earth don't you live at Folkestone? I must try and get away and perhaps we can meet in London town or somewhere?

... Philip was due to leave for France with his Brigade last Tuesday, but I have not heard yet that he has actually gone, though I presume he has. ... It's rather boring down here really though I try and think it isn't. I wish you were here to go walks with: we might have such a cheery time. ...

Marjorie to Toby

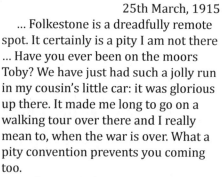

Edwinstone
Torquay
25th March, 1915

... Folkestone is a dreadfully remote spot. It certainly is a pity I am not there ... Have you ever been on the moors Toby? We have just had such a jolly run in my cousin's little car: it was glorious up there. It made me long to go on a walking tour over there and I really mean to, when the war is over. What a pity convention prevents you coming too.

... I have to go home on Saturday as our voluntary hospital at Ware has been put to use and Nurse Secretan is one of those who mind twenty convalescent soldiers.[19] I did night duty for a week before I came here; it was very weird and ghostly going round in an enormous empty old house to see everyone was safely asleep. The other nurse had to shake me at intervals to keep me awake. Next week I will be cooking during the day; much more in my line.

... Before I marry anyone I should like to see him asleep! You say the only way to enjoy life to the full is to share it with someone. I quite see that everything is dull alone, but must you

Marjorie Secretan in VAD uniform
....

19 This hospital was in The Priory at Ware, Hertfordshire, now the offices of Ware Town Council.

share all things with one person? Because what happens when he is shot by the Germans? ...

I thought Philip must have gone as I heard that Division was off. I was sorry to see his friend A. C. Lonsdale[20] had died. Reggie is again at Headquarters with a little Singer car. Humphrey was at Hill House last weekend and missed his train home on Sunday night! He still thinks he doesn't get enough exercise. "These marches are nothing" he says.

Toby to Marjorie   Folkestone
                                                                                        27th March, 1915

Torquay sounds quite attractive ... I have always liked the idea of the moors though I can't say I know them at all, nothing beyond a nodding acquaintance with Dartmoor. The idea of the walking tour appeals to me very much! Thank you, I should like to come immensely! ....

I think I shall try to get home for the weekend of the 9th or the 16th. I wonder if by any chance you could come to Bovingdon too. Mother was down here last week and suggested asking you, so she evidently thinks you are a nice person for me to know! ... I've such lots to talk about and we might even get a single at tennis. ...

                                                                                            Bovingdon
                                                                                        6th April, 1915

Isn't this disease of mine the most foolish thing you ever heard of? I am as fit as ever and what slight rash there was has quite gone again, so I suppose it's all over. Anyhow I am going out and leading a normal life again. The doctor thinks I ought to consider myself infectious for another week but owns that the risk of anyone catching it now is quite minute. So I suppose I must continue to live the solitary existence. I am horribly bored by it. I think you might have come and nursed me! ... Philip's battery have had a shot at the Prussians!

Marjorie to Toby   Hill House
                                                                                        18th April, 1915

If it is really all the same to Mrs Dodgson, I would like to come on Thursday as it means one day less of night nurse, a horrid job, which falls to me this week again. I will motor over about tea time ...

So glad the measles are so slight. But how can you expect me to waste my nursing talents on such a foolish complaint. You must develop something much more interesting to stir my professional zeal.

We have just been into Suffolk for a night and now I have to go on night duty. Think of me these next few nights, when you are snugly dozing off, hurrying about chilly passages, an unwelcome bearer of medicines and milk; or at 4.30 a.m. wrestling with a kitchen stove which won't light. I will be dreadfully sleepy on Thursday!

....

20 Lt Arthur Carr-Glyn Lonsdale, 6th Bn KRRC, was attached to the 2nd Bn Royal Scots Fusiliers. He died on 10th Mar. 1915 at the age of 23 and is buried at Rue-Petilion Military Cemetery, Fleurbaix. He was the son of the Rev J. H. and Mrs. Katharine Lonsdale of the Further House, Wimbourne, Dorset. He was a scholar of Eton and Radley and an undergraduate of Trinity College, Cambridge.

Hill House
29th April, 1915

I am afraid I am most terribly silly, but I always told you so, so don't say you weren't warned. I didn't mean to write to you but things took such an uncalled for turn last night. My family are too dreadful; listen to this. I got home rather weary and very sad about 7.00 p.m.

I somehow felt Uncle Basil's eyes on me directly I came in, which I didn't want at all as there was a choke in my heart and I knew I couldn't stand much. However it really would have been alright if it had not been for a stupid old letter which I got after dinner. You know I am responsible for the well being of certain Belgians here and while I was away there has been a fine bust up over them, all my fault unfortunately, and this letter put things pretty strongly.

Of course I don't care a pin for anything like that in the general way but last night it was the final straw and I started crying. Uncle Basil was fearfully surprised to see his self-possessed niece sitting on the edge of the sofa in tears, and read the letter and said he knew it wasn't that, it was you. ... He was most awfully nice and I said I had not meant anyone to know I cared. He said if only I would bring my troubles to him, he would do everything in the world to make things easier for us. Of course he does not know I am telling you and he won't either. I don't quite know why I am telling you myself, but I somehow feel I would rather you knew: you won't mind will you? Myself I don't see it makes much odds. It will make it easier for me here: I had no idea Padie [her Uncle Basil] could be so sweet. I have always laughed at people who can't hide their feelings, but it seems I am worse than anyone. Even the Belgian lady, whose ruffled feelings I had to go and smooth, said *"Mademoiselle a les yeux si belles ce matin. Que c'est arrivé?"*

Isn't it glorious today? ... <u>Damn</u> the war. Those silk stockings are ripping. I want you very much. I expect you know how much.

At about this time in mid-April Toby and Marjorie became unofficially engaged but decided to keep the news to themselves for a while.

Toby to Marjorie   Bovingdon
29th April, 1915

Oh, Marjorie, it has been such a glorious day and so utterly wasted. The house felt lonely and dull last night when I got back, but I have missed you ever so much more all today and my one perpetual thought has been how nice it would have been had you still been here: what a splendid walk we might have had, and many other "might have beens". ...

... I can hardly believe that this time last year I was so unhappy, sometimes I can scarcely believe it is true and that it isn't some dream from which I have to awaken. But these last few days with you were real and I shall never forget them. Ever since that day we walked in the rain the world has seemed a kinder place and now it is all new, wonderfully new. You have given me back the power to love. Just think what that means dearest and, Marjorie, I do love you and I want to tell you so and to hear you say you want me too in that elusive voice of yours, whose accents I have been trying to capture all day. I do love it when you are talking to me all alone like that. I hear the real Marjorie speaking then, don't I?

London is a stupid place sometimes and it was so yesterday when it came to saying good-bye. I felt quite paralysed. Afterwards I was afraid lest you thought I was cold, but you know me better than that; still I wished I had come and seen you off and not bothered about my silly old train. I dare say you thought I was rather an ass at the theatre, but I never have been able to listen to "Butterfly" with composure, and yesterday, when every sense was quickened, it was worse than ever. ...

Friday: Yes, I certainly was surprised to see your handwriting this morning and to tell you the truth I was rather nervous. I was afraid you had found out you didn't care after all and had written to tell me so at once! Then when I had read your letter I can't express what I felt, only I longed to come to you at once. I know and I understand exactly what you felt that evening. Marje, I can't bear the thought of you unhappy even for an evening. ...

I have had rather a pleasing piece of news today from Maidstone. I am detailed for a month's course at the Staff College, Camberley, commencing May 6th, and the adjutant has persuaded the CO that it isn't worth while my going all the way to Maidstone just for those few days, so he has extended my leave till then, and I shall go down to Camberley direct from here. ...

Staff College
Camberley
Surrey
6th May, 1915

This is rather a pleasing spot and the grounds in which the College stands look cool and green, while the lake is particularly alluring on such a hot evening as this. ... I foresee a strenuous time of it here ...

I got badly ragged when I got home and you would have been highly amused by some of the conversations between Mother and I, could you have overheard them. ... She put a number of leading questions ... which I parried with some adroitness and complete self-possession! ...

Marjorie to Toby   Hill House
                                                        8th May, 1915

I am a wee bit sad that I have not been able to get to London to get something I want to send you for your birthday. It will have to wait till I can get away from the hospital, which there is no chance of all next week. Meanwhile many, many, many happy returns and ones not spent in Camberley but much more sociable places. Twenty-six is a fearful age, I am so glad you get there such a nice long time ahead of me.

I was awfully pleased to find your handwriting awaiting me when I came down this morning. It was dear of you to take the trouble to write directly you got there and I am so glad you did. It looks a fine place and I expect you will really enjoy it. ...

... The Uncle was ripping when I said we were going to let things rest as they were and said he did not mind whatever we liked to do ... . He is a sportsman, and I am ever so glad you like him Toby; he does certainly not think you a villain but keeps calling you a "very nice boy". ...

PS I have written a most chatty little note to Mother, closing the topic of me and my affairs for the present as quite beyond setting straight by anyone outside. ...

Toby to Marjorie

Green Lodge
Bovingdon
Sunday 16th May, 1915

... Only a few short months ago I didn't seem to care much what happened to me. The war was rather a welcome diversion from hopeless thought and if I went under it didn't seem to matter much and was a simple solution. But now life has become so precious: I love it and I want to live. The spring has pushed its way up the trees, making everything new and green: your love had come into my life and made the whole world a new and wonderfully beautiful place. As I was in the woods this morning, humming with life and listening to the cuckoo calling in the distance, and all the little queer noises close at hand, it seemed utterly incredible that people should be killing each other, so hopelessly unreasonable, that I could not understand why anyone tolerates it for an instant. Why? Why, when nature makes the whole world so beautiful, should we befoul it all like this? ...

Staff College
Tuesday 18th May, 1915

The weekend prospect is not developing well as we are having an extra strenuous day on Friday and Saturday so that there is no chance of getting away till the 12.15 train on Saturday, which means I suppose that I shan't reach Stanstead Abbotts much before 2.40. There is nothing official about Whit Monday yet but I should think they ought to give us that. Do you really think I can come for the weekend (Saturday night, anyhow)? Uncle will be asking me my intentions soon! Anyhow I want to come ever so much and to be alone with you, even if it is only for a Sunday morning. ...

Marjorie to Toby

Hill House
19th May, 1915

It is perfectly horrid of the staff college not to let you off till 12.10 on Saturday but never mind, we must make the best of the time we do get; and of course you are coming here .... Uncle Basil was ever so pleased when I said you were coming; very surprisingly pleased. He kept saying "Good, good, my dear. I'm very glad". Hasn't he told me he would do all he could do for us? ... It's just splendid to think you are coming. Be prepared for tennis. ...

I loved your letter written from Bovingdon. It makes me awfully glad to think of you being so happy. ...

Hill House
24th May, 1915

The Gods are on our side again in according me another day's holiday, which with the Uncle ... away golfing, means a whole afternoon of idling in the garden. So I am following your bidding and writing "very soon". It is just a perfect day again and a terrible sin for you to be working in far away Camberley. I am sitting in the shade of the big gorse clump above the pond where you get the very best view of the garden and the deserted tennis court. There is a glorious smell of May from the wood and a nice rustling in the trees. My faithful companion Timbo [the dog] is curled up beside me, very glad of my unshared company for a change! ...

I do hope Toby wasn't very unhappy last night. I did hate his going and the evening was far from cheerful here. Mr ... chaffed me gently about deserting him all day and then came up and whispered "Many congratulations, my dear, he's a very lucky boy!"

... You are a dear, Toby; but you know the war hangs over everything like a dark cloud and when anything else goes wrong it dips down and covers up everything; and it takes a long time to escape again. Because there is no escape really – that's the point – it's something we have got to go through with and banish it from thought and speech as we may, it will come back. It is curious how one little thing going wrong will bring all one's forgotten troubles rushing back in horrible strength. It's especially like that with the war and the prospect of you going to the front. ...

Toby to Marjorie   Staff College
                                              25th May, 1915

... I spent a sweaty Whit Monday – no other adjective will do: the heat in these parts was intense and we were out doing a scheme from 9.00 till 3.00 p.m., during which I felt completely fuddled and quite unable to concentrate my mind. I played tennis till 6.00, then a lecture and another after dinner. Today has been ripping too and rather fresher. ...

Marjorie to Toby   Hill House
                                              26th May, 1915

... If I can escape serving King and country in the hospital I am going on a boat on the Broads for a fortnight in June. It ought to be rather fun – books and bathing.

Dear Toby, I do love you and I do hope you have not missed Marjorie too much this week. I want you ever so much, but it's ever so nice knowing you are there all the time. I am almost forgetting what it was like without you. You have made the world such a different place and such a much much nicer one. ....

Toby to Marjorie's father, Herbert Secretan   Weston-Super-Mare
                                              6th June, 1915

Dear Mr Secretan,

I believe Marjorie has already written to you so I am not going to say much now except that I think I am a very lucky person and that I do hope our ideas meet with your approval – in which case we shall be indeed extremely happy.

I should like to write you an eulogy about your eldest daughter but as people under these circumstances are proverbially supposed to be silly, I refrain with much difficulty, thereby proving I hope that though I've lost my heart, I haven't lost my head!!

It will be nice if we can come to Bennetts End on Tuesday and I am looking forward to seeing Humphrey again whom I have not seen since last summer.

Yours very sincerely
Francis Dodgson

Engagement photograph of Toby Dodgson and Marjorie Secretan with Marjorie's parents, Mary and Herbert Secretan, at The Dells

Toby to Marjorie   8th Yorkshire Regiment
Bramshott,
Hants
10th June, 1915

... It was very hot and steamy in London yesterday which was not at all conducive to the making up of one's mind; still, I did manage after a while to get the ring and I do hope you will like it. It is a pearl with some little diamonds round it. I hope you won't think the pearl sticks up too much, but anyhow it can be reset easily if necessary. I am longing to give it to you now and if possible I shall try and get away Saturday week, the 17th. I shall be vaccinated in the hopes of being ill with it! The trouble is that after the 10th we start our firing and as that goes on all Saturdays and Sundays it knocks all leave on the head.

It's very hot down here but otherwise very pleasant and the huts are excellent. All our men have their rifles now and they are also going in batches on a week's leave, so it really looks rather like business. It is rather pleasant and cheery being back with the Regiment again and that did a good deal to counteract the depressing effect of saying good-bye to you. ...

Marjorie to Toby   Hill House
12th June, 1915

... Oh Toby I am longing to see that ring. I do hope you will get away on the 19th and also that you will be very bad after the vaccination! Pearl and diamonds round sounds just what I would love. I thought of you in hot old London on Wednesday. I picked an enormous amount of pinks and sent them down to Mrs Dodgson. Then I dropped heavily back to hospital work. I am awaiting the news to spread round there, it ought to be rather amusing.

Most of the neighbourhood who have heard so far are quite electrified, but it has not penetrated everywhere yet. ... I have had some awfully nice letters from aunts and people, which I am busy answering. Now that people do know I really don't mind a bit, in fact it's rather fun and I am so glad you also are pleased things turned out as they did. Anyhow we have pleased both our parents and Uncle by making it public and that is a great thing. ...

Toby to Marjorie   Bramshott
14th June, 1915

... I have had quite a sprinkling of congratulatory letters which I will keep for you to see but luckily not many people know my address. ...

... I am afraid I can tell you nothing definite about next weekend as it is so uncertain exactly which day the ranges will be free for my Company, but personally I think it is very unlikely that we shall get to Longmoor before next Monday, but even so it is doubtful if the Colonel will give me leave again so soon. ...

... Oh, Marje, I do love you so much and it seems months since I last saw you, though it isn't even a week yet in reality. Oh, to have this time last week back again now. I long to feel that you are actually close to me again, that I can talk with you and play with you, and then be serious for a moment and feel your warm kisses that mean so much happiness and express the sweetest thing in the world – your love for me. And you will never know how highly I prize that and how wonderfully you have changed everything. ...

Marjorie to Toby   Hill House
24th June, 1915

... How goes the shooting? Think your Company will account for many Huns? Dearest, I am longing to see you again. The photos have brought back again so vividly our times together on Saturday and Sunday. Three quarters of me was sound asleep on Saturday evening so I have a very hazy impression of those two hours, only a sweet remembrance of how nice it was to be kissed and cuddled and not to bother about anything else in the world.

Toby, your ring is just glorious. I remember so well what you said, that I could look at it and think you love me, and indeed I do; and often when the thoughts of you are pushed far away by outside things, I catch a sparkle from the little diamonds and the picture of you rushes back into memory, so insistent and so familiar that I have almost spoken to you in real life across all the miles that separate us. The pearl reflects all sorts of things, it's such a glorious deep colour, so dark and peaceful after the glitter of the diamonds all round. ....

... The latest is that the Uncle and I are to motor to Folkestone on Saturday to see a cousin who has just arrived at Shorncliffe with the Canadians.[21] ...

....

21   Pte George Richardson, Marjorie's first cousin, had come with the Canadian Expeditionary Force *en route* to France. Shorncliffe Camp near Folkestone was the main depot in Britain for the CEF and thousands of Canadians were billeted in the area.

Toby to Marjorie   Longmoor Camp
                                                                      24th June, 1915

With any luck not much more than a week now before you come down here. I do
want you again so much, the last time was so terribly short. ... Darling, you know I
am very sorry if anything I said or did to tease you really hurt and that it was quite
unintentional and simply due to lack of knowledge as to how things I say may affect
you. ...

It is a strenuous life here: up at 5.30 a.m., then on the ranges in the morning
from 7.00 till 1.00 and shoals of musketry returns to be sent in before the evening.
Oh such silly, stupid army forms! ...

                                                                      Bramshott
                                                                      7th July, 1915

It is dreadfully dull now that you have gone and to make matters worse I felt
quite seedy yesterday. ... I do miss you so and after such happy hours as we had
together there seems very little to live for now that you are no longer here. ...
Marje, my darling Marjorie, I have been so miserable without you. Nothing can
fill the aching emptiness I feel within me when you are gone. I have been reading
some Rossetti; he must have understood wonderfully well what it must be to love
someone very dearly. ... Philip arrived in London yesterday and came down here
last night: he looks very fit.

                                                                      Bramshott
                                                                      8th July, 1915

I do hope you will be able to come up on Monday for the "bust" in Town: it will be
such a rag and it is most important you should see your future brethren-in-law. We
only thought it all out this afternoon and Philip suggested your coming before I said
anything about it. ... Mother is to arrange rooms for us at some hotel and is going
to let us know the address, so I shall go straight there as soon as I get up to London.
Philip looks awfully fit but decidedly altered – rather older, I think. ...

Marjorie to Toby   Hill House
                                                                      13th July, 1915

I have just got home again. They motored me down which was very nice. We took
Guy to Stortford first and then dropped me here. It was a splendid treat of Philip's:
at least it would have been if you had been there. I should have enjoyed meeting
them so much more. They both congratulated me very nicely but I could think
of nothing to say except a foolish smile. Philip does look well and quite fat! The
artillery seems a comparatively safe job compared to most. ...

No, I was not surprised at your lack of philosophy when you wrote before;
I rather believe your philosophy is only skin deep and is routed without much
difficulty by keener feelings. I hated to think of your feeling so lonely and if you
do go on like that I shall have to seize Uncle Basil's housekeeping funds and come
down to Bramshott and take a cottage and have you to supper every night. And then
there will be a scandal in the Regiment and you will be sorry you ever had anything
to do with me. I hope you are quite fit again. I don't believe you were as flourishing
as usual while I was there. ...

Written from the hospital at Ware: Stanstead Abbotts
                                                                     14th July, 1915

Here you are, Toby dear – all the photos. They came this morning so I am sending them along at once as I know you will be keen to see them. ...

... Toby, I do love being engaged. It's <u>such</u> fun being welcomed everywhere with congrats. People seem so grateful to us for providing them with some good news, and I like getting all sorts of nice letters. What are you feeling about it? After all the world is very kind to us and I think in war-time you escape a great many of the heavy jobs and so called witticisms that an engagement usually creates. Does anyone know with you yet? It has not reached the hospital. I hear from Esmé we are very popular at home. She says you have always been very much approved of, so my choice is considered very excellent. ...

We had a grand set out in the garden today with the patriotic service and I couldn't help liking being met with congratulations and smiles all round. Everything seemed so golden and happy and, I can't help it, I do like tripping round in a pretty frock (the pink one today) and being the centre of attraction for once in a way. And then they had a sort of service and Uncle Basil spoke as I had no idea he could speak. He generally hesitates rather, but today he went straight to the point, speaking in reference to the war of course. He brought a lump in my throat by speaking of the sacrifice the war means to the women ... .

... When I think of you and your love and all you mean to me there is no gloom anywhere. There's nothing but happiness and trust in you. All the thoughts of you are so beautiful. I'm so happy inside, I can't possibly express it. I can only keep saying over and over to myself: "I love him, I love him". You have come into my life and made me really live for the first time. You can't think how much more sensible I am to all kinds of sounds and sights since I grew to love you. ...

Do you realise the clock is chiming 1.45 a.m. and the other nurse slumbers peacefully. Do you also realise I have written to you three times in 2½ days and all about myself, so you must be soon quite weary of my writing. Never mind, I don't care one bit if you <u>are</u> tired of it because I don't believe you are.

All love, sweetheart ...

Toby to Marjorie   Bramshott
                                                                     17th July, 1915

I got down to Liphook at 7.30 – quite a good train – after a peaceful journey and thank goodness I had the carriage to myself all the way, so that I just sat there dreaming away over the twenty-four hours that had just passed. Wasn't it a beautiful evening? It got finer and finer as we came south. My darling, you were so unutterably sweet all the time that we were together and the time we had at least could not have been better, so that I couldn't feel too sad.

When I got up to the camp it turned out to be what I thought on the way down – those damned Welsh miners.[22] The orders are somewhat as follows: as the Brigade

....

22 On 15th July the South Wales miners rejected the new wage rates that had been accepted by miners in other regions and 200,000 men went on strike. This action posed a serious threat to Britain's command of the sea, and therefore national survival, as coal was needed by the Royal Navy. Toby's reaction was typical of that expressed by men at the Front. The strike ended on 20th July after the intervention of the Minister of Munitions, Lloyd-George, who declared the coalfield a 'controlled' industry under the Munitions of War Act, thus rendering the strike illegal. (Wilson, *The Myriad Faces of War*, pp.223-4)

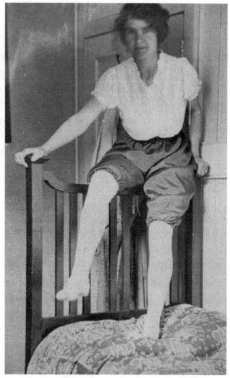

Toby Dodgson on the garden seat at "Hill House", 15th July 1915

"Second lines of defence!" Marjorie Secretan, 23rd July 1915

may be required for special duties, no officers will go more than five miles away and must leave their address; men will remain within bugle call of the camp; on the assembly sounding, units will fall in in full marching order, twenty rounds ball ammunition per man to be served out, etc. All the morning no one was allowed to leave the camp at all. Needless to say there is a good deal of suppressed excitement, all the men here seem to be absolutely against the strikers. ... Meanwhile there is absolutely nothing to do but stand by and wait, which I might have done equally well with you! Thank goodness there is always a humorous side to everything and the mess has been quite lively this evening. The Colonel, who is a man with a very quiet sense of humour, has been thoroughly enjoying the spectacle of his dismayed Subalterns creeping back, one by one, from their various haunts. No one had put a wrong address in the leave book which seems to surprise him very much! But his chief joy is that the Brigadier had taken the weekend off and he declares that the Brigade Major was laying 5-to-1 that the telegrams would come back with "Not known at this address" on them. I was playing bridge with him after dinner and, having greatly chaffed us all the evening, he finally gave us a little comfort by announcing that a notice had come round that the two Companies that were not going to Longmoor for musketry would arrange to send as many officers as could be spared on a week's leave. Think of it, one whole long week together. Oh, my darling, wouldn't it be glorious? ...

Toby wired Marjorie on the 22nd July to say that he had been granted a week's leave. She found him at home when she got back. The next day she recorded in her diary: *"Did photos in spare room. Motor came to fetch us to Bennett's End. ..."* On Sunday 25th July they motored to Marlborough to stay with friends, and returned to Hertfordshire the next day. On 27th July she reported: *"Telegram to recall him tonight - very depressing. Went for walk, got very wet ... Toby left at 9 pm."*

Longmoor Camp
Wednesday [late July, 1915]

... I am very bored at being back here and it seems such a short while since I went off with bubbling spirits in anticipation of a happy week with you, darling, and now it is all over. Oh, everything is so flat. What a blessing it will be when the war is over and we can really enjoy ourselves without feeling all the time that dark clouds are hanging about everywhere. I did enjoy every moment with you this last time and it is so ripping going about with you. I think that morning on top of Martinsell [a hill south of Marlborough in Wiltshire] was best of all. I felt very close to you up there. ...

Longmoor Camp
9.00 p.m. – 1st August, 1915

... We expect to finish here on Tuesday and will probably return to Bramshott the next day. The latest rumour is that we shall not stay there after 16th August, as another Brigade is coming to do its musketry and we are going back into the neighbourhood of Folkestone. But I should doubt its being true, as I think we shall be going out at the end of the month. Anyhow I shall not be sorry to see the last of Bramshott. Do let me know if Humphrey has really gone and where to. He must be very tired of me but what a pity he didn't say anything that night as I could easily have seen myself off. I remember now thinking at the time it was rather strange he didn't suggest you dining with him or anything. I must write him a line and tell him not to be so beastly considerate next time, though it was jolly of him. ...

8th Yorks Regt
Bramshott, Longmoor
3rd August, 1915

I had such a nice evening yesterday with the Beslys.[23] They have just got a new gramophone and he was very anxious for me to hear it and so took me over to dinner. It is a great joy and they have such a good and interesting lot of records. Isn't it simply ripping of them to think of asking you down for the weekend? I nearly squealed with joy when they suggested it. They have got a very nice house and quite near the camp. You simply must come.

....

23 Lt E. M. Besly was a fellow officer who was wounded on 31st Mar. 1918 and taken prisoner. After the war Maurice Besly put his musical talents to good use. Between 1923 and 1928 he was Director of Music at Queen's College, Oxford. He wrote orchestral music, songs and an operetta. In his latter years he worked as a solicitor. He died in 1945.

Bramshott
6th August, 1915

... I returned from Longmoor on Wednesday evening with the very devil of a cold in my head. I spent a perfectly horrid day yesterday, blowing my nose and trying not to feel like a suet pudding. This morning, as I felt no better, I stayed in bed where I am still, feeling stuffy to a degree and my nose so sore I scarcely dare to blow it any more. Did you ever know anything so feeble, and in summer time too, to be shut up in a wretched hut, devoid of everything except necessaries and only damnable little buzzing flies for companions?

I believe we shall stay here now until we go out, as no one seems to have heard any more about us moving anywhere. Kitchener is coming to inspect us on the 13th and we ought to be absolutely ready to go by the 20th, when we shall start "standing by", but as no unit has ever been known to get off in under three weeks from that time, it looks as though we might expect to go at the beginning of September. ...

Marjorie to Toby

Hill House
10th August, 1915

I am very thrilled over next weekend and there will be much weeping and gnashing of teeth if it doesn't come off. It would be splendid to get Monday, and yes, do let's go to the Queen's Hall. I have looked up the programmes and it looks awfully good that night, mostly Wagner. ...

Bring your bathing dress and we will have an early dip in the river. Oh, how I have pined for a swim these stuffy days! The river looks so cool as I toil past it on my bike to the hospital. Last week I got soaked through nearly every night as I came home about 10 o'clock: so it's me should have had the cold really. ... Dear old thing I am just counting the days till we meet again. ...

Toby to Marjorie

Bramshott
17th August, 1915

Heavens! What a life of contrasts! I could scarcely believe when I awoke this morning that I was the same person who only yesterday was so happy and far removed from everything unpleasant. I would have given anything to have been able to lie in bed this morning, and yesterday it was the easiest thing in the world to throw the bed clothes off and jump out.

Dearest Marje, we did have a good time, didn't we? I loved every moment of it. Thank goodness you are to come down here on Saturday, because otherwise I should be feeling very miserable. ...

Thursday: We have been inspected by the King today and had a grilling time of it as the inspection ground was about ten miles from here in the neighbourhood of Frensham. The whole Division was there and it was quite an impressive scene. We left here at 6.00 and did not get back till 4.30 – and such a hot day. Princess Mary was there on horseback, really looking very attractive. She is evidently escaping from Mama's influence! ...

On the 20th August, the HQ of 69th Infantry Brigade received orders that the Brigade was "to hold itself in readiness to embark for overseas. All officers and men [were] recalled from leave."[24] Toby Dodgson wrote the following farewell letters to his mother, Helen, and to Marjorie's mother.

Toby to his mother   Bramshott
                                                              24th August, 1915

As the future is so uncertain and one must of necessity run risks, I am writing these few lines before we leave England just in case the Fates decree that I should fall before the Hun. I write them to you, Mother dear, although I feel there is no need as I know you understand very well the sort of thing I would wish. Having nothing of much value and practically no money (!) I have not bothered about a will. But I think there is sufficient money standing to my credit at the office to pay off what little I may still owe. I should like Marjorie to have my books and there is a certain amount of music ... which I should like her to have. As regards Marjorie, if you could see your way to leaving her a portion of the money that would have come to me, I would be very grateful. She is one of the very best and I can't tell you how she has cheered up these last months and changed the aspect of everything for me. But this last request I must leave entirely to you to do as you think best.

It will depress me horribly if I see anyone wearing black! ...

Toby to Marjorie's mother   Bramshott
                                                              26th August, 1915

Dear Mrs Secretan,

Thank you so much for your letter and all its good wishes. I am so sorry that your weekend with Marje down here hasn't come off, but I never thought we should be out before the end of the month and I think we are quite the exception getting off straight away without any false alarms. We cross tonight and go I believe via Folkestone.

It has been simply ripping having Marje down here these last few days [staying with the Beslys], and all this summer in spite of the old Army I think we have managed to have a very good time. I certainly have never been so happy before. It is beastly having to go away like this, but there is always the coming back to look forward to and that will be a really great day.

Ever your affectionate
Toby

At 4.15 pm on 26th August the 8th Yorkshires marched out of Bramshott Camp to head for Liphook station and entrained in two parties. Marjorie took a number of photos of the Battalion on the march and of Toby's company entraining. On arrival at Folkestone Harbour, the Battalion embarked immediately.

....
24 TNA WO 95/2183

Toby about to entrain at Liphook Station, 26th August 1915

"Seven in each please." Entraining at Liphook Station. Toby is standing with his back to the camera, 26th August 1915

Chapter 4

Philip Dodgson

March to November 1915

Philip Dodgson had left for France with the 7th London Brigade RFA, part of 47th Division, on 17th March 1915.

His first letter to his mother Helen:

[near St Omer]
20th March, 1915

Dearest Mother,

    I am sorry I haven't written earlier but have not had much chance. We had a most luxurious journey to Southampton. We crossed over to Le Havre by night. I

Philip Dodgson

slept most of the way on a sofa in the Captain's cabin. It was a tiny boat from the Clyde and we were packed tight. The guns, horses and wagons went on a large ship. Our little one arrived very quickly. ... Le Havre is a loathsome place and quite wore my feet out. We went into camp for one night about six miles out of Le Havre, in tents; it was bitterly cold. ... Yesterday we got in a train at midday and stayed in it for nineteen hours. We went through Rouen. The poor men were in ordinary trucks with hay – twenty in each. We haven't had clothes off since we left and only one wash. We're all dead tired.

    I have talked more French today than ever before, as I had to arrange billets; it is excellent practice. It is most interesting being out here, though even where we are it is hard to realize what is going on not far

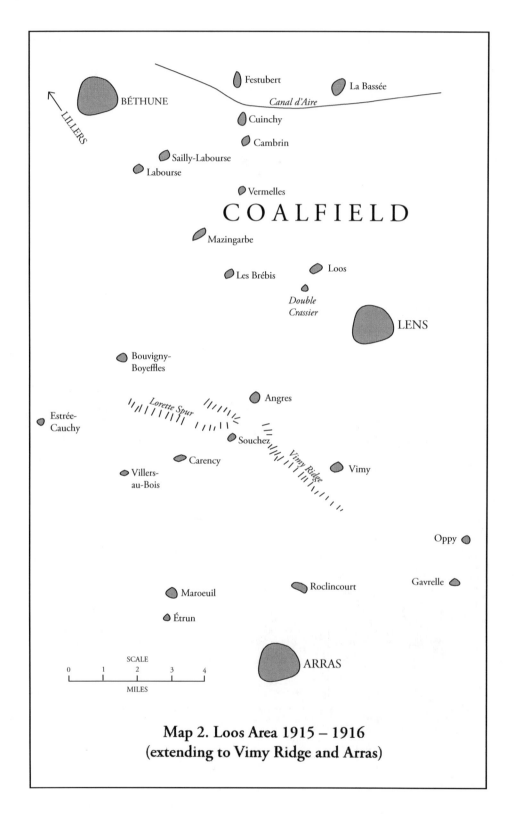

**Map 2. Loos Area 1915 – 1916
(extending to Vimy Ridge and Arras)**

ahead. The weather so far has been good, but cold – this morning there was a hard frost. It is extraordinary how everything here is given up to war: you never see anything else on the roads.

<u>Next day:</u> Have had an excellent night – slept on a mattress in Marryat's room.[25] We all feed together, six of us, in the Town Hall. How well the French cook, even quite poor people.

Ever your very loving
Philip

Philip to his brother Guy   [Auchel, west of Béthune]
27th March, 1915

... We have now been here for a week in a coal-mining district. I am living with some men in a room belonging to the mine, which is normally used for washing miners. Unfortunately the hot showers are not working though the officers can get baths elsewhere in the mine, and we manage to get all the men baths once a week. Living is wonderfully cheap – about two francs a day – with priceless omelettes and wine. ...

I expect to go up the firing line for a few days next week. Everybody is in awfully good spirits out here, but what a ghastly time they must have had during the winter. ... I struggle very hard with French.

Philip to his mother   [Auchel]
29th March, 1915

I am afraid it is a long time since I wrote and I believe it takes a long time for our letters to get home. I spend a large part of my time dealing with other people's letters, which is excessively dull except in a few cases. ...

We are still in the same place. All the officers of the Brigade have now been up to the firing line except Pilditch and self. We have been left out as the junior officers. ... We are having a quiet time. The weather is glorious, but this east wind is biting cold. ...

At present I don't think there is anything I want. A smallest-size Primus stove would be useful, also a small kettle. ... It is such a comfort to make a cup of tea quickly and anywhere.

The Bishop of London is out here and held a service today which some of us went to. We also had a church parade yesterday. I am afraid it was rather a surprise for some of us to hear next Sunday is Easter. One is so out of touch with these things. ...

Philip to his brother Toby   7th London Brigade, RFA
2nd London Div, BEF [Auchel]
30th March, 1915

... Considering this village was already full of infantry when we arrived, we have done quite well for ourselves. All the men with a few exceptions are in a large *"école des filles"*. There was great consternation among the Teachers and Taught when

....

25 Capt (later Maj) Ronald Marryat had been the Adjutant to the Brigade since May 1911. He was a Regular soldier. Philip Pilditch described him as "a born soldier all over, with a strong personality and a keen sense of humour. When he commands a Battery, I think I should like to serve under him, but he would keep one moving pretty briskly." (Pilditch diary, p. 25)

they arrived in the morning to find the place packed with men. The horses are all out in the open and, considering how bitterly cold the wind is, there is very little sickness among them.

I am now on Bde HQ Staff as orderly officer. A good job. HQ and 19th Battery are messing together here. ... It is most monotonous country – flat as a board. ...

I wonder how you are getting on and whether you will be out here soon. It is hard to realize even now that it is all going on. What a relief it will be when it is all over. ...

Philip to his mother   [Auchel]
5th April, 1915

... The parcel from the stores has come and is most acceptable, especially the chocolate and cake. At present, and so long as this kind of war goes on, we do not want the emergency type of eatable, as we can without difficulty get more than enough to eat. Cakes and chocolate, cocoa and sweets are most acceptable. Also, if you could manage it, a bit of pressed beef would be ripping, as we so seldom get a decently cooked bit of meat here – the French don't seem to know how to do it. ... I had a letter from Guy. I hope you manage to get him or Toby for Easter. ...

We are still in the same place and are getting very tired of it. We have now been here for a fortnight. We have a shocking day today, the worst since we left England. It has not stopped raining. We have fortunately got the staff horses under cover among the works of the mines. The Batteries are still in the open, poor things, up to their necks in mud. ... It is extraordinary what a little time one gets to oneself out here. I suppose it is turning in at nine o'clock which makes the day so short. ...

I wonder if you know just where we are. Guy will probably inform you. I don't think his Regiment censors their letters as conscientiously as we do. His lot, from all accounts, are doing awfully well out here.[26] We are not in the slightest danger at present. ...

[Cambrin, between Béthune and La Bassée]
8th April, 1915

... We rode up to have a look round where we are to come to, as a fact I'm there already, not very far from the Proosians [sic] now. I have come on ahead with the telephones and the rest come up tomorrow. ... I am very glad you wrote what you did about Guy. As a matter of fact, Marryat was talking about that point only a few nights ago – he was saying that there was a direct responsibility on senior officers to look after the junior ones, and I think he's quite right. ... Our HQ (i.e. the Col,[27] Adjt, self, doctor[28] and interpreter) are sharing the same house.

....

26   Guy's battalion, the 1/1st Hertfordshires, had arrived in France on 6th Nov. 1914 when it came under command of 4th (Guards) Brigade in 2nd Division. It was the only Territorial battalion ever to have been brigaded with the Guards and earned itself a fine reputation and the nickname 'The Herts Guards'. It adopted the practice of numbering its rifle companies rather than lettering them from the Guards. Guy did not come to France with them until 1917.

27   Lt Col Charles E. Chambers TD "a Volunteer and Territorial officer of long standing and, I should judge, amongst the most able of his kind. He is one of many Etonians in the Brigade and by profession a schoolmaster." (Pilditch diary p. 25)

28   Dr Spurgin RAMC "a quaint old cuss, very devoted to the Colonel and the Brigade, and always *'au grand serieux.'* Looks like Mephistopheles." (Pilditch diary p. 25)

Guy Dodgson

In letters between members of the Dodgson family it is obvious that Guy had some problems. Whether these were military or psychological is not evident and family records do not clarify this.

Philip to his mother   [Cambrin]
13th April, 1915
... One gets used to the thought of destroying property out here. It is hard to realise that people are really slaving all and every day to make things and money. It certainly is a novel sort of life. If you want a bit of furniture you just hunt about the neighbouring houses until you find it. ...
An order has suddenly arrived that no upper lip is to be shaved.[29] This undoubtedly means the war will soon be over. Mine has not been scraped since 16th March, and I'm told it is growing well and is a success. ...

[Cambrin]
18th April, 1915
I think this morning will stand out in my memory as one of the days of my life. For the first time I have looked out over the British and German lines. I spent the whole morning in one of the observation stations. I went up with Maj Crozier: his name is in the last list of DSOs.[30] He is such a delightful man and has done splendidly out here. He observes from a hole in the roof of a high house; it is the last house before one actually comes to the trenches and you get a splendid view right over and beyond the German lines. ...

I spent from 9.30 until one o'clock looking through glasses. It is like a huge maze trying to follow the ins and outs of the trenches. I saw a considerable number of our shells fall in the German country and they also put three heavy shells close to our house, so we had to go downstairs until it was over. It is really frightfully exciting when you hear their shells coming.

....

29 Moustaches were compulsory at that time. The Divisional History refers to 1st Corps Routine Orders dated Apr. 12th 1915 which stated "**Moustaches**. It is observed that of late the provisions of King's Regulations regarding the shaving of the upper-lip have been disregarded. . . . Any breach of these regulations will be severely punished in future." The History observes that "The most farcical apologies for a moustache were adopted, cut as close as nail-scissors would clip them. We never heard of any punishment. Perhaps that was not strange in an army whose King wore a beard, whose Prince of Wales, with clean-shaven face, was then serving with them, and whose greatest wars, from Wellington's backward, had been fought clean-shaved. Before long formal permission was given to shave the upper lip if you liked." (Maude, *The 47th (London) Division*, p. 21)

30 Maj Baptist Barton Crozier, 56th Battery RFA. His DSO citation read 'Rendered valuable service in observing our artillery fire during the actions of 10th and 11th Mar. 1915, at Givenchy, whilst exposed to the enemy's heavy rifle fire and our own shrapnel. He has been conspicuous for gallantry and coolness under fire throughout the campaign.' (*London Gazette*, 15th Apr. 1915)

... Our cook is getting on very well considering he has never done it before. I find I often have to say the same sort of things you do at home to your cooks. We have really got quite a decent Mess now. The meat we get is usually splendid.

... I see [General] French has given us a few words in his dispatch. The Country just now seems more interested in drink than the War. Seems rather foolish to cause ill-feeling by forbidding it. More practical to deal seriously with those who get drunk. As for those who strike, they ought to be tried by District Court Martial and shot. What do you think?

[Cambrin]
24th April,1915

... You must have had a very jolly weekend with Guy at home. ... How funny it sounds to hear Toby talking of tennis, though I daresay I will be sending for a racquet soon.

I think Asquith ought to be shot if he really said we had got all the ammunition we wanted: it is impossible to have enough in a war like this. Lloyd George seems to be quite strong and energetic.[31] It is a mistake to be so over-optimistic. It will take a lot of shelling to dig the Germans out. ...

I have been having a most interesting time laying wires up to the observation posts, etc. The Huns have been rather full of hate today, mostly frightfulness (we call it "frightfulness" when they shoot without seeing where their shells fall).[32] I'm sorry to say we had our first casualty to day and that was among our HQ staff. They were shelling a house directly on the opposite side of the road to our billet. Two or three of our men, thinking they had finished, went across to pick up souvenirs and almost at once another shell came and hit one of them – he was killed on the spot. He was my groom and such a nice boy.[33] I of course saw more of him than the others and he will be a great loss to me. I felt awful when I saw what had happened, but of course one has to try and treat these things as unavoidable, though this case could have been easily avoided – it was merely want of thought. Everybody, on the whole, is awfully careful up here, including myself. It is marvellous how accurately they shoot. Thank goodness I don't mind hearing shells coming nearly as much as I feared I might. I have had some fairly close now. If they are a little distance away, it is quite amusing watching them, but I always get as much under cover as possible. ...

....

31 The so-called 'Shell Scandal' arose after the Commander in Chief, Sir John French, confided his view to *The Times* correspondent, Charles Repington, that the failure of the Neuve Chapelle offensive in Mar. 1915 was due to a shortage of munitions. The resulting scandal led to the downfall of the Liberal Government on 25th May 1915. Asquith remained Prime Minister but formed a new coalition government and appointed David Lloyd George as Minister of Munitions. The war diary of 7th London Brigade RFA recorded that on 3rd May 'Pending inquiry into state of ammunition the Brigade was stopped firing.'

32 'Hate' was slang for a bombardment. The term derived from the 'Hymn of Hate against England' which was composed in 1914 by the German-Jewish poet Ernst Lissauer (1882-1937). The hymn was distributed throughout the German Army, taught to German schoolchildren and performed at concerts. It was seized on by the British propaganda effort as further evidence of German cruelty and bullying.

33 The war diary records that 1312 Driver Bernard John Wyms was killed that day. He was the 19-year-old son of Mrs C. Wyms of 268 Munster Road, Fulham and is buried in Cambrin Military Cemetery (grave A 22).

[Cambrin]
29th April, 1915

... I can't imagine why anyone can suppose the War will be over in June. The various opinions out here on the move to the Dardanelles are very mixed – on the whole against it, when it is obvious we want all the strength we can get here.[34] No good winning in the Dardanelles if we are beat here. ...

We have been the victims of an act of frightfulness. The poor old horses caught it this time. A shell landed among some of the horses which were in a town about three miles back – it killed four of them but fortunately never touched a man though they were crowding round the cook-house only ten yards away – marvellous escape as it was a very powerful shell. ... It looked as if they were really trying for us, but I think it more probable they were going for the road which is used a great deal during the day. There is nothing to be alarmed at in this sort of thing as they are small shells and we are all right indoors even if they do hit the house, unless one is very unlucky. I don't imagine you worry much; if I thought you did I wouldn't tell you anything. Some people seem to worry terribly judging from the letters the men write back. ...

[Cambrin]
7th May, 1915

... If only some people could take a trip over here under the guidance of Messrs Cook and see a bit, then the Country might realize there was a War, and what we're up against, and how much the French people are giving up, how willingly they do it. Our interpreter simply revels in our guns demolishing the buildings in the German lines...

[Cambrin]
12th May, 1915

... The 2nd London Division has now become the 47th Division. I am sorry as there was a certain distinction about our old name. Now we shall be merely one of the crowd. I am afraid we feel a bit bitter about Kitchener's Army when we think of all those beautiful new guns they have got at home, and they are merely playing with them.[35] The men have done splendidly out here but they have not been given much assistance by those in authority. However, I suppose we ought to be thankful to be out here at all. ...

PS I wonder if you are keeping my letters. I would rather like you to, as they would form a sort of diary for me afterwards.

....

34   The Anglo-French landings on the Gallipoli peninsula took place on 25th April in an attempt to force Turkey out of the war.

35   Territorials frequently resented Kitchener's New Armies which often received new equipment (such as 18 pounder guns) in advance of Territorial Force units. This was compounded by the erosion of the Territorial identity through changes of unit designation. Pre-war Territorials in particular resented the fact that TF divisions (which had existed before the war) were given higher divisional numbers than war-raised divisions of the New Armies.

[Cambrin]
17th May, 1915

... I am glad to see the papers and official reports have been frank and have told you that last Sunday (the 9th) was a failure[36] except in as far as it helped the French, which I believe must have been considerable. We have kept the Germans well awake all last week and we started off again at them on Saturday night.[37] ...

[Cambrin]
19th May, 1915

... We are still out of everything here; it is rather beastly having it all going on so close and not taking part. Unfortunately the weather has been all against us since Monday morning; it has been very misty and the ground is very muddy and slippery which adds greatly to the difficulties of the infantry. However, things are moving slowly, though I wish the papers wouldn't be so excessively optimistic – every inch has to be desperately fought for – the expenditure of ammunition is beyond imagination; you can't realize it until you've seen it. I think the Government are being too feeble for words – every MP ought to be out here for a bit and realize what it is like. With them I would have all Trade Union Officials, and they could all go in the front fire trench and be shelled by the Germans and then, just to rub it in, we would telephone down that the guns could not retaliate as ammunition must be economized – then they would realize. Things aren't really quite as bad as this, but it would be good for them. The 19th Battery has been on the edge of this show and even there in one day they fired four hundred shells. ...

I got my hair cut today, which is rather a comfort. I also got a shampoo which was much needed – sleeping on the floor, which I am now really used to, makes one awfully dirty. ... I'd give a bit to get on a bed again between clean sheets. ...

[Cambrin]
27th May, 1915

... I was walking with the Colonel [Chambers] this evening and we met General Barter who is GOC 47th London Division.[38] He seemed very happy and he said that the attack of the London Infantry was a great success. I am so glad, as it is splendid to think they have really done something on their own. The Territorials are doing splendidly, which of course bucks us up very much. ...

....

36   The Battle of Aubers Ridge, 9th – 10th May 1915. Haig's First Army attacked either side of Neuve Chapelle in an effort to secure the ridge. Because of a lack of ammunition the preliminary bombardment was not heavy enough. The Germans were able to emerge unscathed from their dug outs to man their trenches and inflict 11,000 casualties on the BEF. British gains were negligible.

37   The Battle of Festubert had opened on 15th May. The 47th Division took part from the 24th until the end of the battle on the 27th. First Army incurred 16,000 casualties for a maximum advance of 1,300 yards.

38   Maj Gen Sir Charles St Leger Barter, KCB, CVO, commanded the 47th (London) Division Aug. 1914 to 29th Sept. 1916. He was commissioned into the army in 1875 and saw active service in several late 19th century campaigns and was wounded in South Africa. He was an instructor at Sandhurst (1884-86) and was CO of the 2nd Battalion Kings Own Yorkshire Light Infantry. He completed four years as GOC Poona Brigade in India in June 1913. He had a reputation as a ladies' man and spoke fluent French.

[Noyelles-les-Vermelles]
2nd June, 1915

... I have quite a good bit of shell which I will try and get off to you. It is a bit of one that fell close to our old house and will give you a good idea of what a high explosive shell does. The things gongs are made out of are the cartridge cases of our 18 pound shell, also the French 75 mm gun. It makes us pretty sick to hear Kitchener's Artillery coming out with the 18 pound gun, as in practice of course it will put them before us as their equipment is more efficient[39]. I'm afraid in my unpatriotic self I sometimes almost wish that the men would prove less efficient.

There's no doubt they have been given all the chances possible, and they ought to be good. The French seem to have done well in getting Souchez and it should make a difference.[40]

[Ames]
9th June, 1915

... I am most interested to hear about Toby and Marjorie, but not altogether surprised. Ought I to write and congratulate or shall I know nothing about it? I would so like to have a talk to you about it; it seems so strange to think of Toby engaged. I should think Marjorie will do him rather well, though I have never felt very impressed with her. It must be very amusing to see them going about together. ...

[Ames]
13th June, 1915

... We have all had a beastly disappointment. We had every good reason to believe that as we were resting we would get a few days' leave. However, for some unknown reason, it has not been approved of. I think it is a bit hard as there is nothing to do here and everybody is getting a bit sick of this monotonous existence. We used to think it dull at Bovingdon, but it's nothing to this; it's so dull never being able to speak to anyone who isn't a soldier, and also of course we never get a day off even. Heaven only knows how long we shall be here. ...

[Ames]
17th June, 1915

... I have had a letter from Toby – he seems very happy. Are there any prospects of Toby's Division coming out yet? He has said nothing about it in his letter. We have orders just now to be ready to move at an hour's notice. It would be upsetting except that we are now so used to being kicked out and pushed about without warning. One can hardly realize what a business a move in England was, but of course here the men are all billeted in barns together and they don't all have to have a single bed each. The 19th Battery are coming down here tonight so I'll see something of them for a bit. ...

....

39 At this time the 47th Division RFA was still equipped with the obsolete 15 pounder guns. It was re-equipped with 18 pounders in Nov. 1915.

40 The French Artois Offensive launched on 9th May 1915 captured the Lorette Ridge and also the village of Souchez at the foot of the northern end of Vimy Ridge.

[Lapugnoy]
27th June, 1915

An application for a week's leave has gone in for me today and as you can imagine I am fairly keen for it to go through. This, however, is doubtful and I am not looking on it as a certainty, and you mustn't be surprised if it fails. Pixley has applied too, so if his goes through we will travel together.[41] We have asked to go next Thursday, 1st July. Pixley has asked some friend to lend us a car to Boulogne. If this succeeds, we arrive in London the same day about nine o'clock...

I believe Marjorie will be with you at Bramshott. It is so hopeless trying to fix up anything when I don't know when I will arrive, and also I feel so uncertain if I will get home at all. ... I must also see Guy and Toby. ...

[Lapugnoy]
30th June, 1915

I have had no reply yet to my application for leave so I shall take it that I'm not getting it, and you must too unless I turn up before this letter reaches you. I can't tell you what a disappointment it will be to me if I don't get it. ...

[Lapugnoy]
1st July, 1915

Gott strafe that d----d Staff!!! They have been and sat on my leave. They have made a ridiculous order that only one officer from each Brigade shall be on leave at the same time. This probably means that I shall not get home before October. I can't tell you how disappointed I am, though I'm beginning to feel resigned to it. Today has really been rather a joke for those not concerned. At 12 o'clock our car duly turned up. As our leave had not come to us Pixley and I decided to try and go to it. We first of all motored to Béthune, where we telephoned our Divisional Artillery Staff. They told us they had forwarded our leaves and we could get them from the Divisional Staff. We set off with great expectations and I boldly went in to Divisional HQ, hoping to see old Foot.[42] Unfortunately he is on leave. I saw his understudy who gave me the sad news with which I started this letter. You can guess there has been some hate against the Staff – d--n them. We tried to overcome our sorrow by having the best luncheon that Béthune could produce. ...

Philip did, after all, get a week's leave in the first half of July.

[Grenay]
14th July, 1915

What a glorious week we have had; and I wouldn't have missed it for anything and I don't think we could have used it better. I enjoyed every minute. We had quite

....

41   Stewart Edward Hewett Pixley was an Old Etonian and a bullion broker in the family firm of Pixley & Abell in the City of London. He was commissioned into the 7th London Brigade RFA on 5th Aug. 1914 and finished the war as a Major. (TNA WO 374/54359) Philip Pilditch described him as "a quiet charming fellow with a very sound knowledge of gunnery." (Pilditch diary, p. 26)

42   Lt Col R. M. Foot, Royal Inniskilling Fusiliers, was a staff officer (AA and QMG) in the 47th Division until 7th Feb. 1916 when he took the same role in the 62nd Division. *The History of the 47th Division* fondly recalls (p. 5) that he 'had a passion for paper' and that 'he loved to have everything done decently and in order and in quadruplicate'. On 3rd Nov. 1917 he was promoted to Brigadier General and took the role of DA and QMG in II Corps. He was awarded the CMG.

an uneventful journey. What a splendid send-off we had. The sea was perfect. We went across on a very small paddle-steamer, absolutely packed. The train on this side was very slow. Got to Béthune about eight o'clock. ...

The Brigade has moved and the batteries are in action again. ... I believe we are in quite a decent spot and it's a relief to be doing something again. ...

[Grenay]
28th July, 1915

... A Kitchener Division is coming in.[43] They are a fine lot and full of self-confidence, but they are already I think treating the Boche with a little more respect than they did at first, and it is wise on the whole to do so.

I am glad Toby has had some leave. I'm sure he will have made the best of it. How horribly critical things are in Russia: I am afraid a great deal depends on the result of the great battle now proceeding.[44] Some people seem to think a winter campaign may be saved if the Russians can save Warsaw and beat the Germans, but I am afraid we are stuck here for a good while yet. ...

[Gosnay]
10th August, 1915

... We seem to have had a small success at Hooge, but that is miles from us.[45] We are on the extreme right of the British line, or were before we came out to rest. ...

We had our Sports yesterday, and on the whole it was quite a successful afternoon. We were honoured for a short time by Sir Douglas Haig.[46] ...

Your "canteening" sounds rather strenuous, at least from a travelling point of view, but I suppose to do anything like that is not very possible in Bovingdon! ...

[Lozinghem]
26th August, 1915

... I hope for your sake and for Toby's that those last few days won't be such a ghastly rush as ours were. I don't think it is possible – I expect on the whole they will be all glad to get out – they must be sick of training – and after all to come out here is what everybody joined for. I only hope they will come to France and somewhere near us. Will you let me know the number of his Division? I was awfully interested in all Guy's news. ...

....

43   Philip Pilditch identified them as the 15th (Scottish) Division: "The men, especially the infantry ... look a very good lot. The artillery are armed with 18 pdrs. It is no good complaining but it does seem ridiculous that while hundreds of these guns have been used in England for the last six months for training (probably under quite archaic, pre-war conditions) we might have been using them here on the Germans, and saving Lord knows how many of out infantry's lives." (Pilditch diary p. 135)

44   The Gorlice-Tarnow Offensive of May 1915 by the Central Powers led to the expulsion of Russia from Russian Poland by mid-1915. The Eastern Front was pushed hundreds of miles into Russia, removing the threat of a Russian invasion of the Central Powers.

45   The German flamethrower attack of 30th/31st July captured a small part of the British front line near Hooge in the Ypres Salient. All the ground lost was recaptured by the 6th Division on 9th August.

46   The Brigade war diary for 9th Aug. records, "Brigade sports on racecourse at Hesdigneul. General Sir Douglas Haig and General Rawlinson attended." (TNA WO 95/2717) Haig recorded in his diary: "After lunch I attended some sports of the artillery of the 47th Division and saw some artillery driving competitions. They really did very well. ... All seemed cheery and happy." (TNA WO 256/5)

[Lozinghem]
30th August, 1915

... How strange it is to think Toby is now in France. I wonder whereabouts he is. I expect being engaged didn't make it easier for him going off. I am glad he's come to France and not to the Dardanelles. ...

[Bois des Dames, near Marles-les-Mines]
2nd September, 1915

... I've had a letter from Toby but apparently they censor their officers' letters, so he told me absolutely no details about their journey or anything. Do tell me anything you can about him. I have no idea where he is. ...

[Bois des Dames]
9th September, 1915

... We are still in our stubble field bivouac, a place of great safety. We are just within earshot of the guns. The last few days have been glorious and it has really been quite a joy living in the open and all the mud has dried up.

I can't hear any mention at all of Toby's Division, so it doesn't look as if he can be anywhere in these parts. ... Toby's surroundings did not sound up to much. It sounded rather unnecessarily uncomfortable, but of course everywhere is hopelessly overcrowded. I think they really should clear out all the civilians as the villages are packed with them – mostly refugees. ...

I had a letter from Guy telling me about his machine guns. I think he is rather lucky to get sent on the course, as I should think they are much the most interesting thing to do in the infantry; and leave every weekend doesn't seem so bad. ...

[Bois des Dames]
12th September, 1915

... I had a letter from Toby yesterday. He is unfortunately just too far for me to ride and see him but I expect we will meet sometime later on. ...

The Zeppelins seem to be having the time of their lives over London. Everybody seems to have seen them. I'm afraid there must have been a great many casualties. The worst thing about it is that we seem quite unable to retaliate in any way. ...

[Bois des Dames]
19th September, 1915

... I think the waste and extravagance is in every way a scandal; the fact of our spending £5,000,000 a day could have been reduced by a half if they had conscription instead of bribing men into the Army. ...

[Haillicourt]
24th September, 1915

Just a line to let you know we are all well. There is no news that I can tell you, but it looks as if things are going to hum a bit, so it's possible the mails may be irregular. It's sickening I can't tell you anything. ...

15 pounder gun of the 19th County of London Battery RFA in a covered position near Maroc, autumn 1915. The officer is probably Lt R. E. Burgess who is known to have served with the battery at that time. (Photo courtesy of Stuart Arrowsmith)

The British attack on 25th September was the Battle of Loos. Of the two Corps taking part, the one in the south of the line was IV Corps, commanded by Lt Gen Sir Henry Rawlinson. His three Divisions in the attack included the 47th (London) Division which was on the right flank adjacent to the French Army. The landscape is fairly flat, though dotted with coalfields and slag-heaps. Initial optimism that the attack might lead to a breakthrough was not fulfilled because of inadequate artillery support and an unfavourable wind direction which did not assist the British use of gas. Other factors were the reserve divisions being held too far back and insufficient cooperation with the French forces.

Philip to his mother [Les Brébis]
27th September, 1915

At last I can write a sensible sort of letter. The battle began on Saturday: you will no doubt have seen this in the papers. Thanks to our old [15 pdr] guns, the Artillery of this Division has been left out except for one Brigade and a few other guns. We were in reserve on Saturday morning, seven miles back, not even knowing that they had begun. ... We got orders to move up on Saturday afternoon. We had an awful march: it rained all the time and the roads were crowded and blocked with various Kitchener ammunition columns. The result was we didn't reach our destination till about seven o'clock. The wretched men had to doss down in a stubble field, poor devils. We managed to find an *estaminet*. However, they didn't leave me in peace. Just after we had finished a meal an order came in for me to go up to the Infantry as FOO. I had to find the 1/20th London Battalion who had made the attack and were holding the front line there. It sounded a pretty fine job, but the anticipation was the worst part. It was a beautiful moonlight night. It was very weird walking down the road to the trenches where, the day before, it would be fatal to show your head. I had a telephonist with me. The road went right through the English trenches, across "no man's land" and through the German trenches.

The RAMC were hard at it fetching in the wounded. As long as I was on the roads I was all right as I had a map, but after a bit it was obviously wise to get into a trench and then we began to lose our bearings. However, I eventually found the Infantry HQ at about 12.30. They were settled in, in the cellar of a house quite close up to the Front – and beastly cold and uncomfortable it was as I only had a mackintosh with me. I came across three wounded men on my way up – I could not do anything for them myself, so I reported them to the RAMC. There was a beastly row all night and we got no sleep. All Sunday the shelling was incessant and being where we were we heard the German as well as our own, so that with a few machine guns going the noise was pretty awful. The house we were in was on the south side of Loos on the slopes of Hill 70, and as the Germans were above us on the hill you can imagine there was some sniping. We had a more or less uneventful day – our infantry were not intended to advance further and they held on splendidly. Our fear was that, being in an advanced position, we might be put in an awkward place if the people on our left retreated. We had our first scare about 8 o'clock in the morning when we saw a certain battalion, not Territorial, come legging it back down the hill. We thought at least the Boche were after them. However, the Colonel of my battalion went out with his Sergeant Major and stopped them and reorganized them.[47] We afterwards found that there was no reason for their leaving the trenches. I suppose they got in a panic. I was beastly sorry for the men – they had been badly led in an attack the evening before and it was the first time they had been to the Front. After this we all got cheerful and optimistic again, but about 2.30 we got a message to say that the people on our left could not hold on and were retiring. It sounded inconceivable but we soon realized it was true for we could see them coming back in lines.[48] It seemed as if the London Infantry would have to retire and then, just to cheer things up, a Kitchener battery started to shoot at us and just over us, thinking there were Germans where we were. ... Quite unexpectedly I was relieved and set out for home. ... My telephonist, who stayed up after me, came back with hair-raising stories of German charging and all that, but I think he imagined a good bit. I have heard this morning that the London Division are holding their old line on the hill and that some dismounted cavalry regained most of the ground lost by the Division on our left.[49] At any rate, I was not sorry to leave. The London Division again did splendidly. The Battalion I was with were a most awfully good lot. Although they had had no sleep for two nights and had suffered heavily, they were quite cheerful and game. They are the Blackheath [and Woolwich] Battalion.

....

47 These were almost certainly men from a unit of the 21st Division which had moved into the line on the left flank of the 47th Division overnight on 25th/26th Sept. The British *Official History* (p. 314) records that during that morning 'survivors of two companies of the 8th East Yorkshires and stragglers collected by the 1/20th London continued to hold a position astride the Loos Crassier in touch with the left of the 47th Division south of Loos.'

48 This is probably the retirement of the 21st Division which had been rushed into an attack on the German Second Line at Hill 70 at 11.00 am on 26th Sept. During the course of that afternoon units of the 21st Division withdrew in some disarray. There is disagreement in accounts as to whether it was a retirement, a retreat or a rout. This was their first time in action, and the exhausted men had suffered heavy artillery fire, the loss of senior officers and heavy casualties. The British *Official History* (p. 335) describes them as 'sheep without a shepherd' who rallied when given firm leadership.

49 Following the partial evacuation of the Hill 70 trenches, part of the 3rd Cavalry Division, as the only available local reserve, was sent forward on foot to reinforce Loos and the British trenches on the slopes of Hill 70.

I had a beastly walk down again. The German trenches were very shallow and packed with our infantry. In addition there were wounded trying slowly to find their way back. I did not have hardly anything to do myself during all this, it being almost impossible to keep the telephone going, but I saw a good deal – enough to last me a good long time. It has also filled me with admiration for our Infantry. From all accounts we have had a better day today and it is really looking as if we may get a move on. Our Adjutant was sent up to Loos today to look for guns. He has just returned with the news that he has found seven there in addition to any so far reported. ...

I wonder if you have had any news of Toby. ... They are still pushing on here and we hope by now we have got Hill 70 – it is important as it overlooks Lens and also commands our present lines.

[Haillicourt]
30th September, 1915

I'm afraid things here have come to a standstill. We hope it will only be temporary. The French seem to be getting on all right, but I feel somehow the Germans are not so strong in front of them; also I believe the Germans hate us more than the French. There is no doubt this is a fearfully difficult part of the line to get through. There are such an enormous number of straggling villages and so many of these big mines. ... The weather too has been all against us.

I had another beastly night last night. I more or less volunteered for it, so cannot complain. I was sent up to Loos with two limbers to fetch down a couple of German guns. I got there at midnight. It was an extraordinary scene – the place is an absolute ruin, far and away the worst I have seen. It was quite deserted except for straggling parties of infantry and wounded. Everyone seemed lost and no one knew where anybody else was. I found nobody to meet me. I waited and waited till after 3 o'clock. I then began to get anxious as it was necessary for me to get back by dark as, if it were light, I would have to have gone in full view of the Germans – with obvious results. I had fortunately found out where the Infantry headquarters were, so about 3.30 I went up there to see if they knew anything. Luckily they had just received an order for me to go home, which I did feeling very disappointed and cross. When I got back I found that the 1st Division had taken the guns before us, although our Infantry had captured them. Then the officer who was getting them out went home by a different road from the one I went in by and, to cap everything, the telephone was broken down. That was how we were kept hanging about all that time. I have got no trophies out of Loos – my memory will do for a souvenir all of my life. I am glad to have seen it all, but I'm not anxious to go again.

[Labeuvriere]
4th October, 1915

... I expect you will have had my second letter telling you of my trip to Loos. It was one of the creepiest experiences I have had. It was so absolutely silent as far as human beings went, except for parties of infantry who all seemed lost. The London Division were relieved on Thursday and our Infantry needed it as they had been in the trenches since Friday 24th September. Although up till now they have not appeared in any accounts in the papers, they did splendidly. On the Saturday they made the attack on the right, and although the papers seem to think the new Army

Division on our left took Loos, they only took half of it, as our own 141st Brigade took the south part of Loos. They pushed on and held the right flank of the advance from our original line in front of Marles-les-Mines to a point east of Loos on the slopes of Hill 70. On the Saturday the two other Divisions did splendidly too. It was however on the 26th that the London Infantry especially distinguished themselves in spite of the fact that the Division on their left could plainly be seen withdrawing back. They held on most wonderfully and absolutely saved the position: it is absolutely certain if the London Infantry had not stood their ground as they did we should have had to give up Loos and everything would have been wasted. It makes us feel pretty sick that our Infantry are given no credit for all they have done. Gen French's dispatches will be interesting to see how much of the truth they tell. ...

I'm afraid there's no chance of leave for ages. I wish there was: we're all sick of France. I'm feeling especially so as I've just had my field glasses stolen. It's pretty sickening to be treated like this, but these French people would do anything for a franc. It isn't so much the expense I mind but the difficulty of replacing them. For artillery work it is useless unless they are absolutely the best. ...

[Philosophe]
21st October, 1915

... We are still worrying the Boche on this front. We had a wonderful sight two nights ago. Just after dark the Huns got out of their trenches to attack just north of us. All the guns were turned on to him and there was Hell for a bit, and I am glad to say they got it in the neck. It was priceless to see guns blazing away all around. ...

[Vermelles]
3rd November, 1915

I'm so glad you've had good news from Toby. Your description of his surroundings really sounds quite comfortable. I shall make a serious effort to see him when we go out to rest. I expect his Division will be out at the same time as we are. ... If you go and see the guns at Whitehall, would you make a note of who captured all the guns that were taken at Loos and let me know, as it would be interesting.[50] ...

[Vermelles]
HQ 7th London Brigade
[5th November, 1915]

... These old Germans have been funny today. While we were at lunch we heard a big explosion and all the windows shook. We went out afterwards and found that a huge shell had fallen about ¼ mile away. It was the biggest hole I have ever seen, about 12 ft deep and 30 ft across. It must have come at least 17 miles. ...

[Vermelles]
14th November, 1915

... I was so interested to hear that you had been to see the guns. It is good to know they will never shoot at us again. I'm so glad to hear Guy is getting on well. ...

....

50 Guns and trench mortars captured at Loos were displayed at Horse Guards Parade for several weeks. Each piece had a notice saying which unit had captured it.

Chapter 5

Charles Fair

Charles Fair was born in the summer of 1885 at Bexley in Kent, where his father, Robert, was a parish priest. Charles was his father's first child but his mother's seventh. She, Frances, was the widow of the Venerable Edmund Fisher, Archdeacon of Southwark.

The Rev Robert Fair had been born in South Africa where he attended school. He came over to England in the 1870s to take a place at Peterhouse, Cambridge, where he studied Theology and, in due course, took Holy Orders. One post he accepted was that of Sub-Warden to Archdeacon Fisher at Kennington, South London, where the vicarage overlooked The Oval cricket ground. Robert was a good friend to all the six Fisher children. His friendship towards Frances Fisher developed into something stronger: a feeling which she reciprocated. Robert did the only thing a man in his position could do – he returned to South Africa. However, Edmund Fisher died in 1879, whereupon Robert wooed his widow by letter from South Africa. Frances accepted his offer of marriage, so Robert returned to England and the couple were married in St John's Wood in the autumn of 1884. To take on a widow with six children on a clergyman's stipend would barely have been possible had not Frances had private means.

In 1892 the family, augmented now by Charles's sister Helen, moved to Hampshire to the tranquil setting of the parish of East and West Wellow. Charles was sent to

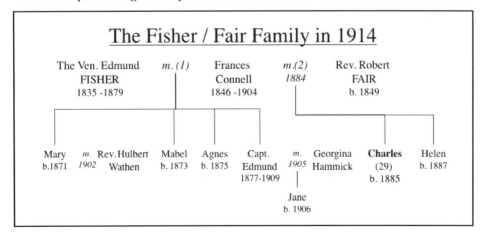

The Fisher / Fair Family in 1914

| The Ven. Edmund FISHER 1835 -1879 | m. (1) | Frances Connell 1846 -1904 | m.(2) 1884 | Rev. Robert FAIR b. 1849 |

| Mary b.1871 | m. 1902 Rev. Hulbert Wathen | Mabel b. 1873 | Agnes b. 1875 | Capt. Edmund 1877-1909 | m. 1905 | Georgina Hammick | **Charles** (29) b. 1885 | Helen b. 1887 |

Jane
b. 1906

Connaught House, a preparatory school in Weymouth, followed in 1899 by a move to Marlborough College, Wiltshire; a school founded in 1843 for sons of the clergy. In the same year the whole family moved from Wellow to West Meon, a village lying to the east of Winchester. The rectory there was large, as was the garden and the combined family of Fishers and Fairs lived in some comfort with indoor and outdoor domestic staff.

The Rectory at West Meon

Charles had a distinguished career at Marlborough where he excelled at the classics, though mathematics was a weak point. He had no less than three years on the College Rugby XV: he was a tall lad of six feet and could move with some speed. He also played on the Cricket and Hockey XIs. Charles, who adored singing, was an enthusiastic member of the choir. Life in the Chapel meant a great deal to him. He would sing in any concert that was organised, whether of the more serious or light-hearted kind. A fellow chorister, though some years younger, was Humphrey Secretan.

When Charles left Marlborough in 1904 to go to Pembroke College, Cambridge, on a Classical Exhibition, it seemed on the face of it to be a really happy life. But two of the Fisher girls had died at an early age and his mother, Frances, died the year he went up to Cambridge. This sad event drew Charles particularly close to his father, Robert, to whom he wrote every Sunday: a habit gained from the practice amongst boys away at boarding school.

Charles's days at Cambridge continued much as they had done in the Sixth Form at Marlborough. Classics and history were subjects he loved and he soon found outlets for his other talents. He sang in the College Choir and played games with his customary vigour. In his last year at Cambridge he captained an outstanding

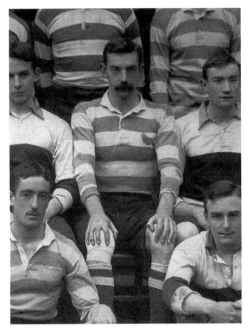

Charles Fair as Captain of the Pembroke College 1st XV rugby team

Pembroke rugby side. Whilst at university Charles decided that life as a schoolmaster would appeal to him. He had two spells teaching at boys' preparatory schools – first at Burnham in Somerset and then at Broadstairs in Kent. In 1912 he accepted a post at Haileybury College, Hertford, an institution he found particularly congenial. He had rooms in College and dined with the other bachelors who, at that time, outnumbered the married men. Apart from teaching classics, he enjoyed coaching games, even finding time to play some club matches on his own account. As at Marlborough and Cambridge he was a committed member of the Choir in the College Chapel.

Life would have continued in this vein had not the Great War erupted in 1914. When the Germans invaded

Haileybury College, Hertfordshire

Belgium, Charles would have just started his summer holidays but he enlisted, despite no previous military experience, as soon as he could reasonably inform the Headmaster he would not be available for the start of the autumn term. On 10th August Charles joined the Honourable Artillery Company at Armoury House in the City, paying his guinea entrance fee. There is no record as to why he chose that unit, but the HAC headquarters was not too far from Haileybury College and some school and university friends had chosen the same Regiment.

The question arises as to why Charles enlisted quite so soon after war was declared. He certainly did not rush to join the Army in a search for adventure or the quest for glory: that was not his style. Part of the answer must lie in the respect and affection he had for his half brother "Ted", a regular soldier, who had fought in the South African War where he was one of the survivors of the Siege of Ladysmith (2nd November 1899 – 28th February 1900). Captain Edmund Fisher served with The 1st Battalion of the Manchester Regiment and after the Boer War he was used as a model for the Regimental War Memorial which still stands in Queen Anne's Square, Manchester.[51] It is said to be a good likeness of him. Sadly Ted's health was never strong after his experiences in South Africa, and he died in 1909 aged thirty-two leaving a widow, "Gina" and daughter, Jane, aged four.

The Boer War Memorial to The Manchester Regiment in Queen Anne's Square, Manchester for which Charles Fair's half-brother Ted Fisher was the model. The sculptor was William Hamo Thorneycroft (1850-1925) and the memorial was unveiled by General Sir Ian Hamilton on 26th Oct. 1908.

His death was a great loss to the whole family and Charles in particular, being deprived of his only brother. Charles would have been appalled by the German disregard of Belgian neutrality. As a good schoolmaster, the bullying of a small boy by a larger and stronger would have been anathema to him. When Charles died many years later his great friend and Haileybury colleague, Major Roy Tennant, who had served in the same Regiment as Charles (though not in the same Battalion) wrote, "Naturally, he joined up at once, for to him it was the only thing a good citizen could do, although military life and ways seemed to him a more uncomfortable joke than anything else."

Few records remain of Charles's days as a Private in the HAC, although he was promoted to Lance Corporal and a photograph survives which shows him in civilian clothes sitting among a squad on the ground cleaning their rifles. After forty-seven days he was discharged to take an immediate commission in the 2nd Battalion of the 19th London Regiment, which was drawn from the working-class Borough of St Pancras. With hundreds of thousands flocking to enlist, there was an acute shortage of officers to lead the newly raised units. A man of twenty-nine with a Cambridge degree behind him, several years' experience of school mastering and a games player

....

51   Ted Fisher is mentioned in *Ladysmith: The Siege* by Lewis Childs, Leo Cooper, 1999 (see pp. 134-139)

Cleaning rifles at the HAC, Aug. 1914. Charles Fair is seated eighth from the right. His moustache is just visible.

Charles Fair

used to captaining sides, the Army chose wisely. Although he often had doubts as to his fitness to command troops in this new role, he was never to let his men or his country down.

In early October 2/Lt C. H. Fair reported to the 2/19th London Regiment at The White City, where the Battalion was commanded by Lt Col Christie. Amongst other junior officers was 2/Lt R. C. G. Dartford, a young man ten years junior to Charles. Dartford had left Haileybury College only the previous July. He was a skilled violinist, a member of the College Gymnastics VIII and, more importantly, one of only two boys in the Haileybury OTC in 1914 to hold the rank of Cadet Sergeant Major.[52] It must have been a strange situation for a master and former pupil to meet on equal terms so soon after leaving the school environment.

....
52 Richard Gordon Charles Dartford, the son of H. W. Dartford of Lisbon, was born in 1895 and went to Haileybury in 1909.

The Battalion moved to Reigate, Surrey, in February 1915 where some time was spent building trenches on the North Downs, part of the defences of London but also useful practice for the Western Front where trench warfare had become an integral part of the fighting. By the end of March the Battalion was stationed near St Albans, Hertfordshire, followed by moves to Coggeshall and Braintree in Essex. On 27th June they moved to a tented camp in a park on the edge of the village of Hatfield Broad Oak. One advantage to Charles of this location was the relative proximity to Haileybury, where he could escape when off duty to meet up with colleagues and even play the occasional game of cricket. The first of his surviving letters to his father is dated 4th July, though what prompted Robert Fair to start saving them is not known. Throughout the next two years, whether in England or in France, Charles wrote regularly to his father and occasionally to his sisters.

Charles to his father Robert   2/19th Battalion London Regt
                                                                       Hatfield Broad Oak
                                                                                      Harlow.
                                                                               4th July, 1915

Dear Dad,
    ... We are all fairly comfortable here and so far I have a tent to myself. It is a nice park with plenty of trees, but not very much air. The whole Brigade is here so there isn't very much room. ...
    Love to all,
    Your loving
    Charles H. Fair

                                                                2/19th Battalion London Regt
                                                                                  Middlesex Hut
                                                                                    Bisley Camp
                                                                            4th August, 1915

    I am getting on pretty well. The course lasts till August 20th. Tomorrow we have an exam on mechanism of rifles and care of arms. I'm afraid I shall do pretty badly: mechanism is not much in my line! ...
    The youngest Woodroffe has been killed and Leslie wounded, though not badly. I am awfully sad about them all. They were such a wonderful family.[53] ...
    The air is very refreshing after Hatfield Broad Oak. I am enjoying the change, but some of the work is rather beyond me.
    Love to Helen.
    Your loving C.H.F.

....

53 The three Woodroffe brothers were all members of the same boarding house as Charles Fair at Marlborough, though not all at the same time. They were all in turn appointed "Senior Prefect". The eldest, Leslie, was a particularly close friend of Charles and also became a schoolmaster – at Shrewsbury. Lt Kenneth Herbert Clayton Woodroffe, 6th Battalion Rifle Brigade, attached to the 1st Welsh Regiment, had been killed in action at Neuve Chapelle on 9th May 1915, aged 23. He was Mentioned in Dispatches and is commemorated on the Le Touret Memorial to the Missing.

St Albans
Herts.
8th August, 1915

... I got through the *viva voce* exam on mechanism and care of arms all right. I was almost too frightened to speak when I first got into the room! I have another exam on Wednesday and three more (one written) before the end of the course. ... They are a nice set of men at Bisley and the instructors are mostly gentlemen who are good shots and have been given sergeants' rank for the purpose of the school.

Woolacombe (on leave)
22nd August, 1915

... I got through the final exam all right and on the whole result was classed as a first-class instructor, which I hope will satisfy the Colonel. I go back to HBO [Hatfield Broad Oak] on Tuesday evening unless summoned back before. ...

2/19th Battalion London Regt
Hatfield Broad Oak
Harlow, Essex
29th August, 1915

... As a result of Bisley I now find myself acting as Brigade Musketry Officer, which is of course a species of staff job, though it doesn't bring in any extra pay nor entail the wearing of a red hat. I don't know how long the authorities will let me hold the post without finding out how very little I know about the subject. Meanwhile it is rather pleasant. ...

Hatfield Broad Oak
3rd September, 1915

... I gave a lecture on Thursday to most of the subalterns in the Brigade, standing under a yew tree just outside the churchyard. Of course as long as I hold this job I am not likely to go abroad until or unless the whole Brigade goes: I don't suppose you will grumble at that. ...

Hatfield Broad Oak
12th September, 1915

... On Tuesday I motored to Bishop's Stortford with the Colonel to a very interesting lecture by a Colonel back from the front. We have had the zeppelins right over the camp three times but I only woke up once and then there was too much mist to see them.[54] Last night they were reported to be quite visible. On Friday I was sent over to the Mimms Musketry Camp near St Albans, as we are sending 250 men there tomorrow for shooting. ...

I was awfully pleased about "Boodles" Woodroffe's VC.[55] It will be a great

....

54 These are the raids on the nights of 7th/8th and 8th/9th September that Marjorie Secretan refers to in her letters (see footnotes 85, 87 and 88 in Chapter 7).

55 2/Lt Sidney Clayton Woodroffe, 8th Battalion Rifle Brigade, was killed in action at Hooge, aged 19, on 30th July 1915. He is commemorated on the Menin Gate. His death prompted Charles Hamilton Sorley, a Marlborough contemporary of Sidney, to write a poem in his honour. (See Appendix I).

help to them all. ... I'm afraid nothing more has been heard of Reid.[56] Yesterday
I actually played cricket for the Brigade against another Brigade. They won by
three runs. I only made one but my hands showed their old cunning in the slips. It
was great fun. ...

The Musketry Camp
Colney Heath
18th September, 1915

... Our hours for shooting are rather restricted as the farmers in the danger area
are getting up a second crop of hay, and so we are to shoot all day on Sunday to
make up. I shall try to get ... to evening service at the Abbey [St. Albans], but that
is at 5.30 p.m. now because of Zeps! The camp itself is very pleasant and pretty
and we are getting on pretty well as regards food. It has been very hot by day and
generally cold by night. We have *reveillé* at 5.30 and breakfast as 6.30 so that most
of our work is over by about 2.00. ...

Hatfield Broad Oak
4th October, 1915

... Yesterday, after church parade, I biked over to Haileybury. It was a lovely day
and the place was looking wonderful. I saw everybody, I think. ... A great many
officers in the 1/19th [57] have been hit. ... They had really the post of honour, as
"Tower Bridge"[58] was their objective.

Tomorrow we go on a four days' trek into Essex, sleeping anywhere, taking our
food with us and returning here on Saturday morning. ...

Hatfield Broad Oak
10th October, 1915

... Yesterday I went to London to see Dartford who was wounded in the face on
September 25th. He is getting on all right and was walking about ... .

(October 13th or 15th)

Just off to S. Walden to make billeting arrangements for the Battalion. Address
for the present: 2/19th London Regt, Rose & Crown Hotel, Saffron Walden. I have
never done anything of this kind before: expect I shall make an awful mess of it!

There followed a telegram from Saffron Walden to West Meon:

15th October, 1915
Probably going abroad very shortly.
Will wire arrangements later today
Fair

....

56   Charles's Haileybury colleague, Capt Charles John Reid, 9th Battalion, The Royal Warwickshire Regiment,
was killed in action on 10th Aug. 1915 at Sari Bair on Gallipoli. He was 41, an Old Haileyburian, and had been a
housemaster for ten years. Another colleague, Lt George Edward Grundy, an assistant housemaster, had served
in the same battalion as Reid and had been killed on 22nd July 1915. Both masters are commemorated on the
Helles Memorial to the Missing.

57   The 1st/19th London Regiment were part of the 47th (London) Division attack at Loos.

58   The nickname for the pit-head winding gear at Loos.

Charles to his father

Rose and Crown Hotel
Saffron Walden, Essex
16th October, 1915

It's a bit of a shock, isn't it, but I don't complain, though everyone thought I had got a job which would keep me with the Brigade. But it is the first time they have asked for captains, and two – Stokes[59] and myself – with two subalterns are going from our Battalion. ...

I shall come to West Meon on Tuesday evening as I can get to Southampton so easily from there. I have to be medically inspected tomorrow by our doctor.

Though I dislike the prospect naturally, there is a certain amount of relief in feeling that one has at last done the whole thing: to be still in England after fourteen months at war is beginning to seem almost a disgrace. I shall see you all either in London, at home, or both.

Love to all, ...

Charles was being posted from the 2/19th Battalion of the London Regiment to its sister battalion, the 1st/19th Londons. The 1/19th was part of 141st Infantry Brigade in the 47th (London) Division and had been serving in France since March.

Charles Fair's letter from RMSS Normannia – Oct. 1915

RMSS "Normannia"[60]
30th October, 1915
10.00 a.m.

We are getting on all right. The boat didn't leave till 6.00 this morning 'though they made us be on board by 12.00 last night. ... We shall reach Havre about 1.00 p.m. ... We had a cabin between the two of us and slept pretty well. The Isle of Wight looked lovely at 7.00 this morning.

No. 11 Base Camp
Havre
31st October, 1915

I hope you got the letter which I wrote on the boat. ... We are at present at our Divisional Base Camp waiting for orders about going up country. We are in huts and quite comfortable. Today I am writing from an hotel at

....

59 James Gordon Stokes was promoted to Captain in the 2/19th Londons on 5th August 1914. In the course of his career he would be awarded the MC (gazetted 19th May 1916) and DSO (gazetted 2nd July 1917) and as acting Lt Col commanded the 1/19th Londons in late 1917 and early 1918.

60 The RMSS Normannia was built in 1911 and survived the Great War but was sunk on 29th May 1940 when taking part in the evacuation from Dunkirk.

Honfleur whither we have come in an excursion steamer to visit the people with whom Stokes used to live while learning French. ... There are amazing uniforms to be seen in all the streets and I expect we have saluted some French sergeants from fear of omitting to salute a General. I helped censor some letters this morning and they were very amusing.

Havre
1st November, 1915

... We had a very pleasant time at Honfleur. Stokes' friends were quite nice people and came down in a body to see us off. We also visited the museum there and a church built by our Henry VI in which are some stone cannon balls fired into the place by the English. This morning we went to some lectures on various trench matters and this afternoon are going into Havre again after tea for a little final shopping.

[Mazingarbe]
5th November, 1915

Arrived at Battalion Headquarters today. ... We go up to the trenches tomorrow – only in reserve, I believe. I keep my Captain's rank. Will write from there if possible. Everyone here very cheerful.

Chapter 6

Philip and Charles with the 47th Division – Winter in the Loos Salient

November 1915 to March 1916

Charles's arrival at the 1/19th London Regiment meant that he was now in the same division as Philip Dodgson. There is no evidence to suggest that either man knew of the other at this stage of the war, or indeed that they would meet in the future. However, it is sensible to publish their letters together from this point forward as they would not have been more than a few miles apart and would have been involved in the same major operations.

The day after Charles arrived, the 1/19th Londons moved into support trenches that had previously been the old German front line position for the battle of 25th September.

Charles to his father   ["10th Avenue", north of Loos] In a dugout
Sunday, 7th November, 1915

... We got into the trenches yesterday. I am in charge of the Company so was a bit worried about the routine, as we are very short of officers. However, I am gradually getting the hang of things. Where we are is very quiet at present. I did have a bit of shrapnel whizzing around today but it had been aimed at an aeroplane and therefore was only an occurrence which might happen in London! We have got a rather fine dugout – once belonging to Germans – lined with wood and steel girders across the roof. ... I expect we shall absolutely lose count of time soon. ...

 Please keep me supplied with refills for my electric torch. ... I think a supply of Bovril tablets and chocolate are the chief necessity: also refills for the "Tommy's Cooker"... The general idea seems to be that the Division will have a pretty good rest after another week or so. ... I haven't succeeded in getting much sleep so far, but it doesn't seem to matter.

[Trench B2]
A dugout, 3" deep in water, with 6" of water and mud in the trench outside
12th November, 1915

We are having our fill of trench life! We took four and a half hours to get to this particular spot through a maze of water-logged trenches. It has rained almost without stopping for four days and you simply can't imagine what we look like. We haven't had our clothes off since Friday and haven't washed or shaved since Wednesday. We are supposed to be relieved on Saturday night, but don't know if the relief will reach us. Our food gets through to us all right and yesterday we had bacon and eggs for breakfast, though the Huns are less than two hundred yards away! It is quite exciting when both sides are using artillery for all they are worth. I am glad I know what it is like: it would have been very difficult to have remained in England all the war and then had to face anyone who had been through it. I get plenty of letters so far, which is a great blessing, but when you are in the actual trenches the newspapers don't appear very often: perhaps it would be a good thing if you could arrange for a halfpenny paper, e.g. "The Chronicle," to be sent out regularly. We keep fairly warm with the help of the daily tot of rum! I haven't yet had occasion to put on the carbolic vest, as our first dugout was quite clean and the present one is too wet to be inhabited by anything! ...

[Lillers]
Sunday, 14th November, 1915

Another extraordinary Sunday! We came out of the trenches last night after eight days there. It was wetter than ever – water in places up to our knees and the soil, being chalk, was crumbling away all the time. The relieving forces arrived pretty late [8 p.m.] and eventually we reached the billets [Mazingarbe], where I had originally joined the Regiment, at 1.30 a.m. this morning, after a four hours' trudge (in full equipment) of which one hour was through trenches of running water about two feet deep and the rest was ground riddled with ancient shell-holes. Today we have moved right back several miles from the fighting – for a "rest" of two or three weeks, we believe. I am lucky so far and we had no casualties in my Company. We are having a new Colonel soon – the fifth since mobilisation. ...

The Division had moved back to the Lillers area as reserve division in IV Corps. It was to spend nearly a month in that area for "rest and mild training."[61]

Charles to his sister Agnes   [Raimbert]
16th November, 1915

... I am getting on all right. ... We are now right back from the fighting and I am billeted in a miner's cottage – clean but humble. We had a really bad time in the trenches as regards weather – even the most experienced hands admit that.[62] The final effort was that the relieving regiment arrived at 9.15 p.m. (after being due at 7.00) and we had a four hours' scramble through water-logged trenches in a plain strewn with shell holes until we reached the billets where we originally joined the

....

61 Maude, op cit, p. 42

62 The Divisional History states 'our worst enemy was the weather' with 'perpetual rain' and 'the November soak'. (Maude, op cit, p.40)

Battalion. ... We expect to be here some time, as the Division has had no real rest since their great deeds on 25th Sept. Will you send out another suit of pyjamas, please? They are useful in billets. Gina's slippers are a great gift.[63] The Government provide us with trench waders now. The French cottages are all right, with the exception of the *cabinets*! ...

    PS My sense of humour, like Gina's, has never failed yet.

* * * * *

On 17th November Philip Dodgson was attached to 47th Divisional Signals for a course.[64]

Philip to his mother   [Marles-les-Mines]
19th November, 1915

    ... It is a relief to be out of it for a bit, though it's wonderful how one gets used to the noise. I went on ahead last Monday with the interpreter to arrange billets. Usually this is a beastly job, as there is generally an awful rush and not enough room, but this time it was all right and everybody is very comfortable. ... We have got our billets in the brewery which, as is usually the case, is the best house in the town as in these parts every town has its own brewery.

    ... I have been sent on a fortnight's telephone course, so am not with the Brigade at present. We spend part of the time actually learning to send messages, lay lines etc., and we also have lectures on elementary electricity and instruments. It all interests me very much and is also very useful. ...

    ... I had a letter from Toby. I'm afraid there isn't much chance of my getting to see him as he is so far away and the days are so short.

    I can't think of any other news to tell you. It is not conducive to writing having about half-a-dozen whistling, singing, chattering fellows all together in a not-very-large room.

* * * * *

Charles to his father   [Raimbert]
21st November, 1915

    ... We are leading much the same sort of life here as we should be at Saffron Walden, except of course there is no social side at all and French cottages are very cold as all the sitting rooms have brick floors. The one real excitement is the arrival of the post. I don't think the authorities much like the name of the Division being put on letters, so perhaps you had better leave that out. ... We had quite a nice church parade in an elementary school today. I had charge of the detachment from our Battalion. We are having a new Colonel, ... a Capt. Hamilton of the Queen's is to command us.[65] He is meeting Company Commanders today.

    ... I am going to have a riding lesson this afternoon!

....

63 Gina was the widow of Charles's half-brother Ted Fisher.

64 TNA WO 95/2717

65 Capt Hamilton was a regular soldier who had been commissioned into The Queens Royal West Surrey Regiment in 1905. Prior to taking command of the 1/19th he had been adjutant of the 1/18th Londons (London Irish). Hamilton was later awarded the MC and promoted to Lt Col.

[Raimbert]
28th November, 1915

Thanks for letters, papers and parcels. I think everything has turned up all right. … We are spending our time chiefly in overhauling kit and equipment – a very boring proceeding. … It has become very cold and we are devoutly thankful we are not in the trenches. Our new CO is getting on well but, like everyone else, he is never allowed by higher authorities to carry on any scheme for more than two or three days without having the entire programme upset. To a civilian – especially a scholastic mind – these changes seem all against producing a good result. Perhaps the idea is to get the men so bored with their "rest" that they are glad to seek the comparative repose of the trenches! We had a long talk from Brigadier Thwaites the other day.[66]

He spoke very straight to the young officers and it was very good. He calls a spade a spade and some of them certainly need it. Unfortunately nobody lays themselves out to instruct so-called senior officers like myself! We have to muddle through somehow. …

* * * * *

At the beginning of December Philip heard that he had been promoted to full Lieutenant.

Philip to his mother   [Cauchy-La-Tour]
3rd December, 1915

Very many thanks for your good wishes. It was quite by chance I heard of it myself, as we hardly ever seem to get a paper lately but Marshall was also gazetted the same day, saw it when he was home and told me last night. I am dated back to August, as it was then that the vacancy occurred owing to Marshall being promoted.[67]

I don't believe I have ever written to thank you for the pheasants which arrived safely and were excellent. … I should simply love a turkey for Christmas, if you think there is any chance of its arriving – only a small one, as we will be in action and therefore not much cooking accommodation.

We had a fairly stiff time on our route march. We moved away on Thursday [1st December] … in pouring rain – it cleared later, however, thank goodness. We went about fifteen miles and then billeted, which was some job as we had to get a battalion of infantry, as well as ourselves, into a small village.[68]

....

66   Brig Gen William Thwaites commanded the 141st Infantry Brigade from 2nd June 1915 to 8th July 1916, having served as a GSO with the 47th Division since 1912. He was promoted to Maj Gen and commanded the 46th (North Midland) Division until early Sept. 1918. He was 'a keen disciplinarian and a popular leader' and an enthusiast for trench raids as a way 'to improve the offensive spirit of the men.' (Maj R.E. Priestley, *Breaking the Hindenburg Line*, 1919) In the 47th Division he was known as 'Ginger Pop Thwaites' as he was believed to be from a family that manufactured carbonated soft drinks. (Henry D. Myer, *Soldiering of Sorts: A London Territorial Officer In The First World War*, unpub. manuscript c. 1979)

67   Capt E. H. Marshall had been transferred from the 19th London Battery RFA to command the 18th London Battery RFA on 16th Aug. Philip Pilditch said: "he was a great character and has great personal influence with the men. They'll follow him anywhere." Marshall was promoted to Temporary Major on 17th Aug., and Philip Dodgson promoted to Temporary Lieutenant on 27th Aug.

68   The Brigade went on a route march from Cauchy-La-Tour to the village of Rincq where it billeted on the night of 1st Dec.

It was some crush, as you can imagine. I had the job of doing the billets. We had *reveille* at four o'clock the next morning and got home about four in the afternoon. There were, of course, fearful muddles and congestions, but they were all quite expected and we managed to see the funny side of it. ... We had a most amusing night. We all just dossed down with the men and the numerous orderlies who visited us during the night all took us for Tommies and you can imagine we heard some interesting things about the Army.

... I hope Toby's leave will pan out better than you expect. I also think Marjorie should arrange for Toby to be alone with you a bit but he of course will be torn both ways. I hope to get home soon after Xmas.

* * * * *

Charles Fair had, in fact, been on the same westwards march further into the rear areas of the BEF. It was a divisional route march, which "was said to have been a valuable piece of training for the staff".[69]

Charles to his father ["In the field", Raimbert]
5th December, 1915

... I haven't been able to write during the week as we have been on a "trek" (by way of resting!) rather like the one we had at home. There was a good deal of criticism of many points by higher authorities but on the last morning I was publicly complimented by name by the Brigadier on the general turn-out of my Company, and the Brigade Major[70] told me afterwards that they were, that day, the best looking Company in the Brigade. I had dinner with the Brigadier on Friday and spent quite a cheery evening. ... Did I ever tell you that a month ago we were reviewed by the Lord Mayor of London?[71] ...

[Raimbert]
11th December, 1915

Many thanks for letters. ... I have also received parcels from Mabel. Her periscope travelled safely and ought to be very useful ... . At present there is some doubt as to whether I shall be able to go with the Battalion, as I have a slight poisoning in my left arm (cause unknown) which the doctor has to cut open this morning. I hope it won't keep me away from the Regiment: it would be so undignified! It was, I think, the first time that a surgeon's knife had ever been used upon me. I recently had to make an expedition to an unknown destination with other officers at 3.00 a.m. on a wet morning. We were conveyed in a London motor bus with the advertisements on the inside still surviving. ...

Last Tuesday I did a very bold thing in going "mounted" on a tactical scheme in the presence of various Generals, etc.! Luckily my horse and I agreed on all essential

....

69 It was also described as "the first and last of its kind." (See Maude, op cit, p. 42-43.) Philip's and Charles's letters do imply a certain amount of chaos, but also that logistical lessons were being learned.

70 Maj B. C. Battye RE was a capable staff officer. On 22nd May 1916 during the German attack on Vimy Ridge (see Chapter 8) the right flank of 141st Infantry Brigade was lost and "at great personal risk [he] undertook a close reconnaissance and was able to locate it." He was gazetted with the DSO on 16th June 1916. (Maude, op cit, p. 55) On 30th Apr. 1917 he became acting GSO 1 in 42nd Div and was promoted Lt Col in 1918, serving as GSO 1 with 34th Div from 10th Aug. 1918 onwards.

71 The war diary for 6th Nov. 1915 records "Inspection by Lord Mayor of London (Sir Charles Johnston)". (TNA WO 95/2738)

matters but I was very anxious, especially as it was partly over plough! However, I didn't hear any scathing comments on my horsemanship and there were certainly others there who were not much better. We have had some shooting during the week on a range improvised against a slag heap near one of the mines. The miners showed a disposition to come over the top and run down the sides.

* * * * *

Philip to his mother [Cauchy-La-Tour]
12th December, 1915

... It is sickening that so few of our men get home on leave. Even now under a hundred men from the whole Brigade have been home, and we've got over 600, so it's a bad lookout for some of them. We are going into the line again this week. I go up tomorrow to look for billets. I have been fortunate enough to get a seat in an ambulance, so I am saved a long and boring ride. I can't tell you how sick we are getting of these same old roads and the weather is too awful. You can't imagine the state of the places the wretched horses have to stand on. Isn't it almost inconceivable to you that nothing has been done to provide decent standing for horses? They ought to have learnt last winter, and they have had all the summer. The Staff have as little initiative as it is possible to imagine. ... If only they would come and see the state of things more often for themselves. The thing is that most of them are from the Infantry and have no idea what looking after horses means. They have an idea the only thing necessary is to pour oats down his throat. They forget he wants a drink sometimes ... absolutely no arrangements are made for watering them. I can tell you I'm getting fairly fed up and will be glad of some leave, which I hope to get soon. ....

* * * * *

At the end of the second week of December, the 47th Division took over the northern part of the Loos salient – the Hulluch sector. This included the quarries and the infamous Hohenzollern Redoubt. The 1/19th Londons moved into the front line on 14th December. Charles, however, was not with the Battalion for the first week.

Charles to his father [In hospital]
14th December, 1915

I have been sent to hospital probably for about a week to get my arm right. I don't think it would have been possible to keep it free from dirt in the trenches or billets. It is an awful nuisance as the Battalion are still rather short-handed. ... I was sent here yesterday in a motor ambulance with one of our subs who has got flu. ... I think parcels have some difficulty in reaching hospital. My servant is here with me. He can do what shopping I require. At present he has gone to try and find the Battalion, which is only a few miles away, to get my letters. I am enjoying myself really – having absolutely no responsibility!

[In hospital]
Sunday, 19th December, 1915

... I expect to be discharged to duty tomorrow or Tuesday. The poison is all out of my arm, but the hole caused by having it cut open is not filled up yet. ... We have a fine day at last. I went for a walk this afternoon with two other invalids and we saw an aeroplane being attacked with shrapnel and apparently taking refuge in the moon which was directly behind it! It was a very strange effect.

... In case my Xmas letters are late in arriving I will send love and best wishes to all in this letter. At least we are more use here than that farcical Xmas at The White City![72]

[Sailly Labourse]
21st December, 1915

This is simply love and good wishes to all for Christmas. I don't know where I shall be. If I am with the Regiment, as I expect, we shall probably be in the trenches. Personally, I hope there won't be any attempt at an Xmas truce in our sector: it throws too much responsibility on the Company Commander. I expect it will be forbidden this year. ...

Charles to his sister Helen   [Labourse]
23rd December, 1915

... We shall be near the firing line but not actually in it on Xmas Day. I think we are going to eat heavily tomorrow as far as circumstances permit. We have moved this morning a step nearer the front than where the Battalion was when I rejoined them. I am to sleep in a room tonight, which necessitates going through all the bedrooms of all the civilian inhabitants in order to reach it! It will be cheerful if they get Christmassy tomorrow evening! ...

Charles to his father   [Hohenzollern Redoubt][73]
Christmas Day, 1915 - 8.15 a.m.

... Yesterday we left our billets at dead of night and got into trenches full of mud. I fell head over heels, with Major Hamilton beside me, in the mud in the first five minutes. We really expected something but luckily nothing happened. We are now sitting in a dugout, very muddy, but having had breakfast – a piece of bacon, some dog biscuits (so called), a bit of cold sausage and some jam. Luckily we had my plum pudding on the evening of the 23rd.

[Labourse]
31st December, 1915

Here we are back for a short rest and I have at last received my Xmas parcels. Thank everyone very much for everything. I think the only things which have failed to reach me are some razor blades from Mary. ...

Starting with 2.00 a.m. on Xmas Eve we have really had the most strenuous week, and certainly the most uncomfortable, of my life. We never knew all Xmas Eve whether we shouldn't be called upon to attack somebody somewhere. I spent the night in quite a good wooden dugout with seven other officers including Stokes. We

....

72 From Oct.-Dec. 1914 the 2/19th Londons were based in the White City. On Christmas Day leave was stopped because of renewed fears of invasion. A "rather dreary day" was enlivened by the sounding of the fire-alarm "just before midnight. Very few had ever heard the call before, and not all of them recognized it, but, of course, everyone had to turn out in various stages of *déshabillé*, and hang about until the 'all clear' was given. Whether there was really a fire or not nobody ever knew." (Eames, F. W., *The Second Nineteenth*, p. 7)

73 Charles' description of Christmas Day 1915 in the Hohenzollern Redoubt can be found in Appendix II.

had a fairly cheery breakfast but my Xmas dinner was one slice of bully beef and a bit of cake! After lunch I had to go and reconnoitre the position to be occupied by my Company for the ensuing 48 hours. They were to follow at 6.00 p.m. under a subaltern but the mud in the trenches was so appalling that they did not arrive at their destination until 4.00 a.m., and even then some seven of them were stuck in the mud all night and had to be dug out in the morning! In the trench itself the mud was in many places nearly up to my middle. There I spent three nights with rain practically all the time. Then we had two days further back during which I scribbled you a line – then one more night right in the front, during which we really had a hot time from the Germans. I am glad to say my Company got off very lightly as regards casualties and only one Officer in the Battalion was actually hit.[74] However, all went well in our portion of the line and we are now right out of things for a few days. ...

After three weeks in the Hulluch sector, the 47th Division relieved the French 18th Division in the Loos sector immediately to the south on 4th January.[75]

Charles to his father   [Les Brébis]
                                                                          9th January, 1916

Excuse the paper.[76] A cellar in a mining village, once unknown but now quite well known through the war, does not provide an opportunity of buying any, and my spare store is in my valise some miles back. We have been in the trenches since Thursday. Two days previous to that we spent in cellars just behind and we alternate between the cellars and the front line trenches. There is practically nothing of this village left except the cellars, as both sides have possessed it in turn. It has been finer lately and these particular trenches are quite dry. But they were made by the French and do not come up to our standard of sanitation or soundness, so that a good deal of literal spadework is necessary. The Boche seem thoroughly nervous of us about here and, except for snipers, we never catch a glimpse of them. Occasionally there is some shelling and we have a few casualties. We had a 4.2 shell drop in our trenches without exploding the other night, so I had to go and inspect it and then place a sentry to prevent the inquisitive from handling it. There is a great rumour among the French that the Kaiser is dead: I suppose it is a periodical rumour at the more festive seasons of the year. ... I had to take over some cellar accommodation from the French the other day. They were very casual and simply straggled away by degrees when we came. The CO never bothered to let his subordinates know when he was going and the last party were too sound asleep to go with the rest. ...

....

74 The Battalion spent one week manning the Hohenzollern Redoubt, with the rifle companies rotating between the front line and the support line. Three other ranks were killed and eleven were wounded. Capt S. R. Jackson died of wounds and 2/Lt Driver was wounded. (TNA WO 95/2738)

75 Maude, op cit, p. 45

76 This letter was written on the reverse of two sheets of the 'Messages and Signals' form (Army Form C. 2121) which was used to send messages between subunits and their parent HQ. One sheet is an old message from Charles to Lt Col Hamilton giving the trench strength of 'A' Company.

Charles to Helen   [Les Brébis]
                                                            13th January, 1916

I have time for once to write. I am not sure it is a good thing as we are all feeling pretty fed-up with existence. We have just finished eight days in the trenches and were due for four days' rest, but for some reason our rest consists in hiding in filthy dirty cellars only about four to five hundred yards from the Hun, unable to walk about in daylight, rather short of food, very short in the temper, shorter still in the wind (from lack of exercise) but not short of money, as there is no possibility of spending it! I have only had my clothes off once this year and haven't had a bath since before Xmas! Altogether we're feeling rather ill-used as the men have worked most awfully hard. We took over a line of trenches which had been occupied for many months by the French, and they devote all their energies to actual fighting and neglect all sanitary arrangements, or even make their parapet bullet-proof. We're all feeling very itchy and one of my subalterns has actually got creeping things innumerable. Hitherto I have escaped, but it can't go on much longer.

Charles to his father   [Les Brébis]
                                                            16th January, 1916

… The parcels for my servant and for myself have arrived and also one or two others, for which many thanks. I have at last changed my clothes (for the first time since New Year's Day, I think) and had a bath for the first time since before Xmas. … This is about as unlike a Sunday as any day can be. There has been some heavy shelling of the artillery in our neighbourhood and our signalling officer had a very narrow escape as a man close beside him was killed walking along the road by a stray piece from a "Jack Johnson".[77] We have had more food than we can eat the last 24 hours. That is always the way: when you are in the trenches things, except letters, never reach you, and when you are out they come in a regular deluge. …

Soon after this letter Charles had a week's leave in England.

* * * * *

Philip to Hamilton Fulton, a friend of the family and solicitor in Salisbury:
                                              [Les Brébis] C/235 Bty RFA
                                                            26th January, 1916

My Dear Hamilton,

Thank you so much for your Christmas letter which I have never answered and again for yours which I received yesterday. I am most awfully glad to hear that Mother is well and happy. We are having some splendid weather just now and are able to enjoy it. About ten days ago we had a fall of snow which is still on the ground. … I've got a top-hole billet which is as cold as it is large. This morning when I got up my thermometer in the room registered eight degrees of frost. The air is so dry that one doesn't seem to feel it as much as one would expect, and the last few days have given us a cloudless sky with glorious sun, as one expects at this time of year in Switzerland.

....

77   A "Jack Johnson" was the British nickname given to large calibre (5.9 inch/15 cm or bigger) German shells which exploded with distinctive black smoke. The name derives from the eponymous black American world heavyweight boxing champion who held the title from 1908-15 and whose nickname was 'The Big Smoke'.

My first night in a decent bed with sheets was fine too and brought sweet dreams of home. I'm afraid there is no chance of my meeting George at present. ...

George Fulton

George Fulton was Hamilton's younger son who had been educated at Marlborough College and Brasenose College, Oxford before qualifying as a solicitor in 1910. He was 29 when war broke out and received a commission in 1914. He was gazetted Captain in the 8th (Reserve) Bn of the Wiltshire Regt on 1st March 1915. By 1916 he was with his regiment on the Western Front.

Philip to his mother [Les Brébis]
28th January, 1916
... Things are so interesting out here just now. ... The Boche has been frightfully offensive during the last few days, and it really looks as if he is going to make a push. What everybody wants to know is where it is coming. Wherever he tries I'm sure he'll run his head against it and will get a nasty knock. According to reports he is bombarding from Switzerland to the sea. ...

* * * * *

Charles to his father [Loos]
1st February, 1916
I have arrived all right at the town where our Brigade HQ and our own transport is. I met Capt Ward[78] – our Second-in-Command – on the boat and, such was our zeal to reach the Regiment that we came straight from Boulogne by passenger train, although the real troop train didn't leave till lunch-time today. The Regt have been having a pretty warm time but so far have been lucky and only one officer has been wounded (slightly).[79] ...

....

78 A/Major Bertrand Thomas Ward had served as a private soldier in the Kimberly Rifles in the late 1890s and as a trooper in the Protectorate Regiment during the Siege of Mafeking. Prior to joining the 1/19th Londons he had served with the Royal Sussex Regt and was gazetted captain on 14th Nov. 1914. He was 2 i/c of the 1/19th Londons in early 1916 before Charles Fair held that role. He was gazetted with the MC on 1st Jan. 1919.

79 The Battalion war diary for 31st Jan. recorded that 2/Lt R. E. Richardson was wounded. (TNA WO 95/2738)

Charles to his sister Mabel [Loos]

3rd February, 1916

... We are here in very draughty cellars, slightly verminous I expect! ... Major Hamilton is now on leave at home for ten days and another subaltern has gone home to get married. I had a letter from Leslie Woodroffe yesterday. ... It is very cold here and quite fine and dry. I grudge the time spent practically underground when the sun is really shining.

Charles to his father [Les Brébis]

6th February, 1916

... We are now back about three miles for four nights' rest, which has begun by half my Company being bagged for a working party about four miles away. This is "rest" and on a Sunday, too. ... You will be sorry to hear that my horse has been killed. A shell dropped right into our transport lines – about two miles away from us – and killed one man, wounded eleven and killed twelve horses (at least, some of them had to be destroyed). I shall have to start riding again on another, and probably fiercer, steed. ....

We have had two wonderful instances of red tape lately:
1. During very heavy bombardment a circular calling attention to a paragraph in King's Regulations re. moustaches.
2. At midnight on 4th February I was awoken to receive a weather forecast for 2nd February!

Charles to Helen [Les Brébis]

7th February, 1916

... We are having four days' rest at the moment and so far it has been more restful than usual. I have slept in a bed two nights in succession. I went this afternoon to try and get a bath with the Field Ambulance but they had used up all their hot water. However, we are having our meals off a tablecloth and there are some deck-chairs in this house! ... For about six hours today I was left in command of the Battalion, but luckily nothing much happened to alarm me. We had some pretty heavy shells drop near our last cellars and several men cut themselves shaving because one dropped so close as to jog their elbows!

Charles to his father [The Double Crassier]

10th February, 1916

I am writing from one of the strangest places in the whole line. We are holding one of the numerous slag heaps which abound here.[80] and from it we get a bird's-eye view of all the trenches for miles around. Provided nothing unpleasant happens it is really very interesting but unfortunately I have, at the moment, only one subaltern and he has never been in a front line trench before; consequently I am a bit over-worked and in fact I have only had about one hour's sleep altogether in the last thirty-six hours. Luckily it is pretty fine, though very cold in the early hours of the morning in our alpine neighbourhood. Stokes is on leave at present and Hamilton has not yet come back.

....

80 The "Double Crassier" was the name given to two parallel slag heaps at Loos.

The Double Crassier, Loos

[The Double Crassier]
13th February, 1916

I have just received a parcel of socks, etc., from Agnes. Please thank the donors and makers. They are very welcome, as we are doing a spell of six days right off in a front line trench. My Company has a sort of post of honour and is probably in a unique position as regards the British front. We are in a long trench on the top of a huge slagheap of a coal mine: the other half of the heap is occupied by the genial Hun. Between us and him there is a great gulf fixed, most of which is barbed wire. It is rather a strain as we are short handed both in officers and men. I have a dugout near the foot. At first I only got two hours' sleep during forty-eight hours and that was broken, but last night I managed to get about three straight off. I am writing this on a Sunday morning right on the top of the heap. We are supposed to be having a practice gas alarm and are patiently waiting to be told by headquarters that we are being gassed. I fully expect to be ill when I put the gas helmet on for the first time as the chemical preparation smells appalling. ...

The 47th Division was withdrawn from the front line on 14th – 15th February and went into Corps reserve in the Bruay area where it was to remain for a month. The 1/19th Londons returned to their former billets in the village of Raimbert.

Charles to his brother-in-law Hulbert Wathen [Raimbert]
17th February, 1916

... We have just come out of the trenches altogether for our month's rest, so no one need worry about me for some time to come unless something very extraordinary happens. ... We are at present in the same billets exactly as we were in November. The people seemed delighted to see us and simply hated the Scotch and Welsh regiments which they have had since we were last here. I don't know whether we shall stay here all our month – probably not. ... It poured all the night we came out, and the next morning we set off for here in the heaviest rain I have ever known. We had a four mile march, three-quarters-of-an-hour's wait on a draughty platform, half-an-hour's train journey and then another four miles in a tearing wind. ...

* * * * *

Philip had a week's leave in mid-February.

Philip to his mother Boulogne
18th February, 1916

... When we got to Folkestone on Wednesday [16th] we found the boats would not run but they could give no definite times, so I couldn't go back to London. ... We got a room at the Pavilion Hotel and went to the theatre and saw quite a good show. We had a glorious crossing: it was beautifully sunny and fresh. Strangely enough I met Toby's Adjutant at Folkestone and crossed over with him. It was sickening I didn't see Toby. They wouldn't let me on to the pier to meet the boat and of course he had to get straight into the train. He certainly scored by being hung up at Boulogne as he must have got to London for lunch. ...

* * * * *

Charles to Helen [Raimbert]
19th February, 1916

Many happy returns of your birthday. I have asked Dad to see about your present. You have probably heard that we have got safely back for our month's rest and are occupying exactly the same billets as before. We have started some riding lessons before breakfast every morning. I hope they will prove really profitable. My new horse is much more active than Silvertail and I don't think he knows what to make of me yet! It is nice to sleep in beds again and I got a bath yesterday for the first time since I left England. But there is always an awful lot of worry in rest. Men are continually going on courses and I hardly get any of my Company on parade, though I have to be responsible for all their grocery and haberdashery. It destroys all interest in the men when you never really see them. We are going to entertain the Sergeants to dinner next week, so I shall probably have to try and sing some of our old Poppy Songs if I can get anyone to play the accompaniments.

Charles to his father [Raimbert]
20th February, 1916

I hope you got letters from me saying we are back from the firing line for at any rate a month. Last night some Zep bombs were dropped on the nearest large town.

81

... We had a church parade this morning – the first since we left here. If anyone is sending out a parcel we should like a cake occasionally and also some marmalade: both are very hard to get here and Army rations almost always produce plum jam. The "Daily Chronicle" has entirely given up publishing any names in the casualty list which is a great nuisance: I suppose it is for economy in paper.

Charles to Agnes [Raimbert]
26th February, 1916

The parcels (two) arrived safely from Fortnum and Mason. Many thanks for them. The contents are disappearing fast. We have snow everywhere and are very thankful to be out of the trenches. They must be perfectly ghastly now and will be worse when the thaw comes.

Charles to his father [Raimbert]
27th February, 1916

... It really seems as if the great German movement has begun at last.[81] I think they find the French easier to attack at first than we are. The French always need something very definite to go for. Our riding lessons came to an abrupt end, but I hope they will begin again soon. Meanwhile you would be amused to see me clanking about in spurs! It is lucky I got my leave as the operations against Verdun have resulted in all leave being stopped as far as we are concerned. Yesterday we went for a route march in the snow and two aeroplanes descended quite close to us. ... A French spy was shot here a month ago: he was a prisoner in Germany but was allowed to come home as being permanently unfit, whereas he was no worse than most others. We have bought two deck-chairs for our Company mess. ... On Tuesday we had a dinner for all the Sergeants in the Battalion. It was quite amusing and very reminiscent of choir suppers.

* * * * *

Philip to his mother [Quality Street]
3rd March, 1916

... The 18th Battery were unfortunate yesterday having a gun hit, three men being killed and two wounded. The sickening thing was that the Germans had shelled the battery really badly with heavy shells on several occasions and had done no harm, but yesterday they just sent over one small shell which did all the damage. I was glad to hear that the men were all killed outright.[82] However, on the whole we've been fearfully lucky. Isn't it extraordinary to think it's just on a year since we first left England. Everything remains so fresh in one's memory. ....

....

81 The German offensive at Verdun had opened on 21st Feb.

82 According to Philip Pilditch (p. 222) a shell exploded in the gun pit of B subsection, 18th Battery in Quality Street, killing 'Sgt Raynor [sic] and three or four good gunners'. 685 Sgt P.G. Rayner was 25 and the son of Samuel and Margaret Rayner of 64 Montague Road, Hounslow. He is buried in the CWGC plot of Vermelles Communal Cemetery (grave 5). Buried on either side of him in graves 4 and 6 respectively are 153 Bombardier Reginald William Cook (age 26, the son of William and Emily Cook of 10, Sherborne Gardens, West Ealing) and 1309 Gunner H. Clarke (age 21).

* * * * *

Charles to his father   [Enquins-les-Mines]
                                                        5th March, 1916

I have very nearly forgotten it is Sunday. We have left our usual billets and are some miles away in a very pretty village among some hills for a few days' training in open warfare – a thing I haven't tried to do since I left Coggeshall! The weather is bad. We had an awful march getting here – about ten miles in blinding hail, snow and rain alternately. Today we have been out doing some manoeuvres by companies. We took our lunch out and in the middle the Brigade Chaplain[83] arrived and held a small service while it snowed on our backs. We have really good billets here. I had a fire in my bedroom last night, which was very welcome as all my clothes were wet through, and they sent me in coffee in the morning! Personally I should like to remain here for some time. ...

                                                            [Bruay]
                                                        12th March, 1916

... We have moved on another six miles and are billeted in quite a decent sized town. In our Company mess we have an open fireplace: a thing almost unknown in this part of France.

... I am thinking of going for a ride this afternoon. We had church parade in a cinema this morning. Tomorrow the Battalion is furnishing a guard of honour for a General. Stokes is to be in command, so everything is sure to be very methodical! The Battalion is really very smart now in spite of the mud. We haven't any idea what our next move is to be.

....

83   Probably the Rev Claud Thomas Thallinsson Wood who been serving as chaplain to the 141st Infantry Brigade since the beginning of the war. He became senior chaplain to the 47th Division in May 1916 and he was gazetted with the MC on 3rd June 1916. (Maude, op cit, pp. 220, 256) During his career he also served as *padré* to the 19th Londons and as chaplain to the Archbishop of Canterbury. After the war he became vicar of Tring.

Chapter 7

Marjorie and Toby

August 1915 to April 1916

The ship carrying Toby Dodgson and the 8th Yorkshires arrived at Boulogne shortly before midnight on 26th August 1915. The Battalion disembarked and marched to a nearby rest camp. It then had one week's training in the Monnecove area between Calais and St Omer.

Marjorie to Toby

Hill House
Stanstead Abbotts, Ware
28th August, 1915

Dearest Toby,

... Oh, my darling, I wish I was back there near you again. They were very precious days and unlike most of our times together seemed very long. When you had gone we bundled into the car again and went to Haslemere and forlornly ate eggs in a tea shop to fill up some time. I was left at the station where I had to wait till 7.40. The last troop train did not go through till 7.30. Such a crowd of people there were – every corner crammed. ...

Oh, "Dodders", shall I ever be able to tell you what your love has meant to me these last four months; how you have filled my life with a happiness which has surpassed all my dreams? Dreams are silly things really when you compare them with actualities and it makes me laugh when I remember how at one time they were the best part of life. ...

I love you always and always darling
Marjorie

Toby to Marjorie

[Monnecove]
28th August, 1915

Dearest Marje,

Here followeth the letter at earliest opportunity and I hope you got the PC all right. Our crossing of the Channel was short and sweet. ... We had rather a long wait on the quay the other side but eventually marched off to our camp (tents), pitched on the downs about three miles away; quite a sound spot. By the time we were all settled down, there wasn't too much time left for sleep. The next day was very hot and we spent it doing odd jobs in the camp which we left that afternoon and continued our journey by train again, packed like sardines and the average rate of progress about ten miles an hour. On de-training we found we had about four miles to march to the village where we are billeted, the men in barns, which are numerous and good. I, together with the other C Coy officers and Besly and Tilly,[84] am at the local pub; such a nice clean looking place, long and low with a simple whitewashed front which is pleasing to the eye. Here we got boiled eggs and the most delicious bread and butter, coffee and some *vin blanc* (1.50F the bottle) all of which we devoured greedily and then retired to bed fairly tired out. Six of us are sharing a loft under the roof, approached by a most dangerous trap door which I quite expect to end my days down, before the shells get at me! ...

Lt E. M. Besly, 8th Yorkshires, about to entrain at Liphook station, 26th August 1915.

I have found all the things we got in Aldershot that afternoon most useful. What a long time ago that all seems, now that we are fairly embarked on the great adventure. I thought of you as we were crossing, creeping home by the last train, feeling rather desolate and very flat. I always think it's worse for those who stay behind on these occasions: the people going away have a certain amount of novelty and excitement at least, and they are fully occupied, which is a great thing. I hope you get something interesting to do during the winter. Are you going to ... carry on at the hospital for a bit?

The country round here is a pleasant surprise; this village is on a slight rise and one sees a large expanse of open undulating land, all well cultivated. The hay harvest, which is for the most part gathered, appears to be a very good one. They seem to have a perfect genius in this part of the world for planting trees in just the right place and one can't help being reminded of the Dutch painters. ...

Ever your loving

Toby

....

84 2/Lt John Tilly was born at Seaton Carew, Co Durham in 1886. In 1905 he entered Pembroke College, Cambridge to study law and was admitted to the bar in Oct. 1911. He enlisted in the Royal Fusiliers on 15th Sept. 1914 but was discharged a week later on taking a commission in the 8th Yorkshires on 22nd Sept. He was promoted to captain on 19th June 1916. He was wounded by a German shell splinter in Munster Alley on 5th Aug. 1916. Captain Tilly's award of the MC was gazetted on 19th Nov. 1917. He died of wounds received during a trench raid in Italy on 8th June 1918 aged 31 and is buried at Barenthal Military Cemetery (grave I.B.1). (TNA WO 95/14643)

[Bayenghem]
8th Yorkshire Regt

I got your first letter Sunday evening and the next yesterday, so the posts have been pretty good. What a darling you are to write so soon: it made all the difference as I've not heard from anybody else yet. ... I think you were splendid [at the station] ... It's a great thing to be able to show a firm face to the world no matter what you may be thinking and feeling really.

We are still in the same village but the weather has quite changed and after some rain storms has turned cold. We have been finding our loft draughty and not too water-tight. ... At first I couldn't bear the idea that there were to be no more cheery weekends, but now we can look forward to the time when we shall have not only the weekends but all the days in between as well.

[Monnecove]
8th Yorks Regt
Sunday 5th September, 1915

... We have been having the most vile weather: it started raining last Thursday and for twenty-four hours it was an incessant downpour. ... The cooking is certainly the best part of this billet. Also I have run out of my pet cigarettes and altogether we have been feeling rather bored with this spot. We get the papers the following day and the letters seem to come fairly quickly but I've not seen a sign of a parcel yet. ...

Marjorie to Toby

Great Amwell House
Ware
Sunday 5th September, 1915

Here are the photos. ... If you do not want to keep them give them to any of the men who are in them, and do say if they would care to have any, because I could so easily do some more. They might like to have them to send home. ... The men in hospital here are always so awfully bucked with photos of themselves. That big one of you _is_ so good, but you mustn't turn your toes in like that: I can't allow it. It is the most perfect reproduction of how you looked all that time at the station. ...

I was delighted to get your letter yesterday and to hear you got mine so soon. Yours only took two days to come. ... It makes all the difference in the world to find one waiting for me when I come in. I get them by the evening post.

I am spending two nights with Olive as Uncle Basil is away. ...

We will have a grand time on Tuesday. The concert includes the Beethoven Concerto in B flat played by Solomon. We have heard of somewhere really wonderful to dine but I shan't tell you until we have been in case it is not respectable. You will get this by then so think of us that night. Only my darling I do wish you were coming. ... Marjorie is bored of London with no khaki escort.

... As you say, it is extraordinary how one gets used to almost anything. I have grown very used to not thinking about the future at all but just thinking simply of what one is doing at the moment. ...

Well, goodbye for today, dear. Remember I am miles more interested in your doings than my own, so tell me all that happens.

Toby to Marjorie   [Oultersteen]
                                                                7th September, 1915
    ... We left the billets we were in early on Monday morning and had a very
sweaty day of it, marching something like eighteen miles. The first part was along
a good straight road, but the going through the towns was a terribly slow business,
perpetual checks and the *pavé*, of which most of the roads are made in these
parts, are perfectly damnable to march on. We spent the night in quite a nice little
[Walloon] village right in the country. My company had quite a decent farm and the
officers had the parlour which was a cheery old room with good wooden beams
in the ceiling. The lady of the house was a jolly sort of body and looked after us.
One thing we are very lucky in and that is the weather. After all the rain we had
last week, Sunday turned out a beautiful day and I went for a delightful walk. ...
Everything was so peaceful and quiet and agriculture so very much in evidence
everywhere, that one could not believe that out there towards the East there was
an ugly great scar across the country. ... We were on the track again this morning
and again the weather was perfect, only very hot, and we must have done another
twelve miles today. The character of the country has quite changed and is now most
uninteresting and not nearly so prosperous looking. Our billet is a very poor place,
squalid and smelly to a degree, owned by a really dreadful old crony who jabbers
and is quite unintelligible.

                                                                       [Berquin]
                                                                8th September, 1915
    Our valises did not turn up last night so we had a rotten night of it. However, I
was so tired that I lay down as I was in my Burberry and went to sleep on the floor,
which is of tiles and damned hard. Things look more cheerful this morning as the
post has come in with your parcel, my cigarettes and a package from Mother. ...
    Today is a splendid day again and we are resting this morning. The guns have
been quite busy but it all seems to come from further up the line. We had a very
scrappy breakfast: dog biscuits and cheese, so we did a little foraging afterwards
and have been amusing ourselves cooking fried potatoes in our mess tins in the
orchard. ...

Marjorie to Toby   VAD Hospital
                                                                            Ware
                                                                9th September, 1915
    Dash! Here I am on night duty and likely to be doing it ten days at least. How I
dislike it; these glorious sunny days to be spent sleeping. However I haven't had a
turn for ages and it's my last one for months. Plenty of time for letters too, though
we are really meant to be darning shirts, etc.
    Talk of you running into danger in the trenches. Read this evening's paper
and see how a Zep visited Waltham and dropped bombs. Think of two maidens
returning by a late train, hearing a noise, and looking out of the window and there,
like the Ghost Ship "sailing comfortably over the stars" was a fine fat Zeppelin. Soon
– Crash! Crash! and we caught a glimpse of falling bombs, our heads thrust out of

the window. Then, splash! one fell into the river quite close at hand as well.[85] The [River] Lea water does not improve coats and skirts and Olive says we shall send in the bill to the Kaiser! The damages were – so they say – two men killed and two poor old women died of fright.

... The concert was grand. I enclose a programme. Solomon was splendid again. The first movement of that Concerto I liked the best; the *adagio* was not so interesting, but the first part was glorious and the end very cheery! He was recalled about a dozen times and eventually played the encore he gave when you were there. ...

What a good thing it is to have Olive to make such jaunts with. ... I shopped at Shoolbred and had my things put down for the Uncle to pay and then I strolled round Liverpool Street while waiting for Olive, smoking a cigarette! You know it's rather awful: I used to be such a "nice" girl and now I am quite changed. I feel an extremely different person since you went and for one thing I don't care one little pin about what I do or what anyone thinks. ...

And now, dearest, what in the world are you doing? Four whole days: no letter from Toby. No, just five days it is. Doubtless you are moving or busy or something, but don't forget you promised to send PCs when you couldn't write. ... I got a very good map at Stanfords.[86] Goodnight, old thing. I like to think you may be having a peaceful night's sleep. Think of me awake all these next nights. Remember I love you above everything and take care of yourself as much as a soldier is allowed to, won't you?

PS There was a bicycle accident in the drive this morning. Damages: me, scratched ankle, bent finger – her, two spokes broken.

VAD Hospital, Ware
2.00 a.m. – 10th September, 1915

But my dear Toby -

WHY GO TO WAR? Stay in beautiful London: AIR RAIDS DAILY. Fine views of Zeps in action. Bombs dropped in all quarters. Numberless casualties and all without crossing the Channel!

Yesterday morning the rumour came: Liverpool Street in ashes. But the truth is one signal box destroyed and some of the offices outside damaged. Also a bomb fell in the road outside Broad Street. Heaps of damage was done behind the Guildhall

....

85 Marjorie came closer to action than she might have wished shortly before midnight in the evening of 7th Sept. as the night of 7th/8th Sept. was that of the third Zeppelin raid on London. Army Zeppelin LZ.74 commanded by Hauptmann Friedrich George had crossed the coast of Essex at 10.40 pm flying westwards. He turned south at Broxbourne in Hertfordshire to approach London by flying down the Lea valley. Thinking wrongly that he was over Leyton, he released 39 bombs to lighten his ship and these fell in the area of Cheshunt and Waltham Abbey. About half a mile north of Cheshunt station the railway runs beside the River Lea, so Marjorie's train must have been very close to the line of bombs. The anti-aircraft gun at Waltham Abbey opened fire at 11.55 pm, but LZ.74 - flying at an estimated 9,000 feet and nearly 40 mph - had passed out of range by 11.59 pm. (Castle, *London 1914-1917, The Zeppelin Menace*, pp 32-34)

86 Stanfords (est. 1853) is the UK's leading specialist retailer of maps and travel books. Its flagship store at 12-14 Long Acre, Covent Garden, was opened in Jan. 1901. Maps of the Western Front were top selling items as many households wanted to follow the progress of the war.

among warehouses and alongside the river.[87] Casualty lists not yet out. But there were 56 killed and injured on Tuesday when New Cross and Woolwich caught it.[88] One explosion was only a few hundred yards from the Arsenal. Everyone round here, except the two night nurses, heard them last night. They came this way, according to hearsay, to travel to London by the help of the Lea, their only guide. ...

What beautiful nights we are having. ... It's so warm and a lovely smell of hay from a belated clover field as I came along. It's horrid having to sleep all day, but *c'est la guerre,* etc. Mrs Dodgson and Guy are coming to lunch on Sunday. ...

She bids goodnight and goodbye to Dodders till this hour tomorrow, wondering how long you can continue to find something to say when you get no answer. I should love to tease you tonight, yes, and to kiss you too.

Toby to Marjorie   [Oultersteen]
                                                            11th September, 1915

I have just received yours dated the 9th – a most refreshing epistle, but it was very careless of you to get so close to the Zeps as that. They really seem to have found the way at last and I hear that quite a large part of the City is demolished! ...

You can have no idea what an effort it is to write letters at all out here. To begin with, the climate is appalling and makes one feel so limp and inert that by eleven in the morning I long to go to sleep for the rest of the day, and secondly there is absolutely nothing to write about. I am bored to tears by the whole affair and in a perpetually bad temper. We are still in the same mouldy farmhouse but, thank goodness, the weather has been fine so that I have been able to spend most of the time in the orchard, where I have also been sleeping. One does nothing once parades are over: what is there to do in this God-forsaken country, except listen to the boom of the guns and wonder? At night when it is still one can hear fire from rifles and machine-guns as well. ...

I loved hearing about the concert and I am so glad you enjoyed it. I don't think I have ever heard the second pianoforte concerto. I know the *Valse Triste* and *Finlandia* very well, also the songs; the Delius and other things I can quite imagine were not very interesting. Oh, I'd give something to hear the strings tuning up now; that and a bath are what I want more than anything just now (with one exception) and I don't see the slightest prospect of either. ...

... Please be a dear and send me something to read. I am tired of those papers and you know the sort of stuff most people out here read. By the way, thank you very much for Punch, but we are having it sent out regularly with the Tatler, etc. ...

....

87   The fourth Zeppelin raid on London took place on the night of 8th/9th Sept. The Naval Zeppelin L.13 commanded by Kapitänleutnant Heinrich Mathy approached London from the north dropping the first bombs on Golders Green at 10.40 pm on 8th Sept. It continued southwards, releasing more bombs over Russell Square, Gray's Inn and Farringdon Statation. At least ten incendiary bombs were dropped in the narrow streets just to the north of the Guildhall. The next target was Broad Street where a bomb hit a bus on the road in front of the station, killing or wounding all the passengers. Other bombs fell around Liverpool Street Station and the southern end of Shoreditch High Street before Mathy headed for home. This raid caused more damage than any other airship raid of the war (valued at £530,787) with 22 people killed and 87 wounded. (Castle, op cit pp. 35-38)

88   She is referring to the third Zeppelin raid (see footnote 85). From Cheshunt, LZ.74 continued southwards over the City then turned towards New Cross, dropping another nine bombs shortly after midnight on 8th Sept. Half an hour earlier at about 11.50 pm on 7th Sept. another Army airship, the Schütte-Lanz SL.2 commanded by Hauptmann Richard von Wobeser, had dropped a number of bombs on Woolwich. In total 18 people were killed and 28 injured in the raid, but damage was calculated at only £9,616. (Castle, op cit pp. 32-34)

[Armentières]
Sunday evening – 12th September, 1915

... We have moved on again today and it has been hotter than ever; wonderful weather, which is lucky as we are bivouacked out in an open field tonight. We are fairly close up now and there is one of our guns hidden within a few hundred yards which makes the devil of a noise when it goes off. It is a good sight to watch our aeroplanes at work and the Huns potting at them: little puffs of smoke all round them, but they never seem to score a hit. It is getting too dark to write any more now ...

8.30 a.m. Monday morning – 13th September, 1915

The guns woke us up directly it got light and we saw a splendid aeroplane duel; our man had a machine gun on board and forced the Hun to descend behind our lines. This interrupted my morning shave and I have just succeeded in cutting a large piece out of my face!

On 13th September Toby's Battalion arrived in the Bois Grenier sector, south of Armentières, for instruction in trench warfare. Like his brother Philip, Toby also wrote regularly to his mother Helen from the Western Front, but fewer of these letters have survived, and some of his comments are similar to those he wrote to Marjorie.

Toby to his mother

[Rue Delpierre]
8th Yorks Regt
16th September, 1915

Dearest Mother,

Just a line to let you know that we are in the trenches amongst the "whizz-bangs",[89] snipers, etc. However, the Hun is not doing very much in these parts apparently and I think he is not keen on trying too much "strafe". The worst part of this life is the lack of sleep, which is very trying.

Would you get me a periscope? ... I only want quite a simple affair – a couple of mirrors on a stick; only it is no good having the mirrors too small, and one wants something not too bulky to carry about. Also I should like my canvas washing basin, but don't send the wooden frame ... I hear from Marje that you had a very good day at home last Sunday. England seems such a long way away from here. I am too sleepy to make much of an effort in the letter line, so excuse this scrawl and this perpetual demand for things.

Your ever-loving son,
Toby

....

89   A term widely used to describe incoming German artillery fire, usually with reference to the 77mm field gun. Shells fired from field artillery travelled faster than the speed of sound, so troops on the receiving end would first hear the 'whizz' of a shell travelling through the air before they heard the 'bang' made by the gun itself. Whizz-bangs were feared as they gave virtually no warning of incoming fire.

Toby to Marjorie   [Rue Delpierre]
                                                              17th September, 1915

You are a dear to write every day as you do and it makes all the difference in the world, especially in these damned trenches. The solid *eau-de-cologne* arrived this morning and is perfectly delicious. ...

We had quite a lively night with much strafing on both sides and consequently very little sleep. There is about 400 yards between the lines, which is more interesting than being jammed close up against the wretched Hun.

Marjorie to Toby   VAD Hospital, Ware
                                                    12.00 p.m. - 18th September, 1915

... Poor old Toby! It must be a rotten existence and I am so sorry not to have been more cheerful about things. It must have been partly feeling ill and all the night work that made me let depression get the upper hand. But everything is all right now and it was just splendid to be woken by Uncle Basil coming into my room at seven o'clock with your two letters. He was so sweet last night, it made all the difference and solemnly produced a bottle of fizz at dinner for his tearful-eyed niece.

... I am so sorry you are having such enervating weather. It's boiling over here too but very lovely. I think I can realise how difficult it is to write letters: poor old thing, the whole affair must be horribly boring at present and enough to make you not want to do anything. No wonder you are in a bad temper. But I shan't let you off letters all the same. Very good for you to have an occupation!

... I hope you liked the book. I couldn't get another decent one anywhere here, but on Monday I am sending you Rupert Brooke's poems.[90] I like them very much; he did so love the feel and the taste and the smell of things. ...

The aeroplane duels must be quite a diversion and most exciting. No more Zeps here lately, but an anti-aircraft gun is now placed over at Amwell in a field, so no wonder they are nervous.

Yesterday I could not get to sleep at all during the day, so this morning I vowed I would not be defrauded again, so Timbo and I set off in the heat of the glorious sunshine and marked the old familiar path over the fields. The country was grand, a feeling of autumn very faintly behind it all, though the leaves have not begun to turn. We passed the hay where you and I sat one morning before breakfast, now grown into a large stack. Then round by the wood and down into the valley by the river, over that open field. It looked very beautiful, the light in the distance was all hazy and I remembered so distinctly the different things we have talked about as we have gone that way before. Once we planned the honeymoon there, do you remember? Then came the little round wood facing the toy farm, and there were the wooden animals grazing in the same old field. ... I climbed the hill on the other side of the wood and came round the other way, past the brushwood pile where he first kissed her, only the brushwood has gone and a fine young plantation has taken its place. All the way I gloried in the feeling that you were about somewhere and probably thinking of me. Isn't it splendid having that lovely summer behind us with

....

90   The poet Rupert Brooke had died of septicaemia on 23rd Apr. 1915 shortly before his unit landed at Gallipoli. His posthumous second volume of poetry *1914 and Other Poems* was published in May. Marjorie had been given a copy of this volume on 2nd Sept. by her friend Olive Naylor.

its memories of all we have done and said and thought together and all the things between us "that only you remember and only I admire". ...

Only one more night of this and then, praise be the Lord, I am going to a Prom with your mother; nearly all Wagner this time, including Parsifal Transformation and Closing Scene. Oh, how I will think of you! ...

Toby to Marjorie   [Rue Delpierre]
                                                                20th September, 1915

I am awfully sorry about the letters but I am sure I acknowledged the photos and told you that I thought the men would very much appreciate them. I am afraid there will always be a gap in my letters whenever we are on the move. ...

You will love the Tristan on Monday and the Ride of the Valkyries, which will fairly gallop you away, while the Rhinemaidens will charm you with their melodious strains in *Götterdamerung*. ... The Liszt concerto I don't know, but he is not a composer I am very much interested in.

... I've thought such a lot about you during the nights out here and longed and longed for you; to feel your arms round my neck and your kisses on my lips. Really, I don't know how one would stick it here if it wasn't for you. I hardly dare let myself think about coming home on leave – a week – what use will that be when I want to hold you tightly for always and always.

Marjorie to Toby   VAD Hospital, Ware
                                                                20th September, 1915

... Hurray! My last night at this job. Tomorrow at this hour I shall be blissfully returning from that concert. ... On Tuesday morning I come on morning work here again for a week or so.

We leave Hill House on 4th October. I am going first to the Lunns[91] at Hastings and another visit before I get home. I hope soon to hear more about this secretary thing I applied for, but the form has only been sent in a few days and of course being a Government department one must expect a long pause! One thing grieves me very much and that is leaving Timbo. I will miss his doggy devotion dreadfully. ...

Toby to his mother   [Rue Delpierre]
                                                                20th September, 1915

Your letter posted on 15th and the parcel of eatables arrived last night, the latter in very good order. Curiously enough I had been groaning a good deal about the monotony of the food here. (It is rather a business to get things up to the trenches.) Things have been pretty quiet here except for mild artillery duels. The weather has been ideal, though it is beginning to get much colder at night. ...

I am getting quite used to being perpetually in my clothes which I have not had off since last Tuesday. No signs of "life" yet!! ...

I heard from Philip again the other day but I'm afraid we are not quite within meeting distance at present. ...

....

91 Lady Mabel Lunn (née Stafford Northcote) was Marjorie's best friend at school. She had married Arnold Lunn, son of the travel-agency pioneer Sir Henry Lunn. Arnold (1888 – 1974) had founded the Ski Club of Great Britain in 1908 and would invent the slalom skiing race in 1922. There is a memorial to Sir Arnold Lunn in Murren, Switzerland.

Toby to Marjorie   [Rue Delpierre]
                                                  21st September, 1915

... If I had known that you wanted me to write every day I would have done it somehow, but it's a fearful strain to write here when one feels that half the things that one would naturally say mustn't be said, and that these are just the things with which the whole of one's mind is occupied, to the exclusion of everything else. The result is that one feels that letters must be hopelessly artificial and unreal, not to say very boring. ... and if you knew how much one's nerves are on the stretch here, and have been during the last three weeks, you would understand. They say anticipation is the worst part of anything unpleasant and I think it's true.

... We are still in the trenches which are becoming very noisy, but I got out for the day today to go to a lecture and practical demonstration on the use of the smoke helmet at a small place behind the lines. I was jolly glad to get away and one got what seemed a magnificent lunch in one of the bars. There was an awful old ill-tuned piano which a heavy-handed gunner insisted on tormenting, the result being an exact imitation of a bad barrel organ. Outside there was an intermittent stream of troops of one sort and another marching over the dreary and hard cobble streets of this half-deserted place. The whole produced a hateful feeling of the melodramatic. ...

                                                         [Rue Delpierre]
                                                  22nd September, 1915

Your letter with the photos and the books and food all arrived this evening. I've not read either of the books, and really I think the Rupert Brooke is rather too good a volume to send here as I fear the odds are very much against any of them getting back to England. ...

We have had a very noisy day today which is very tiring and makes one feel rather more sleepy than usual. What would one not give for the calm and peace of England and you? ...

Toby to his mother   [Rue Delpierre]
                                                  24th September, 1915

Just a few lines to let you know that we are still in the trenches and beginning to feel it is about time we were relieved. Last night there was a thunder storm but, although the lightening was very vivid, it never came really close and the rain, which lasted on and off for a couple of hours, was of a very ordinary kind. Even so, the whole place is a quagmire and I would never have believed that so little rain could make so much mud. It must be the most extraordinary soil, as it was as dry as a bone previously. The result is that we are all smothered in mud and have the greatest difficulty in keeping on our feet owing to the intense slipperiness. What it can be like after a proper spell of wet I can't conceive.

I had a very good letter from Guy last night, telling me all about his weekend and the Prom you went to; also one from Mrs Secretan.. ... This is a weary life and it will be much worse when the winter comes on, but one must go through with it. I often think of your cosy little cottage and the lights and the warmth with a bit of an ache ... but everything comes to an end some day.

Toby to Marjorie   [Rue Delpierre]
                                          Sunday 26th September, 1915

... I am quite sure that all the letters I write are not reaching you, as I am sure I wrote directly we got into the trenches. ... I purposely have not attempted to describe my trench experiences at all yet but I intend to send you an article on the subject when we go out for a rest.

... We are enjoying a comparatively peaceful Sunday with the sun shining, which we are very glad of after the rain and mists we have been having. Yesterday too was a terribly noisy day as there was a show on.[92] ...

My imagination runs riot over food, baths, armchairs, etc. Out here I become horribly extravagant. ... We will have a good time together when it's all over, darling. I believe I shall almost have forgotten how to kiss by then!

                                          [Fort Rompu, NW of Fleurbaix]
                                          2.30 a.m. – 30th September, 1915

An awful hour, isn't it, but I've given up trying to sleep as a bad job and it's rather an opportunity of writing to you in peace and quiet. We were moved out of the front two nights ago, but instead of going back into billets as we had hoped, they have only sent us back to the second line, which is rather more than half a mile behind our former position. Of course it is a good deal quieter here: you are immune from anything except shell fire; nor are one's nerves stretched out to the extent they were, but against all those very good points is the fact that these trenches are only about half made and in consequence there is practically no cover. More than half the men have to bivouac out in the open under a waterproof sheet with a blanket, and there are only two dugouts built so far for us, as compared with six which we had in the firing line. The weather has been vile, soaking wet ever since we came to these trenches, so that every one is thoroughly moist if not actually wet through. And the mud – it defies description – I thought I knew what a clay soil was, but I never saw the like of this stuff. Naturally the weather makes all the digging twice as hard and, Heaven only knows, we have enough to do here anyhow. Certainly, from the point of view of comfort there is no comparison. I had an awful cosy dugout up in the front line with a jolly comfortable bed too, but there one never had the chance of properly appreciating it. Now here, when one could get a decent uninterrupted night's rest, there is nothing to sleep on – ugh! And owing to a muddle with the transport I have not yet got my valise, so that I am still left with just the one blanket that I took up to the firing line, which makes a very poor bed with nothing but the hard, damp clay to support it. ... Yesterday in desperation we managed to fix up a bath in a shattered farmhouse behind these lines. They are a dreary sight, these farmhouses, not much more than a mass of debris out of which arise the remains of the walls supporting the roof, all of which have large shell holes through them and look rather unsafe. Inside they have been utterly gutted, every piece of furniture having been taken. A good deal is to be found in the dugouts: beams have been sawn off; tiles from the floor removed wholesale, together with doors and windows, all of which there is a great demand for, for our amateur homes. In this particular one there are two fairly decent rooms, i.e. they have floors and walls intact. One we use as the officers' cook house and ... the other as a bath house. We found a round

....
92 The Battle of Loos

wooden tub, which after much scrubbing made a very tolerable bath, just room to sit down. The hot water we got from the company cooker. Imagine then, as dusk drew on, your beloved seated in a round wooden tub (no need to blush) in the middle of a desolate room, lighted by one flickering candle, a ground-sheet hung over the entrance in place of a door and another one over the window to hide the eyeless socket and help keep out the reeking damp atmosphere. It was an anxious moment when I took off my clothes, but it's all right – there were no signs of life!!! I did enjoy that bath; you can't imagine what it means to have your clothes on solid for a whole fourteen days.

What you heard about our trenches is quite correct; they are the trenches of the British Army and quite wonderful. I should so like you to see them. …

I much enjoyed your account of the concert and am not a bit surprised that you enjoyed those bits of the *Meistersingers* best: I think anyone would, hearing them all for the first time. When you've heard the opera a few times you recognise at once that the pleasure derived from them is only skin deep compared to the emotions aroused by many other passages. I am delighted about the Beethoven and should have been horribly disappointed if you had not succumbed. …

What do you think of the latest war news? Not too bad, is it? We have been terribly hampered by the weather which is incessantly vile. The morning of that fateful Saturday was terribly misty on our part of the line and quite upset the plan of operations in which we were playing our little part. We thought we really were in for it! …

[Rue du Biez]
2nd October, 1915

… Yes, I love Tchaikovsky's 5th Symphony, even better than the *Pathétique* in some ways. I think Thursday's concert is rather good: you would like the Grieg concerto and the Debussy is very attractive. …

It is simply glorious today, perfectly clear and fresh after just a slight touch of frost last night, and the sun is streaming down, doing its best to make us forget that the drear Autumn is here, that the days are shortening and the leaves turning yellow, when everything has to die. Ugh! I hate it. I loathe the cold unless it be the clear, crisp cold of Switzerland, and I am thinking that darkness on the land from four until eight will be perfect hell out here. Everybody is in tremendous spirits out here over the recent show and one can't help feeling that the Hun is up against something much better than himself. Even so, I don't allow myself to expect anything very speedy or dramatic. Personally, though, I've always said that the end would be dramatic. I expect we shall stay out here six months at least after active hostilities have ceased while they haggle and argue about peace terms. But the Hun has not shortened his line yet, so perhaps that is rather premature. …

[Rue du Biez]
3rd October, 1915

… We are really quite comfortable here; these wooden shelters, magnified rabbit hutches, are not at all bad though they are getting a bit chilly at nights. Anyhow, after the trenches, they seem like hotels, although we have nothing but our valises, some straw, and a decrepit table in them! The cake and walnuts arrived last night.

The former I have not sampled as we still have one going, but it will be very useful tomorrow and the nuts are splendid; they all arrived in the most excellent condition and certainly were very well packed. Thank you ever so much for sending them. Yes, there is one particular kind of sweet I would like sometime when you are in London, made by Fortnum and Mason, hard things like square acid drops only bright green with a crème de menthe taste. ... Mother sends me out food regularly and manages to get the most wonderful things in tins, which are a great success, though I never used to like the idea of tinned things. For instance, this evening I've had a most refreshing dinner – sweetbreads and tomato sauce, cocoa, cake, bread and jam!

... Marje darling, I've got a dreadful longing for you this evening; if only I had you here it would be so cosy. I want that wonderful kiss very badly, my darling; just to feel your arms tight around me once again ... . How perfect! And here we are separated, miles away from each other – it is damnable. Write me a long love letter next time; never mind if it sounds sloppy, I shall understand. You darling, I've such an ache for you, the physical you, this evening: sweet intimate times we've had together keep floating through my mind. ...

[Fort Rompu]
7th October, 1915

... We are still in these mouldy canvas bivouacs about two miles behind the firing line; but I can't remember, now I come to think about it, whether I have written since we left our little wooden hut. We moved here on Monday, but it's only about a couple of miles from where we were before. I hear that Philip has been having exciting times down at Loos, doing observing officer up in the front line near Hill 70. I wonder how your interview went off on Monday. I do hope you get a job in Town; it would be so much more amusing for you when you get your evenings off. I don't see anything much in the news yet to shout about: our diplomats don't seem to have been very clever in the Balkans. I only hope those damned Bulgarians get it in the neck.[93]

We went to the Divisional baths the other day and I can tell you I was not sorry to get the men a real hot bath and plenty of soap! What used to be the local laundry has been well adapted by the military for bathing purposes and they bath over a thousand per day; this includes ironing and disinfecting their khaki while they are in their bath and exchanging all their underclothing for a clean set, so that part of the establishment still fulfils its old functions and is run by a staff of most wonderfully industrious French girls. There is, I fear, a certain amount of laxness as to the conventions, owing to the fact that the washing rooms for clothes can only be reached through the room used as a dressing room by the men, so that a Sergeant has to be stationed at the door and whenever any of the fair workers want to pass through, there is a furious blowing of whistles and shouts of "Cover up!"; all of which I think the immovable natives regard as an absurd piece of prudery; anyhow they seem not a whit embarrassed and the men thought it no end of a joke.

....

93 Bulgaria had entered the war in Sept. 1915 on the German side following the failure of Allied diplomatic efforts to keep her out of the war. Austria and Germany renewed their attack on Serbia on 6th Oct. Bulgaria attacked Serbia on 13th Oct. and her forces interposed themselves between the Serbs and the Allied forces, which had recently landed at Salonika in northern Greece to support the Serbian Army.

... Poor Humphrey, being done out of his bread ration. Our men have also been very short. Personally I don't think they lose much, as the Army bread, by the time it has travelled all the way up here, is like nothing on earth. On the other hand, the local French bread is really excellent and, together with the white wine, is about the only redeeming feature of these parts.

How you must have hated leaving Hill House. I don't like to think of it all shut up, but of course it's much the best thing to do in these times. Was Mr. Richardson depressed about it? ...

... And how does the naïve Marjorie like Hastings? ... Oh, for just one night in London and lights and music, nice girls to look at and a general air of enjoyment in place of this eternal medley of men and horses, motor lorries and telephone wires, everything and all in a sea of mud.

Toby to his mother   [Fort Rompu]
                                                    7th October, 1915

I was very glad to hear some news of Philip as I imagined he had probably not been idle during the recent strafe. We are about a couple of miles back behind the firing line now, resting in nearby canvas bivouacs placed round what was once a grass field but is now only a sea of mud. I think quite the greatest disadvantage of this land is the water which invariably smells of the manure heap. ... Marjorie is down at Hastings now. She is still hoping to get some sort of secretarial work with the Red Cross I think, which will suit her much better than nursing. She sent me a first-rate cake and some walnuts the other day and always writes most regularly which, as the mail is the one good thing in the day to which we all eagerly look forward, is very nice. The tinned meats are a great success, especially the beef and carrot. ...

Toby to Marjorie   [Fort Rompu]
                                                    9th October, 1915

... The post has just arrived with your parcel and letter (6th). The preserved fruits are excellent, especially the cherries and greengages: the lumps of citron I shall attempt to palm off on my friends. ... Hastings sounds quite a pleasant spot. ... The candle is on the point of going out, so I must stop; my pencil has been going in a very halting manner, so perhaps it is just as well. ...

Marjorie to Toby   Albany Hotel
                                                            Hastings
                                                    10th October, 1915

... You had not said before you had moved under canvas. It sounds dreadfully muddy and no wonder you are longing for lights and a sense of enjoyment. Fancy playing football too: what an effort! The description of the baths was very amusing. I do love hearing a bit what life is like out there – ugh! the dirt must be nasty and the cold must be worse than anything. ... Oh, you poor things, it is <u>rotten</u> for you all. As for those Bulgarians, d--n them, what a mess they've made. The Hun must be glorying greatly. Philip must indeed be having an exciting time, I had heard nothing of him as I have not seen Mrs Dodgson of course. I hope you have your cigarettes by now, also the telescope. ...

Yes, I was very sad when it came to the point of leaving Hill House. I have many pleasant memories connected with it, especially memories of you. Padie was sorry too ... but he is going down every weekend you know, so it's not like leaving altogether. ...

I have just loved being here. Mabel and Arnold [Lunn] <u>are</u> so nice. Arnold and I have had two games of golf and won one each, which has inspired him with a horrible keenness. He is quite a beginner and used to be a scoffer at all games. Arguments over the prospect of peace have given way entirely before the burning question of free will or predestiny. Of course I am an ardent believer in the former. In spite of animated discussions for two days no one is one whit removed from their original position.

It's all very exciting. Arnold says I used to be such a "nice girl" but since my engagement there is a bad decline. This is because I advocated the absolutely harmlessness of engaged couples staying at hotels! ...

The following long letter from Toby to his mother gives a good impression of the experiences of a young officer on his first deployment on the Western Front.

Toby to his mother   [Rue Marle]
                                                                    10th October, 1915

I promised to write and try to give you some account of my experiences and what trench life is like. Not being a genius, there is no chance of my succeeding, but however here goes.

You remember the final stage of our march up to the firing line brought us to some fields about two miles behind it where we were bivouacked out in the open. Our Division was to relieve a regular one, and during the two or three days that we spent there we visited the trenches and saw how they ran things and generally spent all our time getting as much information and as many tips as possible from them. We took over trenches from a well-known Scotch regiment and I can't tell you how nice they were and what a lot of trouble they took to help us in every way.[94] They had had an awful time at Ypres and one of the other big shows. They regarded these trenches as a kind of rest cure, and I believe it is a fact that they are considered the best and most comfortable trenches in the British lines. They were known as the "Daily Mirror trenches" at one time who, in their turn, spoke of them as the "Garden City". And it is a literal fact that we have in our section of trench two very fine gardens: real flower beds, actually trimmed with grass and beautiful neat paths for which the wooden trench floor boards come in very handy. There were two standard rose trees and some excellent flowers of which the mignonette was the best.

Well, on the evening we were to take over (it is always done by night) we started for the trenches just as it was getting dark. The country is absolutely flat and divided into a regular chess-board by the numerous roads. These, and ditches half full of water, form the boundaries between the fields, there being comparatively few

....

94 A and B Companies of the 8th Yorkshires went into the front line trenches of the 2nd Battalion, The Queen's Own Cameron Highlanders (81st Brigade, 27th Division) for instructional purposes at 5.00 pm on 14th Sept., swapping with C and D Companies the next day. The Battalion became solely responsible for that section of the line on 16th Sept. (TNA WO 95/2184)

hedges. The land is all cultivated and it is extraordinary how they go on working, even now, quite close up to the firing line. There are endless farmhouses dotted about all over the place and as we marched down we must have passed any number in various states of dilapidation, but generally speaking it struck one how little damaged they were. About half-way there we went through a bit of a village – a long row of squalid-looking cottages still occupied by women and children; then some more of these, black and deserted, the street looking horribly desolate. By now it is nearly dark; the crack of the rifles sounds distinctly nearer and the glare of the flares, shot into the air like small rockets from the trenches, lights up the surrounding country. We turn to the right and are heading now direct for the firing line, past another group of houses evidently occupied by the RFA and very strongly fortified, until we finally reach the beginning of the communication trench. This is by a farmhouse – or, rather, what remains of it – and a more hopeless appearance of utter confusion is difficult to imagine. There are our men filing into the trench from the road which is blocked with transport dumping rations; RE wagons full of timber and wire waiting to be unloaded, and a pair of mules starting to kick and attempting to destroy the last vestige of any order. It is all pitch dark. Everybody is swearing and cursing and no one knows who anyone is or where they are. I stick to the side of the canny Scot who has at length found No. 11 Platoon and is to guide us to our section of the trench. After much halting and waiting, we at length get under way up the communication trench which is, as a matter of fact, more like a miniature Devonshire lane, being on the average quite eight or nine feet broad. The sides are boarded up the whole way, and half the ground space is occupied by the trench floor-boards, indispensable on account of the mud. Every ten or twenty yards it takes a violent turn, first one way then another, so that by the time you've been walking for twenty minutes or so you've not the very least idea which way you are facing. It is a slow business getting the men up with their equipment and full packs, as there is a constant stream of men coming the other way, carrying various impedimenta of the regiment we are to relieve; and tiring too, as the surface is very rough and it takes all one's time not to slip off the boards.

I think what strikes the novice most is why the Huns don't shell that horrible medley disentangling itself at the dumping point, and what an awful mess there will be if one <u>does</u> come!

At last we are in, or rather behind, our sector of the fire trench. I must here state that the word "trench" gives one the wrong idea: these are breastworks really as they are only dug down about a couple of feet and the rest of the parapet, which is on the average about eight feet high, is built up with sand-bags; the result being that at the back one can stand about and look towards one's rear, which is quite open. But close up to the parapet another thick sand-bag wall is built, so that what it really amounts to is a trench built above ground, and it has all come to be greatly elaborated, regular forts being built at some points, dugouts, cookhouses, etc., all being built into and connected up to the main trench by a maze of secondary trenches. So you can imagine that to get one's men into these trenches is no simple matter for the first time, chiefly on account of the darkness. At length, however, the thing straightens out: somehow our men are all in and the Jocks lined up in the rear ready to file away. They go and you realise that this bit of line depends entirely on your regiment.

I am not going to attempt to describe our feelings on that first night, but the men were as jumpy as could be and there was generally a feeling of great insecurity. The trenches are about three or four hundred yards apart in that part of the line, so that there is a large tract of "no-man's-land" consisting of what were once fields with a fair number of trees dotted about. The German snipers were particularly active that night and it was this more than anything else that upset the men who, by about 1.00 a.m., were seeing a sniper in every bush. One man declared that a Hun was creeping about at the bottom of our parapet and had even climbed up and looked over!! Anyhow, everybody was jolly glad to see daylight, but not for long because the shelling started as soon as the light was good enough, and we had learnt to respect shells the morning before when we were going round the trenches. It was just after lunch, which we had had in the trenches, when the Hun started putting a few shells over. The first two went well over and burst amongst some trees about thirty-five yards back. Personally, I didn't mind a bit and was chiefly interested in watching the effect, being inclined to regard the whole performance as a sort of firework display. However, the third shell got the range and burst just behind the trench and caught poor Fenton,[95] who was walking from one dugout to the next. He was badly wounded in the head and died that night. It really was rotten luck. So our Company was short-handed from the very start.

But after the first two days everybody had quite settled down. The routine is more or less as follows:- everybody "stands to" early in the morning before it starts to get light and that is the beginning of the day. When it is bright daylight one carries on with rifle inspection, etc.; then probably breakfast, after which there are working parties to be seen to, filling sandbags, repairing and improving sections of the trench, etc.; then letters to censor – a long and horrible job. After lunch one tries to get some sleep. No time for more!

[front line trenches, near Rue Marle]
12th October, 1915

... I hope you will get Marje to come and stay with you for a bit. I expect she will like to as Hill House is shut up; unless of course she gets a Red Cross job. Guy will enjoy a week's leave: he must be heartily sick of training.

The weather has been much better again this last week and the ground has dried up a lot, but I'm afraid it can't last long. We are in the trenches again now and a little further up the line; a rather more interesting spot too, as the Huns' trenches are only about seventy yards away just here, which seems very close after the respectful distance at which our last trenches were built. We've not had any "Sausages"[96] or bombs over yet but expect to be introduced to these armaments before long. They had a pretty busy day yesterday but I think Fritz is prepared to dig in for a rest. It is a perfect autumn day and it seems a shame to spend it in these absurd trenches. These are much more battered about by the fortunes of war than

....

95 2/Lt William Vernon Fenton died of wounds received from an enemy shellburst when going into the trenches for the first time on 16th Sept. 1915. He was educated at Cranleigh School where he had served in the OTC. A student in 1914, he joined the University and Public Schools Brigade of The Royal Fusiliers before being commissioned into the 8th Yorkshires on 8th Feb. 1915. He was 21 and the eldest son of Mr and Mrs W H Fenton of Heston House, Heston, Middlesex. He is buried at Bois Grenier Communal Cemetery Extension (grave I.6). (TNA WO 339/32532)

96 "Sausages" were rounds fired by small German trench mortars. They were made from lengths of stove piping and were so slow in flight that they could easily be observed.

those we were in before (no flower gardens here). I am sharing a very excellent dugout with another man. It was built by the RE when they were up here a lot sinking a mine, which has since had to be abandoned as they could not cope with the water. This gives one a certain sense of safety, as if we can't mine neither can the Hun. The point is, however, that in consequence this hutch is very well and strongly made and even has a nice stove in it. ...

Marjorie to Toby   c/o Mrs Tosswill,[97] Garlands, Crowborough, Sussex
12th October, 1915

... This is a most glorious spot to have a house – right on top of a hill with a view away across to Beachy Head and on fine days you can see the sea. ... It is wonderful weather, the hot sun streaming on me as I write, but of course it's chilly in the evenings and must be very nasty in tents or trenches. ...

Things seem very lively in the West again, but what a failure and a mess in the Balkans. The latest idea is that Germany will seize a bit of Serbia, make a compact with Bulgaria which will open up the whole of Asia to her, and then offer any terms of peace we like with regard to Belgium, etc.

It was quite sad leaving Hastings, I did enjoy it so. ...

Guy is going to get a week's leave some time soon: oh, when is yours coming? ... Dear old thing, I do hope you get a good long rest from the trenches. I hate to think of you having such a rotten time among your men, motor lorries and mud. ...

Crowborough
14th October, 1915

... I think I really ought to have married a schoolmaster. I like little boys so much. I had a killing letter from a Haileybury boy yesterday including apologies for not knowing my new name. A little premature. ...

Crowborough
16th October, 1915

Your letter dated 13th came this morning. How horrid being back in the trenches. I hope the Hun will be fairly quiet. When there is an extra noisy bombardment you can hear the guns here quite plainly. They say it is because it is so high, as they are not heard on the south coast. We heard them just faintly for about half an hour the other day, but we don't generally hear them except during an attack like that of September 25th and 26th.

Your letter was very sweet. One day we will certainly make up for all this separation and won't we be happy? I will get Rossetti's sonnetts when I am in London next Wednesday and if I don't go near a book shop I will write for one. I am staying on here till Wednesday in the hope of hearing from the Red Cross, because if I have been taken on I want to see about getting a uniform in London. But I can't really believe those marvellously efficient dames have considered me worth having. They said I should hear in about ten days, so I ought to know soon. ...

... I am being frightfully lazy here and doing nothing but reading and going for walks and doing odd jobs for my aunt and am feeling very fit. You would be very

....

97 Jane Tosswill was one of her aunts. Marjorie's mother, Mary, was the youngest of the nine Richardson children and Jane was her eldest sister.

amused over the people here – they are all so prim and conventional. No room for *outré* ideas and no cigarettes for ladies except in the garden hidden by the hedge. ...

I suppose you are in the front line again. I do hope they won't keep you there so long this time. You have been there five days already. ...

Toby to Marjorie [Rue Marle]
16th October, 1915

... I went into the town near here [Armentières] (we are billeted on the outskirts) yesterday afternoon. It is quite a decent sized place: about the size of Guildford, I should think; deserted now with the exception of the military and a few shopkeepers and people who are too poor to go away. The shops (there are about two of each kind open) are quite good, though they charge double for everything, with the exception of Burberry's Agency which charges treble. There is a really excellent tea shop and actually two girls to wait on you. I made an absolute pig of myself over French *éclairs*, etc. Well, what can you expect? It is an awfully strange feeling walking about the place and wondering who all the big houses belong to and what it looks like in peace time. In many of the streets the grass is growing up between the pavements; some new houses, only half built, remain as they were twelve months ago; the railway station is a mass of weeds and looks like an old Roman remain. I would give anything to be here when peace is declared and watch the transformation scene. I was terribly tempted to buy things just for the sake of buying, but we didn't do much more than rag the good ladies in the shops, and Besly insisted on using the second person singular, which never failed!

[Rue Marle]
17th October, 1915

... I wonder how you will like being at home again; rather flat, isn't it? Will you tell Esmé I have not forgotten that I owe her a letter and that a great effort shall be made shortly. I am so glad you are going to stay with Mother. ... Give my love to Mr and Mrs Secretan.

Toby to his mother [Rue Marle]
17th October, 1915

... I got the parcel of food and the oil sheet while we were in the trenches and found them most -------- and comforting. The writing paper came last night. Thank you so much for looking after all my wants. ...

I heard from Philip the other day, but I am afraid there's not much chance of our meeting, at least not until things quieten down. Yes, do send "War and Peace": it is a beastly edition and I never got very far, but it is most interesting, especially in these times. ... We shall soon have been out two months now and I shall start to think about leave before so <u>very</u> long. All peace times seem unreal and far away now but they will come again one of these days and then it will be great.

Marjorie to Toby Crowborough
19th October, 1915

We are still having the most glorious weather. I do hope you are too; it must make such a difference in the trenches. You have been there over a week now and I hope by the time this reaches you, you will be thinking of getting out of them again. I am rather glad I am going home tomorrow as I am getting tired of having no one young and foolish so to speak, to talk to. It will be cheery to have old Esmé again, I have seen her so little lately, and it will be great to hear an orchestra once more on the way. ...

There are some delightful people living next door here, by name Montagu-Smythe. He is an artist and does book illustrations – you may know the name. Although well over age he enlisted in the Artists' Rifles and is a doctor's orderly, which I consider first class patriotism when it means giving up all his work. I was at tea there on Sunday and quite loved him: he took such an interest in what you might be doing. Afterwards his wife told me when he was in Japan he bore the name of "the lady-man" among the Japanese![98] It is curious what a sympathy springs up at once between people who have someone very dear out at the front. (The Smythes have their only son just going.) One notices it directly you meet them and without saying a word about it, it gives you a quick feeling of friendship, which you would never experience towards an ordinary stranger. ...

Do you think a lot about how we are getting on in the Dardanelles and in France and how it will all end etc., or do you just hope you will get a fairly good dinner and a dry place to sleep, and leave the rest? I can't help thinking it will all be so interesting twenty years hence, but at present it's all an infernal nuisance and I wish everyone would leave off. And let Toby and everybody else's Toby come home safely.

Toby to Marjorie   [front line trenches, near Rue Marle]
20th October, 1915

We are back in the trenches again, as you will already know. ... I am so glad the Red Cross are taking you on. I hope you have stipulated that you take a week's holiday directly I get leave. What a bore having to wear a uniform, but that can be discarded when I come home, can't it? Oh, I do hope it will be somewhere in London: it will be so dreary if it is some provincial town. Do you have to sign on for any definite period? Oh dear, why can't I be there to take you to that concert on Friday; surely you cannot resist hearing the "Unfinished"? I certainly couldn't now and we would stay in London and have no end of a time; unknown to the grown-ups lest they should be unnecessarily worried. What a week that will be! ...

Marjorie to Toby   Bennetts End
21st October, 1915

... I am longing to hear how you have been getting on in the trenches this time. Well, here I am home again and very glad to be here. They are all very flourishing and much thrilled over a note from Humphrey to say he has taken a Commission. He gave no reasons, just said the Colonel had sent for him and said the War Office had offered him one again; but we think the final touch was his finding three unwelcome visitors in his clothing! We hope he may come home. Reggie is having

....

98   The moderately well known illustrator Walter Montagu Smyth (1863-1965). His works included illustrations for *Old and New Japan* (by Clive Holland, pub J. M. Dent, 1907). He was the 1912 president of the London Sketch Club who describe him as "immaculate almost to dandyism, always with the prettiest girls on his arm, and still having pictures accepted at the Royal Academy at the age of 100." (http://www.londonsketchclub.com)

a most comfortable time, sleeps in a bed with a stove in the room and can buy anything he wants, lucky devil: I wish you were in a job like that. ...

They are celebrating a day in aid of the Red Cross here. Selling things in baskets from house to house. Mother is hawking her wares at this moment. Edith (the cook) has made you a cake this morning. I hope it will be a success. If so it shall go off tomorrow. ...

I do miss having you in London with me sometimes. We did have some fun together didn't we? I feel very jealous of people who have their khaki officers with them, though there are precious few now, it seems, and those not very much worth the having. What a time we will have when you come back again! ...

Toby to Marjorie   [front line trenches, near Rue Marle]
22nd October, 1915

... It has been a glorious sunny day but it rained last night which has brought the mud back again. And now there is a full moon rising in a cloudless sky but it's all spoilt by the restless rifle and machine gun fire which always waken up when dusk first sets in. By eleven or twelve o'clock it will all be quiet again, except for an occasional shot or two from some persevering sniper. ... I still take a very keen interest in all the various fronts, but one needs a deal of patience these days. All the news is dreadfully negative in character, isn't it? However, I stick to my opinion that when things do move it will be with alacrity, not to say with an almighty rush. The war was started in Serbia and I shouldn't be surprised to see it end there too! ...

Later: ... I have got a dreadful ache this evening: I want you so badly and it seems such ages since we saw each other. I gaze and gaze at your photos but they don't help very much on an evening like this when it is you I need so badly. ...
To be separated under ordinary circumstances would be bad enough, but these conditions accentuate it horribly. But always there is the looking forward to those days we are going to get ... I am just existing for that. ...

[Bois Grenier]
24th October, 1915

We are back in the second line now and I've been very busy all day or I would have written before. A new Officers' Mess and two more officers' dugouts have been occupying all our attention. I think there will be no need for any army huts or bricks and mortar, which we can't afford; a few thousand sand bags and some good timber – the rest we'll do ourselves! It is certainly the only amusing thing out here, this building of primitive huts and cave dwellings. I love building them and get very excited over them; the annoying part is that just as your work is nearing completion you move and someone else gets all the benefit. We found two magnificent old oak beams in a shattered farm close by; things about a foot thick which were sawn out and carried off in triumph for the roof, which is really strong this time and already has over three feet of earth on top of it without showing even the suspicion of a sag anywhere. This time too we have gone in for a fireplace and chimney, our design, which was tested this evening; most of the heat went up the aforesaid chimney, but anyhow it didn't show a sign of smoking. ...

[Bois Grenier]
Monday 25th October, 1915

Alas! the weather is being most unkind: it started this morning and it looks like raining all day, which is the very devil for building operations! You can't imagine the mess it makes of everything and how appallingly uncomfortable it all becomes. You get wet and muddy all over and everything you touch is the same.

Later – 10.00 p.m. ... I am so glad Humphrey has got a Commission. I should think he is certain to get back to England to equip, lucky devil! I should think he will be very thankful to cease being a Tommy: it's no joke out here, I can assure you. ... Well, my darling, as it is rather late I must turn in. I've got a very cosy dugout this time with a fire, but it's beastly lonely. I wish I had you here!

[Bois Grenier]
26th October, 1915

... I hope the inoculation has been a success and that you felt the right amount of illness. I wonder how long the Red Cross will keep you "standing by". I am much looking forward to the cake: nothing has turned up yet, but we live in hope. ...

It has been a perfectly glorious day – bright sun, as clear as anything. Of course the guns must needs spoil it by being exceptionally active. Even our friend over the way, the vile Hun, managed to find a few shells again and join in for a bit; started dropping shrapnel about here before breakfast; rather good shots too, but not very dangerous as you could hear the whole performance from start to finish; small pop from his gun in the distance and the noise of the approaching shell gradually getting nearer, then that peculiar metallic clang and the puff of white smoke in the air. Shrapnel is pretty to watch, especially on a fine morning, and it is a great temptation to stay out and watch it, but I don't on principle – at least when they are dropping as close as they were this morning. Well, as I have to take charge of a darned working party at 6.00 a.m. tomorrow I must go to bed. Come here and let me give you that goodnight kiss you wanted so badly. My darling, I do love you so dearly ...

[front line trenches, near Rue Marle]
28th October, 1915

I was so glad to get your letter last night and to hear that mine have arrived at last. The cake and the caramels are most excellent too. The cold has passed over, thank goodness, but the handkerchiefs will be most useful, as there is still a good deal of nose blowing to be done and the faithful Humble (my servant) gets rather tired of continually washing the half dozen I brought out.[99]

I spent all yesterday up in the front line trench with that working party and by the time I got back, at tea time, had developed a perfectly vile headache, but fortunately I managed to borrow some Phenacetin – stuff I shun – and went to bed. At 7.30 p.m. I awoke quite recovered but did not bother to get up for the evening meal; instead I just had a cup of tea and cake in my dugout, and very warm and comfortable it was. Afterwards I read and reread your letter and lay there thinking about you until I dropped off to sleep – happy because I love you so and in the delightful sense of personal contact that your letter aroused. ...

....

99 13942 Private Joseph Humble of B Company was the son of James and Elizabeth Humble of 22, The Parade, Washington, Co. Durham.

<u>10.30 p.m.</u> I did not have time to finish this this morning, so I just sent you a card to let you know I am still kicking. We are back again in the front tine. It rained steadily all day and is still doing so; as you can imagine, it was pretty rotten work doing a relief on a night like this, as it always entails a good deal of standing about, and the trenches become young rivers which the floor boards may or may not keep your boots out of. I found my dugout leaking in about ten places, all directly above the bed, which contains an artificial pond several inches deep. However, after some labour I have improved the position by slinging a waterproof sheet as a kind of glorified canopy over the bed, which successfully catches all the drops and drains them down to the far end, where they are deposited on the floor. The lake also has been drained and my other ground sheet placed on the top of its site. I don't think I ever told you the tragedy that happened to the ground sheet that shared so many happy hours with us. I dropped a match on it one day and burned a great hole, so I got Mother to buy me another, which is nearly twice as big as the original one. They are splendid things, invaluable out here, and the one with the hole can still do useful work. I couldn't bear to part with him for worlds. ...

[front line trenches, near Rue Marle]
30th October, 1915

... Oh! Marje, I wonder if we shall have altered much when we meet again; won't it be exciting?

So glad you are educating your parents over little things like smoking, but I like the free use you make of my name and will you, please, tell Father that that is one of the things I did not teach you! You seem to be having quite a nice little holiday at home and you must appreciate having plenty of time to read in comfort. ...

Yes, I think we may consider that more than a third of the time has gone by now. Well, I must go to bed. It is too damned cold to sit up any longer. I do loathe the cold. I may say that going to bed here means putting a sand bag over each leg, in order to save one's blanket as much as possible, and lying down in every article of clothing you can find under the aforesaid blanket. Then, by the time you have amassed a little warmth and got off to sleep, you are awoken by a rude hand and find it is your turn to go and wander up and down the trenches, getting cold again till it is time to torment someone else. The going to bed process is repeated, and you get another spell of sleep until "stand to", when you get up and watch it grow light, the most vile of all active service tricks! ...

Toby to his mother   [front line trenches, near Rue Marle]
31st October, 1915

... There has not been much of a cheerful nature in the news lately, has there? Still, there is no knowing how things will turn out in the Balkans. I think it may well be that Germany has taken on more than she can carry through. I am so glad that you have got Marjorie staying with you this weekend. I hope she is looking fit and behaving nicely!!

Marjorie to Toby   Bennetts End
                                                                  2nd November, 1915

... Uncle Basil is coming down for the night. It will be nice to see him again after so long. Esmé has taken up her abode in Selwyn College [Cambridge, to be trained as a nurse] and seems to be settling down quite happily and has written home for a hockey stick. I had a very amusing letter from her this morning ending up "I long to hear you are booked for that hospital on Salisbury Plain. Hope Toby is alive and kicking ... ."

I met Mrs Dodgson in Hemel Hempstead this morning, her arms full of parcels, the largest of which was chicken food and had burst! She was glad to hear your cold had not turned out badly.

Toby to Marjorie   November, 1915

... I believe leave is to start at the end of this month, two officers only from each battalion to be sent away at the same time, but there seems to be some doubt as to how it will be worked exactly. If they just work straight down the list in order of seniority I suppose I should get mine about January, but there is a rumour that one senior officer and one subaltern go each time, in which case it would be the CO and I to kick off. My idea is to stay in London for the week and make headquarters there. I think it's much the best place in the winter and one can go down to Bovingdon, or any other old spot, for the day if necessary. ...

Marjorie to Toby   Bennetts End
                                                                  3rd November, 1915

Padie came down last night and we were all sitting in the drawing room about 9.00 p.m. when in walks Humphrey! Great surprise – he had not known till an hour before he started that he was to come. About ten of his Regiment are getting Commissions. They had to report at the War Office and were offered two days or two weeks and two days leave! Needless to say they unanimously voted for the latter. Today he has gone off to report at his [Royal Fusiliers] depot at Hounslow. He will be gazetted about November 16th and then will have to go to Cambridge for five weeks' training. He has applied to the Royal West Surrey reserve of officers. Really I think he has done himself well over keeping to the ranks. Think of a whole fortnight! He looks awfully well and is full of spirits. We all sat round and fired questions at him. He seems to have picked up many interesting bits of news on the way home. It is nice to have things explained a bit and learn where all the headquarters are, etc. Do tell me what Army Corps you belong to, if you know! He was very far South, with French on either side of just three English Divisions. ...

Your letter, such a nice one, dated 30th, came this morning. You are a dear to understand everything I say so well. I couldn't sit at home this morning, it was so gloriously fine, so I went on a long tramp through the lanes, which are really lovely, so absolutely lonely and hidden away. Some day I must introduce you to them. The leaves are a wonderful gold this year and looked splendid against the blue sky. I read your letter through again out there and your love felt so near and so real.

... How horrid it must be marching up and down the trenches all night, or part of the night. I know that awful feeling of being woken up so well and turned out into the cold. Only I never had to go further than upstairs into the wards. ...

Bennetts End
4th November, 1915

... I have been asking Humphrey endless questions all day and listening to his tales. He has had a very good time and quite sorry to come home. What wasted leave! He has never seen a German or been under severe fire: his worst experience was rats in some of the billets. What luck it all is as to where you get placed and what you have to do. It is horrid to think of those two new Divisions being rushed into action down at Loos.[100] There are deplorable tales everywhere now about our higher command. Humphrey had picked up a lot coming home and there are rumours of great changes, but I expect you know all about it. Humphrey sends his love and says "<u>Poor</u> Toby!" when he hears I write every day. ...

No news from the Red Cross yet. ...

Toby to his mother   [Fort Rompu, NW of Fleurbaix]
4th November, 1915

We came out of the trenches on Tuesday night after a pretty rotten time, as it rained without ceasing during the last forty-eight hours and was still pelting on the night we came out. We had a six mile march to a house. I am glad to say I managed to get a billet as I have been feeling pretty rotten with a perpetual stomach ache. I have been in bed all today and the doctor has been up and given me some pills and told me to eat nothing but slops. He was not our own man, who is ill himself, but a very nice chap from the field ambulance.

How awfully well Philip's Division [47th] has done. ... It is terribly awkward trying to write in bed so I will stop now and write to you tomorrow when I hope to be up.

Toby to Marjorie   [Fort Rompu, NW of Fleurbaix]
7th November, 1915

I am up again now, but don't feel up to much. The weather is raw and cold, with a dark sort of mist brooding over the mud and slush, which is not conducive to good spirits. It has been ripping getting your letters each evening. How nice for you having Humphrey home. He certainly has done well for himself and the five weeks training up at Cambridge will be quite pleasant too, lucky devil.

<u>Later</u>: The Battalion are going into the trenches tonight and the MO thought it was not very wise for me to go straight up after having been in bed until today, so he sent me into hospital, who forwarded me on here to the Divisional Rest Station. I am in an officers' convalescent home – a private house in the town, nicely furnished and very comfortable. I came in a car this afternoon and by then the sun had got through and it was quite a decent day, though still cold. It felt quite strange to be in a car again and reminiscent of the time when one did pleasant things. I expect I shall be here [Steenwerke] for two or three days and then join up with the Battalion again, as I am really quite well now. ...

....

100 The New Army 21st and 24th Divisions, newly arrived in France, had been rushed into action with disastrous results. (See footnotes 47 and 48, Chapter 4.)

Marjorie to Toby   Bennetts End
                                                              7th November, 1915

... We had a good time at Berkhamstead yesterday: two rounds [of golf] both
very close and exciting – one I got beaten and the last all square. The colours of
the leaves in those woods were glorious. At first it was dull and misty but after
lunch the sun came out and made them glorious. I always thought it was the best
place round here in the autumn. How I wished that you had been there to enjoy it
too. ... Tomorrow we are going to London to a play of sorts. Nearly all the plays are
matinées only, which is rather a nuisance. Bother those Zeps!

Humphrey has taken father off for a week and mother is sleeping after her night
work at the hospital, so I have the dining room to myself and am enjoying a quiet
cigarette. I have wanted you so much these last two days to play with again, to
forget we have grown up and going to be respectably married. I want to take your
hand and go wandering through the pretty golden woods and not bother about
anything. Just enjoy the feeling of youth and happiness in the freedom that only an
intimate love can give us ... .

Toby to Marjorie   [Steenwerke]
                                                              8th November, 1915

I must try and gather together the rather disconnected threads of my letters
to you during the last week. I simply couldn't write in that billet: it was such a
depressing place and then being in bed is always a difficulty. I had a room on the
ground floor of a small farmhouse looking out into a most odiferous courtyard,
the centre of which was as usual occupied by a smelly manure heap and a pool
of murky, stagnant water. But the people were really quite kind and did all they
could for me when they heard I was *"malade"*, and the coffee they made was most
excellent. This place is a delightful contrast in every way. We have a warm well-
furnished sitting room, a Mess room and separate bedrooms upstairs with real beds
and real sheets. There is also a paved and enclosed courtyard at the back leading
into quite a large and well-kept garden. The cooking smells excellent and that is
as far as I have got at present, as the MO is keeping me on a milk diet, though I feel
quite all right today. I don't know how long it will take for letters to follow through
to this place – probably some days. ...

Toby to his mother   [Steenwerke]
                                                              8th November, 1915

I am back in an officers' convalescent home ... You can hardly imagine what a
pleasure it is to see a room decently furnished and to have one's meals properly
served on a table with a tablecloth and the right number of plates, etc. ...

Things in the Balkans are getting very interesting, aren't they? I think Germany
will find she has undertaken more than she can manage there, even with the help
of the d----- Bulgars. ... I had a hamper of apples and nuts with no indication as to
who the sender was. I rather suspect them of coming from Hill House, only Marjorie
never said anything about them. I don't expect to be here more than a day or two.
By the way, it is rumoured that leave will be starting at the end of the month. I don't
expect my time will come before January, though it is just possible I might go first
with the Colonel – it depends how they arrange it.

Toby to Marjorie [Steenwerke]
10th November, 1915

I am still in the same spot, but feeling absolutely fit again now. No letters have come through yet, so I am feeling rather lost and it is very tantalising as I know there must be two or three from you by now. I had the most glorious bath this morning in a private house across the road. The people are related to the owner of this place and have placed their bath at the disposal of the officers here; so I went across and was introduced to the family and shown the bathroom by quite a chic *"demoiselle"* who talked very fair English, much to my relief. The bathroom is the best thing I have seen in France: a big room, walls of attractive white tiles and heated with hot water pipes. I just soaked for half an hour and finished up with a cold shower. When I had dressed (complete set of clean undies!) I felt better than I've done for ages.

This afternoon I took quite a long walk to a neighbouring town on a little hill. (It must have been at least 100 ft high!) Oh! the relief of seeing even such a small rise as that, and of getting just a little above the surrounding country. I also heard the whistle of a railway train; a sweet sound that said "home" and I thought of the day when I should be going feverishly to catch the train for Boulogne. It was a very decent town, with a fine open market place and not at all bad shops. ...

I wrote to Esmé the other day and addressed it to Selwyn College, which is I hope correct. I suppose she and Humphrey will be able to see quite a lot of each other. ...

Marjorie to Toby Bennetts End
11th November, 1915

I was so relieved to get yours of the 7th last night and hear you are about to have a few days in a resting place. ... Humphrey has gone away for a couple of nights, also Mother, so I am more or less alone. Father is always invisible in the garden. I have grown so used to being alone all day at Hill House that I positively object to having other people continuously there. Rather lucky, as they always tell you the newly married lady is dull all day and misses brothers and sisters, etc. Having been here three weeks I am beginning to get a little bored and want to be doing something else. I shall certainly start working at the hospital here soon. I hope the Red Cross won't keep me too long, but I expect they will. Old Esmé is having a fine time at her job, the patients keep her in chocolate and biscuits, as far as I can make out, and the last heard of her was escorting a very juvenile lad in the Black Watch to a service at Kings College Chapel who had got a new kilt for the occasion.

I have been ragging Humphrey and telling him he is the only man in the British Army who has not got a girl to write to. He told me confidentially that all the men with him were so surprised he had no one and in fact did not believe it, and he was equally surprised that all of them had. He says he would have no fault to find with life at the front as long as the officers show a common consideration for the men. Apparently his Regiment are most unfortunate in theirs, and his Company Lieutenant is under sentence of death from nearly all his men directly there is an attack. It sounds perfectly horrid. He told me to be sure to ask you if your men have a proper time allowed them for breakfast, as he could never succeed in getting time enough for his men! Also, another point of interest: do officers' servants take their turn at watch in the night? He wanted to know several other things too which I have forgotten. I do wish you could have a camera. Some of his photos are nice and he much regrets not having taken more. ...

I found Mrs Dodgson embarked on "War and Peace". Do you think she will ever get through it? So many people never do. You talked about heredity once. I would like to know where I got my taste for reading from. There is not one of either Secretans or Richardsons as far as I know who are really interested: and it certainly wasn't a cultivated taste. It has always been very boring having so few people who cared about it too. I always thought it would be dreadfully dull to marry anyone who hadn't got the same tastes, but had pretty nearly accepted it as an inevitable evil. ...

Toby to Marjorie [Rue Marle]
13th November, 1915

I rejoined the Battalion yesterday and am feeling perfectly fit. We are in billets again, for which I am not at all sorry, as today it is blowing a regular gale with squalls of driving rain. I was sorry to leave the Home, as we were awfully comfortable there and it was a very pleasant rest. On the other hand there was nothing to do there and it is more cheery to be back amongst people one knows again. I had a jolly good day yesterday. Besly, Wellesley[101] and myself went into the town [Armentières] to do some shopping and have tea. I had a most luxurious haircut and shampoo: there is no doubt that in anything of that sort the French beat us hollow. Then tea, which was a huge success. They have a piano there and afterwards Besly played, which is the greatest of treats, to me especially, and I can't tell you how it affects me after not having heard a piano, let alone any other music, for so long. Everybody felt awfully cheery and sang lustily, much to the delight of the girls in the tea shop. I had dinner with D Company and afterwards we played a small game of Hazard – another thing that I haven't done for about a month. The cards were in great form and the money was changing hands very freely. After having been twice reduced to my last five franc note, I ended up about 150 fr. to the good! ...

... Those billets we were in then were some way from the town but not much more than about a mile and a half behind the line. These are close to the town. We have not been what you might call properly back ever since we came into the firing line, which is pretty rotten. ...

Toby to his mother [Bois Grenier]
18th November, 1915

Just a line to let you know that the second parcel from Selfridges has arrived. I was very glad to get the muffler. The curry and sausages are both splendid things for this cold weather. We have been in the trenches since Sunday and are getting sharp frosts every night, but anything is better than rain. The waistcoat is splendid and fits very well. Thank you ever so much for it. I heard from Philip the other day. He seems to be pretty fed up but is expecting to go out for a rest before long.

....

101 2/Lt Eric George Wellesley was educated at Winchester College from 1909 until the summer of 1914 and enlisted in the 18th (1st Public Schools) Battalion, The Royal Fusiliers on 15th Sept. 1914. Having served in the OTC at school, he was commissioned into the 8th Yorkshires on 19th Feb. 1915 and travelled to France with them in Aug. 1915 as commander of 13 Platoon, D Coy. He was was the son of Herbert Wellesley, a stockbroker. The family was related to the Duke of Wellington. (TNA WO 339/32755)

Marjorie is going to a hospital at Chatham for a month – rather an awful spot, I should think. My boots have not turned up yet, but I am expecting them daily. ...

Toby to Marjorie [Bois Grenier]
20th November, 1915

... We have got definite information about our leave. The first lot are off on the 22nd; the next on the 27th and so on, every five days. We leave here early in the morning and arrive in London, Victoria, at 4.30 p.m. the same day. Leave is for a week, i.e. if you arrive in London on a Monday afternoon, you have to catch the 1.30 p.m. train from Victoria on the following Monday. Jolly good, isn't it? I do hope you won't get ordered off to Chatham now: it will be such a nuisance for you. I see we shall spend the whole of the first morning sending wires and telephoning. Yes, we'll certainly try and get Guy to come up, and I expect Mother will come and stay, part of the time at any rate, in London with us. ... Poor old Esmé! What rotten luck getting a dose of night-nursing like that. ...

Marjorie to Toby Great Amwell House
Ware
20th November, 1915

... I did not write yesterday as I was up in London. It took Humphrey and I nearly an hour to get me to the station as the roads were like glass again. I got those gloves for you and will probably send them along today. They are a present from Marje – no settling up. They are not as soft as I would like but I could not find any better ones. I don't know if you will find them useful. They seem very queer but its Humphrey's idea. ...

Later: ... I have asked Olive to be a bridesmaid and she was very pleased, but wishes it to be understood that the bridegroom may on no account kiss the bridesmaids! ...

The Balkan news is pretty gloomy isn't it and makes one wonder if it isn't going to develop into a ten years' struggle at least. ...

Next week I am going to work at the Hemel Hempstead hospital from 1.00 till 8.00 p.m. I was so dreadfully tired of doing nothing and the matron seems glad of help.

Toby to Marjorie [Bois Grenier]
22nd November, 1915

... I don't think I am going to get off on the 27th, so we must be resigned to the 2nd. (I expect it will go on like this for a long time: it seems the inevitable way in anything to do with the military.) ...

We have just got an unexpected two days in the billets and I had a very pleasant dinner with Besly last night. He had just had some music sent him and, amongst other things, "They wouldn't believe me". We both agreed that it was a jolly good tune and the chorus is full of suppressed "pash". We are back in the trenches again, but only for a short spell, I believe. The weather remains fine, with a hard frost every night. ...

[front line trenches, near Rue Marle]
23rd November, 1915

... Olive will make a lovely bridesmaid, but I am not sure whether the affair will be quite in order and really valid if she starts tampering with the privileges of the bridegroom! ...

There is nothing more definite about leave as far as I am concerned and I've not had a chance of seeing the Adjutant [Capt C. S. Simpson] lately. He and one of the others are going on Saturday. ... I've simply heaps of good ideas that week and we'll just let ourselves go and enjoy it, won't we darling? – and be blowed to the Kaiser and all his great wars. Marje, my darling, I do love you so and I am just longing and longing for the day. I don't feel that I can wait much longer; just think – three weary months. Have you forgotten again how to kiss? I almost feel as if I had, but it will come back quick enough when I see you. ...

[Rue Dormoire]
26th November, 1915

The gloves and the acid drops came last night. Thank you ever so much for them.

... We are out in billets again and I believe for eight days this time. I have got quite a decent room with a bed in it. The weather is rotten: today we had a biting wind and intermittent falls of rain and snow, but the sun is shining brightly now and it is freezing hard. ...

Toby to his mother [Rue Dormoire]
27th November, 1915

The Selfridges parcel arrived last night and the socks look splendid. ... That's one of the best tins of mixed biscuits I've tasted and a great improvement on the old Huntley and Palmers. I am due for my leave on 2nd December but I don't suppose I shall be able to go then as both my Company Commander and 2 i/c are in hospital. However, just in case I do get off, I've fixed up most of the arrangements with Marjorie. I think I told you we were going to stay at the St Ermin's Hotel where Mr Richardson is living. ... Hope to see you before very long.

Toby stayed in billets from 28th November to 3rd December. On 1st December he heard that his leave was to start on Friday 3rd, so he wired Marjorie with this news on 2nd in order to give her a few hours warning.

On 3rd December Toby went to Boulogne. There he had to wait eight hours for a boat and did not arrive in London until midnight. He went to the St Ermin's Hotel at St James's. After breakfast and shopping the next morning, he took the train to Boxmoor, arriving in the pouring rain at 1.08 p.m. He was met by Marjorie and his mother.

Marjorie's account in her diary of how they spent Toby's first leave shows that they were constantly together. For Toby it must have seemed a huge change from the front line. They made the most of these precious few days, living an almost fantasy existence. They stayed in the St Ermin's Hotel – a hotel that describes itself even today as 'an intimate and discreet venue', and to which they would return in the future. They spent their evenings at the theatre or at concerts, and in dining out. They often took the opportunity to catch up with friends.

4th December, 1915:

We all motored up to Hill Cottage together. Toby looked very well and a good deal fatter. ... It was difficult to believe we were really together again. He got into his mufti, grown rather tight. We dawdled away the afternoon, perfectly happy again after those long weary months. ... The best part of the day was after Mrs Dodgson had gone to bed when we had a great time together. He did not go till about midnight. He slept at the Vicarage.

5th December, 1915:

... Toby and I went to Green Lodge to collect some clothes for him. ... and we went round the garden. It was cold and damp, I felt – rather depressing. ... Toby was very sleepy that evening and felt a cold coming.

6th December, 1915:

Mrs Dodgson went to Town early and Toby and I had breakfast together. He was fearfully annoyed because his uniform had not come and was really cross, but luckily we found the uniform on the station and that cheered him up. By the time we were in London he had recovered! We went to the St Ermin's Hotel where Toby took a suite! How grand we felt.

I changed into my new frock which he very much approved of and we went to lunch at Princes. ... We did some good shopping, stockings for my frock. ... Tea alone in the suite was a very happy hour.

Then we went to Queen's Hall where we met Mrs Dodgson. The concert was splendid, the 5th Symphony was played. ... We dined at Les Goblins, quite a familiar place now, and returned to the St Ermin's where we met Padie. ...

7th December, 1915:

Toby had to go into the City in the morning ... and he bought me a brooch for my birthday present. We lunched at the Café Royal with ... Mrs Dodgson. Then Toby and I did more shopping. He bought me a hat at Maison Lewis. ... We went to dinner with Uncle Basil at the Rendezvous and then to see 'More' at the Ambassadors. It was a very amusing show. Afterwards we had a glorious time together. ...

8th December, 1915:

Actually a fine day. We walked across St James Park to Bond Street to look for a nice button-hole for me tonight. Then we went on to see his grandmother. ... Lunch at the Windsor. ... I went up to the Criterion to meet mother and brought her back to the hotel and we four had tea together in the lounge. We had dinner at Les Goblins with Olive ... .

9th December, 1915:

... Guy turned up about 12.30 and Mrs Dodgson, ... all came to lunch. Afterwards we went to see Charlie Chaplin at the New Gallery Cinema. Then Toby and I left the others and he bought me some books. He and I dined together at the Savoy and went on to the opera, coming in late to see "Pagliacci". We met Guy and his mother there. "Pagliacci" was splendid. We had the best evening of all this night.

On 10th December Toby and Marjorie *'had breakfast fairly early'* and packed up his belongings. They took a train to Victoria. Mrs Dodgson, Guy and Padie met them on the platform. ... The train left at 9.50. *'Toby looked so cheery as it went away.'*

Marjorie and Mrs Dodgson went back to the hotel. Marjorie wrote that she felt *'too flat for words'*. They packed up and Marjorie took a taxi to Euston Station. ... They went to see "The Man Who Stayed At Home" - *'a very good piece'*. Marjorie then headed for home ... .

Toby to Marjorie [Boulogne]
10th December, 1915

I must write you a few lines before I go to bed, though I feel so dreadfully sleepy that I can hardly keep my eyes open! We had a pretty rotten crossing as there was quite a sea running and we had embarked on the stupidest little cockleshell which took about three hours, so that we did not get here till nearly four o'clock. We had no chance of getting anything to eat, so you can imagine I was feeling fairly hungry. I wonder I wasn't sick, as I hate embarking on an empty stomach. However, perhaps you could scarcely call mine that, after all the meals we ate together! Just this time last night we were comfortably sipping bubbly at The Savoy. When we reported to the RTO we found that our train would not start until 1.00 p.m. tomorrow. I can't tell you how relieved I felt, but it is rather sickening to think that we are hung up here and not at Folkestone. Anyhow, a good night's rest will be very good for me, as I am feeling fagged out and still very full of cold. ...

[Boulogne]
Saturday 11th December, 1915

I had a very good sleep from 9.30 last night till after 8.00 this morning and then *petit déjeuner* in bed. I do feel better this morning and the cold is not so heavy either. The time of our leaving is again put off till 7.00 this evening. It poured with rain again first thing this morning but looks finer now. I have been thinking of nothing but these last few days we've had together; they were just perfect, but next time I think we'll only spend one, or at the most two, nights in London and the rest in the country amongst the woods and the fields. The days will be longer then and the feeling of the country in March or April is very different to what it is now in December. Anyhow, that is what I feel about it now, though I dare say another three months in Flanders may change my feeling back again! ...

Marjorie to Toby   Bennetts End
                                              11th December, 1915

I can hardly believe you are really gone and that I am back in the same old life as before you came. Everything seems so unreal. I don't seem to belong to things here a bit, and it feels as though it were ages and ages ago since I was up here wildly excited over getting your wire to say you were coming. So much has happened in between. My sweetheart, I can still see the dear look in your face as the train went away, as though it were but a moment ago. I can almost hear your voice very low in my ear and feel your warm cheek against mine. So close you seem, so tantalisingly near and yet just out of reach. I have been so very sleepy all day today, which has made me very dull to what is going on around, and conscious, in a dreamlike way, of your presence. But even as I come to put it into words the dream breaks up and leaves me beginning to awaken to the bitter reality.

... Oh the dullness of returning to the hotel and seeing your room without you and all your things scattered about. I could <u>not</u> believe you were gone. It felt as though you <u>must</u> step out of one of the rooms and put your arms round me once more. But it did not take us long to pack and we went off to Euston. All the way in the taxi I kept thinking is it really possible that you should really pass in twelve hours from this life to that in the trenches. I was ever so glad to have lunch with your mother and Guy and go to that place and not get home until the evening. It made the best of a perfectly damnable afternoon. ...

There is one bright spot on the page here. Reggie says he will be home on Wednesday next for a week. That is really good after a whole year, isn't it? Mother is perfectly delighted. I expect he will be quite different: he was such a lad when he went out. Meantime I promised, before I heard, to begin work at the hospital here, 8.00 a.m. – 1.00 p.m. every morning, on Monday next. That poor Matron will be quite sick of me and my changes of plan. Oh dear, think of having to have had breakfast and be in Hemel Hempstead by 8.00 o'clock on beastly cold or wet mornings.

... Toby my darling, take care of yourself till you come home again. I shall never be able to tell you what that week meant to me. ...

Toby to Marjorie   [front line trenches near La Rolanderie]
                                              12th December, 1915

Very, very many happy returns of the day, though I am very much afraid that this will not reach you by the 15th. I do hope you will have a nice day and I only wish that I could spend it with you. It's a great age, isn't it? And it really is quite time you were settled down with heavy responsibilities around you! ... The whole of that week is like some splendid dream now, and I can scarcely believe that it was ever real. I hope you got the letter that I posted from Boulogne. We did not get away from there until 8.00 p.m. on the Saturday, and then the railway journey took over six hours. On arriving at the railhead we found there was nothing to meet us and so had a long, weary tramp to the transport lines, nearly four miles away. The final straw was finding the farm completely surrounded by water, even on the road it was about two feet deep, and in the fields round about more than waist high, so reluctantly we splodged through it. My boots proved an immediate success and I arrived with quite dry feet. The whole state of the country is indescribable, and they say that the floods have not been so bad for twenty years. ...

On the same day, Marjorie's younger brother, Reggie, had written home:

12th December, 1915

Hurrah! My leave has been changed, and I shall be home for Christmas after all! Send the turkeys out just the same, as the fellows here have been awfully good to me and I want them to have a good time as well as me.

Reggie's mother reported that he came home for Christmas, his haversack and kit bag crammed with shell cases and other souvenirs from the front.

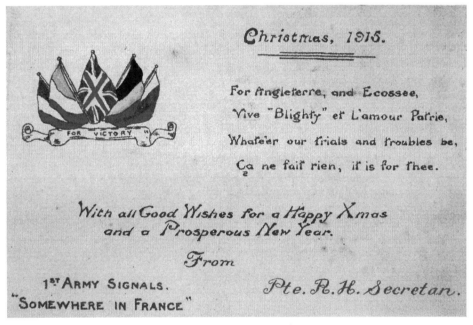

Reggie Secretan's Christmas card from France – Dec. 1915

Marjorie to Toby   Bennetts End
                                                      16th December, 1915

I am getting quite excited over the prospect of a letter from you tonight. There ought to be one, unless Christmas is making merry with the post. Isn't it luck? Humphrey comes home from 24th to 29th, so we shall be quite a cheery party. I am so glad. I was feeling very dismal over the thought of being quite alone with Papa and Mama. It would have been so flat. Uncle Basil has invited me and Reggie to a theatre and to stay with him on the 23rd, which will be very nice; though I don't feel that I want to go back to the St Ermin's without my Dodders. However we are all rather waiting to see when Esmé gets home; and besides Reggie is not here yet, and you never know!

What do you think about Sir Douglas Haig's appointment?[102] Let's hope he will make things a bit different among the Staff. It came quite as a surprise at the last moment. Don't you think things at Salonika look very shaky?[103] I continue to grow in admiration of the Hun and what he accomplishes compared with the awkward corners the Allies seemed doomed to place themselves in. ...

Toby to Marjorie   [La Rolanderie]
                                                          16th December, 1915

... There is not much news: the trenches are in an appalling condition now and need perpetual work on them to prevent them falling to pieces altogether. But the Hun is in an even worse condition than we are, as our artillery never gives him any peace at all. Whatever his diversion in the Balkans may do, one fact remains certain, and that is that at present we are absolutely on top of him here. There will be no truce here this winter. A few days ago, further down the line, a party of about fifty Huns came out and sat down in front of their trenches, making friendly overtures, when they immediately received rapid rifle and machine gun fire for their trouble. ...

                                                          [La Rolanderie]
                                                          17th December, 1915

... Will you do one or two things for me when you are next in London? First, get me a Christmas present to give Ma. I think one of those cases for holding notes would be quite nice. I saw some rather nice ones in black silk with a white stripe and I think the small size would be most convenient for her; and get it with silver and gold corners if you can. Failing, this, I know she always likes scent. Would you pack up whatever you get and send it off to her? ...

I think the hospital sounds most energetic. To start off at 7.30 a.m. these vile mornings is the limit: no wonder you remain very slight! I am awfully glad you have got Reggie coming home. I wonder if he will find his elder sister "gone to the dogs" too. You had better show him the photo book so that he shall make no mistake which Dodgson it is. ...

                                       [front line trenches near La Rolanderie]
                                                          19th December, 1915

... We are up in the front line again now and having a pretty rotten time, as they are dreadfully water-logged but, thank goodness, the weather so far this trip has been pretty decent. ... I have been feeling hopelessly unwarlike and crying peace at any price. The awful stagnation of this trench business is enough to rot anybody's mind and body. You would never believe the dreadful level to which conversation sinks, the utter futility of it and the inane remarks that cause a burst of hysterical laughter.

....

102   Gen Sir Douglas Haig was appointed Commander in Chief of the BEF on 10th Dec. 1915, replacing Field Marshal Sir John French. Haig was promoted to Field Marshal on 1st Jan. 1917.

103   The Allies had landed troops at the port of Salonika in early Oct. 1915. The objective was to help Serbia, but the Bulgarian army prevented any direct link between the Allies and the Serbs. In late Oct. the Allied troops had advanced into southern Serbia. However, in early Dec. 1915, under pressure from the Central Powers, the Allies were forced to withdraw into Greece and set up a defended line in the hills some 14 miles inland from Salonika. The Front remained a relative backwater until 1918.

Today has been particularly evil because, after waiting patiently all day, the evening has only brought the disappointment of "no mail tonight", so we are all more than usually snappy. It is rotten; you can't think how I look forward to letters from you, dearest, nor how flat it is when the post fails and one has to start getting through another twenty-four hours. ...

Marjorie to Toby   Bennetts End
                                                                  25th December. 1915

... It's sickening to think of you having such a rotten time. I expect your cold's made it feel worse lately. I feel quite horrid having everything so nice here, especially as I have not written the last two days; but really I could not help it; we simply rushed about London and had no time for anything. ... I ordered your French grammar and a phrase book yesterday. ... Mother is giving you this one: she said she wanted to send something. I have also ordered the waders. ... I sent a few sweets, etc., from Fortnum and Masons too. ...

We really are lucky: here we are all four at home for a week! Esmé suddenly got leave as her hospital is so empty. Imagine my joy on Tuesday, just as I was starting with a large box for Chatham to have a wire saying it was put off. Fancy the War Office doing anything so sensible! Reggie and I nearly burst with glee and hurried off to London, hastily arranging things just as you and I did. ...

It was a good two days, but I am in sad disgrace as I had no time to get anyone a Christmas present. However I have promised them all two each next year. ...

Reggie has returned laden with souvenirs, shell cases, crucifixes, German spurs, etc., etc. How he carried them all over I can't think. He gave father an enormous bottle of what he thought to be white wine at first, but which proved to be *eau de cologne*! Rather clever of him but of course no one inspected his kit. ...

Toby to Marjorie   [Rue Marle]
                                                              [late] December, 1915

Ever since we came out of the trenches the weather has been perfectly awful, so we are very thankful to be in billets. Christmas Day proved very uneventful and was rather more depressing than usual. I never can raise much enthusiasm over it at home and out here it seemed strangely ironical. ...

You can hardly believe how bored and flat I have been lately, hopelessly inert and terribly disinclined to write at all. I sit down and stick; nothing will come and the effort results in a blank page. I think this life has the most lowering, numbing, even debasing effect on anyone that you can imagine. ...

The Major [OC 'C' Company] and Player[104] are both back and have been getting on my nerves to such an extent that I wanted to yell. Oh, how I loathe having no single place that one call one's own to get away from all these people who are less than nothing to me. Everything about the Army is gross and damnable, and I am utterly sick to death of the whole thing. Yes, things have been quite lively in this part of the world; small raids into the Hun's trenches by night are the order of the day

....

104   Capt Eric Noel Player had attended Bristol University where he had served in the OTC. He was commissioned on 4th Nov. 1914 and was promoted to captain on 16th Apr. 1915. He was killed in action on 6th Aug. 1916 and is buried at Bécourt Military Cemetery, Becordel-Bécourt (grave I.V.31). He was 28. (TNA WO 339/187)

and have been, in many instances, very successful. We've not actually done one yet, but I suppose our turn will come.

We had one very unfortunate incident during our last spell in the trenches, which resulted in the loss of Wellesley. He was sent out on a reconnoitring patrol to inspect the enemy's wire and, having done this quite successfully without being spotted by the Hun at all, he needs must go and start throwing bombs into their trench, after which they had, of course, to make a hasty retreat, at the beginning of which he must have been hit. This all happened at about six in the morning, just before it got light, which is all the more foolhardy, as it was impossible to send anyone out to look for him until the following evening. We spent a miserable day wondering if he was lying out there wounded and able to do nothing. However, the next night no trace of him could be found and the Huns were waiting all ready for our patrol, so it looks as though they must have got him, though whether alive or dead it is useless to speculate. Personally, I shall miss him very much, as I used to see a lot of him and we had many a cheery game of cards together. And the Battalion can ill afford to lose officers such as he.[105] ...

Marjorie to Toby   Bennetts End
                                                              26th December, 1915

... It's only a fortnight since you went but it seems ages and ages. I dare say it is because I have done so many different things and we have been so thrilled over Reggie coming ... .

I had great fun with Reggie in Town. You see he joined the Army directly he left school and went out so soon he has never been about with us since he was considered a child; and he still likes me to conduct him and do all the talking. But I was very firm and made him tackle the waiters and do everything in style. He is an awfully cheery lad. He is going to apply for a Commission, I am sorry to say, as he is so safe as he is, but he thinks no young healthy people ought to take up those kinds of jobs. Of course he could not help it at the beginning, but now he thinks they won't mind his eyesight. He will have to apply though his CO so it is sure to be some time going through. He has given me a very nice map of the First Army area which he had issued to him. He never goes up near you, his work taking him mostly to Béthune and back. ...

Toby to Marjorie   [Rue Marle]
                                                              31st December, 1915

... I and the red-headed Rowley[106] are together in the remains of a farm a few hundred yards behind the front line. There is only one room left still habitable and in that the rain comes through the ceiling, as there is no roof and the only means of

....

105   The body of 2/Lt Wellesley was never found. He was killed on 21st Dec. 1915 and is commemorated on the Ploegsteert Memorial to the Missing. He was 19. Several accounts of the circumstances of his death can be found in his service record. At 6' 3" he cut a distinctive figure in the Battalion and was popular with the men: "he was the pick of the Regiment and anybody in the Platoon would go anywhere for him." (TNA WO 339/32755)

106   2/Lt Newton Rowley had enlisted as a Territorial in the ranks of the London Rifle Brigade in Jan. 1913 before gaining a commission in 8th Yorkshires on 18th Dec. 1914. In civilian life he was a 'Master Printer' from New Barnet in Hertfordshire and was married. He was killed in the attack on Contalmaison on 10th July 1916 at the age of 26. He is buried in Bécourt Military Cemetery (grave I.T.7). (TNA WO 339/17707)

entrance is through the shattered windows, which one has to scale as they are some six or seven feet above the ground. The furniture consists of a few relics amongst which we sit with a couple of candles and a smoky brazier. ...

[Rue Marle]
1st January, 1916

Here we are in a new year and how I wonder what it will bring us; so much is going to happen before this time next year. ...

We have started here well, anyhow. ... Early this morning, our Division carried out a raid on the Hun trenches.[107] We were not detailed to go over the top but were in the reserve line. It was quite successful as all the raiding party got back after entering the Hun's front line and the whole scheme went without a hitch, the conjunction of the artillery being splendid, and must have caused the enemy heavy casualties. The whole thing only took about twenty minutes, though of course it was much longer before the commotion died down. You can't imagine the noise. ...

Marjorie to Toby   Bennetts End
1st January, 1916

... Dearest, I have been thinking of you such a lot these last two days and my heart makes me think of you "Lonely and angry and hating it still". I long to be with you and shake you back into your real self, into the Toby I know and love so well. Don't let yourself be overwhelmed with the beastliness of it all. Let us hope you will win back your £5 with regard to the War ending in 1916 – this year, you know. My God, wouldn't that be grand? To think we have come round to the anniversary of the time I stayed at Green Lodge and we first discovered a mutual interest that ended so gloriously. ...

Toby to Marjorie   [Rue Marle]
3rd January, 1916

... We moved yesterday to another part of the reserve line. We have got a Mess in an old farmhouse where there has evidently been a young genius – all the paper is off the walls and on the plaster are some simply splendid charcoal studies; one, a girl in a columbine dress, nearly life size, is just perfect. I sit there and can hardly take my eyes off it. I wish you could see it, because what struck me at once was that she has a perfect figure, just right, and I believe you would agree too. Then there is another of a rotund and hilarious Major in full chase, the expression on his face is too priceless, and the girl is good too, quite slim. ...

[Rue Marle]
5th January, 1916

... We are still in the trenches, but the weather has been much better these last few days and yesterday was quite sunny, with almost a touch of spring in the air. I am very fed up with the posts, as parcels seem to be taking about ten days to get

....

107   The war diary of 69th Infantry Brigade records "A raid on the enemy's trenches ... was carried out by a detachment of 9th Yorkshires. About 20 of the enemy were killed by the assaulting party. Our casualties ... were 7 wounded, of which 5 were slight cases." (TNA WO 95/2183) This was the first trench raid carried out by the 23rd Division. It is described in detail in the Divisional History pp. 40-42.

here, so I've got nothing to read and I have had such a lot of spare time, which has all been wasted. Reading is about the only thing I feel the least inclination for; I could play cards, only none of the blighters in this Mess play; as for letter writing, it becomes more irksome every day. I loathe the sight of writing paper and envelopes; it's all hopelessly inadequate and clumsy.

It is really awfully sweet of you to write every day and I can't think how you manage it, but I don't want you to if it is an effort … . The perpetual standing about behind mud heaps and sandbags, killing time, being fatted up for the slaughter in the spring. Oh, such a fine ennobling existence! Now I've lost my temper, so I'll shut up.

[Rue Marle]
9th January, 1916

I am afraid you are thinking me a perfect pig, which I certainly was the last time I wrote. I have ordered Whymper's "Scrambles in the Alps" for you as a "pig present". I hope you have not read it already; it sounds such a fascinating book. It may take a little time to arrive, as they will have to find a second-hand copy. …

I was playing bridge round at HQ last night. One, Major Lush of the West Yorks,[108] is our CO now; not at all a bad little man and, though easier in some ways to get on with than old [Lt Col] Stephen, not really a patch on him.

Marjorie to Toby
Bennetts End
10th January, 1916

… I suppose I ought to be in despair over that blighted Red Cross but I seem unable to feel anything but feebly amused. I saw another lady this time; also very nice. She says it's not their fault, it's the War Office. They got out the scheme for women and told the Red Cross to get the names, etc., which they did last October. Having got all the people as desired, nothing happens. No effort was made to send the men into a more active sphere, consequently very few have gone. In addition the WO have reduced the salaries all round. She said they may want us at Chatham at the end of January, but she knew no more. The Red Cross people were very annoyed about it. Also the rule is now made after a month's service you must sign on for a year. Of course I shall chuck it. It is no earthly use for me. But observe the absurdity of having applied on 4th October and on 10th January to realise it is no good. This lady said it had come very hard indeed on girls who had depended on employment for their living and been kept waiting for nothing. Last October I was quite keen to go into a London hospital for three months like Esmé did; if only I had known then I could have done it; but now it is too late as I had pinned my hopes on your getting home before three months elapsed from now. …

....

108   A pre-war regular soldier, Maj Robert F. Lush was a captain in the Reserve of Officers in Aug. 1914. In Sept. 1914 he rejoined the army and became a major in the 11th West Yorkshires (69th Infantry Brigade). He was appointed to temporary command of the 8th Yorkshires from about 1st Jan. until 17th Jan. 1916. In Feb. 1916 Lush was promoted to Lt Col and took command of a battalion of the South Staffordshire Regt.

Toby to Marjorie   [front line trenches, Rue Marle]
                                                          11th January, 1916

... We are in the front line again. The weather is warm and muggy and the trenches a good deal drier than they have been. ...

                                             [front line trenches, Rue Marle]
                                                          14th January, 1916

Last night no less than four letters arrived all in a bunch, dated 5th, 6th and 10th. I just loved them. It is sickening for you about Chatham, but personally I am not so very sorry, as I always had visions of my getting leave and you not being able to get away. No sweets have ever arrived yet, but there is still a chance that they may turn up in a day or two. ...

Aren't Bairnsfather's things priceless? I believe they are to be published separately and I want to get them; they are so expressive of the life out here, so true to life.[109]

Marjorie to Toby   Bennetts End
                                                          14th January, 1916

It is really quite wrong of you to spoil Marje like this; but I love you for it and

although I feel I don't deserve to be given a present, you are a dear to think of it and I shall be so pleased to have Whymper. ...

The last few days I have been going to the hospital again, 8.00 – 1.00, doing what is really Mother's work. This time I am downstairs and have to look after the Tommies. It is perfectly amazing what cures they make. Some of the men have been in hospital over a year and still have great open wounds; but will get well in time. You had better keep away from me when you get wounded or I shall be wanting to practice my inexperienced hand on you! ...

Toby to Marjorie   [Fort Rompu, NW of
                                  Fleurbaix]
                       18th January, 1916

... We have a new Colonel definitely appointed, who appears to be quite a good sort, though I've not met him personally yet. He was in the Navy in

Mary Secretan

....

109   Capt Bruce Bairnsfather was a humourist and cartoonist who was best known for his cartoon character "Old Bill", a curmudgeonly old soldier with a walrus moustache and balaclava. First published in the *Bystander*, Bill was very popular with officers and men in the BEF who identified with his humour and stoicism.

earlier days. Everyone was quite sorry to lose Lush, who really went out of his way to be pleasant. I was playing Poker round with D Company the other night. It's a fine game and has almost entirely taken the place of "Vingty" amongst us. ...

They have started a Divisional theatre now, with a combined cinema and variety show, which I went to last night; really awfully well done and all real talent. There are two Sergeants who are evidently comedians in civil life and they made everyone scream with laughter.[110] It is a great thing for all the Tommies and it was packed full. I seem to have had no time for any reading of French these last few days. Have you got any definite plans, or are you just going to keep on at the hospital in Hemel? Poor old thing, it is a dull life and you have not got anybody much to talk to round about. ...

I had such a wonderful dream last night; that evening before I left England all over again, but oh! the greyness of waking up and finding it was only a dream. It was so sweet while it lasted. ... You can never know how much I need you, how hopelessly wasted all these days are without you.

[front line trenches, La Rolanderie]
24th January, 1916

... We are in the trenches again after quite a good week in billets. We have got another new CO [Lt Col E. L. Lowdell] as the naval man has gone. The General (Divisional) [Babington] thought him too old and apparently wasn't at all complimentary. I've not met the new one yet. ...

P.S. *The Dump* won't amuse you much, I expect, as it is so topical and a lot of it bad at that.[111] Will you pass it on to Mother; she might like to see it and I have not got another copy.

[front line trenches, La Rolanderie]
26th January, 1916

... I think the preparatory school idea is great and sounds much more attractive than any hospital – nor nearly such long hours, decent holidays and probably a nice place. What sort of a screw [salary] will you get? I think you could be a great success, too. It would just suit you and I don't think you would have any difficulty in keeping order, as they always succumb to a pretty face and a cheery soul. My leave is rather a problem and I should hardly think you would get a week off, but then I could come and take the sea air and flirt with you when you were not on duty and you could get a long weekend. Then, with any luck, I could get my leave during the holidays. I must say, the picture of Marjorie as a schoolmistress appeals to me quite a lot.

We are just out of the trenches again and going to the baths this morning. ... I wish they'd send us to Egypt, or anywhere as far as that goes. I never want to see Flanders again. ...

....

110   The concert party of the 23rd Division later became known as 'The Dumps'.

111   *The Dump* was the trench journal of the 23rd Division which was published annually from Christmas 1915.

Marjorie to Toby   Bennetts End
                                                              28th January, 1916

I heard from Humphrey this morning seemingly quite annoyed I am not going to Chatham. Why could I not sign on for a year, etc.? He seems to like it quite well, but says there is nothing whatever to do, crowds of officers and very few men. He was thinking of applying for a transfer into another regiment. ...

Marje has had quite a new scheme in her head this last fortnight. Soon after you went away last August a very old family friend, a Mr Churchill who has a school at Broadstairs, recommended me very strongly to get a post as mistress in a preparatory school, of course for the lowest form. He said there was enormous demand for that, owing to so many masters having gone. ... So I casually made a few enquiries last time I was in London not thinking it would be much good, but last night I had several schools send me quite decent ones wanting a junior mistress. I wrote to one at Deal which sounded the nicest. Mr Churchill wrote again a few days ago and told me the best place to apply in London, so I am going to see if I can find out more tomorrow. I don't quite know what to think about it myself ... . I don't know if I could teach and I am sure I have forgotten how to do long division and fractions. On the other hand it would be quite a nice life, plenty of holidays and some extra cash, and I don't think I can face the prospect of staying here endlessly till the war ends. It's _so_ dull, you see we are all such miles away from anyone and I have been feeling so utterly flattened by it lately. But the great point is, will any schoolmaster give me leave when you get yours. What do you think? ...

Toby to Marjorie   [La Rolanderie]
                                                              30th January 1916

Yours of the 26th came last night. So glad *The Dump* reached you and of course I understand you've had no time to read...

... We had dinner at Lucienne's last night - Besly, Thomson, Adjutant [Capt C. S. Simpson] and Grellet (Captain of D Company)[112] - a very cheery party. Besly has just written a new song and one of the best he has done, I think. I have been feeling ever so fit this last fortnight or so and just longing to kiss someone! I've a lot more to say but no time to say it.

                                                [front line trenches, La Rolanderie]
                                                              2nd February, 1916

... You will be interested to hear that I have been appointed Second-in-Command of B Coy. I don't know whether it will mean a third star; probably not, as they have a nasty way out here of giving you a job without the accompanying kudos. Anyhow it is a change for the better. Of course I was sorry to leave C Coy as I had been

....

112   Capt Reginald Charles Grellet was commissioned into the 8th Yorkshires on 6th Dec. 1914 having enlisted in the Inns of Court OTC on 16th Oct. An exceptionally capable officer, he achieved rapid promotion becoming a Major and 2 i/c of the 8th Yorkshires in May 1917. He commanded the Battalion during the summer of 1917 until he was wounded by a shell fragment at Inverness Copse on 22nd Sept. 1917. (TNA WO 339/3388) He was awarded the DSO "for conspicuous gallantry and devotion to duty. He led his battalion through heavy shell fire, and assisted both in the capture and defence of the furthest objective. By the determination which he inspired at all times, and by his energy, coolness and judgment he raised the highest enthusiasm among his men. As a result of his organisation the battalion within a short period took over and maintained with the highest spirit a new portion of the line under most difficult conditions." (*London Gazette* 27th Oct. 1917, citation 18th Mar. 1918). After recovering from his wound he commanded the Battalion for much of 1918 and 1919.

there ever since the start and knew all the men, but the Mess was awful. Captain Richardson commands this Company - a funny old bird, an awful grouser and a terrific bore.[113] There are only three other members at present: Miller the signalling officer,[114] Oakley (who draws and did those silhouettes amongst other things)[115] and another harmless sub.[116] We are in the trenches again and the weather has gone much colder, though it still remains wonderfully fine...

[La Rolanderie]
5th February, 1916

... We only got out of the trenches last night. We had a Company of the Suffolks, belonging to a new Division just out,[117] in with us for instruction, so I had a busy time and no opportunity for writing or reading. Presumably that Division will relieve us sometime this month. I felt absolutely fagged out last night: a head sore and aching from short, wakeful nights and a body stale and inert. Under such circumstances you can scarcely imagine the physical pleasure of getting one's clothes off and creeping into the welcome fleabag. Of course I feel as fit as anything this morning, especially as it is a grand day, with quite a warm sun ... and I went for a topping ride this morning ...

The dining club is meeting this evening and as the Adjutant [Capt C. S. Simpson] is going on leave tomorrow it promises to be a cheery, if not riotous, evening. I think it is quite doubtful whether I shall get mine before we go back into Corps Reserve. ...

Dear old thing, it is just glorious to think of seeing you again and feeling you kissing and holding me tight in your arms. ... Oh, I'm just longing to be with you, Marje my darling!

[Hallobeau]
8th February, 1916

Just a hasty line to let you know that I may come on the 16th. Of course it may not go through, but anyhow my name has gone in and I will wire you directly I hear anything definite. ... I shall do my best to make sure of catching the morning boat this time and will wire you from Boulogne to the St Ermin's Hotel. ...

[Hallobeau]
11th February, 1916

The leave seems to be going forward, so I am beginning to hope it may be all right. We are having some perfectly hateful weather – very cold east winds with rain and sleet. Thank goodness we are not in the trenches. There is absolutely no

....

113 Capt Arthur V. Richardson was OC of B Company. He was made a captain in the Yorkshire Regt on 23rd Dec. 1914 and posted to the 8th Bn. He was awarded the MC when serving with the Battalion in late 1916/early 1917.

114 Lt F. C. Miller was commissioned into the 8th Yorkshires on 8th Feb. 1915 after service in the OTC at St Paul's School. He was slightly wounded on 10th July 1916 before being promoted to Captain on 28th Feb. 1917.

115 Lt H. L. Oakley was an artist who drew silhouettes and cartoons for The Dump between 1915 and 1918 as well as for The Bystander. He was commissioned into the 8th Yorkshires on 20th May 1915. The War Diary records a 2Lt Oakley as arriving at the battalion on 7th Oct. 1915.

116 Sub = a subaltern. The generic term in the British Army for commissioned officers holding the rank of Lieutenant or Second Lieutenant.

117 The Brigade war diary records: "11th Suffolk Regiment joined the Brigade for a course of instruction." (TNA WO 95/2183) The 11th Suffolks were part of 34th Division, a New Army division which had assembled in France by 15th Jan. 1916.

news. I think I told you that the Admiral is back again; he is a typical sailor and very good company off parade. They had him round to dine at D Coy last night and we played poker afterwards, at which he was very cunning. His remarks on the Kirchner pictures were also very much to the point.[118] ...

Toby was granted leave in mid-February and again Marjorie recorded this happy week in her diary:

> **17th February, 1916:**
> ... I went to Victoria and found the leave train arrived at 12.07. At last it came and I met Toby looking very well, and drenched through with the rough crossing. We went back to the St Ermin's where he changed and then up to lunch at Mrs Dodgson's club. It was bitterly cold. We went and bought the camera at Negretti's and some silk stockings, etc. for me. ... We went to dine at Princes ... then we went on to the Palace ... . Toby enjoyed the show immensely. I believe I did eventually go to sleep about 4.00 a.m!

> **18th February, 1916:**
> ... Then we did some more shopping and had some lunch at Euston and came home by the 1.45. Toby had a room in the adjoining cottage this time – we had a long time together before we went to bed.

> **19th February, 1916:**
> We motored to Cambridge – did some shopping. Toby being very much welcomed in some of his old haunts. Then we had lunch at The University Arms with Esmé and Guy. ... We stopped at Amwell and had tea with Mr and Mrs Naylor and arrived at Bennetts End about 7 o'clock. Mrs Dodgson came up to dinner too and we had a cheery evening.

> **20th February, 1916:**
> A very cold day. We went up to Green Lodge – lit a fire and took some photos in Mrs Dodgson's bedroom. Toby went to sleep after lunch. We just took Toby back to Green Lodge and after tea developed the photos. ...

> **21st February, 1916:**
> ... Toby and I stayed in all day and took photos ... . He was dreadfully sleepy all day but of course we had stayed up very late again.

> **22nd February, 1916:**
> We motored into Hemel Hempstead and then up to Bennetts End on a bitter day and a snow storm. Lunch at Bovingdon and then more photos at Green Lodge. ... I developed them alone and we sat up late again.

....

118 Raphael Kirchner (1876 -1917) was an Austrian illustrator whose erotic sketches of 'long-legged bestock-inged beauties' were popular as pinups in officers' messes. (Holmes, *Tommy*, p. 597)

23rd February, 1916:
Snow everywhere. We spent the morning in the cottage and I took photos out of doors of Toby and his mother. We went up to London by the 3.20 and went to tea at St Ermin's. We have rooms on the 5th floor this time. ... We went to the Rendezvous to dinner and then on to see "Please help Emily" – a very amusing show. ...

24th February, 1916:
This was an extra day which Toby had taken, thinking to catch up his own lot at Boulogne. It was snowing hard. We stayed in the hotel till 11.30 then he went to the City and I went to Negretti's and we had lunch with Padie at his office. ... Then we came up West ... where he met Mrs Dodgson. ... Toby and I dined at Les Goblins and went on to the Shaftesbury. ... It was good to see "Pagliacchi" again and it was very well done. The last evening was very, very sweet. We were both very sleepy.

25th February, 1916:
We had breakfast ... and came to Victoria about 8.45. ... The same sort of crowd on the platforms. The train went off punctually at 9.15. ... It was vilely cold.

Marjorie to Toby   Bennetts End
25th February, 1916

I am afraid you must have had the devil of a cold crossing. It has been so bitterly cold all day. I do hope you will not miss those gloves too much. Poor old thing, having no one to chat to. Marje was a very bad little girl and went back to the hotel and sat on the edge of her bed and shed many tears. She felt so lonely.

Now I am back again I can hardly believe you have ever been here. ...

I had a note from the agency bidding me write at once to the Eastbourne school so I made a noble effort to control my writing and compile a really tempting epistle. Vacancies are coming in galore now. I really ought to get something ...

PS She is <u>so</u> sorry she cried this morning. Very unfair when the passing is just as bad for you. Almost worse when I think what a beastly time you get compared to our existence here. I didn't mean to. All the same I would much rather be bashed up by the Hun than left to live on alone.

Toby to Marjorie   [Steenbecque]
28th February, 1916

I'm afraid it is a long time that I am waiting before sending off a letter. I did begin one at Boulogne, but have mislaid it somewhere, so I must begin again. Of course getting a letter from you today has made me even more conscience-stricken, though as you shall see it is not all my fault. Yes, we did have a vile crossing – frightfully cold and about halfway across came into a regular blizzard with snow, which made the getting into the harbour a very slow business. I spent the night there at the Hotel de Paris and did my best to chase away the inevitable glummers with cocktails.[119] Anyhow I had a very good night's rest and continued my journey the next day about one o'clock, which landed me at my billet about eight that evening, where I was somewhat disconcerted to find that the place was deserted, the Regiment having moved off some days previously. I could find out nothing except that they were expected back the next day, so I couldn't do anything but go to bed. The people at my billet were awfully nice and could not do enough for me. Luckily the next day the Regiment did come back, for which I was glad, as I wasn't very keen on marching a pilgrimage through France trying to find them. That little devil Jennings[120] has got three weeks' leave to get his teeth done - wasn't I a mug, as I did break a great chunk off one of mine some months ago too. ...

No, the week did not seem at all long to me and when I got over here and thought about it all it just felt like one very, very happy day – all over before one realised that it had begun. I did enjoy every moment of it from the time I first caught sight of you on Victoria Station, when you looked just as I had always pictured you would, right up to the very last moment when we said goodbye. I am so glad you liked the camera and the other things. ... Now I am really going to start saving up a few pence just in case the war ends before we expect and there is a chance of getting married, so I don't suppose you'll get any presents next leave, which we will spend by the sea for about 5/- a day! Oh, Marje! It is so dull and lonely coming back here away from all you love most in the world, and a week like that does accentuate it all so. The weather is perfectly vile out here – colder and nastier than it has been the whole winter. I foresee we are going to get damn all in the way of a rest: already I have been rushed off my legs with work since I got back.

[Ruitz]
1st March, 1916

I am afraid letters will be rather erratic at present as we are on the move again – no peace for the wicked! Thank goodness the weather has improved and yesterday was a ripping fresh day with quite a warm sun. There are some quite pleasant hills around here and the march yesterday after the train journey was quite exhilarating. It is a relief to see some decent country after the eternal flatness of our last environments. I am much nearer Philip now – almost directly behind him, I should think – so I hope we may meet after all. It begins to look as though this show of the Hun down at Verdun was the real thing and let's hope it will be his last. The next few months should be full of excitement. ...

[Ruitz]
4th March, 1916

Thank you so much for sending on the gloves and for getting the cards and counters. ... We have actually remained still the last two or three days and, with the exception of an inspection, have had a pretty easy time. I rode into the town

....

119   A feeling of gloom – even depression – was felt by many soldiers when returning from leave. Leave could be disruptive by emphasising the gulf that existed between the Home Front and the front line, not to mention the inevitable sense of loss when leaving loved ones at the end of leave. (See Fuller, J.G., *Troop Morale and Popular Culture in the British and Dominion Armies 1914-18*, p. 73.)

120   Three officers with the surname Jennings – presumably brothers or cousins – were commissioned into the 8th Yorkshires on the same day – 14th Jan. 1915. 2/Lt S. Jennings and 2/Lt T. N. Jennings were both serving with the Battalion in Mar. 1916.

near here [Bruay] yesterday, which is quite the nicest that I have struck since we've been out here. The weather has quite gone to pieces again and we are once more inundated by a heavy fall of wet, slushy snow which is too vile for words, but it can't do the Hun's offensive any good anyhow. ...

[Ruitz]
5th March, 1916

Just a few lines before I go to bed, though there is not very much to write about. It froze quite hard last night on top of all that snow and slush, so you can imagine the state of the roads, but today has been better again with some sun. Besly and I rode over to the town [Bruay] and had a most cheery time – an excellent lunch at an hotel, after which we did our shopping and in the boot shop we came across two of the prettiest girls I've seen out here. Oh, quite charming and full of fun! It is extraordinary how different the people in this part of the country are; much nicer both to talk to and to look at, and much more what one always imagined French people were like. It is hardly necessary to add that we both behaved in an exemplary manner all the time.

We expect to be moving again tomorrow, so don't expect too prolific a correspondence. I feel ever so much fitter and better pleased with life down here. It does make such a terrific difference to have more or less interesting country about one, with some hills and valleys, though I dare say some of one's enthusiasm will leave before long, as I believe it is a pretty damnable part of the line. ...

With the French Army now coming under immense pressure at Verdun, and the BEF growing in strength, the French needed to hand over more of the line to the British. In March 1916 the British front was extended by twenty miles, running from Loos to a point southwest of Arras at Ransart. This extension included the important tactical feature of Vimy Ridge. This operation relieved the French Tenth Army for operations at Verdun. One of the British divisions taking over the line in the Souchez area at the northern end of Vimy Ridge was the 23rd Division. The Division started to move south during the first week of March. The 8th Yorkshires marched into the new sector on 6th March.

Toby to Marjorie [Gouy Servins]
6th March, 1916

... This is probably the last comfortable evening we shall have for some time. We marched away from our last place this morning, with snow falling quite heavily, but after about a quarter of an hour it cleared up and the sun came out and made us very warm. I enjoyed the tramp very much. About half way we climbed up a long hill, which gave us a splendid view from the top, where we halted for lunch on the outskirts of a wood. It looked quite like a Swiss scene and there was a pleasant little *estaminet* where we got coffee served by a young blue-eyed maiden with well formed athletic limbs and a shy smile. We are now billeted in the most extraordinary place that must, once upon a time, have been a fine *château*, but all the windows have been bricked up, every sort of fixture, down to the mantelpieces, removed and generally it looks as though no one had inhabited it for years. It is fitted up with makeshift beds and has the appearance of a very dirty barracks. I am fed up with this snow. It does make everything in such a mess and it came down like anything just as we were getting here. ...

The Battalion took over trenches from the French late in the evening of 7th March. As Toby was soon to find, the new line consisted of shallow, poorly maintained, filthy trenches containing many unburied bodies, and few strongpoints or dugouts.

Toby to Marjorie [front line trenches, Souchez sector, Vimy Ridge]
8th March, 1916

You will only get a very short letter today, as it will be written under rather difficult circumstances. We are again in the trenches and having a fairly thin time of it. All this snow is the limit and makes it bitterly cold. Our present bit of line is as big a contrast to what we had previously as you could imagine. It makes me realise to the full how good and comfortable our old trenches were. ... I heard from Mother yesterday, who was down at Dartmouth. Guy has got a week's leave and is going to join her there. ...

[Gouy Servins]
13th March, 1916

... I envy you your job by the fire these days: it is damnably cold out here. We got out of the trenches a couple of days ago after a rotten time. It was the most arduous time we've had and a great change from anything we'd done before. The weather was awful: we left our billets at about six in the evening with snow falling fast, and were not in position until about 2.30 a.m. and the snow had not stopped even then. It was about a six mile march along the road and then a communication trench over two miles long and hilly at that. We finally found ourselves in a trench (so called by courtesy only) perched on top of a hill [the northern end of Vimy Ridge], with the Boche sitting also on top of the hill about fifty yards, and in some places only ten yards, away. Morning disclosed that we were in "some" position. It looked just like Switzerland and they would have been fine skiing slopes. From where we were we could see a tremendous way, as the ground fell away sharply behind us and to our left, so that we looked right down on top of the line. The trench was the worst thing I've seen: our accommodation for five officers was one hole in the ground, about twenty feet below the ground level, which you had to descend to backwards down a sort of mine shaft. The said hole was certainly not more than 6' x 10' and here we slept and did everything. You couldn't cook, except on a Tommy cooker, and water was very scarce, as every drop had to be carried from the bottom of that damned hill. The men had a rotten time as there were practically no dugouts for them and many of them never got even a drop of hot tea all the time they were in. It snowed again the second day we were in, so thank goodness they relieved us on the fourth night and that was about as bad as the rest of it. We got back to these billets at 5.00 a.m.! Heavens! Bed was nice and I slept without winking from six till four in the afternoon and got up for dinner.

Yesterday Besly and I went over to the *château* at the other place we were at, and damn me if some blasted Hun didn't bomb us from the skies and fairly put the wind up us. We were riding through a village and saw five aeroplanes high up. The first bomb fell quite close and made the most hideous noise coming down. I may mention that this visit was for the benefit of Besly entirely! Anyhow, we do manage to enjoy ourselves when we are out of the trenches, and I have been quite liking the war since we came to these parts: the people are so much more pleasant than those sour-looking Flemish.

<u>Later</u>: We moved again today and are now back where we were before. It has been a splendid day – hot and sunny. It is a treat to feel some warmth in the air.

Have you seen Oakley's silhouettes in *The Bystander* of 8th March? You will recognise Jennings leading his platoon up a communication trench! ......

As Toby had observed, the Vimy Ridge sector was difficult to defend as the Germans looked westwards down the slope from the summit of the ridge over the British front lines, supply routes and artillery positions. However, British observers were unable to see the enemy artillery and approach routes on the far side of the summit as the eastern escarpment drops steeply towards the Douai plain. Since the French offensive of September and October 1915 this had been a quiet sector and the French and Germans had since operated a 'live and let live' approach.

The Battalion had been withdrawn from Vimy Ridge on 10th March, moving into reserve positions at Gouy Servins. The Brigade marched to Bruay on 13th March before taking over the Angres Sector on 19th March. The Angres Sector was the northernmost part of the former French line between Loos and Vimy Ridge.

"Trench Life" - Silhouettes from The Bystander, 8th March 1916. Marjorie believed that Toby's silhouette was the single figure wearing a peaked cap and holding a cigarette near the centre of the right hand edge of the picture

Toby to Marjorie   [trenches, Angres Sector]
                                                              19th March, 1916

It is quite a long time since I wrote to you, for which there is no adequate excuse as we've actually been stationary for a few days, but I've been busy amusing myself. Philip and I have at last discovered each other. He was billeted at a place about three miles away, so we saw quite a lot of each other. ...

... The sun has been splendid and the mud has been drying up and one feels like shouting. On the march yesterday the roads were quite dusty, and it was delicious to be able to lie down in the sun during the lunch halt and eat our sandwiches in comfort. That sort of thing is quite the best part of this sort of life. But everything has been much pleasanter since we came down to these parts and we've been constantly on the move, which is always more interesting than being stuck in one spot. ... We are in the trenches again, but my Company is in reserve in some houses about a mile and a half behind the front line, knocked about a good deal but still habitable.

... Haven't the French been splendid at Verdun? I really think the Hun is nearly at the end of his tether, once the spring comes and the Russians start to move. The Turk, too, must be heartily sick of it. ... I am utterly disgusted with all the bickering over the married men, and why the devil they should think themselves privileged to slink out of it all while other people do the dirty work for them, I never have been able to fathom.[121] ...

Toby to his mother   [trenches, Angres Sector]
                                                              20th March, 1916

You will be glad to hear that Philip and I have met at last. His [47th] Division relieved ours and last week he was billeted at a place only about three miles from us, so he came over to see me one day and I went over there the next. That was well back from the firing line and quite decent country. The Battalion is in the line again now but my Company is in reserve in billets that are fairly intact. I believe these trenches are much better than the last lot we were in. ...

At about this time Helen Dodgson's three sons heard that she was to marry Hamilton Fulton.

Toby to Marjorie   [trenches, Angres Sector]
                                                              22nd March, 1916

I got yours of the 16th all right with the photos ... . I think Seaford sounds rather nice and I've always heard that it was good country. I should have thought you could easily have got up enough botany to grapple with the youthful enquirers after knowledge. Mother and Father might give you practical knowledge and illustrations

....

121 Throughout 1915 there was an ongoing public debate on whether married men ought to volunteer. *John Bull* had been firmly in favour of their doing so in 1914, but in 1915 had advocated that men with dependants should volunteer in 'the last resort' after men without responsibilities. The last attempt to keep alive the voluntary system of enlistment was the Derby Scheme. During the period Oct. to Dec. 1915 men who had not so far volunteered could 'attest' and wait their turn to be called up. Under the Scheme, single men would be called up before married men. However, there was a 'storm of protest' in 1916 as married men who had attested under the Scheme were called up before unattested single men who were only able to be called up after the Military Service Acts of 1916 brought in conscription. (Adrian Gregory, *The Last Great War,* p. 94)

from work in the garden; then during the evenings you could spend two or three hours with text books! ...

[trenches, Angres Sector]
25th March, 1916

Sorry this has not gone off before, but I was interrupted. We are in the front line again and, as luck would have it, there was a heavy fall of snow again the night before we came in, so our spring weather was not long-lived. It was sickening to see all the roads wet and muddy again and now snow on the top of it is the limit. ...

By now Marjorie had accepted a teaching post starting in the summer term at Seaford on the Sussex coast. St Peter's School was a boarding preparatory school for boys.

Toby to Marjorie   [trenches, Angres Sector]
27th March, 1916

... I think Seaford will be quite a good spot for a summer leave if not too overrun by the military. You can find out all the nicest walks and must mark bathing pools. Oh, how ripping it will be to be with you again! I've wanted you so badly. I had a splendid dream three nights ago.

Marjorie to Toby   Bennetts End
29th March, 1916

I have had two letters from you since I came home, the last one dated 25th. It is horrid to think of you in the front line through this awful weather. I was not surprised to hear your burst of spring was short-lived. We have had the most terrific snow storm I have ever known in these parts. When we came back from the canteen last night it was blowing and snowing a hurricane. I had Smut [the donkey] at the inn but thought it better to brave the elements on foot and lucky I did. A kindly farmer from the Green was on the train and he accompanied me. Directly we left the High Road we found the snow getting deeper and deeper and in places under the hedges it had drifted ever so high. It was nearly dark and you could hardly open your eyes on account of the awful wind, so whenever we met a snow-drift across the road we fell in a bump. ... But I really rather enjoyed it, especially when we rounded the corner and met the relief expedition (father) floundering well over his knees, looking like a snowman come to life. ... I like your idea of me studying botany. Do you realise I am hard at work practising hymns ancient and modern? (I have to play one for prayers every morning). Also learning up "*mensa, mensa, mensam*". I <u>was</u> an ass to say I would take Latin. It's an infernal waste of time to make anyone begin Latin until they are twelve at least. I'm waiting anxiously to hear more details of the work and what books they use. I can't do much till I know. ...

Toby to Marjorie   [trenches, Angres Sector]
30th March, 1916

I hope to send this by one of those fortunate people going on leave. I expect you have guessed from the information published in the newspapers a few days ago that that time we had an extra long relief and four rotten days in the trenches we were taking over from the French in the Souchez sector. It was very interesting and at times distinctly amusing. The French are perfectly amazing; so utterly unlike us and they certainly have disadvantages. They are the very dirtiest people you can imagine. I couldn't describe to you the filth of the billets we took over. Their sanitary arrangements are conspicuous both to nose and eye by their absence. Why they don't all contract the most horrid diseases I can't imagine. But our experience of their trenches was a real eye-opener. I was very interested because we went over the country where there was all that tremendously heavy fighting last May, when the French advanced and took Carency, Souchez and the Notre Dame de Lorette spur.[122] It was an eerie feeling, marching down that road where, four or five miles back from the present line, the country is utterly blasted and desolate. It was all so cold and still in the snow, so utterly dead, while everywhere there was that faint smell of decay which we are becoming so accustomed to out here. Souchez, which anyone can see must have been a ripping little place, lying snugly in the valley with a stream running through it and pleasant woods round about, is now nothing more than a heap of stones. There isn't an upright wall. Even what was once the road is now no more than a footpath between piles of bricks and rubbish. The whole valley made a great impression on me; not only were there no houses standing but all the trees were blasted and whole woods reduced to a collection of stumps.

The French guides who met us and showed us the way up to the front line were comical to a degree. The whole performance was reminiscent of some extravagant scene from a comic opera. They jabbered and laughed, lost the way as though it was the most natural thing in the world and explained in dramatic sentences the state of things prevailing in the trenches. "Ne tirez jamais," they kept on impressing on us.

It was not until the next morning that we could see our position. We found ourselves on the top of this damned hill [Vimy Ridge] which was a maze of trenches and shell holes; our front line trench a rotten shallow ditch that exposed you from the waist upwards nearly everywhere, with the most feeble wire in front of it. You can imagine our amazement when, as the daylight came, we saw great fat Huns strolling about not more than fifty yards away and, in places where the listening post reduced the distance to ten or fifteen yards, there was soon a rapid exchange of questions and answers. And it proved to be as the Frenchmen said: no one fired off their rifle, and when they were going to let off torpedoes, etc., the Hun gave us the tip. I didn't like it a bit and felt much more unsafe than if we dared not put our heads above the parapet. Still, there was nothing else to be done until we had deepened the trench and made it reasonably safe. But aren't the French extraordinary? Apparently they just sat there and did damn all; then one fine day, when it suited him, the Hun would play dirty and the Frenchman would get his blood up and fight magnificently. The Hun was very anxious for English newspapers, so they threw him some over for his edification while he supplied our men with cigars, etc. One of their most bitter topics was the artillery: they would kill all theirs if we would do the same, etc. Of course it's all different now and we've had pamphlets galore on fraternising with the enemy from the ------ Staff! Yet, at the same time, they winked at it, knowing that it was the only sensible thing to do under those circumstances and now they try and insinuate that the officers and

....

122 The French offensive in Artois which opened on 9th May 1915. It lasted for five weeks and cost over 100,000 French casualties.

men did not do their duty. I think our Staff are utterly mad. I've never known such sheaves of pamphlets and ridiculous orders come round. Everybody is simply fed up to the teeth with it all. I am at last beginning to think we shall lose the war. Pages and pages of rot about whether a man wears his mess tin in his pack or tied on somewhere else, and a hundred other stupid, footling, similar things. But don't let's talk about the Army – it drives me wild.

We are in support trenches now, about five hundred yards behind the firing line. The Battalion is in the trenches for twenty-one days, two Companies in the front line and two behind, so that we just relieve each other. I shall be very glad when it's over and I hope we may get back to Bruay for a week or so.

... The weather seems to have been as bad in England as it's been out here. I am glad you had a good weekend at Hill House: it is a nice place. I always associate it with you and the beginning of things. This time last year I was just enjoying German measles. When does the term at Seaford begin? ...

Marjorie to Toby   Bennetts End
                                                      31st March, 1916

It was ripping to get your nice long letter of the 27th this morning. It must have been dreadful in the trenches during that awful weather. I do hope you did not get the cyclone on the 29th. ...

Your explanation of long division was most helpful. ... I wish Mr. Henderson would hurry up and send me a few more details as to the work. ...

Yes, Seaford ought to be quite a good place for your next leave and I will at once search out a bathing place. I suppose it is impossible in war-time but it would be glorious if we could find the steeds and ride over the downs. But I fear all livery stables are empty these days of anything but knock-kneed and otherwise decrepit beasts. I should love to go riding with you. Oh! It will be lovely to see you again ...

Toby to Marjorie   [trenches, Angres Sector]
                                                       2nd April, 1916

... It has been gloriously hot here today and it has been very tantalising only being able to see mud walls and a patch of the blue firmament up above. ... I am glad you thought the silhouettes in *The Bystander* good enough, though I don't know how you made one of them into me, as Oakley hardly knew me when he did those, so I've got the laugh of you. ... It's perfectly wonderful how quickly he does them, and he has been doing several more scenes from the front which he hopes *The Bystander* will take. ... There never seems to be any time [to read] these days as we've always had rather congested quarters lately and one can't read with about five other people all talking rot at once. ...

Marjorie to Toby   Bennetts End
                                                       4th April, 1916

It was most interesting to hear all about your taking over the French trenches [on Vimy Ridge]. I had wondered if you were doing so before. Twenty-one days is a horrid long time to be in trenches, even if you do take it in turns to be in the second line. It was quite funny to read about the way the French had arranged things with the Hun and to the unmilitary mind rather sensible. It must have been a nasty shock to you to see them all so close. Were they really very fat? I had no idea the French were such a dirty race. Such dirty billets, etc. must be too disgusting. And <u>how</u> mad you must get with our Staff. ...

I go to Seaford on May 4th. Term begins next day. I don't want to give up the canteen before I go as they are so short of helpers. ... I am trying to get hold of some botany books and must go and get one which tells me more about Henry VIII, etc. I am getting tired of the hymns but shall be quite expert at them. Did I ever tell you I used your lovely bath salts once or twice but Pa and Ma protested so loudly, said they could smell them in the garden , etc., I had to desist. Very annoying!

Chapter 8

Philip and Charles on Vimy Ridge

March to July 1916

As Toby Dodgson had observed in his letter of 20th March, his Division, the 23rd, had handed over responsibility for the defence of the northern end of Vimy Ridge to the 47th (London) Division.[123] The Souchez sector included the commanding Lorette spur, which allowed the Division's guns to take covered positions in the Bouvigny Woods.

Philip to his mother   [Chatelain]
                                                              17th March, 1916

At last Toby and I have met – he is quite close and likely to be so for the present. It is extraordinary how difficult it is to find anybody out here. I went over and had tea with him yesterday and he rode over here today. He looks awfully well, I thought, much thinner than he was. ... The country down here is quite pretty and we are going to live the simple life in a dugout in the middle of a huge wood [Bouvigny Woods]. If the weather keeps good it ought to be all right but I expect water is going to be a trouble. We are absolutely sick of moving. It does seem such a waste of time and work. One sometimes wonders whether those in authority ever think ahead at all. This is about the fourth time we have moved in a month. ..

* * * * *

Meanwhile Charles and the 1/19th Londons were about to move into the trenches on Vimy Ridge.

Charles to his father   [Carency]
                                                              15th March, 1916

We have had rather a disappointment just after I wrote last, as we have been ordered back to the trenches. I suppose it is a distant effect of the Verdun fighting.

....

123   The 47th Division assumed command of the Souchez sector on 16th Mar. (Maude, op cit, p. 50)

We are taking over a very odd part of the line – a bit further south than we have ever been before and in country which is really pretty. We have spent two days in quite a pretty village. It had been knocked about a good deal about a year ago, but we managed to make ourselves pretty comfortable and there were some shower baths in a farmhouse.

We are unfortunately a long way from any shops so we shall be more than usually dependent on food parcels. I received some from Fortnum and Mason yesterday which, I think, came from Gina. ... We are having splendid weather now and I am writing this sitting in the ruins of a farmhouse at 5.30 p.m.

[Carency subsector]
Sunday, 19th March, 1916

... We are back in the trenches, but at present we are getting on all right. The previous occupants had let things slide very much and we have had to put in a tremendous lot of spade-work to get the trenches in fighting order. Major General Barter and one of our Brigadiers have both been round today and are awfully pleased at the work we have put in. The Brigadier told me he didn't believe we could have done so much in so short a time. The German trenches were also in a bad way and there has been a temporary stoppage of hostilities while both sides have been digging and wiring. It has been rather uncanny to see men on both sides walking about in the moonlight in full view of each other. Apparently neither side at present finds its position good enough to start "strafing" the other, and it remains to be seen which side will begin again first. Stokes is ill and is quite likely to go home with enteritis.

We are awfully grieved at the death of Whitby[124] who commanded B Coy. He was taken ill while we were on a trek and went to hospital where he had two operations for appendicitis which apparently proved unsuccessful. He was the only officer who had done continuous service out here with the Battalion all the time except for the ordinary leave.

Charles to Agnes   [Maisnil Bouché]
22nd March, 1916

... We are back from the trenches for twelve days' rest and I think we have earned it. I have never seen men work so hard and we turned an impossible position into a fairly well-defended one. Unfortunately we had some casualties including an officer killed in our lines, though he was not doing duty with us. The comic and tragic sides were most hopelessly mixed during this last term. Imagine us talking to the Germans opposite to us – shooting at each other with Very Light pistols (a sort of rocket!), both Germans and ourselves showed ourselves freely – each side knowing that the other's trenches were as bad as their own. It was practically a truce between the infantry, with the artillery going on as usual and the units on each side trying to kill each other. However, War was "declared" again before we left, though we thought it only right to warn them that friendship was ended and

....

124 Capt James Hornby Whitby arrived in France with the 1/19th on 10th Mar. 1915. He was commissioned into the 19th Londons on 1st Sept. 1914 after service in the OTCs at City of London School and Cambridge University. He died on 16th Mar. 1916 after an operation for appendicitis at Lozinghem and is buried at Lapugnoy Military Cemetery (grave I.F.6). He was 23, a resident of Kentish Town, and had been Mentioned in Dispatches.

to fire a few shots over their heads as a sign. Things were normal for the last two days, but the first four were absolutely uncanny. We collared a deserter who is proving very valuable. They are all absolutely sick of it. Rations are bad. He was absolutely ravenous: they have had no news from Verdun and his wife is starving. His information on local military matters has been checked and found correct in every case, so the rest is probably true also. Now we are in a village, rather dirty but nearly out of the sound of the guns. We reached here at 4.30 a.m. this morning and I slept from 5.00 till 1.00 p.m. I had had about two hours' sleep on an average the six preceding days. We had most wonderful moonlight nights and on the hills we could see for miles. It is one of the most war-ridden parts. I marched through a village in the evening without noticing it – the houses and trees had been absolutely levelled with the ground.

Charles to his father   [Maisnil Bouché]
26th March, 1916

I have received safely and gratefully parcels from Agnes and Mabel and a "Bystander" from Helen. ... We are still out of the trenches.... Yesterday we had a Brigade march-past for the General – in the snow which made it impossible to be at all precise in one's movements. The whole show was thoroughly boring, exasperating and intensely military. ... I have managed to have a bath here, which was very necessary. I generally get my hair cut by a lance corporal in B Coy who is quite adequate. My bed in my present billet is a roll of chicken wire fixed on some boards: it is quite comfortable but has given way once or twice. We are having great difficulty in getting anything washed in this part of the world so that the socks which were sent me were extra welcome. ...

I am going to make another attempt to have a ride this afternoon. Hitherto all my equitation has been for purely military purposes and I generally find some man in the Company whose feet are so sore that I have to give him a lift and walk myself. ...

[Villiers au Bois]
Sunday, 2nd April,1916

We have got the most splendid weather now and I hope you are getting dry also. ... We have several officers ill with flu and other things. I think these Londoners think they are ill far more easily than we should do. They are so used to having a telephone to their doctor and their chemist, instead of being eight miles from both! We are on our way back to the line now and are curious to see whether the same amazing state of affairs exists. Personally I hope not: it is uncanny and uncomfortable and I don't trust any Hun at all.

On Friday I sat as one of a Court Martial on a man in our Battalion for wearing medals he was not entitled to. Later in the same afternoon I took the chair (consisting of a pile of rugs) in the absence, through illness, of the CO at a religious discussion on the question "Does Christianity make a man a better soldier?" I am writing this sitting in a ruined garden outside a partially ruined farmhouse, where we have our Company mess. There is some very good oak furniture still left in the house, guarded by an old woman of about ninety who can neither read nor write and does not ask for any money but only a portion of our rations. We took her over from our predecessors with the other dilapidations!

... We slept last night in a hut where there seemed to be some officers belonging to almost every branch of the service. We are just far enough behind the line for even gunners and cavalry to begin to come in contact with the long-suffering infantry. I haven't got any subalterns with me who have ever been in the line before, so I shall be kept pretty busy.

[Maisnil Bouché]
9th April, 1916

We got out of the trenches in the middle of last night and I crept thankfully between my blankets on a bed of chicken-wire about 4.00 a.m. The weather has been good practically all the time and the trenches are in far better defensive condition now. We had some casualties and were pretty heavily shelled at times, but got out all right. We are very short handed and I got on the average about two-and-a-half hours' sleep in each twenty-four. I had my boots on for a week, all but five hours! Major Hamilton has gone to London to receive his Military Cross from the King and the Adjutant is also on leave: the RSM has got a Commission[125] and the doctor has got a base job, so that our personnel is changing very frequently. It makes everything very difficult.

... I had a letter from Dartford this week. He is back with the 3/19th now and seems to have quite recovered from his wound. It was nice to wake up (at lunch time) today and hear pigeons cooing instead of shells roaring!

* * * * *

Meanwhile Philip Dodgson was some three or four thousand yards behind the front line with the Division's artillery. By now he was acting Adjutant of 7th London Brigade RFA.

Philip to his mother   [Bois de Bouvigny]
6th April, 1916

... I expect Toby will have told you tales of some of the extraordinary things which took place when we first took over this front – the barter of plum jam or cigarettes for a cigar was quite common, and the Germans frequently told our people when their guns were going to fire.

... Could you send me a few packets of nasturtium seeds to sow, as I think they would grow rather well and brighten the place up for a bit – even if we don't stay here, it would be nice for those who come after us. ... I think some mustard and cress would be rather a good idea too.

... If all goes well I should get leave in about a couple of months' time. We listened to a most amusing lecture from our Corps Commander – General Wilson[126] – the

....

125 3369 RSM William James King DCM landed with the 1/19th in France on 10th Mar. 1915 and served with the Battalion in France until 2nd Apr. 1916. He was commissioned into the 8th Battalion of the North Staffordshire Regiment. (TNA WO 329 Medal Rolls 19th London Regt)

126 Lt Gen Sir Henry Wilson was an ardent Francophile and had been one of the architects of the pre-war Anglo-French alliance. He was responsible for the planning which saw the BEF successfully despatched to France on the outbreak of war. He served as GOC IV Corps from 22nd Dec. 1915 until 1st Dec. 1916. In Feb. 1918 he was appointed Chief of the Imperial General Staff (CIGS) and was principal military adviser to Lloyd George in the last year of the war. He was promoted to Field Marshal on 3rd July 1919 but was murdered by the IRA in 1922..

other day – he talked about the situation before the war was declared. ... He was most scathing about everybody in authority. He of course took an extreme military view. He is also frightfully down on England as a whole, in contrast with the French who have given up everything. He instanced how, on the outbreak of war, all their horses were taken from the hunts and all their hounds killed. He said that he didn't think this war would end until England had thrown herself into the war in the same way. He thoroughly appealed to us all when he talked about conscientious objectors and strikes... We want every possible man if we are going to win this war. Old Wilson made us feel pretty strongly about it. It makes one sick that the papers are all allowed to pat ourselves on the back because we now hold one quarter of this front. ... What a relief it will be when the war is over - it seems incredible that it can go on much longer. ...

We had quite an excitement the other morning. While an aeroplane was observing for one of our batteries, a Hun came over about 2,000 ft below ours. Our observer telegraphed that he was going after the Hun and we heard no more. When we saw him in the afternoon he told us that they dived 2,000 ft towards the Hun and shot him as they went past. It must have been a thrilling moment. ...

[Frévillers]
HQ 7th London Brigade RFA
16th April, 1916

I am going to the 18th Battery on Wednesday, so you had better address things there in future. ... All leave is stopped, which is most depressing. I am so fed-up with everything. I heard from Toby and he seems fairly tired of life too. I wonder who isn't? ...

******

Charles to his sister Agnes   [Bouvigny]
15th April, 1916

Many happy returns of your birthday! Dad will see about a present for you. ... I believe we have all to be inoculated again, which is a bore, and the men are naturally very much annoyed. ... I am still waiting to have a bath, as the last really decent one I had was the first week in March. ... I have got quite a decent hut in the woods where we are now. There are two bunks – the other being occupied by Naylor, one of the Haileybury boys.[127] There is also a stove and enough tables for us each to have a sort of wash-stand. The woods are beginning to get quite green. I'm afraid that the flies will be an awful difficulty as the weather gets warmer. We have wonderful circulars sent out as to how to fight them, but most of the suggested materials and remedies are quite out of reach of the trenches. They also say that men's hands ought to be clean before eating or handling food: this is when shaving is only possible at rare intervals! I wish the authorities occasionally visited a front-line trench.

....

127 Lt Henry Morland Naylor was born on 2nd Apr. 1897 and had left school in Dec. 1914 having been a member of that year's cricket 2nd XI. He was commissioned into the 19th Londons on 21st Mar. 1915.

Charles to his father [Bouvigny]
Palm Sunday, 16th April, 1916

... Major Hamilton is still away but Trim, the Adjutant,[128] has returned and some of our invalids also. I mentioned in a PS to Agnes that Dartford is now at Winchester. If he still possesses his motorbike it would be easy for him to come over and see you. ... He plays the violin so well it would be worth asking him over while Helen is at home. I am writing this sitting in my deck-chair outside my hut in the sun. Aeroplanes are buzzing about overhead. The temperature changes with great frequency and it is rather trying for delicate people like me! ... If Colonel LeRoy comes home you'd better ask him to get me an instructor's job somewhere. I don't think it would ever occur to the military authorities that a schoolmaster might possess some powers of instructing. Last night we had a rat hunt in the moonlight and succeeded in slaying one after some exciting chases.

[Bouvigny]
18th April, 1916

I hope this will reach you somewhere about Easter and find you not too tired. ... Yesterday I rode over to a very witty and interesting lecture by [Lt Gen] Sir H. Wilson on the situation immediately before the outbreak of war and the operations up to the Battle of the Marne.[129] He was very sarcastic at the expense of the Liberal Government and Haldane in particular.[130] ... I am afraid we shan't get hot-X buns in the trenches, though we have started having a canteen in the Battalion headquarters dugout and the men can order things like cigarettes, tinned fruit and chocolate by telephone from the front line.

[Carency]
Easter Day [23rd April], 1916

... The weather is appalling here. It rained practically all Holy Week.... We are back in the trenches and they are in very bad condition – knee-deep in places. One evening it was pouring and I was nearly up to the knees in water, when a breathless messenger reached me with a typewritten message to the effect that all ranks are forbidden to pick and eat watercress! There is a derelict roller just behind my trench so we can get the pitch in order for Bank Holiday, if the Hun will let us! ... Major Hamilton is back, but not very fit, and at present is resting at Brigade HQ. ... I hope you don't still read "The Express". The article on trench life and the evolution of the officer are utterly different from anything I have ever come across!

....

128 2/Lt (later Capt) Edward Joseph Trim was from Southwark and had enlisted in the Grenadier Guards on 28th Sept. 1914. After being commissioned into the 19th Londons on 26th May, 1915 he arrived in France to join the 1/19th on 4th Oct. He was awarded the MC on 4th Nov. 1916. (TNA WO 374/69512)

129 Wilson's style of lecturing made a lasting impression on those who heard it. Capt Beaumont Tansley, a gunner in 236th Brigade RFA was also in the audience and noted in his diary a "lecture on *'Days before the War'* ... extraordinarily funny with dirty stories!" (IWM Tansley papers, Tansley diary, 17th Apr. 1916,)

130 Wilson had been critical of aspects of Viscount Haldane's defence reforms that had been implemented during 1906-12 by the Liberal Government that came to power in 1905. He believed that the reforms were not radical enough. He was acutely aware of German preparations for war, and belived that the British voluntary system would not be capable of providing an adequate response. He advocated conscription but British political opinion, however, remained firmly opposed to conscription until 1916. (See Ch. 5 of Jeffery, *Field Marshal Sir Henry Wilson,* 2006)

* * * * *

Meanwhile, Philip Dodgson had been posted back to a battery of guns after his time as Adjutant.

Philip to his mother
[Bois de Bouvigny]
18th London Battery
7th London Brigade RFA
22nd April, 1916

Your parcel of eggs and seeds has arrived safely – thank you so much for them – not one of the eggs was broken; isn't it wonderful? Since they arrived the weather has been so awful that it's not been possible to plant the seeds. ... I changed over [to the 18th Battery] last Wednesday. The life is an absolute contrast. One has more physical discomfort but, on the other hand, one is relieved of a great deal of worry. As Adjutant you are never free, and I did at times get sick of it, but for certain reasons I'd like to be back. I'm getting £11 extra pay for the time I was Adjutant, so that's not so bad. ...

I am finding my trench coat most useful. Do you remember the little things I left out of my mess tin – cup, plate and several little boxes? If you could find them, will you send them as they would be most useful for this sort of existence? ... I would also like another of the smallest sized Primus stove: they are collapsible and fit in a box. ... It is such a comfort to be able to hot up some tinned meat during the day and have a hot drink. ...

Easter Day: After yesterday's awful rain we have a glorious day today. We had a Communion Service here this morning which I attended. It's the first time we've been for ages. Leave is also on again, so we are all happy at present. I've taken to smoking again so could you send me, about once a fortnight, two ¼ lb tins of Waverley smoking mixture, coarse cut? ...

We've had a party of sailors on a visit today. They have been out here for four days, spending today with the Artillery.[131] I think conditions of life out here have been a bit of an eye-opener to them. We had the officers with us to lunch: they were so nice and interesting. They have thoroughly enjoyed themselves. I wish in the same way they would send us for a trip to sea.

[Bois de Bouvigny]
18th London Battery
7th London Brigade RFA
27th April, 1916

I think it is a most splendid idea your marrying Mr Fulton. I am sure you will get on awfully well with him. Of course I can hardly remember him, but you have seen a good bit of him lately, haven't you? Of course it will alter things for me and Guy a bit, but with things uncertain as at present this need not be considered. I am sure you will be ever so much happier. You must have had an awfully lonely time during the War. I can't imagine what it will be like having you living at Salisbury with Mr Fulton... but I think in every way it's best for you to be settled. ...

....

131 Personnel from the 63rd (Royal Naval) Division were attached to units of the 47th Division during the spring of 1916 so that they could learn "the ways of war on the Western Front". (Maude, op cit, p. 60) The war diary of the 1/19th Londons reports "1 W[arrant] Officer and 6 Royal Naval men attached to Battalion from 21st to 22nd [Apr.]." (TNA WO 95/2738) The 63rd Division had previously served in Gallipoli.

I think I will be almost certain to be able to get leave at the beginning of June; that is, if leave is still on.

I have been attached to the Infantry as a liaison officer for forty-eight hours and come in for a fairly active time. However, all is well and very few casualties. ... I shall try to see Toby when we get out. The weather is being glorious, but one feels the heat a bit at first. ...

* * * * *

Philip's description of 'a fairly active time' refers to the explosion of a mine under the 47th Division's trenches on 26th April. The Divisional History records: "Our front line was broken by the explosion, but the crater was immediately seized, and the near lip consolidated. Rifle fire from the 1/17th and 1/18th [Londons] protected the consolidation and prevented any counter attack. The crater was called New Cut Crater."[132] The 1/19th Londons were in the midst of the action, and Charles described it in his next letter home.

Charles to his sister Mabel   [Estrée Cauchy]
                                                                                  28th April, 1916

I hope Dad got my Field Service Card all right. I sent it because you seem to have a pretty good idea whereabouts we are and would see from the papers that there has been a certain liveliness in these parts. Our time in the trenches had a pretty exciting finish, as the Germans blew up a mine on the last evening just between our front line and theirs. It did quite as much damage to their line as ours. Luckily we had an idea that it might go up, and we had made preparations accordingly. If, as is possible, the Boche thought they were going to attack they had a bitter disappointment. Whenever a mine goes up all the artillery on both sides who are anywhere in the neighbourhood lay on for all they are worth. This time it was an awful sight. My Company was having its turn "in support", so that we were not in danger from the actual mine itself. I was standing in my trench when I suddenly saw a column of earth and smoke rise in the air followed by a sheet of flame of the most appalling size. I at once ordered all my Company into their dugout, and rushed for my telephone to communicate with Battalion HQ. Immediately the most appalling crash of artillery began and every kind of thing streaming over us. All telephones except mine broke down, so that I was the only Officer who could communicate with my CO. In the next half hour we could do nothing. At every sign of a lull I dashed up into the trench to see how my lot were faring and to try to get an idea of what was going on in front. Then came a short lull and I had to call for a volunteer to go to the furthest Company for news. Two men went up (I loathed sending them). Thank goodness they got there and back all right. I never thought to see both unhurt again. Presently "runners" in various stages of collapse began to reach me and I could telephone through what news I could gather. Then I moved twenty-five men to the front line (under orders) and had to organize a party with picks and shovels to work on a new trench round our side of the mine crater. The rest of my Company I used for keeping up a connection till the telephone wires were repaired, and for carrying up extra ammunition and bombs. The CO and Major Ward visited me during the evening. I felt pretty useless really, but we fulfilled

....

132   Maude, op cit, p. 51

all the duties of a support company quite adequately and the men were simply splendid.[133]

Charles to his father [Estrée Cauchy]
30th April, 1916

Thank you and all for letters and sausages which are a great success. I haven't much to add to my long letter to Mabel which no doubt you found interesting. The weather is splendid and we have been having a fairly peaceful time. Unfortunately, I have been the only officer in my Company ever since Wednesday and have hardly had a minute to myself, as we had to get ready for an inspection this morning by the Major General [Barter] commanding the Division. Such things are generally pretty wearing for Company commanders, but today luckily all was *couleur de rose*. He told me that my Company was quite excellent in every way: the men had certainly worked very hard to get cleaned up after a very dirty tour in the trenches and deserved all the praise they got. I gathered (privately) from Maj Hamilton that the Company, for the moment, stands out above all others in the Brigade, which is pleasing for an entirely un-military man! Then the General went off to inspect our transport and I was left in command of the Battalion (Stokes is away). I started to take them home and immediately had to pass the Corps Commander [Lt-Gen Sir Henry Wilson]! The Adjutant told me afterwards that he said we were the finest looking lot he had seen for ages. This afternoon I went to a church parade at the Hospital here. It was held in an orchard and they actually had a harmonium and Easter hymns.

* * * * *

Philip to his mother [Le Comte]
1st May, 1916

... I'm so glad to hear you are so happy. However, you are wise not to get married too quickly, as there must be heaps for you to arrange. I shall of course do my best to get leave then.

... We came out of action last Saturday – as you say, things have been fairly active in our part of the world. What the Boche is up to we don't know, but he is behaving very like he did at the end of January and beginning of February. He seems to have plenty of ammunition too. ...

Later: Have arrived in my billet, so thought you would like to know a bit about it. I share it with the other Subaltern in the Battery.[134] We've got an awfully decent room in a farm. I sleep on a camp bed with sheets. ... My stable companion and I are getting on most awfully well together.

... I have been lucky to get a Section at once in the Battery. My show consists of two guns, four ammunition wagons, about sixty horses and as many men. It's a bit of a job getting to know them all. ...

....

133 On 26th Apr., when the Battalion was occupying the front line in the Carency subsector, the Battalion War Diary records, "Enemy exploded a mine at 7p.m. destroying part of our line and made a small attack. We consolidated our side of the crater and held it... 2/Lt W. J. Isaac and 1 OR killed, 12 ORs wounded." The Battalion was relieved later that night and went into billets in Estrée Cauchy. (TNA WO 95/2738)

134 Probably 2/Lt O. Edwards the junior subaltern of the 18th Battery at that time.

[Le Comte]
9th May, 1916

... I have seen some more of Toby. He is now only about four miles away so I rode over to see him the day before yesterday and had tea and dinner with him. What a nice lot of officers they are in the 8th Yorks. Toby came over to see me yesterday but unfortunately I was in bed, which was rather boring for him as I would have liked to have shown him round the Battery. I came off my horse yesterday morning and landed on my head and was stunned for a few minutes, but no damage is done although I'm being kept in bed for a couple of days as a precaution, though I still have a bit of a headache. I have really rather enjoyed a day in bed: it's the first I've had for years. I've heard nothing definite about my leave yet. Unfortunately the Captain of the Battery went down with measles yesterday, which means we will be short of officers for some time.[135] ...

* * * * *

Charles was also thinking about leave.

Charles to his father   [Bouvigny Woods]
2nd May, 1916

It is just possible that I may get home on Saturday this week – May 6th. Don't count on it too much, but if Mary can stay on at West Meon to see if I come – keep her. ...

He was indeed given a week's leave but was soon on his way back to France.

Charles to his father   The Grand, Folkestone
13th May, 1916,
5.45 p.m.

You will have heard that Gina's energy and persistence was rewarded at last. We all dined and went to the theatre together. Here we are at Folkestone: the boat doesn't leave till 7.30 p.m. though we left London at 7.50 a.m. I went to Canterbury and had lunch with Camilla [Friend] and spent about two hours with her. She seemed well and the baby is very fat. ...

[Fresnicourt]
17th May, 1916

I seem to have had no time since leaving Folkestone. We had a very quick passage... We had a good sleep at a hotel in Boulogne and eventually reached our quarter-master's stores at 11.00 p.m. on Sunday: slept in a tent there and rejoined the Battalion on Monday morning. My subs are still away and I am awfully busy. This morning I have to defend in a Court Martial a man in my Company who is charged with attempting to desert.[136] This afternoon I umpired a cricket match.

* * * * *

....

135 Almost certainly Capt W. G. Coates, at that time 2 i/c of the 18th Battery.

136 1719 Pte A. Sear – a pre-war member of the Battalion – was tried by Field General Court Martial for "attempting to desert HM service". He was found guilty and sentenced to two years Imprisonment with Hard Labour which was commuted to three months Field Punishment No. 1. (47th Div A&Q war diary extracts TNA WO 154/69)

Philip to his mother
[Le Comte]
18th Battery
18th May, 1916

... I'm afraid there is not much chance of my getting home for 1st June, as we still have no leave and they won't give me a special leave. There are several officers who have not been home since last December, so it would be rather hard luck on them. I shall hope anyhow to get home about the middle of June – perhaps for Guy's birthday. I don't believe any unit has ever had so little leave as we have had. I had a letter from Toby saying he was starting for England on Saturday: so he is lucky. ...

We had a "spit and polish" inspection yesterday by GOC Division [Brig-Gen Cuthbert].[137] We turned out quite a good show for him and he made quite a complimentary speech to us, in which he said that the 18th seemed to be the smartest battery. You will see how they have been chopping up the Territorial Force. They have now added insult to injury by altering our name. This Brigade has been called by its name for nearly ten years. We have now been given the number 237th which is junior to the latest-formed Kitchener Brigade, and of course anybody not knowing us will consider us as such.[138] ...

* * * * *

Charles to his father
[Carency subsector]
Sunday 21st May, 1916

... We are back in the trenches again now. The weather is very fine but rather hot and the flies are beginning to be a nuisance. ... I found a letter from Leslie [Woodroffe] waiting for me when I got back. He can ride and had done a sixteen-mile march. Stokes has got the Military Cross for his work the night the mine went up. He is the first of the old 2/19th officers to get anything. ... Most of our subalterns have now returned and the dugout is rather crowded. At the present moment there are four Haileyburians in this one. I forgot to mention that Stokes has got a home appointment. He did not ask for it himself: his family worked it somehow, as he is the only male in the firm who understands the business and his father is suffering from something incurable. ...

On 21st May the 47th Division was attacked on Vimy Ridge with the brunt of the German force falling on 140th Infantry Brigade. Four hours of intense bombardment preceded an infantry assault at 7.45 pm while "a barrage on Zouave Valley ... practically cut all communication with the front." The Londoners "were driven out of the front trench, across two supports, into a line half-way down the slope."[139] Despite limited counter-attacks over the next forty-eight hours the Germans were left holding most of their gains. Charles and the 1/19th Londons were on the fringes of the action.

....

137 The War Diary records for 17th May 'Inspection in Marching Order of Brigade by GOC (Gen Cuthbert).' (TNA WO 95/2717) Maj Gen Barter was on leave and Brig Gen G. J. Cuthbert CMG (GOC of 140th Infantry Brigade) was acting GOC.

138 This is a further indication that the Territorial Force was losing its special identity (see footnote 35, Chapter 4).

139 Maude, op cit, p.53

[Diéval]
27th May, 1916

Many happy returns of the day! You will be glad to hear that we are right back – hardly within sound of the guns – and are likely to remain so for some time, barring accidents. As you probably know, there has been quite a big show in our neighbourhood with very heavy fighting. Though we were in the front line we were just on the edge of the storm and had few casualties.[140] The Germans did not attack on our Battalion front, though part of the Brigade were right in the thick of it and did wonders against very heavy odds. The bombardment was terrific on both sides. It is described as being far heavier than at Loos last September. We suffered a great deal of unpleasantness from lachrymose shells and my eyes were quite bad on Sunday evening. The bombardment then lasted about eleven hours – from 4.00 p.m. on Sunday until 3.00 a.m. on Monday morning. I'm afraid that a good many men whom I know slightly in the Division were hit. You will see that our Brigadier was wounded.[141] We got away from the line on Thursday night [25th May]. I have been acting as Second-in-Command while Major Ward has been on leave and Major Hamilton and I had to move pretty quickly as we were the last to leave the trenches at 2.30 a.m. and about one-and-a-half miles of our way lay across the open and day was breaking. We floundered on breathlessly over the mud, trying not to imitate Lot's wife. The mud was awful and I fell down three times. When we at length got on the road we found a man with a badly sprained ankle being helped along by a Sergeant Major. We were still in full view of the Hun if the light improved, so I stayed behind to help the man along and we eventually reached a ruined village (where I had left the Battalion when I came on leave). We put the invalid in a dressing-station and then trudged on; reaching a village we know well, where the Battalion had a rest and a sleep. (I had one-and-a-half hour's sleep only.) Then we set off on a twelve mile trudge and got here about 9.30 p.m. It is a really pretty place but the accommodation is poor at present. ... The butter arrived in perfectly good condition. ...

PS Get yourself a present.

* * * * *

After the 'trying days' on Vimy Ridge, the Division was withdrawn for a fortnight's rest in Corps reserve in the Diéval area, southwest of Bruay.

Philip to his mother   [Brias]
29th May, 1916

Just a line to bring you my very best and sincere wishes, and I do hope you will be very happy. I am most awfully disappointed that I cannot be with you on 1st June, and that I have not seen you before, but it can't be helped so it is no use worrying. ...

We are having quite a good time at present. The Boche, having got what he wanted [i.e. a better position on Vimy Ridge], is leaving us more or less alone, and

....

140   The Battalion's casualties for the period 21st – 25th May were: officers – 1 wounded; other ranks – 2 killed, 2 died of wounds and 13 wounded. (TNA WO 95/2738) However, the 47th Division's casualties during the same period were "63 officers and 2,044 other ranks killed, wounded and missing." (Maude, op cit, p. 56)

141   Brig Gen Thwaites was wounded at 11.30 pm on 23rd May 1916 (TNA WO 95/2734)

you needn't worry about me as we are in a quiet position. We are doing quite well too in the way of food, as the gardens in a demolished town nearby are coming to life and we are getting some fresh fruit which is a great change. The weather too is glorious. ... Write and tell me all about everything when you have time, and an address to write to you.

* * * * *

Charles to his father   [Diéval]
4th June, 1916

... We have had a really very pleasant week. We have got up early and done practically all our work before dinner and had the afternoon free for rustic cricket. In the evenings we have continued riding classes for mounted officers. Yesterday we had a match against the 6th London Field Ambulance. They beat us by 29. I made five. It was very fine and we had tea on the cricket field. In the evening we had an open-air concert: quite a successful day and about as un-military as a day in France can be. ... About 3.00 a.m. this morning I was woken up by some troops passing through, who enquired at my window whether I sold beer, being apparently under the impression that I was the French proprietor of an *estaminet*.

* * * * *

Philip to his mother   [Barlin]
8th June, 1916

I feel quite ashamed at not having written to you before. I was thinking hard of you at one o'clock on 1st June until I remembered you had put your clocks on an hour and I was late for your wedding.[142] It was stupid of me. The cake arrived safely and was much appreciated both as a remembrance of you and also as cake, of which we have not had much lately. We were also prevented drinking your health here on the proper day as we had a bit of a show on that evening.

It was splendid Toby getting such good leave. I have seen him twice since he got back. ... I hope by now you are feeling happier about the Navy.[143] How magnificently they did! ... The Russian news also is most hopeful, and we are all feeling quite optimistic about the many peace rumours which are floating about. The news about Kitchener came as a sudden shock.[144] It was a tragic end and it is sad that he cannot see the result of what he has done. ...

* * * * *

Charles to his father   [Diéval]
10th June, 1916

I think the enclosed may interest you for the family book. It was in "The Chronicle" at the beginning of this week. "Ginger" is the real name of one of

....

142   Daylight Saving Time was introduced on 21st May 1916.

143   A reference to The Battle of Jutland (31st May/1st June) which was the largest naval battle of the Great War and a strategic victory for the Royal Navy. After the battle the Imperial German Navy took to port, never venturing out again.

144   Lord Kitchener, Secretary of State for War, was travelling to Russia on a diplomatic mission when HMS Hampshire on which he was sailing was sunk by an enemy mine west of the Orkney Isles on 5th June.

our Privates and the account of his deeds is pretty accurate.[145] Apparently they can't get on without us in the front line, for we have just had orders to leave our comfortable billets and go back there again shortly. It is a great disappointment, but I suppose we are lucky to have had a fortnight out. During this week I have been re-inoculated. ...

On 12th June the Division moved slightly to the north to the Angres sector between Vimy Ridge and Loos, where it stayed until the end of July. The Divisional History recalled "it was a peaceful time but for an elaborate programme of bluff operations which ushered in the Battle of the Somme. The artillery did most of the demonstration, but infantry also played a part in the form of raids, a new kind of amusement..."[146]

[Angres]
13th June, 1916

I am most awfully grieved to see that Leslie has died,[147] apparently from his old wound, but I know no details. It is like losing a relation after his being my best friend all these years. It is awful to think that all those three are gone. They stood out by themselves amongst all the brothers I know for character and brains. Some day I shall try and get Mrs Woodroffe to give me one of the many books full of Marlborough snap-shots which Leslie took twelve years ago. ... I had just finished my letter to Agnes when I saw it in Saturday's "Morning Post". ...

[Bouvigny Boyeffles]
18th June, 1916

... I rejoined the Battalion on Friday and only had twenty-four hours in the trenches, so that with luck I shall just get my birthday before we go in again. Birthday letters have begun to arrive. The weather was quite rotten while we were at the Gas School. ... I had a letter from Leslie's cousin, Gambell, in the 2/19th.[148] According to him, Leslie was sent out here again by a mistake and was wounded almost as soon as he arrived and died a day or two later.

This morning we had a voluntary church parade and celebration in an orchard. ... Dartford has rejoined us and seems very well and is very useful. It is a pity he can't bring his violin out here with him. ...

....

145   4700 Private Ernest Ginger had enlisted in the 19th Londons in late May 1915 and arrived in France to join the 1/19th on 28th Oct. 1915. He was awarded the DCM for his actions on 6th May 1916 when the Battalion was in trenches on the eastern foot of the Lorette spur. His citation read: "For conspicuous gallantry. He was buried by the explosion of an enemy mine, but, on being rescued, assisted in the rescue of other men under heavy fire. When attacked by hostile bombers he engaged them single-handed and drove them off." (Supplement to *The London Gazette*, 31st May 1916, p. 5412). He served in France with the Battalion until 25th Aug. 1917.

146   Maude, op cit, p. 58

147   Captain Leslie Woodroffe, 8th Battalion Rifle Brigade, was severely wounded at Hooge in July 1915, after which he was awarded an MC. He did not return to the Front until June 1916. He was wounded on the day of his arrival and died three days later on 4th June 1916, aged 31. He is buried in Barlin Communal Cemetery Extension (grave I.J.66).

148   Lt Dennis Clayton Gambell was commissioned into the 2/19th Londons on 17th May 1915 and served with that battalion in France, Salonika and Palestine until he died on 30th Apr. 1918, aged 23. He is commemorated on the Jerusalem Memorial.

[Angres]
25th June, 1916

... Some more parcels have turned up since I last wrote – one from Harrods... and one from Fortnum and Mason. ... I have got Dartford attached to my Company, I hope permanently. I had a letter from Mrs Woodroffe earlier in the week. ... Naylor, one of the Haileyburians, is being sent down sick to the base: I hope he will get home. He is only 19 now and has been out here since the beginning of October. ...

* * * * *

Philip eventually had a week's leave in late June.

Philip to his mother   [Barlin]
A/237th Battery
30th June, 1916

I hope you got my wire all right from Boulogne. I had an unexpectedly rapid journey back. We went straight on to the boat at Folkestone and we came in from Boulogne the same evening and I joined the Battery yesterday mid-day and everybody is very well and in excellent spirits. I enjoyed my leave enormously and I want to thank you and Hamilton again ever so much for the ripping time you gave me. I thoroughly enjoyed every minute; even coming away was not so bad, as it is a great thing for me to have seen how happy you are. ...

* * * * *

By early July the officers and men of the 47th Division were aware of the opening on 1st July of the Anglo-French offensive on the Somme over forty miles to the south. However, it would be over two months before the Division would become involved in that battle.

Charles to his father   [Fosse 10]
2nd July, 1916

... I had simply no time [to write] all this week. We were in the front line for most of it and I reckon that during four days and nights I had an aggregate of about seven hours' sleep. We had been specially chosen to do a little business with the Hun and of course it was done to the letter.[149] There are many of them who will never trouble us again and much valuable information was got. I had a mild, unheroic part to play. I had some excitement of course, but the chief personal interest was in digging out one of my Company who had been badly buried. It was a case of getting some very heavy baulks of timber off him and then simply piles of chalk. We had to do it lying or crouching as, if we had stood up, we should have been in full view of the enemy. Personally, I lay on my face once we had got the timber off, which we had to do standing up with two men clinging to my waist to add extra weight. Then we simply

....

149   The 1/19th Londons had been chosen to carry out the first trench raid by the 47th Division. The War Diary recorded that on the night of 27th/28th June1916 the Battalion "Carried out raid ... on German front line destroying about 60 of the enemy and bringing back one prisoner." (TNA WO 95/2738) This was one of a large number of raids carried out by the BEF in June 1916 all along the front with the intention of obtaining up-to-the-minute intelligence on the German Army as well as distracting the Germans from preparations on the Somme sector.

burrowed like dogs with entrenching tools and our hands. Once we got him free enough to get his head up and give him some brandy, it was only a question of time, and he will recover.

Everyone is awfully proud of the Regiment and the day after we came out Generals of various sorts came to thank us. Things seem to be really moving at last [i.e. on the Somme]. We can do with a continual supply of socks for the men: they are always necessary. ...

[Souchez]
9th July, 1916

... The weather has been awful until today and we are over our knees in mud and water in many places. The trenches are quite as bad as they were any time during the winter. I am writing this in a dugout about 100 yd from the Hun. I hope he is equally uncomfortable. The roof is so low that I am bent very nearly double and I haven't washed or shaved for 48 hours. ... I had a letter today from Lemprière, the Haileybury doctor, who is getting very tired of being in France.[150]

PS Will you get me a new shaving brush, please? I think trench mud disagrees with mine: it is getting very bald. ... We had quite a good concert twice during the early part of the week in a Church Army hut.

* * * * *

Philip had spent a few days in early July attached to one of the infantry battalions of the Division.

Philip to his mother   [Barlin]
6th July, 1916

... Since I last wrote I have done my turn with the infantry in the trenches. I was with them for four days and had quite a good time. The officers I was with were a genial lot which makes so much difference. Except for a few raids things have been more or less normal here. ... We seem to be getting on well down South [on the Somme] and the prospects seem hopeful.

We are at present working hard on our garden and we have dug out some of the borders and have planted out some carrots and lettuces. This afternoon we have made a rustic seat and are paving in front of it with bricks (so we shan't get our feet wet). ...

I forgot to tell you we found a magnificent copper in this farm and we have also found a big zinc bath, so we can get splendid hot baths – water from the well in the yard. ...

....

150   Dr Lancelot Lemprière (1872-1947) was an Old Haileyburian, and was appointed as medical officer to the College in 1903 after education at Worcester College Oxford and Manchester University. He remained in that role for 35 years with a break for service as a captain in the RAMC during the Great War. He served initially with No. 18 General Hospital but spent the largest part of his war service with 13 Field Ambulance (5th Division) from 23rd Nov. 1915 to 8th Sept. 1917. He was awarded the OBE and the Médaille des Epidémies for his war service. (Obituary in *The British Medical Journal*, 27th Sept. 1947, pp. 510-11; WO 95/1540 13 Fd Amb War Diary)

[Aix-Noulette]
A/237th Battery
10th July, 1916

... As our pastime we still work in our garden and are also having good fun with the rats, of which there are plenty. My cat is on the point of having a family. It is rather a nuisance as they may be expected hourly now. ... Things are still very quiet here, though the news on the Somme continues to be favourable to us.

Let me have any news you get of Toby. I don't know where he is.

[Aix-Noulette]
13th July, 1916

... We are all well and still quiet here. Everybody is very hopeful. I had a PC from Toby yesterday saying he was well.

* * * * *

Charles to his father   [Bois de Noulette]
16th July, 1916

... Since last writing to you I spent a night in hospital owing to some grit in my eye, which it took four doctors and a dose of cocaine to remove. I am quite all right now and for the moment we are out of the trenches in huts in a wood on a hill. I am temporarily acting as Second-in-Command again. Hamilton has applied to have me permanently in that capacity but I don't think it will be granted, as there are other people senior to me. It would be very nice in many ways, though I should become very careworn whenever he was away! Also, my knowledge of military laws and etiquette is very nearly nil! Meanwhile, it is a rest not to have the care of a Company, though I have plenty of odd jobs of an indefinite character. One night I went out in charge of a large working-party in a new trench. The Huns were only about 100 – 150 yd away and there was some wire in between, but they did not seem to take much notice of us. There is some talk of my going to deliver a lecture to the officers of the Division. ... Dartford is back with us again now.

[Noyelles-en-Chaussée]
6th August, 1916

We are well away from all fighting areas for a bit. I don't suppose it will last long, but it is very pleasant. We are working hard and have done some long marches – starting very early in the morning and avoiding the hottest part of the day as far as possible. I am still Second-in-Command and likely to remain so. My name has been recommended for the temporary rank of Major while holding the position! I will let you know if you have to alter my address to correspond! I saw that Champion (Haileybury) had become a Major before he was wounded.

I have a splendid billet while we are here, shared by Dartford and our Irish doctor.[151] The latter is very amusing. The garden is very English, with roses and vegetables and little box hedges. ... I am to have a new horse. I am very fond of my old one but she isn't quite stylish enough for my new position.

....

151   The RMO was Captain Lionel Glover Pearson MB RAMC (TF) who had qualified as a doctor in 1912 after studying at the University of Durham and clinical practice at Leeds General Infirmary. He had arrived in France with the 1/19th Londons on 10th Mar. 1915 and was promoted to Capt on 28th Apr. 1915. He served with the Battalion until at least July 1918.

Chapter 9

The Champion Brothers

The Champion referred to in Charles's letter of 6th August 1916 was Major **Carl Champion**, a Haileybury colleague of Charles. Carl had joined the staff at that school in 1910 as a science teacher. With his initials of C. C. he was inevitably nicknamed 'Cheesy' by the boys. The two friends had first met at Pembroke College, Cambridge, in 1906 when Charles was starting his last year.

Carl Champion was born in 1887, the eldest of three boys who lived with their parents at Blackheath, their father working in "shipping in the City". Carl went as a boarder to Clifton College, Bristol, but did not really enjoy his experience there. This may have been in part the effect of his father's death on Christmas Day during Carl's first holiday back from school. He was only fourteen years old at the time, while his younger brothers, **Alan** and **Eric**, were eleven and five respectively. Carl felt a measure of responsibility towards his siblings, Eric in particular. Their mother moved the family to Silverdale in North Lancashire and in time sent the younger boys to Rugby School. Carl, when in Lancashire, developed a great liking for the seaside golf links adjacent to Morecambe Bay and even greater fondness for the Lake District. Both locations encouraged a love of ornithology. When he was old enough to drive

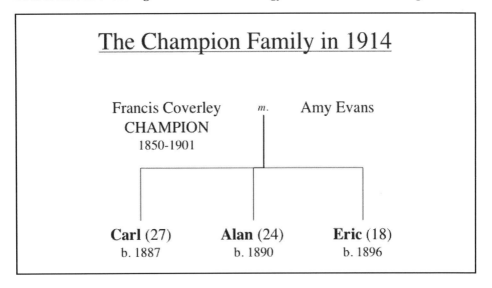

The Champion Family in 1914

Francis Coverley
CHAMPION
1850-1901   *m.*   Amy Evans

Carl (27)   **Alan** (24)   **Eric** (18)
b. 1887   b. 1890   b. 1896

a car, he found the un-tarred mountain passes an irresistible challenge for his small Singer.

Following the outbreak of war Lord Derby made a number of recruiting drives in Lancashire. On 3rd September 1914 at a meeting at the Theatre Royal St. Helens, Lord Derby and Sir David Gamble, the Mayor, made an appeal for volunteers for a new battalion of The South Lancashire Regiment. Over one thousand men enlisted overnight. They became the 11th Battalion, The South Lancashire Regiment, known locally as 'The St Helens Pals' and formed part of Kitchener's Fourth New Army (K4). Carl was commissioned on 29th September 1914 and joined the Battalion before the end of the month at Sutton where Pilkingtons, the glass manufacturers, had placed one of their works at the disposal of the Army. Alan Champion soon joined his brother, having received his commission on 17th October. Eric was still at Rugby School in September, but so keen was he to join his elder brothers that he left school in December, thereby sacrificing his chance to captain the school cricket team in the summer of 1915. Eric received his commission on 5th December 1914.

St Helens newspaper article about Lord Derby's appeal for the St Helens Pals – Sept. 1914

In February 1915 under the heading "The Pals Depart for Bangor" *The St Helens Reporter* recorded that 1,250 men under the command of Lt Col Sir John Harrington,[152] had left for North Wales. Among the officers on parade were listed: Lt C. C. Champion, Adjutant; Lt A. T. Champion, o/c E Company and 2/Lt E. O. Champion.

On 10th April 1915 the original Fourth New Army was broken up so that it could be used for replacing casualties in the first three new armies (K1 to K3). Its units were converted for training and draft finding purposes and some were moved into other divisions. By 14th May 1915 the St Helens Pals had been transferred into the

....

152   Lt Col Sir J. L. Harrington KCMG, KCVO, CB was a retired major of the Indian Army. After leaving the Army he served as High Commissioner to Ethiopia from 1903 to 1909.

Carl Champion

30th Division which they joined near Grantham.[153] They began training in the grounds of Belton House.

At this time the Battalion was converted from a normal infantry battalion into a pioneer battalion, one of which was attached to each division. This was a sensible move in view of the experience of many of the men who had previously worked in the Lancashire coal mines, on the railways and in other heavy industries. Carl Champion readily adapted to this change. He was a man who, at home, had his own workshop and maintained his own car. When applying to go to Cambridge University, under the heading of "possible career" he had stated "engineering". The Battalion became known officially as the 'St Helens Pioneers' and no longer the 'St Helens Pals.'[154]

No battalion war diary was written for this period but Carl recorded on camera many aspects of their training. The more obvious features were digging trenches, rifle shooting on a local range

Alan Champion (standing, right) by Carl Champion's Singer car at Grantham

....

153   Major A. F. Becke, *Order of Battle of Divisions, Part 3b – New Army Divisions (30-41) and 63rd (RN) Division*, 1945. On 27th April 1915 the Fifth New Army (K5) was renamed the Fourth New Army and its six divisions were renumbered. The 30th Division was part of the original Fifth New Army and had previously been called the 37th Division.

154   The exact date at which the Battalion was rerolled from normal infantry to pioneers is unknown. However, it is likely to date from after the break up of the original Fourth New Army in April. The first references to the 'St Helens Pioneers' in the local paper are in June 1915.

and map reading. The more specialist skills were illustrated with men building simple bridges and laying light railway lines. Carl had his Singer with him, so he and his fellow officers could escape to nearby towns or golf courses. On 30th July Alan married Katherine Malcolm at Scotforth, near Lancaster, with Carl as his Best Man.

Carl Champion at the wedding of his brother Alan to Katherine Malcolm, 30th July 1915

In September the St Helens Pioneers moved to Salisbury Plain for final training before they set sail for France, landing at Le Havre on 6th November, with the strength of thirty officers and a thousand other ranks. They were stationed in the southern part of the British zone in France and were soon acclimatizing themselves to their allotted tasks maintaining roads, railways and bridges. Their work was under the direction of the CRE, the senior sapper officer in the Division. Companies were often well separated from each other. On 16th May 1916 the CO was replaced by Lt Col H. F. Fenn, DSO,[155] who remained in command for two years. Captain Carl Champion was appointed Major in June 1916 and Second-in-Command of the Battalion with effect from 14th April 1916.

....

155 Lt Col Harrington had gone back to England on sick leave. Lt Col H. F. Fenn DSO had previously served with the 21st Royal Fusiliers.

'C' Company of the St Helens Pioneers digging trenches near Grantham, 1915. The huts in the background suggest that these trenches may have been dug near their camp in the grounds of Belton House.

St. Helens Pioneers trestle bridge building at Larkhill

Chapter 10

Marjorie and Toby

April to June 1916

While Philip Dodgson and the 47th Division were on Vimy Ridge, Toby and the 23rd Divison were slightly to the north in the Angres sector.

Toby to Marjorie   [trenches, Angres sector]
                                                                              13th April, 1916

I expect you are getting impatient again at not getting a letter before this. We are only just out of the trenches and had a strenuous time, as two of the officers out of the Company were away. ... A series of short and broken nights is most demoralising and does not make for letter writing. I was in a bad temper and very irritable, but your letter of the 8th which I got last night quite revived me. ...

Marjorie to Toby   Bennetts End
                                                                              17th April, 1916

I was so pleased to get your PC two days ago. I am horribly afraid there is some show on in France. Such enormous casualty lists, and everyone on leave has been recalled. It makes one very anxious. One poor girl whom I meet at the canteen was expecting her husband just after you went back and it was put off and put off until he finally appeared for ten days on Thursday last – only to be recalled on Saturday. I do think we have been lucky as far as leave goes. Those two weeks have made all the difference to these long months since last August. There are some sweet memories to dream through and hold a promise of good things, which more and more than make up for the loneliness and heartache of separation. ...

Toby to Marjorie   [Divion]
                                                                              18th April, 1916

I couldn't write before as we've been on the move during the last few days. We are just out of the trenches and well back from the line; just in time too, as the weather is being vile – a perpetual gale and great storms of rain. Our leave is all stopped again, so I foresee that it will be considerably over the three months before I get my turn. ...

[Laires]
22nd April, 1916

... This can't be a proper letter, as it is late and I feel very weary as we've been on our legs all day from 8.00 a.m. till 6.00 p.m. this evening. We got back to this little place a few days ago and very nice it is – quite out of the world, surrounded by fine, high, rolling country which reminds me rather of the Wiltshire Downs, only every inch of it is cultivated. We are doing manoeuvres and so far they've not given us a moment to ourselves, which is pretty rotten after a long spell in the trenches. My hair is longer than that of most musicians and I am badly in need of a bath, which I don't see much prospect of getting. The weather has been vile: bitter cold winds and perpetual storms of rain, so we have not been able to appreciate the country much yet.

[Laires]
23rd April, 1916 [Easter Day]

I am awfully fed up with life as we are having a stinking time doing manoeuvres (so-called). Today we shall have done the best part of ten hours parades by the time this evening's night operations are over. I think everybody is looking forward to the time when we get back into the trenches away from all this tommyrot. ...

[Laires]
Monday, 24th April, 1916

At that point the writer's great brain fell asleep and bed was indicated in no uncertain manner. I am just back from a tactical exercise with the Brigadier, which wasn't bad fun. It is a topping day and I enjoyed the riding.

The post has just come with your letter of the 21st.... The same post also brought me some very good news, which you have probably already heard by now. I am so glad Mother is going to marry again, as I think it is quite the happiest thing that could have happened, and Mr. Fulton is an extremely nice man. Curiously enough, I was going to say something to you about it in this very letter, as I had imagined something of the sort might be in the air from things Mother has said once or twice in her letters. Well, darling old thing, I must set to and write some letters of congratulations. I wish you and I were going to be married on May 20th, don't you? But never mind, our turn will come and then we'll have a better time than any of them. ...

Toby to his mother   [Hersin]
28th April, 1916

Your parcel arrived only yesterday and it was quite wrong of you to send a letter containing such good news in such a slow way! I had a very nice letter from Mr Fulton a couple of days ago. Of course I wasn't very surprised. I thought your increased interest in your income, etc., portended something! I can't tell you how pleased I am because I know how much happier it will be for you to have a home again and it need make no difference between us. It has always been beastly to think of you sitting alone in that little cottage, and even after the war it wouldn't have been much better as Philip and Guy will both probably find something to do which might have necessitated them going away. But I shouldn't bother about "after the war" at present: the end looks to be a long way off yet and one can't possible attempt to arrange anything – after all, Philip and Guy are quite grown-up and sensible. ...

Leave has started again and, as far as I can tell, I ought to get mine about the end of this month. I heard from Philip two or three days ago and he is also expecting his about then. He had not heard your news then, so I don't know what he thinks, but I hope I may see him shortly as we are not very far away from each other. Of course Salisbury is rather a long way away but under present conditions that doesn't matter much, does it? We had quite a pleasant week back at a delightful little village in very nice country, and the weather during the last four or five days has been too glorious. I am having a very strenuous time as we are so short of officers again. What with people sick and away on courses of instruction, it is extraordinary how they dwindle down to nothing. ... Well I must stop, though I don't feel that I have said half that I want to. I think if you could arrange your marriage somewhere between 20th May and the end of the month it would be the most likely to fit in with my leave. ...

PS You've quite taken the wind out of our sails!

Toby to Marjorie   [Hersin]
                                                              29th April, 1916

... We are having a rotten time or I should have written before this. This new Brigadier that we've got is a perfect fiend, a regular slave driver, and he never has a good word for anyone; nothing is ever right.[156] Everybody is fed up to the teeth. It is knocking all the spirit out of the men and demoralising the officers. God, they are fools. We've not a chance of winning the war and they had much better make peace on the best terms they can. That little village, Lavies, that we were at would have been delightful if only we'd been left in peace, as it was right out of the way; no motor lorries or noises and the people were charming. I had a room in the local *estaminet* "Au Vin Blanc" and they brought me coffee in the morning and couldn't do enough.

My Company Commander is going on leave today, lucky devil, and I am left alone with the Company, all the other [officers] being either sick or on courses of instruction, so don't expect much in the way of correspondence. We are in some miners' cottages near a pit [Fosse 10] which is just behind Bully: not altogether a healthy spot, as the Hun likes to drop nasty great shells on the mine which, however, is still worked by night. We are supposed to be here till the 2nd and then go back to Bruay for a week and then trenches once more. ...

                                                                          [Hersin]
                                                              30th April, 1916

... I heard from Mother yesterday and apparently the marriage is fixed for 1st June. ... I quite foresee that my next leave is going to be very complicated, as of course I must be in Town for that. ... I hope this will catch you before you leave for Seaford. Good luck, old thing, and I do hope you get on well and like the life. Mind you write and tell me all about it. ...

....

156 Brig Gen Thomas Stanton Lambert of the East Lancashire Regiment took over as GOC 69th Infantry Brigade on 8th Mar. 1916. He was promoted to Maj Gen and became GOC 32nd Division on 31st May 1918, commanding it successfully through the 100 days. He was awarded the CB and CMG.

[Fosse 10]

1st May, 1916

... Well, I wonder if the little boys are going to be good and how long it will be before they are all in love with you, lucky little devils! I never had a supple nymph with beautifully shaped legs to teach me. And don't imagine they don't notice that sort of thing, because they are all devils! ...

[Fosse 10]

3rd May, 1916

(This letter arrived long after it was written, the bearer having forgotten to post it.)

... We are still in the same place and expect to move on Friday now and, according to present rumours, are to return to relieve Philip's Division on about the 15th, which is not too good as that's a vile bit of the line. Still, it's good to think that I may get leave in about three weeks' time, isn't it? You must look about and see where I am going to stay in Seaford. Is there a good hotel, or would rooms be more convenient? I think the latter are usually best in those sort of places: the hotels are so often dear and bad. But I don't want a landlady with any scruples. ...

I am so glad you liked Mr Fulton. It's funny that he should know all your family. What a change it will be. I shall be sorry not to have a home in Bovingdon: it's a funny, cheery little place and I can't picture Ma living in The Close at Salisbury! Oh, damn and blast the war! I wish it would stop so that we could settle down: I am sick of wandering over the face of the earth. I long to get back to something rational. ...

Marjorie to Toby

St Peter's School,

Seaford, Sussex

5th May, 1916

You see I'm safely landed here and still alive so far, but the boys do not come till this afternoon. I got here about 4.30 p.m. yesterday and found a very nice matron, a Miss Layton, who does the housekeeping, etc. She really seemed extremely nice and it will make all the difference having her here. She is also new this term. She showed me all round. I have a little room upstairs looking out towards Eastbourne, a lovely view. It is a very small room but quite nice and I have a writing table and a book shelf and plenty of nails to hang photos of Toby on. He looks at me from all sides! There are two other masters besides Mr Henderson but they are not here yet. I had a long *tête à tête* with him after dinner and he told me all about the work, etc. My brain reels with instructions. It seems all right except that I have to give them a quarter of an hour scripture every day. He most particularly asked me about hymns as his last governess played so many wrong notes!! I fear he will get even more from me. He is <u>such</u> a schoolmaster. Oh, absolutely typical but I believe he will be quite nice when shaken out of it. Anyhow I hear he is long-suffering and ready to help and advise. His eyes were pinned on my ring; so when he said I was certainly to go away for one weekend during the term I said it would be most convenient if I could go when my fiancé was home. He said, "Yes, of course!" and changed the subject. ... I shall be very virtuous and do all I can out of school and not bother to take extra time off, so that he will be well disposed when you come home. Oh, dearest, I wonder when that will be. ...

Toby to Marjorie [Divion]
10th May, 1916

... Thank you ever so much for the things from Fortnum's. I have got so much food now I can't cope with it all at once, as there is no one else in the Company at present. I had six others in to feed last night in the hopes of reducing the bulk somewhat before we move. The eggs from Bennetts End arrived unbroken and are most excellent, also the cake. ...

[Bully Grenay]
12th May, 1916

I wish I could send you some definite news about my leave, but I shan't know for a few days yet. The Adjutant [Capt C. S. Simpson] and I are hoping to go together and I was talking to him last night about it. I am hoping to get ten days ... .

Toby had some leave in late May, during which he and Marjorie made plans to get married on his next leave. Once again, Marjorie recorded these days in her diary:

22nd May, 1916:
Toby arrived in the little car just as we were starting supper. I rushed out and met him. It was good to see him and looking so splendidly well and sunburnt. We soon got my box and drove down to Mrs Moore's house, Longdown, where I had taken rooms. We took the boxes up and then went into his room where he kissed me hard, again and again, and I said "There, is that better?" It was. ... He had bought me such a present, a whole box full of undies – most beautiful ones. I had to try on these when we went up to bed, and then, best of all, he came into my bed with me. It was a great big one and I wore a wonderful nightie he had bought me. The fresh sea air came in right on to us and we were absolutely happy. It was a long time before we went to sleep.

23rd May, 1916:
I had to get up early to go to school. Then he came to fetch me and we motored off to Wilmington and climbed up The Long Man. We had a nice sheltered place for lunch. I went back to school for one hour and then Mr Henderson came in and let me off. We went back to Longdown and played about till bedtime and again had a glorious happy night.

24th May, 1916:
Again I had to go to school but he fetched me and we took our lunch to a nice spot along the Eastbourne road. ... We were back at school at 3.00 as we had to fetch my form down to tea. We took four of them first. They clung on all round the car. Then he left us on the beach and went to fetch the other five. How they enjoyed themselves! We were in fear they were going to fall into the water but all went well and we took them back to Longdown to tea. Toby chuckled over their hearty

appetites – afterwards, very reluctantly, they were conveyed home and I hurried into respectable clothes to go to supper at Eastbourne. We went first to Birling Gap and Beachy Head and peered timidly over the edge. It was a beautiful afternoon. ... We had supper with friends, and Toby was in very good spirits. We started home soon after ten but had to stop almost at once to clean out the carburettor. Then right up on the downs we had a puncture. It was awfully dark and it delayed us a long while. How glad we were to reach Longdown at last and tumble quickly into bed.

On the same day Toby wrote to Marjorie's mother:

Dear Mrs Secretan,

I am writing for Marjorie who is still busy putting wisdom into the heads of Davis Minor and others! I think Mother is arranging to have us at Bovingdon for the weekend so we shall see you at the tea fight on Saturday. ...

We are having a simply ripping time and Mr Henderson is being awfully nice about Marje getting off. He is such a nice man and I like him because he seems to thoroughly appreciate Marje. She is evidently a great success.

I am having all her form out to tea this afternoon so I must go out and buy up the local confectioners.

Yours affectionately, Toby

Marjorie's diary continues:

25th May, 1916:
Toby fetched me after school and we took our lunch out above Cuckmere. It was a lovely day though rather chilly. The surroundings are beautiful up there ... . He brought me back to afternoon school and then I biked down to Longdown where we had tea and just flirted till we went up to school to supper. That was a funny evening and Toby was completely done in by the terribly stodgy suet pudding. Afterwards we went up and talked to Miss Layton till about 9.30 when we went home and began the best part of the day.

26th May, 1916:
I biked up to school and Toby motored off to London. ... School went very slowly and I took the little game and at last went off to London by the 5.30 train. He met me in mufti and we dined at Scotts and then went to the Coliseum ... . We slept at the St Ermin's but he had not been so clever over the rooms as I was. However we got on very well and enjoyed it as much as ever.

27th May, 1916:
We did not do much in the morning. Looked at the dressing case they are giving to Mrs Dodgson for her wedding present. We went to lunch at the Carlton ... and then took the car and motored down

to Bovingdon. It was a lovely run – a hot sunny day and the country was so green and beautiful. We reached the cottage ... and found a tea-party in full swing. Mr Fulton was there and also Mother. Everyone seemed very pleased to see Toby. ... We told his mother how we meant to be married on his next leave, also my Mother and they were both so pleased. When everyone had gone Toby and I went and found our respective lodgings which were not in the same house and changed for the evening. Supper in the cottage with Mrs Dodgson and Mr Fulton was great fun and we had the pianola afterwards. At last Toby and I walked off to our beds but we had a little chat first down a queer little green lane.

28th May, 1916:
... Toby and I went over to Bennetts End. We sat under the little chestnut tree and had milk and cake and we took some photos. ... Motored back to golf links and then lunch at Hill Cottage. Toby and I went up to Green Lodge afterwards and took a lot of photos. We had to hurry back and pack, have tea and catch a train to London. Then we went back to Seaford, had an hour's wait at Lewes and reached Longdown about 9.30. Mrs Moore had supper already for us and Toby had brought back a bottle of fizz. Oh, it was good to be back there, all by ourselves and we had the best of suppers. That fizz made my head quite funny. How he laughed when he saw it and his eyes were so bright. "You're absolutely in my power to night" he said and I was so glad. I will never forget the lovelight in his eyes and the colour of his curls all ruffled by my hands. I asked him not to leave me and he came and helped me undress and when I came back from my bath, there he was in his pyjamas just waiting. Sleep was very sweet that night. We kept waking each other up with kisses and the morning came all too soon.

29th May, 1916:
I had to hurry up to school on my bike and got back about 12.30. We had lunch indoors as it was not very promising and then set out with bathing dresses for the far end of the beach. There we erected a wonderful tent with his mackintosh sheet over the bolder of a breakwater and then began to think how chilly it was for bathing. Toby insisted however, as he had taken so much trouble over that tent, but further operations were delayed by a company of soldiers coming down to have a dip just near us. We had to wait till they had gone and then about 4.00 p.m. we rather shiveringly undressed and got into the water. It was awfully cold and fairly made us shriek. We did not stay in long, but it was lovely and warm once we were out and we hurried back to Longdown for tea. Toby wanted to stay indoors and flirt but I dragged him out for a walk on Seaford Head and it was a beautiful evening. The sea looked glorious. We came back to supper and had a happy evening together. ...

30th May, 1916:

After school we took our lunch and walked to Seaford Head. ... We came down the cliff and went along the rocks underneath it, where it was warm and sunny. We sat a long time in a little cave and then came back to Longdown and I biked up to school. What was my delight to find afternoon school was over! I flew back and surprised Toby who was just lazing in the sitting room. We had tea and then did a little shopping in the town and went upstairs to pack. The packing progressed slowly – we just lay about on the bed and flirted and laughed. It was all such fun. This was our last evening in Seaford. We went up to bed as early as possible and kept saying how glorious it had been here.

31st May, 1916:

Toby went off early to catch the 8.20, snapping a photo of me as he drove off. I came back to school and caught the 1.20. It was very slow and I did not get up until 4.30. Toby met me, very wrath at having had to wait so long. We went to tea at Rumpelmeyer with Padie but it was a great rush as Toby had to go off to a business meeting. In Piccadilly I bought a 21st birthday present for Reggie. I went to the Regent Palace Hotel and found Mrs Dodgson and Guy and Toby. We went to Les Goblins to dine and then to a terrible play. ... Poor Toby! Gloom had been hanging over him all day and this was the final straw. He was furious and became more and more depressed. ... When we got back to the hotel he seemed to cheer up a bit and practised conducting his mother up the aisle in his quaint little way, up and down the passage. He came into my room to say goodnight. "We shall have to be good tonight" he said and I felt very miserable. He kissed me and said he was feeling happier and then went to his own room.

1st June, 1916:

Today began badly. Toby slept very late and I had to very nearly drag him out of bed. Then breakfast was an awful meal. Guy was with us. The serving was deplorably slow which made Toby more and more gloomy. Mrs Dodgson and Mr Fulton married at St James' Church. Toby gave her away. Lunch at Jules, dined at Scotts. *"A Kiss for Cinderella"* – a lovely night.

Toby to Marjorie

The Grand Hotel
Folkestone
3rd June, 1916

This absolutely settles it: with or without the consent of your parents we will be married next leave! Oh! I am so bored here without you. The boat does not sail until 1.00 p.m. Think what a nice cheery time we might have had here together.

What think you of the naval news?[157] Not too good, is it? There seems no doubt that we got the worst of it, though it is very hard to make out how much damage we really did the Hun, who of course will never admit anything that we don't know for certain. ...

Dear old thing, I wonder how you are feeling – not too sad, I hope. I keep thinking over those days together at Seaford: they were far and away the best. ...

Officers' Club, Boulogne-sur-Mer
4th June, 1916

Just a line to let you know that I am safely across the Channel. This is quite a sound spot and fills a much needed want. It is ever so much better and cheaper than the local pubs. I hope to find the Regiment tonight, if the leave train doesn't take about twelve hours and land me at Béthune at midnight, as it does sometimes! ... It is vile coming back here again and the better one's leave is, the worse it becomes. ... Really we managed to get a lot done, didn't we? But the time at Seaford was best of all. I just loved it. ... D--- the b------ war! Cheerio, old thing!

Toby to his mother [Roupigny]
6th June, 1916

I got back to the Battalion yesterday morning and found everyone very cheery and in very good form. We are back resting for a few days and who should turn up in the afternoon but Philip, which was very nice. He stayed to tea and of course we had a tremendous gossip. I told him all about the wedding ... . He doesn't think he will get his leave for about another month.

... What do you really think about me getting married next leave? Of course I should like to, but I think it will be rather difficult to arrange unless I can get away during the beginning of September, which is bound to be uncertain. Marjorie will be back at school again and I don't want her to give that up. ...

Marjorie to Toby St Peter's, Seaford
6th June, 1916

I have just had your letter from Boulogne and was ever so pleased to hear again so soon. I am so glad you found somewhere nice to stay this time and hope you had a fairly decent journey back to the Regiment. The censor had opened your letter – impertinence! Thank goodness the papers have not recorded so much energy on the part of the Huns lately on the Vimy Ridge. ... It is glorious thinking over all the time you were here. Last week at this time <u>we</u> were busy packing up at Mrs Moore's. I'm so glad you look back on the days here as the best, because I do absolutely: it was all so peaceful and undisturbed and just perfect being quite alone together. ...

Toby to Marjorie [Lorette Spur]
10th June, 1916

... We went into the trenches a couple of days ago, but not the front line. I came back to the transport lines yesterday, which is very pleasant, especially as there

....

157   The Battle of Jutland (31st May/1st June). Although the Royal Navy won the battle (see footnote 143, Chapter 8) it had in fact lost more ships.

has been a heavy thunderstorm with deluges of rain. Otherwise things have been extremely quiet around here.

Wasn't it rotten luck about Kitchener? So damned hard that he shouldn't see the end after having done so much. The Russians once more seem to have made quite a useful push.

I came back to find everyone very optimistic out here and talking about the war being over before next winter, but I still don't think so personally. All leave has been cut down to seven days again. Isn't it stupid? It will mean an awful rush if we are to be married in so short a time, and only about three or four days' honeymoon! I am so glad you are thinking out some cunning schemes for the trousseau. ... Marje, it's just splendid to be loved by you. ...

The 23rd Division was withdrawn from the Vimy Ridge area and joined GHQ Reserve on 16th June. The 8th Yorkshires were withdrawn from the front line positions on the Lorette spur on 13th June and arrived at billets at Estrée Blanche on 16th June. There it spent a week refitting and training. A new Commanding Officer, Lt Col P. E. Vaughan, had taken command of the Battalion on 15th June.[158]

Toby to Marjorie   [Estrée Blanche]
                                                                  17th June, 1916

I have just had yours of the 14th, so the post has been pretty good, hasn't it? ... I don't think you need make all that fuss about a trousseau and you will just have to buck up and not be lazy when the holidays come. I never saw such a girl: always grumbling because there is nothing to do at home and now still grousing when a task awaits that should send a thrill all over you! ...

I forget now whether I told you that Besly has got his job and went off four or five days ago. I rode into the neighbouring town to see him off. He is a dreadful loss as there is no one else in the Battalion with whom I can have quite the same delightful, intimate conversations (much to your relief, I suppose!). We moved again yesterday and are now in quite a nice village [five] miles south[-west] of the town where Reggie spent most of his time [Aire-sur-la-Lys]. I have got about the best billet that I've had since I came out here – a large bedroom looking out on a piece of garden with an orchard beyond, and the people are extremely nice and hospitable.

Aren't the Russians putting up a good show? It really looks as though they may give the Austrians a damned good hiding. I think you are immensely pessimistic about Verdun. Anyhow, it's a virtual win for the French, whether the Hun gets it or not now. I believe we shall see the whole affair take a very different complexion before long. No time for more as I must go and feed. ...

Marjorie to Toby   St Peter's, Seaford
                                                                  18th June, 1916

The days go round so quickly it seems a long time since I wrote to you. I have had a game of tennis ... with three other petticoats down at the club here. It was quite

....

158   TNA WO 95/2184. Lt Col Philip Edmund Vaughan was a regular officer formerly with 1st Bn the Worcestershire Regt (24th Infantry Brigade, 23rd Division). At the outbreak of war he was a Reserve Captain in receipt of retired pay. He took command of the 8th Yorkshires on 15th June 1916 but had previously held temporary command from 21st Jan. to 2nd Feb. 1916

good fun, excellent courts and they played quite well. I panted like a steam engine. It is sad to contemplate but I suppose my best tennis days are over. I don't believe you ever get back to where you were if you drop a game for a year or two. They were most anxious for me to join the club but I am not inspired enough to fork out a guinea. We had a glorious time on Thursday: the whole lot went over to Cuckmere to prawn, armed with paddling shoes and nets. Of course it meant a half-holiday, which I can assure you I appreciate every bit as much as the boys do. One gets dreadfully tired of lessons. A new boy arrived yesterday, such a shrimp – only 7½, can't read of course. He naturally falls to my lot. It will be rather difficult fitting him in with the others.

Toby to Marjorie   [Estrée Blanche]
                                                                  22nd June, 1916

   We are still in the same village and have had a very pleasant time here. The weather has recovered itself these last days and it has been very jolly having our lunch out each day, and we've not been messed about. The CO we have got now is a good fellow. No one outside can realise what a relief it is to have someone at the head who knows his own mind and his job, and is a gentleman.
   I am so glad you have been playing tennis again, but what on earth is all this rot about supposing that your best tennis days are over? I just sat down and roared with laughter when I read that! You just wait till you go into proper training. ...

The Battalion left Estrée Blanche at 9.00 am on 24th June and marched to Berquette where it entrained at 12.30. The destination was near Amiens, almost sixty miles to the south.

* * * * *

Since returning to the Front early in 1916, Marjorie's younger brother Reggie had continued to write home enthusiastically about his life in the Army. He was still serving as a despatch rider in First Army signals.

Reggie to his mother   [Aire]
                                                                  24th April, 1916

   The weather is still glorious and we are bathing every day in the river. I am in the workshops here and am having a good time and jolly good experience as we are always working on our lorries, as soon as one is finished in comes another, most of them are Daimlers and Singers, I am quite an expert on the latter!

                                                                  [Aire]
                                                                  27th April, 1916

   Sgt Walker and I are settled in the back room of our pet café here writing letters, whilst madame is cooking us a couple of pork chops, onions, apple sauce, and fried chips, a splendid dish! We often come in here for a little supper, the people are so nice to us, the only drawback is that we have to embrace "mother" on both cheeks before we go, a terrible proceeding: we always dread it.

[Aire]
17th June, 1916

Thank Heavens my Commission is going through, the inevitable has happened: Sgt Walker, Sams and three others of my best pals have been transferred to form another signal company that has just come out here. Nobody knew a thing about it until 9 o'clock last night, and at 9.30 this morning they were off! We all feel wretched as they have been the men that have made this place what it is; especially me, as they were my special friends, I always used to go out with them, always together, then suddenly we are parted. It will be rotten without Walker, my best pal that I have ever had: how I miss him! But of course we felt very proud that they should have chosen our fellows out of all the DRs in France.

* * * * *

Reggie's brother Humphrey had meanwhile spent the first few months of 1916 with the 3rd (Special Reserve) Battalion, of The Queen's (Royal West Surrey) Regiment at Chatham. However, he was posted to the 2nd Battalion of The Queen's, joining them in France on 22nd May 1916.[159]

"Awaiting Ship for France" Humphrey Secretan (centre) and brother officers of The Queen's (Royal West Surrey) Regiment outside The Grand Hotel, Folkestone, before crossing the Channel, c. 20th May 1916. On the left is 2/Lt E. F. G. Haig. On the right is 2/Lt Gerard Rimington Bower who was killed in action aged 19 with 1st Queen's on 15th July 1916 and who is commemorated on the Thiepval Memorial.

....
159   The war diary records: "Joined: 2/Lts Secretan and Haig with 67 other ranks." (TNA WO 95/1670)

Chapter 11

The Somme

July to October 1916

In his letter home on 2nd July, Charles Fair's comment that, "Things seem to be really moving at last", was a reference to the opening of the Battle of the Somme the previous day. After lengthy preparations and a week-long artillery bombardment, the Battle began on 1st July. Eleven divisions of General Rawlinson's Fourth Army attacked at 7.30 am alongside two divisions of Third Army which took part in a diversionary attack at Gommecourt to the north of the main assault. The total frontage of the BEF's attack was fourteen miles.

The choice of the Somme for the Franco-British offensive was determined by the fact that it marked the junction between the French Army and the BEF. Britain, the junior partner in the coalition, was under increasing political pressure to shoulder a larger burden of the fighting on the Western Front. The joint offensive was conceived with one objective being to help relieve pressure on the French Army at Verdun. The Somme marked the first time that the BEF had played the leading role in an Allied offensive on the Western Front.

The 1st July 1916 would in time become notorious as the "worst day" in terms of casualties in the history of the British Army. For modest gains – a penetration of one mile on a front less than four miles wide - the BEF suffered 57,470 casualties, including 19,240 killed and 35,493 wounded. For the BEF, the day was the nadir of the entire war, but from then on it showed evidence of a genuine 'learning process' with improvements in organisation, command, tactics and equipment as it evolved into the war-winning force of 1918.

* * * * *

Of the nine young men in this story, four – the three Champion brothers and Humphrey Secretan – were involved in the 1st of July attack. Humphrey was the only one to have gone 'over the top' as part of an attack. Unfortunately no letters of theirs survive to tell us what they saw and felt about that infamous day. However, war diaries and regimental histories do at least allow a brief description of their involvement.

The 30th Division, part of XIII Corps under Lt Gen W. N. Congreve VC, was on the extreme right of the British line adjacent to the French Sixth Army which shared the attack. Carl Champion and his brothers Alan and Eric were with 11th South Lancashires, the St Helens Pioneers. Carl had recorded in his diary that during the days leading up

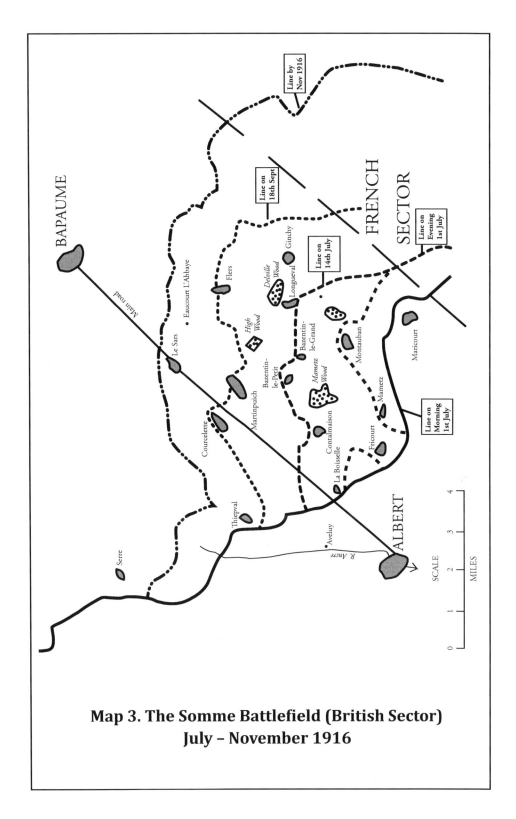

**Map 3. The Somme Battlefield (British Sector)
July – November 1916**

to the offensive, the Pioneers had built a temporary POW cage at Grovetown to house any Germans taken prisoner in the offensive. On the day of the attack the Pioneers created saps in the trenches to enable the infantry to have an easier passage as they surged forward from their positions around the village of Maricourt. To the left of the 30th Division was the 18th Division under Maj Gen Ivor Maxse, who had trained his men to advance behind a creeping barrage. The artillery in this sector, aided by French guns, had been more effective than elsewhere in destroying German barbed wire. The 30th Division was the most successful of British divisions on the first day of the Somme battle. When the attack went well the Pioneers hastily linked the British communication trenches with those vacated by the Germans at Montauban. This village had been captured by 11.00 am and in the afternoon Montauban Alley to the north of the village was in British hands. Although the St Helens Pals had sustained 190 casualties, the three Champion brothers were unharmed. On 4th July Carl noted that 1,350 German prisoners passed through Grovetown.

To the west of the XIII Corps on 1st July was the XV Corps under Lt Gen H. S. Horne. On the right flank of this Corps, opposite the German held village of Mametz, was the 7th Division commanded by Maj Gen H. E. Watts. The overall plan was that this Division, together with the 21st Division on its left, should out-flank the strongly held village of Fricourt. The objective of the 7th Division on 1st July was Mametz village and the high ground to the east along the Mametz-Montauban road.

Humphrey Secretan in trenches near Mametz shortly before 1st July 1916

Lt Humphrey Secretan's Battalion, the 2nd Queen's Royal West Surreys, were part of the 91st Infantry Brigade on the right flank of the 7th Division. 2nd Queen's were in support to the 22nd Manchesters. The Battalion had spent late May and June in and out of the trench system facing Mametz so was familiar with the ground over which it would attack.

At zero hour, 7.30 am on 1st July, the 22nd Manchesters advanced and captured the German front and support trenches at Bulgar Alley, south-east of Mametz. The Queen's then moved forward and occupied the German front line trench. At 9.50 am 'A' Company and Humphrey Secretan's 'C' Company continued their advance northwards and occupied Bulgar Alley and Bucket Trench whilst under machine gun fire from Mametz and Danzig Alley, "suffering numerous casualties."[160] Soon after 1.00 pm 2nd Queen's entered the eastern end of Danzig Alley and was able to bomb

....

160 Wylly H.C., *History of The Queen's Royal Regiment, Vol. 7*, p. 102

westwards towards Mametz. By about 4.00 pm all four companies were consolidating and reorganising in Danzig Alley. By 7.30 pm the Battalion had pushed forward into Fritz Trench[161] which it secured by making three strong points. "Machine guns (91st MG Coy) and Lewis guns [were] placed to sweep the whole front... Rations and water arrived during the night."[162]

The 91st Infantry Brigade had advanced about 1½ miles by nightfall on 1st July. Mametz itself had been secured by about 5.00 pm by other units of the Division. The XV Corps had taken about 1,600 German prisoners but had suffered some 8,000 casualties.

The 2nd Queen's resumed their advance at 11.00 am on 2nd July, taking new positions some 600-700 yards further north in Cliff and White trenches. The Battalion consolidated this position, holding the front line in this sector for twenty-four hours while the focus of operations shifted to the capture of Fricourt to the west. It was relieved on the afternoon of 4th July and went back to bivouacs at Minden Post before marching to billets at Buire the following day. During the first four days of July the Battalion had suffered 320 casualties to all ranks.[163]

* * * * *

Over the next few weeks, Toby Dodgson, Philip Dodgson and Charles Fair would all play their parts in the Battle. Guy Dodgson remained in England throughout the Battle as he was serving with one of the reserve battalions of the Hertfordshire Regiment.

Reggie Secretan was still serving with First Army Signals some fifty miles to the north of the Somme and would play no part in the Battle. However, he had been thinking about taking a Commission and had written home to that effect:

[Aire]
8th July, 1916

... Now about a Commission, if I take one in the RE it will take ages, so I thought of trying for one in the Herts Territorials. They have been out here a good time, and as I presume their reserve is in Hertford, I could often pop home on a motorbike. I have seen the Herts out here. They are a smart lot of chaps, and I should like to be out with fellows from our own part of the world. I want to do a bit more than I am at present, and see more of the War.

So that he would be readily available to attend officers' training, Reggie was posted home in August, when he was attached to the ASC at Woolwich Dockyard. He told his parents afterwards that he was lucky to get away as he had a court-martial hanging over him. His mother described the circumstances: "It appears that one night when out on a round on his motor bike he was stopped by an irate Colonel who damned him sky-high because he had his lights on, and said that he must have been warned at a certain point to put them out. Reggie politely, but firmly, said he had not come that way, and had not been warned. The next day his Captain told him all this had been reported, and that if he admitted he had been wrong he would be let off with a

....

161   This trench ran just past the northern end of the present day CWGC Danzig Alley Cemetery.

162   TNA WO 95/1670

163   Casualties for 2nd Queens 1st-4th July were officers: 6 killed, 7 wounded; other ranks 40 killed, 226 wounded, 41 missing. (Wylly H.C., op cit, p. 103)

slight punishment, otherwise he would be court-martialled. Reggie said he had not done wrong, and he was not going to say he had, and he preferred a court-martial. However, no more was heard of it."

* * * * *

The 23rd Division, which included the 8th Yorkshires and Toby Dodgson, did not take part in the 1st July attack as it was in reserve to III Corps. On 24th June the 8th Yorkshires had detrained near Amiens and marched to billets at Bertangles six miles north of the city where they spent a few days training.

Marjorie to Toby

St Peter's School
Seaford
26th June, 1916

My Darling Old Thing,

I am wondering very much if events are going to move in France. Everyone seems to expect it. I wish you had explained where your little village is. I take it it is behind the lines which is a great blessing. I'm so glad you all appreciate a new Colonel … . It must make a great difference. …

By the way – it's early yet but do you mind one way or another if I am married in white and a veil or in a hat, etc.? I don't know at all where or how it will all take place but I would like to know your opinion. My aunt nearly had a fit today when I said I might be married in an ordinary frock and said you would not like it, so I want to know. Of course we can't decide anything till I hear what Pa and Ma think about how it is going to be done. …

Ever so much love and kisses.

From Marjorie.

Toby to Marjorie

[Bertangles]
27th June, 1916

Darling,

I got yours of the 22nd yesterday. I knew where Reggie was and please allow me to know where I am, or rather was! We were all rather sorry to leave that village, as the people were nice and friendly and the wenches *très chaudes*! I speak from hearsay, of course.

We have had some drastic changes in the officers' staff of B Coy, with excellent results: (1) Our mess cook is cook no longer, he having seen fit to get blind drunk while we were out on a field day, so that when we got in, ravenously hungry, it was only to find what was to have been our dinner sitting forlornly on the stove, burnt to a cinder. So he once more stands in the ranks and has to content himself with the food of the Atkins[164] – silly fool. …

(2) The once-faithful Humble has fallen from his high estate and likewise lost his job - a fat and comfortable one. He, on the morning that we left, failed to wake me till 5.45 a.m., at which hour all kit was ordered to be packed and taken to the Q.M. stores. And then, when I told him off, he was most impertinent, for which latter

164 'Thomas Atkins' was the generic name for the common British soldier. The exact origins are subject to debate but appear to date back to the seventeenth century. It was used as a name in specimen forms published in War Office regulations in 1815.

offence there was nothing for it but to return him to duty.[165] I have now got a lad named Alton, who is going to be a success I think. He is a nice quiet person, more refined than most of them, nice looking with the deepest brown eyes.

Our move here was a lengthy affair with a ride in the puff-puff and a good long march each end. On the way I saw two of the most charming maidens in the world, who were engaged in serving out hot tea to the Atkins at one of the stations *en route*. It really gave me quite a shock as I went up to get the men back into the train, just before going on, imagining the ladies to be some worthy people doing their bit, when I heard the dulcet tones of a really beautiful English girl and, looking up, was instantly captured. The vision was, unfortunately, necessarily momentary but the impression remains and will do for a long time. But we will get on, as I expect you have heard enough of that! ...

I am so glad that the trousseau is progressing but, to be quite honest, I think it will be some time before you need it, as there has been no leave since I came back and we have a great many officers to go now, owing to all these new arrivals. Still, I dare say we shall be married in peacetime after all. Today I have had some splendid asparagus and a cake from Bennetts End, and also a very nice letter from your Mother.

We are rather crowded up in this village and beds are scarce, but luckily I have one and am sharing a room with Tommy (Capt Thomson[166]). Yesterday we went into the town not far away (Amiens) and had a very good time – excellent shops, where I was able to get some luxuries for the mess, including a magnificent duck pasty and some *pâté de fois gras*. We finished up with a good dinner and some bubbly and came away feeling very pleased with life.

If only the weather would dry up – pouring again this morning. It really is sickening. So long, old thing; I'll try and write again as soon as I can.

Marjorie to Toby   St Peter's, Seaford
                                                                       29th June, 1916

I was very glad to get a PC from you this morning. You will send me lots, if things are really going to be lively in France, won't you? You were a juggins not to tell me where you were when you last wrote, but I believe I have said this before! One can't help feeling awfully excited to know if we really mean anything serious or if we are only relieving the pressure on Verdun. I heard from Reggie this morning who was also quite thrilled over everything and says Humphrey is at the hottest place. His [Reggie's] Commission is a long time going through. ...

Here we have begun to say "four weeks tomorrow". The term is going very quickly now. The first whackings took place this morning! Some of the biggest boys for bad Latin. They rushed to tell me about it: "I had four of the best", etc. No one

....

165 Officers' servants had a relatively comfortable and safe existence. They were normally left out of battle before a battalion went into an attack. 13942 Private Joseph Humble of B Company paid with his life for this lapse of duty. He was returned to the ranks of a rifle platoon and was killed a few days later on 10th July 1916, age 26. He is commemorated on the Thiepval Memorial.

166 Arthur Ravesby Thomson, 27, from Putney, had enlisted on 17th Aug. 1914. Having served in the OTC at Bath College, he was commissioned into the 8th Yorkshires and was promoted to Captain on 16th Apr. 1915. He returned to the UK on sick leave in Aug. 1916 and spent the rest of the year and much of 1917 recovering. He was awarded the MC for his part in the Somme, but does not appear to have returned to the Battalion. (TNA WO 339/14641)

seems to take it at all seriously. There is no news. At least, I can think of nothing but what is going to happen in France. ...

St Peter's, Seaford
2nd July, 1916

I was awfully pleased to get your letter of the 27th. We are all fearfully excited over the news. Humphrey is in the strafe on the Somme. He also wrote on the 27th but I had his letter some days ago, saying he was going into the trenches the next day and that his lot were going to attack. He said all he dreaded was the wait beforehand with the guns going overhead and he must have had a good many hours of it. I am wondering so much what happened to him. We shan't hear for a day or two. I am sorry you have moved south. I hoped you were to remain well away from the centre of affairs, which is evidently not very far from where you are now.

Do you think we really shall make the Hun move this time? One can hardly believe it possible, but the Lord forbid another standstill and another winter in the trenches. We can hear the guns so plainly here. I lie in bed at night and listen to them and wonder what you are all doing ... .

I have been out over the Downs with my bike today. The most glorious scenery all around and all so peaceful, but always I could hear the distant rumble if I stopped to listen. I thought all the time of you and what a lot of jolly things there are waiting for us to do. Yes, that wedding will most likely not be this September but you never know. Perhaps you will get a handy little wound which may require treatment at home. ... Well, there is only one subject now and you know more than I do about that, so no more now. Remember, I love you always. Thanks so much for the two PCs. I am fearfully glad to get them frequently. I do wonder about Humphrey. Goodbye Sweetheart.

The 8th Yorkshires had started their move to the battle on 1st July when they marched to bivouacs ten miles to the east at Baizieux Wood. The next day they marched to billets at Albert.

Toby to Marjorie   [Albert]
2nd July, 1916

My Darling Old Thing,

I got yours of the 26th yesterday and am glad to hear that you are still fit. ... I don't feel equal to discussing marriage problems until after the great push: it all seems such a long way away.

You can imagine how bucked up we all were yesterday to wake up and find a real summer day at last – blue sky and sun shining. Everyone is as keen as mustard, and I've never known the men in such good spirits.

The 23rd Division arrived in the line under III Corps on the evening of 3rd July. It took over trenches in the Tara-Usna and Bécourt area. Attacks by other divisions to the east of the Albert-Bapaume road had not been a success but Generals Haig and Rawlinson were determined to press on. III Corps was ordered to capture Bailiff Wood and Contalmaison but again little headway was made. The 23rd Division was engaged in minor operations on the 4th and 5th July to clear the Germans out of the remainder of their front line system in the Horseshoe Trench area. On the 6th and 7th July the Division failed to take Contalmaison from the south.

[Belle Vue Farm]
7th July, 1916

So sorry this has not gone off before, but we've literally had no time. This pushing is the most strenuous business. Unfortunately the weather has been awful the last three days – torrents of rain, and the trenches are about back to winter conditions.[167]

Our Brigade did a bit of a push yesterday and bagged about two hundred Boche,[168] who seemed only too glad to give themselves up. Richardson and another officer in this Company got wounded – nice little ones that will just take them back to Blighty. Several pieces of shrapnel fell on me too, but none with sufficient force to make a puncture.

The mail has been rather disorganised and today was the first chance we had of seeing a paper hearing how things are going. I was very pleased to get yours of the 2nd too, and hope Humphrey is all right. ...

Bivouacking in the rain is a rotten job, but cheerio! Let's hope for the best.
Always your
Toby

Toby to his mother

[Bécourt Wood]
8th July, 1916

Dearest Mother,

I was so glad to get yours of the 1st two days ago and to hear that Philip had had such a good leave. I'm afraid there is no chance of us meeting each other again at present. As you will see from the papers the "push" has started. After the first two days, which were real summer ones, the weather has been perfectly awful – rain, rain and always more rain – and the trenches are as bad as in mid-winter. It doesn't improve bivouacking either, so you will understand that letter-writing is rather impossible, but I will try and write a proper letter directly we get back under cover for a night. ... Best love to Hamilton.

Your ever-loving Toby

The Official History for the 8th July 1916 records that: "at 5.30 pm, a Fourth Army conference of corps and corps artillery commanders was held to discuss the next operation, and also the attack on the enemy's second position, Longueval-Bazentin-le-Petit. General Rawlinson issued the operation order for the latter but left the date to be fixed later, as it depended upon the preliminary operations and also upon the weather. He was determined not to launch the main attack unless conditions were sufficiently good to profit by the advantages of British superiority in the air."[169]

....

167 Thunderstorms on 4th July were followed by intermittent showers on 6th July and half an inch of rain on 7th July.

168 On 5th July, minor attacks by the other battalions of 69th Infantry Brigade succeeded in clearing out the Germans who were still clinging on to parts of their first line trench system. The whole of Horseshoe Trench had been captured by nightfall. Over 180 prisoners and two machine guns were captured by the Brigade during the day. (TNA WO 95/2183)

169 British *Official History 1916 Vol. 2*, pp. 42-43

The attack on the second position was that which would take place on the 14th July. Sir Douglas Haig had discussed the plans for this with Rawlinson and the three corps commanders of Fourth Army. Haig "was still insistent that Trones Wood, of which only the southern extremity was held, should be secured to cover the right, and Mametz Wood and Contalmaison to cover the left, before the main attack."[170]

Contalmaison sits on the top of a spur projecting from the main Pozières ridge which commands the Somme battlefield. The village overlooks the western edge of Mametz Wood and dominates a dry valley to the south-west.

On 8th July the 23rd Division received orders to capture Contalmaison on the 10th. By now it had secured positions in Peake Wood and Shelter Alley, which would make an attack from the west feasible. It was recognised that the village, if captured, could be used to support attacks on Mametz Wood. Bailiff Wood had been taken on 9th July. The officers and NCOs of the 69th Infantry Brigade, which included the 8th Yorkshires, spent the 9th July in reconnaissance and in studying maps, aerial photographs and detailed intelligence information. This was to "ensure that every man should reach his appointed objective and there should be no delay in effecting consolidation after capture."[171]

Contalmaison was reduced to heaps of rubble by the morning of 10th July as it had been shelled for two days and nights. It was "frequently hidden in a cloud of black smoke, great fountains of debris rising up above it at times as the heaviest shells fell among the ruins."[172] It was occupied by about 600 men.

On the morning of 10th July the soldiers made their final preparations before going into battle. They had their last chance to write home and Toby sent a field postcard. At 11.00 am 69th Infantry Brigade moved from Albert. Each man carried two days' rations and water bottles. They expected to be able to replenish their water-supplies from wells in Contalmaison. The assault troops each carried four bombs and two sandbags.

The plan was that two battalions of the Brigade would assault the village with 9th Yorkshires on the left and 8th Yorkshires on the right. The advance would start from Horseshoe Trench, some 1,200 yards from the German positions, crossing the dry valley to the west of the village. Meanwhile two companies of the 11th West Yorkshires would secure the left flank - Bailiff Wood - then bomb along the trench which ran eastwards from the northern edge of the wood.

A heavy artillery barrage would cordon off the village from counter-attacks. The artillery of 23rd Division was to concentrate on the village, and would recede by lifts of 200 yards as the infantry advanced. On the flanks artillery from two more divisions would bombard trenches and routes the Germans could use to reinforce the village.[173] In addition III Corps heavy artillery was to provide additional bombardments on the German second line positions which were another 1,000 yards behind Contalmaison.

....

170   Ibid, p. 43

171   Headquarters 69th Infantry Brigade Report on Operations 10th and 11th July 1916 (TNA WO 95/2183)

172   'The Other Side of the Hill - No IV, Mametz Wood and Contalmaison' in *The Army Quarterly*, Vol. 9, 1924-25, p. 247

173   34th Divisional artillery (reserve division of III Corps) bombarded Contalmaison Wood and the trenches to the north of the village while 21st Divisional artillery (reserve division of XV Corps) bombarded Pearl Alley and trenches to the east.

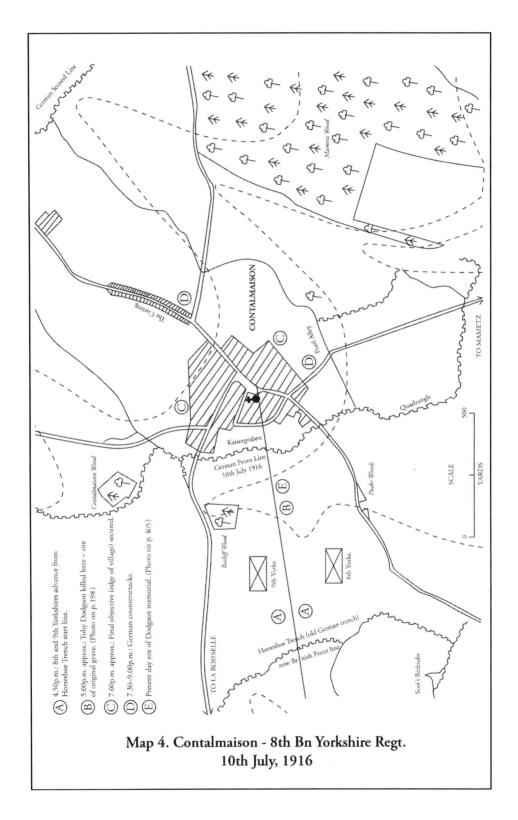

German Second Line

Mametz Wood

The Cutting

CONTALMAISON

Pearl Alley

TO MAMETZ

D

C

D

Quadrangle

C

Kaisengraben

German Front Line
10th July 1916

500

Contalmaison Wood

E

Peake Woods

SCALE

YARDS

B

0

Bailiff Wood

9th Yorks.

8th Yorks.

A

A

Horseshoe Trench (old German trench)
now British Front line

TO LA BOISSELLE

Scot's Redoubt

Ⓐ 4.50p.m.: 8th and 9th Yorkshires advance from
    Horseshoe Trench start line.

Ⓑ 5.00p.m. approx.: Toby Dodgson killed here – site
    of original grave. (Photo on p. 198)

Ⓒ 7.00p.m. approx.: Final objective (edge of village) secured.

Ⓓ 7.30–9.00p.m.: German counterattacks.

Ⓔ Present day site of Dodgson memorial. (Photo on p. 405)

**Map 4. Contalmaison - 8th Bn Yorkshire Regt.
10th July, 1916**

At 4.00 pm the artillery barrages started. One German account describes the village under bombardment: "One dugout after another collapsed, one machine gun after another was destroyed, the cellars of the château were full of wounded … scarcely more than a hundred men escaped to the second position."[174]

Exactly as planned, at 4.30 pm 11th West Yorkshires began their assault to clear Bailiff Wood. They swept through the wood and wheeled to the North to occupy their objective trench and so protect the left flank of the main assault.

From 4.30 pm parties of Germans were observed escaping from Contalmaison. Between 200 and 300 were reported to have been driven out of the village by the British artillery. "Two restless days and sleepless nights, constant alarms, constant shelling and fighting and repairing trenches and dug-outs had completely exhausted them."[175] Machine gun and rifle fire was brought on them and many became casualties.

At 4.50 pm the main advance started. The infantry advanced in quick time in extended order over a distance of 1,200 - 1,500 yards. The assault formation consisted of four waves per company, which were followed by waves of searching and consolidating parties. The advance was directed by the right hand man of 9th Yorkshires, with Contalmaison Church as the axis. Toby Dodgson had taken a position on the left flank of the 8th Yorkshires on this central axis. At first they took few casualties.

When the alarm was given by the German defenders, it had little immediate effect. According to one German account, "only one officer and fifteen men … appeared above ground, and these occupied some ruins at the end of the village, but the air was so full of smoke and the dust of the crumbling ruins that the advance of the British could scarcely be seen."[176] As the advance continued, 9th Yorkshires soon came under accurate German artillery fire in the valley but by 5.20 pm they had reached and occupied the Kaisergraben without opposition. However, 8th Yorkshires came under even heavier fire on descending the slope of the valley 500 yards West of Contalmaison and suffered casualties from machine gun and rifle from the front and the left flank. Toby Dodgson was hit and seen to fall at about 5.00 pm at the foot of the slope.

At 5.25 pm the 8th Yorkshires reached the Kaisergraben. This trench provided little cover as it was only "two or three feet deep with no parados on the enemy side." The ground was "a quagmire of shell holes, wire and debris and the men were compelled to advance in small groups by rushes a few yards at a time. Only the gallant leading of their officers and personal qualities of their commander backed up by the courage of all ranks could have surmounted such difficulties in the face of a continuous hail of bullets and shrapnel."

However, 8th Yorkshires suffered in the last part of their advance in the fifty yards between the Kaisergraben and a garden hedge bordering the houses of the village. A small number of Germans (the officer and fifteen other ranks mentioned above) emerged above ground, and opened a burst of fire which caused many casualties in 8th Yorkshires. Four officers and over 100 other ranks became casualties in a few

---

174 *Schlachten des Weltkrieges. Somme-Nord Vol. I*, pp. 206-7, quoted in Edmonds, *Military Operations France and Belgium 1916 Vol. 2*, p. 56

175 'The Other Side of the Hill,' p. 255

176 War diary of 122nd Reserve Infantry Regiment, quoted in 'The Other Side of the Hill,' pp. 255-6

moments.[177] By this time, 8th Yorkshires had been reduced to an effective strength of five officers and 150 men. However they captured as prisoners of war a number greater than their own strength of unwounded men. The War Diary of 69th Infantry Brigade records that in total the Brigade captured eight officers and 160 unwounded men, 100 wounded men who were pulled out of dugouts, and six machine guns with ammunition.[178]

At 6.00 pm Germans were seen escaping to the North. "Unfortunately the buffer springs of many of the 18 pounders gave out so that the artillery could not take proper toll of the Germans in retreat."[179] Also at this time the Germans counter-attacked the road junction in the centre of the village. This was driven off by 8th Yorkshires. The two battalions consolidated their position during the rest of the evening and fought off further counter-attacks.

The British Official History considered that "the casualties suffered by the Brigade...in the assault on Contalmaison were heavy, but not excessive considering the importance of the operations." Its losses were 39 officers and 816 other ranks killed, wounded and missing.[180] This represented roughly half of the attacking force. Of these, 8th Yorkshires lost twelve officers and 347 other ranks.[181]

* * * * *

Among those "missing" at Contalmaison was Toby Dodgson. It took a few days before his mother, Helen Fulton, received the official news. She wrote to Marjorie on 17th July:

Helen Fulton to Marjorie   The Close, Salisbury
                                                             17th July, 1916

Dearest Marjorie,

I have had a wire from the War Office saying this, "Regret to inform you that Capt Dodgson ... was reported missing on 11th July. This does not necessarily mean he is killed or wounded. Will report on further news immediately."

Oh, Marjorie, I'm afraid I have no hope, but I ought to hope I know. I have written to the War Office ... and to the Red Cross to know if they can tell me any further news, but "missing" is so hopeless. I don't know whereabouts he was. I wish I was near you and could be with you. I had a letter from Philip this morning, written on 13th saying he had had a card from Toby the day before saying all was well. We are trying to telephone to the Red Cross who are said to know all things. I shall go up to the War Office tomorrow and will let you know at once if I hear anything further. Send me a line if you feel you can. Oh, my dear, I am so sorry for us both. God grant he may be only "missing".

Yours,
Helen

....

177 TNA WO 95/2183 and The Other Side of the Hill.

178 TNA WO 95/2183. One of the machine guns is displayed in the Green Howards Regimental Museum at Richmond in North Yorkshire.

179 British *Official History 1916, Vol. 2*, p. 56. The inability of the recuperator springs to stand up to repeated wartime firing was the one basic design flaw of the 18 pounder QF Mark 1 field gun that was in common use in mid 1916. (*British Artillery Weapons and Ammunition 1914-18*, I. V. Hogg and L. F. Thurston, 1972)

180 War diary 69th Infantry Brigade (TNA WO95/2183). These figures were also given in *The 23rd Division*.

181 Based on figures given in the war diary of 8th Yorkshires (TNA WO 95/2184 subsequently stated in *The Green Howards in the Great War 1914-19*) but modified after analysis of *Soldiers Died in the Great War*.

Philip to his mother Helen   [Aix-Noulette]
                                                                20th July, 1916

Your letter has just arrived with the uncertain news of Toby. I am so terribly sorry about it and I know how awful the suspense must be for you, and I feel it very keenly too. I am afraid nothing I can say will be of any comfort to you except that I am trying to find out where the 23rd Division are, and I shall try and get to them and find out all I can for you – at the same time it is doubtful if I will be able to do this. I feel sure by now you will have heard from somebody in the Battalion of the circumstances, and they will probably be able to give you an idea as to what has probably happened to Toby. One is apt in a case like this to jump at once to the worst conclusions, but I do not think it is necessary. … I have not given up hope at all that he may be a prisoner of war. I am afraid this is a very poor letter, but it is difficult to write under the circumstances. … It is the greatest comfort to me to know you have Hamilton with you. … All quiet here, so don't worry about me.

                                                                [Aix-Noulette]
                                                                23rd July, 1916

I received your letter of 20th today and was so glad to hear from you. It is hard that you haven't been able to find out anything about Toby. I had a long day yesterday trying to make my way to the 23rd Div. I've got our General's leave to go, and have raised a motorbike. All that remains is to find out where they now are and that is not easy. … According to your accounts the 8th Yorks had a hard time. I think there is every probability that Toby may be a prisoner, and it would be extraordinary if either one of the wounded or somebody in the Battalion cannot say anything about him, although of course in the noise and smoke it is easy to get lost. For the present, until we get more definite news, we can only hope for the best. …

On the 18th Marjorie had recorded in her diary that Toby's mother was *"making all enquiries. I bathed in the afternoon, a lovely day and I believed that he is alive".*

"I am losing hope," Marjorie recorded on 21st July. *"They say he cannot be a prisoner, but I can't realise it."* She was *"feeling more hopeful again"* on 23rd July. However, on 24th she received *"a letter from his orderly saying he was killed but I can't yet believe it."* She did not write anything in her diary over the following few days, except the entry *"I don't remember these days: they were awful."*

Finally, on 28th July, Helen Fulton received a letter from Lt Col Vaughan, the CO of the 8th Yorkshires, saying Toby was definitely killed on 10th July. Lt Col Vaughan wrote:

> "It is with the deepest sympathy that I write to you to say that I fear there is now no doubt whatever that your son was killed in the advance on Contalmaison.
>
> The ground that we advanced over was quite open and the Battalion did magnificently, led by your son and Capt Thomson.
>
> The advance was without cover, and advantage was taken of the numerous trenches and shell holes, and your son was evidently killed and buried in one of the trenches or shell holes, for we found no trace.

He died gloriously, leading his men, and he lies with many others of his Company in the torn and shell-swept valley just south-west of Contalmaison."

Philip to his mother [Le Ponchel]
6th August, 1916

I have received your letter containing Colonel Vaughan's letter. What a good straightforward letter he wrote, but it did come as a shock to me too, although I thought I had already given up hoping. How I wish I could have a talk with you. It is so difficult writing and it has been a bit hard at times having nobody to talk to here. ...

Helen did not receive War Office confirmation of her son's death until 4th August, on which day Lt Col Vaughan[182] wrote to her again:

> "We are back in the line and I have found out that your son's body was found and buried by the burial party. It was found, as we had thought, in one of the shell holes and I have marked the place with a rough wooden cross. I have shown on the back of this where his grave is. It will, I feel sure, be a comfort to you to know that his body was found."

Philip to his mother [Lanches]
10th August, 1916

At the moment I feel thoroughly in the dumps, partly I think to bodily fatigue but chiefly, like you, to having no-one near to whom I can talk about Toby and you. I do think of you so much and Marjorie too and I'm so sorry for you both. I can't tell you how I have felt having no woman to ever talk to about things. Women are so much more sympathetic. The average man never seems to think of anybody else's thoughts and, if he does, he doesn't seem to be able to talk. I do feel it would be such a comfort to have a good talk with somebody who really knew Toby and knows you, but this is of course impossible. ... The more I think of Toby the more proud I feel of him. Thank goodness we met out here as often as we possibly could have done, and I wrote him a letter just about that time. ...

I've just been thinking how Toby really wanted his money dealt with and I think probably he would like us to treat Marjorie just like one of ourselves and divide it up amongst the four of us instead of between us three. ...

Do you ever see Evelyn Fulton? She seems such a nice girl.[183] I often think of that glorious week of leave. ...

More information about how Toby died was provided by one of his own men, Private B. Angus, in a letter to Marjorie:

....

182 Maj (Acting Lt Col) P. E. Vaughan was gazetted with the DSO on 22nd Sept. "for conspicuous gallantry in action" at Contalmaison. He later went on to command the 6th Worcesters. He died on 5th Dec. 1918 and is buried in the family vault at Llanfihangel Ystrad (St. Michael) Church, Cardiganshire. He was 40 years old and married.

183 Evelyn was Hamilton Fulton's niece.

Yorkshire Regt
Ballyvonare Camp
County Cork, Ireland

Dear Miss Secretan,

... I was with the Yorks when we left Liphook two years ago and I have had the misfortune to get wounded twice, of course not too serious.

Well, to give all the help I can give you in regards Captain Dodgson. Our first advance began on the 8th July. Of course we came through alright with a few casualties. Of course we never sleep one hour from the 1st up to the 10th where we caught pretty hot. We were ordered to take Contalmaison at all costs and we had to advance over 1,000 yards of open ground. We arrived at [the] front line trench at 5.50 p.m. then we mounted the parapet at 5.55, every man as calm as water in a cup. Captain Dodgson leading and encouraging his men on like an old veteran, never once faltering, all this going on with our men falling on all sides but we had to get that village and we meant to have.

But just about 100 yards from the goal Captain Dodgson got hit in the head. Then we gave him a drink and made him as comfortable as it was possible under the circumstances. He wasn't dead then, but later on in the evening after we got the village, someone passed word up the line that Captain Simpson,[184] Hume-Wright[185] and Captain Dodgson had been killed, but I can tell you Captain Dodgson got hit leading his men over the open front.

Hoping you will accept my greatest sympathy during your sad bereavement. ...

The following was written by Private A. Maughan,[186] who was Toby Dodgson's servant for a time. Private Maughan had been wounded on 10th July and had been evacuated to England on 14th July.

Holnest Red Cross Hospital, near Sherborne
Dorset

I hope you will excuse me for taking the liberty of writing these few lines sympathising with you through the death of Capt Dodgson. I feel it my duty to tell you how much he was loved by the NCOs and men that were under him while he was in command of B Coy. Although he was killed you can rest assured that he did not throw his life away through carelessness, as he was known to be one of the coolest headed officers in the battalion.

I was in the officers' mess all the time that he was in B Coy. He was the president, as you will no doubt know, and I was caterer.

....

184 Capt C. S. Simpson, the Adjutant, is buried in Becourt Military Cemetery, Becordel-Becourt (grave I.S.10). He was 25.

185 Lt (Acting Capt) Maurice Gabriel Hume-Wright was 21 and originally from Ireland. He was the son of Maj Gerald and Elizabeth Hume-Wright and lived at Ash Vale near Aldershot. Educated at Wimbledon College, he enlisted in the Hampshire Yeomanry on the outbreak of war. He was commissioned into the 8th Yorkshires on 4th Nov. 1914 and promoted to Lt on 29th Dec. 1914. He is also buried in Becourt Military Cemetery. (grave I.T.9)

186 16814 Private Anthony Maughan had arrived in France with the 8th Yorkshires on 26th Aug. 1915. He was a coal miner from Usworth in Co. Durham and had enlisted aged 19 in Sept. 1914, less than three months after his marriage. After recuperating he served with the 7th Yorkshires in France (Mar. – Dec. 1917) but survived the war. (Service record in WO 363 on ancestry.co.uk)

I have never seen a man so cool as he was when we made the attack. I saw it in the paper about his death, so I will close.

Marjorie saved all her letters from Toby and had them typed up into two leather bound volumes. She wrote in pencil at the end of the second volume:

> *My love came back to me*
> *Under the November tree,*
> *Shelterless and dim.*
> *He laid his hand upon my shoulder;*
> *He did not think me changed, or older,*
> *Nor I him.*
> [Frances Crofts Cornford (1886-1960)]

Despite the tragic loss of her fiancé, Marjorie continued teaching at St Peter's School, Seaford, until the spring of 1917.

* * * * *

The capture of Contalmaison, along with that of Mametz Wood on 11th July meant that an attack on the German second line was now possible. This line ran from the Albert-Bapaume Road, in front of Bazentin-le-Petit Wood and the village of Bazentin-le-Grand and east to Longueval. Haig and Rawlinson developed a plan to penetrate this second line, with XV Corps being ordered to capture Bazentin-le-Grand and the adjacent woods.

The 7th Division received orders on 12th July to resume offensive operations on the 14th. This attack would be led by the 20th and 22nd Infantry Brigades with the 91st Infantry Brigade being held in divisional reserve.

Humphrey Secretan and the 2nd Queen's had spent a week reorganising and refitting at Buire-sur-l'Ancre, a village five miles southwest of Albert. The Battalion had received reinforcements of nearly 300 men on 9th and 10th July before marching back to near the old (1st July) front line on 11th July. There it started to prepare for the attack. On 12th July "all officers [were] taken up to German craters from where the situation and all prominent landmarks in the promised land were pointed out to them."[187] The 13th July was spent in preparation, with ammunition being issued at 6.00 pm. At 9.00 pm the Battalion marched to a position north of Mansell Copse where it bivouacked.

The offensive opened before dawn on 14th July with a brilliantly executed initial attack. No-man's-land was some 1,200 yards wide on 7th Division's front, so the assaulting troops of 20th Infantry Brigade crept forward in the early hours of the morning to deploy about 400 yards from the German front line. The darkness concealed their approach. Further surprise was achieved by omitting any preliminary bombardment: although the guns had registered on the German positions, they were to hold their fire until five minutes before zero hour.

The attack opened at 3.25 am, with the leading waves of the Division only 100 yards short of the German front line when the barrage opened. These leading troops

....
187 TNA WO 95/1670

rushed the German line just as the barrage lifted onto the second line. By 5.00 am the 20th Infantry Brigade had secured its objective which allowed the 22nd Infantry Brigade to pass through. Bazentin-le-Petit and Bazentin-le-Grand Wood were secure by 4.00 pm

Meanwhile, the 7th Divisional artillery had pushed forward and taken up new positions in Flatiron Valley and Caterpillar Valley. The remaining battalions of the Division, 2nd Queen's and 1st South Staffords, were still in reserve, and had moved up in the late morning "to a position east of Mametz Wood, where they dug in under heavy shell fire... Here they remained for over six hours, enduring the German bombardment with slight casualties and waiting for their chance."[188]

At 5.35 pm the 91st Infantry Brigade received orders to capture High Wood with 2nd Queen's forming the right of the advance. The advance started at 7.00 pm and was supported by Indian cavalry on the right flank. "The country ahead was a refreshing sight, green pasture land unscarred by shell-holes and broken by an occasional hedge while High Wood was in full leaf, not a tree as yet damaged by shell fire." The 1st South Staffords on the left flank of the advance were held up by machine gun fire, and orders were issued to the 2nd Queen's "to push on hard for High Wood, hoping they would be able to get into the wood and outflank the troublesome machine guns."[189]

The Divisional History continues: "Advancing in four lines 150 yards apart on a front of 350 yards [2nd Queen's] made splendid progress. As they came on they dislodged the Germans in the shell-holes, a few of whom stopped to surrender or be bayoneted; the majority bolted, giving good targets to the Queen's, who shot them down from the standing position, knocking many over. About 700 yards from the starting point – they had covered the distance in ten minutes – the Queen's took three field guns at a hedge, and half an hour later the leading lines reached the edge of the wood."[190]

The Battalion "plunged into the wood... It was thick with dense undergrowth, in which it was hard to see twenty yards ahead, so direction was difficult to keep, but there were not many Germans in the wood, not enough to prevent the Queen's from pushing through to its eastern edge, which was reached before 9.00 pm. There they proceeded to dig in, having three companies along the SE edge and part of the NE edges, with B Company in reserve." That night was spent in consolidating the position and in fending off a counter-attack from the Germans who were still in possession of the northern part of the wood.

However, the next day it proved impossible to drive the Germans out of the wood which was heavily shelled by both sides. British shells fell among C and D Companies of 2nd Queen's.[191] The British position in the wood now formed a pronounced salient which would be difficult to hold and to resupply. The decision was accordingly taken to evacuate the wood.[192] 2nd Queens were withdrawn to near Mansell Copse in the

....

188 Atkinson, C. T., *The Seventh Division, 1914-18*, p. 289

189 Atkinson, op cit, p. 290

190 Atkinson, op cit, p. 290

191 Wylly, op cit. p. 104

192 The 7th Division's rapid and unexpected success on the morning of the 14th July meant that High Wood was lightly defended at that time. It has been claimed by some historians of the Battle of the Somme that if the attack on the wood had gone in several hours earlier then the whole wood might have been captured that day. This would have avoided the two-month struggle for the wood. This remains one of the most hotly debated 'what if's' of the Battle.

early morning of 16th July.

Between 14th and 16th July the 2nd Queen's had suffered over three hundred casualties.[193] One casualty on the 14th July was Humphrey Secretan who, in or near High Wood, had received a wound to the leg. By the 16th July Humphrey had been taken as far back as the 8th General Hospital at Rouen, from where he wrote the following letter to his sister Esmé, who was by now working as a VAD at Reading Hospital.

Humphrey to his sister Esmé   28th July, 1916

Thanks for your letter which I have just got. The nurses' hours are not so bad I find now. They are on duty from 7.30 a.m. to 7.30 p.m. but getting afternoons and late mornings off a good deal when there are only six or so in a ward for thirty as there are now; but when the wards are full as they were when I first came they had to stay all the time except just for meals and had to work pretty hard. The two VADs in our ward do dressings just as the sisters do and are quite good; they have been in Malta before this.[194] The night staff is rather thin: one sister and two orderlies for three wards or huts as they are of thirty each. However they seem to get on all right. Everyone has to be washed and all beds made by 7.30 a.m. and the doctors in the wards by 9.00 a.m. so there is a bit of a bustle I can tell you. ...

I am very disgusted to see how pleased everyone is I am wounded! No one sounds a bit sorry! Aunt Emma said she was glad to hear it was very serious! ...

Humphrey was awarded the Military Cross for his actions on 1st July, 1916. The citation, as reported in *The Surrey Times*, read: "for conspicuous gallantry. When all the officers of his company had become casualties he took command and did fine work capturing a position."

Humphrey to Esmé   [The hospital at Rouen]
3rd August 1916

Thank you and father and mother for their letters and congratulations. I'm afraid I don't approve of medals, but did not know my name had been sent in until it was too late to protest. I did nothing except what I get 7/6 a day to do. However it seems to have pleased all relations. But really it's nothing to get excited about as survivors always get one provided the Battalion has done all right. ...

Well, since the 1st I can walk with a limp. The hole has filled up but there is still a patch which a sixpence could almost cover where the flesh is raw ... which I give four days before I shall be well. I do not know where I go but am going to try for a week at a convalescent home to get fit again. I feel quite fit but I expect I need a little exercise. They send us to Dieppe from here, so hope to go there. ...

Humphrey had recovered sufficiently from his wound to be discharged from hospital on 15th August. The war diary of the 2nd Queen's Royal West Surreys notes that he

....

193 Total casualties in this period were: one officer and 47 other ranks killed, 10 officers and 211 other ranks wounded, and 47 other ranks missing (TNA WO 95/1670)

194 Malta was known as 'the nurse of the Mediterranean' during the Great War as thousands of allied troops were evacuated to hospital there from the fronts in Gallipoli, Salonika and Palestine.

195 TNA WO 95/1670

rejoined the Battalion on 18th August. It also notes that on 23rd August he took over the duties of assistant adjutant from Captain J. B. Hayes MC.[195] The 7th Division had been out of the line since the action at High Wood in July.

Humphrey to Esmé   [near Mericourt]
                                                                                    27th August, 1916

Thanks very much for the socks and letter which arrived safely. ... Gold stripe is not up yet and I think it very absurd unless they have one for years out here as well.[196] Blood money I am not entitled to unless three months in hospital. Glad Ren [Reggie] has turned up.

The gymkhana went off jolly well. Our Colonel won several prizes but he rode my horse in the jumps and came a cropper and the horse has sprained his neck.[197] (I had a horrible thing to come over here on.) There were a lot of fellows watching the gymkhana, Generals galore. ...

The six weeks' rest started on the 18th July and is now over. We have just moved up to a bit nearer and I fancy our Division is in the line. We may not be wanted but I expect we shall have a go. ...

The 7th Division had indeed gone back into the line at the end of August with the task of clearing out the Germans from the corner of Delville Wood and the villages of Ginchy and Guillemont. The 2nd Queen's entered the support line on the night of 29th/30th August. A German counter-attack on 31st August saw companies of the 2nd Queen's being sent forward to reinforce the front line. On 1st and 2nd September the Battalion made unsuccessful attempts to capture a stoutly defended German strongpoint on the Eastern corner of Delville Wood. Meanwhile, the Division had captured and lost Ginchy on the 3rd and 4th September. The Queen's made a final abortive attack to capture the strongpoint in the late afternoon of 7th September before being relieved early the following morning.[198] The Division was withdrawn to a reserve area about 25 miles northwest of Amiens.

Humphrey to Esmé   [Huppy]
                                                                                14th September, 1916

... We are very comfortable here in the *château*, parquet flooring in the bedroom. We could have a nice dance, only the children are tinies. Monsieur is very affable but does not introduce us to the family who seem to be locked up all day long. I have never seen the children go out yet at all. There is a big town [Abbeville] here about six miles away, but we are not allowed in yet, so I cannot say what it is like.

....

196   The 'wound stripe' had been introduced under Army Order 249/16 dated 6th July 1916 and was a two inch long brass strip which was worn vertically on the left forearm of the jacket. One was awarded for each occasion on which the wearer had been wounded. In soldiers' slang they were known as "Gold Stripes." Overseas Service Chevrons were not introduced until Dec. 1917.

197   The war diary for 25th Aug. 1916 records "2.30 pm, 91st Infantry Brigade Gymkhana. Heats run off in the morning. Lt Col Longbourne 2nd in Open Jumping on *Ivanhoe*." (TNA WO 95/1670)

198   This week of minor attacks had cost the 2nd Queen's over 180 casualties (officers: 1 killed, 7 wounded, 1 missing; other ranks: 49 killed, 114 wounded, 16 missing). (See the combined war diary entries for 1st and 6th Sept. in TNA WO 95/1670.)

Letters have been coming very funny lately. I got one from Marje dated 2nd a day after one dated 9th and "The Times" did the same. I hope R[eggie] has been helping in the garden a bit. ...

* * * * *

Meanwhile, Charles Fair and Philip Dodgson had been well away from the July fighting on the Somme as the 47th Division was still near Vimy Ridge. However, on 1st August the Division started marching southwards. The gunners, including Lt Philip Dodgson, came into action on 13th August in support of the 15th Division in front of Martinpuich, where they remained for a month, firing almost incessantly and suffering several casualties. Charles, with the 1/19th Londons, did not reach the battlefield until September.

Charles to his father [Noyelles-en-Chaussée]
13th August, 1916

... We are still in the same place as when I last wrote but shall probably move shortly. I don't think the censor would object to my saying that I recently rode with Col Hamilton to visit the battlefield of Crécy. It was quite a peacetime expedition. We saw the memorial to John of Bohemia and his knights and we stood on the spot from which Edward III watched the battle.[199]

Please excuse my paper: we are too far from shops to buy any at a moment's notice. You will have to address me as "Major" in future! I am wearing the insignia of that rank and also receiving (I hope) the emoluments while holding the position of Second-in-Command. ...

[Gorenflos]
19th August, 1916

... I am writing this on Saturday, as I don't expect to have time tomorrow. The weather has broken at last and we have had a lot of rain. ... We have had a very vigorous fortnight's training here and I hope it will prove profitable. ... We have spent two days in Crécy forest. It is a very fine place and reminds me of Savernake [a forest near Marlborough, Wiltshire]. ... The news continues to be good from all sources. We hardly ever get our newspapers up to time now, so that you probably know far more about things than we do. I am gradually getting accustomed to my new rank but it takes some doing. ...

Charles to his sister Mary [Gorenflos]
19th August, 1916

Very many happy returns of your birthday! ... We are just about to move from our pleasant quarters. We have been here a fortnight and, though it has been a very busy time, we have heard practically no sound of guns. I expect we shall have our fill of that shortly. I have heard recently from Mrs Tennant at Freshwater [Isle of Wight]. ... I do long for the sea. Every letter I get now from anyone seems to

....

199 The Battle of Crécy (26th Aug. 1346) took place at Crécy-en-Ponthieu, nearly fifteen miles NE of the mouth of the River Somme. It was one of the most important battles of the Hundred Years' War. An Anglo-Welsh army led by King Edward III defeated a much larger force commanded by King Philip VI of France.

come from the sea. I do hope you will make the acquaintance of Mrs Hamilton [his Colonel's wife]. They were only married four months before the war began and there are no children. The butter arrives all right and is much appreciated.

Charles to his father   [Bresle]
24th August, 1916

... We are still trekking and at present I am writing this under a piece of sail-cloth in a cornfield – after breakfast. ... We see Boche prisoners working in the roads: they look very contented and healthy. ... The weather is much cooler since the rain but the flies are getting bad. ...

[Bresle]
26th August, 1916

... I am writing this on Saturday as I am going off tomorrow morning, before daybreak, on a sort of Cook's Tour of some of the places which have become famous of late [the southern section of the Somme battlefield]. It ought to be very interesting and instructive. ... We are still bivouacked in the same spot. ... I hope we shall not get a wet day as the water will inevitably run down the hill into my tent. ... The flies are still very troublesome and the men are so like children that it is only by much strafing that we get them to take the most ordinary precautions. ...

[Bresle]
3rd September, 1916

... Another blow has fallen, as [Lt Col] Hamilton is definitely leaving us to return to his own regiment (he was only attached to us). He doesn't seem to want to go in the least, but it is an order. It seems to me absolute madness to have a change like this just at this moment. In his place we are to have a Col Tew of the East Surreys:[200] he seems a good soldier from his record, but nobody could take Hamilton's place and personally I shall feel absolutely lost. The weather has improved again after having been very bad at the beginning of the week. Our bivouacs were nearly washed away and we have had to crowd the men into any barns and lofts we could find.

[Bresle]
10th September, 1916

... We have had a busy week but are moving forward again tomorrow. Don't expect to hear from me for a bit as we shall be pretty busy. I am glad to say that Hamilton has got leave to stay with us a bit longer. I had a day off in the middle of the week and five of us had an expedition to a largish town in the neighbourhood. We had tea and dinner there and actually did some shopping. I hadn't been inside a barber's shop since I was last on leave! ...

On 10th September - some eight weeks after Humphrey Secretan had taken part in the first attack - the Germans were still holding most of High Wood. The British

....

200   Lt Col H. S. Tew CMG of the 1st Bn East Surrey Regt (5th Division) did not reach the 1/19th Londons and does not appear to have served with any other unit within the 47th Division. (He is, however, listed as being attached to the 19th Londons in the Oct. 1917 edition of the *Army List* but this may be an administrative error.)

merely held the southernmost corner. High Wood and the ridge upon which it sits dominate the battlefield south of the Albert-Bapaume road, and these positions formed the core of the German third line.

General Rawlinson conceived of a major offensive - the biggest since 14th July - that would require three corps to break the German position. The attack was set for 15th September and would be augmented by a new weapon intended to break the deadlock of trench warfare – the tank. III Corps would be on the left flank of the offensive, and 47th Division was allotted the task of capturing High Wood with the support of four tanks.

The world's first tank – the Mark I – was a brilliant innovation which could flatten barbed wire and which could withstand rifle and machine gun bullets. Equipped with either machine guns or 6 pounder guns, it was capable of providing close support to troops attacking German trenches. However, the Mark I had a top speed on level ground of only 4 mph, so would not be capable of breakout and exploitation on the battlefield – a role for which cavalry were still required. Although its rhomboidal shape allowed it to cross trenches, it was still prone to 'ditching' in difficult ground or getting 'bellied' in deep mud.

The attack opened at 6.20 am on 15th September with two brigades attacking the wood. 141st Infantry Brigade was on the left. The 1/17th and 1/18th Londons advanced into no-man's-land but were held up by machine gun fire. Heavy fire came from concrete emplacements inside the southwest edge of the wood. These two leading battalions took heavy casualties.

At 7.00 am the 1/19th and 1/20th Londons left their assembly trenches and pushed forward under heavy fire from the left flank. They found that the preceding battalions had been unable to gain ground. The result was that elements of all four battalions of the Brigade were now hopelessly intermingled in the British front line trenches and the communication trench. At this point Lt Col Hamilton "left his HQ to restore order. To do this he clambered out of the communication trench calling upon men to follow and was killed almost immediately by a machine gun bullet."[201] The adjutant Captain Trim assumed temporary command of the battalion while the men were being reorganised and the trenches were being cleared of dead and wounded.

The problem for the attackers was that little British artillery fire was landing on the defenders of High Wood, so the German resistance was much stronger than expected. This was because of the unwise decision to send the tanks supporting the 47th Division into the wood, rather than in outflanking movements. The wood had been an artillery target since July and by now was a tangled wilderness of smashed tree stumps: a tough obstacle for a Mark I tank.

Of the four tanks that were sent to attack the wood, two became ditched in the British front line or no-man's-land. The third found the going so rough that it turned right out of the wood, lost direction, and ended up opening fire on British troops before ditching in the British front line. The fourth tank, through a combination of luck and skilful driving, crossed the German front line and shot up a small group of defenders. It proceeded to the support line and shot that up too before its engine failed and it was abandoned by its crew.

The attacking infantry were thus deprived of the close support that the tanks could have provided. However, they were also deprived of artillery support as a

....

201 TNA WO 95/2738

decision had been taken not to put down artillery fire on the routes that the tanks should have taken through the wood. This meant that 100 yard wide lanes would be left in the barrage for the tanks. Also, the British and German front line trenches in the wood were so close together that bombardment was difficult. It was therefore decided to commence the barrage 150 yards beyond the German front line to avoid hitting British troops. The attacking infantry therefore had to deal with heavy fire from unbombarded German machine gun positions.[202]

At 10.30 am bombing attacks were organised under Lts Crump and Chandler of the 1/19th to work along the southwestern and northwestern edges of the wood.[203] At about the same time 140th Trench Mortar Battery laid down a hurricane bombardment on the German positions in the northern corner of the wood. These actions finally broke the will of the German defenders who began to surrender in batches or withdraw from the position.

At 12 noon Charles Fair was sent forward from Brigade HQ and assumed command

of the 1/19th Londons.[204] The units of the 141st Infantry Brigade had become so mixed up and "disorganised from loss of leaders" that they were "temporarily formed into a composite battalion" under Lt Col Norman of the 1/17th Londons.[205] High Wood was reported clear of the enemy by 1.00 pm.

Philip Dodgson and the 7th London Brigade RFA covered the attack by the 47th Division's infantry. During the afternoon of the 15th September "some of the batteries began to move up in support, the first being the 19th London Battery under Major Lord Gorell, who brought his battery up into the shell hole area immediately behind High Wood."[206]

Charles to his father   [Bazentin]
19th September, 1916
I haven't time to describe the battle of 15th September properly. I am all right, but Col Hamilton was killed. I feel as if I had lost a brother, we have been so constantly side by side in every sort of corner for nearly eleven months.
I was not allowed to come up to the

Lt Col A. P. Hamilton MC (CO 1/19th Londons), left and Lt Col W. H. Matthews DSO (CO 1/20th Londons)

....

202 For these and other weaknesses of the plan to attack High Wood see Robin Prior and Trevor Wilson, *The Somme*, pp. 235-6

203 TNA WO 95/2738

204 TNA WO 95/2738

205 Maude, op cit, p. 65

206 Maude, op cit, p. 65

very front line till he was hit, as all 2nd-in-command officers were kept back in case of casualties to the COs. He was rallying all men of all battalions after the first direct attack on the wood had failed and, as he led them over the top, a machine-gun bullet killed him. It was just like him to dash in like that but it was not really his job and we feel that he has thrown himself away. ... Of all the soldiers I have ever known out here he was the finest and he was one of the most absolutely lovable men I have ever come across – of the same type as Leslie Woodroffe.

We lost heavily in officers killed and I lost my servant – Prewer. The last thing he ever did was to bring me (unasked) some supper. The Regiment did simply magnificently and were really worthy of Hamilton and his training. It has thrown a very heavy responsibility on me but we are getting along all right at present. Today we hope to go right back for a few days' rest, but the Hun must be kept on the run if possible. Too busy for more.

The capture of High Wood had come at a high price: the 47th Division had lost over 4,500 casualties.[207] Of the officers of the 1/19th Londons, not only was Lt Col Hamilton killed but so also were all four Company Commanders and five junior officers; another died of wounds. Eleven officers killed and only one wounded in a single battalion in one action was a proportion of dead to wounded that Charles thought was possibly unequalled. Of the other ranks, 294 were killed, wounded and missing.[208]

In just two years Charles had risen from a private in the HAC to acting CO of an infantry battalion – a very depleted one, but one which was still full of spirit. The Battalion war diary records that they remained in the captured wood for thirty-six hours and then moved back to Bazentin for two days and Bécourt for three.

Private Prewer's grave, London Cemetery, Longueval

Charles to his father [Bresle]
24th September, 1916

We are right back now for a short spell at the same place whence we started before moving up to the line. Everyone seems enormously proud of what the Brigade, and our Battalion in particular, has accomplished. At any rate we did what many others have failed to do and took a place which has cost many thousand casualties and which is the last of the really high ground which the Germans

....

207 Maude, op cit, p. 67

208 TNA WO 95/2738. For other ranks casualties were 66 killed, 5 died of wounds, 206 wounded and 16 missing.

occupied in this part of the world. We had a pretty rough time and lost many of our very best. I still feel very strange and lost without Hamilton and the others, but on the whole we are in splendid spirits and are receiving new drafts almost daily to make us up to strength again.

We had to spend an extra three days in trenches of sorts for the purpose of burying English and German dead and identifying the former where possible – a very grisly job, but the men stuck to it splendidly.[209] We had a great reception when we rejoined the rest of the Brigade yesterday and marched in with our band playing. Today we had a sort of commemoration service for those who had fallen. I read the lesson and chose the hymns – 274; 291; 197; 437. I also made a short speech to the Battalion before the service began. We are now very busy refitting and reorganizing. I am very well indeed and am nearly rested.

Now that we are so far from any sort of real civilisation I'm afraid I must ask for some of those carbolic vests to be sent me regularly – say one a week, as I have at last fallen a victim to things creeping innumerable. ...

PS I think it would really be much better that you should retire soon. I can't suggest where you should live at all, with my own movements so uncertain.

There is no record of the speech Charles made or what lesson he chose, but the hymns were particularly apt. The first three were subdued but providing solace, no doubt reflecting the mood and needs of his men. A display of jingoistic patriotism would not have suited the occasion.

> 274 "Through the night of doubt and sorrow ... Brother clasps the hand of brother, Stepping fearless through the night."

> 291 "Oft in danger, oft in woe ... Fight nor think the battle long; Soon shall Victory wake your song."

> 197 "The King of love my shepherd is ... In death's dark vale I fear no ill, With Thee, Dear Lord, beside me."

> 437 "For all the saints who from their labours rest ... "

Though Charles probably did not think the men, largely drawn from St Pancras and Camden Town, were particularly saintly, he was well aware that they had performed heroic deeds. The fourth hymn is splendidly rousing and was ideal to lift the spirits of the survivors who would be in action again soon.

The service was almost certainly taken by the *padré* of 141st Infantry Brigade, Rev David Railton.[210] He was the man who, in 1920, wrote to the Dean of Westminster with the suggestion that one "unknown soldier" should be buried in Westminster Abbey. The idea was taken up with such enthusiasm that one body was indeed

....

209 The war diary records: "Burial party of 1 officer and 15 ORs supplied for High Wood" (19th Sept.) and "Large burial parties for High Wood" (20th Sept.) with further parties being provided on 22nd and 23rd. (TNA WO 95/2738)

210 The Rev. David Railton had been appointed as an acting chaplain, 4th class on 6th Jan. 1916. He was 31 and married. Prior to his appointment he was the vicar of Folkestone. He served initially with the 34th Division before being appointed as *padré* to the 141st Infantry Brigade in Apr. 1916. (IWM 80/22/1 and TNA WO 374/56017)

interred there at a national service led by King George V on Armistice Day 1920. David Railton also suggested that the Union Flag to cover the coffin should not be a new one but a flag that had seen service in the field. He volunteered one he had in his possession, so it is probable that "The *Padré's* Flag" that still hangs today in Westminster Abbey near the tomb of the Unknown Warrior had been used to cover a makeshift altar for that service on the Somme in September 1916.[211]

Today, on the roadside in front of the south-western edge of High Wood stands the memorial to the 47th Division, a stark reminder of the sacrifice made by the men from London. Nearby is the large London Cemetery. The grave of Charles's batman, Private Frederick Prewer, aged just 21, lies just inside the entrance to the cemetery along with many others from the Division.[212] Lt Col Hamilton MC lies buried in Flatiron Copse Cemetery near Bazentin-le-Petit.[213]

Although the infantry of the 47th Division had been withdrawn from the line, the artillery remained in action. Philip Dodgson was now in the area where his brother Toby had been killed a few weeks before.

Padré of 141st Infantry Brigade The Rev. David Railton MC. (Photo courtesy of Andrew Railton)

Philip Dodgson to his mother [Mametz]
24th September, 1916

As you have already found out there is no harm in my telling you that I have found the spot where Toby was buried and I know you will be glad to hear that I have made a good solid white cross and put it on the grave. The cross is quite plain and has a white rail round it, and looked very nice. I got one of the Battery fitters to make it, and our cook who is by trade a sign-writer painted it for me. ...

I am at present feeling very lost without my servant, who was a most loyal and

....

211 The *Padré's* Flag was dedicated and placed above the tomb on Armistice Day 1921. Representatives of the 47th Division were chosen to place it in position at the dedication ceremony. (Maude, op cit, p. 76)

212 3276 Pte Frederick Prewer of 'A' Company had enlisted in Nov. 1914 and arrived in France with the 1/19th on 10th Mar. 1915. He had previously been wounded at Givenchy on 22nd May 1915 and rejoined the battalion the following October. He was the son of Mr and Mrs Frederick James Prewer, of 22, Prince of Wales Crescent, St Pancras. (grave 1A.A.12)

213 Lt Col Arthur Percival Hamilton MC was 32 and the son of the late Maj P. F. P. Hamilton, RA, and Mrs Hamilton, and the husband of Kate Hamilton of 42, Eaton Square. (grave VII. I. 2)

Toby Dodgson's original grave with wooden crosses. Bailiff Wood is in the background. Photo taken by Humphrey Secretan

attentive person. A few nights ago the Boche gave us a doing with gas shells.[214] We were all quite all right in helmets, but next morning my servant about eleven o'clock absolutely collapsed, gasping for breath and more or less unable to move. I am afraid it is doubtful if I will see him again, though I believe he is certain to recover all right. The gas they use now seems to have a delayed effect, which explains the above. ...

Philip Dodgson to his mother

[Mametz]
A Battery RFA
237 Brigade
29th September, 1916

... The British Nation seems to be quite unbalanced as far as Zeppelins are concerned. To a casual reader of the papers it would seem that the destruction of one Zeppelin was of more importance than everything else put together. I suppose it is natural as it is only by reason of the Zeppelins that large numbers realize there is a war at all. When it comes to spending hundreds of pounds on a memorial of the spot where the Zeppelin was brought down it is getting rather absurd. It is bad enough giving the man who brings the thing down money, especially as he also got the VC.[215] What about the airmen out here who run greater risks almost every day? ...

....

214 The war diary for 237 Brigade RFA reports that on 21st September while the Brigade was at High Wood "Batteries very heavily shelled all night with gas shells – Lt S. E. Pixley C Battery and two men (C and A Batteries) gassed." (TNA WO 95/2717)

215 Lt William Leefe Robinson of the Royal Flying Corps shot down a Schütte-Lanz airship (not a Zeppelin) over Cuffley, Hertfordshire, on the night of 2nd/3rd Sept. 1916. Robinson was awarded the Victoria Cross and £3,500 in prize money. This was the first award of the VC after an action in the UK.

The 1/19th Londons had little time to reorganise at Bresle. A draft of 250 other ranks was received on 24th September and these men had to be integrated into the rifle companies which were now led by four young subalterns. As acting CO, Charles Fair was shouldering a huge responsibility.

The Battalion moved back into the front line late in the evening of 28th September. The front at that time was nearly a mile to the south-east of Eaucourt L'Abbaye. Two parallel trenches – the Flers Line and Flers Support – were cut by the front line, with the BEF occupying the southernmost sections of the two trenches, and the Germans vigorously holding the remainder.

Meanwhile, on 28th September General Rawlinson set out his further intentions for the Fourth Army. He wanted to straighten the line in front of III Corps by capturing Eaucourt L'Abbaye – a large farm sited on the remains of an old monastery - together with the Flers Line as far as the village of Le Sars. This would provide a better start line for the next major offensive. The date for the assault on Eaucourt L'Abbaye was fixed for 1st October.

On 29th September the 1/19th attempted to bomb along the Flers Line and Flers Support. However, "after two hours heavy fighting, the brunt of which was borne by the bombers, all parties retired to their original position. [The] enemy appeared to be holding this point in great force and was exceptionally well supplied with bombs."[216] The bombing attack was resumed at 4.00 pm the next day, the Battalion cooperating closely with the New Zealand troops to the right. By 7.00 pm the Germans had been "pushed back about 300 yards" in each trench and new blocks established.

Having improved the position, the offensive opened on 1st October. After a preliminary bombardment starting at 7.00 am, the Division started its advance at 3.15 pm with the troops following a creeping barrage. The 1/19th were on the right flank. Two tanks in support silenced German machine guns in the ruins of Eaucourt L'Abbaye allowing parties of the 1/19th and 1/20th Londons to rush through the village and establish a line to the north. The Division spent the next three days consolidating the position as parties of Germans were still holding out in parts of the Flers Line and in the village, and these prevented direct contact with the advanced elements

Charles to his father   [The Flers Line]
Somewhere during a lull in the battle
Monday Morning? 2nd October, 1916

I have been having the most amazing week of all this amazing time. We have been almost continually in action since Thursday night. I had orders not to do anything rash with myself, owing to the scarcity of senior officers in the Battalion. Consequently for a good part of the time I have been directing the Battalion from a telephone on a very narrow staircase in one of the trenches from which we have driven the Hun. I am pretty tired, but things are going well and the men are simply splendid. It is a bit of a strain to have the responsibility of devising schemes for ejecting the Hun or facing his counter-attacks, and I only hope I shan't let the whole

....
216 TNA WO 95/2738

Capt R. C. G. Dartford MC. (Photo courtesy of James Dartford)

British Army down. Dartford[217] is my eyes and ears to the outer world and is simply splendid.

I will write when I can, but I have lost all count of time, especially since they put the clock back an hour in the middle of the battle. This was followed by a request for a return showing how many men have been inoculated during the last year. ...

The Flers Line was finally secured on 4th October. The Battalion was relieved in the early hours of 5th October and withdrew to the Quadrangle trench system near Contalmaison (see Map 4). Since 29th September during the actions on the Flers Line and in the attack on Eaucourt L'Abbaye, the battalion had suffered further casualties of eight officers and 297 other ranks.[218]

[The Quadrangle]
6th October, 1916

I'm afraid my last letter will take ages to reach you as the postal facilities were not great. We are now about two or three miles back in comparative comfort and reasonable safety. We spent six nights in our last part of the line and our efforts had resulted in pushing the enemy so far back that, by the time we came away, we had actually got some of our artillery forward to places where you couldn't walk in daylight when we first arrived there. The Regiment kept going splendidly till the end in spite of mud, discomfort and other horrors indescribable. I am most awfully proud of them. We have had a special message of thanks and congratulations from the General, of which I hope to send you the original copy for the family book. I have now handed over the command to no less a person than Reggie Friend[219]! It is an odd freak of fortune. Of course our Brigadier [McDouall[220]]

217 Dartford, aged 20, had been appointed Adjutant to the Battalion and was awarded the MC for his part in the Somme fighting. A report in his service record described him as "an able officer with good professional knowledge. Power of discipline and leadership good." (TNA WO 374/17931)

218 Casualties were: officers - 2 killed, 6 wounded; other ranks - 38 killed, 3 died of wounds, 221 wounded, 35 missing. (TNA WO 95/2738)

219 Lt Col Reginald Friend was well known to Charles. His wife Camilla was a distant relation of the Fairs and Charles's third cousin. He was a regular officer, formerly with 1st Battalion The East Kent Regiment (The Buffs) and was from a landowning family on the Isle of Thanet.

220 Brig Gen Robert McDouall was commissioned into The East Kent Regiment (The Buffs) in 1892. He served in South Africa and was awarded the DSO in 1901. At the outbreak of war he was a Major with 1st Buffs, and took over as Acting Lt Col of that battalion on 15th November 1914. He was appointed to command 141st Infantry Brigade on 19th Aug. 1916. (Maude, op cit p. 232)

comes from the Buffs, which explains it. At present he has to rely on me for most things of course. I am awfully glad to have him and to be relieved of the strain of commanding, especially as our present Company commanders are all boys. ...

[Franvillers]
8th October, 1916

I hope my letters from the thick of things have reached you. We are still in the reserve trenches from which I last wrote and are fairly comfortable, with some prospect of going further back. I have nothing to add. Reggie is settling down well: he is a good soldier, I am sure, but he has not the wonderful personality of Hamilton. Under the circumstances we have done very well, as a regular soldier who is also a gentleman is rare in these days and the fact that he is a friend of the Brigadier ought to prove useful to the Battalion. It is funny to see Camilla's handwriting appearing on the mess table. It is awfully wet and I fear the Huns will have had time to make themselves comfortable for the winter.

The underclothing from Mary arrived all right and I have got some wonderful khaki pyjamas bought by the *Padré* at a French shop in Amiens. You ought to keep all newspaper cuttings relating to September 15th, 16th, 17th and also to Sept. 29th, 30th and Oct. 1st to 4th inclusive. Most of the newspaper headlines of the latter period actually refer to the doings of our own Brigade. The subalterns who have known me for a long time tell me that they used to chuckle to hear me (knowing my views on things military) becoming more and more military in my language during the time that I had command of the Battalion! I have had some wonderful letters from Mrs. Hamilton: I wish I could help her.

The capture of Eaucourt l'Abbaye allowed several batteries of the Divisional artillery to come over the High Wood ridge and take positions in the open country half a mile to the north of the wood. From there they helped to cover the gallant but unsuccessful attacks on the Butte de Warlencourt by the 47th, and later 9th, Divisions.

Philip Dodgson to his mother   [Mametz]
6th October, 1916

Just a line to let you know we are all fit and well. Have just heard from my servant who is in Bath. If you know anybody there could you ask them to go and look him up ... . He has been pretty bad, but I hope the gas will not permanently affect his throat and lungs.   I have not yet got anybody to replace him. ...

We have procured a flat-iron and with this seem to have defeated the lice, thank goodness.

[Eaucourt L'Abbaye]
12th October, 1916

... I am fearfully sorry to hear you are worrying about me because I promise you there really isn't any need. You have only got to look at the lists to see that the number of RFA casualties is not very great, especially when you consider the immense amount of artillery we've got. At the present we're living in dugouts. We came into this position and found no work had been done at all. As you can imagine, when a battery settles down in a bare plain with no cover at all there is plenty of work for the first night. Marshall slept in a trench with four sheets of corrugated iron over him and Edwards[221] and myself made a bivouac out of a cart cover. The next day we set hard to work and converted a shell hole into a Mess 12 ft by 6 ft ... The next day Edwards and I made ourselves a dugout. We have made it by widening a trench and covering it with curved sheets of corrugated iron. With the aid of sandbags and corrugated iron one can always make oneself comfortable if you take the trouble. ...

By 9th October the 47th Division was relieved. In its fighting on the Somme the Division's casualties were 296 officers and 7,475 other ranks killed, wounded or missing.[222]

* * * * *

In the aftermath of the July 1916 fighting the 11th South Lancashires (The St Helens Pioneers) had often been on the move and were twice placed under the command of divisions other than the 30th, their work often being to improve the communications on land captured from the Germans. On 1st October Carl Champion recorded in his diary, *"Went to High Wood and attacked [Eaucourt] L'Abbaye"*. He must have been close to Charles Fair though probably neither man was aware of the fact. The Battalion remained broadly in the same sector of the Western Front for many weeks. In November Lt Col Fenn was on leave, which meant that Carl was temporarily in command of the Battalion, though his only written comment was, *"Slept in the CO's dug-out"* – presumably one of the perks of his temporary status.

* * * * *

After one week's rest northwest of Amiens, the 7th Division had received orders to entrain for the Second Army area on 17th September. Humphrey Secretan and the 2nd Queen's moved north to Bailleul, arriving on the morning of 18th September. The Battalion took over trenches in the Douve Sector (south of Messines) on the 19th and remained there until it moved into Brigade Reserve at Red Lodge in the afternoon of 27th September.

Humphrey to Esmé   [Red Lodge]
                                                                                                      28th September, 1916
    ... We are very comfortable here. The hut we are in now has several holes in the roof, said to be made from shrapnel, and we found a bullet embedded in one of the supporting posts. The wood we are in is behind a hill and of course at night a few bullets come over. I have been into a neighbouring town to have my teeth seen to and also get a bath, which was rather nice.
    A game of bridge commences now, so must stop. All the new officers can play – joy!

....

221 Lt Oliver Edwards had enlisted in Fulham as a gunner into the 7th London Brigade RFA on 14th Sept. 1914. He had previously served for four years in the 2nd Glamorgan RGA and had reached the rank of corporal. He was appointed Acting Sergeant on 12th Dec. 1914 and was commissioned on 12th June 1915. He was 38, of independent means and had married in 1913. (TNA WO 95/22185)

222 Maude, op cit, p. 73

Humphrey was promoted to the rank of acting Captain on 5th October. The Battalion went back into the front line that afternoon, and spent the next few weeks alternating spells in the line with periods in reserve. The 7th Division remained in this sector until the beginning of November when it received orders to move to the Second Army training area west of St Omer. The 2nd Queen's marched to Meteren via Steenwerck on 2nd and 3rd November. However, it did not remain long in this area, as the 7th Division had been recalled to the Somme to join the Fifth Army. The Battalion started to march southwards on 9th November.

Meanwhile, the Somme offensive was finally grinding to a muddy halt with the onset of winter. The last major phase of the Somme was The Battle of the Ancre from 13th to 18th November. The offensive had cost the British Empire the huge total of 419,654 casualties.

The 7th Division arrived too late to take part in this final stage of the Somme. However, 2nd Queens took over a part of line in front of Beaumont Hamel on 24th November. As the Divisional History records, although "the heavy fighting had died down the position was far from stabilised and the section could not be reckoned 'quiet.'[223] Unfortunately none of Humphrey's letters from this period survive. Some idea of the appalling conditions is given by an unnamed officer quoted in the Regimental History: "surely without exception the most unpleasant bit of line on the Western Front ... a stretch of mud which quite outdid anything that Flanders could produce. In most places it was literally impassable and everywhere it was knee-deep. ... In addition the enemy sprinkled it with shells, while his snipers, operating from higher and drier ground, were active and deadly. Both for danger and discomfort it was hard to beat."[224]

The Battalion spent the next few weeks in and out of the line near Beaumont Hamel but was fortunate to spend Christmas Day in billets in Louvencourt.

....

223 Atkinson, op cit, p. 324
224 Wylly H.C., op cit, p. 108

Chapter 12

October 1916 to March 1917

On 14th October the infantry of the 47th Division marched into Albert to entrain for the North. They did not reach the Ypres Salient until the 17th and 18th. The 7th London Brigade RFA marched north with its guns to take up position on the Hill 60 sector south of Ypres.

Philip to his mother Helen   [Ypres]
                                                    23rd October, 1916

... Since I last wrote a parcel of beans and apples has arrived. They were beautifully fresh and very welcome. Yesterday two parcels also came, one with biscuits and tinned partridges, and the other with cake, powder and soap. Thank you so much for them both. Although I have almost exterminated the vermin I still find one occasionally, so the powder will come in useful after all.

                                                            [Ypres]
                                                    31st October, 1916

... I don't know yet what I am going to do after the war and whatever I do, I don't suppose I'll make any money out of it. I feel I can't go on and waste my life in the City and I equally feel I don't want to go abroad. The question is whether it is possible to make a living by growing anything in the country. ...

We are all getting colds – mine at present is in my head. I think they are coming from the damp, and feet so often wet. I want so badly to get home and buy some winter clothes. It is very difficult to know what to do in memory of Toby. I personally would like to put a brass in the church, in any case. As far as I know I am nowhere near George [Fulton]. ...

                                                            [Ypres]
                                                    11th November, 1916

... I have received the pants and vests and I am very thankful for some warmer clothes.

Our Captain was going on leave today but has been stopped by our General. You can imagine how Generals who stop people going on leave are loved! It's sickening for the individual and also puts us all back and we've had little enough in all conscience.

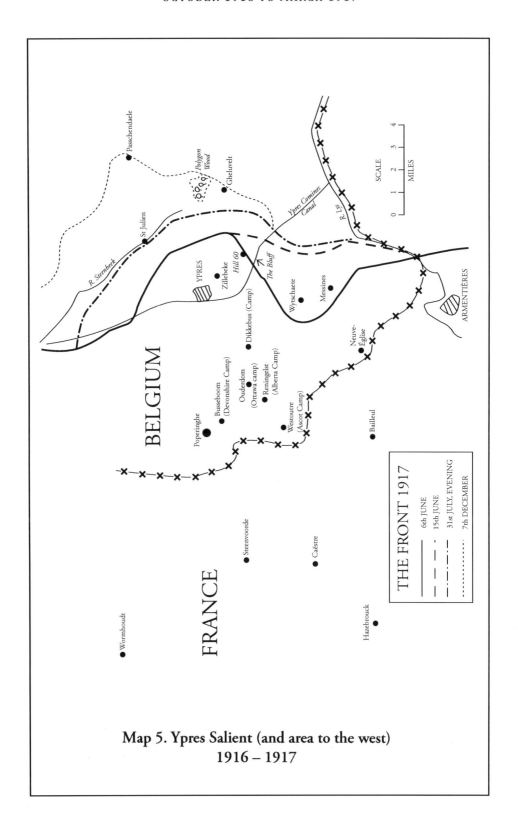

**Map 5. Ypres Salient (and area to the west)
1916 – 1917**

I forgot to thank you for the gloves. They will be most useful. So far the weather has not been very cold but the wet is very bad…

[Ypres]
A/237 Bty RFA
21st November, 1916

… There is a chance I may arrive in England on leave on Saturday. It was the greatest surprise of the war to me when I was told my name had gone in, and I now don't know why, as it isn't my turn. Anyhow, don't reckon on it until you get a wire from Boulogne, though it is practically certain I will come. If by any chance you are in Town, it would be ripping if you could come to Victoria. … If you are at Salisbury I would like to go down there with you to start with. … My clothes are more or less in tatters but you will have to put up with that. The pheasants arrived and we had them for dinner last night: they were magnificent and appreciated.

A week's leave followed for Philip.

* * * * *

Charles Fair was amongst the 47th Division infantry who travelled northward by train.

Charles to his father

[Longpré]
15th October, 1916

Just a line to say I am all right. We are on the move again, northwards presumably. I hope you have got several letters from me by now. Post is still very erratic. I want a winter waistcoat. Can anything be done about sending me one? Perhaps Hulbert could get one. I wonder if Agnes and Camilla could arrange some definite scheme about food parcels for our mess so as not to clash or leave long intervals followed by a rush of edibles.

I am writing this at a wayside *estaminet* whither I have been sent for the purpose for de-training our Brigade, but they are already twelve hours late in arriving![225] Sunday is nearly always a detestable day in this country.

[Busseboom – Devonshire Camp]
22nd October, 1916

Thanks very much for two letters received during the week, also for letters from Agnes and some very succulent and nourishing parcels from Fortnum and Mason. We eventually reached the so-called end of our journey yesterday. In the middle of the week we stayed three nights at quite a nice farm [near Steenvorde] and now we are right up north among places with unpronounceable names – at least, you might be able to pronounce them from your knowledge of kindred tongues[226]- I can't. It has turned most awfully cold and has frozen the last two nights. The men have not yet been issued with blankets, which seems bad.

....

225 This journey took twenty-five hours. The war diary records that the Battalion entrained at Albert at 8.30 pm on 14th Oct. and detrained at Longpré at 9.30 pm on 15th Oct. (TNA WO 95/2738)

226 Flemish has similarities with Afrikaans, which was well-known to Robert Fair from his years in South Africa.

They do some wonderful things to British soldiers which, if done by us to German prisoners, would give the House of Commons food for conversation for months to come. During the week our men had to spend ten hours in trucks, in which there was reminiscence of horse to a depth of several inches – and this, after fighting two of the hardest fights in the war!

[The Bluff]
29th October, 1916

... We have been living in huts all this week but moved further forward again today. Reggie [Friend] is on leave[227] and I am supposed to be going home when he comes back, but at present all leave has been stopped for those who are this side of the Channel. I expect the rough weather has caused trouble in the minefields.

It is awfully wet and cold, but we have got back the surplus winter kit which we left behind before going down to the south. It includes a suit of mine which would be all right if cleaned, so I am sending it home. ...

I believe there is a pair of brown shoes of mine at home which might be re-soled in case I come home. ...

I have bought two or three footballs for the men, but the ground is practically under water. On Friday [27th October] we were inspected by Plumer (who relieved Mafeking, didn't he?).[228] He seemed pleased with what he saw and asked me a good many questions. ... I am in command again until Reggie returns.

[The Bluff]
5th November, 1916

A year ago I joined the Battalion. It is the first time that any combatant officer has completed a year without being evacuated sick or anything else as, even when I was in hospital with my arm, I never left the Divisional area. I suppose I ought to be very thankful, but at the present moment I am feeling thoroughly annoyed with fate. The General[229] tells me that Reggie has discovered he had some heart trouble and will not be returning yet. This means my leave is postponed indefinitely and I am left with the responsibility of an almost brand new lot of officers in the line, to say nothing of the men.[230] Also my youthful Adjutant [Trim] is badly in need of a change. Things are fairly quiet at present: they generally are when our Division first comes anywhere!

... Mrs Hamilton has sent me two parcels lately. Please thank Agnes for one from her. Somebody has got a poor estimate of the size of my feet and I have had two or three pairs [of socks] lately which are too small. We shall need a continuous supply for the men all through the winter. The foot question is very difficult and any officer is liable to be court-martialled at any time if one of his men suffers from "trench

....

227 The war diary records that Charles took over as acting CO on 25th Oct. (TNA WO 95/2738)

228 The war diary records: "12 Noon - Battalion inspected by GOC Second Army." (TNA WO 95/2738) Gen Sir Herbert Plumer had performed well during the Boer War after which he was promoted Maj Gen at the early age of 45. A meticulous planner and capable general, he was very popular with the men who gave him the affectionate nickname 'Daddy Plumer'.

229 Charles is probably referring to the Brig Gen commanding the 141st Brigade [McDouall] rather than the Maj Gen commanding the 47th Division [Gorringe].

230 The Battalion had received reinforcements of eight officers and 136 other ranks between coming out of the line on the Somme on 8th Oct. and the end of that month. (47th Division A&Q War Diary, TNA WO 95/2707)

feet". It rains practically every day and when it doesn't rain it blows very hard. There are trees constantly falling. ...

I have received the coat safely from Aquascutum and it is doing good service. ...

We are now at present making our headquarters in a partly ruined *château* where there is a small lake and a boat.[231] It would be very nice indeed in summer, but it is a bit damp now. ...

[The Bluff]
12th November, 1916

... We are still in trenches – very wet ones – and I wish very much that there was some chance of Reggie coming back. It looks pretty hopeless. What have you done about getting help at Xmas? I am having a great many difficulties just now. For some reason our part of the world is continually besieged by Red Hats asking questions. They are a great nuisance! ... We are very much amused to see that our chief benefactor (Felix Cassell)[232] and a member of this Regiment has followed up his appointment as Judge Advocate General by having twins! We are wondering how all these events will affect our regimental Xmas presents! ...

The *padré*, David Railton, had been on leave in early November, and described his return to the 1/19th Londons in a letter to his wife on 14th November:

> "'Last night when I arrived the transport officer (Maclagan) greeted me with "Many congratulations, *Padré*." I said I had luckily escaped all the traps of the Boche – submarines, mines etc. "No," he said, "MC." I replied "Well, I knew you would have some joke, old Mac." "No, its no joke, it came out in Orders last night."
>
> I then went up the line with the transport. Fair and all the others greeted me the same way, and Fair actually pinned the Military Cross ribbon on. I took it off saying, "Well I must wait until it is gazetted." "No, you mustn't" said Fair, "put it on at once, it was sent for you from Headquarters."
>
> Well, it is a strange fact. Why I have received the honour I do not know. I suppose it must be for High Wood... God alone knows how little I deserve it compared to so many of our combatant officers and men. And yet they seem to be really pleased that I have got it..."[233]

....

231 Battalion Headquarters was at Swan Château.

232 Sir Felix Cassell was MP for St Pancras and was commissioned into the 19th Londons in Aug. 1914. He served with the 1/19th in France from 10th Mar. 1915 until 6th Aug. 1915. He was appointed Judge Advocate General on 7th Oct. 1916, a post that he held until 17th Sept. 1934. Lady Helen Cassell was responsible for running welfare funds providing parcels for 19th London men overseas. After the war Sir Felix served as President of the 19th London Old Comrades Association. (Service Record TNA WO 374/12795, St Pancras Gazette 14th Aug. 1914, Memories, June 1921 pp. 114-5)

233 Railton letters IWM 80/22/1, quoted in Moynihan, *God on Our Side*, p.71

Charles to his father [Devonshire Camp]
19th November, 1916

... We got back from our long tour in the trenches at 4.30 this morning and I turned in about 6.00 a.m. and slept till 1.00. This afternoon the [Brigadier] General came round and told me to put in an application for leave as from next Wednesday 22nd, and he would see what could be done. If the Division grants it I might be getting home on Thursday this week, but I have had so many disappointments that I am not building too much on it. We had three pretty hard frosts during this week: then some snow and then torrents of rain and the state of the mud is beyond description. The camp we are in is the same as where we were when RF went on leave: it is far dirtier and in worse repair than when we were here before. I think I shall catch pneumonia, except that it seems very difficult to catch a cold out here! Yesterday I thought that I should go off my head trying to conduct a telephone conversation using code words throughout on behalf of three other battalions in the Division, whose affairs were being conducted by young and inexperienced subalterns.

At the end of November Charles returned to England for a week's leave. By chance, Philip Dodgson was on leave at about the same time.

* * * * *

In August Reggie Secretan had been sent to the 9th Officer Cadet Battalion[234] at Gailes, in Ayrshire, where he found his Company Commander was Major Henriques of the Queen's Westminsters who had been billeted with the Secretans in September 1914. After being commissioned into the Hertfordshire Regiment on 19th December, Reggie had leave over Christmas and was able to spend it at home.

* * * * *

After their respective leaves, both Philip and Charles returned to their duties with the 47th Division near Ypres.

While Philip had been on leave, the 237th Brigade RFA had been broken up as part of a wider reorganisation of the artillery brigades of infantry divisions.

Reggie Secretan as a newly commissioned officer

....

234 By early 1916 the reservoir of potential officers with experience in the OTC was drying up and the War Office was being forced to broaden its requirements. "In an effort to standardise training, Officer Cadet Battalions were established in Britain, with twelve in existence by June 1916. These ran a four months' course." (Messenger, op cit, p. 314) Twenty-one infantry OCBs were in existence by the end of 1916.

During the night of 27th/28th November its batteries and HQ were incorporated into the 235th and 238th Brigades RFA of the Divisional Artillery. The two halves were respectively re-named the C/235 and C/238 Batteries.[235] When Philip returned he found that he was now part of C/235 Battery.

Philip to his mother [Boulogne]
6th December, 1916

... We left Folkestone this morning and had a lovely crossing. Our train leaves here at midnight and we shall arrive about breakfast time – splendid arrangements, don't you think? I quite enjoyed the theatre last night. ... I had a good bath when I got in. It does spoil the pleasure being alone, doesn't it? I want to thank you and Hamilton so very much for the lovely time I had. I enjoyed myself the whole time, but especially I loved being at Salisbury. It was so beautifully quiet and peaceful and on the whole I think one feels more inclined for that and I am sure it does one good. Somehow in London one never seems to have a quiet minute. I think your house at Salisbury quite delightful. ...

[Château Belge]
17th December, 1916

... This is to bring you and Hamilton my very best wishes for the New Year and Christmas. Let's hope we may have peace before Christmas comes again. Perhaps now the Boche have offered peace they will soon be asking for it.[236] I sincerely hope so.

I am sending you with this a small Xmas present in the form of a tiny piece of Brussels lace, which was made locally by girl refugees from that city. ... I expect the Belgians are sharp enough to "do" us pretty well over it. Anyhow I hope you will like it. I have also sent Evelyn something similar. ...

I am glad Guy is being able to arrange things as he wanted to do.

[Château Belge]
26th December, 1916

The turkey and sausages were simply delicious and we all thank you most awfully. It was a great success having it sent cooked and the bird was an excellent one. The gloves have also arrived safely. I have not yet given them to the men but I know they will be most awfully glad of them.

We had quite a jolly evening last night. ... I personally was feeling quite tired and have got a rotten cold in my head which makes me feel rather miserable.

* * * * *

....

235 A/237 Battery and half of C/237 Battery became the new C/235 battery commanded by Maj Marshall. (TNA WO 95/2717 War diaries 237 and 235 Brigades RFA.)

236 On 12th Dec. the German Chancellor, Bethmann Hollweg, had called for peace in a speech in the Reichstag. Politicians in the Central Powers were becoming pessimistic about the longer term military and economic prospects and wanted to negotiate from the position of strength of being firmly lodged on Belgian and French territory, as well as the recent victory over Romania. However, the peace note was arrogant in tone and was not acceptable to the Allies. Its failure paved the way for the German decision in favour of unrestricted submarine warfare.

Charles also wrote home to his family after his leave:

Charles to his father   [*en route* to Hill 60 Sector]
3rd December, 1916

All goes well and I am writing from the billet of our transport officer. I shall rejoin the Battalion in the trenches tonight. ... I had an easier time with Mrs Hamilton[237] than I expected and she was very full of questions. ... I motored to Haileybury on Thursday and saw everyone. ... *(Charles goes on to give an account of a day in London on the Friday when he did some shopping, had lunch with a friend in a little French restaurant in Soho and went to the Coliseum in the afternoon. In the evening he went to the Criterion Theatre in Piccadilly Circus to see "Daddy Long-Legs" with his sister Mary and brother-in-law Hulbert.)*

On the boat I met our Brigadier[238] and shared his state-room. He brought me up in a car which went very badly and we didn't get here till midnight. I am feeling a bit weary – leave is a tiring business, but there are several domestic matters I must see to here before going up to the trenches. It is fearfully cold and looks as if it might snow any minute.

[Halifax Camp]
10th December, 1916

... We are now out of the trenches for a few days in huts which are fairly comfortable but damp and draughty. The post has been very barren lately and I have not yet received the Fortnum and Mason parcel ... . I should like to see one of the proofs of my photograph if it can be sent out. The actual photographs themselves will have to be my Xmas presents this year. Please debit to me all postal expenses incurred thereby. We are hoping to be out of the trenches for Xmas. At any rate, it couldn't be worse than last year when we spent it at the Hohenzollern.

[Hill 60 Sector]
17th December, 1916

Thank you and Agnes for sundry letters and parcels including the glove-mittens from the school children. They are really very good: I wore them this morning while doing my rounds and they made my hands so hot I had to take them off. We are in the trenches and have had a pretty rough time including, unfortunately, some casualties.[239] We hope to go out tomorrow, all being well. ... We are trying to give the whole Battalion roast pork and beer sometime during the festive season. Needless to say, the actual beer will be the gift of the present Commanding Officer! I believe I am to be sent on a six days' course for COs on December 31st, if I can be spared. I hope it may enable me to fill some of the most obvious gaps in my military knowledge. We are not much excited about the change of Government.[240] We have

....

237 The widow of the CO, Lt Col Hamilton MC, who had been killed at High Wood on 15th Sept.

238 Brig Gen Robert McDouall, CB, CMG, DSO, (1871-1941) joined the East Kent Regiment (The Buffs) in 1892 and had a distinguished record in the Boer War. He was appointed GOC of 141st Brigade on 19th Aug. 1916.

239 The Battalion went into the trenches at Hill 60 on 15th Dec. The next day 2/Lt H. B. Marr and three other ranks were killed and three more other ranks wounded. Another man was wounded on the 19th Dec., the day the Battalion was relieved. (TNA WO/95 2738)

240 Lloyd George became Prime Minister of a new coalition government on 7th Dec., taking over from Asquith.

learnt to distrust all politicians. If they could import some of the French Staff I think it would be a good thing. ...

[Devonshire Camp, Busseboom]
19th December, 1916

I expect I ought to write my Christmas letter today, as it can't be posted till tomorrow and the intervention of Sunday before Christmas Day may cause it to be late. We are still in the trenches as I write but we are hoping to go out tonight. We ought to have gone out yesterday and it is especially annoying to have been delayed, as I believe we are to be inspected by Haig on Thursday and it will leave very little time for the men to get themselves cleaned up at all.[241] I am sad to think it will be the last Xmas at West Meon and that I shan't be at another choir supper. ... I have heard nothing more of Reggie Friend. I have just received a card of greetings to the Battalion from Major General Thwaites, formerly our Brigadier. ...

[Devonshire Camp, Busseboom]
23rd December, 1916

I think all my Christmas things and letters have turned up. Thank you and all for them very much. I have had a sort of disappointment today as I have had orders to go tomorrow (Xmas Eve) on the course to which I was originally going on the 31st. It is a pity as I shall not be with the Battalion for Xmas but shall be, presumably, among complete strangers at the Second Army Central School. ... We are having lots of rain and it is blowing a gale. Pieces of corrugated iron fly about in all directions. I have got to catch a train two miles off tomorrow morning at 6.18, which is a cheerful way of beginning Christmas! I am going to sleep in a chair in front of the Mess fire.

[Woodcote Farm]
31st December, 1916

Thanks for the various letters which I found waiting for me at our Transport lines, where I arrived last night and where I am writing from now. I rejoin the Battalion tonight in a ruined farm. I enjoyed my week at the Second Army School more than any time I have had in France since the summer. It is a great wrench to come back to mud and water and shells. I am glad you got through Christmas all right. ... The numerous Scotchmen in our Battalion[242] are much excited about their "Hogmanay" tonight.

....

241 Haig inspected the billets of the Brigade on Thursday 21st Dec. 1916. His diary entry for that day reads: "Rain was falling heavily, so I cancelled the parades ordered for the afternoon and said I would visit troops in their huts... I had lunch from the lunch box in one of the huts at 141st Bde HQ. Maj Gen Gorringe met me after lunch and accompanied me round the hutments of the 141st Bde. Everything is in much better condition than last winter." (TNA WO 256/14)

242 This is evidence of the British Army broadening the pool from which it selected officers. Although the 1/19th was a London Battalion, by the end of 1916 a significant minority of the officers were Scottish. These included 2/Lt D. Provand (who had been killed at High Wood on 15th Sept.) and Lt W. C. Maclagan, the Transport Officer. Typically they were junior officers who had been commissioned from early 1916 onwards, after prior service in the ranks of regiments such as the Highland Light Infantry or the Glasgow Yeomanry. Typically they were Grammar School educated rather than having the Public School education required of officers commissioned in 1914.

The New Year dawned with the news that both Charles and Philip were amongst those listed for decorations for their work near High Wood in the previous September. The London Gazette of 1st January reported that Charles had been awarded the DSO and was also Mentioned in Dispatches, while Philip was awarded the MC "for gallantry in saving transport under fire".

Charles to his father [Ypres-Comines Canal Sub-Sector]
5th January, 1917

Thank you and all for letters and congratulations. It was a bit of a shock and I fully realise that the compliment is meant for the Regiment and not for the individual – it is only the official way of saying that the Battalion has done well. We are rather disappointed at the few honours which have come to the Division, but otherwise practically everyone I know above the rank of subaltern seems to be in the list. ... My post is rather a heavy one just now and with so many letters I haven't time to write much. I have not received the ribbon yet and I refuse to buy it out here – it is the business of the Government to provide these things. As a further incident in my career I'm afraid you must, for the present, address my letters to: Lt Col, etc.!

[Ypres-Comines Canal Sub-Sector]
7th January, 1917

All the excitements of the week have nearly put my Sunday letter out of my head. There is absolutely nothing to mark Sunday today. We are still in the trenches, but hope to go further back tonight, though still well within reach. In fact the *château* by the lake, of which I spoke once before, has been receiving a lot of attention from the Huns lately.[243] I have had a great many letters during the week. ... I suppose you saw that I was Mentioned in Dispatches along with all the other DSOs. The letters "MC" appeared after my name and may have mystified you. They can only have been a misprint and, if right, would have meant the award of an MC prior to the DSO, which I have no reason to believe, has been so! I have got the "bit of ribbon to stick on my coat". I suppose that, in the wonderful Army system, I shall receive it three or four times from people of varying importance. I have received orders today to style myself Lt Col and wear the badges of such while commanding the Battalion. Of course, if R[eggie] F[riend] comes out, this practice will cease, and in any case all my military titles are quite ephemeral.

[Ypres-Comines Canal Sub-Sector]
14th January, 1917

We haven't had much of a post for the last day or two. Consequently I haven't had much news from home. The stream of DSO letters has practically ceased. We are back in our old trenches. They are almost washed away and the water and mud are over my knees in places. It is very cold. Last night I was up in the front line at midnight and my trench coat began to get absolutely stiff round the lower ends before I got back to Battalion headquarters. It is bad enough for us and I can't imagine how the men manage to stand it. I'm afraid a great many will go to hospital before we get out of the line again. Dugouts are falling in everywhere. I have never

....

243 The Battalion was relieved by the 1/20th Londons on 7th Jan. and moved into reserve at Swan Château. It went back into the trenches in the Ypres-Comines Canal Sub-Sector on 12th Jan. (TNA WO 95/2738)

heard from Malim[244] about the DSO, which is very odd. I had a ... letter from ... Dartford who is drawing up a list of technical terms for the Portuguese in their own language[245]. I do wonder what the people of West Meon are saying about our departure. I should like to get another leave before the move takes place.

The Brigadier is still in England. His substitute – Hawkes, a Colonel in the Royal Welsh Fusiliers[246] – is a good man though not the genial spirit that McDouall is. Most Staff officers seem to regard us as personally responsible for the weather and its effect upon the trenches. They are a curious race, nice individually but absolutely bound hand and foot with red tape.

* * * * *

Philip Dodgson also wrote to his family on his receipt of their congratulatory letters as he had been awarded the MC in the New Year's Honours:

Philip to his mother   [Château Belge, nr Ypres]
                                                  C/235 Bty RFA
                                               8th January, 1917

First of all I must thank you for the records and music, and also for the honey and prunes which have come today and the "Bystander" which has already started to come, and lastly for your letter and the kind things contained in it, but I hope you realise that for everyone who gets a prize there are many who deserve one. I am awfully disappointed Marshall is not included as no one more deserves distinction, and I would of course have liked to see Pixley and Edwards[247] get something. I believe you are wondering that I did not mention it to you when I was at home, but I promise you it came as a complete surprise to me. ...

I am awfully pleased to have got the MC but I feel quite bashful about sticking up the ribbon: it seems such self-advertisement. I have had quite a lot of letters and such a nice one from Eleanor.[248] Guy wrote by first post and I almost got his letter before I knew myself. ...

Pixley has now left us and has gone as Captain to another Battery, so there are just three of the old lot left now. We scarcely ever see Gorell or his Battery now.

---

244   F. B. Malim was the Headmaster at Haileybury College from Jan. 1912.

245   Richard Dartford had been attached to the Portuguese forces in France. He could speak Portuguese as his school holidays had been spent in Portugal, where his father worked in the wine trade. Dartford remained with the Portuguese until the end of the war and was awarded their Order of Avis. He joined the Colonial Office in 1920 and served in Morocco for ten years. In the Second World War he served as a major in the Intelligence Corps. He died in 1988. (TNA WO 374/17931)

246   Brig Gen McDouall was on a month's leave from 28th Dec. 1916 to 28th Jan. 1917. Lt Col W. C. W. Hawkes DSO commanded the 1/4th Royal Welch Fusiliers (the pioneer battalion of the 47th Division) from Feb. 1916 to 27th Mar.1917. (Maude, op cit, pp. 86, 234)

247   Lt O. Edwards was awarded the MC later in 1917.

248   Eleanor was the wife of Hamilton's son, George Fulton.

... Col Peal has of course lost his job and is in England.[249] This is some of what the breaking up of the Brigade means: the destruction of all *esprit de corps* seems to be the object of all Army administration nowadays, and all the old promises that men who joined together would be left together have gone like many other scraps of paper. ...

Philip to his brother Guy   [Château Belge]
                                                              C/235 Bty RFA
                                                              10th January, 1917

It was very nice of you to write off so quickly. Yours was the first letter – in fact you nearly brought the unexpected bit of news to me. I knew nothing of it till it was read in the papers. I have had quite a lot of letters and Mother seems in very good spirits. We had a very ordinary Christmas; that is we didn't take much notice, as unfortunately the War doesn't stop on these occasions, and we had to stick to the usual routine. However, we managed to get quite a good dinner. Mother sent us an excellent turkey and proper sausages, and then plum pudding. I am afraid there is extraordinarily little to write about. ...

Philip to his mother   [Château Belge]
                                                              C 235 Bty RFA
                                                              17th January, 1917

... I know you will be sorry to hear Gorell has been killed. He was wounded, not seriously, the day before yesterday and died apparently from shock the next morning [16th January]. We all feel it most awfully as we are all such good friends, and there are now so few of us left together who came out with the old 7th Brigade. They are burying him today but, as someone had to stay in the Battery, I remained. ...

                                                              [Winnezeele]
                                                              C 235 Bty RFA
                                                              30th January, 1917

... Leave for the present is stopped except for Staff officers. It is this sort of thing which makes for that good feeling between Staff and others: it's they who arrange the leave and they who get it. I believe, however, the stoppage is only temporary. ... Gorell's battery was quite close to us and he was near us when he died, and it is everybody's regret that no one saw him till too late.

....

249 Lt Col Wilfrid Evelyn Peal started the war as a Territrorial Major commanding the 20th County of London Battery RFA. Philip Pilditch described him as "a very sound Battery Commander. Keen and serious." He commanded that battery until Nov.1915 when he was promoted to Lt Col commanding 7th London Brigade RFA (later 237th Brigade RFA). As Brigade Commander, Pilditch described him as "untiring and conscientious... No trouble was too great for him, no detail too small, from systematic absorption of the ever-growing masses of correspondence and operation orders etc., to the daily journeys to batteries and wagon lines, which he carried out with absolute regularity and tremendous energy." He held that appointment until the Brigade was broken up at the end of Nov. 1916. He returned to France in Sept. 1917 and was awarded the DSO in 1918 whilst commanding 123 Brigade RFA (37th Division). He was wounded in Oct. 1918. (Pilditch diary p. 262, Maude, op cit, pp. 235-6, London Gazette 1st Jan. 1919, TNA WO 374/52935)

On 20th January Philip's friend Philip Pilditch had recorded these events in his diary:

> "While I was at Divisional Artillery HQ the most horrible news came in. Poor old Gorell was dead: Gorell whose Battery I had been in for over a year and whom we felt was invulnerable. Poor fellow. It does seem hard after all the actions he went through and all the narrow escapes he had. The horror and amazement of it left me dumb and incredulous.
>
> The funeral at Poperinghe was in a snowstorm and, like all military funerals, was solemn and moving to a degree. The remnants of the Officers of the Brigade were there. We carried the coffin with a Union Jack wrapped round it and his DSO nailed on the outside. The 19th Battery black gun team drew the limber; Gorell's famous black horses he was so proud of. It was a bitterly cold day, with a cutting east wind and scudding sleet and snow."

Lord Gorell was 35 and was buried in Lijssenthoek Military Cemetery (grave IX.B.20). Philip Pilditch reflected further in his diary on 30th January:-

Major Lord Gorell DSO

"Poor Gorell's funeral was a sad business, and the only thing which relieved it at all was the gathering together of all the old spirits of the 7th London Brigade. After the funeral we all had tea together at Cyril's, the new little restaurant in Poperinghe,[250] and though at heart we were all dismal enough, we managed to be pretty cheerful externally.

Gorell, I heard, was hit by a piece of 4.2" shell which burst not far off him as he and his signallers were walking along the 'Marshall's Walk' duckboards from the Hill 60 front line trench, after doing a wire-cutting shoot for a raid. He was hit in the shoulder and, though taken down fully conscious and pretty cheerful to the Railway Dugouts and Shrapnel Corner, he appears to

....

250 Cyril's was a favourite restaurant of officers and was usually known as Ginger's after 'the flame-headed, tart-tongued daughter of the house.' (Holmes, Tommy, p. 592)

Lord Gorell's funeral cortège, 17th Jan. 1917. (Photo courtesy of Stuart Arrowsmith)

have been left there till the evening, on a freezing day! If our Brigade had still been in being, he would have been taken to Poperinghe without any delay and perhaps his life might have been saved. It is too horrible to think of. He died the same night, not, I think, in great pain. The doctors say it was chiefly shock. Most fatal shellwound cases where the actual wound is not in a vital place, are said to be caused by shock, but the exposure must surely have taken away what little chance there was of his recovery. No one in our Brigade seems to have known of his being hit or where he was, and it seems extraordinary that any man, much less one of his calibre who simply could not be replaced, should be left for hours in January to freeze on a stretcher in the open.

So ends a short but brilliant career, and the most original character in the Brigade, one of the most lovable and interesting I have ever met, is taken … Perhaps the keenest and most energetic of all the officers who left England with us…"

* * * * *

Back in England, Reggie Secretan was enjoying his first weeks as a junior officer. At the beginning of January he had been posted to the 3/1st Battalion of the Hertfordshire Regiment at Halton Park Camp near Tring in Hertfordshire, which was not far from his home in Leverstock Green.

Reggie to his mother   1st Reserve Battalion Herts Regiment
                                          Halton Park, Tring
                                          January, 1917

All is well, I met my friend on the train, and together we journeyed up here in a very smart car! Found the Adjutant, who was very nice to us, he presented us to all the others, and so far they seem a very nice lot. ...

At present there are more officers than men, so expect that for a few days we won't have to do much. New recruits are arriving daily, so as soon as we have a complete Company we shall commence work.

I hope to be home on Saturday or Sunday to get the bike, but of course to the Col to get some more kit!! ...

The camp is two miles from the nearest station which is not nice but with the bike it should be alright.

I am sharing a very nice room with another fellow, who seems alright, so am quite comfortable. My servant who is an old soldier informed me that I could get a blanket in the usual way (!!) if I required it, so he is evidently just the right sort for a servant.

Reggie to his father   Halton Park
                                                        15th January, 1917

I arrived back here quite safely after rather an adventurous journey!! Just before I got to Berkhamsted there was an awful crash!! The box had come off, and burst open, but luckily nothing fell out!! I got back after that quite alright, with box bound round with yards of cord; so all was well, except the roads were awfully bad, and I had a hard job to stick on the old bike.

It has snowed here ever since I got back, and is very cold here to the hands and feet, but we are getting more work to do now, 38 more recruits this morning. Also there are 12 of us who are going through a general course for a fortnight, trench warfare all next Saturday afternoon!! Also night operations this week, such nice weather for it. ... What is Philip's address?

PS Twelve of us have just seen the CO. He informed us that he has had to send in our names as available for overseas, as they are calling upon all available officers, have heard nothing more. Will let you know as soon as possible, but they always give us leave and a complete week's warning.

Reggie to his mother   Halton Park
                                                        25th January, 1917

I have just received the rest of the articles from the Army & Navy Stores which you sent on, so feel quite complete now; also the shoes, so if the slacks turn up I hope to have all I want.

All the fellows here say that we are almost certain to get a day's notice before catching the leave train from Waterloo, so I shall wire you as soon as I know. ...

On 26th January his parents had a wire from him – "Home today, leaving Monday." His mother went up to London with him on Sunday and saw him off early on Monday morning. There were other officers going too and Reggie was in excellent spirits.

* * * * *

In the early months of 1917 the 47th Division remained in the North. The Infantry alternated between camps set well back in the flat and featureless landscape west of Ypres and front line locations near the Railway Dugouts, The Bluff (beside the Ypres-Comines Canal) and Hill 60 Sector. In these months there were no major offensives in the area by either the British or the Germans. There were, however, many artillery exchanges and trench raids: the front line could hardly be said to have been quiet.

Both Charles and Philip continued to write home regularly.

Charles to his father   [Devonshire Camp, Busseboom]
                                                                      21st January, 1917
     Thank you and Agnes for letters and for a parcel of socks and foodstuffs. It is most bitterly cold and the snow still lies on the ground, but we are back in huts for eight days,[251] so ought not to grumble, though we simply dread the effect the thaw, when it comes, will have upon the trenches. Naylor rejoined us today but does not look very well.[252] I still think he is growing too fast for this job. I have not heard again from Reggie [Lt Col Friend]. I believe that all sorts of new regulations are to come into force on 1st February as regards temporary and permanent rank in the Territorials, which will quite likely result in my becoming a Captain again, or even lower, so you must be (seriously) prepared for any abrupt change in my position. I shan't mind so much now that I have a ribbon on my chest as a proof that I've not been entirely a failure.
     ... Did I tell you that we recently had a visit (in the trenches) from some civilians – miner's delegates – who came out, I suppose, in order to be able to buck up the would-be strikers at home about the perils of their fellows out here.[253] I think it is a good idea, but it was odd to see blue serge suits and white collars in the trenches.

                                                              [Devonshire Camp, Busseboom]
                                                                      25th January, 1917
     Reggie [Friend] returned last night and has resumed command; consequently I am now a Major again! Of course I don't mind a bit ... . The cold is appalling, the only good thing about it being that it is dry – until the thaw comes. Will you send out a pair of brown boots which are in my room? I think they were recently resoled, just

....

251 On 18th Jan. 141st Infantry Brigade went into Divisional Reserve with the 1/19th at Devonshire Camp. The Battalion carried out specialist and Company training, as well as three route marches around the surrounding villages and Poperinghe over those eight days. (TNA WO 95/2738)

252 Lt H. M. Naylor (see footnote 127, Chapter 8) had left the battalion to go to England because of sickness on 28th June 1916. He returned to the Battalion on 21st Jan. 1917 and, apart from leave, stayed until 18th Sept. 1918.

253 This may have been a delegation from the Miners Federation, or possibly a broader group including delegates from shipbuilders, railwaymen and transport workers' unions. By Nov. 1916 the South Wales miners were threatening to strike again as the mine owners were threatening to cut wages to reduce the price of coal. On 11th Dec. a union leaders' conference in Merthyr Tydfil passed a number of anti-war and anti-conscription resolutions. The strike was averted through government intervention. However, many unionists remained opposed to the war.

before I was on leave. We go back into trenches tomorrow.[254] Quite possibly dugouts will be less draughty than huts! They can't be colder. We have done some quite decent marches on the hard roads and the band has performed heroically in spite of the fact that their mouthpieces have got frozen every time they stopped playing.

[Railway Dugouts]
28th January, 1917

Thanks for a letter received on 26th and for some parcels with socks, butter and some other things. ... We are back in trenches again. Luckily our HQ dug-out is pretty warm and I brought everything up I could carry. We expected some liveliness on the Kaiser's birthday (yesterday) but what there was came from our side. ... I suspect that I have a touch of lumbago as the small of my back is very painful. The Brigadier [McDouall] is due back. His understudy [Hawkes] is, I think, a good deal better suited to trench life, though not so genial a person. We are doing rather shorter tours in the trenches now that the weather is so cold, but as our time out is shortened too it doesn't make much difference. I hope the population of Germany is feeling the pinch. We are all right for food. There is plenty of it and the men get three hot meals a day even in the trenches – plus tea or soup during the night. I think I could do with half-a-dozen more handkerchiefs: they disappear rather easily when washed in Belgian cottages. Naylor rejoined us last Sunday but he doesn't look very well. I have heard from Malim at last. ...

[Hill 60 Sub-Sector]
4th February, 1917

The cold continues but at least the trenches are dry. The ground is so frozen that it is impossible to drive any stakes into it. We are still in trenches, but certainly our dugouts are warmer, in many cases, than huts. I haven't had a bath for a fortnight and haven't had my clothes off for eight days.

... I have heard no news of R[eggie] F[riend]. The Brigadier has ordered me to resume my Colonel's insignia as soon as we get any definite information. ... One day this week all our HQ officers appeared to be temporarily poisoned by something, as three of us were violently sick for the whole of one morning. Unfortunately, I had to take the Major General [Gorringe][255] round my trenches at lunch-time. I don't think I can have been quite at my brightest. ... I am not very pleased at the ribbon appearing in photos taken before 1st January. It looks fishy and also the ribbon is not in quite the orthodox place. It is cleverly done.

* * * * *

....

254 On 26th Jan. the Battalion relieved the 1/7th Londons in support of the Hill 60 subsector. Battalion HQ and one company were stationed at the Railway Dugouts, Zillebeke, with most of the rest of the Battalion at Belgian Château. (TNA WO 95/2738)

255 Maj Gen Sir George Frederick Gorringe, KCB, KCMG, DSO, commanded the 47th London Division from 2nd Oct. 1916 until 1919. The War Diary for 2nd Feb. records "Major General and Brigadier visited our frontage and were pleased with things in general." (TNA WO 95/2738) Gorringe was "a large, arrogant, tactless, officious man, he was often loathed and distrusted. ... He was, however, a relentless commander, cool under pressure and calm in a crisis." (http://www.warstudies.bham.ac.uk/firstworldwar/research/donkey/gorringe.shtml) His rhyming nickname among the London Territorials - 'Blood Orange' - reflected his unpleasant personality.

Reggie Secretan, having left England late in January, was travelling to the Ypres Salient to join the 1/1st Hertfordshire Regiment. All the following letters were written to his family, mostly to his mother.

30th January, 1917

When we arrived at Folkestone the boat was waiting for us, so we were told to get our kits and embark. We all hunted for our kits, everybody found theirs except me. Only a few more minutes before the boat left, so I dashed back to the RTO, he said I was not to leave till I found it, so I got numerous orderlies to search for it, anyhow I was not going to be left behind, so dashed on at the last moment! When we were away I hunted through hundreds of valises all exactly like mine, but I was rewarded for I found it – what a relief! We had a splendid crossing, three destroyers for escort, so we felt fairly safe, but it was so dreadfully cold. Once at Boulogne we reported to the RTO, and found our train left at 4.30, it was then 2.45, so we had a nice dinner at the Hotel Folkestone but the bill – Oh!! Ten francs each! We found the train would be late but we did at last get off at 8.30, and arrived at 10.30 (Rouen). We were told by the RTO to get rooms where we could for the night; immediate stampede of forty-six officers to get the twenty rooms left in the town, you may well guess that I was the first to arrive at the Hotel Maurice where I at once secured our rooms, the rest had to sleep in railway carriages at the station, it must have been awfully cold as England is quite warm compared with this! The next morning we went out to the camp – Oh, the camp! – all canvas, the Tommies are sliding in the lines, but we have splendid news, we four are to go to the 1st Herts, we are very lucky indeed to get there, they are up north. We find we are the only ones who have been out here before, so we shan't be here long. I know where we are going, it is in the area where I was dispatch riding, which will be very useful, as I know the country well [The Ypres Salient].

1/1st Hertfordshire Regt
` 2nd February, 1917

... I was Orderly Officer yesterday and was horrified at the state of the camp. I had up four NCOs for filthy tents, etc., the Orderly Sergeant with me was a fresh fellow, he was furious, we had a regular field day of it! Last night was the coldest I have ever known, I was quite warm in my valise, but the blankets were encased in ice!

The War Diary of the 1/1st Hertfordshire Regiment for 3rd February records that "2/Lts E. M. Paul, R. H. Secretan, E. A. Taylor and F. S. Walthew joined the Battalion from England."[256]

....

256 TNA WO 95/2590. All four officers were commissioned into the Hertfordshires on the same day, 19th Dec.1916. 2/Lt Frederick Selby Walthew was captured on 31st July 1917 and spent the rest of the war in a POW camp in Heidelburg (2/Lt F. S. Walthew papers IWM 84/34/1). 2/Lt Eric Maclean Paul was left out of battle on 31st July 1917, but appears to have survived the rest of the war with the Battalion. 2/Lt Edward Algernon Taylor was killed by a sniper on 11th Feb.1918 whilst out on an afternoon patrol. He was 38 and the son of Henry A. Taylor, of The Retreat, Bishop's Stortford, Herts. He is buried at Fins New British Cemetery, Sorel-Le-Grand (grave IV.B.6).

Reggie to his mother   [Wieltje subsection]
                                                            5th February, 1917

We arrived at the station at 8.45 a.m., the train was in, so we clambered in, and there we waited till 6.30 p.m.! It did at last start, and we spent the night [2nd Feb] at a nice officers' rest house, quite free, except two francs for breakfast. After this we had a good journey to the town where the Regiment was resting [Poperinghe], found a cart for our kit, and a fellow to show us the way, the first people we had met since leaving England who seemed to expect us! ... We were just going to have tea when an orderly came in post haste with orders for us to join the Battalion at once before it left for the line. ...

That night [3rd Feb] we spent in reserve about a mile behind the trenches in awfully nice dugouts along the banks of a canal [Yser], which is all frozen over, so we spent the next day in glorious slidings on the ice, and getting ready for the trenches. Everybody seems very cheerful and nice in the Company I am attached to, and we have awfully good dugouts with beds, tables and looking-glasses, but as we had come away in such a hurry I had left a lot of warm things behind and had only my trench-coat to sleep in, our valises had not come up, I was awfully cold that night, twenty degrees of frost outside! At about 5.30 p.m. next day we fell in and marched up here [Ypres trenches, towards St Jean].[257] My time of duty was from to 2.00 to 4.00 a.m., all very quiet except for a Boche machine gun travelling along the parapet, so we had to keep our heads down.

                                                    [Canal bank, near Ypres]
                                                        10th February, 1917

We are out of the trenches for a bit,[258] we got back about 7.30 p.m., and just as we were going to bed I had to take a party of fifty men back again to shift sandbags, I did not get back till 4.00 a.m., so my night's rest was not as I expected, but will get one to-night, if I have any luck! I shall be glad of some sleep, it was so cold in the trenches, none of us could sleep a wink. The food is very good indeed, it makes all the difference when in the trenches.

                                                    [Y Camp, near Poperinghe]
                                                        19th February, 1917

We are back here for a rest now after many miles of marching.[259] I found my servant had left my cap behind in the trenches, so I borrowed a push-bike and went all the way up there again and got it! ... We will be here for several weeks and are having a sport's rest, i.e., a lot of football, running, etc., which will be very nice, much better than drill!

....

257 On 4th Feb. the war diary records "The Battalion relieved the 16th Notts and Derby in the Wieltje subsection." (TNA WO 95/2590)

258 On 9th Feb. the war diary states, "The Battalion was relieved by the 1/1st Cambridgeshires and moved back to dugouts on the Canal Bank near Ypres." (TNA WO 95/2590)

259 On the night of 14th/15th Feb. the Battalion went into the front line in the Wieltje subsection for 48 hours. It withdrew to the Canal Bank dugouts during the night of 16th/17th Feb. On 17th Feb. the war diary records "The Battalion was relieved by the 5th Loyal North Lancs Regt and proceeded by train to Poperinghe and marched from there to 'Y' Camp." (TNA WO 95/2590)

[Y Camp, near Poperinghe]
21st February, 1917

I expect to go on a Lewis Gun ... Instructors' Course, if I work hard I may get a good job with the Battalion as I haven't a platoon on account of the large number of officers.

We had the [Brigadier] General [Bellingham] to dinner tonight; it was rather a "*faux pas*," as the cocoa after dinner had salt in it instead of sugar. We did not realize it till the General had had a good mouthful!! Then we knew all about it!! ...

[Y Camp, near Poperinghe]
23rd February, 1917

We had such a nice dinner last night, all the stuff that arrived too late for the General!...

[Y Camp, near Poperinghe]
26th February, 1917

We have had a nice time here, our Company was in the final for the football, but lost, I longed to play, but it would have meant another man's place, and they are so keen on it, such a change for them to get a bit of football. We are soon going up again into the trenches, but in a different spot, which will be a nice change. The other day I had to go on a fatigue with a lot of men laying drain pipes across a well used ploughed field, the mud was half way up one's legs in places, I was jolly thankful for the boots, but it was rotten for the men.

[St Lawrence Camp, near Poperinghe]
[undated but believed to be 2nd March, 1917]

To-day we had an inspection by the General of the Corps[260], it was awful, as the unfortunate men had to polish up all their equipment and make it look like new, they only had very short notice, I was furious, also I was up in charge of No. 5 Platoon which only came out of isolation last night on account of a case of diphtheria, of course they all had long hair, their equipment not complete, etc., so at 10.30 last night I was to be seen routing out the hairdresser, then the men to have their hair cut, but after a bit they took it as a huge joke, with the result that they all had it cropped close! My horror on seeing them the next morning, they all looked quite bald! Anyhow, the General noticed the lack of hair in the platoon and inquired if they had had any skin disease on their heads. Immediate collapse of me and Platoon Sergeant! I hope to have a platoon of my own soon, a very nice one, the men come from round King's Langley, practically all our Company come from around us, which is nice.

....

260 On 2nd Mar. the war diary records "Inspection of the Battalion by Lt Gen Sir T. L. N. Morland, KCB, KCMG, DSO, commanding X Corps." (TNA WO 95/2590) Thomas Lethbridge Napier Morland had joined the Army in 1884 and served in six campaigns in West Africa between 1898 and 1909. On 8th Oct. 1914 he was appointed GOC 5th Division, and was promoted to command X Corps on 15th July 1915. He commanded X Corps through The Somme, Messines and Third Ypres before being appointed as GOC XIII Corps on 12th Apr. 1918. He commanded that Corps with "some success" during the Hundred Days offensives of 1918. His obituary in The Times (25th Apr. 1925) says that he passed through the Great War "almost unnoticed," but was "well liked" and considered a competent Corps commander.

[Volckerinckhove]
5th March, 1917

I have been sent down here. We are billeted out in the village. The four of us from the Herts are in a farmhouse with a very nice old lady to look after us. We all have beds with sheets, and our room has a glorious fire in it where I am writing this now. She is a dear old soul [Madam Monsterleet], and has an autograph book where all the officers who are billeted with her have to sign their names. We had a most profuse welcome!

I am on the Lewis Gun Course with two other officers, and about a dozen men, we are all treated the same as the men, so they are all very keen to be better than us, awfully pleased if we can't answer a question and they can! We had an amusing journey down here by light railway along the side of the flat roads. A man fell off, but he got up and began running after us and caught us up at the next station, very red in the face! He tried to catch us up once before and almost succeeded, amid great excitement, all the Tommies leaning out and shouting encouragement to the driver to put on more speed, everyone betting as to whether he would catch us up before we stopped.

* * * * *

Philip Dodgson, meanwhile, was with the 47th Division artillery. Although this Division was not far from the 39th Division in the Ypres Salient, Philip's battery was resting and refitting about ten miles due west of Poperinghe. On 21st January 1917, 235 Brigade RFA "moved to rest" and "Brigade HQ was established at Winnezeele."[261]

Philip to his mother

[Winnezeele]
C/235 Bty RFA
5th February, 1917

... We have periodical falls of snow which keeps the country white. We went over the other day to a town nearby [Cassell] which is most picturesquely situated right on the top of a hill. We had tea in a restaurant with a most glorious view, and with the snow we felt as if we were in Switzerland. ...

[Winnezeele]
C/235 Bty RFA
11th February, 1917

... We all feel out here that the people of England generally have given up extraordinarily little owing to the War. One of our men went home the other day to make munitions at Talbot's motor-works. He will be clothed by the Army and wear khaki but expects to draw about £5 a week. How can this be reconciled with his pay out here where he draws about 10/- a week, suffers considerable discomforts and hardship, and risks his neck – a thing no munitions worker ever does? It is this sort of thing which makes us think the War is a good thing for the people of England. There seem to be a lot of successes reported from GHQ. I think the Boche in France may look forward to a fairly warm time. ...

....

261 TNA WO 95/2717

In mid-February 235 Brigade RFA moved back to dugouts at Château Belge near Ypres so that it could provide support to the 47th Division's infantry in the front line.

[Château Belge]
C/235 Bty RFA
7th March, 1917

... We are working more or less like slaves as usual: dig, dig, dig. I find it horribly exhausting but by doing it oneself one gets more out of the men. ... I am walking down to the Battery tonight. They fixed up a game of bridge and I shall probably stay to dinner as it's a three mile walk. One gets a horribly strenuous life at times but I don't seem to get any thinner. ...

It's horribly cold again with a biting east wind: no day for standing about. Leave is apparently quite off at present. ... As to when the War will end, I won't volunteer an opinion. Everybody out here I think is confident of the final result as we appear to be well superior in munitions, etc., although the old Boche can put up a good show when he tries. One imagines that his fellows must have a fairly nervous time in the front line, as we do give them hell sometimes, and he never knows when it's coming. ...

* * * * *

Meanwhile Charles Fair and the 1/19th Londons had been serving in the 47th Division's front line trenches.

Charles to his father   [Hill 60, Right Sub-Sector]
11th February, 1917

... Two or three nights ago there was a heavy bombardment for about half an hour[262] and some people thought the Germans were going to attack us – I didn't – but we had everything ready and our newest men behaved well. Somebody said to one of them, "Well, how do you like it?" and he replied, "Well, Sir, I don't know if it's dangerous but it's a damned fine sight!"

It seems today as if the thaw is coming at last: the sun is much warmer and the ice is melting in places, but the wind is still north-easterly. It is rather difficult to get water now and I daren't think of the sources from which our washing water has come lately. I haven't heard again from Reggie [Friend]: I suppose he is still at Boulogne.

We seem very seldom to be out of the trenches on a Sunday: it is generally a fiercer day than any other in the week. I have had two rather bad falls on the miniature glaciers which abound, but no real damage was done. The post has been very erratic lately owing, I suppose, to the frost and I have had no letters at all on several days. It will be sad when the West Meon butter is a thing of the past. I wish I could squeeze in another leave before the move. ...

....

262 The war diary for 9th Feb. records "9 pm. Enemy started heavy bombardment of our front, support and reserve lines which continued for 30 minutes. Our guns retaliated strongly, particularly on his front line. No infantry action." (TNA WO 95/2738)

[Devonshire Camp, Busseboom]
18th February, 1917

... The weather has quite broken up and mud abounds everywhere.[263] Reggie [Friend] has come back again and seems pretty well. He seems to like damp and muggy weather. He and I are going to dine with the Major General [Gorringe] tonight. The other night we had a little dinner of all the old 2/19th Officers who are still out here. ... Yesterday we had a great soccer match against another battalion whom we heavily defeated.[264] In the evening we had an entertainment from a party belonging to a neighbouring Field Ambulance. Are you going to be at West Meon for Easter? ... I heard from Turner that they had a half-holiday at Haileybury in my honour! ... At present all leave is stopped in these parts: I think that the frost has thrown the transport arrangements out of gear in many places.

[Bluff Tunnels]
25th February, 1917

... We are back in the trenches.[265] Reggie ... tried to get me some leave but the Division would not sanction it. I think some people have managed to get it pretty cheaply, though as a matter of fact there is none in these parts for anyone at present. It has turned quite warm and the mud is appalling. There has been a good deal of activity in these parts and a considerable number of Boche will be living like princes at our expense for the rest of the war[266]...

[Dickebush Camp]
4th March, 1917

... We have had a few peaceful days out of the trenches in some quite good huts which we had not visited before. For once we have been unhindered by the Staff. I see no prospect of leave... We are rather puzzled by the German retirements. I don't think it will make things any easier for us. The Mesopotamian business sounds better.[267] The Field Card which I sent to Agnes was only an acknowledgement of a parcel: it did not signify any liveliness. There was an account of a raid by one of our Divisions: it was a very fine performance, but we only played a very humble part in it. We are expecting Stokes to arrive any time now. He will have to lose his majority and command a Company. We are well up to strength now and many of our Somme wounded have returned. ...

....

263 War diary, 18th Feb.: "Very mild. Frost and snow completely disappeared." (TNA WO 95/2738)

264 War diary, 17th Feb.: "Football match against 1/20th Battalion. We won by 7 goals to nil." (TNA WO 95/2738)

265 On the night of 23rd/24th Feb. the 1/19th Londons relieved the 1/20th Londons in the Left Section of the Canal Subsector. (TNA WO 95/2738)

266 On the night of 20th Feb. the 1/6th Londons (140th Infantry Brigade, 47th Division) had carried out a battalion strength raid. This was one of the largest raids carried out by the BEF during the entire war, and it holds the record for the number of prisoners captured in a single raid. The 1/19th war diary records "Battalion raid by 1/6th Battalion, our C Company in immediate support, also they provided escort for prisoners. Raid very successful, 1 officer and 113 other ranks taken prisoner, our casualties slight." (TNA WO 95/2738) This raid is described in detail in the Divisional History. (Maude, op cit, pp. 89-92) Another major raid was carried out by the 41st Division immediately to the right of the 1/19th's trenches on the night of 24th Feb.

267 Following the Second Battle of Kut in Dec., British forces had advanced to within fifty miles of Baghdad by late Feb. 1917.

Chapter 13

The Hindenburg Line and Arras

March to May 1917

In his letter of 4th March Charles said that he was "rather puzzled by the German retirements." In February and March 1917 the German Army on part of the Western Front withdrew to a new position. This retirement had taken the BEF by surprise.

In late September 1916, the Germans had started construction of a heavily fortified trench system some miles behind the existing front line. It ran from south-east of Arras to the high ground north-east of Soissons on the River Aisne in the French sector. The Germans called it the *Siegfried Stellung* and their High Command intended that it would form a strong defensive position to which their armies could fall back if required. To the British it became known as the Hindenburg Line. The Line consisted of a series of defensive zones at least 2,000 yards wide. An outpost zone, 600 yards wide, would be thinly held by defensive outposts and machine gun positions. Behind that was a main "battle zone" which included the first and second trench line systems and mutually supporting machine gun positions. Concrete bunkers deep underground would protect large bodies of troops from artillery bombardment. The whole system was protected by thick belts of barbed wire.

In late 1916 the German High Command reviewed its strategic situation and the results of actions in 1916. The German army had suffered massive losses of nearly one million men killed, wounded and missing in the offensive against Verdun (February-November) and in the defensive on the Somme (July to November). The High Command realised that Germany could not afford another year of such losses and resolved to spend 1917 on the defensive on the Western Front. Instead, the Central Powers would focus on the Eastern Front to knock Russia out of the war. The German Navy would also attempt to starve Britain into defeat through unrestricted U-boat warfare.

The German High Command therefore took the decision to withdraw behind the more easily defensible Hindenburg Line. Orders for the withdrawal were issued on 4th February. The retirement, known as Operation Alberich, was carried out in great secrecy. Preliminary withdrawals from some advanced positions, such as the

Ancre on the Somme, had begun as early as 18th – 22nd February. However, the main withdrawal began on 16th March and was largely completed four days later. The new line shortened the front by twenty-five miles, freeing up fourteen divisions which the Germans could use to form a strategic reserve.

As the German Army withdrew, it adopted a harsh "scorched earth" policy: wells were poisoned, trees were felled to block the roads, villages were razed to the ground, bridges and other infrastructure were blown up and countless booby traps and mines were left behind. As the BEF followed up behind the retreating Germans, the pioneer battalions were much in demand to make good the damage, improving communications and water supplies, as well as constructing new forward trenches in the evacuated area. The Champion brothers were soon involved, as their pioneer battalion, the 11th South Lancashires (St Helens Pioneers), was already near to the evacuated area and was pushed forward as soon as possible.

On 18th March the war diary of 11th South Lancs records: "First news of the enemy's retirement ... which took place during the night, was received in the morning. All the work was immediately stopped and the Battalion stood to, pending the arrival of fresh orders." The Battalion was ordered to repair "roads behind the old German Lines [which] had in several places been blown up. Temporary tracks were made round these spots while the craters were being filled in... Several booby traps were discovered and rendered harmless." On 22nd March the Battalion "marched to new billeting area in Blairville which had been evacuated by the Germans. Before leaving they had blown up all buildings likely to provide shelter for our troops, but with the material strewn about the village the Battalion was soon able to provide accommodation for itself. Work was continued in making the roads passable for traffic where they had been blown up by the enemy."[268]

The only one of the letter-writers in this book to take part in the actions that pursued the Germans to the Hindenburg Line was Humphrey Secretan. Unfortunately none of his letters from this period survive. However, he took a number of photographs whilst he was serving with his Battalion, the 2nd Queens Royal West Surreys, part of 7th Division.

The Battalion took part in an unsuccessful two-battalion attack on Bucquoy on 14th March. Its next action was an attack on Croisilles, a village just over a mile to the west of the Hindenburg Line which was "about the most important of the minor actions fought in the course of the German retreat."[269]

The 7th Division had been tasked to clear the Germans from the villages of Croisilles and Ecoust which were protected by "well-wired trenches forming an advance line of resistance to the Hindenburg Line."[270] The 91st Infantry Brigade was the left assaulting brigade, with 2nd Queens being the left flanking battalion having Croisilles as its objective. The attack was set for 5.15 am on 2nd April. With good artillery preparation and support, the village was cleared by 2.30 pm that day and the Battalion was relieved that evening. It suffered losses of four officers and twenty-five other ranks killed, and three officers and forty-two other ranks wounded.[271] Most of those killed were buried near where they fell and the row of graves was

....

268 TNA WO 95/2323

269 Atkinson, C. T., *The Seventh Division*, 1914-18, p. 369

270 Field Marshal Sir Douglas Haig's dispatch of 31st May 1917

271 Wylly, Col H. C., *History of the Queens Royal Regiment, Vol VII 1905-1923*, p. 111

2nd Queens graves in Croisilles British Cemetery, after 2nd April 1917. Four officers and 22 other ranks of 2nd Queens are buried in row A of the cemetery. (Photo taken by Humphrey Secretan)

photographed by Humphrey Secretan. These graves formed the first row of graves (Plot I, Row A) in what would later be known as Croisilles British Cemetery.

* * * * *

Philip Dodgson commented on the German retirement in his next two letters home.

[dugouts near Château Belge, Ypres]
C/235 Bty RFA
17th March, 1917

Today is the second anniversary of landing in France and I hope it is the last we shall celebrate out here. What an age ago it seems since you saw us off at Berkhamsted, and yet I can remember it all so clearly. There was a certain amount of romance coming out then. We've got splendid news from the Somme again today as a sort of birthday present: Bapaume[272] and many other villages in our hands and a wide advance by the French. The news is unofficial but we hope it is true, and I think it probably is. They also seem to be doing good work in Mesopotamia and, though we were alarmed by the first rumours of this Russian upheaval, it seems now that even that has been brought about by the best of motives. ...

....

272 Bapaume, which lay just to the east of the 1916 Somme battlefield, was captured on 17th Mar. by the 2nd Australian Division.

[dugouts near Château Belge, Ypres]
C/235 Bty RFA
22nd March, 1917

... There is no chance of any more leave, I fear – isn't it sickening? Of course it is far worse for the men, some of whom haven't had leave for eighteen months. We are still playing quite a lot of bridge and chess too: they are both splendid for taking one's thoughts completely off the War. We had an awful shock last night. We suddenly got an order to put all clocks on an hour, and so officially summer has started at least a fortnight before we expected and the weather is still quite cold. ...

I had a letter from Marjorie yesterday, and was very glad to hear from her that her brother had found Toby's grave, as I was so frightened lest it might have got lost. It is now of course well out of range. The news from that part of the world was quite exciting, but the Germans seem to be resisting strongly now, though I think he will go back further. On the whole I think most people are optimistic about his retreating, but at the same time we all think he is doing it with the object of making himself stronger for an offensive elsewhere. The Boche seem to be behaving as badly now as they did at the beginning [of the war],[273] and they deserve the worst. Likewise the Tyneside strikers[274] and, to an extent, those who are so weak as to allow them to strike. We are all disgusted to read about it.

[Château Belge]
31st March, 1917

... I can't remember if I thanked you so much for the sandwich case and flask. I hope the latter won't lead me to drink. The event of the week has been the departure of our General [Brig Gen Spedding], and I don't think anybody is very sorry. He had the reputation of being rather mad, and he certainly was most eccentric and uncertain.[275] We now have a Territorial General – the first "Gunner" General they've made, I believe.[276]

I am sorry I wasn't with you today to April Fool you! As it was, I spent the day having a good strafe at the German trenches, and had quite a successful shoot. It really is most fascinating and it bucks one up no end when things go well. Of course

....

273 In addition to the wholesale destruction of the evacuated region, over 125,000 able-bodied French civilians were deported to work for the Germans elsewhere. These examples of German "frightfulness" gave the Allied propaganda machine plenty of new material.

274 Industrial relations worsened in 1917 with more days lost to strikes that year (5.5. million) than in 1915 and 1916. (De Groot, *Blighty*, p. 118) Engineers working in munitions and armaments factories on Tyneside had been on strike over wages because of the rising price of food. The dispute was settled on 23rd Mar. after an offer from the Ministry of Labour to the Amalgamated Society of Engineers was accepted. (*The Times,* 22nd and 24th Mar. 1917)

275 Philip Pilditch (Diary, pp. 254-5) described Spedding as "an extraordinary and eccentric character" with "unsurpassed powers of annoyance and invective". Pilditch wrote "it is impossible to regard him as other than a most difficult man to get on with, whatever his undoubted qualities of personal pluck and energy... Tact and encouragement were methods he had no use for. ... The result was that many otherwise peaceful periods were turned into absolute nightmares of trouble and worry, and when hard fighting was in progress the Germans were often the less troublesome and less relentless enemy. I was not alone in this situation and many another harassed Adjutant and Battery Commander would bear witness to my words. ... His departure was hailed by many with considerable relief, especially by those who could respond more readily to reason than to 'ginger'. To me it seemed almost as great a blessing as the end of the war itself."

276 Brig Gen Edward Nathan Whitley, CB, CMG, DSO, TD was one of the few Territorials to become a Brig. He was appointed BGRA 47th Division on 31st Mar. 1917. Haig's diary for 22nd Mar. 1917 notes him as a Territorial and a "very first rate Gunner". He was gazetted with the DSO on 1st Jan. 1918.

one does not see many Germans under the present conditions, but we know he is in his trenches all right. It is such a change nowadays to what it used to be: we can now use practically as much ammunition as we like instead of in days gone by having little. ...

* * * * *

Meanwhile, Charles Fair was not far away with his Battalion, the 1/19th Londons.

Charles to his father   [Devonshire Camp, Busseboom]
8th March, 1917

We are out of the trenches for about a week, with luck.[277] Had a rough welcome here as, while we were having a meal in the mess at about 1.00 a.m., the hut in which R[eggie Friend] and I sleep caught fire and burned to the ground along with a neighbouring one. R has lost everything except just what he was wearing. I saved all that had been in the trenches with me, but have lost my valise, books, new breeches, tunic, Sam Browne belt, underclothing, two pairs of brown boots, leggings and various small things. We are going to see what we can get out here. I have plenty of socks (parcel arrived in nick of time) and a complete change of underclothing (fortunately at the wash). Almost the saddest loss is my diary for this year and I think for last, too. Please send me a 1917 one as soon as you can. We had a big job to save other huts and I got pretty wet standing on the roof while the water froze on me as I used it!

I don't seem any the worse except for a bruise or two and broken nails. Don't send anything till I see what I can get. I have written to Dodson [my tailor in London] to hasten tunic. Boots will be the greatest difficulty: luckily I had a pair of army boots on.

[Devonshire Camp, Busseboom]
11th March, 1917

... I haven't much to add to my letter re. the fire. The chief difficulty is to replace my brown ankle boots. Will you send the tunic recently cleaned, if you have not already done so; also will you see if I have an old tunic with XIXth buttons? If so, I want the buttons sent me – in any case there are some on my military greatcoat which would do. Our regimental buttons are not procurable out here. I got a ready-made tunic which fits pretty well. As regards underclothing I am all right. Please send one suit of pyjamas. The weather is now quite warm and spring-like. We are still out of the trenches. ...

The Division lent R[eggie] and myself a motor to assist our shopping. I dined with the Artillery Brigadier[278] again the other night: he is a Haileyburian and his ADC also. No leave of any kind seems likely to come our way.

PS There should be a pair of trousers to match the tunic: please send them. I enclose the receipt.

....

277 The war diary for 7th Mar. records "Battalion relieved by 1/24th Battalion and moved into Divisional Reserve..." (TNA WO 95/2738)

278 Brig Gen Edward Wilfred Spedding, CMG OBE went to Haileybury in 1881 and left school in 1885 to join the army. He was commissioned into the Royal Artillery in 1887 and served in South Africa with the Imperial Yeomanry. He had been appointed BGRA 47th Division on 5th Feb. 1916.

[Railway Dugouts, Zillebeke]
18th March, 1917

Thank you and Agnes for letters and for the diary: it will do to go on with but I should like one with a more solid cover though about the same size. My 1916 one was, after all, not destroyed as it was in my haversack and I think I can re-write practically the whole of this year from memory. We are back in the trenches and according to present arrangements shall be in them for about four weeks without any relief at all,[279] which is an awful thought after going through the whole winter here without a pause. It is a bad thought that I shan't see a bath before the middle of April! It is a good deal drier on the whole, but the nights are very dark just now. … At Winchester … I should like to have the room at the top of the house if it is available. I have quite enough of living low down and even under the earth. If I do get any leave the Army has granted me two extra days' leave for the purpose of visiting the [Reserve] Battalion at Winchester. … I should need a lot of new clothes before attempting to appear at Buckingham Palace. We are all very much excited about Russia.[280] All the military authorities seem to think that it is a good thing. Personally, I hope it won't prevent the Prince of Wales from marrying one of the Russian girls: they look very nice in their photos and there is nobody left for him. Stokes has not arrived: he was delayed by his sister breaking out with measles. There is a case of mumps in our Battalion. It would be an unromantic thing to have in wartime.

Luckily Charles was on leave by the first week in April and his next letter was written in London, but not before he had had a telegram:

> Your attendance is required at Buckingham Palace on Wednesday next, 4th April, at 10 o'clock a.m. Service Dress. Regret that no one except those to be invested can be admitted to the Palace. Please telegraph acknowledgement.
>
> Lord Chamberlain, London

Charles to his father   17 Eccleston Square, London S.W.
4th April, 1917

The deed has been done all right. I met the Wathens at Victoria underground at 9.30 a.m. and we went to the Palace. I delivered up hat, coat and stick in the hall. Then there was a wait of about forty minutes during which the Lord Chamberlain explained the ritual. Then we were put in line according to rank and decoration and marched one by one into a smaller room where HM was standing. Another official read out each name in turn. Then the recipient advanced to the Lord Chamberlain, then turned to the left and bowed to the King. Then we advanced two or three steps and the King hung the decoration from a hook which had been previously pinned

....

279 On 15th Mar. the Battalion went into the support positions for the Hill 60 Subsector, with HQ at Railway dugouts. It moved up to the front line in the Hill 60 subsector in the evening of 26th March and did not come out of the line until 8th Apr., when it moved back to Devonshire Camp. (TNA WO 95/2738)

280 Tsar Nicholas II of Russia had abdicated on 15th Mar. 1917 following eight days of protests, strikes and mutinies which marked the start of the Russian Revolution that ultimately led to that country's withdrawal from the War.

in the tunic. He shook hands and said, "I'm very glad to give you the DSO." Then, after another bow, we marched out (singly to the right). In the hall more flunkeys had cases into which they put the decoration and, having pocketed it, I came away. A photographer was on duty all right, but the chances of it actually appearing in the papers is remote. Had a v. good time everywhere. ... Leave London tomorrow morning, all being well.

PS Mary will bring the trinket with her.

Charles returned from leave and the Buckingham Palace investiture to rejoin the 1/19th Londons.

Charles to his father   [Devonshire Camp, Busseboom]
Easter Day [8th April, 1917]

I eventually reached the Transport lines of the Battalion yesterday afternoon. I spent one night at the port of disembarkation and one about twelve miles from here. We had a lovely crossing but Friday was a most awful day. Luckily I found a gunner whom I knew and we travelled up together. The Battalion is just about to emerge from the trenches so that I am not actually rejoining them until they do.[281] Rumour says that we are going some way back at last and I think that this time it is true. So far they have been very lucky in my absence.[282] They say that Reggie Friend is very well. ... and Stokes and Baker[283] have rejoined. ... Will you ask Mary to buy me a folding rubber bath – the only thing which I seem to have forgotten? She can get it on her return journey at Aquascutum, or some such place. Price should be about 25/-. If they will send it by post it will get here quickest.

* * * * *

Meanwhile, Reggie Secretan had successfully passed his Lewis Gun course. He returned to his Battalion, the 1/1st Hertfordshires, on 12th March in Ypres just as it was about to depart for the front line near Hooge.

Reggie to his mother   [near Hooge]
14th March, 1917

I got back at 7.30 p.m. from the course and found heaps of letters for me. On the way up we spent the night at an officers' club [Poperinghe]. It's a wonderful place, the club: one can get splendid meals there; it's very comfortable and very cheap; it's

....

281 The Battalion was relieved in its position in the front line of the Hill 60 subsector on the night of 8th/9th Apr. and moved back to Devonshire Camp. (TNA WO 95/2738)

282 The Battalion had suffered very few casualties during its long tour in the trenches from 16th Mar. to 8th Apr. inclusive. In this period five other ranks were killed or died of wounds and approximately twenty-five other ranks were wounded. (Data calculated from *Soldiers Died in the Great War*, CWGC records, and TNA WO 95/2738) This is fewer than the number of men evacuated through sickness.

283 Capt George William Baker was the second son of Thomas and Mary Baker of Bewdley, Worcestershire, and worked in London for the GPO. He was born on 10th Jan. 1885 and attended Bewdley Grammar School and Birbeck College. He had served for 4½ years in the ranks of the 15th Londons (Civil Service Rifles) before transferring to London University OTC. At the outbreak of war he was on annual camp with the OTC on Salisbury Plain and was commissioned into the 19th Londons on 3rd Oct. 1914. He served alongside Charles Fair in the 2/19th Londons until he was posted to France to join the 1/19th on 30th Apr. 1915. He left the Battalion on 5th June 1915 when he was invalided home suffering from the effect of Lyddite (explosive) fumes. A slow recovery, much of which was spent on light duties with the 3/19th in England, meant that Baker did not rejoin the 1/19th until 2nd Apr. 1917. (TNA WO 374/3340)

a great blessing to us when we are out for a bit. We had to leave for the trenches at 7.15. We had to dash around and get all we wanted into our packs before we moved off. I had to take my platoon a good way away from the rest of the Battalion. Well, we started all right, but we had an awful time of it, none of us knew the way, and it was too dark to use a map, well we stumbled along the right route somehow...

Reggie to his sisters, Marjorie and Esmé   [near Hooge]
                                                        14th March, 1917

My Dear Marje and Puss,

I had a nice letter from Mother the other day, when she was staying up at Seaford with you, I am so glad she was up there as she must have needed a little rest of some sort. She told me that you were very well which is good news, also all the school news.

I heard from Philip, and he seems fairly cheery, he told me that he had found Toby's grave. It's very nice to know where it is, as of course you can realise the difficulty, there are such thousands of them, and such a lot "To an unknown soldier". It's awfully sad.

Well I have just come back from a Lewis Gun Course where I had a splendid time. We were all in a dear little village miles and miles away from the war, with lovely church bells and very nice people.

I shared a billet with Hickley[284] whom I think you know. Well we had an awfully nice one ... with a glorious fire and nice sheets, it was splendid after blankets, and the old woman was very nice to us. I was not on the same course as Hickley but we were together a lot, and I find I like him very much indeed. There is something in common between us, so we are firm friends now. ...

Well, after that delightful rest on the course, we arrived back after having spent a night at the Officers' Club in a certain well-known town around here (!!) to find that the Battalion was just off for the trenches, so we had to dash about and get the things out of our valises that we wanted, then set off. Oh that journey was the limit, a cross-country route; pitch black and nobody knew the way. Well we got here alright, but only two men had managed to keep dry above the knees. The ground was full of shell holes, which were of course little lakes of black mud. ... I had to go first, with disastrous results, I arrived here at 11.30 p.m. with my platoon and was a mass of black slime up to my waist, it had gone through everything, it oozed out of my pockets when I moved. Well we got into a large dug-out a long way down to discover the floor was about 6" under water, but one could sleep above it, duck boards being provided. My dug-out, which of course is the best, has a bed firmly fixed to the wall, just where there are several drips, so writing this I am helped by a steady drip-drip! Well of course bed was out of the question for the present, so I took off all my clothes and dressed myself in numerous sandbags!! You would have laughed to see me. So I settled down to await the rations, and I thought my troubles were over, but alas no...!

In came Roberts (my servant) with a terrible look on his face. He then began to explain that by the time he had got to the ration dump our three bags of crockery

....

284   2/Lt Richard Trollope North Hickley was educated at Winchester College and joined the 1/1st Hertford-shires on the 6th Jan. 1917. He was the son of Leonard and Sybil Hickley of The Hill, Much Hadham, Hertford-shire.

and food had been taken and three others left, which he had brought along. We searched the bags, but they only contained potatoes, cauliflower and pots and pans. Also our primus was nowhere to be found, and to put the lid on the whole thing, the man who was sent to get a sandbag full of coal came back alright with sandbag, but when opened – BRICKS!!

Oh how we laughed: there we were, forty feet under the ground, me with no clothes on, only sand bags tied on with odd bits of string, and water doing a steady drip-drip-drip down our backs. Well, I felt like crying one moment, then laughing the next, as it was so awfully funny. Well of course the men were very much amused, but without asking three volunteered to go and search for my rations. They arrived back – muddy but victorious – they had got mine and someone else's, also three bags of coal. They were pleased; so was I!! So now my clothes are drying in front of a glorious brazier outside, and we have got soup and chops with potatoes and cauliflower for dinner, so all's well that ends well.

We have a cat here in my dug-out, which apparently lives here, which is very nice as it keeps away all the mice and rats. Besides it's an awfully nice one, spotlessly clean and very pretty. At present it's sleeping on my bed, after having devoured our condensed milk.

Reggie to his mother   [St Lawrence Camp, near Poperinghe]
                                                         18th March, 1917

This afternoon I went for a ride with another officer here. It was great fun, as my horse would only do exactly what the other one did in front. I didn't come off, but provided plenty of amusement for my company! It's been a lovely day; it was grand to get a good canter.

Yesterday we went to a theatre run by one of the divisions out here. ... The place was packed; it was awfully good, and made me feel quite homesick.

At last we have a couple of fast aeroplanes up here, and had the satisfaction of watching several of theirs brought down, one in flames, after having seen several terrible deaths because our men were in machines not half as fast as the Hun ones. It was grand to watch just those two fast ones take on six Boches right over our heads, one came down in flames and two crashed, the whole line cheered, it was grand! The mince pies were awfully good, but don't send out anything if it will affect your rations, as we are very well fed out here.

                                                    [Observatory Ridge Sector]
                                                         22nd March, 1917

I came up in advance and took over the position for the Company, and in doing so had rather a hot time of it, as they were shelling fast and furious. You would have laughed to see me and Sergeant doubling for all we were worth across a hundred yards of very, very muddy and shell holed ground, to the shouts of encouragement of the Tommies safely in their dugouts! But all went well and we evidently provided some good amusement for the troops. It is the first time they have done such a thing here, but they had good reason for it, it will occur again.

Well, the rest of the Battalion arrived in the early hours of the morning, and we were fairly starved, with no prospect of dinner for about a couple of hours, when the mail arrived, and then I spotted a large parcel for me, we fairly tore it open and devoured the lovely seed cake, it was splendid, we did enjoy it, also the sweets. I hope to get a letter from you tonight, oh, how we love letters from home!

[Ypres]
29th March, 1917

We are out again after a very exciting time, the Boche had a raid on whilst I was on duty [between Zillebeke Lake and Hooge], but we drove him off in great style![285] We had a fellow died of wounds, and five wounded in our Company. ... The men were very good, all the NCOs very calm and collected, and our Lewis Guns very good, one fellow will get a medal if I can help it, he fired all through the barrage, it was grand! They never reached us as we were all ready for them, it was splendid, I'm so glad I was in the thick of it. The Brigadier [Bellingham] came round the next day and was very pleased with us, as there had been raids on the other Brigades and ours was the only one where the Hun failed to get in; there must have been very heavy casualties. ...We arrived in our billets at 4.00 a.m. this morning, had porridge and eggs and bacon, and went to bed and got up for tea! I have already earned the name of being the heaviest sleeper on record, no one can wake me when I am really tired, they gave it up the other night, and someone else took my turn of duty, they all thought I must be ill, how sick they all looked when I explained that I was always the same!

3rd April, 1917

I am now miles and miles away from the battalion, learning all about the Stokes Gun, good billets and food, and a nice lot of fellows. Glorious sunshine this afternoon. The sweets are very nice, but you must not send out so many in these times, I can manage quite all right. ... Yesterday we played the Instructors at football, but lost, though it was very amusing, as the greater part of the ground was under water!! I managed to get the one and only goal for the officers, great excitement!

* * * * *

April 1917 saw the resumption of offensive operations by the Allies on the Western Front. In the BEF's sector the Battle of Arras opened in a snowstorm on 9th April with an assault by fourteen divisions. The main assault was by General Sir Edmund Allenby's Third Army, which attacked the German positions immediately surrounding and to the south-east of Arras with a force of ten divisions. However, in order to secure the Third Army's left flank it was essential to secure the tactically vital feature of Vimy Ridge which had been in German hands since 1914. This task was entrusted to four divisions of the Canadian Corps under Lt Gen Sir Julian Byng – part of General Sir Henry Horne's First Army.

The first phase of the Battle of Arras finished with the BEF having achieved much more than it had after the first day of the Battle of the Somme nine months earlier. Most significant was the successful storming by the Canadian Corps of the heavily defended Vimy Ridge. In one of the most brilliant operations carried out by

....

285 The war diary for 25th Mar. records: "On the night 25th/26th Mar. the enemy attempted to raid our trenches after an intense barrage. They were repulsed by Lewis Gun and rifle fire before reaching our trenches." (TNA WO 95/2590)

the BEF on the Western Front in the Great War, the Ridge was taken according to the timetable and held. Closer to Arras on the Third Army front, XVII and VI Corps made advances of between two and three-and-a-half miles. On the right flank of the Third Army VII Corps captured the strongly fortified village of Neuville Vitasse at the northern end of the Hindenburg Line. Many lessons had been learnt from the Somme and successfully applied.

None of the letter-writers in this account was directly involved in the opening phase of the Battle of Arras. However the Champion brothers with the 11th South Lancashires (St Helens Pals) were involved, as the 30th Division of which they were a part was the central assault division of VII Corps. Carl Champion noted in his diary that he had watched the attack going in, and later visited areas previously held by the Germans. On the afternoon of 9th April the Battalion moved forward into the former front line of the battlefield to repair and build roads suitable for lorries.

The individual companies were often widely separated and working on separate tasks, so the three Champion brothers may not have seen very much of each other. Besides which Eric, the youngest, had had heart trouble or, perhaps, a nervous breakdown and had spent some weeks back in England. However, *"heard Eric in France"* was a diary entry by Carl for 24th April and when the Division was pulled back from the Front there was an entry, *"Alan came to dinner"* on the 26th and, on 5th May, that Carl had played bridge with him. Finally, *"Eric came"* on 6th May: the brothers were together again.

* * * * *

Charles Fair and Philip Dodgson – both serving with the 47th Division – had remained in the Ypres salient during the remainder of April 1917. Charles had marched twelve miles to Steenvoorde with his Battalion, the 1/19th Londons, on 11th April where it spent two weeks in Corps Reserve.

Charles to his father   [Steenvoorde]
21st April, 1917

...The weather has improved a bit and we have been able to put in some useful work. Unfortunately practically all the land is under cultivation and I suppose the damage we do will ultimately be paid for by the British taxpayer. Naylor has now joined us at Headquarters as assistant adjutant and signalling officer. Sheppard ... has gone to help in the Brigade Office. ... The new regulations are gradually coming out in the Gazette as affecting temporary rank in the Territorials. I shall probably appear as reverting to Lieutenant. It will only mean that I shall have to go through a form of being appointed "acting" instead of temporary. I don't think I shall have to refund any pay: if Cox try to make me I shall fight it. The rubber bath has arrived and is a great success. I don't think I told you that Railton – the *Padré* – has left us.[286] His successor – Graham, by name – is a Trinity College Dublin man – and a gentleman – which is something in these days.

....

286 Railton had left 141st Infantry Brigade in March 1917 and then served as Senior Chaplain to the 19th Division. He left the army in Jan. 1919. After the war he was appointed vicar of Margate and served with the TA until March 1922. (IWM 80/22/11 and TNA WO 374/56017)

On 26th April the Battalion left Steenvoorde and marched east to the Divisional Area where it went back into camp at Busseboom.

Charles to Helen   [Devonshire Camp, Busseboom]
                                                                      28th April, 1917

... We are back now in the camp where the fire took place. I don't know how long we shall be here. Reggie [Friend] is hoping to go on leave on Monday so, if you write to Camilla during the week, you may get some news of us. It is still very cold but dry. ... I see that I have, at last, become a real Captain but relinquish the temporary rank of Major: that only means that I shall have to be reappointed acting Major, which is what I have always imagined myself to be. Anyway, the application goes in tonight so that it won't make any difference. I am going to try and arrange a little Haileybury dinner with some of my ex-pupils while R[eggie] is away.

Meanwhile, Philip was with the 47th Division's artillery which was providing support to the troops in the front line. He did not have the opportunity to pull further back from the front that month.

Philip to his mother   [Belgian Château]
                                                                        C/235 Bty RFA
                                                                      19th April, 1917

... I am afraid I cannot tell you where I am for obvious reasons. I am sending you a small souvenir from what we've come to call "our Farm". As a matter of fact, the daffodils are almost out. Wonderful, isn't it, the way these things come up in spite of all they've gone through. No, I have never received the eggs and the socks. How sickening it is! They must have got lost, I'm afraid. I could well do with some more socks, and eggs would of course be a real luxury. Isn't the news splendid? This last battle of Vimy and Lens is particularly interesting to us, as we were for so long in those parts and of course know the country very well. It really is the biggest victory we've had so far and the Boche cannot afford to lose two hundred guns every week. Even if he does destroy Lens with all its mines it will be a great gain for us, as he won't be able to use the mines himself as he did previously. From the Lorette Heights we used to be able to see in the distance all the mines and factories working. ...

                                                                      [Belgian Château]
                                                                        C/235 Bty RFA
                                                                      27th April, 1917

... Our Wagon Line have now started a concert party and give a very good show. Most Divisions run a show of this type, but I think we must be the only Battery. We've got a beautiful girl – one of the drivers dressed up! This is of course quite an excitement and needless to say one of the attractions! We've put the cinema away for the summer, so now have concerts with the band. ... There is no doubt all these things are very valuable for keeping the men happy and contented: I think ours are more so perhaps than in any other unit we've come across. ... I am so glad you are going to have a service for poor old Toby. I'm afraid it would be useless for me to think of leave for the present, much as I would like to be there of course.

... I think there is a possibility of my meeting George Fulton. Is he still with the 6th Wilts? I think we've got plenty of books, thank you very much. One doesn't get much opportunity to settle down and read. ...

* * * * *

Reggie Secretan was also in the rear area of the Ypres Salient with the 1/1st Hertfordshires. On 11th April the Battalion "moved to tents and few huts in 'C' Camp [between Poperinghe and Vlamertinge] ... and remained here till the 28th, employed on constructing a new railway close by."[287]

Reggie to his mother [C Camp, near Poperinghe]
12th April, 1917

Isn't the advance splendid! We all long to be in it, but don't think we ever shall. At present we are making a railway for our advance, but I am going up for a week in charge of a party for a Tunnelling Company, a good job, miles under the ground and quite safe [near Zillebeke Lake].

The weather is rotten, snow and rain nearly all day, with very strong winds. I wonder when spring will really come! Won't it be grand when the old Hun goes back all along the line. We are thrilled at the thought of it!

[C Camp, near Poperinghe]
17th April, 1917

Yes, our Company [No. 2] did very well in the raid;[288] that's why I'm very pleased with life, for if they had got in, the Brigadier [Bellingham] would have wanted to know the reason why. I forgot to tell you that though my platoon did all the fighting that night we had no casualties. Weren't we lucky?

I have just come back from the tunnelling job. We were working last night, and at 9.30 p.m. I received orders to catch a train at 10.30, so we had to fly back to our billets and dash off as quick as we could, I had a terrible time of it. It was pitch dark, and when about half way through what is left of the town [Ypres] we got mixed up with a lot of lorries that were loading up bricks, there were about eighty of us, and when we were well mixed up the old Hun began a strafe! Well to start with a man sprained his ankle, so I had to send for a stretcher for him, and whilst we were struggling about in the mud trying to get past lorries all over the road, with bits of shell flying about, I heard awful groans and shrieks coming from the rear of the party. I dashed back expecting to find somebody hit, but instead one of our fellows was lying down in all the mud with cramp in his stomach!! It was really the limit, we could not do anything with him, so had to send for another stretcher to get him away. At last we got going again, and then I had a bit of ill luck, a piece of shell flew past me and embedded itself in the sleeve of my British warm, if only I had been half an inch further back I would have caught it in my hand, and ten to one be in Blighty by now! I am fed up about it, only half an inch! I have got the piece that almost brought me home again and will send it to you. Well we at last got to the train and safely off, arrived at our so-called station and set off for the camp with a guide to show us where we were to sleep. I saw all the men safely in bed, then was

....

287 TNA WO 95/2590
288 The raid of 25th/26th Mar. – see footnote 285.

led back to my hut, it was a good ten minutes' walk through a wood. Well I got there to find the valise had not arrived, so I waited for a bit, then tried to find the way back to show Roberts (my servant) where to bring the valise, I found him all right, but on account of its being so dark I could not find the way back to the hut, so there we were, 2.00 a.m., nowhere to sleep, and quite a stranger to the place! Roberts thought he knew where our Company HQ were, and after having walked into an unlimited number of huts we found our Company HQ full of my friends all asleep, so I had the valise put under the table, the top being engaged, and at last got into bed! However, one of the fellows is off on a course, so I shall get his bed, and not have to live in my little hut out in the woods, miles from everywhere!

[C Camp, near Poperinghe]
19th April, 1917

... My report came through from the Army School today. 'Good, qualified as instructor,' with the Brig's congratulations written across it, if I had got a 'VG' I should have had a job down the line, so I am glad I didn't.

The weather is awful, rain and snow all day, and heaps of mud all over the place. We are in a wood in huts, and the few men in tents, and as they get wet every day it's rather rough on them, but they are all in good spirits. Isn't the French news glorious?[289] I can see the end in sight now, and so can the Government, for at the end of this month all whisky is to be stopped!

[C Camp, near Poperinghe]
28th April, 1917

I have a good piece of news for you. I am off on a month's course, which is very interesting, all about the new fighting which we all hope to have soon[290]; also we get riding every afternoon! It will be the same place as I was on my first course [Volckerinckhove].

Back in England, Reggie's sister, Marjorie, had left St Peter's School, Seaford, on 3rd April and on 30th April had started teaching part-time at a small private school, run by a Mr Gladstone, in London.

* * * * *

The only letter-writer in this account to take part in offensive operations in May 1917 was Humphrey Secretan. His unit, the 2nd Battalion The Queens Royal West

....

289 The Nivelle Offensive on the Chemin des Dames, which had opened on 16th Apr., turned out to be an almost unmitigated disaster for the French, triggering widespread mutinies in the French Army.

290 New tactics based on lessons learned from the Battle of the Somme were introduced to the BEF in the spring of 1917. These lessons were encapsulated in two seminal documents, the sixty-page SS135 'Instructions for the Training of Divisions for Offensive Action' (Dec. 1916) and the 15 page SS143 'Instructions for the Training of Platoons for Offensive Action' (Feb. 1917). SS135 stated that 'offensives should start with a creeping barrage closely followed by the assault troops, snipers, Lewis guns and Stokes guns which should work together for mopping up enemy positions, especially neutralising machine gun positions'. SS143 stated that each platoon should be self-contained with its own integral fire support. The platoon was to be divided into a small platoon HQ plus four fighting sections. Each section had its own specialism: bombers (whose role was to use hand grenades to bomb along trenches), a Lewis gun section (gun crew and additional men to carry the spare ammunition drums), riflemen (with a sniper and scout) and rifle-grenadiers (known as the 'infantry's howitzers'). SS143 marked a vital change from the tactics of 1st July 1916 involving riflemen advancing in lines, to the modern infantry tactics of fire and manoeuvre at platoon level. (Sources: Griffith, 1994 and Palmer, 2008)

Surreys, part of the 7th Division, next went into action in early May as General Sir Hubert Gough's Fifth Army attempted to secure the village of Bullecourt.

The ruins of Bullecourt formed a heavily defended fortress embedded in the Hindenburg Line. On 11th April Gough launched an attack on the village using the 62nd and 4th Australian Divisions. It was a disaster for a number of reasons: despite securing a foothold in the village it could not be held and the troops were evicted. The Australians alone lost 3,500 men of which almost 1,200 were captured.

Gough was undeterred and determined to try again. Just as the Battle of Arras was petering out further north, the Second Battle of Bullecourt opened on 3rd May and over the next two weeks seven British and Australian divisions were sucked in. Bullecourt was to become notorious for the ferocity and brutality of the hand-to-hand fighting among the ruins and dugouts.

On 7th May the 7th Division gained a footing in the south-eastern corner of the village. That evening 2nd Queens moved into the Ecoust area in support. Running to the north and east of Ecoust is a railway embankment which had formed a formidable defensive line for the Germans in the 2nd April assault on Croisilles and Ecoust. Now well behind the British lines, it became a place of refuge and 2nd Queens occupied several dugouts in the embankment while they were preparing for the assault on Bullecourt. Humphrey Secretan took several photographs of officers and men in this location, of which most were probably his own D Company.[291]

2nd Queens in dugouts Ecoust Railway Embankment From left 2/Lts Gardner, Short and Pinchbeck

2nd Queens in dugouts Ecoust Railway Embankment From left Capt Driver, 2/Lt Gardner outside Coy HQ

....

291 Five more of these photos have been reproduced on pp. 208-212 of *Walking Arras* by Paul Reed.

2nd Queens in dugouts Ecoust Railway Embankment. From left, standing, Lover, seated,
Hampton (S/6714 Pte Ernest Lover who had been mentioned in the War Diary on 4th July 1916)

On the 9th May the 2nd Queens went back for a night to Mory. They returned to
Ecoust on the 10th, and on the 11th were in position to clear the village as part of an
attack by the 91st Infantry Brigade. The Battalion attacked at 3.40 am on 12th May
with A and B Companies leading, C Company following up and D Company in reserve.
The objective was only about 400 yards away and this was achieved by 4.15 am by
following under the cover of a creeping barrage. Having secured the objective, the
2nd Queens remained there until the early hours of 15th May.

In its attempts to secure Bullecourt, the 7th Division had suffered losses of 128
officers and 2,554 men killed, wounded and missing.[292] Losses in 2nd Queens were
two officers and thirty-two other ranks killed, four officers and 121 other ranks
wounded, and ten other ranks missing.[293] The village was finally completely cleared
by the 58th (London) Division on 17th May.

* * * * *

While Humphrey was fighting at Bullecourt, his younger brother Reggie was still on
his month's training course at Volckerinckhove to the west of the Ypres Salient.

Reggie Secretan to his mother   [Volckerinckhove]
6th May, 1917

The first week here is over, the weather could not have been better, boiling hot
all day, not a cloud to be seen, so we have had a hard time of it drilling out in the
open, and riding. The latter is great fun and I have made good progress, it will be
great fun after next week as we will go over the country in a sort of steeple chase,

....

292 Atkinson, C. T., *The Seventh Division, 1914-18*, p. 392.

293 Wylly, Col H. C., *History of the Queens Royal Regiment, Vol VII 1905-1923*, p. 112

my old horse is called Peggy, and in her time was a very good hunter, she can still jump beautifully. ...

[Volckerinckhove]
7th May, 1917

Your last parcel was forwarded down here, the cake you made yourself was praised up to the Heavens, they all said it was the best they had had for ages, it cut three others out which were on the table! ... Last Sunday I had a glorious time. By arrangement, a DR came out here, and I settled him in my billet for the day, and I was off on his bike to see all the old fellows, I had an awfully nice time, they had not seen me for nearly a year! I am going again next Sunday, and I hope to see W which will be great.[294] It was awfully nice to be on a bike again out here, it's the only thing that I feel unhappy about here, being away from mechanical things, as you know it's the first time since I first went to Oundle. ... I do wish all the infantry were on motorbikes or cars, but I shall have to content myself with Lewis Guns! I am getting along fine with the riding, we go across country, and jump ditches and fences, it's great fun, especially as several of us keep on falling off, as yet I am the only one who has not done so, but most of the credit is due to Peggy, my old mare, we are already great friends. Last Saturday the General Course took us on at hockey, and we won, the first time on record! I got a cut across the knees and am all bandaged up, and could not drill, but strange to say I could ride all right!

[Volckerinckhove]
14th May, 1917

Last Sunday I went again and saw all the old DRs and had a glorious bathe with them all, it was grand! ... All the DRs said how changed I was, much fatter! I am much stronger and fitter, in very good training, as hard as nails, and fearfully sunburnt. The riding is glorious, we have changed horses today, and I have got the best jumper, its great fun, clears five-bar gates!! You should see me hanging on for dear life!

[Volckerinckhove]
22nd May, 1917

Last Saturday we had a voluntary ride; it was glorious all over the country, with all sorts of jumps! My horse, Patsy by name, is easily the best jumper in the School, very fast, and always very fresh, she loves the country rides, but the School does not interest her a bit. I hope I shall be able to keep her.

The weather is glorious, too hot to do much work, but the Army evidently does not agree with my idea!

Oh those Russians! I am afraid they have let us down, I can't tell you more, except that the Hun is twice as strong on our front as he was a month ago! But our artillery is splendid.

At the end of his month's course Reggie rejoined the 1/1st Hertfordshires who were far from the front, at Wormhoudt in France.

....

294 Probably Reggie's friend Sergeant T. Walker of the MTASC.

Reggie Secretan to his mother   [Wormhoudt]
                                                                30th May, 1917

Here I am, miles away from the line on our way back to train for a short time. We are on a three days' march and have just finished the first one, eighteen miles with full pack all through the heat of the day is no stroll I can assure you, but we did very well, only two of our Company fell out, and considering they had just had a rough time of it in the line it was jolly good. No one in my platoon fell out, but I had to carry a rifle for one fellow, and lighten the pack of another to keep them going.

Thank Heaven I am fit, as it took some doing you can guess. I am quite alright except that my feet are about double size, but they will be all right to-morrow, they lasted me out, which is the great thing.

* * * * *

The 47th Division spent May 1917 in the Ypres Salient. The gunners and the infantry were preparing for the summer's offensive operations. Both Philip, with 235 Brigade RFA, and Charles, with the 1/19th Londons, spent part of the month far to the rear for training and rehearsals.

Philip to his mother   [nr Ouderdom]
                                                                C/235 Bty RFA
                                                                9th May, 1917

... We are leading a very irregular life here. We go to bed very late as a rule and, as you can imagine, we get up at a time to correspond, which means breakfast at 10.30 a.m. and so on. Hasn't the weather been glorious, and even this stricken land has a look of freshness about it. I haven't come across George [Fulton] yet, but have not had much time to look for him. I wonder if he knows what Division I am in. It is so difficult to find people out here, even when you are quite close to them. Today is the second anniversary of our first battle. One can't help wondering at all the changes that have taken place since then. What an age ago it seems! I suppose the War will end some day! ...

Philip to Guy   [nr Ouderdom]
                                                                C/235 Bty RFA
                                                                12th May, 1917

I am ashamed I have not written to you for so long. I received your letter safely and also the cheese. Thank you so much for sending it. It was very good indeed and much appreciated. In desperation I did send off a Field Postcard the other day. I wonder how you have been getting on with your march, somewhat warm, I expect. I do think walking in this heat is a most exhausting occupation. However, on the whole, it's been glorious the last fortnight. We are fortunate in being near some water. I can get an excellent bathe; the water has got so beautifully warm. I wonder if you were able to get leave to be with mother for Toby's Memorial Service. She said nothing about it, so I suppose not. Mother told me you expected to go to the 3rd Battalion.[295] Have you ever had any interest in Machine Guns? It always seems to me the MG Corps have rather a nice independent time out here, and they have a few horses ... .

....

295   The 3/1st Battalion of The Hertfordshire Regiment at Halton Park Camp, Tring, Herts.

Philip to his mother [nr Ouderdom] C/235 Bty RFA
13th May, 1917

Just a very hurried line to let you know I have received yours enclosing the copy of the Memorial Service. I was so glad to have it. I thought of you so much and did so wish I could have been with you, but it was not possible. ...

We are fortunate here in being near a beautiful piece of water in which excellent bathing can be had. It is not very deep and the water has got lovely and warm. We are working very hard – building! We are wonderfully comfortable but one's work isn't finished at that. ...

[Zillebeke] C/235 Bty RFA
25th May, 1917

... I'm so sorry I've been so terribly slack about writing to you. I believe it must be nearly a fortnight. As a matter of fact I've been fearfully on the go of late. For the last week we've had the Battery out of action in the Wagon Line,[296] and we did what he could to make the best of it and give the men a good time. We had mounted and dismounted sports, football matches, and concerts in the evening. So, on the whole, they had quite a good time but a week is a very short time. I myself quite unexpectedly have come down to the country and am not with the Battery for a few days. Marshall and I are together here with about half-a-dozen telephonists and we also have horses with us. ... We have a most delightful little village to ourselves and it is so beautifully quiet and peaceful one really hardly can believe there is a war going on such a little distance away. We are in glorious country with quite big hills and valleys, and after so many months on end in that flat desolated country it is a most welcome change.[297]

Marshall really arranged for me to come down here for a rest as leave was impossible.

... We are living in a little farm looked after by one woman and one girl. ... It is wonderful how the women work in this country.

[Lock 7, Ypres-Comines Canal]
C/235 Bty RFA
30th May, 1917

We are on the point of re-joining the Battery. We have had such a lovely quiet time and feel ever so much better for it. The weather has been glorious too and we've slept out in the orchard every night. We are putting up for a night at two towns on the way back I think.

....

296   The war diary records that on 18th May 'C/235 and one section of D/235 withdrew to wagon lines.' C/235 Battery reoccupied its position in Zillebeke on the 24th.

297   Philip had been detached to train with one of the Infantry Brigades of 47th Division that would be involved in the upcoming attack at Messines, as he would be taking the role of Forward Observation Officer. Judging by his comments on the topography and distance, this training area was probably near Tilques in the hilly area to the west of St Omer in France. The War Diary for 235 Brigade RFA records that on 12th May "a party consisting of Maj Clifton DSO, 2/Lt Robinson with seven telephonists accompanied 140th Infantry Brigade to Tilques for training." (TNA WO 95/2717) Rehearsals were a key factor in the success of the offensive. The Divisional History records "The two attacking brigades were given opportunities for rehearsing their attacks, and had a few very pleasant days in the Steenvorde area at the end of May." They trained over "taped out courses" and "found the enemy's trenches almost identical with those that had been laid out for them to practise over." (Maude, op cit, p. 97)

... I forgot to tell you a few things I meant to in my last letter. Firstly, Marshall was again Mentioned in Dispatches. We are all sick that he hasn't been given the DSO. He has done so splendidly out here and deserves it far more than many we know who've got it. ... By the way, many happy returns of 1st June! I shall probably drink your health in something, even if it's only boiled shell-hole water.

Meanwhile, during the first fortnight of May, Charles and the 1/19th Londons had been in Divisional Reserve at Busseboom, south east of Poperhinge.

Charles to his father   [Devonshire Camp, Busseboom]
6th May, 1917

We have had a pretty uneventful week as regards matters military. R[eggie] went on leave last Monday and must be having splendid weather. The Battalion is at present divided into two halves for the purpose of doing pioneer work – carpentry, digging and all sorts of jobs. This morning I am going to visit the other half seven miles away.[298] I am hoping to get a lift on a passing motor lorry. ... It has been very hot and dusty during the week. We have got out our cricket paraphernalia, including a matting pitch, and some of our young bloods have been displaying their powers.

[Devonshire Camp, Busseboom]
13th May, 1917

Thank you and all for letters and for the weekly parcel. Our butter seems to be the only kind which can stand up in the present heat. We are expecting Reggie back today or tomorrow. He has been awfully lucky in the weather. We are, at the moment, still in our old camp but move to a rather more forward area tonight.[299] ... There has been a fair amount of rustic cricket during the week, but I haven't played myself.[300] The day before yesterday I had a visit from two Haileyburians – both ADCs in the artillery. ...

[Left Section, Canal subsector]
20th May, 1917

... We are back in trenches now – very nearly in the same place as before.[301] It is very hot again and the aroma is everywhere very unpleasant except just about dawn. I received three pairs of very nice socks from Elsie. Mary sent me a large consignment made by good workers at Woodford and intended for the men. ... We are all rather pleased that a small amount of regular leave seems to be reopening. It will make a lot of difference to the men who have been out a long time. We all

....

298 The Battalion provided numerous working parties while it was at Devonshire Camp. The War Diary for 1st May states, "Battalion engaged in pioneering work as per previous days." On 4th May it records "Half Battalion (C and D Companies) moved into dugouts in Ramparts in Ypres for special work." That half returned to Devonshire Camp late in the evening of 10th May. (TNA WO 95/2738)

299 The War Diary records that on 13th May "Battalion HQ and C and D Companies moved up to Canal Reserve Camp at Dickebush". (TNA WO 95/2738)

300 The War Diary states, "Cricket during afternoon and evening" for every day between 2nd and 12th May inclusive. As well as "Officers v Officers' Servants" and inter-company matches, the Battalion played Brigade HQ (twice), and a battalion of The West Yorkshire Regiment (twice). Results are not recorded. (TNA WO 95/2738)

301 The Battalion went into the front line at The Bluff by the Ypres-Comines Canal on the night of 19th/20th May. It spent a week there before being relieved on the night of 25th/26th May and moving back into camp at Ouderdom. (TNA WO 95/2738)

consider that it is a direct result of the American Navy taking a hand. I believe that our second line has been in action but we have not yet heard any news of them[302].

[Ottawa Camp, Ouderdom]
28th May, 1917

Many happy returns of your birthday, in a more tranquil atmosphere. Will you help yourself to a birthday present – probably you will want something for your new study. Did you take or receive from me my rent for the current year? If not, please take it now. ... We are most awfully amused at some of the "mentions" in Haig's latest dispatch. One officer who is still officially on our list is mentioned, but he is so inefficient that he has not been in the trenches since the summer of 1915 and ever since I have been out here he has been in charge of the Divisional Laundry![303] Did I tell you that I had a visit from Champion the other day [22nd May]? He discovered we were in the same neighbourhood at last and walked eight miles in order to have tea with me in the trenches! Friendship could go no further. I don't know which is to be your last Sunday at West Meon. I suppose you remember that the first text on which you preached there[304] was "What doest thou here, Elijah?" I have heard nothing of Roy Tennant and the other Battalion (the 2/19th London).

* * * * *

On 17th May the Champion brothers moved north to Flanders with the 11th South Lancashires (St Helens Pioneers) in order to help with preparations for forthcoming offensive operations. On 20th May it arrived at Palace Camp near Dickebush. The rest of the 30th Division relocated to the Ypres Salient in the days that followed. The Battalion spent the last ten days of May building roads and light railways in the Dickebush area.

On the 21st May Carl wrote, *"Eric in for gramophone at night",* while the following day he added, *"Met the QM of the 1/19th London Regiment; went and saw Fair".* This meeting of friends, recorded in greater length by Charles Fair in his letter of 28th May, took place in a short, gentle valley inaptly known as "The Ravine". Four days later Carl left on leave for England, where, as on previous leaves, he probably called on friends at Haileybury.

On 31st May the St Helens Pioneers moved into the *école* on the eastern edge of Ypres.

....

302 The sister battalion, the 2/19th Londons, had been involved in fighting on the Salonika front. A major Allied offensive, the British part of which was the First Battle of Doiran (24th/25th Apr. and 8th/9th May 1917), made little impression on the Bulgarian defences.

303 This lighthearted comment for family at home smacks of hearsay, and Charles is perhaps being unkind to the officer concerned. The 47th Divisional Employment Company managed the baths and laundry which were "admirably organized" by Capt A. F. Robinson. (See Maude's *History of the 47th Division*, p. 221). The baths and laundry 'contributed greatly to the comfort of the Division'. Many letters home testify to the restorative powers of a bath and a clean change of clothes. Until the institution of the OBE in 1918, the Mention in Dispatches (MID) was the only way in which an officer doing an important but non-combatant job could be rewarded. *The London Gazette* shows that Robinson was MID on three occasions 25th May 1917, 25th May 1918 and 19th July 1919 and was later made an OBE. Robinson had in fact served in the front line with the 1/19th Londons. He was one of the original contingent of the Battalion which disembarked in France on 10th Mar. 1915. According to the diary of another 1/19th officer, Capt Waterlow, Robinson had served with B and D Companies, but by the time of the Battle of Loos on 25th Sept. 1915 was in charge of ammunition resupply to 141 Infantry Brigade. He was promoted to Maj. on 24th Aug. 1920.

304 In 1899

Chapter 14

Messines and Passchendaele

June to August 1917

(see Map 5)

The city of Ypres is overlooked by higher ground to the east and south. This had been occupied since the First Battle of Ypres in 1914 by the Germans who had continued to strengthen and fortify their positions. The low ridges gave the Germans a significant tactical advantage in that they were able to observe and fire upon the British troops in and near Ypres.

From the summer of 1917, the BEF under Haig had to take the major responsibility for Allied actions on the Western Front. The French Army was in no state to take part in major offensives as it had been weakened by mutinies after the failure of the Nivelle Offensive in April. Meanwhile, on the Eastern Front, Russia was collapsing into revolution. Haig believed that the most effective way of keeping pressure on the Germans on the Western Front would be for a Flanders offensive. The immediate objective of this would be to capture the high ground overlooking Ypres, thus relieving pressure on the city.

On 7th May, Haig presented his plan for the Flanders offensive at a conference of his Army commanders. The operation would be split into two phases. The first phase was an attack on the Wytschaete-Messines ridge in June by General Sir Herbert Plumer's Second Army. The second phase would take place a few weeks later and was designed to capture the Passchendaele Ridge and Gheluvelt plateau to the east of Ypres. General Sir Hubert Gough's Fifth Army would be responsible for this phase. The capture of the Messines Ridge had to be achieved first in order to ensure a secure defensive right flank for the second phase. It would also provide more 'elbow room' south and south west of Ypres for the assembly of the artillery and troops required for the second phase.

The Battle of Messines would open on 7th June with nine infantry divisions from three corps in the assault. The 47th Division would be the central attacking division of X Corps which formed the left (northern) flank of the attack. The Division would attack from its front line positions near the Bluff, and would have to cross the obstacle of the Ypres-Comines canal.

From 21st May, the battle was preceded by artillery bombardment and counter-battery fire during which the British artillery was attempting to neutralise the

German artillery. Charles experienced the artillery battle from the front line trenches with the 1/19th Londons.

Charles to his father   [Left Section, Canal Sub-sector]
3rd June, 1917

I suppose this will be the last Sunday letter I shall write to West Meon. ... I expect I shall miss the choir unless you make sufficient friends with someone at Winchester to get me a seat in some choir when I feel inclined. We are having a very hot time in the trenches in every sense[305] and I suppose things must go on getting hotter for a bit. Naylor has got mumps, so don't be surprised if I get them too. It is an awful waste of fine weather to spend so much of it more or less under-ground. ...

Meanwhile, Philip with the 47th Division's artillery had been playing his part in the artillery duel.

Philip to his mother   [Lock 7, Ypres-Comines Canal]
C/235 Bty RFA
6th June, 1917

... The weather is glorious and one couldn't wish for anything better. We are fearfully busy,[306] so I hope you'll forgive any more. Will write again as soon as I can. ... Give my love to Guy if he is with you and thank him for his letter. I hope he is quite fit again now.

However Philip didn't actually remain with the guns during the battle. His friend Philip Pilditch had recorded in his diary on 5th June: "Unfortunately both Marshall and Dodgson are going as liaison officers (FOO) with the Infantry during the attack. I don't envy them."

The Battle of Messines commenced at 3.10 am on 7th June with the detonation under the German front line trenches of nineteen mines containing nearly one million pounds of high explosive. Advancing behind a creeping barrage, the infantry assault rapidly overcame the stunned German defenders. The crest of the ridge was held by mid-morning, and all objectives were taken and secured according to plan. Messines was a model set-piece attack which reflected meticulous planning and preparation.

Philip Pilditch recorded in his diary for the 7th June: "This afternoon I heard Philip Dodgson had been wounded during the attack on the White Château. Directly I heard about P. D. I got on old Jack in the thin kit I was wearing owing to the heat and dashed off all over the place to see if I could find a trace of him. I went to three Casualty Clearing Stations and all the Aid Posts I could hear of, but could find no sign of him. In some of the dressing stations near Dickebush men were being patched up temporarily or lying about awaiting attention, British and German alike. It was a pathetic scene and all animosity between the two races seemed to have disappeared

....

305 The war diary from when the Battalion went into the line on the night of 31st May/1st June until it was relieved on the night of 4th/5th June records continuous fire by British artillery 'all day and night' as well as plenty of retaliation from the German artillery. Casualties for this tour in the trenches are stated as 13 other ranks killed and 2/Lt W. McNichol and 25 other ranks wounded. (TNA WO 95/2738)

306 The war diary for 235 Brigade RFA for 1st to 6th June inclusive reports "wire cutting and bombardment of trench system was continued daily... Harassing fire on enemy's communications was maintained throughout the night." Practice barrages were carried out on 3rd and 4th June. (TNA WO 95/2717)

under the strain of common pain and misery. The organisation of the RAMC in a battle such as this is a marvel nowadays."

Meanwhile, Charles had been at the rear of the battle zone. The 1/19th Londons were in reserve for the attack, as the 141st Infantry Brigade had been tasked with following the leading brigades and occupying the German front line trenches once those brigades had passed through.

Charles to his sister Helen   [Swan Château]
                                                                         10th June, 1917

I am all right so far and, as far as I know, Reggie [Friend] is too. The Regiment is right in it, but I am at present only on the fringe, as they don't take both CO and 2nd-in-command into action nowadays.[307] It is a wonderful victory, but there is a lot to be done yet. ...

Charles to his father   [Swan Château / Bluff Tunnels]
                                                                         10th June, 1917

As far as we can make out all goes well. I had a note down from Reggie [Friend] last night. We are sending them up everything we can and hoping that they may be relieved before long. I expect you get news more in quantity and quicker in transit than we do: we generally have to wait for the London papers to hear what is going on anywhere except in our own particular sector. ... Let me know as soon as you are really at Winchester in order that I may notify your change of address to all concerned. ...

PS Keep all copies of "The Times" referring to present operations.

                                                     [Ascot Camp, Westoutre]
                                                                         15th June, 1917

We are all well and right away from the trenches – can only just hear the guns. R[eggie] has stood the strain well. Stokes and Baker are all right. We hope to be back for at least ten days, so you can settle in peace [into Winchester].

                                    * * * * *

Meanwhile, at the beginning of June, Reggie Secretan and the 1/1st Hertfordshires were still at Wormhoudt in France, about twenty miles west of Ypres.

Reggie to his mother   [Wormhoudt]
                                                                         3rd June, 1917

Now about those cakes you send me; ... remember I don't want them if things are short in England. I can quite well do without if necessary. The last one was awfully good. We are having glorious weather, but a bit too hot, as the drill is stiff now, especially for me, as I am training a platoon as well as Lewis gunners, it takes all my time as I have to work out a programme for the next day after a hard morning's work, but all rests are the same, the great thing is to give the men a rest, as being continually under fire is very trying. I am afraid I am getting very hard-hearted

....

307   As 2 i/c Charles had been 'left out of battle' (LOB) along with a cadre of about 10 per cent of the strength of the Battalion. This would form a cadre around which to rebuild the Battalion in the event of heavy losses. By 1917 this was a standard procedure for an infantry battalion going into an attack.

out here, one has to be, as everyone is so casual about death, but what's the good of making a fuss about it? One can't when you have to give lessons on bayonet fighting!! The whole time out here we try to instil into the men's minds that death is quite a small matter! It's a funny world we live in now! I went to early service this morning, just about a dozen of us, in the open under some trees close to the men's billet: directly it was over, there we were teaching them to kill! ...

The War Diary of the 1/1st Hertfordshires states that on 3rd June "The King's Birthday was celebrated by a parade at Wormhoudt."[308] Another officer, 2/Lt Frederick Walthew, recounted the plans for the parade in a letter home: "We are celebrating the King's Birthday tomorrow by selecting 100 men from each battalion of the Brigade and saluting the French and British flags. It ought to be rather a fine show... Bet the French people get excited! We are also having the company [No. 2] photographed afterwards, but I don't suppose it will turn out very well."[309] Reggie and his platoon were indeed photographed that day.

Reggie Secretan (seated, centre) and No. 8 Platoon, 2 Company, 1/1st Battalion, The Hertfordshire Regiment, Wormhoudt, 3rd June 1917

The Battalion and the 39th Division had not been involved in The Battle of Messines, but Reggie was well aware of the successful British advance on that part of the Front.

Reggie to his mother   [Wormhoudt]
                                                                7th June, 1917

You will have seen the papers, it was a grand show – I hope the beginning of the end! I have a platoon of my own now [No 8 Platoon], an awfully nice one too – all from Hemel Hempstead and Berkhamsted – some of them know our house. I hope to keep it as I think I should prefer it to Lewis gunners, as you see more of the men,

....

308 TNA WO 95/2590

309 Lt F. S. Walthew, letter to his uncle, 2nd June 1917 (IWM 84/34/1)

which is the great thing. The weather is beautiful, and the crops could not be better, every bit of ground is cultivated. The whole village turns out to work in the fields all day, including schoolboys under the master; they commence at 5.00 a.m. and work till 7.00 p.m. They are grand, the whole lot of them. ...

[Wormhoudt]
10th June, 1917

All has gone splendidly and casualties were slight; also cheery news regarding the morale of the Boche – it's only his artillery that's saving him, but a time will come when that will fail him, just you wait and see!!

I have just discovered that we have not been training but having a rest, and our training commences soon, so we will be full of beans when we do get a chance to have a go at him! The men have loved the stay down here in lovely country. ...

[Bayenghem-les-Seninghem, near St Omer]
14th June, 1917

We have just finished our three-day march, and are settled down for a bit. We are back where I was in January 1915, and our Company HQ are in the same house that I once lived in, awfully strange! The old lady was of course delighted to see me, so you may guess that I am quite all right! There is not much room to sleep here, so two of us slept out in the field, just in our valises, it was awfully nice. ... So glad things are all right at home in the way of food, I think the old U-boats are finished, America has helped a lot, but I doubt if they will be over here in time, I expect it will be up to us to finish it with the French![310]

[Bayenghem-les-Seninghem]
17th June, 1917

The weather is fearfully hot, and as we are billeted in a little village in a valley, we suffer from it rather, after the morning's work, which nearly kills me! After the morning's work I get into some thin shorts and a vest and lie out in the orchard, get cool, and then go and have a bathe in the stream, so you can see that we are having a good time, except for the work in this awful sun. ... Now don't worry as we will be quite all right for a long time, and we are all very happy and content here. No hope of leave yet, I hope the next leave will be Peace!

* * * * *

The three Champion brothers were meanwhile to the east of Ypres with the 30th Division which had not been involved in Messines. The War Diary for June of the 11th South Lancashires recorded that, from the 8th to 13th, they were very heavily shelled with gas or HE and most of the casualties suffered were sustained in billets. Carl Champion did not return from leave until the 9th. In his diary for the 11th he wrote, *"Eric killed this morning. Buried under sycamore tree near north-east corner of*

....

310   The USA had declared war on the Central Powers on 6th Apr. 1917 following the German campaign of unrestricted submarine warfare. However America had a small professional army and had to recruit a mass citizen army from scratch. This meant that there would be few American troops on the Western Front until the summer of 1918.

the school" – followed by a map reference.[311] This bald statement does not reveal the grief that Carl felt for the loss of his twenty-one-year-old brother, for whom he had an almost paternal affection since the early loss of their father. At the back of his diary he recorded in moving terms a dream he had later of Eric. Carl was left for decades regretting that, as a senior officer in the Battalion, he had not done more to shelter his brother from harm. For the rest of Carl's life a portrait of Eric hung in a prominent position in the Champion household.

Eric Champion

Eric Champion's grave at Bedford House Cemetery.

On 12th June the Battalion suffered twenty-six casualties in their billets. This led to a shift on 13th June. *"Moved to the Railway Dugouts in the evening. I stopped to see them all out"* recorded Carl. These dugouts, lying to the south of Ypres, were built into a railway embankment, no doubt reinforced by railway sleepers and steel tracks and so, in theory, gave some protection. Digging deep tunnels in the water-logged Flemish landscape was not an option. For each of the next few days Carl wrote in his diary, *"Shelled most of the day".* The hoped-for rest in their new location was not forthcoming. *"Heavy calibre shells: between 13th and 27th fifteen dugouts were smashed in. Gas shells also were sent over on two nights."*

In the absence on leave since 24th June of Lt Col Fenn, Carl signed the Battalion war diary at the end of the month, the last paragraph of which read, *"During the month the Battalion suffered a very large number of casualties, one Officer being killed, one wounded and died of wounds later, and three other Officers wounded, one*

311 2/Lt Eric Osborne Champion of C Company was later re-buried in Bedford House Cemetery south of Ypres. (Enclosure No.2, Grave II. A. 23)

of whom is still on duty. Other Ranks: killed 17, wounded 88, wounded still on duty 38. These figures do not include gas cases or shelled-shock cases." Compared with many an infantry battalion these figures are not unduly high, but for Carl, as he signed it, the *"one Officer being killed"* was his brother, Eric.

* * * * *

Philip had been wounded at Messines. On the 9th he cabled his mother: "Wounded in head – not serious – am at Stoodley Knowle, Torquay". He wrote to her from there several times over the next few days.

> Stoodley Knowle
> Torquay
> 20th June, 1917
>
> ... I'm going on very well and there is no need for you to worry about me. I am getting up for a bit today and hope to get out in the garden, weather permitting. ... I'm sorry to hear Guy is going out so soon. I hoped to see him again before he went, but it does not seem now as if it will be possible. I expect you will drink his health in something before he goes, and when you do you must drink a little bit extra for me. I expect on the whole he will be glad to get out and when he gets there I am sure he will be surprised to find how much one is able to enjoy oneself and life is taken so much less seriously out there than it seems to be in England. They seem to have so many petty restrictions for officers in this country ... .

Philip Dodgson (left) with nurse at Stoodley Knowle

> Stoodley Knowle
> 21st June, 1917
>
> I hope you will have a very cheery time in Town. I am sick I can't be with you. Has Guy written to the Colonel of the 1st Herts to let him know he is coming out? If not, and he knows the Colonel, it is a good thing to do; and ask the Colonel to write to the Base and ask for him. I shan't write Guy a separate letter, so please give him my love and I hope he'll have a good journey and he finds somebody he likes to travel with. Tell him if he ever finds himself near the 47th Division to go and look up the Battery ... he will be sure of a welcome. ...

Stoodley Knowle
25th June, 1917

I have just been before the Medical Board and they have recommended me for
three months' convalescence. I have got so long owing to my eyes. I went down this
morning to see the oculist who, after examining me, found that my actual eyes were
very good but there is a weakness in some muscle connecting the two with the
result that I get a double view of things. This of course makes my sight indistinct.
He says it will get all right of itself but will probably take some time – hence the
three months. This will be a ghastly long time if I get stuck in some out-of-the-way
place. I will probably be here for some time yet. ... Do you know if there is any
convalescent home for officers near Salisbury? I shall get so horribly bored if I don't
get to a place I like. ...

Philip was transferred to a convalescent home at Wilton House, near Salisbury. His
comment that he was to have three months' recuperation was an underestimate, as
he did not return to the Western Front until the end of November 1917.

* * * * *

On the same day that Philip wrote to his mother from Stoodley Knowle, his younger
brother Guy, who was now twenty-two, had at last landed in France and was on his
way to join the 1/1st Battalion of the Hertfordshire Regiment.

Most of Guy's letters were written to his mother, Helen (now Mrs Fulton).

17th Infantry Base Depot, Calais
25th June, 1917

... The Mess is a hut and we three are sleeping in a tent. Luckily our valises have
turned up all right, so I shall have a comfortable night. So far, of course, conditions
are very much as they were in England. The <u>great</u> piece of news is that we, all three,
have been posted to the 1st Herts Regiment. Isn't it splendid? I have had a letter
from the Adjutant [Capt Milne] tonight saying how much he hopes I shall get to the
1st Battalion. ...

Calais
1st July, 1917

... They don't give you very much time to yourself in this camp. We go on parade
every morning at 8.00 and don't get off until about 5.00 in the afternoon, and then
there is usually something in the evening as well. So far I have learnt nothing new.
They seem to treat all officers, whatever service they may have had, as if they had
only just got their commissions. ...

Calais
3rd July, 1917

... We are not allowed to fire blanks or make any noise for fear of disturbing the
inhabitants. ... How splendid Philip getting on so well and three months – that's a
blessing anyway. Does being convalescent mean he can be at Salisbury? ...

Calais
5th July, 1917

Just a short letter to let you know I'm still safe and at the base, for how long I don't know – probably another four or five days. Anyhow I have nearly finished this so-called "Training" of which I am heartily tired. It seems so pointless and is exactly what I have been doing all the time in England. ...

Calais
9th July, 1917

You must have had rather fun with Philip; it's such ages since he's been home for any length of time. Let me know if he does get to Wilton. As you see, I'm still in the land of ink, though I don't expect to be much longer. ... I received preparatory orders yesterday telling us to be ready to go up to the 1st Battalion, but that may be anything up to four or five days. ... The only thing I have done today is to censor men's letters all this morning. Poor things! They are frightfully funny, some of them; nearly all of them very sentimental and usually madly in love with somebody! They don't hesitate to put their innermost thoughts on paper! ...

* * * * *

Meanwhile, on 21st June the 1/1st Hertfordshires had moved to Serques about five miles from St Omer and had started training for the forthcoming Third Ypres offensive.

Another subaltern in Reggie Secretan's No. 2 Company, 2/Lt Frederick Walthew, described the training: "In this district a full scale model of the section of the line to be attacked had been prepared, woods being shown by branches of trees, and dummy trenches indicating the German positions. Day in and day out the troops were put through the part to be played by them in the attack, advancing first in artillery formation, then extending at a given point, which represented the crest of a ridge at the southern end of Kitchener's Wood, on which was situated the famous Falkenhayn redoubt, and continuing in extended order to the line of the second objective, where in due course the barrage would be picked up."[312]

Reggie to his mother   [Serques]
24th June, 1917

... When we arrived we found nowhere to sleep except on the mess room floor, which is brick, so three of us took our valises out into the back garden and went to sleep on the path, it was all very nice till 7.00 a.m., when I woke to find it raining hard! ... Breakfast was at 10.30, so we had to dress and wait around, but we were determined that the others should not sleep if we couldn't, so the rest of them were all pulled out amidst very strong language! ...

[Poperinghe]
30th June, 1917

We go in tonight for about a fortnight, and expect we shall spend most of our time in working parties and such like horrid things! My platoon Sergeant [Walker] is off on leave today, after eighteen months out here without it, he's an old 1st Battalion man and has never been touched, so he has done very well, he's
....

312 Lt F. S. Walthew in Notes for *Hertfordshire Regiment War History 1913-23* (Herts CRO 26821)

a splendid fellow. At present it is raining hard after our glorious weather, which is rather a blow.

[Canal Bank, Hill Top Sector, Ypres]
6th July, 1917

We do nothing all day here as we can't, so breakfast is about 11.00 a.m., which is just the time it always should be! After lunch we sleep, if possible, till teatime, after tea aeroplane fights are watched carefully till dinner, then we are on fatigues most of the night, we generally get back about 2.00 or 3.00 a.m. and try to sleep, if the Hun is polite enough! We are all well and flourishing, but miss our exercise after our hard training, we all long to go and dash about the country, which is not at all advisable around our part!

Guy Dodgson eventually joined Reggie Secretan with the 1/1st Hertfordshires. Their letters describe the build-up to the forthcoming offensive.

Guy to his mother
1/1st Herts Regt
[Hill Top Sector]
12th July, 1917

I have arrived at the 1st Battalion. I am at present back in reserve some way behind the line and am likely to be for some time. I went up yesterday for a kind of "Cook's Tour" of the trenches where the Battalion is. ... Everything was quiet, for which I was devoutly thankful. ... I wish I could tell you more. ...

[Haule]
18th July, 1917

... We have been on the move[313] and have come right back to quite a nice little village for a few days. ... I have got on so far very well with the Battalion and everybody has been very kind to me, though there are a good many fellows I don't know at all, but on the whole they are a genial crowd. ...

I am so awfully glad Philip is going to Wilton after all. It will be ripping having him so close. Give him my love and thank him for his letter next time you see him. ...

I have seen Reggie Secretan and had one or two talks with him. He is quite a cheery person and rather like Esmé to look at. Unfortunately, we are in different Companies. ...

Reggie to his mother
[Haule]
19th July, 1917

We are now miles away thank Heaven, as we had a very rough time of it. I had no casualties in my platoon, but the Company had three killed and eight wounded, we also had an awfully nice officer wounded. He was awfully fed up about it. We had a lot of gas too, but we had no casualties, as we had made the men practise the precautions, it's an awful death, as he's using some stuff now that smells like roses, and has no effect at all until three hours after, but it wasn't a quarter of what

....

313 The 1/1st Hertfordshires had been relieved on 16th July and marched to C Camp near Poperinghe. The next day it "marched to Poperinghe station and entrained to Watten where it detrained and marched to billets at Haule, arriving [at] 7.00 am [on the] 18th." (TNA WO 95/2590)

he got!! I was on duty all one night with H.; an awfully nice fellow. [The Germans] gassed and shelled us all night, then three separate bombardments, we thought it was coming every time, but I think he had only got the wind up, as his shelling is very random now. ...

I have had a young fellow up from the base, he has been out here for ages, but could not get up to the Battalion, because he was under age, he arrived up one day hoping to see his brother, who was killed on the rest [No. 4 Bridge, Yser Canal], awfully hard luck, and when he came out of the line he asked to see me, and so he came along and asked if he could join my platoon, as he wanted to be in Bilby's[314] section, as he wanted so badly to account for his brother's death, isn't it grand of him! I am sure he will get his chance some time!!! ...

Guy to his mother [Haule]
20th July, 1917

... Thank you so much for sending the snap-shots of Toby's grave. How very nice it looks. Perhaps someday you will be able to come out here and visit the place yourself. I am afraid I am nowhere near. ... Have you twigged where I am? I tried to tell you in my first letter from the Regiment, though I could only suggest. ...

[Z Camp, Vlamertinge]
24th July, 1917

... I am now more or less where we were when I joined the Battalion, though in a different camp. It's some few miles behind the line but we can distinctly hear the guns. It's really wonderful how life goes on behind the lines. Our nearest town [Poperinghe], which is about five miles from the line, is extraordinary. One can go down there and get a really excellent dinner with all things necessary to drink! There are three or four Officers' Clubs[315] and quite a number of shops. There is a ceaseless stream of traffic going through the main street. ...

PS Could you send me some [sheet] music? Light stuff, fairly up-to-date and some sentimental songs that everybody knows.

[Z Camp]
25th July, 1917

We are still in the same place, although it was rumoured that we were to move today to a camp a bit nearer the line. ... I expect you have had plenty of rumours about the great doings that are going to take place before very long [preparations for the Third Battle of Ypres]. ... The Battalion is taking part but I personally shall not be in it, so there is absolutely no cause for you to worry. ...

Reggie to his mother [Z Camp]
26th July, 1917

... Guy Dodgson and I had a glorious bathe together before we moved up here. Sgt Walker has just returned off leave, it was grand to see him again, he is a splendid

....

314 2216 and 265340 Cpl Joseph Edward Bilby was killed in action 31st July 1917 and is commemorated on the Menin Gate.

315 The best known club in Poperinghe was Talbot House 'Toc H' which was open to all ranks. Skindles, a few yards further down the same street, was the best known club exclusively for officers.

fellow. I should just love to see the garden, it must look grand now.

Quite a large number of men are on leave now from my platoon, including my servant and two NCOs. I expect we will be up by the time this reaches you!!

Guy to his mother [C Camp]
29th July, 1917

... We have again moved, not very far this time and only two hours' march to another camp nearer to the "war". I remain here tonight together with other unfortunates who, for various reasons, are not allowed to fight the King's great battle. ... You will have seen in the papers about the tremendous artillery work going on. ...

1st August, 1917

... I am now away from the Battalion, together with nine or ten other officers who are not in this show [the opening day of Third Ypres]. We are back in quite a nice little village and the best of it is that I have been lucky enough to secure a billet with an enormous bed. ... I wish I could give you news of what is going on here but I can't for two reasons: firstly, we know nothing for absolute certainty and secondly perhaps it is rather early to say anything.

* * * * *

In early July, Reggie's brother Humphrey was well away from the Ypres Salient. After the Second Battle of Bullecourt, the 2nd Queens and the 7th Division had been withdrawn from the line to rest and refit behind the Bullecourt-Croisilles sector of the Front during late May and June. In early July, 2nd Queens were at Saint-Léger, between Arras and Bapaume.

Humphrey to his mother [Tangier Camp near Saint-Léger]
9th July, 1917

I got the cake from Harrods quite safely and it is quite nice, although not so good as the old sort. Could you please order me one a week rather larger than the one you sent out and in a tin, please?

I told you I think about our first tour in the line and about going back to billets in a village. Well, while there we had a few shells over and then my Company [D] had to go up again into the line for two nights owing to a little reshuffling. While we were there, the Battalion was shelled again without casualties and now they have had to move back into the camp not so far away but safer as we are in a field of thistles. The least rain turns everything into mud. Most of the men would prefer to chance the shelling and keep dry. I don't expect they will keep the shelling up forever. ...

Humphrey to Marjorie [Tangier Camp near Saint-Léger]
10th/11th July, 1917

Thanks for your letter. I was so glad the photos came out. I actually took two of the grave[316] and one looking towards Contalmaison, but as Father never sent me any of them I presume they did not come out. This one is very clear. That is Bailiff

....

316 The photo he is referring to is that of Toby Dodgson's grave on page 198 – see Point B on Map 4

Wood in the background. The helmet has always been there, it was not marked in any way but I am sure it must be his. We are too far away now to go over there, but if we go back for a rest I might be able to get it. The edging, where you can see it is broken, I repaired.

The line is much quieter now and we have got proper trenches and all. We have just had to move out of some lovely billets because the Boche suddenly took to shelling them every night and now are in a camp which is not nearly so nice. Most of the men would prefer to chance the shells and keep dry. Just had a line from Reg. He seems quite happy but is in a warm corner, I fancy. ...

Humphrey to his mother   [Tangier Camp near Saint-Léger]
                                                        12th July, 1917

... I forget what I said in my last letter. I told you of our return to the village to a very nice new billet and of our extra tour in the line. While we were there the Battalion had orders to leave the village for a camp on account of the shelling. We are now a little further from the Boche right out in what would have been a hayfield had it been manured and weeded but now is nearly all thistles. We were very sorry to leave the village and some would have preferred to risk the shelling as the weather has been very bad lately and camps are then not nice. We have the companies separate and have built a lot of small bivouacs to hold ten men each. You can stand up inside and the men like them very much, especially as the ones we rig up temporarily you can only lie under. These have to have two bivouac sheets instead of one. We have got tables outside so they can have all meals out of doors. The officers have two tents and a mess is going to be built, the camp will be a permanent one. We go from there to the trenches and back again, changing over with the same people each time. ...

Billets of D Company, 2nd Queens, Tangier Camp, July 1917. (From left to right: Abbaerley, Durrant, ?, White, Theobald)

The 2nd Queens went into the trench system again on the night of 12/13th July.

Humphrey to his mother   [trenches NW of Bullecourt]
18th July, 1917

Thank you so much for sending the cherries. They were so good and we all enjoyed them awfully. ... We are now back in reserve [trenches] ... about 1,600 yds from Fritz, but it is very quiet where we are and tonight they are bringing the gramophone up for us. The gooseberries were lovely too; ... Marje sent some gooseberries a few days later as well. ...

We have had quite an exciting time in the line this tour. Our "old friends" did a raid.[317] The preparations had been going on for ages; nearly every General within fifty miles had been to see them in training. Gradually more men were put into it and of course it was well advertised. ... The barrage opened but those of them who went over the top were all back within ten minutes and nothing was done at all. Another raid which took place on the same night not far off was successful and they captured several prisoners and blew up a dug-out which the prisoners said contained two platoons.[318]

Of course we got the retaliation for our barrage but luckily none of our Company got hit. My officer on duty had a lucky escape. He was knocked right down but not touched. Our trenches were only slightly damaged and we soon had them straight. The observation is very good from where we are and it makes it very interesting as we often have an opportunity of killing a Boche. Once we actually saw thirty and turned a Lewis Gun on them. The artillery of course gets lots of practice.

The Huns had a heavy trench mortar up this time which went off with a terrific noise, but on the second day it blew itself up, much to our delight.[319] You can always see them coming but the noise is so terrific that we never much care about them. We had a dug-out for company HQ in a sunken road. Last time we were in the line it was very quiet there indeed, but now they seem to shell the place rather a lot. One man of the regiment next door got buried just before we left and when they dug him out he was dead.

The banks of this road are full of buried men from a previous battle, and now they shell us these are continuously coming out of the side and the smell is unpleasant at times. After three years' of war we have just woken up to the fact that these battlefields are full of stuff which if salved can be put to good use and now at last the salving of different stuff is properly organized. I hope it will reduce our expenditure. ...

....

317 The neighbouring battalion of the 91st Infantry Brigade, the 1st South Staffordshires, carried out a raid on the evening of July 14th. Only two men succeeded in entering the trenches. Little damage was done and no prisoners were taken. (Atkinson, op cit, p. 399).

318 The 2nd Gordon Highlanders (20th Infantry Brigade) carried out a more successful raid on the German trenches just north of Bullecourt the same evening. (Atkinson, op cit, pp. 399-400) Humphrey's description of the results is fairly accurate.

319 The 2nd Queen's war diary for 14th July reports "Heavy TM firing on Dog Lane between R.10 and R.16 taken on by 4.5" howitzers and seen to explode." (TNA WO 95/1670)

[near Ervillers, north of Bapaume]
19th July, 1917

Thanks very much for your letter of the 15th. The parcel containing cake and sandwich arrived quite safely while we were in support on the railway bank [NW of Ecoust]. We are now in the camp [Tangier] we built for two days, then go back to [the] railway for two days for fatigues, then back here for four days and then back to the line for our four days in front line and four in support. These two extra days in the line for fatigues are a new idea and means we get less rest of course. However, we don't do so badly out of it.

Leave is rushing round again, but six new fellows arrived while I was away last time so they all come in front of my next turn. One mother has just written to me to ask if I will give her son a month's leave to help with the haymaking! ...

[trenches NW of Bullecourt]
4th August, 1917

... We are out of the front line now on the railway embankment [near Ecoust] but have to go back again tomorrow night instead of being relieved, much to our disgust. However in a few days now we shall be right out of it. ...

I got Marje to choose me some records for the gramophone and she has got some beauties. ... It has been very wet for the last four days but this evening seems to be clearer.

* * * * *

Charles and the 1st/19th London were nearly thirty miles to the west of Ypres during the last fortnight of June. The 47th Division had been withdrawn from the line after Messines for rest and reorganisation. It took three days to march to a rest area south west of Hazebrouck.

Charles to his father   [Caëstre, S of Steenvoorde]
17th June, 1917

Nothing to add to my last letter. We are on a trek – westwards for a change! We hope to arrive somewhere tonight and stay there at any rate for a week. It is awfully hot, and the men are very tired. All the same, we didn't have a single man fall out by the way yesterday, though another Battalion had about fifty. I shall be lucky if I spend my birthday [20th June] out of the trenches for the second year in succession.

[Blaringhem, SW of Hazebrouck]
24th June, 1917

... The Brigadier [McDouall] seems to think I may be going to Aldershot, but I have heard nothing official about it yet. We are having a really pleasant time, though I fear it will soon be over. We are full of preparations for a Divisional Water Carnival. We have had preliminary stages of Company and Battalion heats for various swimming races.

Now the representatives from the different Brigades are to compete on Tuesday. We have got three representatives out of seven for the Brigade, which is pretty good.[320] We haven't been able to have any cricket as the ground is all either hay or under cultivation. We have had strawberries a few times. I wonder if you are at Winchester at last. ...

The Battalion spent twelve days having "a most enjoyable rest" at Blairinghem. The war diary for 27th June notes that a concert was held in the boys' school: "Concert very amusing. Major Fair DSO and 2/Lt Sheppard MC each sang."[321] The Battalion left the village on 30th June to return to the Ypres Salient.

Charles to his father   [Alberta Camp, Reningelst]
                                                                                1st July, 1917

Thanks for your first letter from Winchester just received. I am glad that you are apparently settling down so well. ... I think a few visits from the 19th officers will reduce the amount of wine for which you cannot find a resting-place. Our period of rest is over and we are back practically in the old haunts. We expect to be in the trenches again very shortly.

I have heard nothing more at all about Aldershot, so conclude that it was a false alarm. ... We accomplished our trek both ways without losing a man, which was pretty creditable. ...

Charles "and the Company Commanders reconnoitred trenches [in the Ravine] preparatory to taking over" on 2nd July.[322] However he did not stay with the Battalion in the sector for long but left for England to attend the Senior Officers' School at Aldershot.

This School had been set up in October 1916 with the aim of training majors and senior captains who had to pass the course before being allowed to command a battalion. Up to three hundred officers attended each course. The School was commanded by Brig Gen R. J. Kentish[323] who had established a formidable reputation as an innovative trainer of officers and NCOs. Kentish had set up the first officers' school in the BEF – in Third Army – in October/November 1915.[324] His 'absorbing interest' was the teaching of leadership and morale.

Charles found himself in syndicate C4 with nine other majors, three captains and the senior officer of the syndicate, Lt Col McCordick.[325] Much of Charles's notebook

....

320   The war diary for 23rd June notes "Completion of Battalion swimming contests during the morning to select men to represent Battalion at Brigade Sports. Brigade swimming contests during afternoon to select men to take part in Water Carnival arranged by the Division. We won 100 yards backstroke, 440 yards race and diving contest." (TNA WO 95/2738) The Carnival was "held in the canal at Blairinghem" on the afternoon of 26th June, and was "a great success. They were enjoyed not only by the members of the Division, but also by a great gathering of the local inhabitants who came from all the villages around." (Maude, op cit, p. 104)

321   TNA WO 95/2738

322   TNA WO 95/2738

323   Brig Gen R. J. Kentish CMG DSO (1876-1956) also commanded 76 Brigade, 3rd Division in July 1916 and 166 Infantry Brigade, 55th Division from Mar. 1918 onwards

324   *This Foul Thing Called War: The Life of Brigadier General R. J. Kentish CMG DSO,* Basil Kentish, Book Guild, 1997, pp 61-66

325   Lt Col Frank Case McCordick was a Canadian officer from St Catherine's, Ontario. He initially commanded the 35th (Reserve) Canadian Infantry Battalion which embarked at Montreal on 16th Oct. 1915. After the Senior Officers' School he commanded the 18th Battalion CEF (Western Ontario Regiment) in the 2nd Canadian Division and also served with the King's Own Yorkshire Light Infantry.

from the course survives and his notes give a good idea of the syllabus he covered on certain days, as shown in the incomplete list below.

11 July	Organisation of an infantry battalion
12 July	The attack (*his notes suggest that fire control was of particular emphasis*)
13 July	The attack, continued
16 July	Preparation and delivery of a lecture (by Brig Gen R. J. Kentish)
17 July	Topography – map symbols
18 July	Orders and messages, including the sequence for giving orders; topography – contours and sketching
19 July	Protection (i.e. sentries and outposts)
23 July	Orders and messages – Part II Orders
27 July	Advanced guards and points about outposts
28 July	Military law
30 July	Advanced guards and rear guards; battalion organisation
31 July	Esprit de corps; Field General Court Martials
1 August	Offences and punishments
13 August	Tactical map marking, enlarging maps, and the use of the compass
15 August	Use of the compass by night; using the sun to navigate
22 August	Field engineering – trench construction
27 August	Inspection of regimental transport
28 August	Methods of dealing with offences
29 August	Tactical use of the Lewis gun and machine gun

Charles's detailed notes frequently reference Field Service Regulations, Infantry Training, and the new tactical manuals which drew on the lessons of the Somme and the spring of 1917.[326] His notes also include observations which are drawn from his own and his instructors' experiences.

Just before he started the course, Charles wrote to his father from his sister Mary's house in Essex:

Woodford, Essex
8th July, 1917

... I go to Aldershot today ... I shall be there two-and-a-half months and then get a fortnight's leave before going out again. I hope to get most Saturday nights off and shall come to Winchester on 14th July. You had better fix up to go to Harrogate towards the end of this month, as I shall go to Haileybury on the 28th for the last Sunday of term. ...

Charles did indeed go to Haileybury College to attend the end-of-term concert. Here, for the first time, he met Marjorie Secretan who quite often visited the College as her uncle, Basil Richardson, was a member of the Council (the governing body). She knew a number of the staff and their wives. Afterwards Charles escorted Marjorie back to Hill House at Stanstead Abbotts.

....

326   For a further explanation of the changes in tactics see also footnote 290, Chapter 13.

Marjorie to Charles

Hill House
Stanstead Abbotts
Ware, Herts.
1st August, 1917

Dear Major Fair,

... Yes, Saturday evening is good to look back on: everything combined to make it most cheery; the music especially, and a general air of liveliness. It must have been a very pleasant weekend for you as a contrast to life in the trenches. I enjoyed it immensely; in fact it came as a wonderful surprise that, after the sadness of this last year, life could suddenly resume such a rosy aspect.

I think it would be very jolly to meet again; although [I am] not in London every day now, it's quite easy to get up if you ever have a free afternoon. But perhaps I shall see you down here again, only I am going away on 13th August for about a fortnight and I don't suppose you will be here before then.

I'm afraid you would smile at my amateur efforts over the small boys; but, as you say, it's very interesting seeing how they develop and why and so on. It's a most puzzling thing to me why so many schoolmasters become so hopelessly – well – like a schoolmaster, if you know what I mean, as they get older. Or is this merely an outsider's point of view?

Yes, my uncle remembers you quite well. We succeeded in waking him up on Saturday night and he greeted me on Sunday morning with, "And who were you with last night?"!

Yours sincerely,
Marjorie Secretan

* * * * *

While Marjorie and Charles were enjoying one another's company, they could not have known that under the command of General Gough the British Fifth Army, which included Reggie Secretan and the 1/1st Hertfordshires, was about to launch another major offensive in the Ypres Salient. This offensive was the Third Battle of Ypres, but would become known in the popular imagination as the Battle of Passchendaele.

The British objectives were to capture the higher ground which dominated the area around the Belgian city and, more distantly, to clear the Germans from the Belgian ports which were used as bases by U-boats. A further aim was to distract German attention from the French section of the Western Front, where the French Army was still recovering from mutinies earlier in the year.

Reggie hinted in the following letter to his mother that a large scale operation was imminent:

Reggie to his mother

[C Camp near Poperinghe]
29th July, 1917

We are still in quite a nice place, I will do my best to let you know how I am going along, but please don't worry too much as its going to be awfully difficult, and I daresay it will be all in the papers by the time this reaches you! I have got a good job and I think my luck will hold as it has done up to now. I am awfully bucked with life, and the men could not be better.

Later: I had to stop for a bit. I told you we had had glorious weather, well, today we moved off under a glorious sun, and just before we reached our camp [Vlamertinghe] it came down dogs and cats, I have never known it rain so hard before!

Well, we arrived at our camp to find that it consisted of bivouacs, most of which were under water, so we had to wait a couple of hours out in the rain before it stopped, then we were able to drain them and get in, but we are all right now and hope it will be a good day. Well goodnight, Ma, and rest assured your son will be all right.

As Reggie had observed, the weather had broken on the 29th July. Heavy rain persisted in the forty-eight hours before the battle, and almost one inch of rain fell on 31st July, the first day of the offensive.

An attack on the low-lying landscape east of Ypres would have been demanding at any time but the heavy rain, plus the disruption by artillery shell holes to the natural drainage, made the landscape particularly difficult for advancing troops.

* * * * *

Carl Champion at this time held the rank of Lieutenant Colonel. He wrote in the war diary of the St Helens Pioneers a description of the difficulties faced by the Battalion.

> **Work of the Battalion on zero day** (31st July, 1917)
>
> The work on zero day, allotted to the Battalion, consisted of opening up tracks to captured territory for the passage of guns and transport, and of constructing strong points, in conjunction with the REs, a short distance behind the new British Front Lines.
>
> Under ordinary weather conditions the actual task of making fresh tracks and maintaining the old ones would have produced no insurmountable difficulties. To lay out "Fine Weather Tracks" in torrential rain proved to be quite another proposition. Very quickly the tracks became little more than quagmires, and work upon them had to be confined to pegging them out, clearing them of barbed wire and other obstacles and filling in or bridging old trenches. A shortage of hard material for filling in the shell holes and trenches added to the difficulties. Furthermore the parties working were shelled persistently.

The BEF not only had to contend with rain soaked terrain but also an enemy who had learnt from the Somme in 1916. The Germans had altered their defensive tactics by not having a "front line", but a succession of strong points in depth. These strong points, often pillboxes made from reinforced concrete, had overlapping fields of fire. Subsequent lines of defences were stronger still. Behind the battle zone, and safely out of artillery range, the Germans held counter-attack troops.

The 1/1 Hertfordshires were part of 118th Infantry Brigade in 39th Division. This Division was on the left flank of the British advance which was the responsibility of XVIII Corps. The Corps Commander, Lt Gen Sir Ivor Maxse, was particularly well-known for the thoroughness of the training of his men.

The 39th Division was tasked with capturing three lines of German defences in its sector. The two leading infantry brigades, 116th and 117th would lead, taking the German front line and, 2,000 yards behind that, the second line positions. Following behind, the 118th Infantry Brigade would pass through and capture the German third line position a further 2,500 yards on.

The forward elements of the two leading brigades would stop at the ruined village of St Julien and the line of the Steenbeek stream. The Steenbeek was a major ten-foot-wide obstacle, with five-foot high banks. There was some dead ground on the eastern side of the Steenbeek.

From the Steenbeek the land sloped gently upwards to the third line position at the top of the ridge, which itself was a spur off the main Pilckem Ridge. The top of the ridge was about sixty feet above sea level. This slope was dotted with a number of concrete German bunkers including a large bunker at Maison de Hibou and another called the Springfield Pillbox.

Running a little short of the objective line was the Springfield Road. Beside it, in 2 Company's route, sat the Springfield Pillbox. This was demolished after the war, but a description was made by an officer who fought there a few weeks later. "It was a strongly built pillbox, almost undamaged; the three defence walls were about ten feet thick, each with a machine gun position, while the fourth wall ... had one small doorway - about three feet square. ... the interior [was] in a horrible condition; water in which floated indescribable filth reached our knees. Everywhere was dirt and rubbish and the stench was nauseating."[327]

Lt Walthew of No. 2 Company described the training in the weeks before the battle:

"Every man in the battalion taking part in the attack had it impressed upon him that the barrage, under cover of which he would advance, would be of such intensity that it would be impossible for anything to live in front of him, for a depth of 1,000 yards, and that consequently no hostile attack would be met with for some hours after the capture of the objective.

To this end the Battalion was trained to advance from their "jumping off" position across the Steenbeek Brook at a steady walk, rifles slung, and bayonets fixed, right up to their objective, the Green line; when this was reached they would proceed to consolidate, establish connection with contact patrol aeroplanes by means of flares, and push out patrols and outposts to the crest of the ridge some 50 to 100 yards farther on, for observation, etc. assisted by tanks. In the event of any uncut wire being met with, which was not considered likely, the tanks would breach it to enable the infantry to pass through.

Special emphasis was laid on the fact that nothing in the shape of delay on the flanks was to hinder the advance, and additional stress was brought to bear on this point at a special Corps course on the battle held two or three weeks prior to the attack, at Volckeringhove. It was recognized that there was a possibility that one or two intrepid German machine gunners might remain under cover and in action, in spite of the barrage, and might conceivably hold up the advance, on a limited front, until they could be dealt with by tanks or other means. As this was reckoned as an improbability, and as anyhow the action would be very local, it was not considered advisable to delay the general advance, especially as the success of an attack of this

....

327 Edwin Campion Vaughan, an officer in 8th Warwicks, used the Springfield Pillbox as his headquarters on 27th August. (E. Campion Vaughan, *Some Desperate Glory*, pp 225-6)

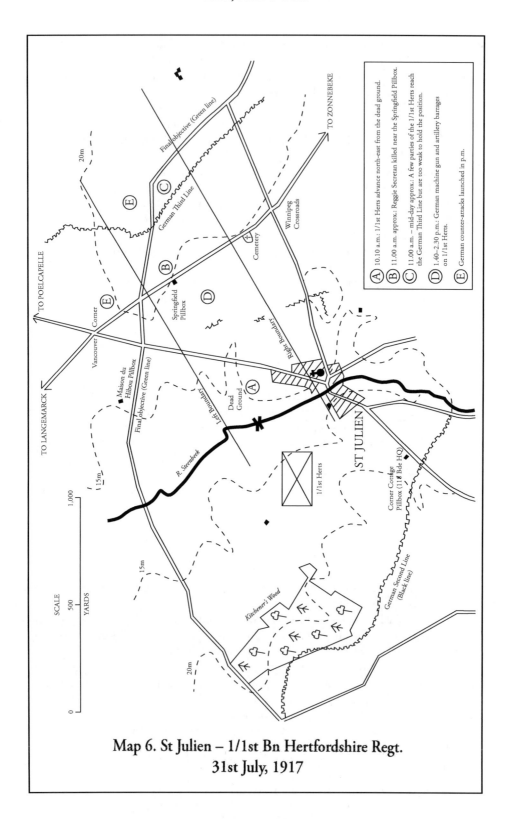

Map 6. St Julien – 1/1st Bn Hertfordshire Regt.
31st July, 1917

nature depends primarily upon the close proximity of the infantry to the creeping barrage."[328]

Lt William Thompson of No. 1 Company recalled the final hours of the Battalion before going into action: "The Battalion was bivouacked the night previous to the battle on the outskirts of Poperinghe. Shortly before dusk the Regiment left its quarters, per platoons at intervals, the gallant major (Phillips) stationed at a corner of the camp bidding good luck to each as it passed. A thick mist, after a heavy rain, hung over the landscape as the regiment made its way up to the position it was to occupy prior to the attack. It was dark as the battalion approached the Canal Bank (Ypres), and here encountered a heavy gas barrage. Gas helmets were obliged to be worn: this rendered it difficult to keep in touch and in the right direction. By midnight the regiment was in position (left of Irish Farm) for the attack at dawn. But for a little intermittent shelling, the night passed without incident, and the casualties were few."[329]

The Fifth Army and the 39th Division began the attack at 3.50 am as dawn was breaking. As 118th Infantry Brigade was not taking part in the initial assault, all ranks received a hot meal. At 5.30 am the 118th Brigade advanced, with the 1/1st Hertfordshires moving forward in four lines behind 116th and 117th Brigades for which everything went to plan. By 6.30 am 118th Brigade was established just to the west of the German second line (the Black Line).

Lt Thompson's account continues:
    "Here the regiment had some considerable time to halt while the artillery was doing its work. At this period the enemy had no doubt realized the loss of their second line and were putting down a heavy barrage upon it.
    Sections were lying in shell holes getting what protection they could, while that gallant officer, the *padré* of the brigade (the Rev Popham), came amongst us. There he was; I can see him now, as he sat in the shell hole passing his cigarettes around and chatting to the men, amid the din of the battle. Why he should have chosen to be with us, when he could have been with either of the other battalions, who knows? He knew the regiment had the place of honour that day, as the Brigadier had previously told us, and he was going to be with them.
    From this point the battalion slightly altered direction, and officers were now engaged taking their new bearing. There stood the colonel, compass in hand, ascertaining that all officers knew their direction, leaving nothing to chance, as was always his way. It was an anxious wait on this second line, with the shelling all the time increasing in intensity."[330]
    The Battalion resumed its advance to St Julien and crossed the Steenbeek. Several platoons were able to make use of dead ground on the eastern side of the stream to shelter whilst they prepared for the attack on the German third line (the Green Line). "Up till this time the casualties had been very slight indeed."[331]

....

328 Lt F. S. Walthew in Herts CRO 26821

329 Lt W. Thompson in Herts CRO 26821

330 Lt W. Thompson in Herts CRO 26821

331 TNA WO 95/2590

At 10.10 am, exactly on schedule, the Battalion resumed the advance. 2/Lt Ritchie of No. 2 Company described the attack:

"We advanced according to schedule, in two waves the counter barrage being very heavy: the ground was very sticky, half way up to our knees, and men were going down right and left. Our left flank was entirely in the air. During one of our two-minute rests I brought up No. 5 platoon in line with No. 6 as we could not cover the front.

Captain Lowry was now reported hit and the whole company was now in one line and there appeared to be nothing between us and the enemy. When we reached the St. Julien - Poelcapelle road Lt Head and I each had about five men left. There was a hedge running more or less at right angles to the road. Head took his lot up the left side while I went up the right. I do not think anyone saw Head or any of his men again.

About 200 yards on there was a row of Block Houses held by the enemy, so I tried to work round them. I was carrying my Lewis Gun as the Lewis Gun section was knocked out except one man, but the gun was choked and useless. While trying to get at these Germans I got knocked out.

When I came to I found I had no NCOs left so I sent Private Atkins on with the three remaining men. At this time we were a bit behind schedule. I could see 2/Lt Secretan further on the right, the counter barrage still being unpleasantly heavy.

Going back I got in touch with the Black Watch who were certainly behind time, and I think that it was in the gap on our left between us and the Black Watch that the enemy came down and cut us off. Most of our dead and dying were lying between the road and the Steenbeek, which was where we suffered most of our casualties."[332]

Reggie Secretan was killed at about 11.00 am near the Springfield Pillbox. Reggie and his platoon had stopped to shelter for a few minutes in the shell holes near the road. He then sprang up, shouting "Come on No. 8!" and waving his arms to encourage his men forward. Survivors from his platoon recounted that "a German officer with a bandaged head, and some men, ran out from behind the redoubt." They saw the officer aim at Reggie who "fell forward on his hands and knees, and was killed instantaneously." He was twenty-two.

No. 3 Company on the right succeeded in penetrating further into the German positions. The war diary records: "About half way to the objective some of No.3 Coy came upon a German strong point which they gallantly charged, capturing or killing most of the garrison and sending the remainder back as prisoners. On reaching the enemy wire this was found to be practically undamaged (except in one place) and very thick. 2/Lt Marchington[333] and a handful of men of No.3 Coy got through the only gap and got into the enemy trench and killed a lot of Germans." [334]

However, by this time the Battalion was far too weak to hold its gains and there was little effective supporting artillery fire. The war diary continues "The remainder of the Battalion, being unable to get through the wire and suffering severe casualties from enfilade MG fire and the Germans making a strong counter attack from our left flank

....

332 2/Lt Ritchie was the only surviving officer of No. 2 Company. (Herts CRO 26821)

333 2/Lt Eric William Marchington was commissioned on 27th Nov. 1915 and was wounded on 31st July 1917. He was awarded the Military Cross for his actions on that day.

334 TNA WO 95/2590

about this time, had to fall back having suffered exceptionally heavy casualties. The remnants of the Battalion subsequently dug themselves in ... on the west side of the Steenbeek."[335] The last man across the stream was the chaplain, the Rev Edgar Popham.

The CQMS of No. 2 Company, Gordon Fisher, had seen the Company off that morning. That afternoon he was bringing up some rations for the Battalion and found Brigade HQ. "They were in an underground German concrete pillbox [Corner Cottage] just in front of St. Julien. I went down the stairs, saluted the Brigadier [Bellingham], told him who I was, explained the position and said, 'Could you give me any instructions, sir, that would help me to find the battalion?' He just stood and looked at me. We were both standing on the steps, and the pillbox was rocking like a boat in a rough sea with explosions. After a while he said, 'I'm sorry, Quarters, I'm afraid there isn't any Hertfordshire Regiment.'"[336]

The 1/1st Hertfordshires had indeed been wiped out. The war diary records that the Battalion had lost twenty officers and 459 other ranks killed, wounded and missing. Only 130 other ranks remained.[337] In other words, over three-quarters of the other ranks and every officer that had gone 'over the top' that morning had become a casualty.

The Battalion was withdrawn from the line on 5th August and moved into bivouacs at Reigersburg Château.

* * * * *

It took a few days before news of casualties reached families at home. A letter written to Reggie by his sister Esmé was returned, with the envelope stamped "Killed in Action." She was a nurse in a hospital in Reading and had written:

Reading
4th August, 1917

My Dear Podger,

Of course I've been horribly worried ever since I saw the news in the paper and had your letter, but hope and pray that you are all right. I long to hear as you don't know what a lot I think of my Podger, but am sure your luck will hold out and you will come through this d----d war safe and sound. ...

I will do my best to cheer them up at home. I write often, but I'm sure poor Ma is fearfully worried.

Convoys [of ambulances] are at last beginning to arrive, but no bad cases so far; only turn-outs from the French hospitals. But I'm sure we shall be very busy before long. ...

How rotten for you this weather; it must have made the ground impossible, especially as it's very low and marshy, isn't it, where all the fighting is? It rains here all day and oh! so cold.

Well, good luck, old man; all my love and good wishes,

Yours ever,

Puss

....

335 TNA WO 95/2590

336 Gordon Fisher recounted his story fully in Lyn Macdonald's *They called it Passchendaele* (pp. 121-2 of the Papermac edition, 1983)

337 See the entries for 31st July and 2nd Aug. 1917. (TNA WO 95/2590)

The whole Secretan family was greatly distressed by the news of Reggie's death, his mother Mary in particular. She received numerous letters of sympathy from Reggie's fellow officers and men in his platoon telling her what a fine and popular officer he had been. (Several of these are included in Appendix IV.)

Charles must have seen 2/Lt Reggie Secretan as reported killed in the casualty lists from the battle in the national papers. He wrote to Marjorie as soon as he had heard the news.

Charles to Marjorie   Senior Officers' School
Malplaquet Barracks
Aldershot
7th August, 1917

Dear Marjorie (I can't be stiff and formal when you are in trouble: please do the same if you will.)

I only got your two letters both together this morning. What can I say? I am so awfully sorry. It is doubly hard that you, who have suffered so much already, should have this too. Just too when, as you said in your first letter, the world was beginning to look brighter again. I would do anything if there was anything that would be any good. It is one of the hardest things in the war, I find, to be unable to help when you want to. Your letter came just as we were going out for the whole day on a scheme. I'm afraid I didn't give my mind to the scheme much because of your news. I expect this will take a long time to reach you, but I don't know your address. I will write again when I know it, if you would care to hear. I must see you again the first chance there is. I haven't pledged myself after the 18th at all, and practically all my Wednesdays are free.

A mere letter when anyone is in trouble is so very little, but this one brings all the sympathy that a letter can.

Yours ever,
Charles Fair

Marjorie to Charles   Hill House
11th August, 1917

Dear Charles, (although I will never rise to it when I meet you!)

It was kind of you to write as you did. It was only too true about Reggie, as you will see in the paper this morning. It was in that first capture of St Julien on the 31st, I believe. The only comfort is that he was shot and killed outright. But it's heartbreaking for my poor parents. They hadn't heard when I went over with the news on Sunday. It's so awfully hard, as you say, to see other people suffer and to be so powerless to help. Of course I'm doing all I can for them and shall spend the holidays there. I'm just here for the night to collect my things. My address there is Bennett's End, Hemel Hempstead. When it's someone you have known from his babyhood one realises so acutely the years of toil and love that go to make up a brave life and then it's smashed up like this at the very start. The only consolation I have ever found is that the joy one has in the companionship of anyone you care about far outweighs the sorrow of their death. It's very nice of you to be so sympathetic: I think you told me you'd had a bad time over something yourself, so you will understand.[338]

....

338 She is referring to the death of Charles's mother in 1904.

You dropped the conventions over my name and now I'm going to take you at your word about "doing anything that would be any good". What I would love you to do later on is to take me to one of the promenade concerts at the Queen's Hall, which I see begin on August 25th. I love music and hardly any of my friends do and it's so flat going alone. I foresee awful difficulties over getting home afterwards, etc., but perhaps if we both turned our brains that way we might do it somehow. If you like, I'll meet you in London on Wednesday week. The only thing is, I can't stay up late as our house at home is three miles from a station and it's awkward getting back. However, we could at least have tea. Write to me at home and say what you think.

Yours very sincerely,
Marjorie Secretan

Marjorie recorded in her diary for 11th August that she and her mother went to Hertford to attend a memorial service for the men in the Hertfordshire Regiment who had been killed in the Ypres Salient.

Marjorie to Charles   Bennetts End
                                                         Hemel Hempstead
                                                          15th August, 1917

Dear Major Fair (Quite forgot – too lazy to rewrite letter!),

Thanks very much for your two letters. I am glad it's all right about the 22nd. I shall probably be up early in the day, so will come along to Waterloo for the 3.08 and you will find me by the board that tells you the arrival platforms. ... It will be great fun fixing up a visit to the Queen's Hall and, if it's a case of getting home late, I can always go to Hill House for the night, where it's no bother getting up from the station. Yes, this station is Boxmoor and we only have a small pony trap to get out to our house, so I don't like to be late home as Mother or Father have to meet me – the groom of course having gone in the Army.

How lucky for you, getting a fortnight's leave in September. That's a rare event nowadays, isn't it? My next term [teaching in London] begins on September 24th – a long time away. Curious how one has come to live solely in the present. I've quite given up thinking of anything till I get there. No, I don't know that book – it sounds very attractive – perhaps we might have a look at it on Wednesday, though I don't know why you should give me a present. It's very kind of you.

Totland Bay sounds a delightful spot. I quite agree with you about the downs: they have a wonderful charm all their own, but I've never been to the Isle of Wight. I'm glad you had such a cheery time there – you made me quite jealous! Of course I did not mind your writing again – why ever should I? The only letters worth having are the ones people want to write. Well, *au revoir* till Wednesday.

Yours,
Marjorie Secretan

* * * * *

When the Third Battle of Ypres opened Humphrey Secretan was still far to the south near the Bullecourt-Croisilles sector of the Front with 2nd Queens and the 7th Division. Humphrey did not hear the news of his brother's death until several days after his family at home. It is poignant that his mother Mary would have received this letter from him nearly a week after she had been told.

Humphrey to his mother   [Berles-au-Bois, west of Ervillers]
                                                                            10th August, 1917

... Glad Reggie was not in the push but he is bound to get a dose sooner or later. We can only hope for the best. I haven't heard from him lately but have only just written. ...

We did our two days' extra in the front line and had rather an anxious time as we were expecting the Germans to do a raid. We were very unlucky over casualties. One night a shell pitched near a sentry and wounded the NCO in charge of the group very badly and the sentry died half an hour later with a piece of shell in his body.[339] I had been talking to them in the very spot only half-an-hour previously. After we had sorted out the stretcher bearer to attend to these two, I went into the trench and found a man buried with only his head out – snoring hard. We dug him out and found he was unwounded although the shell had dropped almost on top of him but [he] was badly concussed. I haven't heard yet how he got on. ...

Well, we came back and spent two nights and one day at the old camp [Tangier, near St Leger]. The next day we went for a route march and are now in a French village with two weeks' training before us: not a rest exactly, but a relief.[340] Do you remember last June when I cycled over to see the old 10th [Royal Fusiliers]? Well, I am back in the same house ... . Then there were no civilians, but now nearly all have come back so we can get our fill of eggs, butter, milk and vegetables. ...

Humphrey to his sister Marjorie   [Berles-au-Bois]
                                                                            11th August, 1917

Yes, poor Reggie was in it as you thought. It has been my constant dread for days and now the worst has happened. The favourite of all of us. Poor Mother, how she loved him: he was all in all to her. She will be a long time getting over it. How I wish I was at home. Find out all you can from the Depot and let me know. I might get a chance to visit the same place perhaps soon.

We are far from the line now for a week or two. ... Glad you like ... [Charles] Fair. No I didn't take part in any raids, only sat and got the shelling in retaliation – safer by far. The rain must have been awful up north poor devils. I shall never find a friend like him [Reggie]: how I adored him. ... I only hope I don't get taken for the parents' sakes but life is not worth living now. ... Love to Uncle Basil.

Humphrey to his sister Esmé   [Berles-au-Bois]
                                                                            12th August, 1917

Yes, as you say, poor darling Reg was right in the middle of it all. Oh, how we shall miss him, he must have been the favourite of all of us, and poor Mother will be so upset. I had been dreading it all along as soon as I heard he was in it. What shall we

....

339   According to the war diary, D Company's trenches were shelled on the night of 6th/7th Aug. One casualty was recorded. (TNA WO 95/1670)

340   7th Division had two weeks "for refitting and intensive training" prior to a move to the Ypres Salient. The Division was able to train in the old trench systems from the 1916 Somme battlefield and work on new tactics to counter the new German defensive tactics that the BEF was experiencing at Ypres. (Atkinson, op cit, pp. 403-405)

do without him? He was always the life and soul of us all. No details ... so far ... I am doing what I can to find out something. It makes you wonder whether this war is worth it. We entered it to help Russia and Serbia and the first is letting us down and the last is a lot of cut-throats. How I wish Reg had stopped with the motorcyclists. He did right to leave I know, but oh, how I wish he was still alive, if only he had been wounded. You must feel his loss terribly: you two always got on so well together. I wish I could get home, but here there is no one to talk to about him and you have to carry on as if nothing had happened. ...

Humphrey to his mother   [Berles-au-Bois]
22nd August, 1917

... Leave is quite out of the question. Sorry I have not written quite so often lately, but I have been so busy and also felt I could not write about everyday life here, but now I will start again. I have written to Dad. You must all pull together at home. Don't worry about me: I am miles from harm, nearly fifteen, and very well. ...

* * * * *

Meanwhile Guy Dodgson and the left-out-of-battle cadre had rejoined the 1/1 Hertfordshires. The Battalion was being rebuilt from the few survivors of the attack of 31st July. On the 7th August it arrived at Thieushouck near Caëstre for a week of rest and refitting. His letters from this period show that he was trying to find out what had happened to the Battalion and Reggie Secretan on 31st July.

Guy to his mother   [Thieushouck]
7th August, 1917

... The weather has at last improved, thank goodness. It was too awful a few days ago – persistent rain day after day and the mud, even back where we were, was appalling. I am afraid there is no doubt about Reggie Secretan. He was killed rallying his platoon for the final assault – at least, that is what I have been told. ...

[Thieushouck]
12th August, 1917

I got your last letter written from Bovingdon yesterday. How lovely it must be to be down there again. ... My Company is at present billeted in a farmhouse with some really very nice people who do all they can to make us comfortable. The four of us – Leslie [Gold][341], Hickley, who I came out with, and a fellow called White[342] – live in one of their rooms. It's extraordinary how little one sees of other fellows out here except those in your own Company. Here for instance we are a good two miles from HQ, where the other Companies are. We have not yet had any satisfactory information as to what really happened to the Battalion on July 31st but, as far as I can tell, they got up to their final objective, which was in a line with the village of Langemarck and then they found the wire uncut and the Germans who were holding the line fired on them with machine guns. I think there is no doubt that

....

341 Capt Leslie Guy Gold had been commissioned into the Hertfordshires on 15th Sept. 1914 after having served as a Cadet Corporal in the OTC at Radley College. He was promoted to Captain on 1st June 1916 and was wounded later in 1916.

342 2/Lt F. E. White was commissioned into the Hertfordshires on 15th Oct. 1915.

most of them lost their lives in this way, as there were very few wounds from shells. Reggie Secretan must have been killed in this way, I think. I have written to Marjorie and said what I could to cheer her up, and today I have heard from her, though not in answer to my letter. ...

You sent me a splendid selection of music. Thank you so much for it. ...

On 14th August the Battalion was bussed to a camp at Ridge Wood nearer the front line.

Guy to his mother   [Ridge Wood]
16th August, 1917

I have had your two letters since you knew the news about the Battalion. Thank you so much for them. As you say, it is rather a bad beginning for me, but you cannot imagine how cheerful everybody is even under these circumstances. To me it is nothing short of marvellous. Leslie, who has been out nearly three years now and knew all those fellows so well, is as cheerful as anything and keeps everybody on the go. I am sure I could never be quite like that, I am sorry to say. I suppose it comes from having too much imagination. ... If you look in the "Daily Mirror" and "Daily Mail" of 15th August you will find a short appreciation of what the Regiment did, written by the ubiquitous Beach Thomas.[343] We all feel very proud and it certainly is high time that we had some kind of public recognition. ...

I had a letter yesterday from Humphrey Secretan wanting news of Reggie. I answered by return and told him what I could, which was not very much. ... Rather an odd coincidence, he said he had just had a small draft of Herts men sent to his Battalion (2nd Queen's), some of whom knew me and had in fact been up before me as "criminals", as he could tell by my signature on their conduct sheets.[344]

[Ridge Wood]
19th August, 1917

Just a short line as I may not be able to write for a day or two. I am going to the war! But to a good bit of the line, as far as I can gather, where there is not much going on and one sits more or less still, acting as a sort of garrison. ... For the last few days we have been in tents just behind the line in quite a pleasant wood and have had a very easy time – only two hours parade a day. ...

I have seen one or two quite interesting things since we have been here. A tank came waddling along yesterday – the first I had seen – and there is a big gun quite close, which I went and had a look at the other day and watched firing; thereby nearly getting the drums of my ears smashed. ...

....

343   William Beach Thomas (1868-1957) was one of the five selected journalists allowed to report the war from the Western Front. An extract from his Daily Mail article is included in Appendix IV. The journalists had to accept military censorship over what they wrote which meant that an optimistic spin was put on military setbacks. Front line soldiers naturally tended to become cynical towards the more purple prose that appeared in the daily newspapers. Thomas later admitted that he was "deeply ashamed of what he had written" about the disastrous first day on the Somme in 1916 as he knew it to be untrue. He was knighted after the Armistice.

344   Each soldier's service record contained a conduct sheet which was a form designed to record offences and punishments. Offences could range from minor misdemeanours to major crimes. The form also included comments as to whether he was of good character and on his sobriety. The service record followed him as he was posted from one unit to another.

On 19th August the 1/1st Hertfordshires went into the Klein-Zillebeke trenches in the front line.[345]

* * * * *

Humphrey had meanwhile obtained second-hand news of his brother's death from Guy.

Humphrey to Esmé   [Berles-au-Bois]
22nd August, 1917

Thanks so much for your letter. I think you ought to stay on at [the War Hospital in] Reading. The loss is awful to Father and Mother, but think of the others who have lost sons and brothers. If all left their work we could not get on with the war. Marje will have been a help to them and perhaps you can meet Dad in Town some days for lunch for a bit. I enclose a cheque for your fares as it will be a drain on your pay if you do it often. ...

Yes, it is awful to think that all the best of England are getting killed while the dodgers can keep away from harm. COs [conscientious objectors] will make me madder than ever now. I have a rough idea of where he fell from Guy Dodgson, but no officer has seen him dead apparently. I never dare hope, but I never believe men after a show like that. However we should know definitely soon, as the ground must be in our hands again now. ...

PS Don't mistake what I have said, there can be no hope, but I shan't believe him dead until I have found his grave or body.

On 28th August, after two weeks at Berles-au-Bois, 2nd Queens marched westwards to Pommera, a village nearly five miles east of Doullens. The next morning it marched one mile to the station at Mondicourt and entrained at 2.30 pm.[346]

Humphrey to Esmé   [Mondicourt, east of Doullens]
29th August, 1917

I hope you have settled down by now and definitely decided to stay at Reading. I feel sure Father will be all right and I see they are having visitors now at Bennetts End so that they will always have company now. There is another fellow from my company in the war hospital at Reading, a medical case. ... He was Second-in-Command of the Company. He can talk a dog's hind leg off and ... is quite a nice fellow. He can tell you where [we] have been lately.

We are on the move now so I don't know where we shall be soon. At the present moment we are in the train at the station [Mondicourt] which I left when I came home to get my Commission. There were several tears shed when we left the village where we spent two weeks. ... Marje has just let me know that Reg was seen to fall near Springfield Road, so I shall soon be able to fix the spot exactly. ...

The 2nd Queens detrained at Hopoutre near Poperinghe at 9.30 pm in the evening of 29th August and marched to Ottawa Camp, Ouderdom, arriving at midnight.[347] The Battalion and the 7th Division would soon be playing their parts in the Third Battle of Ypres.

....

345 TNA WO 95/2590

346 TNA WO 95/1670

347 TNA WO 95/1670. Ottawa Camp is described as "spacious but dirty and quantities of flies."

Chapter 15

Charles and Marjorie

August to November 1917

In the late summer of 1917 Charles and Marjorie continued their correspondence and their growing friendship flourished. Charles was still attending the Senior Officers' School at Aldershot.

Marjorie to Charles   Eastbourne
                                                                19th August, 1917

I will be going home tomorrow, so will probably be able to bike to the station on Wednesday, which means I needn't get home quite so early and will make it more worth your while coming up to London.

I am sitting on the beach and much appreciating a sight of the sea again, even though it is bounded by parades and street-lamps and the inevitable crowd that invariably display themselves at these fashionable so-called pleasure resorts. It is really warm and sunny under a breakwater and I am thinking how pleasant it would be to spend a week or so in some really attractive seaside place with nothing to do except bathing and walking and other delights. Unfortunately there is no one here with a sound pair of legs, as Beachy Head looks very alluring and I should love to get up there.

I am probably going to lunch with Mrs Naylor on Wednesday and will come from there to Waterloo. I will try to be punctual but if I'm a minute or two late don't think I've failed you...

Charles to Marjorie   Aldershot
                                                                24th August, 1917

This may be a long letter before it is finished, so you had better keep it till you have absolutely nothing to do. I rather like to write a letter which goes on for a day or two. Do you ever do that? I don't do it often! We have had a most exhausting day

– out on a scheme[348] from 8.45 a.m. till 3.00 p.m. and then another lecture from 5.45 till 7.15! Tomorrow will be a bad morning beginning with the exam paper and then two hours' ceremonial drill. Also they have had the bad taste to give us a problem to be studied during the weekend! I hope to goodness they won't do the same on 1st Sept. If you are going to stay that night in London, what will be the chances of seeing you on the Sunday? It would be so awfully nice if we could manage to spend that together too, but I am dreadfully afraid of your becoming tired of the sight of me. I really must stop now and go to resume my studies: I very much doubt whether I shall manage to keep awake!

Marjorie to Charles   Bennetts End
                                                      24th August, 1917

Thanks very much for your letter. We certainly were not very bright about the Queen's Hall! As to that Saturday, if you really have nothing to do on the Sunday, will you not come down with me to Hill House after the concert and spend the Sunday there? I did not like to suggest it before as I did not know whether Uncle Basil had the house full, but he was here last night and said he would be so pleased if you would come. I think there is a train about half past ten, which would do alright. They don't usually have a very interesting programme on Saturdays, so I am rather keen to see what it will be. We haven't much choice about the day in any case.

Yes, I got home quite early and must have been pretty well asleep by the time your train left Waterloo. Oh, those spelling faults, I won't be able to give your name as a reference next time I apply for a post. I'm really very apologetic over the DSO, but somehow had an idea it was MC, though I ought to have known the ribbon. I think the Haileybury gossip must have informed me of it but, like many other things, it had got pushed out of my mind. Anyhow, I offer a very late congratulation.

I hope the exam will go off satisfactorily. It was today, wasn't it? I am glad you enjoyed Wednesday, it was very cheering. We have a great many acquaintances in common anyhow.

Charles to Marjorie   London
                                                      25th August, 1917

Your letter came just before I came away for the weekend. I should simply love to come back with you next Saturday. It is delightful of you to think of it and most awfully nice of your Uncle to approve of it as a suggestion. ... We haven't yet decided how we are going to spend next Saturday afternoon. It will rather depend on the weather, won't it? I got the programme of the Queen's Hall today. It doesn't look too bad as far as I know anything about it. ... The exam wasn't very terrible, but they have very meanly set us a problem to work out during the weekend. If they do the same next week you will have to help me with it! We have a nasty looking programme for the week, so if I arrive a mental wreck don't be surprised. I hope this long scrawl hasn't been too much for you. ... Please write again soon.

....

348 Probably a 'tactical exercise without troops'. Students would have been given a tactical problem to study on a piece of terrain near Aldershot, and would have had to develop their own solution which they would then have had to present back to the instructors. The problem might have been, for example, to devise the plan to attack a village as if they were in command of a battalion. This would have tested their understanding of tactics, logistics, and their ability to write and transmit orders to officers below them in the chain of command.

When Charles met Marjorie on 2nd September he proposed marriage to her and she accepted.

Marjorie to Charles   Bennetts End
                                                                3rd September, 1917

My Dear Charley,

I hardly know what to say to you. I still feel I must be dreaming and that I shall wake up and find you are not really there at all. It is rather like stepping suddenly out of a cold, dark winter into the warm sunlight, so that all I can do is to sit still, rather dazedly, and enjoy the bright light. But it's oh! so splendid to feel happy again and to see other people happy about me, too. Father and Mother are sweet about it. Father nearly had a fit when I told him on the way up in the pony cart. All he asked was what you looked like and did Uncle Basil like you! Then, did you smoke!!! But he's awfully pleased now that he's really taken it in and says as long as I'm happy he doesn't mind what I do. I do love seeing my mother really glad about something again and of course she is prepared to give a very warm welcome to anyone who knew "Dick".[349] The Saturday scheme is quite approved of, so I shall expect you by the 6.10 from Euston. Meanwhile your letter to father is eagerly awaited.

I went to what I thought looked a really artistic photographer in Bond Street and he will do his best to let me have the proofs by Saturday.

I didn't get up here till 4.30 p.m. and now the post is just going, and anyhow I feel horribly tongue-tied, but I do love you, Charley and I'm ever so happy: you are a dear.

All my love,
Marjorie.

* * * * *

Meanwhile, Guy Dodgson was still in the Ypres Salient with the 1/1st Hertfordshires.

Guy to his mother   25th August, 1917

... I came down from the trenches the night before last. We were up there [the Klein-Zillebeke trenches] four days and on the whole things were not as bad as I expected.[350] The trenches <u>were</u> bad, mere slits in the ground with no cover or communication, but we had good dugouts (formerly Hun and therefore of the very best and made of concrete). It actually had a bed therein, which added greatly to our comfort. We are now back about two-and-a-half miles in shelters – old trenches with quite good dugouts but surrounded by our guns, which makes things rather noisy! ...

....

349   Henry Richardson (Dick), another of Marjorie's uncles and a housemaster at Marlborough College, Wiltshire.

350   The 1/1st Herts went into the front line (Klein-Zillebeke trenches) on 19th Aug. and were relieved on 23rd Aug. suffering casualties of one other rank killed and two missing during the four days. They moved into Brigade Reserve. (TNA WO 95/2590)

[Ridge Wood]
27th August, 1917

... It poured with rain last night[351] and I had one horrible moment when I woke up and heard an ominous drip, drip and found it was all over my clothes!! The dugout not being as water-tight as I had thought. The rain has stopped this morning and it's quite a nice day with a certain amount of sun and things are beginning to dry up and, as I write, I can see my beautiful blue vest fluttering in the wind on a clothes line! But despite such minor discomforts as rain and mud this place seems the epitome of comfort after the line and the feeling of absolute safety is so extraordinary, though we are still quite close. However, the Boche has been very considerate and has not worried us at all, which is really very odd of him as the whole area simply swarms with our own guns and they keep going pretty well the whole time. This is our last day here and tonight we are going back for four days about three miles into a regular camp.[352] ... I wonder if by any chance you saw "The Gazette" of 24th August: all our promotions, etc., according to this new scheme, were in – a whole column of them. I don't quite understand how the scheme works, but I think it is based on the length of commissioned service. Anyhow, they appear to wish to exalt me once more to Captain, which worries me a lot. I don't want to be promoted in the very least, and shall do my best to get out of it. This probably sounds silly when you read it, but you know what I mean. It isn't fair on other fellows, and besides I still have so much to learn about the job out here.

[Mount Sorrel]
2nd September, 1917

It's no good – I have got to be a Captain, and today my arm is once more adorned with three stars and much braid. I have asked the opinion of several people and they all seem to think I should be very foolish to try and give it up. I suppose, in a sort of way, I am very lucky. ...

The weather is still pretty beastly and the ground never gets a chance of drying up, with the result that the roads and tracks are in an awful state of mud and slosh, which is made all the worse by the tremendous amount of traffic there is in these parts. Has Philip any idea where his Division [the 47th] is nowadays? I wish you'd ask him and, if I ever got near them, I would go and look them up. ...

* * * * *

Charles to Marjorie's father, Herbert Secretan   Aldershot
3rd September, 1917

Dear Mr. Secretan,

I hope you have got Marjorie home by now and have heard our news, and I do hope you will be able to give it your approval. I can only say that I love her with every bit of good that there is in me and I will do everything that a man can do to make her happy. I think it all began with my admiration for the pluck with which she has faced the troubles that the war has brought her. She will have told you that

....

351 The 26th and 27th Aug. were exceptionally wet days in the Salient with a total of 35 mm of rain being recorded.

352 The 1/1st Herts were relieved by the 14th Hampshires and moved into Divisional Reserve near Ridge Wood. (TNA WO 95/2590)

our present plan is for me to come down to you for next Saturday night and talk things over properly. All the time I have been in France my father has had Power of Attorney and has been acting for me, and as I have only seen him once since my return I am a little bit vague about my financial position, but my income from all sources is something over £600 a year[353] and of course all the time I am in France I am hardly spending anything. In addition, my father is of course still alive, and there are some other sources from which I shall ultimately benefit. I think it is only right to mention this in my first letter, but your approval and consent is after all what really matters.

Yours very sincerely,
Charles H. Fair

Charles to Marjorie
Aldershot
3rd September, 1917

My Darling,

I just wrote those two words and then sat and looked at them for quite a long time while trying to realize that I have the right to use them. It is all so tremendous and wonderful that I am a little bit lost still, though I am walking about inches taller from sheer pride and happiness. You dear, wonderful little person. It will take more than a life-time to pay it all back to you, but I will have a tremendous try. God grant I may never make you regret it for a moment.

I hope you have got home all right and been photographed. I have been scribbling to my sisters every spare moment I have had today so far, and I have just finished my letter to your father. (These Mess pens are awful for writing an important letter!) It is perfectly lovely again today and we have had rather a slacker time than usual, luckily, as I am only just beginning to return to normal sleep and appetite! I hope you are too, but I don't believe you were as bad as I was! I now wait anxiously for approval from both sides. I can't hear from my own people except by telegram before Wednesday. My whole heart and mind is too full of you to write to anyone intelligibly. I simply love you with every little bit of good there is in me, and it will grow on getting bigger and bigger. This must catch the post now. Take care of yourself, my darling, and write.

With all my love,
Charles

Aldershot
3rd September, 1917
10.00 p.m.

It was a very hurried and dull letter I wrote you this afternoon (I had so many to write) and so I am writing again now. I want you every minute I am away from you. Our weekend was so absolutely wonderful for me in every way. If only we need never be away from each other without our both consenting to it. Surely, after all that has happened, Fate will some day be kind and let me try to make you absolutely happy so that neither of us will have to sit alone with our thoughts. I am doing it tonight – as far as a crowded officers' quarters will allow! – and I have only got one thought which runs through and through my head. My darling, I can never be worthy of you, but it is something to have a very definite thing to try to
....

353 This is approximately £32,500 per annum in 2010 based on Bank of England data for retail price inflation.

live up to – the man you would like me to be. All today I have been finding the few people here who jarred a little bit when my nerves were on edge are quite bearable people really, and when my instructor told me privately that he had specially recommended me I nearly embraced him on the spot! I am so awfully glad I told you so much about myself: it isn't easy to talk about things which are past and really over, but it would be hateful to think there was anything which you might hear from other people and not quite understand, because I hadn't told you myself. Anyway, there is only you whom I love like this in the whole of my world and the whole of me is absolutely yours to do what you like with. I feel so relieved that my future seems to have gone beyond me to control because you have got to do it now! I am going to stop here and go on tomorrow. You mustn't expect me always to begin another letter an hour or two after the last, but this is rather special, isn't it?

Goodnight, my precious darling!

Wednesday

This will be rather a scramble to catch the post. We have been out all day in the sun and on the heather. It was absolutely lovely. If only you could have been there too it would have been simply heaven. I found your dear letter when I got back. Thank you awfully, darling, for writing when you had so little time and your head must have been simply whirling.

I believe the best train leaves London 6.05 and arrives 6.45. Is this right? It will be only three days more by the time you get this. All my love, darling …

Marjorie to Charles   Bennetts End
                                                         4th September, 1917

Isn't it a perfectly lovely day again? I am sitting out of doors in the sun and just loving it; everything seems all happy and merry again and I have your letter by me telling me that it's you and your love that have filled the world with sunshine again. No, of course I will never regret it for a moment: on the contrary, I shall always remember how you came into my life when I was tired and lonely and made it all splendidly worthwhile. You won't grow too many inches taller, will you? Or I will never be able to reach you! I love to hear of you so happy and I am just living for next Saturday when I will see you again.

I do hope your sisters will approve. Do collect a bigger photo of you if you can; in fact I want all you can find, and Uncle Basil was asking for one too. I have written to my brother and Toby's mother, and my mother will see Esmé today and tell her. Father is too funny: he has just asked me quite concernedly if you are good-tempered! I said I would ask you! I think I am faintly amused over the way we have taken our relatives into our confidence. It's so absolutely correct and as it should be done. Father and Mother are both quite nervous at the thought of meeting you. However, Father says nothing matters to him as it's me that has to marry you.

I was surprised to get your letter so soon as this morning and ever so pleased you wrote at once. I hope your work won't suffer through it all. Write again soon. Like the little boys, I might say "and the rest of the page will do for kisses" but you must imagine them.

Goodbye, darling …

Charles to Marjorie   Aldershot
                                                          4th September, 1917
                                                                 10.00 p.m.

It was a very hurried finish that I put to my last letter this afternoon, and
tomorrow there will be hardly a moment to write at all. We shall be out from 9.00
till 3.00 and then I am rushing down to Winchester to have dinner with Mabel
and Agnes and possibly my father, if he can get back then instead of on Thursday.
I had a wire from Winchester tonight asking if I could possibly bring you with
me tomorrow, but as I have got to get back here tomorrow night I don't see how
that could have been managed. I shall have to rely on your photographs and the
eloquence of my language to paint them a proper picture! Oh, my darling, I love you
more every day and it is awfully hard to think of anything else at all. There ought
to be a fresh vocabulary invented for people like us, because the ordinary language
seems so poverty-stricken. I'm afraid my letter to your father may have sounded
cold and business-like: did it? It is hard to be natural in writing to someone you
have never seen. I have been looking up the Sunday trains from Boxmoor. They
don't look very promising and I expect I shall have to spend Sunday night in London
and come here by the early train on Monday morning, unless it would be possible
to catch a later train by going to St Albans. But I don't mind a bit as long as I get
every possible minute with you, and I shall want you to meet me the following
Wednesday, the 12th, in London, if you can, and we will do some shopping together.
... I wonder what your own people's ideas are as to when we should be married.
Personally I think it is entirely a matter for you and them to decide. It is those who
must be left at home who have to think of all possibilities and I will be guided by
what you and they decide. I do hope your photograph will be good and worthy of
you. I will see if there are any large ones of me left at Winchester and if not I will
order some more. ...

I don't at all like your being anywhere east of London during the air raids. It will
be especially horrid if you have to go to and fro on the Great Eastern: it is such a
target for them. Take care of yourself, my darling.

                                                                Aldershot
                                                        6th September, 1917
                                                               5.00 p.m.

... It is such absolute heaven to have you for my own. I heard from your father
by the same post just to say that he gave his approval. I do think it's so good of
everyone to take me on trust. ...

My father is frantically excited and longing to see you, but true to his own
traditions he waives all claims upon me or my time where you are concerned. He
absolutely lived up to that in his own married life: in fact he never saw his own
people again after he married, as they were all in South Africa. So you need never
fear that he will grudge me to you for a moment and I know you will love him for it.
My sisters simply pelted me with questions and Helen, who was not at home, put in
her share over the telephone. I know they are all prepared to love you at sight and
I don't suppose they will be able to help themselves. ... Only just over 48 hours and
I shall be with you again. I long for you every hour of the twenty-four, my darling.
If only we need never be parted again. But a man's proper place is at the Front. I

travelled with an attractive Belgian officer yesterday, whose home is in Antwerp, and I thought to myself more than ever that it is worth it all a million times to keep you safe and free from even the sight of a German. If anyone offered me so-called a "safe" job now for a bit, I think that after nearly two years at the Front I would take it for your sake, but I will never seek one for myself and I know you will say I am right. However, we won't let the thought of parting cloud our happiness, will we? I do wonder what you and your people are thinking about our getting married. ...

Charles to his father   Bennetts End
9th September, 1917

We have settled to be married on Tuesday week, September 18th, in London. Can you suggest where and start making some arrangements for us? Would any friend of yours lend a church? I shall have to see about the licence, but I don't imagine there is any difficulty for soldiers in these days. Of course, you will marry us: I shall get a subaltern ... as Best Man. Please give me all help and advice as you can. ... We are having an awfully happy time. I am getting on well with my future in-laws! We think of going to Devonshire for a week's honeymoon, leaving time for a flying visit to each home before I go out again. We are both coming to you next Saturday for two nights, and then I propose that you and I and Mr Secretan all meet at Essex St on the Monday (17th) to see that everything is in order.

Charles to Marjorie   Aldershot
10th September, 1917

It was a very hurried little note I dashed off to you this morning, simply because I wanted you so awfully badly. I found a letter from Esmé waiting for me, which was most awfully sweet of her: it is going to be answered tonight and I am also going to write to Humphrey. I had such an awfully nice letter from my cousin Camilla Friend (whose husband is our Colonel) that I am sending it to you with this. I do hope I shall soon be able to let you know what church we are going to be married at. Oh my darling! I am simply counting the hours till you belong to me and nobody else. It seems so poor a language when I can only go on saying, "I love you", but as long as you know that I am yours, body and soul, it is all right. I told your mother I had been playing a little tennis to soothe my nerves! It was rather delightful to play again. I have written to "The Tors Hotel" [Lynmouth, North Devon]... I do wish I was a rich man and could simply shower things upon you. Anyway I am going to give you what I like this once, because we shall be engaged for such a short time that I shall have hardly any opportunity of giving you anything before we are married! Will Esmé get up on the Monday? ... If she is a bridesmaid, you must help me choose her a present. I have been looking up dressing-cases in catalogues and I think I can get you a crocodile one: you'd love that, wouldn't you? ...

* * * * *

Meanwhile, Guy Dodgson and the 1/1st Hertfordshires were safely behind the lines.

Guy to his mother: [Chippewa Camp, Reninghelst]
9th September, 1917

... I have just had a letter from Marjorie telling me she is engaged to a Major Fair and I have written back at once to congratulate and say how glad I am. I expect you think the same as I do: that it is quite the best thing that could happen from her point of view but personally it is quite incomprehensible to me, though I don't think I know very much about these things!

We came down from the trenches last night and had to march about eight miles to get here[354] and I felt a little bit on the tired side when we got in. However, it was worth it as this is a priceless camp with really excellent accommodation – separate cubicles and beds; quite like a camp in England. ... It was extraordinarily nice to get a bath this morning and clean clothes. ...

News of the impending wedding had obviously reached Humphrey Secretan too:

Humphrey to his mother   [Zuytpeene, near Cassell]
14th September, 1917

... Am so excited about Marje's wedding. I can remember exactly what he [Charles] was like.[355] ... I wouldn't write to the GRU[356] any more. They will let you know in due course but that won't be for a good while yet. Don't send any more fruit as we can get plenty here. Melons and pears are in season now. ...

Tomorrow we shall only be about six miles from the place I was first billeted at in France and visited again last October. Just got the letter from Father. Today we have been into the town and had a look round. There are quite a lot of those WACs about doing jobs men used to do. I passed what I thought was a POW camp and found it was one of theirs. Lots of barbed wire about!

* * * * *

Charles to Marjorie   Aldershot
14th September, 1917
5.30 p.m.

... I simply hate to think of you wearing yourself out over the beastly licence. I do hope to goodness it is all going to be all right now and that you are safely resting at Salisbury. ... It is an awful nuisance that we are being inspected by [Field Marshal] French[357] tomorrow morning and there is just the chance I might miss the train. ...

....

354   The 1/1st Hertfordshires had been in support trenches in Brigade Reserve in the area of Larchwood Tunnels and were relieved on 8th Sept. by the 14th Hampshires, moving into Divisional Reserve at Chippewa Camp. (TNA WO 95/2590)

355   Charles and Humphrey had been contemporaries at Marlborough College. Although Charles was the elder by three years, they had sung together in the school choir.

356   The Graves Registration Units eventually developed into the Imperial War Graves Commission and thence into today's Commonwealth War Graves Commission.

357   Field Marshal Viscount French of Ypres became Commander-in-Chief of British Home Forces in Dec. 1915 after he had been replaced as C-in-C on the Western Front by Sir Douglas Haig.

I never heard from the original best-man and have got one, Maj Woolley, of our Division who is here. He is tall, fair and very charming.[358]

Charles graduated from his course at the Senior Officers' School at Aldershot on 15th September. His confidential report by the syndicate commander survives and says:

> "A determined, cheerful and energetic officer, keen on his work and anxious to improve his knowledge. His appearance is smart and soldierly. He is a man of the world. His powers of imparting knowledge are good. His military knowledge is fair. He knows his drill and handles his troops well on parade and in the field. He has shown great keenness in his work during this course and has made good progress.
>
> He is in my opinion fit to command a battalion in the field at once. He is a good type of officer, who knows both how to command and look after men."

The School Commandant, Brig Gen R. J. Kentish signed off with the comment "an excellent officer. Fit to command a battalion at once."

Written by Charles on their wedding day –
London
18th September, 1917
9.00 a.m.

I hope you slept decently and are not awfully tired. I woke at 5.00 a.m. – otherwise all's right with the world and it is going to clear up and be fine. My precious little queen of my heart, I love you with every atom of my soul and I'll simply slave to try and make you happy always. I am sending round Woolley's present to go with the other things. There are millions of things to tell you, but they must wait till I get you away. Only a few more hours.

All my love, darling, for always

Marjorie and Charles were married that afternoon at St Michael's, Chester Square, by his father Robert assisted by the Reverend Hulbert Wathen, Charles's brother-in-law. Charles's eleven year old niece Jane, daughter of his dead half-brother Ted Fisher, recalled that the reception was held in a nearby hotel but a combination of wartime shortages and the lack of time meant no wine or champagne was served. A photograph of the happy couple appeared on the front page of the "Daily Mirror" the following day.

Having taken two days to reach Lynmouth, travelling by train and spending their first night at a hotel in Clifton, near Bristol, the honeymooners spent a week in North Devon, where they explored the coastline and went walking on Exmoor.

....

358 Maj E. J. Woolley MC was serving with the 1/22nd Londons which were in 142nd Infantry Brigade. His MC had been awarded on 14th Jan. 1916.

Charles Fair and Marjorie Secretan's wedding photo. This picture was printed on the front page of the Daily Mirror, 19th Sept. 1917.

Charles to his father

The Tors Hotel
Lynmouth
Lynton, N. Devon
20th September, 1917

Just a line to say that, except for a few minor anxieties as to cabs, everything has been plain sailing and we are thoroughly enjoying ourselves. The place is looking very lovely and quite comes up to our expectations. We were much amused at our picture in the press.

Charles and Marjorie left Devon by train on the 27th and called on his father, Robert, at Winchester. On the 28th they met Marjorie's mother in London before travelling on by train to Folkestone.

While the happy couple had been in North Devon, Humphrey Secretan had written three letters to his mother. His Battalion, the 2nd Queens Royal West Surreys, were in the Ypres Salient with 7th Division.

Humphrey to his mother

[Boisdinghem]
21st September, 1917

Thanks very much for your letter of the 17th with all the news [about Marjorie's wedding]. ... I should say Puss [Esmé] would have looked very nice in her uniform. We are still in the same rest billets and are having schemes every day. Last night we had a rugger match against the RFC. They won rather easily as our side had had no practice at all. This morning we have been up very early and had a practice attack in the dark and so have got all today off with nothing to do. ...

[Boisdinghem]
25th September, 1917

... We are nowhere near the fighting. Yes, it is really a good advance as the objectives have been taken and held this time.[359] In fact the Staff have arranged things very well. If only Reg had been in this one instead. His crowd were there but I do not know if the Herts actually fought or were only in reserve. I hope Reg used

....

359 This is a reference to General Plumer's successful operation, the Battle of the Menin Road, which opened on 20th Sept. This was a carefully prepared 'bite and hold' attack (where the objective was limited to what could be captured and successfully held). Such attacks did not outrun the supporting artillery and the objectives were typically taken and held according to plan.

to wear his identity disc in the proper place. We may have something now as we are slightly beyond where he fell.

I am so glad the wedding went off well. I got the 'Daily Mirror' – thanks. I had been told about it but had not seen it. ...

We expect to leave here shortly. ... The weather is lovely and we are out doing field days which are quite interesting. Lots of Generals about and the C in C [Field Marshal Haig] turned up one day.[360] I got an umpiring job one day which is rather fun, and today we were the skeleton enemy. It is quite a science now attacking a place, and success entirely depends on the amount of time spent explaining details to all ranks.[361] If everyone knows exactly what to do the show will always be successful. There is quite a shortage of water now in our village which is rather a nuisance. We haven't had a bath for quite a long time. ...

[Boisdinghem]
27th September, 1917

... The wedding seems to have gone off well. What is Marje going to do when Chas goes back? Will she have a home or is she going on with school work? There is no reason for her to chuck it all up, I suppose.

We are still in the same billets doing training. We are having lovely weather, and long field days which are quite interesting. Can you send me out a spring for a Decca gramophone? Mine has just broken and we have bought one from a French shop but it is not nearly strong enough and we can't play the records quick enough. I don't expect our rest can last much longer now; we have been out for such a long time. ... I expect the garden is lovely now with all the autumn flowers out. My leave is getting nearer again but if all goes well I can hardly get it before Nov. or Dec. and lots of things can happen by then.

All the men are having a bath this morning. We have borrow[ed] a copper and so it is not so bad but rather slow work. Luckily it is very hot and so the bath being out of doors does not matter.

We are playing a game of rugger this evening against the RFC who beat us the other day. I expect we shall get a bad beating again. The ground is a bit too hard for my liking.[362]

....

360 Haig's diary for 24th Sept. records: "Soon after 10 am I motored to Etrehem ... and I watched the 7th Division carrying out an attack practice on the ground between Zudausques and the high ground west of Wisques. The latter represented the Passchendale ridge. I had a long talk with Maj Gen Shoubridge [GOC] ... and the brigadiers commanding the attacking brigades (Green 20th Bde and Pelly, 91st). The latter is quite young, a Brevet Major really. The enemy's defensive system was a copy made from photos of actual ground near the Passchendaele ridge. A considerable number of 'pill boxes' were represented by square enclosures formed of canvas walls and garrisoned by three or four men with blank ammunition. All this arrangement gave our troops good practice. I spoke to many platoon and section leaders, and was much struck by their intelligence and knowledge. I thought the system of training good. All ranks seemed to be very keen and greatly interested in the scheme. There is no doubt but that the training has a direct effect on reducing the number of casualties suffered in a battle." (TNA WO 256/22)

361 By this stage of the war training for a major offensive often included showing the men map models of the ground over which they would attack. Once the plan had been explained, officers and men would rehearse the attack by walking over a piece of ground which had been carefully prepared to resemble the objective, e.g. by using tape to mark the outlines of woods and other features.

362 September had been an exceptionally dry month in the Ypres Salient. An inch of rain had fallen on 6th Sept. but the remainder of the month saw negligible rainfall.

I have just heard that there has been another attack last night, apparently a success.[363] We are not there, so don't worry. ...

Much love to you and Father

＊ ＊ ＊ ＊ ＊

Meanwhile, Guy was not far away with the 1/1st Hertfordshires.

Guy to his mother [Ascot Camp, Westoutre]
15th September, 1917

As usual we have been moving about rather a lot – two days in one camp – and now we are under canvas in quite a good place. There is grass in the field and the tents don't let in the rain. The weather has been glorious, so much so that yesterday some enthusiastic spirits arranged football between the officers and sergeants, in which I was inveigled into playing. I nearly burst! The sun beat down and I was playing outside, which means a lot of running about. I also had a large, fat sergeant opposed to me! However, we got through all right and we managed to defeat the sergeants. ...

[Ascot Camp, Westoutre]
17th September, 1917

... We are still in our moderately comfortable camp with the green grass, but tomorrow is the last day as we are moving forward again. I shall be rather sorry to leave this place as we had quite a good time here. I found a fellow I knew the other day who has a motor for his particular job, and he took three of us over for dinner to a neighbouring town. The dinner was rather funny. We asked for champagne but were politely told that champagne was *defendu*! Heaven only knows why. One could have any amount of anything else. Well, we then bespoke some red wine but when it arrived it was so icy cold that it was quite undrinkable. So we asked for it to be warmed. We waited about ten minutes and then it came back absolutely hot!! I think the good people had put the bottle in boiling water. However, we quite enjoyed it and anyhow it is a change to eat off a china plate instead of everlasting tin. ...

[Corunna Camp, near Westoutre]
28th September, 1917

At last I can write to you, but really the last eight days it has been quite impossible. We have had rather a brute of a time and everybody is exhausted. At the beginning of the show one of the Brigades in our Division attacked and our Brigade was in support.[364] Luckily we were not wanted. But the next night we had to go up and take over the line,[365] which was rather horrible: no proper trenches and nobody knew anything about the country. I can't attempt to describe it – absolutely nothing

....

363 The Battle of Polygon Wood opened on 26th Sept. and was another successful 'bite and hold' attack.

364 The 39th Division took part in the opening of the Battle of the Menin Road on 20th Sept. in which 117th Infantry Brigade attacked at dawn with 118th Infantry Brigade in reserve. (Edmonds, *Military Operations France and Flanders 1917, Vol. 2*, pp. 261-2)

365 The War Diary of the 1/1st Hertfordshires records that on 21st Sept. the "Battalion relieved 16th & 17th Bns Notts & Derby Regt in right sub section Bulgar Wood sector as soon as it was dark, taking over the line captured and consolidated on the 20th." (TNA WO 95/2590)

left except a few tree stumps; not a sign of a road or a house and not a square yard that hadn't been shelled. The most horrible part of the whole thing was trying to find your way about this country – no tracks left and no time to have had any made. Everybody lost their way in a most terrifying manner – myself included. However, it's over now and when I see you I will tell you all about it. George [Fulton]'s Division [the 19th] attacked on our right and I believe did very well.

[Corunna Camp]
29th September, 1917

... I know you will be glad to hear that I have got a Company of my own, anyhow for the present, though I can't say for how long I shall remain. I am no longer with Leslie. The officers who were in the Company were all slightly wounded while we were up the line and I now have two fellows with me who have only just joined.[366] I also was slightly wounded! Don't be alarmed: it was only the smallest piece of shell which had the impudence to strike me on the left wrist, just making a small hole. I didn't even leave the line but just had it bound up and now it's practically healed. I only tell you this in case my name appears in the casualty list and you might have rather a shock.

We are now having a very peaceful time and everybody really needs it. You can't think what a relief it is to get back to ordinary country again. One gets so tired of seeing nothing but destruction and desolation all round.

I had an interesting letter from Philip the other day and I will write to him soon. Will you tell him that he is quite right about my position? Z[illebeke] is the place but I don't think he would recognize the country now. ... George's Division is in the same Corps as us. I am hoping to be able to see him sometime.

* * * * *

By the 29th September Charles was on his way back to the Western Front, Marjorie having seen him off at Folkestone, according to her diary. His Battalion, the 1/19th Londons, had left the Ypres salient on the 22nd September and by the 25th was at Roclincourt, just north of Arras. It remained in this area for four weeks, moving forward to hold the front line in the Oppy Wood sector east of Arras. Charles rejoined the Battalion on 30th September and thereafter wrote to Marjorie every day, and sometimes twice a day. She wrote to him very regularly, though fewer of her letters have survived the hazards of the Western Front. Marjorie returned to her uncle's house at Stanstead Abbotts and continued with her part-time teaching job in London.

Charles to Marjorie   [Boulogne]
29th September, 1917
6.15 p.m. (Summer Time)

I hope you have had as easy and quiet a journey as I have so far. I keep looking at my watch and wondering where you have got to. You did understand, didn't you, that I simply couldn't trust myself to talk that last two hours we were together. Everything that I wanted to say at the finish simply stuck and had to be left unsaid. You were so brave and splendid and I am so awfully proud of you. I've never hated anything like leaving you. It was far worse for you, in a way, because I began to
....

366 2/Lt Claude Stewart Ringer and 2/Lt Frederick Ernest Allen joined the Battalion on 29th Sept.

meet friends at once. Woolley was there on the boat and we are sharing a room here tonight and not going on till 11.00 tomorrow morning. ... It is a perfectly lovely evening. ... Nothing can ever spoil the memory of our wonderful days together, my darling, and I already begin to feel what a wonderful help it is to me to have you and know that I can write to you about anything and everything. Our love is so perfectly wonderful and seems so part of the Infinite, that sometimes it makes me simply gasp when I think about it. ... I hope to get this off tonight. ... I am simply longing for my letters from my wife. I looked back at you once as you went alone up the street: I daren't do more. Take care of yourself, my own precious darling.

All my love always ...

> In the train
> 30th September, 1917
> 12.15 p.m.

... It is just about twenty-four hours since I left you and Heaven only knows how long it seems. I had quite a pleasant evening really with Woolley and two others, helped considerably by a very good dinner with "something with a bubble in it"! It is a perfectly lovely day again and the sea is absolutely blue, though I'm afraid we have left it now for good. Our carriage is a very dirty second class with seven of us in it and we don't expect to reach anywhere till night. Our destination is rather vague but a vast way from where I left the Regiment. ... My arms simply ache for you. But it is making such a difference to know that we love each other so tremendously and that life can never be really empty again. I can never repay you for it all, Marjorie darling, but I will try desperately hard to be the man you think me, especially out here where so much is against the grain even apart from the horrors of it all.

> [Roclincourt]
> Later, in bed, 11.30 p.m.

Here I am, back with the Battalion, being chaffed by everyone and feeling very faintly merry and bright. ... We don't go into the trenches for a day or two and I am in a tent – d----d cold!! ... Goodnight, my darling.

<u>Monday:</u> Another heavenly day. ... The Brigadier [McDouall] came over himself to renew his congratulations, which was awfully kind, and the Sergeant Major made a little speech! ... It is so wonderful to have you to live and fight for. They [the Battalion] all seem very well and have had marvellously few casualties considering what they have been through since I left.[367] We shall be in the trenches by the time you get this. There seems some doubt as to whether I shall remain a Major for the present! But I hope for the best.

----

367 Although the 47th Division had spent the summer of 1917 in the Ypres Salient, and had spent time holding the front line, it did not actually go 'over the top' during the Third Ypres Campaign. During July, Aug. and Sept. 1917 the 1/19th Londons suffered total fatalities of five officers and 47 other ranks. (Calculated from *Soldiers/ Officers Died in the Great War* and CWGC records.) A total of 124 men were evacuated wounded in those three months. (TNA WO 95/2707 47th Divison A&Q War Diary)

Marjorie to Charles

Hill House
1st October, 1917,
6.30 p.m

We had another air-raid last night.[368] There is a pretty considerable noise round here on these occasions as there are a good many guns within a small radius but, beyond small pieces of shrapnel falling, no damage is likely to occur. The star shells are a wonderful sight. The barrage round London is quite terrific, I believe, and is the cause of many broken windows, etc. My small boys [at the school in London where Marjorie taught] greeted me with long tales of how they spend a couple of hours in the cellar every evening. I have only four of them as the other three have retreated to the country while London is so lively! The bigger boys were quick to greet me with, "Good morning, Mrs Fair!" ... I only had one-and-a-half hours there; just time to discover they had forgotten all I taught them last term.

I was greeted most heartily by a village friend who had been shown "The Mirror" which occasioned vast excitement down the street which was once my district. Mr Turner came to call yesterday. He said none of the masters [at Haileybury College] knew about our marriage until they returned, so of course they had not written. They are going to combine together to give you a present and he asked me if I approved of a rose bowl. I did, very much. It would look awfully nice on our dining table. It is rather amusing meeting other people and being congratulated, but I do wish you were here too: it falls a bit flat alone. ...

Charles to Marjorie

[Beverley Camp, near Roclincourt]
2nd October, 1917

In two days at most your letters should begin to arrive and they will make such a difference. ... Letters from England seem to be taking four days now instead of three. It is still gloriously fine and hot in the daytime, though pretty cold at night as we have not yet got blankets and are sleeping in tents. I am managing to keep warm by wearing all my underclothing under my pyjamas! ... I never mind lying awake: I just go over in my mind all the lovely times we have had together and make plans for the future, if Fate is kind. I do hope the air raids aren't troubling you. They don't seem to be doing much harm. We shall be in the trenches by the time you get this. The only thing that really matters which I seem to have left behind is my air-pillow.

... Mind you let me know how much the season ticket and the furs cost. You must be photographed by someone in them so that I can see how they look. I do want to hear about your reception at Haileybury as "Mrs Fair". ... My servant has never turned up: I can't think what he can be doing. I have never seen him since I left the hotel to go to St Michael's, Chester Square! That is just a fortnight ago. ... Take care of yourself, my darling.

[Beverley Camp]
3rd October, 1917

It is very lonely work waiting for your letters to begin to arrive. ... Yesterday we were inspected by the Major General [Gorringe] and made a really good show. He seemed pleased to see me back. We are just thinking about going to trenches again – never a pleasant thought, but I believe these are dry, which is something! ... There

....

368 Gotha bombers raided London on the night of 30th Sept./1st Oct., killing 14 and injuring 38 people.

293

isn't an hour when I don't thank God for you and the difference you have made in my life.

My servant has turned up at last. He got held up for a night in England (he says)! They don't seem to know what to do with me at present and I shall very likely have to mark time as a Captain for a bit: it will be rather a bore, if it comes to that, but if I hadn't gone home I shouldn't have you, so what does anything else matter?

[Oppy]
In a deep dugout
4th October, 1917
6.30 a.m.

Post seems dreadfully slow and I am still waiting for my first letter from you. It is pretty sure to arrive today, but it does seem ages since I left you. We are right back in the trenches now. ... Yesterday evening my first prowl took me within about twenty-five yards of the Boche. He is pretty quiet at present but, as we always stir up strife wherever we go, I don't suppose the period of peace will last very long. ... Your photograph sits very proudly on the shelf in our sleeping room, flanked by my shaving soap and the bottle of Anzora Cream! It is so splendid to be able to write to you every day and know that you belong entirely to me. ... We shall probably be here several days as far as I can make out. We have plenty of men, and they seem a pretty good lot, though a fair number are new to the job. ... I am rather worried by your being so much within reach of the air raids. One Private in the Battalion had his wife and child killed on 30th Sept. Their pictures were in the front page of "The Mirror" on 1st October.[369] We applied for special leave for him and he goes home today to arrange for his other children. I shall see red if I hear there have been bombs at all near my little wife. ... Your flask has already done noble work and is at present full of rum! ... What a contrast this room is to our room at "The Tors". I can hardly believe I am the same person. But I am, and I bump my head more than ever on the dugout roof because my pride has made me so much taller! ... Here comes my morning cup of tea (plenty of sugar), so I must stop. I hope this will catch the post that goes out tonight so that you won't have a blank day, as generally happens when we first go back into the trenches. Take care of yourself, my own Marjorie.

[Oppy]
5th October, 1917
10.30 a.m.

Your first letter of Sept. 30th came yesterday, and I am so happy at getting it. I am awfully glad you got back in decent time from Folkestone, but it is horrid that

....

369   The front page of The Daily Mirror for Monday 1st Oct. 1917 has the headlines "11 Killed and 82 Hurt in All Districts Raided" and "Brave Boy Hero's Magnificent Air Raid Exploit" above pictures of a Mrs Hall, her baby and two sons. Text below the pictures recounts that: "A deed of splendid heroism was performed by a boy during the progress of Saturday's air raid. Mrs Hall and her six children were seated in the lower back room, when a bomb fell in the garden, killing Mrs Hall and one of her sons. Ernest, the eldest boy, with great presence of mind, rescued the baby uninjured from [the arms of] its dead mother. No other children were injured, and the front of the house was not damaged. The husband is at present serving in France." During the Gotha raid of that night a bomb fell on 34, Mortimer Road, Hackney, killing Mabel E. Hall aged 32 and Percy H. Hall aged 6. Her husband was 615853 Private Edward Ernest Montague Hall of the 1/19th Londons and they had married in 1907. He was born in Hoxton and originally enlisted in Hackney as 210395 in 25th Battalion, The Rifle Brigade. Tragically, Private Hall was killed in action on 8th Aug. 1918 and is buried in Heath Cemetery, Harbonnieres (grave VIII. G.16).

the raids should come right over you like that. My darling, of course I didn't think you were taking our parting casually. I was just awfully proud of my wife. ... This morning I got up at 5.00 a.m. to go round the line and got back about 8.00. It had rained during the night and was very slippery. It is rather tiring going round before breakfast, but I had some tea before I started and more with a Subaltern halfway round, which I am sure would please your mother! ... Your first letter as Mrs Fair certainly received full marks from me the moment it came! ... All round the trenches and everywhere I keep thinking of you, Marjorie darling. ... Take care of yourself. ...

[Oppy]
5th/6th October, 1917
Midnight

Your second letter arrived this afternoon. It is simply glorious to get them and have them to look forward to every day. Nobody can realise what a difference you make to every minute of my life. ... I think the Haileybury present to me is perfectly splendid and I am so glad you have settled ... what you would like it spent on. ... I have just come in from a night tour round the trenches. It was all very quiet except for a few rifle grenades. The moon looked down on us and the horror of it all always seems very incredible on a quiet moonlight night. ...

9.00 a.m. Quite a good night, except once when I woke myself up saying, "Oh! My darling!" when I heard someone else move and thought it was you! It was rather a bitter moment. I am awfully fit really. There is no prospect of getting our clothes off in less than eight days from when we came here and possibly not for a fortnight. The next time I come home I shall have to be well disinfected somewhere on the way. ... At present things are so quiet here that it seems uncanny, and I can't believe it will last long. I do hope Humphrey is all right: have you heard from him lately? Everyone is very enthusiastic and optimistic about the fighting in the north.[370]

[Oppy]
6th/7th October, 1917
Sometime after midnight

I have just come back from another nocturnal ramble. It has been a pretty wet day and the trenches are beginning to resume their normal appearance. I'm afraid it is the beginning of winter. I nearly had a fight with one of our own men, as each of us thought that the other was a Hun. ... There was no letter from you today, but the CO didn't have one from Camilla either so I expect the raids upset the post a bit. There is only about a quarter of an inch of candle left, so I think I had better go to bed. It only means taking off my boots and wrapping myself in a horse blanket, but even that is better done with some light! ...

Sunday, 10.30 a.m. ... Your *eau de cologne* is proving a great success. ... We expect to be in the trenches for about another fortnight, so we shall be pretty dirty by the time we come out. It has turned very much colder and I shall soon have to start winter clothing altogether. Have you done anything yet about Humphrey's gramophone? ... I haven't heard from anyone else at Haileybury yet. I expect they

....

370   The Battle of Broodseinde opened on 4th Oct. It was another successful 'bite and hold' attack which reached the crest of the ridge east of Ypres. However, it did not attempt to each the village of Passchendaele on the summit of the ridge, and that village would not be secured until 6th Nov.

are still stunned by the shock. I believe that Lemprière is somewhere in this part of the world and I shall try to find him. We have a gunner officer with us now who is in Philip Dodgson's battery, but he doesn't know him personally.

Charles to his father [Oppy]
7th October, 1917

I haven't had a line from you yet since I left England: in fact a half sheet from Agnes is all I have had from Winchester. ... Could you send me out the fleece lining which I wear under my Aquascutum in the winter? ... Marjorie seems to be settling down to her work all right. I have had two letters and a parcel from her. She writes every day, but the post takes much longer now, either because we are in a different part of the line, or because the air raids have worried the postal authorities. Stokes is still on leave. I don't know what is to happen to me when he returns, as his seniority and his service entitle him to be the 2nd in command as he has been during my absence. Baker is also on leave, which does not seem very difficult to obtain now. ... Since I came back we have been awarded one DCM, three Bars to MM and four MMs, all for deeds done during my absence.[371] Everyone in the Division seems to have seen our photograph in "The Mirror". It was the first, and only, intimation to most people. The Haileybury masters have presented me with a cheque for about £20 ... the subscriptions were strictly limited owing to the war, but even so it seems a noble present after only two years' work there. ... We are simply miles from any inhabited town. That is the worst of living in re-conquered territory.

Charles to Marjorie [Oppy]
8th October, 1917
10.15 a.m.

Your two letters of the 2nd and 3rd arrived together yesterday, which was a great luxury and very much enjoyed. Evidently it saves a day if they are posted in London. ... The powers that be are much the same as usual. We have got at least nine jobs on hand, all of which are marked "priority", which means they're supposed to be tackled first! Yet they don't provide us with the necessary material. My bed consists of two layers of rabbit wire covered with a layer of sand bags. It is really quite comfortable. I have a horse blanket and a mackintosh to keep me warm at present. The Adjutant sleeps just above me, like a cabin, and on the other side of the dugout are two other subalterns. Your photos look proudly on this weird scene lit by two flickering candles. The CO says that the photo was very obviously taken after we were engaged because you look so bucked with life! ... Have you been able to swank in your First Class carriage in front of any of your friends? I hate to think how you've been bothered by the raids. ... We have several more days in trenches yet.

....

371   The War Diary records that a DCM was awarded to 610037 CSM G. Bayley on 6th Oct. Maj Gen Gorringe presented the Bars to MM (613604 Cpl W. Kaill, 610576 Pte A. Crow, 613628 Pte A. Jennings) and MMs (611127 L/Cpl F. Hibbart, 612815 Pte W. Pace, 610511 CSM G. Barney, 612180 Pte W. Storey) when he inspected the 1/19th Londons on 2nd Oct. (TNA WO 95/2738)

[Oppy
9th October, 1917

... I hope you are really hearing from me regularly. We received orders yesterday that the Colonel is to go to England for six months' work with the Training Reserve Battalions. I am very glad for his sake and Camilla's, but a little bit envious! I am not likely to get command of the Battalion, as the man who did my job while I was away – Stokes – is really senior to me, and there are also others in the Division with some claim. I don't really mind: my time will come and, at any rate, I am certain now to remain at least a Major. I should chiefly like command because I have been so long with the Battalion out here and I know you would be so pleased. Also it would give us more £ – s – d! But ex-Private Fair has no false pride about playing second string to anyone, provided he really is senior and probably a better man. After all, there aren't many Colonels of thirty-two! ... The men are keeping wonderfully fit and cheery at present, but we are all getting in sore need of a bath: I have only had two – in my rubber bath – since I left you and the last of these was a week ago. Your *eau de cologne* is a great help to dugout life! ...

I have written a good many thank-you letters ... . We are looking forward to the first consignment from Fortnum and Mason. ... The Colonel has taken down your address and if he and Camilla are in Town he says he will ask you to meet them for lunch or something. ... I shall be single-handed until Stokes comes back from leave, so perhaps my letters will shorten. That won't mean I think of you a bit less. Take care of yourself, my darling.

* * * * *

Meanwhile, further north, Guy Dodgson was in the Ypres Salient, with the 1/1st Hertfordshires.

Guy to his mother   [Swan Château, Ypres]
9th October, 1917

We have now once more moved rather nearer "the war" than we were, though not in any fighting capacity. We are here for the purpose of supplying sundry working parties to help with the endless work that is inevitable after an advance.[372] It isn't really a bad job and of course infinitely preferable to the line but, as it happens, we aren't very comfortably quartered. I am living in what was once a gunners' dugout but the men have only got bivouac sheets and, as it has suddenly turned horribly cold, it isn't very cheery for them. We moved yesterday and they actually gave us a train to bring us here. Unfortunately, just as we were marching here from the train, it started to pour with rain, which made getting in rather an uncomfortable business. However, we've been so blessed so far as regards the weather that one really ought not to complain. I am getting on quite moderately well with my Company, though it's rather a strain at times: there seems so much to think about. ...

....

372 The War Diary records that on 4th Oct. 1917 the Battalion "Moved up to camp near Swan Château 2,000 yards south west of Ypres under orders of 1st ANZAC Corps in order to work on railways under the 5th Canadian Railway Troops. From 5th to 13th [Oct.] 500 men were employed daily on the railway lines between Westhoek and Zonnebeke; from 14th to 17th [Oct.] only half the battalion was employed daily." (TNA WO 95/2590)

I am so sorry my name ever appeared in the papers. It is too stupid and I do hope you haven't been very worried, though I am afraid you may have been. ... The weather is still rather vile and it still persists in raining, which makes things rather unpleasant. However, everybody is very cheerful, including myself, and after all, I think if you look at things in the right light, there is a certain amount of enjoyment to be got out of this life.

PS I think I might tell you that I am about a thousand yards from the most famous town of the war [Ypres].

[Swan Château, Ypres]
10th October, 1917

... I am off today on a new job. I am going to live with Brigade Headquarters. I don't quite know for how long; probably about a fortnight, as it is quite a temporary job. I don't think there is any harm in telling you what I'm going to do. I am going to be Brigade Intelligence Officer!! What I have to do I haven't the remotest idea and I am hoping it won't be anything that requires too much intelligence. Anyhow, I shall have a nice comfortable time. ... I am not particularly keen on going, and on the whole would rather stay with the Regiment. ...

On 11th October the war diary of the Brigade records "Capt G. Dodgson [joined] for duty as Bde Intelligence Officer."[373] Brigade HQ at that time was just inside the French border, about twelve miles southwest of Ypres.

118th Infantry Brigade HQ
[Berthen, France]
11th October, 1917

... I got down here last night and have got more or less settled in, though it is going to take me some little time to get accustomed to the atmosphere of Red Tabs! They are really very nice and the General [Bellingham] is one of the best and moderately young. He was a splendid sight last night fox-trotting with the Staff Captain to the strains of a somewhat wheezy gramophone! Of course everybody tells me I am extraordinarily lucky to have got this job, even if only for a short time. I have got a cubicle to myself instead of sleeping five in a somewhat smelly dugout, and the meals are very good. Last but not least, we are a nice long way away from shells and beastly things of that sort! But somehow I'd rather be with the Battalion. I have grown so bad at getting to know fresh people and think I must be growing shy in my old age! ...

[Berthen, France]
12th October, 1917

... I am afraid I have very little news for you. ... Here I am pretending to be very busy and surround myself with quantities of maps and official correspondence and try to look very wise, but really there is very little to do, though I think there may be rather more in the future...

* * * * *

....
373 TNA WO 95/2589

Humphrey Secretan in Glencorse Wood, Oct. 1917

Marjorie's diary entry for 9th October included: *"Heard Humphrey wounded"*. On 4th October her brother Humphrey had, in fact, been severely wounded in his left thigh and, to a lesser extent, in his left arm and elbow. The 2nd Battalion, The Queen's Royal West Surreys was moving up for an attack east of Ypres, beyond Polygon Wood, this action – the Battle of Broodseinde – being a phase of the Third Battle of Ypres. The CO was away and the 2i/c was killed. Humphrey (OC of D Company) took over the Battalion but was badly wounded within half-an-hour.

He was evacuated by ship from Boulogne to Dover on 8th October and taken to a war-time London hospital in Grosvenor Street, where Marjorie visited him on the 11th and 12th. As she was teaching in London, her visits became quite regular. Humphrey was also visited by his other sister Esmé when she had time off from Reading Hospital where she was nursing. Humphrey remained in hospital for several weeks. On 22nd November Marjorie recorded, *"Took Humphrey out in a bath chair"*. It was not until December that he was sufficiently recovered for Marjorie to write on 7th, *"To the Coliseum with Humphrey"*. He never returned to the Western Front.

* * * * *

Charles Fair was east of Arras in the Oppy area with the 1/19th Londons.

Charles to Marjorie [Oppy]
10th October, 1917
9.00 a.m.

... I hope to goodness my letters are arriving all right now. I have written every day and only missed posting one the day I spent in the train. We are still pretty quiet here: in the same old spot. ...

Later: I went round about 9.30 a.m. Got back here and did some necessary work and then, as so often happens, the General [McDouall] appeared and wanted to go round with me. However, I managed to short-circuit him and am now writing just before lunch. We have discovered there are quantities of sugar-beet growing all round these trenches. We are boiling them and eating them cold. They taste exactly like beetroot and are a great addition to the table. ...

[Oppy – support trenches]
11th October, 1917,
3.00 a.m.

I am awfully thankful to hear that my letters have begun to arrive at last. It does bring us ever so much closer together, doesn't it, and makes those wonderful days seem not quite so far away. ... My dearest, the world is so different now that I always have you to turn to and think and dream about. I have put your photograph where it is the first and last thing I see each day. I find myself wandering in there at all sorts of hours just to look at it.

[Oppy – support trenches]
12th October, 1917,
9.30 a.m.

... We are still in trenches and still being rained upon. I am getting very dirty. Your *eau de cologne* is a splendid help. ... The Major General [Gorringe] came round yesterday and, to my great surprise, congratulated me and wished us <u>both</u> (very emphatically) every happiness. It is considered rather remarkable as he is a confirmed bachelor and said to be a misogynist!

We have shifted our quarters and have not gained by the exchange. Your husband can't stand upright anywhere in the new place! Of course we feed, read, work and write entirely by candle light. Those little collapsible candlesticks I bought at the Army and Navy at Aldershot are proving awfully useful. Our mess is about two-thirds the size of your sitting room. Three of us sleep, wash and live in it. At meals we are joined by three others. There are two wooden beams sticking up through the table and it takes some juggling to hand the plates round without accidents.

<u>Later</u>: I have been out for three-and-a-half hours, tramping round trenches and haven't very much time before the post goes.

[Oppy – support trenches]
13th October, 1917,
10.30 a.m.

... Stokes arrived back yesterday and took command. He is a good fellow and we shall get on all right. ... You haven't said anything at all about Humphrey: I do hope he is all right. ... I hope you will never know what it is to have the same clothes on for ten days or more without taking them off. I have only had mine off for the first three nights since I left you! By the time you get this we shall have been married a month. ...

[Oppy – support trenches]
13th October, 1917,
5.00 p.m.

Your letter about Humphrey being wounded has just come and I am so dreadfully sorry for him and for all your anxiety, my precious little wife. I do hope you have got later and more reassuring news, perhaps from himself. I have written immediately to his CO asking for a line about him, as I think he is Tim Longbourne[374] who was at Marlborough with me. I thought I might get some details from him which wouldn't reach you. It is horrid to think of your being worried, and I not there to help. ... Our doctor says it probably means that either his leg or his arm is broken. Anyway I do hope that he will be sent to London so that you can see him whenever you want to. ...

Sunday – 8.30 a.m.
14th October, 1917

Writing in our "summer-house" – a fearful and wonderful erection above ground outside our dugout. I am waiting for breakfast. A perfectly lovely morning – when war and horrors ought to be impossible. Your parcel from Fortnum has arrived. After some discussion we decided that the pickles are hardly necessary as we get them as a ration from time to time. Instead I suggest an occasional tin of real marmalade. All your other items receive full marks from me! I am hoping to go down to the Transport Lines today for twenty-four hours to have a bath and see to one or two matters affecting the well-being of the Battalion. ... I heard from Lemprière – fearfully envious of my amazing luck! I believe he is somewhere in these parts and I shall try to see him. I had an unpleasant job last night – though it wasn't so bad in the end. We had some men putting wire in an absolutely ruined village and I went out to see how they were getting on. We fell about at every step in the dark, always expecting to find ourselves falling down a well. Luckily the Boche was very quiet and only a few machine gun bullets whistled overhead. ... Take care of yourself, my dearest, and try not to worry too much about Humphrey.

[Oppy – support trenches]
15th October, 1917

I was so awfully relieved to get your letter of the 10th yesterday saying that Humphrey was in London and doing well. I do hope everything will go all right with him and that you will be able to see as much of him as ever you want to. ... I am writing from a cellar at our Transport Lines. I came here in time for lunch yesterday and go back to the trenches this afternoon. I had a splendid bath at our Divisional baths in a real enamel bath with nobody else waiting for it. The colour of the water when I had finished was quite unspeakable. I had the luck to get in touch with a man who was a Captain in my Company two-and-a-half years ago and we had a dinner party of five at the nearest Officers' Club, which was most cheery, your husband standing the wine! They all drank to Mrs Fair's health in which, oddly enough, I joined! ... I quite enjoyed my ride down from the trenches, though I nearly took a toss through a stirrup leather breaking.

....

374 Lt Col Francis Cecil Longbourne DSO commanded 2nd Battalion The Queen's. He was two years above Charles at Marlborough and left school in 1899 to join the Army, serving in South Africa. He was promoted to Brig Gen in 1917 and took over as GOC 171st Infantry Brigade, 57th Division on 23rd Sept. 1917. He was wounded on 5th Oct. 1918, was awarded the CMG and *Legion d'Honneur*, and was Mentioned in Dispatches on thirteen occasions.

[Oppy – support trenches]
16th October, 1917
10.00 a.m.

I was so relieved to get your letter yesterday – the one written after your first visit to Humphrey. It is everything that he is not dangerously hit, but probably bad enough to be at home all the winter. ... I came back to the trenches after my twenty-four hours holiday which I thoroughly enjoyed. I hope we may be relieved before long, but dates are always kept secret as long as possible. We ate one of your tins of brawn today and it was given full marks. It is very lovely again today. Yesterday evening I rode and walked up with our transport officer. It was dusk and so we came over the open, though it was still light enough to see a good way. When we got into the trench area he produced (in pieces) a weapon which was not originally designed for killing Huns. We then spread our party out, and the result is an addition of a hare and a partridge to our larder! It was a quaint proceeding in steel helmets and with box-respirators on our chests! ...

[Oppy – support trenches]
17th October, 1917,
10.00 a.m.

... Your parcel with the walnuts and other things and also the F & M parcel arrived all right. It is dear of you to take so much trouble. ... Things are still pretty quiet and much drier here. We hope to go out for a short rest before long: I will let you know directly we are out of the trenches. There are all sorts of domestic jobs which the Second-in-Command has to see to, which quite honestly bore me to tears! ...

I haven't seen Humphrey's name in the casualty list yet. ... You haven't said anything about Esmé in any of your letters. I hope she will have been able to go up to see Humphrey. ...

[Oppy – support trenches]
18th October, 1917,
8.30 a.m.

... We are on the move at last and I am going ahead to see to things for the Battalion. I will put in a line when we reach our destination. ... It will be a relief to get out for a bit, though everything has been wonderfully quiet – almost uncanny! I am writing rather under difficulties, as the usual turmoil of packing up in a confined space is going on. ...

[Maroeuil]
18th October, 1917,
9.15 p.m.

We are billeted in a village which suffered a fair amount from shell-fire at one time, but many of the houses are still all right.[375] I am sharing a room with the Assistant Adjutant: the furniture is all rough work done by ourselves and our predecessors. My bed is just bits of board nailed together, with a mattress of chicken-wire, which creaks horribly. It is really quite comfy and I have my valise

....

375 The War Diary records that at mid-day on that day "Battalion relieved by 1/23rd Londons and Brigade went into Divisional Reserve, 1/19th Battalion being billeted at Maroeuil. Reached billets by motor lorry at 3.00 p.m. Men's billets good, officers' poor. No cooking accommodation for the men at all." (TNA WO 95/2738)

and blankets and pyjamas – a great joy. We shall be here about a week, I suppose, and are hoping to get up some concerts and football for the men. Things were so quiet in the trenches that we did jigsaw puzzles sometimes in the evening. Will you send me something to read in your next parcel, please darling? ...

[Maroeuil]
19th October, 1917,
12.30 p.m.

... NO post today, which is damnable as it makes three days this week that I haven't heard from my beloved and I'm very especially hungry for those snapshots! Your parcels meet with great approval in the mess. From all they hear of you I think it more than probable that all the celibate officers will want an introduction to Esmé at an early date! ...

[Maroeuil]
19th October, 1917,
10.00 p.m.

... This evening we had a concert by an ASC concert party, but unfortunately it was not at all good. Stokes was not there so I had to stop to the end in order to go round and say a few kind words of thanks to the performers. ... Today we have eaten one of the *Gruyère* cheeses which you sent and they are a great success. ...

[Maroeuil]
20th/21st October, 1917
10.00 p.m.

... It has been a very lovely day and I have spent it chiefly in fussing about canteens, recreation rooms, footballs and so on. I went for a short ride before tea. There was a lovely new moon as I came back. ... I am a sufficiently important person to have some choice as to when I come on leave (provided it is due), so you will let me know what time will be the best in every way, won't you? We shan't have to fix up our second honeymoon in such a hurry as our first! ... We are hoping to have a whole month out of the trenches sometime before Xmas, but I shall not believe it till it really comes off: we have had so many disappointments. ...

Sunday – Midday
21st October, 1917

Just come back from church parade at which I read the lesson! ... This afternoon we have got a soccer match against the ASC.[376] It is getting quite cold for standing about without a coat and today I have got on my cardigan waistcoat for the first time. The civilians are returning to these parts now pretty fast. Some of them have hung on all the time. The chief drawback is the number of *estaminets* which they wish to open. In this village alone there are sixty-three! I know I shall get cashiered some day. I get so angry with the Staff and their ways. Get Humphrey to help you with ideas for your F & M parcels. ...

....
376 "Church parade in YMCA tent limited to 300. Football match v. ASC, won (5-0)." (TNA WO 95/2738)

[Maroeuil]
21st October, 1917
9.00 p.m.

... I hear there has been one or more raids on London. Darling, I don't much like you being there for the night when there are likely to be any. I am so looking forward to the new professional photograph of you. Remember, I can't have too many photographs of my wife: I would like to have my hut and my dugout papered with them – all different. ...

It was very lovely this afternoon. We watched a football match (which we won easily) for a bit and then went for a walk. Then I went and aired my best French with the worthy lady who is catering for our Officers' Dinner on Tuesday. We shall probably be back in the trenches again by the time you get this. ...

[Maroeuil]
22nd October, 1917
6.00 p.m.

... I have had the best day since I left you. I was taken up to Lemprière's village in a car about 11.00 a.m. and found him almost at once. We had lunch and tea together and went a real country walk on the hills in lovely sunshine, with leaves and berries of all colours everywhere. Of course we talked a lot about you and it was nice to have someone who knew you, and really appreciated my amazing luck, to talk to. He is very much altered by his moustache and professes to be very bored with the quietness of his existence! I think most of us would be quite willing to change places with him. They do live in comparative luxury and can always be clean. Their clerks have six stoves in one room and there is only one stove in the whole of this village. ... Our road today took us through some of the villages where we used to be billeted in the early days of 1916, which was quite interesting and recalled many strange scenes. ...

[Maroeuil]
23rd October, 1917
11.00 a.m.

A pouring wet morning: impossible to do anything much. We have got our Officers' Dinner tonight and most of the morning I have been wrestling with the accounts of various regimental funds, at which I am perfectly hopeless. We shall, I expect, be back in the trenches again by the time you get this.

[Maroeuil]
24th October, 1917
11.00 a.m.

... I was so delighted to get the snapshots at last. Some of them are quite good and they are all very precious and bring back such heavenly memories. ...

Our Officers' Dinner last night was quite a success. Darling, if anyone was asked now who is the most lively and consistently cheerful officer in the Battalion, there would be the same answer from all and it is all through you. ... This evening I am going to deliver a lecture to the Brigade School for young NCOs on "Leadership". It will be rather amusing to get on my legs again in the old way. ...

[Maroeuil]
24th October, 1917
9.30 p.m.

... There was no letter from you today but the London Sabbath always makes one day go wrong in the middle of the week, so I hope to get two tomorrow. The subaltern who shares my room – Barclay[377] – goes on leave tonight. It is only just three months since his last, which is pretty good work. It is getting very cold and draughty in these billets which have all suffered more or less from shellfire in the past. ...

[Maroeuil]
25th October, 1917
7.00 p.m.

... I am so glad you saw Naylor and liked him. Unfortunately we shall be in the trenches when he comes back and, as he goes on a course at once, it may be some time before I see him, which will be dreadfully tantalising. I simply long to talk to someone who has actually seen you since I have, though the thought of it makes me long for you even more, if that is possible. I have been out all day reconnoitring trenches again. I came back from them alone to where I had left my horse and groom. There was a tremendous wind blowing but lovely sun, and I sat down under a half-ruined railway bridge with three derelict trucks still on it. ... If all goes well we shall hope to get a month out of trenches before Xmas, which knocks a big hole in the time. ... The time as a whole goes awfully slowly, but each day in itself goes fairly quickly, except that all the morning I am looking at my watch and counting the time till the post arrives!

[Oppy]
26th October, 1917
9.30 p.m. In the trenches

Your letter and the book have just reached me (dated 22nd). ... By the same post I had a letter of congratulations and good wishes to us both from Champion: he is still out here. ... Today we came up part of the way in motor lorries. ... It was also simply pouring. We then tramped for about two hours to our trenches. The weather has become very bad and all the familiar discomforts of the winter are with us.[378] ...

Marjorie to Charles   Hill House
26th October, 1917
6.00 p.m.

It has been such a glorious day today; wonderful blue sky and the leaves turning all sorts of colours. Now the moon has risen and we are anticipating the Boche in the air. It has been so nice having a holiday. I spent the morning lazing about among my books and then this afternoon walked up to Haileybury to retrieve my

....

377 Lt William John Barclay, a stockbroker's clerk from Catford, had enlisted in the ranks of the 20th Londons on 7th Aug. 1914. He was wounded at Loos on 25th Sept. 1915 while serving with the 1/20th Londons. He was commissioned on 14th Dec. 1915 and spent the next 11 months with the 3/19th Londons in England before joining the 1/19th Londons in France on 14th Nov. 1916. (TNA WO 374/3855)

378 The War Diary records "Weather very bad and trenches falling in at many points." (TNA WO 95/2738)

walking-stick from the Malims. I found Mrs Malim recovering from an attack of flu and helped her pick and arrange flowers in the Chapel vases. She is always very affectionate to me and calls me "Dear"! ... I wouldn't stay to tea with her as I have a bit of a sore throat and I didn't want to stay out late. I ran most of the way home, most energetic like, but I felt so bucked with life and pleased to be walking about the country again. What fun it will be when I can come home to our home on these occasions and find a harassed schoolmaster just returned also from afternoon school. Darling, do you see any prospect of the war ever ceasing? I don't! These beastly old Huns must have lots of go left in them to start this Italian push. It's rather a bad affair, isn't it, and makes one curse the Russians very heartily. ...

I say, Charlie, oughtn't we to be thinking about your famous dinner on the 10th? Will you give me sometime a list of the people who will be there? Do send suggestions as to what you want sent out, as my mind always goes a dead blank whenever I get inside Fortnum's. Don't laugh, but I must be terribly in love. The other day, when I got to Liverpool Street, I offered the ticket collector your letter instead of my season [ticket]! Then I went on to the pillar box and posted my hankie and took the letter along in my pocket! This story is not to be repeated in the Mess. ...

Charles to Marjorie   [Oppy]
27th October, 1917
7.00 p.m.

... The trenches are suffering from the weather and it took me three hours to go round this morning. I shall be going round again about midnight I expect. Things are not as quiet here now as they were. Naylor has arrived back from leave but I haven't seen him, as he is going on a course tomorrow. I have sent a note down to him that he is to be sure and write me an account of his meeting with you before he goes. Today we have had an extraordinary succession of visitors – twenty-three officers, one after another, of all sorts and ranks, came in between 10.00 and 2.00.[379] My sleeping place was awfully cold last night and the draught simply whistled up through the meshes of the "chicken wire". ... Have you heard anything of George Fulton? ... I hope Humphrey is still going on all right. Did I tell you that I saw Woolley for a moment yesterday? It is nice to have three people in the Division now who know Marjorie and can appreciate a little my perfectly amazing luck. ... Eight weeks ago we were having dinner at "Les Lauriers" – one eating a hearty meal, the other imagining that the lobster or something was bad! What a perfectly marvellous evening it was. Do go up to Haileybury again soon and visit my rooms and take away anything you like that belongs to me. After all it is all yours now as much as mine. ...

[Oppy]
28th October, 1917
11.30 p.m.

Three letters from you today, as the missing one has turned up! It was obviously written on the 20th, but the postmark at Stanstead Abbotts was 23rd! I have never had quite such a lovely budget as today's. Three letters from you, and all of

....

379 The War Diary records "Battalion lines visited by numerous parties of staff officers and representatives of various units." (TNA WO 95/2738)

them long ones, a letter from your mother (an awfully sweet one), one from Dad, one from Helen and, not least in importance, one from Cox[380] to say that in spite of marrying a very expensive wife my balance there is £419 (not to mention my balance at Lloyds)! It really has been a good day for the trenches, darling, and I did love all those very precious letters from the little queen of my heart. It is sweet of you to write such long ones and I love to know your thoughts and dreams as well as your doings. ... It almost frightens me to think how perfectly stupendous will be our happiness when we meet again. Dearest, I have just come in from my nightly tour round the front line and over and over again, as I stumbled round corners and pulled my feet out of the mud, I had the glorious feeling of pride that I am Marjorie's husband. Tomorrow (Monday) if all is well, I hope for a little change as I am going to attend a sports meeting out of the trenches to arrange a football competition in the Division, to be played off by degrees during the winter. ...

Charles to his father   [Oppy]
                                                          28th October, 1917

... We are back in the trenches again and for the most part they are awfully wet and muddy. We hope not to stay in them for very long. McDouall[381] has gone home for six months like Reggie and we are commanded by one, Erskine, a Scots Guardsman – no longer young.[382] Yesterday we had an extraordinary influx of visitors – 23 in all, varying from the Divisional Commander [Maj-Gen Gorringe] down to a Captain in the Sanitary Section. I have sent in a request to the Brigade that such visitors should take back salvage with them! ...

Naylor has just been home on leave and went to see Marjorie – more, I think, out of curiosity than anything else! She was very glad to have first-hand information of us. He told her in an optimistic manner that my next leave would probably be about Xmas which is, of course, impossible. If all goes well I might get home in the middle of January. ... It is two years tomorrow since Stokes and I at last succeeded in crossing the Channel. ... I have told Marjorie to raid my room at Haileybury and remove any books which might interest her. I had a letter from Champion a few days ago: I believe he is now in command of a Pioneer battalion.

Marjorie to Charles   Hill House
                                                          29th October, 1917

I had another letter this morning, also dated 24th, which was written before the one I had yesterday. Darling, I am so glad you liked the photos; they certainly are a very dear remembrance. Today we have taken the "fur" ones but it's too late in the year for snaps and, by the vigorous way in which Aunt Emmie jerked the shutter, I fear me they have not a great chance of success. However, let's hope for the best. Dear old thing, I am so glad you are so cheery and just love to hear of you livening

....

380 Cox & Co. were agents and bankers for officers in the British Army.

381 Brig Gen McDouall CMG DSO returned to 47th Division after five months, taking over as GOC 142nd Infantry Brigade on 1st Apr. 1918. He held that role until the end of the war. He was Mentioned in Dispatches seven times and was appointed CB in 1919 and CBE in 1920. He retired in 1924 and died in 1941.

382 Brig Gen James Francis Erskine, CB, CMG, DSO, MVO commanded 141st Infantry Brigade from 26th Oct. 1917 to 2nd Jan.1918, though he was away on sick leave from 16th Dec. A Scots Guardsman, he had served in the Sudan in 1885 and South Africa in 1900-02. From 1911-14 he commanded a brigade in 52nd Division and from Dec. 1915 to Mar. 1917 had commanded two brigades in 11th Division. He was 55 at the time of this letter.

things up. If the others attribute it to me, so much the better. It's good to have done it (though quite unintentional!)

I have been up to see your rooms. Mr Headley was most kind and allowed me to perch on chairs with very muddy boots, so as to examine the [photographic] groups more closely. What a lot there are. I was awfully interested. Now do tell me what exactly you were in. I know the Marlboro' footer XV and also cricket XI. I see you played tennis for Pembroke. But I still feel rather vague as to what else you did at Cambridge. ...

Charles to Marjorie   [Oppy]
30th October, 1917
8.30 a.m.

... I am writing from our Transport Officer's billet – a ruined house which he has repaired. I came down for the meeting about a Divisional football competition and stayed the night. We have rigged up a cellar quite comfortably as an officers' hotel. It is all whitewashed and coconut matting on the floor, and three bunks. I had a splendid night and a bath and am just off up the line again. We are already beginning to think about Xmas and have bought some pigs and geese to fatten up for the men's dinner. There is a great rumour that leave is to be a fortnight long in future! Wouldn't that be glorious! ... You would have laughed this morning to see your husband in pyjamas, boots and a waterproof, scrambling about in a ruined village in search of a certain very necessary place of retreat! I wonder if such a figure had ever been seen in the street before!! It is blowing most awfully hard today and a steel helmet is an awful thing to wear in a wind. ...

[Oppy – support trenches]
30th/31st October, 1917
6.00 p.m.

I didn't have much time to write to you this morning before coming up the line again. We seem likely to be in trenches for ages this time, but it is really true that leave is to be a fortnight long during the winter and there is to be far more leave for the men than ever before, so everyone is feeling quite bucked, in spite of the bad news from Italy, which is a blow. However, I put no faith in anyone except the little Frenchmen: I really do admire them and the women of the French working and middle classes. However, we never write much about the war, do we? When Dartford wrote to me he said that, considering that the war had brought me a DSO and a wife, he thought I ought to regard it as a pretty good war! It was very tantalising not to see Naylor: I did so want to have first-hand news of my precious little lady. ...

... We have got a new Brigadier [Erskine]. I shall miss our old one very much. I am beginning to feel rather a back number in the Brigade. I am the only officer left of the rank of Major and upwards who went down to the Somme in August 1916. The rest have either drifted home or become casualties. A Fortnum parcel arrived today – a very welcome sight – also a parcel of socks from Gina and one from Winchester. We can never have too many socks for everyone. ...

31st October

A lovely morning and lots of aeroplanes about: one, nationality unknown, has come down within sight of us – shot down by another, I think. ...

The "bad news from Italy" to which Charles referred was the near collapse of the Italian Army at the Battle of Caporetto. On 24th October, 1917, a combined force of Austrian and German troops launched a heavy attack in the north-east of Italy at Caporetto. The unsuspecting Italians were driven back a considerable distance as far as the River Piave. This reverse made the Allies decide that some British and French Divisions would be needed to stem the Austro-German advance. Some were indeed sent but they did not include the 47th Division.

* * * * *

Meanwhile Guy Dodgson was serving as Battalion Intelligence Officer with the headquarters of 118th Infantry Brigade in the Ypres Salient.

Guy to his mother   [118 Infantry Bde HQ] [Fairy House]
15th October, 1917

Brigade HQ have now moved and we are living most awfully comfortably. The place is a farmhouse where the General and his Staff live and the rest of us live in very good huts built round the house. The Mess is one of the best huts I have seen, with beautiful red wallpaper inside and chairs and a proper fireplace. One really wants a fire these days as it's getting awfully cold at nights. ... How beastly for Philip having to go to some reserve battery: I know exactly what he feels. ... I am afraid you will miss him when he goes to Luton. I'm afraid I haven't seen anything of George, though we have been in the same Corps. Now I hear my Division [39th] is being moved into another Corps. ... Personally, I would much rather have a Company than this job on Brigade HQ. I hate having no men with me. I think Company Commander is one of the most enjoyable jobs one can have. ...

[La Clytte, 8 miles southwest of Ypres]
27th October, 1917

... I think the Brigade is going into the line again quite soon and our days of comparative ease are numbered. I shall go and live with HQ in those horrible tunnels – a beastly place, though safe, and of course infinitely preferable to the front line. ... We've got a lovely day today and I'm sitting writing with the door of my hut open and the sun pouring in, and it's really quite hot on my back. Yesterday was appalling and it never stopped raining all day till the evening. Then it cleared up just in time to let the Boche come over and drop a few bombs.

The Brigade took over a section of the line on the night of 28th/29th October and an advanced Brigade HQ was set up in the Hedge Street Tunnel.[383]

....
383 TNA WO 95/2589

[Hedge Street tunnel]
31st October, 1917

I'm afraid I haven't written to you for the last few days, since we've been in the line. But, as I thought, there has been rather more for me to do than there was before. As I imagined, we are living in the tunnels where we were before. ... I think this Italian business is altering things a good deal on this front and I think it will effectually put a stop to too much "offensive spirit" here. It's a bad business, isn't it? I suppose everybody will crumble until England is left single-handed against the Germans! ...

[Hedge Street tunnel]
2nd November, 1917

... I have had a little trip up to the line this morning and got there and back with no mishaps of any kind. Luckily it was a misty morning and there was very little going on on either side, but I have never seen the country look so desolate with the mist hanging about among the tree stumps and everything grey and horrible. I found the Battalion on the whole very cheerful, though the conditions they are living under are none too comfortable. However, they are getting some sort of trenches dug and those they <u>have</u> dug are moderately dry. ...

[La Clytte Camp]
5th November, 1917

A most splendid piece of cheese arrived yesterday. Thank you so much for it. It is being so appreciated by everybody and the General loves it! I am sure I have gone up points in his estimation since its arrival. ... We are out of the line again. We came out the night before last, travelling down in lorries about 2.00 in the morning and we are now in the same place as we were before. ...

[La Clytte Camp]
7th November, 1917

We are moving our quarters again tomorrow. I am rather sorry as we are very comfortable here and I have a lovely bed, entirely surrounded by sand-bags <u>inside</u> the hut as well as outside. I feel beautifully safe when the Hun comes over and drops his beastly bombs. ... It isn't so much the danger of the things as the frightful nuisance of continually having to put one's lights out and take cover. I only hope we annoy him as much as he does us. ...

* * * * *

Charles to Marjorie   [Oppy – support trenches]
1st November, 1917
11.00 a.m.

Another quiet night, luckily, and I slept awfully well. ... Result – an enormous breakfast: porridge with Ideal Milk – two fresh herrings – an egg – marmalade sent by my wife! The largest breakfast I have eaten since we left "The Tors" I think. ... We are always deep in problems of how to keep the men fit during the winter. I find it desperately hard to become really interested in diet, though occasionally I have a bright idea! I do hope Humphrey is still going on all right. It is splendid that he is sure to miss this beastly winter. We seem to be really in it now and it is my third out here. I am writing amid rather distracting surroundings as one of our carpenters is doing some work in the dugout and, in addition to the noise of his saw, he occasionally spits violently upon the instrument. ... At first I thought he was doing it to lay the dust! For the moment our trenches are quite dry and I am going about in ordinary ankle-boots and puttees. We are working feverishly at drying-rooms and kitchens in preparation for the really bad weather of which we have had some foretaste already. I wish some of the business members of your family would give me some lessons in book-keeping: I get awfully tied up with canteen and other accounts. I always used to put them right by dipping into my own pocket if necessary, but now that I have a very smart wife to look after I make desperate efforts to find a balance on the right side. ...

[Oppy]
1st/2nd November, 1917,
9.30 p.m.

... I wonder what you are doing with all my letters. I am keeping a special haversack for yours in my valise, but I shall have to destroy the envelopes in order that it may not become too bulky, though I shall hate doing even that. I find that our new *padré* is engaged: I don't know her name. He is quite nice and not above laughing at little risqué stories and remarks. ...

Marjorie to Charles

Hill House
1st November, 1917,
5.30 p.m.

You really are spoiling me horribly with this delightful plan of sending an extra note to School for a surprise. ... It is splendid to know how much you love my letters, dearest. ... Mother told me about your correspondence with her. She thinks you are everything that could be desired by way of a son-in-law. You know she always brought us up to believe that she did not consider all her geese to be swans (like most Mamas)! But just lately she has turned quite sentimental about me ... .
... The raid was very disturbing to Londoners last night, but we never had a gun firing here.[384] ... Humphrey says your Battalion must have another name besides 1/19th: all London regiments have. Has it? I said it hadn't.

Charles to Marjorie

[Oppy Red Line – support Battalion]
2nd November, 1917
6.30 p.m.

I had a splendid post today – all the three letters you wrote to me during your long weekend. I was simply absorbed in them for ages. It was great to hear all about your visits to Haileybury ... It really did bring you so near again to picture you in my own room. Of course you were allowed to stand on the chairs in your muddy boots; why, they are really mine! ... It would be a blow if they sent us to Italy. Of course there are the wildest rumours as to who is going. I expect the sending of troops there will be political rather than military in its intention. ...

....

384 A Gotha raid on Kent, Essex and London killed 10 and injured 22 people on the night of 31st Oct./1st Nov. 1917.

3rd November – 1.00 p.m.

Five weeks gone now since I left you. Time is getting on: if only my leave really comes off in January. It is a typical misty November day and we have been walking about in the open quite freely. We have a great passion for salvage in the Battalion and manage to collect all sorts of weird things to send back, all of which is saving money for the tax-payer.[385] ...

Marjorie to Charles   Hill House
                                                                2nd November, 1917

I'm just back from quite a cheering afternoon. I went to hear the London String Quartet at the Aeolian Hall. It was good to hear some strings again; I've tried to go so often lately, but been prevented. They played a Beethoven Quartet and a Haydn, which was a real treat, especially perhaps the former. I met Mr Hylton-Stewart there, also alone.[386] He came and sat with me and let me look over the score to the Haydn which he had procured. He has got this Quartet to come down to Haileybury to give a concert there on 8th December: a good move isn't it? He asked me how was "the Brigadier or Colonel or whatever he might be by now"! ...

I went to Fortnum's and said the parcel of the 19th had not turned up, and they assured me it would, saying they're getting fearfully busy now, Xmas rush already beginning. Darling, we really ought to start thinking about sending out anything for the 10th soon. ...

Humphrey has been out of bed twice for a short time, so feels he is really getting on.

No more tonight, darling, but all my love. Oh, what fun it will be when you and I can go to concerts together: it always takes two to really enjoy anything, as I believe I remarked to you the first time we met. Anyhow, I thought it.

Charles to Marjorie   [Oppy Red Line – support Battalion]
                                                                3rd November, 1917
                                                                     5.30 p.m.

... I am getting very anxious for the new photograph of you, dearest. I can't have too many: I should like to have my walls papered with them, all different! This afternoon we had a visit from one of our Divisional Staff who, twenty years ago, was at Connaught House, Weymouth, with George Fulton and me, and afterwards

....

385   The War Diary for 3rd Nov. records that "Fog in morning enabled much useful salvage work to be done." (TNA WO 95/2738) Salvage was ultimately collected, cleaned, sorted and sent back up the supply chain by the salvage detachment of the 47th Divisional Employment Company. The Divisional History states that "the activities of the salvage party ... were varied and ubiquitous and ... rendered real service in the cause of economy." (Maude, op cit, p. 221)

386   Bruce Hylton-Stewart was the senior music master at Haileybury College.

reappeared at Pembroke.[387] ... I am hoping to go and dine at their mess before long. I am composing a list of those who are likely to attend the dinner on December 10th, if all goes well. Woolley of course will be there, if possible – the only outsider. ... We are all very anxious to know who will be sent to Italy. Personally, I have no wish to go there at all, though some people say they would be glad of the change. But then they haven't got Marjorie waiting for them on the other side of the Channel. ...

Oh, Marjorie darling, I am counting the days to when it will begin to be possible really to talk about leave. We have so much lost time to make up, haven't we? ...

Charles to his father   [Oppy Red Line – support Battalion]
                                                                           4th November, 1917

Thank you and all for letters and a parcel containing socks and other things. The weather has cheered up and the trenches are reasonably dry, though the foggy weather gives additional cares to us and the enemy, increasing the chances of gas attacks. We are likely to be in the trenches for some little time yet. Today we are sending the men back, a few at a time, to get a bath. I had one earlier in the week. ... They have put me on a committee for arranging a Divisional football competition during the winter. The chairman is A. J. Turner,[388] the Essex Cricketer (brother of W. M. Turner of Totland): he is on our Staff.

Charles to Marjorie   [Oppy Red Line – support Battalion]
                                                                           5th November, 1917

Two letters from you yesterday of the 30th and 31st. You will know by now that the missing one and the parcel from Fortnum turned up after a bit. Your parcel of kippers arrived yesterday and was a great success. ... Things were pretty noisy here yesterday and both sides got a bit cross with each other. However, we came off lightly.[389] It is two years ago today since I first joined this Battalion out here and, except on duty or leave, I have not left the Divisional area. It is extraordinary how fit most of us keep.

....

387   Charles had elsewhere identified this officer as Capt Julian Ito Piggott MC who served as GSO 3 (Intelligence) to the 47th Division from 9th Apr. 1917 to 5th Apr. 1918. His award of the MC had been gazetted on 4th June 1917. Piggott was born in Tokyo on 25 Mar. 1888 while his father, the barrister Sir Francis Piggott, was serving a three year term as adviser to the prime minister Hirobumi Ito while the Japanese constitution was being drafted. After Pembroke, Piggott played cricket occasionally for Surrey from 1910 to 1913, hitting 84 against Oxford University at the Oval in 1910. He was commissioned on 6th Oct. 1914 into the Corps of Interpreters and was immediately attached to HQ 22nd Infantry Brigade (7th Division). From 15th Sept. 1915 he served as an ADC in the 41st Division. After the 47th Division Piggott served as a GSO 3 (Intelligence) at GHQ. He was promoted to Major in Dec. 1918 and served as GSO 2 with the Military Governor's Staff in Cologne until he was demobilised in June 1919. In the 1920s Piggott served as British Commissioner in Cologne of the Inter-Allied Rhineland High Commission. He was made CBE in the New Year Honours 1933 and died in 1965. (Maude, op cit, p. 231; Obituary, *Wisden*, 1965; TNA WO 339/38736)

388   Lt Col Arthur Jervois Turner, DSO, RA (1878-1952) served as GSO 1 of 47th Division from 17 Nov. 1916 to 21 Feb. 1918. (Maude, op cit, p. 230). Turner was a regular soldier who had served in the Boer War. In his spare time he batted for Essex in 77 matches between 1897 and 1914, scoring 4,053 runs. He also played rugby for Blackheath and Kent. He retired from the Army as a Brigadier having served as GOC 150th Infantry Brigade, 35th Division for the final months of the war. He was also awarded the CB, CMG and Croix de Guerre. (Obituary, *Wisden*, 1953)

389   The War Diary for 4th Nov. records "Successful raid by Brigade on our right. Enemy retaliation very slight." (TNA WO 95/2738) The Divisional History states that this was a major raid by about 500 officers and men from 142nd Infantry Brigade, in which over 100 Germans were killed and much damage was done to the German front line trench. (Maude, op cit, pp 116-7)

My motto is to sleep and eat whenever I get the chance in the trenches and to keep as clean as possible. If we do go out for a month before Xmas, we could do with any magazines or illustrated papers you don't want for the men's recreation room. We have started a barber's shop in the trenches. This morning it was again misty and I have been wandering about in the open with the sergeant cook and a small party of men collecting turnips, swedes and beet planted, I expect, by the far-seeing Boche in anticipation of being still here when they were fit for consumption. We are collecting enough to give the men some every day and, at the same time, start an emergency store at our transport lines.[390] I hope you have heard from Woolley by now. He has changed his battalion, although remaining in the Division. ...

So glad Humphrey is going on all right ... .

[Oppy Red Line – support Battalion]
5th November, 1917
6.30 p.m.

... Woolley has just been in to tea in our dugout – quite unexpectedly. He never received your note – was it in the parcel with the *eau de cologne*? Consequently he couldn't imagine who his unknown admirer could be! ...

Our Battalion has no pet name. There are a few of our battalions which have those. The official title puts St Pancras in brackets after the word "London" but we never use it. I don't think the 6th, 7th, 10th, 17th or 20th have any fancy names either. ...

... I hope Hulbert [Charles's brother-in-law] is in good form for your visit: he can be so awfully amusing and he is a most unconventional *padré* in most ways. ... We have got another American officer attached to us for a few days. It is quite amusing and helps to pass the time. This is just a little letter to greet you at Woodford.

[Oppy Red Line – support Battalion]
6th November, 1917
10.30 a.m.

... My bed in the trenches is also made of chicken wire – about four inches from the ground – rather draughty. I have a horse rug and my mackintosh over me and put each foot in a sandbag, which generally keeps them warm. I have my waterproof sheet underneath. It is always the most difficult part to keep the draught out from underneath. It is pretty cold now at nights. I have got a woolly sweater and a Balaclava helmet for the very cold nights. My chicken wire is very narrow and <u>very</u> creaky whenever I am restless, and oh! I do long all the time for "The Tors" and all that that meant! Today I am hoping to go to another football meeting, which will make another little change and I shall lie in wait for the post in hopes of a letter from my lady. It has become, of course, an absolute joke in the mess the excitement of the Major when the post is due and his language when there is no letter from his wife! The other day the Adjutant had me badly by coming in with the letters and giving all the others theirs and only handing me "The Times" when there were really <u>two</u> letters from Marjorie all the time. ...

....

390 The War Diary for 3rd Nov. even records that "large supplies of beet, turnips and swedes collected for immediate consumption and for future use by being returned to the transport lines at night." (TNA WO 95/2738)

[Oppy Red Line – support Battalion]
7th November, 1917
10.00 a.m.

No letter yesterday in spite of my waylaying the postman at a bleak and muddy spot and breaking the seal of his sack! There were no letters from England at all. I went down to the meeting and had tea at the Officers' Club where I met an OM – G. C. Turner[391] – who was at Marlborough with Humphrey. He belongs to our Division, but was home wounded for a very long time. He had seen our wedding in the paper and wondered if you were Humphrey's sister. ... They sent me back part of the way in the car and I came the rest of the way on foot alone. It was awfully dark and very muddy. I stumbled along among shell holes and light railways and trenches and wondered often if I could be the same person who had just seven weeks ago been spending his first night with Marjorie. ...

(A short interval at this point, as the Adjutant wants me to sing "The Perfect Day" with him as a duet! A good thing to do at 10.00 a.m. on a wet morning in the trenches. I wonder if he dreamt again that he was on patrol in Piccadilly) ... .

[Oppy Red Line – support Battalion]
8th November, 1917
9.00 a.m.

... It is a lovely day at last but we aren't always pleased with that as it generally means more aeroplanes and more shelling. I am much harassed just now by having to try and bend my brain to the problem of Christmas for the men. I never have the least idea how many nutmegs a battalion will require and whether they should cost 2½d or £1 each! Now, darling, about December 10th: we shall be about twelve to fifteen, I expect. ... I want you to try and supply the following part of the menu by sending from Fortnum or elsewhere. ... Of course I can get most of the *pièce de résistance* out here. Will you send material for:

Soup (mulligatawny will do)
Savoury (those tins of lobster you sent once made an awfully good savoury)
Dessert (some dried fruit, etc.)
1 bottle orange liqueur brandy
1 bottle cherry liqueur brandy
(I can get Benedictine here without difficulty)
Box of cigars (I know nothing about them!)

I have made arrangements for chickens, ducks, or both, and we can always get fish. The sweet is generally a difficulty, but we can probably manage some species of omelette. Of course, wine is easy to get. I shall be broke for the time being, but it will all be in honour of my little lady and we will drink her blessed health very lustily. ...

....

391   Capt (later Maj) George C. Turner, of the 1/23rd Londons, was an Old Marlburian who joined the staff of Marlborough College where he later became Headmaster. He was awarded the MC on 3rd June 1918 whilst attached to the 1/21st Londons. After the war he collected material and wrote a large part of *The 47th (London) Division 1914-1918.*

[Front line - Oppy left sub-section]
8th November, 1917
6.00 p.m.

... It is awfully wet again now and I propose going round the line about 5 o'clock tomorrow morning. If no officer from Headquarters ever goes round at that very beastly hour I feel sure that both the men and the officers in the actual front line picture us as always sleeping soundly in a deep dugout. How badly I need a proper bath and a change. ...

[Front line - Oppy left sub-section]
9th November
11.00 a.m.

Went all round at six this morning. Rain and mud everywhere. However, I had quite a good night and was not too cold. By mere chance I left a candle burning in our sleeping place, ready for Stokes to come in, and from where I lay it was just lighting up Marjorie's eyes and hair in the photograph I like best, and looking at it and loving it I fell asleep. ... The horrid old Boche is getting noisy in these parts: we can hardly blame him, as our Division never gives him any rest anywhere. In about another fortnight I should like some more *eau de cologne* if you could send me some. ...

[Front line - Oppy left sub-section]
10th November, 1917
10.00 a.m.

Darling, your husband was a sorry sight when he reached his dugout about midnight. Rain caught us halfway round and I hadn't got a mackintosh. The trenches were falling in everywhere and the mud was up to my knees in places. Barclay – our bombing officer, and one of the best – was with me and we fell about in all directions, cursing and laughing alternately. Finally, we got back and my tunic was wet through in places to the skin. However, I took it right off, also my boots and socks – luckily I had on those knee-covers – and simply gulped down hot tea with rum in it. I don't think I am any the worse, but those poor devils, the sentries, were having a rotten time, though we manage to give them something hot every four hours now that winter has really set in. ...

[Front line - Oppy left sub-section]
10th November, 1917
9.45 p.m.

... Your husband thought he was wet and dirty last night, but tonight beats anything seen since Xmas 1915! I went round at 5.30 this evening and it took three hours. Even then I missed out a bit. The water and mud is clean through my breeches and there is no chance of taking them off tonight, so I am sitting in them rather squishily! I sat down in the trenches four or five times. It was so dark we had to feel our way. The water was over my knees in places and the smaller men

are getting stuck in the mud. It is quite one of the worst nights I remember.[392]
However, we hope for a change very soon: in fact, if all goes well, I am off tomorrow
to billet for the Battalion. Oh, I shall be thankful to get these wet and filthy clothes
off. Darling, it is very sweet of you to be making the socks: don't let them be a
bother to you. I shall love to have them whatever they are like. Your flask has been a
tremendous help all this long, wet time and is generally full of rum! ...

* * * * *

Meanwhile, Guy was still in the Ypres Salient with the headquarters of 118th Infantry
Brigade.

Guy to his brother Philip [Scottish Wood Camp]
8th November, 1917

... We were in the line about five days ago for six days and we had rather a
beastly time – a rotten piece of the line – and the old Boche was very offensive at
times. He is altogether too warlike for my liking and sends over too many of those
blinking shells. I find my job quite moderately interesting in the line and I manage
to get to know quite a lot about what is going on, which as a Company officer one
never does. But out of the line there is very little doing and I get a little bit bored.
After all, I don't think this country offers sufficient amusement for one to have <u>too</u>
much time on one's hands. ... Mother tells me you are fairly bored with Luton and
I don't wonder. I know so well the way they mess about in England is too sickening
and it all seems so pointless. Of course it may be different in the Gunners but I don't
expect it is. When will you be coming out again? For many reasons I don't want you
to come out here again, though it would be very nice to meet you out here. As far as
I can tell, leave for me is now in sight but exactly when I can't say. ...

Guy to his mother [Bde HQ - behind Tower Hamlets/
Bodmin Copse sector of front line]
13th November, 1917

Many thanks for your letter of today talking about my arrival. I quite agree, it is
far better to have things [travel arrangements] more or less settled beforehand. ... I
will send you a wire from Folkestone and then you will be able to judge what time I
shall be in London. Do come up if you can possibly manage it and I should love you
to meet me, though it would be an awful fag for you. ...

Guy was on leave in England during the latter part of November and early December.

* * * * *

Charles to his father [Maroeuil]
11th November, 1917

... The weather has been very bad and trenches worse than any I have seen for
two years. Luckily I have left them today for some time, I hope. We are hoping to

....

392 The war diary for the 11th Nov. records that the weather was so bad that one other rank died of exposure.
(TNA WO 95/2738) This was probably 613515 Cpl Ernest Bernard Murphy who 'died of disease' and who is
buried nearby in Orchard Dump Cemetery, Arleux-En-Gohelle (grave VIII.A.9).

have a real "rest" soon and Stokes has sent me out to make arrangements. Today I had lunch with an OM – L. C. Gamage (of Holborn) – who is an Adjutant in our Division.[393] I last saw him in High Wood [in September 1916] when we quoted Homer together. He was wounded soon after. ... I was most awfully wet and muddy last night. The mud came right through my breeches and I had to sleep in them: it took me three hours to get round the front line in the dark and I nearly shot an officer of another battalion who was rather slow in answering my challenge. The trenches had fallen in so badly in some places that we were practically walking on the top, part of the way. I am just about to have my first bath for a fortnight. I have been wearing the same underclothing for sixteen days. I did once actually find a missing garment when I undressed after a week in the trenches! ...

Charles to Marjorie   [Maroeuil]
                                                              11th November, 1917
                                                                    6.00 p.m.

   I am safely out of the trenches and with luck may not go there again for some time. I found such a lovely long letter from you waiting for me, dated the 7th and containing an adorable tiny snapshot of Marjorie, which I simply love. ... You know I feel a sort of strange reverence for Toby's memory partly because, tho' he didn't know it, he died to give me the greatest happiness I shall ever know, and partly because Marjorie loved him, and that is enough for me in everything. ... If we really stay out of the trenches for a month that will knock a big hole out of the time still remaining before I can consider myself qualified to go on leave again. People are getting away so splendidly punctually now that I <u>might</u> be able to come at the beginning of January. ...

                                                                    [Maroeuil]
                                                              12th November, 1917
                                                                    6.00 p.m.

   ... It has been a simply lovely day here and I have been very busy getting things ready for the arrival of the Battalion tomorrow evening. I have ridden more than a dozen miles and my horse simply loves a touch of frost in the air. I get so awfully angry at the <u>continuous</u> comfort in which the Staff live, most of whom have never seen a trench and never intend to. <u>They</u> can get materials for deck-chairs, beds, arm-chairs and tables, while we have to beg and steal to get anything to sit on at all or eat our meals off. This is no exaggeration as I have been doing it for two years now and <u>everywhere</u> we go we have to <u>make</u> our own simple furniture, while those who stay behind the lines have more or less perpetual homes and make themselves really comfortable. However, it is good to be out of the trenches at all and it is more than good to be Marjorie's husband. ...

   Awfully busy today, dearest, getting ready for the others. Lovely sunshine all the morning. Just having a drink at the place where we had our Officers' Dinner three weeks ago and where I hope to give mine in Marjorie's honour on December 10th!

....

393 Capt Leslie Carr Gamage MC had been two years below Charles at Marlborough where he played rugby and hockey for the College. He was a scholar of Exeter College, Oxford and a solicitor. He was adjutant of the 1/24th Battalion, The London Regiment and his award of the Military Cross had been gazetted on 1st Jan. 1917.

[Maroeuil]
14th November, 1917
Lunchtime

Everyone got here all right last night and seemed very pleased at all that had been done for them in the two days available. Your husband has only got one virtue, darling, that for some reason men will work damned hard when he asks them – perhaps because he is able to produce some comic stories under most circumstances. This morning I have been awfully busy over various domestic details. ... I have the *padré* sharing my room at present: he is a good fellow (drinks beer and port and does <u>not</u> smoke!). He is also engaged ... .

[Maroeuil]
14th November, 1917
6.30 p.m.

A rather angry husband this evening because, for some reason, the post corporal omitted to call for our outgoing letters and consequently the one which I wrote to you this morning is still here. It was the only one written by the whole Mess today and I have started this one before anyone else has started one at all! I have had a busy but profitable day in the interests of the Battalion (and we'll hope of the Empire!) but oh! these military details bore me more and more intensely every week that passes. I started being bored with soldiering on August 7th, 1914, and nothing I have seen or done since has caused me to alter my opinion. However, I mustn't grumble on my pet grievance, darling, especially when we are just starting our "rest". ...

<u>Later</u>: Good temper quite restored, sweetheart, as the *padré* made some remark which had a *double entendre* for our naughty minds and the more he tried to explain the deeper he floundered. Result – your husband and several others lying about in limp and speechless heaps. Thank God for the power to laugh! My sense of humour has never failed me yet. ...

[Maroeuil]
15th November, 1917
Lunchtime

Another lovely day of sunshine but much mud. I had rather a bad night last night, starting with neuralgia and going on to bad dreams, or at least intensely irritating ones of a boring military nature. There are great rumours that what you dread most will come off.[394] I hope they are only rumours, but one never knows. Everything is rather tense everywhere now, I think.

... By the way, darling, if you have not already sent the things for December 10th, hang them up for bit: I don't altogether like the rumours of moving. ...

[Maroeuil]
16th November, 1917
2.00 p.m.

I'm afraid I wrote a rather depressing letter to you yesterday, but still it looks as if our fears are likely to be realized. It will probably postpone my leave a bit,

....

394 The possible move to Italy.

but not indefinitely I think. If it does happen, darling, I know you will face the disappointment as bravely as you faced our parting, but still it hasn't happened yet. We are having quite decent weather and are getting reasonably clean by degrees. Inspections by all sorts of people are in prospect. How I hate them: they are to my mind militarism and Prussianism rampant! ... I think I dislike everything military more and more every day. ... It will be an awful pity if we have to leave this place in a hurry, as we really have made it pretty comfortable. We have painted and papered the dilapidated room in which we have our Mess and have bought curtains and tablecloths and had six chairs made and upholstered by our own men. All of this would have to be left behind if we really move from here. Your ginger in the last F & M parcel was a great success.

[Maroeuil]
17th November, 1917

I'm afraid that which I hinted is really going to happen. It is a bad blow for us and many others like us, dearest; we can only try and make the best of it. If you get a sudden stopping of my letters you will know it is because we are on the move, though you know that I will never miss an opportunity of sending you a line even if it is only a field postcard. ...

[Maroeuil]
17th November, 1917
7.00 p.m.

... We don't know yet what is going to happen to us, but anyway I think it is very unlikely that I shall get home as early as January now, though leave is still going on here and going well too. I wake up early these mornings, generally in a frenzy of rage and then, if there is light enough, I can just see Marjorie's photograph and I know that <u>everything</u> is worthwhile as long as she loves me and even though we are separated in this beastly way I wouldn't be anyone else in the world.

... Did I ever tell you we caught a Boche during our last tour in the trenches? I hear that he was a Pole – thoroughly fed up and ready to give away all sorts of information, but of course we have to pass him to higher authority to examine.[395] Oh, those damned Italians; why on earth can't they look after their own country? I have long been convinced that the little French man is the only ally worth fighting for. I am so awfully glad that Humphrey is able to get up for a bit now and it will be nice when you can start going about together. ...

[Maroeuil]
18th November, 1917
11.30 a.m.

... It seems certain that we are going to move right away and it <u>is</u> hateful as far as one can judge at present. I have got a competition with the *padré* as to which of us can find a silver lining first. He is engaged, you know, and was expecting leave in about three weeks' time. To add to my rage I have had my British warm stolen from the passage outside the Mess last night. I'm afraid there is no hope of getting

....

395 The War Diary for 13th Nov. records: "A deserter came into our lines in the early morning." (TNA WO 95/2738)

it back and, unless I can manage to get a cheap one through the Ordnance people tomorrow, I look like having a chilly time with only a mackintosh for our journey. ...

[Maroeuil]
19th November, 1917
Mid-day

I am still in the same place and everything seems to be in a most uncertain state. My schoolmaster's soul always rebels against changes and upheavals: I do like to stick to a time-table in work, but be absolutely unfettered in play. We <u>are</u> an extraordinary nation! This afternoon I am riding over to watch a match in the Division Football Competition, which goes serenely on its way in spite of alarms and excursions. Our Dinner last night was quite a success and tonight we are hoping to have a Battalion concert.[396] I have been over to the nearest Ordnance Store and bought a new British warm – awfully good and fleece-lined – only 35/-!

[Maroeuil]
20th November, 1917
12.30 p.m.

No English mail today; therefore a blank day for your husband. We seem really about to start on our long, long trail though we haven't got definite orders yet. ... We have had a good many minor worries during the last week as well as the main one. However, it will pass. I am never out of sorts for more than a day or two at a time. We had quite a good Battalion concert last night and some of the turns really made me laugh a lot.

... I have had to destroy the envelopes of your letters to make more room in my haversack. It went to my heart to do it, but it really does make more room. ...

I wonder if my 10th December [Dinner] will be held! Never mind if your parcels are on the way; we will carry them about with us somehow. When does your term come to an end?

[near Étrun]
21st November, 1917
5.30 p.m.

There is no post in or out today as we are on the move, but I hope this may get off to you tomorrow. We haven't moved very far – in fact our moving at all was only (in our eyes) a maddening bit of red tape, as we are in sight of our old billets and, instead of the Mess which we had spent time and money upon and made really comfortable, we are in very draughty huts with very few stoves (not being Boche prisoners!) and looking out on an absolute sea of mud. ... We are all very much excited about recent events in these parts. We have had no part in them at all, but we could hear the noise in the distance. ...

....

396   The War Diary for 19th Nov. records: "Football match v. Divisional HQ (lost 2-5). Battalion concert in the Lace Factory." (TNA WO 95/2738)

Chapter 16

Cambrai and Bourlon Wood

November and December 1917

Charles's remark about "the recent events in these parts" was a reference to the Battle of Cambrai, which had been launched the day before (20th November) by the Third Army under General Sir Julian Byng. Advances in artillery techniques since 1916 had meant that the BEF was able to mount a short but intense artillery barrage without registration. This 'predicted-fire' barrage lessened the advance warning, taking the Germans by surprise. More important was the need not to churn up the ground and so impede the mobility of the nearly 400 tanks taking part. Initial success on the first day of an advance of three to four miles on a six-mile front led to bells being rung in London, but this initial euphoria was somewhat misplaced: the Germans responded quickly and the anticipated breakthrough did not occur. On the left of the advance was the tree-clad hill of Bourlon Wood, which looms over the lower ground towards Cambrai and which had been largely occupied by British infantry of the 62nd Division.

Charles to Marjorie [near Étrun]
22nd November, 1917

I think I was, perhaps, premature in my prognostications [about a move to Italy]. We are still in the same neighbourhood from which I have been writing lately. Nobody seems to know what is in front of us at all, or what our destination is. It is trying for us in every way to be in such a state of uncertainty, but it is for you that I mind, darling: I know you will not worry more than possible and as soon as anything is clear I will of course let you know, as far as regulations permit. ...

The mud, even out of the trenches, is very bad now. Please excuse a short little letter, my darling. I love you so very dearly, but things are too uncertain to be able to write much more for the moment.

Marjorie to Charles Hill House
23rd November, 1917

I had two letters today, the last dated 20th announcing your intentions of an imminent departure. It's very depressing. I'm not at all philosophical about it. ... I will expect a parcel from the Front with extra kit. Why didn't you send my letters

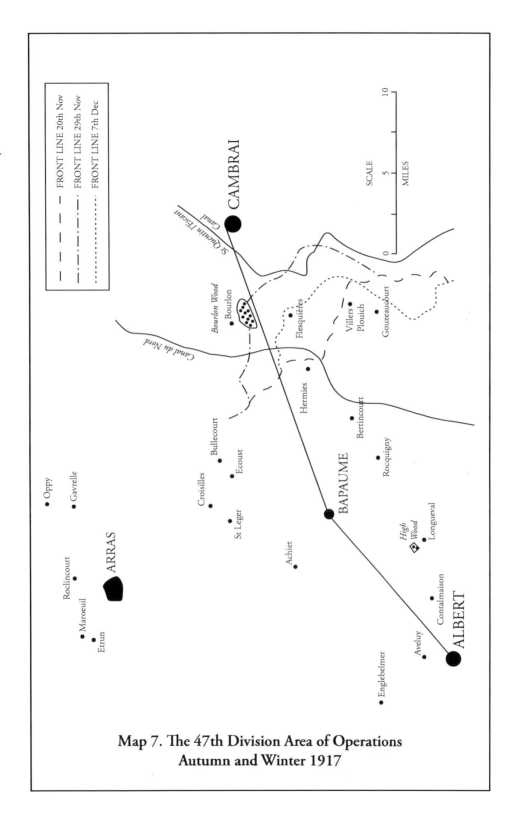

Map 7. The 47th Division Area of Operations
Autumn and Winter 1917

FRONT LINE 20th Nov
FRONT LINE 29th Nov
FRONT LINE 7th Dec

CAMBRAI

St Quentin l'Escaut Canal

Bourlon Wood
Bourlon

Flesquières

Villers
Plouich
Gouzeaucourt

Canal du Nord

Hermies

Bertincourt

Rocquigny

Bullecourt
Ecoust

Croisilles

St Leger

Achiet

BAPAUME

High
Wood
Longueval

Contalmaison

Aveluy

ALBERT

Englebelmer

ARRAS

Roclincourt

Maroeuil

Etrun

Oppy

Gavrelle

SCALE

MILES

0   5   10

along with it? They will soon become an enormous weight to carry about. ... I have sent a parcel from Fortnum's every week; so let me know if they still arrive. ... Darling, I didn't mean to give the impression I was bored at Woodford – it was only the 1½ hr in church! Otherwise, I love being there and getting to know a little more of them [Mary and Hulbert Wathen]. Of course I was lonely: I pretty nearly always am, except when I'm working. ...

I came down on the train tonight with Mrs Wright, Mr Ronald and Mr Hylton Stewart [all Haileybury staff]. We had all been to the String Quartet concert, but I was late so did not discover them. ... Darling, it's so jolly the way all the Haileybury folk are so friendly and it's all because they are your friends. Miss Secretan was no one, but Mrs C. H. F. a most important being. Mrs Wright begged me to come again too. Poor Mrs Wright: she had just seen her second boy off to France for the first time, and Jack had gone off too. I know so well how she felt. ... I am making a vast effort to remember (with no success) that I have the best man in the world for my sweetheart. I forget that (a) he is away; (b) no prospect of leave; (c) I am darned tired of the lonely life.

Charles to Marjorie   23rd November, 1917
2.00 p.m.

I am away from the Regiment for a day or two and so am still without your letter. ... I think our <u>very</u> long trail is definitely "off" which is something gained, but I expect we are in for something pretty vigorous. ... Meanwhile, I am here on an unpleasant job, but in very pleasant surroundings. Two of our subalterns have got in to a rotten scrape about two girls at a place where they were on a course and away from the Regiment, with the result that they are in for a Court Martial. I have come here to speak for their character with the Regiment and give them a leg up generally. We are all very much distressed about it and one of them is a simply splendid chap. Of course a convivial evening was the real cause of it. I came over in a motor ambulance and quite enjoyed that part of the outing; also I am sleeping in a bed with sheets for the first time since September 29th! It is a treat. I expect to re-join the Battalion tomorrow, though goodness knows where they will be by then. ... Everything in this little village is quite peaceful and the people so kind and my room so clean. ...

24th November, 1917
7.00 a.m. In bed!

... The Court Martial on those two boys[397] takes place this morning. Personally, I believe they are innocent – after having a talk with them yesterday. Till then I expected to find that they had been foolish at any rate, but now I think the whole thing is a put-up job and I have great hopes that they may get off. It is quite possible that the cases may not get finished today. I should like another night in a real bed,

....

397 Lt H. Ferguson and 2/Lt Sydney L. Batte were tried under Section 40 of the Army Act which concerned acting 'to the prejudice of good order and military discipline'. (TNA WO 90/8 Judge Advocate General's Office: Officers' Courts Martial Records, abroad). Batte had enlisted in the ranks of the 19th Londons on 28th Sept. 1914 and arrived with the 1/19th in France on 10th Mar. 1915. He was promoted to sergeant before being commissioned in the field on 5th Nov. 1916. He had served continuously with the Battalion in France until he died of wounds on 19th Jan. 1918. He is buried at Rocquigny-Equancourt Road British Cemetery (grave IX.D.21). (TNA WO 374/4733)

but I want badly to get back to receive Marjorie's letters, as I haven't had any for three days. ...

It is very wet and blustery and, as far as I can make out, the Battalion is trekking onward ever onward. Goodness knows where I shall find them when this business is over. I seem to have been in an absolute whirl of uncertainty for the last ten days – a sort of nightmare from which I have not yet woken up. ...

25th November, 1917

7.00 a.m. Again in bed!

The Court Martial went on so long yesterday that I had to stay another night here. The two boys were both acquitted; in fact, there were some pretty strong remarks made about the case ever having been brought up at all. It was trumped up, I think. Of course all the village knew about it and the people at my billet said that if anything had happened to the officers the ladies in the case would have been whipped by their gentle sisters among the local population! We all walked into the nearest town and had dinner to celebrate our success. Goodness knows where we shall find the Battalion today. I know they are still trekking about and we shall probably have an awful job to discover them. ...

What news of Esmé? I am not sure I should know her again if I saw her – our acquaintance has been so very brief. ...

<u>Later</u>:

[Achiet]

November 26th

10.00 a.m.

Reached the Regiment all right last night after a roundabout journey. Found four letters from my beloved. I hope you are feeling more cheerful now, darling, about our future: things are not too bad, though inclined to be exciting. ...

[Rocquigny]

26th November, 1917

Mid-day

I just put a hurried note at the end of my last letter to say that I had re-joined the Battalion. It was a wearisome journey and I only managed to finish it at all by calling at Divisional HQ to ask for a car to take me the last part of the way. It is fearfully cold and there has been a raging gale for three days, which generally means suspension of traffic in the Channel and no post! ... Goodness knows what we are in for but for the time being, at any rate, I don't think <u>those</u> fears will be realized, but I honestly don't know and only hope for the best. ...

[Rocquigny]

27th November, 1917

9.15 a.m.

I can't help feeling a bit depressed today. The Regiment is not with me and I am left behind with a certain number of others to be fetched if wanted. It is simply <u>hateful</u> seeing them go off and knowing they can't <u>all</u> return. Also, it is a bit of weather as bad as anything I have ever seen. All last night it snowed and blew and now it is simply pouring and has been so for several hours. We got up soon after 5.00 a.m. and I am now waiting to collect the remnants. I haven't any idea what sort of place we shall be housed in, or whether I shall be sent for later on. Anyway, I don't see how any post is going to reach me for some days. But, however beastly it all is here, I would far rather face whatever is in store in these parts than go right away, as we feared. It is astonishing how the weather always turns against us when we look like having a really good show. A Fortnum parcel arrived yesterday – cutlets and various potted meats. I thought that the poor devils going forward had better take most of them, as their rations are likely to be a very uncertain matter. I seem to have been living in a constant nightmare for the last ten days and I can see absolutely no end to it yet. I don't know what I should do if it wasn't for you, Marjorie darling. ...

It is sometimes desperately hard to believe that we <u>are</u> winning the war, isn't it, and today is one of them. We ourselves practically always beat the Boche, but other people don't seem to. I am so glad you have seen Mrs Tennant and I am awfully relieved to hear that her husband has been out of the latest Palestine fighting.[398] She is so absolutely wrapped up in him and he has never seen his daughter who is just over a year old. ...

<u>Later</u>: 8.00 p.m. in a truck (previous occupants probably horses!) I have written to you from some fairly odd places, darling, but this beats them all! We got into this wonderful railway conveyance at 12.30 p.m. and at present have gone 1½ hours. We are fourteen officers in this truck, all from different battalions. ... If it wasn't for being separated from the others and not knowing what is ahead of them or me, I should be rather enjoying it. Your flask (full of rum) is in my pocket and I have got my knee-covers, British warm and the fleece lining from my mackintosh, so I am quite warm and when I finish writing my wife's air-pillow is just handy to prop up my head on my haversack, which bulges with her letters and photographs. ... I had a letter from Mary again yesterday. You have made great conquests at Woodford, darling, as I knew you would and she thinks it is so brave of you to face Sunday in a vicarage without me! ... I hear that George [Fulton] has gone as Second-in-Command to a battalion of the Cheshires. ...

[Engelbelmer]
28th November
6.30 a.m. in bed

Just arrived! It was quite a short journey but took simply ages. Such a nice billet, darling, but I hate the contrast between me and wherever the others are.

[Engelbelmer]
28th November, 1917

... We have no news of the others yet and can hardly expect it. I do trust they won't have too awful a time. This village has been knocked about a little but my bedroom has obviously been rebuilt and papered. It has a brass-railed single bed and a little table. ... I must be sparing of my notepaper till I find somewhere I can buy some more. ... There is an English cemetery which I penetrated today, but I didn't see any names I knew. I have moved about so much during the last week or so that I feel quite bewildered. There is no sign yet of any leave re-opening. I hope

....

398 Charles's Haileybury colleague Maj Roy Tennant was with the 2/19th London Regt in Palestine. The British Army was advancing on Jerusalem which fell on 9th Dec. 1917.

there will be some before long: it makes the whole difference to everyone's temper. The mud even here, well away from the trenches, is simply appalling. ...

[Engelbelmer]
29th November, 1917 -
9.15 a.m.

Not very much news as yet. I am still in the same place and enjoying my billet, but we are pretty short of everything and practically no chance of adding to our stores or receiving any post, but we are, for the time being, well away from the trenches, though I can't believe it can last for very long. ...

No rations arrived yesterday, but again my thoughtful wife came to our rescue.

[Engelbelmer]
29th November, 1917
6.00 p.m.

I believe we have at last managed to arrange for our letters to get posted, so that probably, after you have had no letters from me for a few days, you will get a whole pile at once. I am still in the same spot from which I last wrote. This afternoon I went for a walk with Fox.[399] He is the Company Commander who had a son and heir arrive on 25th October. It was really quite a nice walk and not too muddy. I believe we are within a ride of where Toby is buried and, if only I had my horse, I would try to go over and find the spot.

Until this point, the 47th Division had not been involved in the Battle of Cambrai. However, on the night of 28th/29th November it took over the Bourlon Wood sector from the 62nd Division. It had been a difficult relief for the Division since the Germans were shelling the wood. As 2i/c Charles had been left out of battle.

[Engelbelmer]
30th November, 1917

Your husband is getting dreadfully impatient for a post which it seems almost impossible to get before I rejoin the Battalion. I do hope my letters are reaching you all right: they have been given to all sorts of odd people to stamp and post. This morning Fox and I went for another walk – quite a nice one, and mostly along the edge of some woods which were practically unspoilt by the war and must be very pretty in summer. I thought so much of our lovely walks together, darling, in those heavenly days last September. ... This afternoon we have organized a cross-country race of about two miles for the men here. Your portly Major will not take part! ...

[Engelbelmer]
1st December, 1917
8.00 a.m.

We have been sent for to the Battalion. I don't know what has happened or what is wanted, but hope that things are not bad. ...

....

399 Capt Harold Fox had been commissioned into the 19th Londons before the outbreak of war. He joined the 1/19th in France on 13th May 1915 and returned sick to England in Sept. 1916. He returned to the Battalion on 8th May 1917 and his MC was gazetted on 1st Jan. 1918. He was taken prisoner on 24th Mar. 1918.

What had actually happened to the 1st/19th Londons is best shown by quoting the war diary which is in Charles's own hand-writing. It would have been written a day or two later from information supplied by the survivors:

> **28th November**: During the night the wood [Bourlon] was bombarded with 7.7s, 4.2s and 5.9s. At 11.30 p.m. the enemy put over gas shells, mainly of the tear variety. The gas bombardment lasted until –

> **29th November** at 2.15 a.m. when it slackened until 6.00 a.m. when a heavy bombardment was put up around the wood on the Bapaume-Cambrai road. SOS was put up on the left of the wood and our Artillery opened fire. Shelling slackened about 8.00 a.m. During the morning hostile planes flew low over the wood, which was followed by shelling of the wood. From 3.00 p.m. to 6.00 p.m. heavy bombardment of gas shells and HE. Men were sick and their eyes affected. 2/Lt Kemp and Lt Axford went to the Aid Post gassed at 7.00 p.m. Heavy shelling of the wood began at the same time. 11.30 p.m. further bombardment.

> **30th November**: 3.15 a.m. shelling ceased. Men were arriving at the Aid Post all through the night and were sent down. At 9.00 a.m. the MO visited all Companies and reported 50% gassed badly and should be evacuated at once. Capt Baker, Lt Sinclair, Lt Smith and 2/Lt Morrison passed through the Aid Post gassed, B Coy thus being left without any officers. In the early afternoon Capt Welch and Lt Gilchrist also passed through, C Coy also being left without officers. The CO visited all Companies and found only 10 NCOs and men all badly gassed in C Coy trenches and about 30 NCOs and men in the same condition in B Coy trenches. At 6.00 p.m. the MO had to retire gassed, followed by 2/Lt Butler and Lt Barclay. During the whole of this period intermittent hostile shelling of the wood continued.

> **1st December**: Remainder of D Company who were in support to 18th Battalion came back under Lt McNichol with 2/Lt Batte and joined the remainder of the Battalion in A Company's trench, Lt McNichol assuming command of the joint company. Intermittent shelling all day. During the night the Battalion was withdrawn to Hindenburg Support Line which was reached about 4.00 a.m. next morning (2nd December).

Of the fifteen officers and 600 men who had gone into Bourlon Wood, only six officers and 61 men (with six Lewis guns) were able to retire unaided on 2nd December. This meant the Battalion had suffered a casualty rate of about 90 per cent. Those wounded by HE or gas, having gone through the aid posts, went on to the Casualty Clearing Stations. The more serious cases were taken further back to the Base Hospitals at Rouen or Étaples on the Channel coast. Although the majority of these wounded men would eventually recover, a total of 47 officers and men died of gas at Étaples, almost within sight of England. They are buried in Étaples Military Cemetery which is second only to Tyne Cot Cemetery, near Ypres, in the number of British war graves. As it lies further from the Western Front, Étaples is less visited but the cemetery is a particularly beautiful and moving place. Another thirty officers and men are buried in St Sever Cemetery and Extension at Rouen.

* * * * *

Although not present in the fighting around Bourlon Wood, Philip Dodgson had arrived in France after recovering from his wound and was on his way back to join the 47th Division.

Philip to his mother

Hotel de Paris
Boulogne
30th November, 1917

You will see from this that I have arrived safely. We had an early lunch at Folkestone and crossed over this afternoon. It was lovely and fresh on the sea but not rough, for which I was thankful. ... I am going straight up to the 47th Division. As you can imagine, I was very pleased when I heard of this as I hated the idea of going to Havre. It does feel strange to be back in France again, and at present I can think of hardly anything else but what a glorious time I have had, and I do want to thank you and Hamilton for all you've done ... . It was just hateful having to say goodbye to you all, but I loved you coming to the station, and I hope you found a good breakfast waiting for you. The train went off very suddenly, didn't it? But perhaps it was best. ..

* * * * *

The remains of the 1/19th Londons, plus the reinforcements Charles had brought with him, had taken up a new position in the old German support line, some miles back from Bourlon Wood.

Charles to Marjorie

[Hindenburg support line]
2nd December, 1917,
4.30 p.m.

I am back with the Battalion after very many weary hours of trudging and making enquiries. We are pretty well in the thick of things and it is not pleasant. I will try and find time to write you a proper letter later on, but at present it is rather difficult to do so without saying things that I shouldn't. I haven't yet had your letters, as all the post was packed up when I passed by it, so I have heard nothing for practically a week. I do hunger for news of you and it is awfully tantalizing to know that there are several letters knocking about France for me somewhere. Things are very noisy, darling, and we are awfully busy.

[Hindenburg support line]
3rd December, 1917

... I am writing from an old Boche dugout and it is fairly comfy but damnably cold. Things have been a bit quieter today, but the others had some pretty rough

times while I was away from them and those that are still here look most awfully
tired. At the present moment (6.00 p.m.) we don't know if we are going to spend
the night in the draughty dugout or literally in the open air. The night before last
I and three others tramped about from 9.00 p.m. till 2.30 a.m. trying to find our
transport in a big wood and finally gave it up and lay down in a wooden hut on
some thin laths of wood. We lit a fire, but it was desperately cold and of course we
had been very hot while tramping about for five hours and more in the mud. Also, I
fell all my length in the muddiest part of the wood and got pretty wet. ... Last night
I slept side-by-side with the Adjutant on bare boards in a Boche cubbyhole. A rat
squeaked between the boards and suddenly jumped through onto us. We leapt out
in terror (much worse than a shell!) and that spoilt our night's rest again! ...

[Hermies]
4th December, 1917
4.00 p.m.

We are out of the trenches at last, though not very far away as yet. The Battalion
has had a rough time but I am so awfully proud of them, though I feel horribly
mean to have only been with them at the finish. Many of my friends are not with
us now but, as regards officers, there are not any killed or dead that we know of.
They did splendidly in most difficult circumstances. We are now busy getting things
straight again and hoping for a little rest, which may give us the chance for our 10th
December dinner after all. If there is half a chance, we shall have it, though with
diminished numbers. ...

I forgot to tell you that, in my wild chase after the Battalion, I passed within half
a mile of Toby's grave. It may have been a little fanciful but, as I passed the village,
I raised my hand in a salute to his memory because I owe him you, darling, and
nothing can ever repay that debt to his memory. I don't know whether Mrs Fulton
is the sort of person who would like to know this: if you think so, tell her. It was
awfully interesting passing through the battlefields and seeing the places which I
suppose helped me to get my DSO.

* * * * *

Philip Dodgson was now back in the same area with the 47th Division artillery.

Philip to his mother

[Metz]
C/235 Bty RFA
4th December, 1917

I am at present with the Divisional Ammunition Column, having arrived here
yesterday. ... The journey was on the whole pretty beastly though it was fortunate
the weather was fine, but it was cold and some wretched person took my coat
on the way and didn't return it, so I was fortunate I had that Jaeger waistcoat. I
had some difficulty in finding the Division as they had been moving about. The
train journey up from Boulogne took twelve hours, which was boring. Fortunately
we had provided ourselves with sandwiches and biscuits. We were deposited at
midnight in a ruined town and the only accommodation was two draughty huts
crowded with officers lost like ourselves. We stayed there Sunday night as well, and
came on here by lorry yesterday. ...

I walked up to the Battery with Pixley today: it's about four miles, so we've had a good walk. I only got as far as the horse lines and missed Pilditch, but found him here on our return. They seem to have had a very thrilling time these last few days. ...

Everybody seems to be in pretty good spirits, personally I just long for the end of the War. I am afraid the glorious time I've just had in England hasn't made me any keener on this life. ... All this beastly Censor business completely puts me off letter writing, so this is a very dull letter, and I wrote Evelyn an equally dull one this morning; but when you mayn't say where you are or what is going on, and these are the only two things of interest to write about, it does make letter writing difficult. I feel awfully fit in myself and am eating tremendously. I think this frosty, sunny weather is very healthy.

I saw both my horses today looking very well – but I am sorry they didn't recognise me!

* * * * *

Charles to Marjorie   [Bertincourt]
5th December, 1917
3.30 p.m.

We are getting a bit further away by degrees, but the others have had a most awfully rough time and we are pretty short-handed. Now a crowning blow as Stokes has got to give in and go to hospital with eczema and throat trouble, and I shouldn't be surprised if he went home. This, of course, leaves me temporarily in command.[400] It is the third time I have had to carry on in another's place and I'll manage to do it again, if I go mad in the attempt. At present Sheppard, the Adjutant, is all right and I hope to goodness he will keep so. We shall be a tiny crew for 10th December but we <u>will</u> celebrate it somehow! It is a sad business but I have fared worse and everyone is so splendidly willing and helpful. Darling, I <u>am</u> so proud of my Division. They are never much to look at but for enduring sheer hell they can't be beaten. ... My dearest, I shall need <u>all</u> your help in these times which lie ahead to keep me worthy of the Regiment and of your

Charles Fair as Second-in-Command, sketched by 2/Lt J. W. D. Muff-Ford

....

400   The Battalion war diary for that day records "Reorganisation continued. Lt Col Stokes DSO MC, Lt Mc-Nichol, Lt Axford went to hospital suffering from gas poisoning. Maj C. H. Fair DSO assumed command." (TNA WO 95/2738)

wonderful love. Any letters of mine might be reaching you on your birthday from now onwards. I couldn't think of you more than I do already, but I shall be even extra loving and grateful to Fate when that day comes along. What tons of love we are saving up, aren't we, for that next meeting? I expect I shall be awfully busy for a long time now, so don't mind if my letters seem scrappy and pre-occupied. I haven't the least idea what will be our next move in the dark. Latterly we have hardly been able to see the wood for the trees! I love you more every day, sweetheart.

Marjorie to Charles Hill House
5th December, 1917

I had three letters this morning ... the last mentioning you had been called to join the Battalion. As there was that fearful attack on the 3rd, I can't but feel horribly anxious and I know I won't be able to hear for a day or two how you got on. Thank goodness you were out of the Friday show. I don't know what I should do if it were not for my work. The little boys occupy my entire attention all the morning and by the end of the day I am usually only too ready to fall asleep and forget it all. ...

If you should get near Contalmaison any time you will find Toby's grave all by itself in a valley a little to the south-west of what was the village.

It is wonderful how regular your letters have been up till now. I don't think I have ever been more than two days without one and very seldom that. I shall probably not go to Seaford after all unless I hear from you (that) you are safely through the fighting before Saturday. I would be worrying all the time lest there was news of you here. ...

Charles to Marjorie [Bertincourt]
6th December, 1917

Your letter written on 30th November has just come together with one from Humphrey. I'm so glad he is getting on so well. We are still where I wrote from yesterday: I don't know for how long. Anyway, I see no prospect of any "rest" here as, whether we are fighting or not, the Battalion has got to be entirely reorganized and to a certain extent re-equipped, and there are very few of us to do it. I only hope to goodness I can keep fit, as I seem to be almost the only link between the past and the present, except the Adjutant, and he is none too well. Darling, I can't tell you how you and your love are helping me. I have got a tremendous job to face and I know you will expect me to do it and that is such an incentive. ... Did I tell you that Woolley rolled into our dugout the other evening? He has had a rough time but is still quite immaculately turned out. I hope you will soon let me know that you have bought that wristwatch, darling. Surely I ought to send some more money to cover my Fortnum parcels? That original £5 deposit must be used up by now. Does brother Humphrey think I am very extravagant for not being as Spartan as he is? ...

[Bertincourt]
7th December, 1917,
11.30 a.m.

The work of reorganisation goes on slowly, but it is rather sad and depressing to have to do it for the third time in my career out here.[401] The difficulty is that there are so few people to put in positions of authority. I told one or two of our subalterns who were likely to go to London, to let me know what hospital they are sent to, as so many of them come from Scotland and they might find a visit from Mrs C. H. F. cheering! I'm afraid we shan't have much opportunity of taking breath before we are wanted for something or other again. Last night we had some bombs dropped in our neighbourhood, but they are a minor discomfort! As long as the post continues to come, I can put up with anything! We are going to try and raise a Dinner on the 10th, but I greatly fear we shall inevitably be back in the trenches by then.

Later: ... It is rather cheerless here now, darling, – only three of us left out of that very cheery Mess of a month ago, but I'll see the thing through somehow, because I know you expect it of me. Your letters are more valuable than ever if it is possible. ...

Marjorie to Charles   Hill House
7th December, 1917

No letter today, but I did not expect it. I think I must take the next train to the Kaiser and tell him this simply can't go on. Picture to yourself your wife waking with rather a heavy heart tearing, her furs and long coat flapping, to the station of a morning, somewhat absorbed in divers pursuits all day, and returning up this hill of an evening almost afraid to go in for fear what news may have arrived during the day. And so on... day after day, world without end – Amen!

Today I went to the Coliseum with Humphrey. He gets about easily and is recommended for a seaside hospital and electric massage. Tomorrow we are lunching together and going to "The Invisible Foe". I can't go to Seaford until I know about you. Isn't it odd to think we have never been to a play together, I mean just alone together. Oh! How jealous I am of all the girls I see with their khaki-clad escorts.

Charles to Marjorie   [Bertincourt]
8th December, 1917
3.30 p.m.

... No letter from you today, nor any post at all – always a bad blow. Darling, I can't help feeling lonely; our merry Mess of eight or nine is reduced to three and I fully expect the Adjutant to go to hospital tomorrow. The last three weeks has been a very heavy strain on him. Your husband is almost too fit for this war! Except for occasional neuralgia, I am really perfectly well – the only officer in the Battalion who has been out a long time and is still really well. ... Unfortunately, I see absolutely no signs of a change of scene for us, and all round here everything is frightfully desolate. Also we have, at present, a rather aged Brigadier [Erskine] who never smiles. Thank goodness your husband can still see the funny side of things – nothing has ever yet robbed me of that. Luckily, in our present quarters we

....

401 The Battalion was by now greatly under strength and had been organised into two rifle companies instead of the normal four. Charles had previously reorganised the Battalion twice on the Somme in late Sept. 1916 (after High Wood) and in Oct. 1916 (after the actions on the Flers Line).

have a good brick fireplace and plenty of logs. If only we could share the firelight with a sofa, or even one big comfy armchair between us. ... We have got four or five fresh officers who seem quite nice and willing, but I miss the old lot dreadfully, just as I did after the Somme last year.[402] The frost has broken and the mud is rapidly becoming worse than ever. ...

[Bertincourt]
9th December, 1917
2.00 p.m.

... We are still in our ruined village and thankful for small mercies. If we are still here tomorrow, we are going to meet for dinner and drink my beloved's health, though catering for a real Dinner has been practically impossible and, in addition, our Mess Sergeant has not returned from his leave as we had hoped. The rain is simply streaming down. This morning we had a church parade in a cinema hut and, when it was over, I said a few words to what is left of the Battalion about keeping

things going and so on – not an easy task when one's heart is feeling very heavy. We are pretty well organized now as regards the men we <u>have</u> got, but I am dreadfully afraid of the Adjutant [Sheppard] having to go to hospital: he is such a splendid boy – one mass of grit and very good-looking. ...

This morning I went for a very wet tramp over some fields to find a small rifle range and came back very cold and depressed, but all clouds went when I found your two letters, my darling. ...

Charles to his father   [Bertincourt]
9th December, 1917

The remnant that is left has led a fairly quiet life since I last wrote, tho' I suppose it can't last. I think I told you Stokes has had to leave us and I am once more left in command. Unfortunately Sheppard, the Adjutant, is pretty seedy and I fear he will have to go down for a bit too. Otherwise – apart from the worry and occasional neuralgia – I am quite fit. We managed to get together quite a good scratch concert last night,

The Adjutant, Captain J. J. Sheppard MC. He had enlisted in the 19th Londons as a private soldier on 1 Sept 1914 and had served at Loos as Signal Sergeant. He was commissioned in early 1916 and as a Lt-Col commanded the 1/19th Londons for a time in 1918.

....

402   The Battalion war diary records that on 4th Dec. 1917 "2/Lts [W. W.] Wilson, Clark, Harper and Cunningham joined [the] Battalion." (TNA WO 95/2738)

which cheered up the men. Today we are ordered to have a 'Thanksgiving Service" – what for, is not quite clear – perhaps those amazing people who rang joy-bells in England can explain. I am feeling very much incensed against our friends the Staff: we had the hottest corner of all that trying week, but the only Staff officer who visited us was the newest of the lot. Perhaps he had not had time to forget what the regimental soldier's life is like. The frost has broken and the mud is getting worse than ever. We have a Mess which is far too large for our reduced numbers. It is in a patched up French house, but it has quite a good brick fireplace and the *débris* of the village gives an unending supply of firewood.

... We were for some days without a doctor, ours having become a casualty,[403] until I met one whom I knew in the road and obtained permission to keep him.

Charles to Marjorie   [Bertincourt]
10th December, 1917
6.00 p.m.

Our departure was postponed for a day at the last minute and we are really having a little "do" tonight after all! We shall be eleven and I will send you the

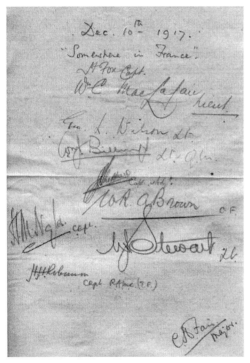

menu and the names of those present. Sweetheart, you <u>have</u> altered all the world for me when I look back to the lonely bachelor of this day a year ago. Everything is rather gloomy still and I expect to be in the front line tomorrow night. ... Wilson[404] has just come back from his leave and I have been thanking him for telephoning to you. Naylor has also just rejoined after his long absence and I have been hearing all about his visit to you – but that seems dreadfully long ago. I have got to write a letter to the fiancée of one of our officers who has died of wounds. I am so sorry for them, knowing what they have missed by not being married. Darling, a certain amount of leave is reopening, so we must hope for the best, but I'm afraid the CO is off to England, so I can't say at all when I am likely to have any chance.

Signatures of officers attending the dinner in Marjorie's honour on 10th Dec. 1917

....

403 Capt W. Fotheringham MC MB, RAMC had retired gassed on 30th Nov. His MC was awarded on 2nd July 1917 and a bar to his MC would be awarded on 1st Jan. 1918.

404 Lt George Logan Wilson MC was from Lewisham and had served in the ranks of the 20th Londons before the outbreak of war. He was a sergeant when he went to France with the 1/20th Londons in Mar. 1915. He was commissioned on 14th Dec. 1915 and served with the 3/19th Londons in England until he joined the 1/19th Londons in France on 17th Nov. 1916. His award of the MC was gazetted on 27th July 1917.

Charles enclosed a sheet of paper with the signatures of all those present at the dinner party.

Charles to Marjorie   [Bertincourt]
11th December, 1917

... I am still in the same little ruined village from which I have written for the last five or six days. I haven't yet had to go up, tho' I have actually packed up once or twice and last night we <u>did</u> have something like a dinner at which our health was nobly drunk. The *padré* insisted on making a little speech in which he said (apparently quite innocently), "Major Fair has found, as we all do in this country, that he can't get on without a woman"!![405]

There are rumours, alarms and excursions every day but I see no chance of quitting this undesirable neighbourhood yet. Two Fortnum parcels from my very attentive wife reached me today. You do spoil me, darling. I am for the moment in charge of all sorts of odd bits of regiments – rather a difficult task in a way. ...

[Bertincourt]
12th December, 1917
3.30 p.m.

I am still in the same place, thank goodness, though we have had to lend a Company to some other people who are more in the heart of things. It is reasonably fine and I have just been on quite a nice little walk with the doctor whom we have got with us for the time being, our own having become a casualty ten days ago. We are gradually getting news back from some of our casualties: two of the subalterns have died in hospital,[406] I am sorry to say. ... I wish I saw some chance of my getting away early in January: I don't, now that the CO has become a casualty. We are sleeping six in a rebuilt French cottage. Really quite comfortable and I have a little table on which Marjorie's photos stand looking at me so sweetly all the time – the last thing I look at at night and the first thing I see in the morning. Darling, the more I look at your photos the more proud I am of my wife. I have seen lots of photos of wives (and others!) belonging to men out here, but nobody who can be compared at all to my Marjorie: she is so sweet and I do love her so utterly.

Interrupted here by arrival of your little letter dated 7th December. Poor little darling, I do hate to have you so worried and all about me, but there is something sweet in it all the same (can you understand that?) to feel that I do matter so much. ...

* * * * *

Philip to his mother   [Metz]
C/235 Bty RFA
12th December, 1917

... I am still in the DAC. I am very annoyed that the Staff has made all this difficulty about my going back to the Battery. I saw the Staff Captain today who told

....

405 Almost certainly the Rev W. R. A. Brown (see footnote 420, Chapter 17) who was given to a humorous turn of phrase.

406 Lt F. W. H. Smith and 2/Lt Joseph Morrison had both died on 4th Dec. and they were followed by 2/Lt Gavin Wilson Sinclair (7th Dec.) and 2/Lt A. E. W. Kemp (10th Dec.).

me that he thought I should be going in a few days, but the General [Bellingham] hadn't quite made up his mind! As it turned out, between you and me, I'm not altogether sorry as they've had a beastly uncomfortable time lately, practically living in the open through all this cold weather – but it annoys me to think that they should make a favour of sending me back to my own Battery. ...

I am living with Pixley in a small wooden hut which used to be used as a gas chamber and so, having been made more or less gas-tight, is now fairly free from draughts, the weather being pretty severe. ... It makes us long for the good old days when we used to have billets. We had a try the other day to get back to a civilised town to do a little shopping, and I also wanted to stop on the way to go and see Toby's grave. We got a lorry all right here but unfortunately the roads were so congested with troops that it took us four and a half hours to get half way, so we had to have lunch and come back. If I can manage another day I shall do so. ...

Guy had also written to Helen on his way back to the Front the previous week:

> Hotel Burlington
> Dover
> 4th December, 1917
>
> I sent you a PC yesterday that we were going across at twelve o'clock, but we are still here. I don't quite know why, but I believe it was something to do with the wind making sailings impossible. Anyhow, we expect to cross today. It is very cold but a lovely day and it ought to be ripping on the sea. We have had a very comfortable night at this hotel, though it is rather a nuisance being held up like this.

> [Eecke]
> 7th December, 1917
>
> I got back the day before yesterday in the evening after a rather tiresome journey. I think I wrote and told you they kept us a day at Dover and after that we slept a night at Calais, where the worthy Boche dropped bombs on us with no great effect; though causing me to spend a good part of the night in the cellar. Then we had a slow railway journey and finally arrived about six in the evening. But the news on arrival amply made up for the beastliness of the journey. The [39th] Division is really going back for a rest. We start going back tomorrow and go to within ten miles of the sea, so it really is something worth having and we shall be a nice long way from the war. ... We expect to stay back about three weeks, so we shall get Christmas in civilization. ...

The 1/1st Hertfordshires and 118th Infantry Brigade relocated to the hills to the south of Calais.

Guy to his mother   [Alincthun]
11th December, 1917

... I think I told you we are now right back and really miles from the war. We came here almost directly after I got back. ... Brigade HQ are in a large *château* where we live in great comfort. I have a fire in my bedroom! It really is lovely down here. The country is hilly and rather like Hertfordshire, with any number of little, winding lanes and villages and the weather is splendid with frosts at night and clear, sunny days. It really is a magnificent existence and I wouldn't mind spending the remains of the war under these conditions. I believe we are to spend Christmas here. ... The only bad part is that the battalions are rather a long way away: the Herts are about six miles away and it's rather difficult to get to see them. ...

[Alincthun]
14th December, 1917

I have had several letters from you since I have been back but I am afraid I have been rather lazy myself about writing. Perhaps it is the effect of this gentlemanly life of ease we are leading now. Everybody is enjoying it. ... I spend a good deal of my time riding round on a horse visiting people, which I think you will agree is a good way of carrying on the war. I went into the town yesterday to see a bit of life and succeeded in grossly over-eating at dinner! I succeeded, however, in getting a piano for the time we are here, so that ought to cheer things up a bit at Christmas. The next idea is to get some nurses to come up and give a dance in our *château*. ...

* * * * *

Charles to Marjorie   [Bertincourt]
13th December, 1917,
6.00 p.m.

... Everything is still absolutely uncertain here, but we are gradually getting things straight again. I am sorry to say that Baker[407] – one of our Captains – has died in hospital as a result of the recent action. He was one of the best and a great friend of mine and we got our Commissions the same day. It is simply hateful writing letters to the relations of those who have gone under. Baker and Morrison[408] were both engaged and one of the other subalterns was married. Try not to worry too much about me, darling: I am keeping quite well and reasonably cheerful. The news of the fall of Jerusalem is really cheering: I do wonder if Roy Tennant is there now. Your scholastic husband was able, without looking it up, to tell the Mess the exact year when it was last in Christian hands.[409] ... Woolley came in to tea today. He had a very rough time last week and, thank Heaven, he came through all right. He seems quite all right again now and enquired much after you. ... At present we are doing very well as Xmas parcels keep arriving for Stokes and, as he is not here, we open them and greedily consume the contents!

....

407 Capt George William Baker (see footnote 283, Chap 13) died at No. 8 General Hospital Rouen on 5th Dec. 1917 of gas received at Bourlon Wood on 1st Dec. He was 32 and is buried at St Sever Cemetery, Rouen (Officers' Plot B, grave 3.17).

408 2/Lt Joseph McLaren Morrison was a shipping clerk from a skilled working class background in Glasgow. He had originally enlisted in Aug. 1916 under the Derby Scheme as a trooper in the Lanarkshire Yeomanry. He was commissioned into the 19th Londons on 27th June 1917. He had disembarked in France on 21st Aug. and joined the 1/19th on 20th Sept. He was engaged to Miss Helen Lawson and is buried in Étaples Military Cemetery. (grave XXVIII.D.8)

409 The previous Christian rulers of Jerusalem were the crusaders who lost the city to Saladin in the siege of 1187.

[Bertincourt]
14th December, 1917
4.00 p.m.

Your letter written on the 9th has just come. I am so very glad your anxiety has died down a bit and that you have been enjoying yourself with Humphrey. Do enjoy yourself every chance you get, dearest. ... Where is Humphrey going for his treatment? ... I want to meet him again so much: we shall talk an awful lot of Marlborough and Flanders shop, I expect! ... Please thank Uncle Basil for the cutting about the Lord Mayor (and himself!). We didn't see him, though he did see some of our Division – a good thing, too, as one of his predecessors kept us waiting three hours on a muddy field two years ago. I am still in our little re-built cottage and revelling in a real open brick fireplace with Yule logs crackling. I don't know how long one can dare to hope that such comparative comfort can go on. It is sad that nearly all our buglers and drummers have become casualties and consequently, when next we march, it will be a very silent proceeding. Leave is at present rather restricted – preference being rightly given to those who had a bad time in the last show, but I think the end of January might find me coming. ...

[Bertincourt]
14th December, 1917

I forgot to say that one of our very nicest subalterns is now at home suffering from gas poisoning and, if you can find time to call in on him, I know he would be so pleased.

Lt W. J. Barclay,[410]
Ward C4, No. 3 General Hospital,
Wandsworth. S.W.

In the next bed is one of our *padrés* – named Monro – an Old Marlburian.[411] They are both feeling pretty rotten, I think.

....

410 Barclay (see footnote 377, Chapter 15) spent until May 1918 on sick leave but does not appear to have re-joined the 1/19th Londons on the Western Front. He was gazetted with the MC on 1st Jan. 1918 and Mentioned in Dispatches in May 1918. (TNA WO 374/3855)

411 The Rev Robert Elliot Monro, the Church of England chaplain attached to 141st Infantry Brigade, had been gassed at Bourlon Wood. (Maude, op cit, p. 220) He had been six years ahead of Charles Fair at Marlborough and was also the son of a vicar. He had been ordained in 1905 after graduating from Hertford College Oxford and was appointed vicar of St. Matthias, Bethnal Green in 1913 and Chaplain to the Forces in 1916.

Chapter 17

December 1917 to January 1918

(For 47th Division operations in this period, see Map 7)

After the casualties suffered at the Third Battle of Ypres and at Cambrai, the British Army was short of men at the end of 1917. This situation would be exacerbated as the BEF took over more of the Western Front from the French in January 1918. American troops were eagerly awaited. Meanwhile, on the Eastern Front the Russians had accepted an armistice with the Central Powers on 16th December 1917. This would give the Germans the potential to reinforce the Western Front with Divisions transferred from the Eastern Front.

After Bourlon Wood the 47th Division withdrew to reorganise and refit. The infantry of 141st Infantry Brigade, which included Charles and the 1/19th Londons, relocated to an area near Albert on the 1916 Somme battlefield. The gunners of the 47th Division RFA, including Philip Dodgson, did not move so far to the rear so that their guns could support those Divisions now occupying the front line.

Charles to Marjorie   [Bertincourt]
15th December, 1917.
11.30 a.m.

Your birthday and a "very, very much in love with Marjorie" husband is thinking of you all the time and blessing every power there is for his wonderful little wife. … I wonder if you, like me, plan out over and over again every minute for the first twenty-four hours whenever we do meet again. I do, from the moment when I step out of the train and hug you in my arms, and go through everything we will do, in my mind, over and over again, practically every night before I go to sleep. I whisper it all to you, darling, and love to feel that perhaps you are whispering back to me all across the sea and the mud and the shell-holes and horror. …

Charles to his father   [Bertincourt]
15th December, 1917

… I had a Christmas card for the Battalion from Thwaites, who was our Brigadier till July 1916 and now commands a Division. … Our new Brigadier [Erskine] (who, incidentally, is rather old) shows distinct signs of breaking up. There are very few of the old gang left. I hope to have an opportunity during the next week of trying to find the graves of [Lt Col] Hamilton and others who were killed last year. ...

Charles to Marjorie   [Bruce Huts, Aveluy][412]
                                                         16th December, 1917
                                                         5.00 p.m.

A very bad tempered husband today, though on the face of it he ought to be pleased. We are at least right back at last – rather further than the place where Toby is buried. <u>But</u>

    (a)   No post for two days.

    (b)   It is snowing.

    (c)   I had only three hours sleep last night.

    (d)   We are in the worst camp I have ever seen.

This is what "they" provide as a rest place for men who have unquestionably gone through hell: huts which are utterly un-weatherproof – walls splitting apart – floors full of holes (your husband has fallen through the floor of the Mess three times already!) – three bunks for a whole Battalion to sleep on – two tables, two forms: this is all the furniture. No washing water within a mile. The CO sharing one of these luxurious palaces with eight other officers. This is all to my mind an absolute disgrace to all concerned. How can we buck up the men (who badly need it) either in mind or body in such a place? Every time anyone walks across the floor the candles fall over on the table and between the cracks in the floor we can see the refuse of the last inhabitants! I hope I am not unduly grumbling, but it is maddening to see, as I have done over and over again, the luxury in which many of the mighty and their underlings live and the poor devils who fight their battles and die for them have such places as these given them for a long-promised "rest". ...

Later: A ray of light at last – a late and unexpected post bringing a very sweet letter from my lady, written on the 10th. Darling, you always cure me when I am in a bad temper, and you know nothing really matters as long as you love me. It has absolutely cheered me up, though my feet are so cold I could almost cry and my head aches rather badly in consequence. It is snowing hard. ... Your socks and two handkerchiefs have just come. Thank you awfully, sweetheart. I love them and I know the socks will warm my toes tonight.

* * * * *

Meanwhile, Philip had returned to his battery of the 47th Divisional artillery.

Philip to Helen   [Metz]
                                                         C/235 Bty RFA
                                                         16th December, 1917

... I joined the Battery on the 13th, stayed two nights at the wagon line and came up to the guns on Friday. I am sorry to say our Colonel [Lt Col Gordon DSO] was

....

412 Just north of Albert

killed on Wednesday and our Senior Battery Commander was also wounded.[413] The Colonel is a great loss to the Brigade…. These casualties mean changes: Pilditch is going to command the Battery of the wounded Major, and Pixley is coming to us as Captain.[414]

… We are living fairly comfortably here except, as I said before, very crowded. We are down an old German dugout: it's at least thirty feet underground. It really consists of a shaft down at each end connected by a passage about four feet wide underground. It's pitch dark, of course, quite safe and moderately warm. … It's very nice for us that the Boche is so industrious … though I suppose he makes the Belgians do a lot for him.

Yesterday was a glorious sunny day. The Major and I spent most of it walking round to find the best places to observe from. It's very interesting work and I thoroughly enjoyed it. We saw a few Germans strolling about, but unfortunately were not in communication with the guns. I am afraid I mustn't tell you where I am. I heard that George's Division is somewhere round here. I've written him a line, so perhaps we may meet. …

* * * * *

Charles to Marjorie   [Bruce Huts, Aveluy]
17th December, 1917
7.00 p.m.

… I began to write this letter, but was interrupted by an OH … who has just joined our Division and is living in huts beside us. He was in my form in 1913 and was out here as long ago as Loos. I do love meeting these boys and the public school element was so refreshing among the weird and impossible officers we have now[415]. Whatever the faults of the system, the result is perfectly wonderful in producing men who can do wonders as leaders, however young and inexperienced they are. The cold is simply fearful: I took the Major General [Gorringe] all round this beastly camp today, and he said he would try and get us better quarters or, at least, the material to improve it. It is a gloomy spot in which to recuperate and there is so much to be done I haven't any hope really of leave for another month or six weeks. …

[Bruce Huts, Aveluy]
18th December, 1917
5.30 p.m.

This is really my Christmas letter, though I'm dreadfully afraid it may arrive late. Anyway, it brings oceans of wishes and love and kisses. I just live and fight

....

413   The war diary for 12th Dec. records "4.30 pm. Lt Col A. C. Gordon DSO killed by an odd shell which also wounded Maj E. R. Hatfield DSO. This occurred on B/235 position. Maj A. J. Cowan assumed command of Brigade." Gordon's burial at Ruyaulcourt Military Cemetery (grave G.10) is recorded the next day. (TNA WO 95/2717) Lt Col Adrian Charles Gordon DSO was 26, the son of Charles and Florence Gordon, and had previously been Mentioned in Dispatches.

414   The war diary for 16th Dec. records "Capt P. Pilditch to command A/235 as A/Major Lt S. E. Pixley returned from hospital to C/235 as Second-in-Command and as A/Captain."

415   In 1917-18 the majority of newly commissioned officers in the British Army were not from the traditional public school background. These new officers included men from the working classes, particularly skilled men or those with supervisory experience. In 1914 most such men would not have been considered as suitable officer material, but by the later stages of the war had gained hard-won leadership experience in the ranks. The officer corps had become increasingly meritocratic.

and work and pray for my darling to be well and happy and everything else seems to come a long way after that. ... We are gradually making our huts a little less draughty but they seem likely to fall down any moment in this piercing east wind. It is simply fearful in its iciness. ...

Today Naylor and I walked into the nearest town [Albert] and had tea at the Officers' Club beneath the shadow of a Virgin in a rather eccentric position. Humphrey has probably seen it[416]. Yesterday I discovered a splendid and uninhabited camp half a mile away which I at once applied for. We shall probably not be allowed to have it as it is "not in our area". Red tape is simply the outside edge, isn't it? The camp has not been occupied since 7th November, and it is quite the best I have seen for ages. ...

[Bruce Huts, Aveluy]
19th December, 1917

... Will you try and call on one of our Company Commanders in London, darling. He has had a very bad time from gas shells and I think he has pulled himself through by sheer pluck and grit. He has rather a curious voice but is a most cheery and amusing soul and his people live down at Dunmow. This is his address:

> Capt Claude Welch,[417]
> 1/19th London Regt,
> 2nd London General Hospital,
> St Mark's College,
> Chelsea. SW

It would be quite easy to see him. The cold is still awful but thank goodness the wind has dropped. ...

According to Marjorie's diary she visited Captain Welch ten days later.

Charles to Marjorie

[Bruce Huts, Aveluy]
20th December, 1917
7.00 p.m.

I have been simply awfully busy during the last twenty-four hours. I have delivered two lectures and strafed all sorts of people, including some of the Staff! I am feeling awfully fit now and quite rested. If only I could see that I was going to be with my beloved soon. The snow is quite deep in places and the trees which there are here are looking so pretty. It is still awfully cold. I am sending you today one of our Divisional Xmas cards. Owing to our recent moves, [there are] only a very limited number of them and I have only kept one for myself, or rather for my wife. We are hearing by degrees some news of those who have gone home. Stokes seems

416   The golden statue of Mary and the infant Jesus on top of the Basilica of Notre Dame de Brebières was hit by German shellfire in Jan. 1915 and knocked to a horizontal position. The leaning Virgin became a familiar image to British troops.

417   Capt Claude William Welch was commissioned in Aug. 1915 and served with the 1/19th Londons on the Western Front from 4th Dec. 1915 to 22nd July 1916 when he returned sick to England. He served with the 1/19th again from 12th Oct. 1916 to 30th Nov. 1917 by which time he was OC 'C' Company. The Battalion War Diary for the 30th Nov. records that Capt Welch passed through the Regimental Aid Post early that afternoon. He was awarded the Military Cross on 31st Dec. 1917. After he had recovered he was attached to the 18th Middlesex from 20th Sept. 1918 to 26th Feb. 1919.

47th (London) Division Christmas card for 1917

to be getting on all right. He is somewhere in London. I hope my wife realizes I am drawing another 4/- a day whilst I am in command of the Battalion! ...

[Bruce Huts, Aveluy]
21st December, 1917
2.00 p.m.

... It's the last day of your term, isn't it? ... We are still in our draughty camp, though it is a good deal more comfortable than when we came here. I think I must be a nice CO! I have just got one officer a nice and absolutely safe job as Adjutant of a school, and tomorrow I am sending our Adjutant on leave. He only came back on 21st October, but he is still suffering a bit from the gas and needs a rest, so I have worked it for him. He has promised to try and see you – Capt Sheppard. He has a bit of a cockney accent but he is a simply splendid boy and nice looking. I shall be awfully jealous of him, but he does deserve his luck. He is by way of being engaged.
...

We are trying to give the men a bit of an Xmas dinner, but of course all our original plans were spoilt by our move. The best we can do at present is roast pork, apple sauce, pudding, cigarettes and beer. But each man will have a parcel provided by the worthy folk of St Pancras and Camden Town. They are very good to us. I can't help feeling that the mere fact of someone making peace will prove very infectious, even though we may not consider it a good time for us. Still, there is no doubt that they can't go on demanding impossibilities of the fighting men of all nations and, if the winter is a hard one, the working classes in all countries on both sides will probably kick a bit. The post bugle has just sounded, so I will stop.

[Bruce Huts, Aveluy]
22nd December, 1917
2.00 p.m.

Just a line of <u>very</u> fondest love to you, which I am sending to be posted in England by Sheppard – the Adjutant – who goes on leave tonight. He is very lucky but he does deserve it and I only grudge him the chance of seeing my Marjorie, which he says he is going to do. Sweetheart, I want you simply desperately: it is so cold and I am rather lonely in the Battalion and Brigade and it <u>is</u> uphill work rebuilding a Battalion. ...

PS It is, of course, quite forbidden to send letters home in this way!

[Bruce Huts, Aveluy]
22nd December, 1917
6.30 p.m.

... I have just been to see Sheppard off on his leave. I trudged back alone with only the moon, stars and snow, everything looking like an Xmas card and did so wonder what my beloved was doing. ... I did feel jealous of Sheppard, but he has splendidly earned his leave. ... I don't know how long we shall be here. I live in constant fear of the camp being burned down (in which case I should have to pay!). The men are so awfully careless in spite of all orders and precautions. ...

Marjorie to Charles

Bennetts End
Hemel Hempstead
23rd December, 1917

A perfectly glorious morning! Mother got one of her village friends to bike down to Hempstead to fetch the letters and he brought no less than four from you. ... Darling, it is so splendid: I have read them over heaps of times already. ... You do spoil me over the presents, sweetheart. Thank you ever so much for the £10. What fun buying some books! I have a list of one or two my soul has been pining for for some time. And stockings must certainly be included, for your very especial benefit. Next time I go to Town there will be some shopping! ...

My darling, how perfectly disgusting that you should be given that hateful camp to go to for your rest. It is a shame when your men have been having such a hard time. Poor things and, as your say, it must be the very limit to keep their spirits up in such surroundings. It makes me shiver to read about it. What a heavy husband I have got to fall through the floors! ...

<u>Later</u> – 5.45 p.m.: ... Darling, you are so sweet to me. I do love you for it. Certainly the best way to be happy is to be pleasing the one person you love best. I simply love seeing your eyes all shiny with happiness. Oh! Aren't the nights cold? I bury my face in the pillow and try to pretend it's that warm comfy place on the curve of your arm that I know so well. ... I am so glad to think you are out of the way of the shells for a bit. That was a nice, loving Xmas letter you wrote on the 18th, darling, and it has come two days before the time. Aren't the posts good? Your wife is very happy. She is so acutely aware of the difference between last Xmas and this. She was so very miserable then and now she just clutches the memory of you to her heart and thanks God she came through it all right. ...

Charles to Marjorie   [Bruce Huts, Aveluy]
23rd December, 1917
7.00 p.m.

A very tired but very, very loving husband and, in a sort of way, a contented one because, though in a sad way, he has really been in touch with Marjorie today. I have found Toby's grave, darling. The roads are so frost-bound that I gave up hope of riding over to look for it, so after lunch today I took Fox and set off on foot. It was a long tramp but we first got there while there was still enough light to search. I knew nothing, except you had said it was south-west of the village and I had seen the photograph. The last mile or two we steered straight across country and came almost straight on to it. It is quite all right, very easy to find, both the crosses standing quite upright and the wire round it and the other grave, on which I couldn't read the name: was it Toby's orderly? You can understand, darling, the mixture of thoughts that ran through my head as I stood there. I think you were very present with me. I had taken a white card and I tied it on the cross with this on it:

From Charles and Marjorie Fair
Xmas, 1917

It is well away from the roads. All around is every sign of war, but today the horror was all concealed by the snow and in the mixture of light – half sunset, half moonlight – it looked weirdly beautiful. I suppose you know what is on the crosses. The one at the head has just the name, regiment and date. The other has the same and, near the bottom, "Translated from the warfare of the world into the peace of God". I copied that down and then we just saluted and came away. Somehow I felt a strange feeling of comfort, my darling, because at last even all those miles away from you I had been able to do a little thing for someone you loved, and something that I knew would please you. You will tell Mrs Fulton that the place is quite unharmed, won't you? We had really rather a wonderful walk back, facing the lingering sunset, with the snow crackling under our feet. Part of the way led across the old, original No-man's Land, and there we were nearly up to our knees. It is still desperately cold, but the things we promised the men for Christmas have come, so I do hope they won't have too miserable a time; of course I had to put my hand in my pocket a bit. ...

Charles to his father   [Bruce Huts, Aveluy]
23rd December, 1917

... The cold is intense. The snow is anything from four inches to three feet deep and the roads very slippery indeed. We had hoped to move into a better camp for our "rest", but as usual red tape was too much for us. However, we have been fairly successful in getting Xmas fare for the men and I hope they won't have too bad a time. We are giving them dinner at midday and having our own – all the officers together – in the evening. There is a Church Army hut in the nearest village where we are to have a service. ... My shaving brush was frozen as stiff as a poker this morning. I woke Naylor up by attempting to spear his cheek with it.

... Our aged Brigadier [Erskine] has broken down, as I prophesied, and his place is being taken by Col Mildren[418] – a Territorial and a very good fellow who has always been with the Division. I hope he will keep the Brigade permanently. I don't require "The Chronicle" any more, but "The Tatler" gives amusement to so many that I will keep it on for the duration! Stokes is now at Millbank, I believe. He has come down to Major and I am, of course, drawing some extra pay as long as I remain in command. ...

* * * * *

Philip to his mother   [Metz]
B/235 Bty RFA
23rd December, 1917

Your letter written on the 16th arrived yesterday, so the posts are still very slow and I believe mine are taking a long time too, as Evelyn told me she hadn't had a letter for ten days.

... I'm glad Guy is having a comfortable time for Christmas. I can't remember Marjorie's new name: will you tell me when you write? We never see a newspaper now, not for the last week anyhow. Could you write and order "The Times" to be sent out to me every day? ... We have a lot of trouble with envelopes, as they get stuck down with the damp. I think it would be a good idea if you could enclose two or three each time you write. We are fearfully short of candles having to use them all day. We are all becoming experts at prolonging the life of tiny bits of wick with odd bits of grease. We are now dependent on a little paraffin with a bit of string sticking through the lid for wick. However, all these little things afford amusement and pass the time. ...

* * * * *

Charles to Marjorie   [Bruce Huts, Aveluy]
24th December, 1917
6.00 p.m.

I have been out all day in the snow on a tactical exercise, rather as we used to do at Aldershot. It was awfully cold, but not too bad as a change from the ordinary routine. So like the Army – they graciously took us out six to seven miles in a motor lorry and then, at the end of the day, we had to trudge home through the snow on foot, when there were heaps of details about Xmas still waiting to be seen to. However, everything seems to be working out all right for tomorrow. All the parcels for the men have come. The worthy people of St Pancras and Camden Town are not only paying for most of the dinner but everyone has received from them also a tin of sausages, a tin of 50 cigarettes (do you want mine?) and a tin of cocoa and milk, which I consider is a very noble present at the present rate of prices. ... Darling, you would have smiled, a little tenderly, I think, to see the pace at which your Major walked home today hoping for a letter from Marjorie: poor Naylor got left so far behind that he didn't arrive for more than an hour after his CO! What a nuisance
....

418   Brig Gen Erskine had gone on sick leave on 16th Dec. Brig Gen W. F. Mildren CMG, DSO was a pre-war Territorial and a director of the Amalgamated Press. He was Lt Col commanding the 1/6th Battalion, The London Regiment in 140th Infantry Brigade until late 1917. He was appointed acting GOC 141st Infantry Brigade on 18th Dec. 1917 and was promoted to Brig Gen, being confirmed in that role on 2nd Jan. 1918. He commanded the Brigade until the end of the war. (*The War Illustrated*, 2nd March 1918)

Humphrey being sent right up to Blackpool. We can hardly go right up there if he is still there when I come home. ... We have our own dinner tomorrow evening at 8.00 p.m. In the middle of the day we are simply having a cold bite of something so as to be able to look after the men. My dear love, I want you and long for you in every possible way every minute that we are parted. I do really think that, if nothing very unforeseen happens, I might get home about a month from now ... .

[Bruce Huts, Aveluy]
Christmas Day, 1917
6.30 p.m.

What a very clever little lady my wife is! Two letters from her on Xmas Day, dated 20th and 21st, was far more than I had dared to hope for. Thank you ever so much for them, sweetheart.

... I think the men are pleased with our efforts for them today. ... We had only sandwiches for lunch, but are having our dinner this evening. ... Oh, my dear, dear love, of all the love and longing which is going home today there <u>can</u> be none greater than mine: I only want to be allowed to spend my life in serving you and making you happy. ... You wonder if you look after <u>me</u> properly: why, my darling, there isn't a man out here whose wife gives her husband so much thought and care and, if you never sent me a thing except your dear letters and all the love they bring, I would still be blessed above every man in the world. ...

* * * * *

Philip to his mother   [Metz]
B/235 Bty RFA
26th December, 1917

... You'll notice a change of address for me. I've been put to this Battery in the same Brigade as Captain. It's only acting rank, but I keep it so long as I'm doing the job. I'm jolly sorry to leave the old Battery, but it could not be avoided except by refusing promotion, and it would obviously have been wrong to do that. ...

We had a thoroughly cheery day yesterday. The weather was splendid: bright and sunny, and we had quite a good [Christmas] dinner – soup, tinned lobster, an excellent turkey, plum pudding and sardines-on-toast, with champagne and port to drink. So we did pretty well as far as food goes. We played a rubber of bridge afterwards and then walked out to visit another battery at about eleven o'clock. It had been snowing but was bright moonlight when we went out. It all looked so pretty and peaceful. However, we went past the guns and each shot off a round at the Hun as our contribution to his Christmas dinner.

I had a letter from Marjorie the other day. I haven't seen her husband yet, as he is not near us at present. ...

Evelyn sent me such a lovely tin of honey. It's simply delicious and a great treat after rationed jam. ...

* * * * *

Meanwhile, Philip's brother Guy was still attached to the HQ 118th Infantry Brigade, 39th Division who remained resting and training in the hills southwest of Calais.

348

Guy to his mother [Alincthun]
21st December, 1917

... I really have had rather a lot to do lately. I have been running some Brigade sports: footer, running and so on, and it seems to have taken up most of the time. We had a tug-o'-war competition this afternoon, which the Herts won in some form. They are going to compete in a divisional competition. It's an awfully good thing and the men get quite keen on it and anyhow it is something to do in these out-of-the-way little villages. I was down in the town last night and thoroughly enjoyed a good dinner and comfortable night. It gets rather cold, though, in our *château* at times. ...

[Alincthun]
27th December, 1917

We have had quite a heavy fall of snow, about eight inches, and the country is looking beautiful, though I hate it really as it makes it so absolutely impossible to get about and I should imagine it makes the forward areas even more than usually unpleasant. We had a great time this afternoon and went out tobogganing. The snow being very soft, we didn't manage to get any very great speed on but it was very amusing. ... For a couple of hours or so I quite forgot there was such a thing as a war. It has done me a lot of good and helped me to get over the effects of Christmas! We had a very cheerful Christmas dinner and shouted songs round the piano afterwards. I would very much have liked to have gone to the Battalion for dinner but we decided that, if everyone went to his Battalion, one wretched individual would have to stay at Brigade HQ to answer the telephone. ... I shall not be altogether sorry to leave this *château.* There is something rather depressing about a large, uninhabited, half-dismantled house miles from anywhere and surrounded with snow. However, you will think I am grumbling and not appreciating my luck in being so far back. I have not heard from Philip yet though I wrote to him for Christmas. ...

* * * * *

Charles to Marjorie [Bruce Huts, Aveluy]
27th December, 1917
9.00 p.m.

... Today I went out on a reconnaissance (quite unnecessarily) all the afternoon for a possible tactical scheme. We were walking for well over four hours, except for a quarter of an hour when we looked in at that billet I had a month ago. ... I hinted to the Brigadier today that leave in January would be acceptable, and he seemed quite willing: it remains to be seen whether the Major General will think the same. ...

Marjorie to Charles Bennetts End
27th December, 1917

... I was simply delighted to hear you were feeling a bit rested and had got that camp more comfortable. I do hope that means the men had a better Christmas than might have been expected. How did their dinner go off? How I would love to hear you giving a lecture; it sounds such a grand sort of proceeding. Splendid that you are drawing extra pay and I dare say you will be glad when you come to pay the bills incurred during leave. ... We are all sitting in the drawing room, Marjorie on the sofa with a horrid blank beside her, resting after our usual bridge exertions. Our diversion today was tea at the vicarage ... . They lost their only son in the war, who was by way of being a great friend of mine. Your sock is getting on and is much admired by Father. Humphrey rags me a lot about you, keeps on saying, "Poor Charles! If only he knew!" ... I bury my face in the pillow and whisper your name over and over and pray and pray that you may come back to me before long. I do wish I had a baby.

I had a card from Maj Woolley this morning. I see the names Welch and Maclagan[419] of the London Regt Mentioned in Dispatches. Are these your friends? ...

Darling, it's rather a sad time here. Poor old Mother can't get over Reggie's death a bit. He was always so much her favourite. I dare say in some ways Humphrey and my coming home accentuate his loss. I remember last year at times I nearly disliked Reggie for being here when my Toby had gone. Oh! How curious everything is. How little did I dream then of what this year would bring. My darling, I owe so much to you and I will never be able to repay it, but I will make you happy. I know I can and I shall love you more and more as the years go by. ...

Charles to Marjorie
 [Bruce Huts, Aveluy]
28th December, 1917
7.30 p.m.

Two lovely letters from you today, for which thank-you ever so much. Such a cold and busy husband, darling. It was so cold last night that the damp socks, which I took off when I went to bed, froze stiff on the floor during the night! Today we had some men shooting on an improvised range in the neighbourhood, and the wind was so cold that I simply gasped whenever I had to face it. At this moment the snow is coming down hard and is finding its way through the many cracks in our hut. We have patched it a good deal, but it is by no means weather-proof yet.

... The Rev W. Brown[420] went to a *padrés'* meeting yesterday and returned saying, "Yes, I found the teashop: the girls were excellent, but their prices abnormal"!! He certainly has the most wonderful gift for things one would rather have expressed differently. Your letters have now reached nearly one hundred. Oh, my darling, they make absolutely all the difference and no day can be quite blank or wasted when I hear from my beloved. I shall probably be ill soon, as I eat such an enormous amount in my endeavours to keep warm! MacLagan has got himself into a nice warm billet and is ministered to by a young French widow – very dangerous, I call it. He has promised to introduce me as his chaperone! What an earth can it be like in the trenches? I know a bit, because I have been there in weather like this.

....

419 Lt William C. Maclagan was commissioned in the field into the 19th Londons on 5th Mar. 1916 after service as a private soldier in King Edward's Horse. He served with the 1/19th from that date until 31st May 1918 and was Transport Officer for the battalion. His award of the MC was gazetted on 11th Mar. 1918.

420 Capt The Reverend Wilfred Roland Alexis Brown, RAChD was a fourth class chaplain (Church of England) attached to 141st Infantry Brigade. He was captured on 24th Mar. 1918.

[Bruce Huts, Aveluy]
29th December, 1917

... Your little letter written on Xmas Eve has just come – an unexpected joy as I thought it would be more delayed on the way. ... My dearest, the cold is simply terrific. I can't think how I managed to get on without you. ... Today we got up at 6.30 a.m. for a sort of field-day. There are three huts between mine and the Mess and yet my moustache froze between the two places! It was really a very lovely morning once the sun rose, but I am a bit tired after tramping about in the snow from 8.00 till 2.00. ...

Marjorie to Charles
Hill House
29th December, 1917
7.30 p.m.

How clever you have been about letters! I had one this morning before I left home and found one waiting for me here. Do try to get me one at Winchester where I go on the 7th for three nights. Darling, the one I had this morning told me of your walk over to Toby's grave. I am so glad to know it stands quite unharmed. The little cross next to it is the one erected by the Graves' Committee and they tell me it marks the actual place he was buried. When the others were put up the state of the ground forced them to put them just to one side. I can well imagine the scene, the snow covering the destruction all round and afterwards that wonderfully red sky. Darling, do you realise that just when you were there I was coming home from St Albans facing that same sunset and very keenly alive to my love for you and the peace and content you have brought back to me. It was very, very sweet of you to go and I appreciate it very much. Somehow I am very glad his grave stands all alone. He always detested anything in the way of a churchyard and said he meant to be buried in a field. He was a dear, and how he loathed soldiering. He would be the first to appreciate your generosity towards him. I will be sure and tell his mother next time I write that you have found his grave and all is well.

Sunday - 10.30 a.m.

... I ordered another Fortnum parcel yesterday. I want to know if you approved of the honey and oatcakes: you ought to have had it by now. Then I ordered you those pyjamas. After leaving two shops with my nose in the air, I at last encountered some I thought would do. While I was closely inspecting a pile of them, another portly major took up his stand next to me and began to look at some wondrous silken underwear. I was considering what size you might wear when the assistant embarrassed me horribly by saying in strident tones, "If you would measure the gentleman round the waist, Miss!" Darling, I do hope you will like them. ...

Then I went off to Chelsea and discovered Capt Welch, robed in a dressing-gown and green spectacles. He was very chatty and it was so nice hearing about the Cambrai show. He was much better and expected to be getting about in a few days, but he had a bit of a cough. He was really awfully good in telling me as much as he could of what had happened. What a terrible lot of casualties the Battalion had. I hadn't realised how utterly depleted it must have been when you got up to them. He seemed quite surprised anyone got back from the wood at all, owing to the German advance in other places. It was nice talking to someone who knew you, old thing. He said Col Friend was coming to see him. I am now looking forward to meeting Capt Sheppard on Thursday. ...

Charles to Marjorie   [Bruce Huts, Aveluy]
30th December, 1917,
4.00 p.m.

... It is still awfully cold, but the thaw seems to have begun and I expect everything will soon be mud again. This is our Sabbath but I have had no time to myself all day. I simply insist upon having time to write to my wife, otherwise I should be simply impossible to live with. There are all sorts of rumours of another move for us but so far they haven't come to anything. ... I can't help feeling a bit lonely in the Regiment these days and there is a most awful lot to be done in getting it back to its old standard and I have so very few experienced people to help me. ... I wonder if Humphrey has gone to Blackpool yet. I do wish it wasn't so far away. You will miss your little outings with him. I should love to spend a day once more that was absolutely unmilitary. ... If I don't get home soon I shall be absolutely in rags. I can't get any things from the Ordnance stores which are big enough for me. ...

Charles to his father   [Bruce Huts, Aveluy]
30th December, 1917

... We have carried out various tactical schemes in the snow and they leave me so sleepy in the evenings that I never can get any reading or writing done except what is absolutely necessary in the way of business. I have been up to my eyes in all sorts of things connected with the reorganisation of the Battalion. ... The cold has been simply fearful. The damp socks, which I took off over night, were like two pieces of board in the morning. When Sheppard comes back from his leave I shall begin to see about trying to get some myself: I have been back over three months now. ...

Charles to Marjorie   [Bruce Huts, Aveluy]
31st December, 1917

... We are still being absolutely frozen and I fear our period of rest, so called, may come to an end any minute now. The wind simply pierces me through and through. I have only three times in the last fortnight had any meal without wearing my British warm. The supply of fuel is very inadequate, though there is really plenty about. On the occasion when I visited Lemprière I saw clerks in the employ of the high and mighty with three stoves in one hut, while we who fight their battles for them have to shiver in our overcoats indoors while we are "resting". The prospect for leave doesn't look so good again now. It is a nuisance sometimes to be the only officer who is invariably perfectly well! ...

[Bruce Huts, Aveluy]
1st January, 1918,
6.00 p.m.

Such a good post today – two letters from you and the Anzora cream. ... I am so awfully glad you are going down to Winchester, darling: I know they are longing to have you and get to know you better. I expect you will have to submit to going to the cathedral once with Dad. If you are very wise, you will suggest going into the west end just to listen to the music for a bit and then coming out, and it really does sound lovely from there. ...

As soon as Sheppard comes back I shall try and get something definite settled about my leave. The worst of being the CO is that your leave has to be approved by the Major General, whereas a mere Second-in-Command simply goes when the CO can spare him. Naylor is getting very agitated about <u>his</u> next leave, but I tell him he certainly isn't going to see you again before I do! He is acting Adjutant in Sheppard's absence but is really far too casual.

My dearest, I wonder what 1918 will bring for us two. I don't think it can bring me anything more wonderful than 1917 – you and your love. ...

Marjorie's diary for 4th January records that she had had lunch with Captain Sheppard in the Piccadilly Hotel.

Charles to Marjorie [Bruce Huts, Aveluy]
2nd January, 1918
6.00 p.m.
... The thaw seems to be arriving by degrees, but it is still most awfully cold. We had the Major General round to see us this morning. He seemed awfully pleased with our work on the camp and particularly with our culinary arrangements. You would have laughed to see him and your Major learnedly discussing the price of carrots, bully beef rissoles, and oatmeal scones. The men really are being fed very well and this village, though partially ruined, manages to produce beer which is quite like the genuine article! I shall be quite a learned housekeeper by the time this war is over. ...

* * * * *

On 31st December 1917 Guy Dodgson, the 1/1st Hertfordshires and the 118th Infantry Brigade moved once again to the Ypres Salient.

Guy to his mother [Canal Bank, north of Ypres]
1st January, 1918
Here's wishing you the very best of luck in 1918! May we be celebrating next New Year together somewhere and the war a thing of the past. ... We have been on the move and you know what that means, continually packing and unpacking and rather a lot of worry this time. The roads have been in such an awful state owing to the frost that transport has had an awful time, especially motor lorries, any number of which have got ditched and stuck on hills unable to move either way. I spent most of yesterday going round the country in a lorry collecting stuff that had been left behind. It wasn't particularly pleasant as we got stuck four times and had literally to push the blessed thing with the help of chains under the wheels. We ended the tour by colliding with an ambulance coming round a corner. Luckily we were going very slowly and no damage was done. But I was glad to get back, as the stupid driver had lights that wouldn't work and for about two hours we were driving in the dark with a loaded lorry and a road only partially cleared of snow. ... We are in exactly the same place as the Battalion was before 31st July where Reggie Secretan was killed. It's such a contrast between the hilly country round Boulogne and the horrible, flat

mess of Belgium with the long, straight roads with the inevitable avenue of trees.

We had a very cheery evening last night (New Year's Eve). We happened to strike a billet with a piano and, what is more, a beautiful damsel who was only too willing to sing to us.

I wonder if women get as tired of their own sex as men do. I had a letter from Philip soon after Christmas and he seems to have had a pretty rotten time. ...

[Canal Bank, north of Ypres]
6th January, 1918

I have had rather an interesting day today and been out most of the time with the General. We went up towards the line and over the exact ground which the Battalion went over on the 31st July. It is of course all very much altered and roads and camps have been made that were never there before, but one can still see the main features quite clearly. The old lines of German trenches are quite distinct; some in quite good repair even now, others absolutely bashed in. The line runs a long way in advance of where this Brigade went on the 31st and we were able to get to where their objective was. We were able to make out the remnants of the wire that held up the Herts and got them into such an awfully tight corner. [See Point C on Map 6] It was rather pathetic. I know you will be glad to hear that this is quite a quiet sector. We go into the line tomorrow for eight days and I hope to have quite a good time as our HQ are decent – a huge Boche erection of concrete, really quite a house with about eight rooms. ...

[Alberta Camp, Reninghelst]
9th January, 1918

... Here we are again, once more up the line and the ground covered with snow and freezing hard every night. It thawed the night we came up, which made everything very unpleasant and muddy, but it froze again the next day. It is really far preferable, as it is at least hard and clean, even if it is cold, and one can walk about without getting covered with mud.

... When the sun comes out even this deplorable country looks quite nice. ... What do you think about peace? I think most people here think it is coming in the not-too-far-off future. The General is firmly convinced it will be within six months and I must say I think things are pointing to it. Anyhow, it is being talked about and there are bound to be conferences and rumours and muddles generally before it comes. I should rather like to be in the line the day it is actually declared and see what happens. I suppose an order will come round, cold and to the point, "Hostilities will cease at 6.00 p.m. on such-and-such a date" and we shall solemnly get out of our shell-holes and shelters and pill-boxes and march back. The Boche will do the same. Or do you think we shall rush frantically across No Man's Land and cheer and shout and fraternize with the Hun and have the inevitable drink with him? Probably neither; things never are what you imagine, but what a day it will be! I believe the first thing they are going to do in France is to close all the pubs, but they will certainly be broken open!

* * * * *

Charles to Marjorie   [Bruce Huts, Aveluy]
                                                          3rd January, 1918

... Today has been very lovely – bright sun all the time after a little fresh snow in the night. I have been awfully busy all day. Things seem to crop up unceasingly: I have never looked like reading a novel all the time we have been "resting" though of course I might have done so if I didn't like going to bed so early. ... By the time you get this we shall probably have moved again, but I don't know where. I wish we could settle down somewhere and know what our programme really is. Last winter was pretty muddy and uncomfortable, but at least we carried out a very fixed programme which hardly varied for several months. Did you see our Major General [Gorringe] got a KCMG in the New Year's honours? Colonel Mildren, who has been commanding our Brigade for the last three weeks, has definitely got the job now. I am very glad, as he is not <u>too</u> military, being himself a Territorial who came to France with the Division and has been with it ever since. ...

                                                          [Bruce Huts, Aveluy]
                                                          4th January, 1918

A very sad husband writes to you today. You may have seen that another Haileybury master – Purser[421] – has been killed. He was just about my age and we lived together on the same staircase for that last happy year before the war. He was brilliantly clever, very good at games and the most splendid company at all times. I was most awfully fond of him. We met, just for a few minutes, on a Victoria platform the day I last landed in England. It is a bad loss for everyone who knew and loved him. It is colder than ever, I think, and we are on the move again, which doesn't tend to cheer us up. I have just detailed a subaltern for leave who hasn't seen a trench since August and whose total service in France during the war (as far as trenches is concerned) amounts to about ten weeks. Isn't it sickening? One of those officers who were home for six months exchange has got married and has taken a house for himself and wife at Colchester, where he is temporarily attached to a Reserve battalion. Still, I would far sooner be Marjorie's husband in France than anyone else's husband anywhere else in the world. ... Your letter about your visit to Welch has just come. Thank you awfully, sweetheart, for going to see him. ... Now I am longing to hear from Sheppard about his lunch with you. He is due back in two or three days now. It will be desperately cold travelling about and I expect by the time you get this we shall be in the trenches again. ...

                                                          [Bertincourt]
                                                          5th January, 1918,
                                                          8.00 p.m.

No post today as we have been on the move: an awfully cold journey and it will be really awful in the trenches and worse still when the thaw comes. We are spending a night in the place where we had our Dinner on 10th December – nearly a month ago. Our three weeks' "rest" went far too quickly. It is rather rotten that we haven't had a whole month out of reach of shells since August 1916 and we <u>know</u> that other people get far more than we do. I am simply longing to get Sheppard

....

421 Lt Frank Dulcken Purser RNVR was on the staff at Haileybury for only four terms before enlisting in the Nelson Battalion of the Royal Naval Division. A scholar of Uppingham School and Trinity College Cambridge, he was killed age 29 on 27th Dec. 1917. He is buried in Villiers-Plouich Communal Cemetery (grave B.1).

back and hear all about his meeting with my lady. I am rather worried at our prospect for the next few weeks, darling. We haven't yet anything like recovered from all that Welch told you about and, though we are all pretty fit, that doesn't make up for other matters. We had a telegram last night to say that Welch had got an MC for his work that day: he has really earned it over and over again. He is quite one of the bravest people I know and seems to find war quite interesting! People like that are so wonderful: I do hate soldiering so and to return to the neighbourhood of past troubles is always depressing. I had quite a fright this morning, as my Sergeant Major and I were watching the departure of our transport and the frost was causing difficulties: he put his foot on a spoke in the wheel and the mule started suddenly. I can't think why his leg wasn't broken. I thought I heard it crack and I rushed and threw all my weight in the opposite direction. Luckily he only wrenched the muscles a bit. I can't afford to lose him. ...

[Bertincourt]
6th January, 1918

... My leave doesn't seem any nearer yet but I hope for the best. I have spent all today reconnoitring trenches and the cold is simply ghastly! I can't think how we are to endure it at all! Trenches tomorrow night is an awful thought. The great joke today is that the rank of (<u>very</u> Acting!!) Lt Col has been given to your portly Major and your next and following letters must be addressed to Lt Col C. H. F. You know I held the rank for two or three months last winter. Of course I shall have to resign it when either Reggie Friend or Stokes comes out again and I shouldn't bother about having it now only I do want the extra money for you, darling, and I know it will give you some pleasure to address me as such, even for a little while. Oh it <u>would</u> be fun to come home for once as a real CO and make Humphrey and co salute me in public places! What a farce the whole thing is – especially for anyone so utterly un-military as your husband!

... Tonight we are hoping for a visit from Railton, who for many months was formally our *padré* – a great sportsman – who wanted to find me a wife after the war in Switzerland! I always told him I shouldn't want any of his second-hand Swiss goods. I expect he'll rag me a lot. ...

Marjorie to Charles

Hill House
6th January, 1918
5.30 p.m.

What do you think has happened? Marjorie has been to church!!! Do not faint away with surprise! The thing was, they were having intercession services re the war all over the Kingdom so I thought perhaps, if I interceded very hard, you would get leave a little sooner! Seriously though, it was quite a sensible service and I rather liked it. Amwell is such a dear little church. ...

It's pouring with rain now and I do hope my Charlie is somewhere under cover. Once again, that drawer I keep his letters in is full to overflowing. He is a darling to write so many. ...

Charles to Marjorie   [Bertincourt]
7th January, 1918
11.30 a.m.

Just a hurried line before starting off for the trenches. The thaw has come with
torrents of rain and heaven only knows what the trenches will be like. I shall be
more than ordinarily thankful when this tour is over. It is rather worrying not to
have so many of the familiar faces, and now I hear that Sheppard has been ordered
to have an extension of leave, which will further postpone mine, I expect. It will
probably be better to let Fox go the minute he is due and can be spared and then
hope to come myself as soon as he returns. That would make mine come about the
30th. However, we shall see. We can only hope for the best. It will be all the more
wonderful when it comes. I shall have some rough passages before then, I expect. I
think our Staff beat some of their own records yesterday in detailing for some job
poor little Morrison who had died four weeks ago. I <u>was</u> angry and made no bones
about telling them so. I will write more tonight if possible, my darling. I do love you
so very, very dearly.

[Flesquières]
8th January, 1918
11.00 a.m.

I didn't have time to write again last night as I hoped or, to put it more truthfully,
I hadn't got elbow-room as there were eight of us in a little dugout smaller than
your room at Hill House, and three of us had also to sleep there. Luckily we had
quite a quiet night and your husband slept pretty comfortably on a stretcher in the
corner with one blanket and a pair of sandbags to put his large feet in. Yesterday
it was thawing all day, but last night it froze again and today the snow is coming
down as thickly as ever. Certainly those of us who are doing third or fourth winters
in the trenches must have had a very sinful past if this is the atonement we have
to make! I can't think how the men manage to stick it all, though of course there
are practically none of them doing their third consecutive winter. You will be very
jealous to hear that Woolley is on leave <u>now</u>! Of course, it was easier for him to get
away, as he is not in command. How is the Colonel's wife today? Oh, my darling,
what a weird joke it all is! The Army contains no more unmilitary man than your
husband and here he is posing for the time being as a Lt Col! However, I've no doubt
his wife will be very glad to have the spending of the extra £ – s – d! ...

Do you know your letters to me number well over a hundred now? They are all
very carefully kept. I couldn't bear to destroy them until we do, some day, find they
take up so much room that perhaps Joan will seize them when Darby is out and put
them away!! Railton was much amused at my married airs and duly impressed with
Marjorie's photo, and he was fearfully bucked at the snapshot of us two taken at
Winchester. ...

[Flesquières]
9th January, 1918

Two letters from you yesterday, both written on the 2nd (one in bed!) and
bringing the news about the salver from the officers of the Battalion. How simply
splendid, darling! It was an <u>absolute</u> surprise to me: I did think it a little odd that

none of those who were out here at the time except Reggie Friend had given me anything, but I put it down to the speed of our movements and also that I was away all the time the deed was maturing! Of course I shall write to Stokes and as many of the others as I can manage: some of them, as you know, are beyond reach of thanks now. ... I have been prowling about in the snow in the neighbourhood of the front line this morning with [Lt G. L.] Wilson. Coming back we had to make a pretty wide detour as the wily Hun was shelling our more direct route pretty heavily. Even so, we ducked once or twice and little hot bits of shell sizzled in the snow beside us. ... I shall be in rags if I don't get leave soon. There is very little chance in these parts of replacing any clothes. If you hear later on that I am really coming, will you leave that tunic somewhere to have the badges altered to Lt Col – unless I have resigned my rank again before that wonderful day arrives. I think I shall go mad if I ever hear that I am really coming. My hopes rise and sink so. ... The cold is simply fearful – the poor sentries - there is so little one can do to make their lot easier. It is the responsibility which worries me so much. ...

Silver salver with signatures – wedding present to Charles and Marjorie Fair from the Officers' Mess of the 1/19th London Regiment.

* * * * *

Philip to his mother

[Trescault]
B/235 Bty RFA
9th January, 1918

... I don't know how the poor chaps in the front line stick it, and you can just imagine the slipperiness of everything – the roads were just a sheet of ice. ... How pleased Eleanor must be to have George back home so soon. ..... and later: I am going to bed as we can't get the stove to go and it's blowing a regular blizzard outside.

I shall hope to see George on his return. I wonder if you are having this very cold weather. It reminds me of days at Cambridge when we used to go skating. There's a lot of peace talk going on. I was glad to see Lloyd George has at last made it clearer what we are fighting for.[422]

* * * * *

Charles to Marjorie
[Flesquières]
10th January, 1918
1.00 p.m.

... The thaw has come again and everything is indescribably beastly. I had rather an exciting walk this morning as, while I was out visiting some of the Companies, the Boche started dropping shells near my dugout. Wilson and I had to watch for the bursts and listen for them coming and got home by doing short rushes along the trench, splashing in mud and water and catching our feet in broken telephone wires. I shall have a horribly wet and muddy tour somewhere about midnight tonight going round the line. I see no prospect of getting my clothes off for a least another fortnight. I shall be pretty dirty (or worse!) by then. I heard from Welch, but he only made a short reference of thanks for your visit and did not say what lurid details of my past he had revealed to you! Did I tell you that he had got the MC for his share in that damned show? I had a letter from another Aldershot man who was in the same neighbourhood and he told much the same tale as Welch. I am trying to get in touch with Philip Dodgson. I have found out where he is and we shall not be far apart in future, I expect. ... But the horror and beastliness is worth it all for you, darling. After all, we do sometimes realize that if we weren't out here you might be meeting Germans in England, and I have felt the war so much more a personal matter since I had my wonderful lady behind me. ...

[Flesquières]
11th January, 1918
1.00 p.m.

Two splendid letters from you last night which cheered me enormously, but oh! such a weary, muddy husband crawled back into his dugout at 3.00 in the morning. It is simply beyond words, the mud and utter discomfort of the men in the front line. The thaw is worse than anything, and I see no prospect of a bath for another fortnight or so! I am so glad you met Sheppard and liked him. ... I am not feeling very well today: it is probably worry and strain. ... I shall be so thankful to have Sheppard back: Naylor does his best, but he is awfully casual. Alas, we are living in such a muddle in a tiny dugout that things get lost and trampled on with horrible frequency. It seems simply years since our "rest" came to an end. ... I am longing to hear about your visit to Winchester: I know it will have given most enormous pleasure to them...

....

422 On 5th Jan. at Caxton Hall in London, the Prime Minister, David Lloyd George, had given a speech to the Trades Union Congress at which he outlined Britain's war aims "as a means of stiffening war resolve". Although the prime war aim – that of liberating occupied Belgium and France – had never been in doubt since 1914, this speech was the first clear articulation of Britain's position on issues such as the establishment of democracy in Germany, the fate of the German colonies, and the fate of the Austro-Hungarian and Ottoman Empires. (See Wilson, *The Myriad Faces of War*, pp. 545-7)

[Flesquières]
12th January, 1918
4.00 p.m.

... A very worried husband tonight, darling: so many things are going wrong in little ways and the weather is trying for us all. One wretched subaltern (thank goodness he didn't subscribe to our salver!) has had a cheque dishonoured and of course I have got to row him about it.[423] Then some of these conscripts we get now are not too enthusiastic about their job and they need constant watching. Oh! It is a beastly life, but thank goodness I have my Marjorie who loves me and she makes everything worthwhile. ...

The boy who used to be my runner and is now a Sergeant got the DCM to add to the MM for which I recommended him.[424] He was "wounded", in that show. I hope he will get all right: I was very fond of him. I have heard from Sheppard. He much enjoyed his *tête-à-tête* and I did envy him. Oh! My darling, the longing for you is getting absolutely unbearable, and I can only suppose that the reason other people who are separated from their wives for months don't go mad is that they are not married to Marjorie and don't know what absolute happiness is. Eleven days together – good God! – out of 32½ years!

In the middle of this strenuous tour we were asked for a return (marked URGENT) of men who are thatchers or ploughmen!! This in a London Battalion![425] I have been asked for an officer recommended to be trained for the Staff. I am thinking of saying that all mine have too much sense of humour to fill the post.

[Flesquières]
13th January, 1918
10.45 a.m.

No letter from you yesterday, as I more than half feared. I had a bad day altogether, as when I was going round about midnight, I fell into a 7ft trench, unnoticed in the dark, and have strained some ligaments in the left leg so badly that I am a helpless crock in my own dugout! I don't know what is to be done about it: I must see them through this tour, and then I think the doctor will insist on sending me somewhere where it can be x-rayed, as he is rather anxious about the most tender spot just at the top of the fibula. It is an awful nuisance just now. What I dread most is that I shall be sent to hospital in France long enough to lose

....

423 It would have been a disciplinary offence for an officer to write a cheque that bounced. This could have led to a Court Martial for bringing the Army into disrepute.

424 On 4th Jan. the war diary noted the award of the DCM to 610824 Sgt L. Wells MM. Leonard Wells had enlisted in the 19th Londons in early 1915 and his MM had been gazetted on 3rd June 1916. His DCM citation read "For conspicuous gallantry and devotion to duty. After all the company stretcher bearers had become casualties he supervised the evacuation of all cases to the Regimental Aid Post himself, under a very heavy barrage. Also, when acting as CQMS, he conducted the ration parties through heavy fire and was successful in keeping the company supplied throughout the operations. By his coolness, courage and resource he set a splendid example to all ranks." (WO 95/2738 and *London Gazette* 1st May 1918)

425 Charles is perhaps being a little harsh in his judgment. By early 1918 many, if not most, battalions had lost much of their local character as men were drafted in to where they were needed. In fact, in the final 'hundred days' of the war only about 7% of the 1/19th Londons were actually from the St Pancras area, and a further 23% were from London (see Fair, *London Pride*, p.80). By then, the majority of the battalion was drawn from the counties of SE England and many men had initially enlisted in regiments such as The Royal Hampshires and The East Kents. It is therefore possible that by Jan. 1918 a few thatchers or ploughmen might have found themselves in the ranks of the 1/19th Londons.

command of the Battalion, but not a sufficiently bad case to come home. That would be a maddening combination of circumstances. Meanwhile, I am quite helpless and pretty uncomfortable, as the leg has swollen a lot. I am having it massaged by a stretcher-bearer. ...

I thought I had been blown up by a shell when I felt myself dropping through space. It was a jar and I was awfully lucky not to break my leg altogether. Perhaps, in a way, you are wishing I had, oh most loving but unpatriotic wife!

It was a toilsome journey back to the dugout last night being helped along the trench in awful mud by the doctor and another man. Whenever I do leave here it will have to be on a stretcher, I'm afraid. Darling, I was very touched at your having been to that intercession service. ...

* * * * *

Philip to his mother   [Trescault]
                                                          B/235 Bty RFA
                                                    13th January, 1918

... The weather doesn't seem able to settle down. For the last few days it has thawed and everything has been in an awful state of slime, as the rain hasn't been able to get through the frozen ground. However, tonight it's freezing hard again. It's been a glorious day today, but too clear to be really enjoyable! I'm afraid I can't tell at all where Guy is just now. I wish we could meet. ... I'm glad you've seen Eve[lyn]: how does she seem? She hardly ever mentions herself when she writes ... . I'm very well just now and am enjoying having a little more responsibility. ... I had had about enough of a subaltern's job, which consists so much of being alone doing nothing. ...

* * * * *

Charles to Marjorie   [Flesquières]
                                                    14th January, 1918

What a splendid post yesterday – your first two letters from Winchester, the two books (<u>most</u> welcome to your lame husband) and two Fortnum parcels. ... My dearest, I do love to hear of your making friends with them at Winchester. I am longing to hear from them too about your visit. ... Oh! I am so weary and lonely and for the last week nothing has gone right and, if it wasn't for your letters, I simply don't know what I should do. I do worry so about things and I have only slept about six hours in the last four nights all put together. Have you written to Naylor about the salver? ... How is Humphrey getting on at Blackpool? I'm afraid there won't be much chance of seeing him. ...

                                          In a casualty clearing station
                                                    15th January, 1918
                                                          1.30 p.m.

Here I am; surely a most unheroic and undignified casualty, not even qualified for a gold stripe! I don't know what my fate is to be as I have only just arrived, but I am fighting all I know against being sent down the line, for fear of losing the command and postponing my leave! It is rather a treat to be between the sheets again and there is a nice Sister with red hair to look after me – not too young and good-looking, so it's all right! But I do hate having left them when they are short-handed and things are not going too well. Sheppard should arrive back today and I so awfully want to see him if possible. The Brigadier said yesterday that, if I remained within easy reach, he would try and send me on leave as soon as I could walk enough to enjoy it. That would be a splendid plan, if only it could be worked. We have really had a pretty peaceful trip as far as casualties go, but the discomfort and trials of the men are simply beyond words. Since my accident I hadn't seen daylight for nearly three days and quite blinked when I came out of the dugout. We had an exciting beginning to the trip in the ambulance as two shells hit a house within fifty yards of us and I felt so trussed up and absolutely helpless! I do hope this will hasten instead of postponing my leave: it is an annoying injury – full of all possibilities except that of sending me home.

16th January, 1918
Same bed; same hospital
7.30 a.m.

How is the wife of the lame Colonel today? I'm afraid the weather is being perfectly horrid for her to resume her early morning journeys. ...

I don't like being in hospital when I am perfectly well at all. Sister goes through the mystic rite of taking my temperature, and to my great annoyance I was woken up at 4.45 a.m. as if Marjorie's husband was ever ill!! The poor stretcher-bearers found his 14st a bit of a trial yesterday over mud and shell-holes. It will very soon get on my nerves to be perfectly well and yet surrounded by people groaning and coughing. Your two books couldn't have arrived at a luckier moment. ...

16th January, 1918
7.00 p.m.

The accident was more serious than we thought, as the x-rays show a bit of bone broken. I leave for the base tomorrow, Thursday the 17th. Can't tell whether I shall get home yet, but will of course wire or telephone if I do. I am in absolutely no pain. The rotten thing is I drop to Major again with the pay and allowances of a Captain. Never mind, I am bound to get a decent leave when I am convalescent and, as I am perfectly fit, we shall be able to enjoy ourselves as much as ever we can. ...

Charles to his sister   16th January, 1918
Dear Helen,

I am in hospital for a bit, having fallen into a trench and strained some ligaments in my left leg (not the old knee) which has left me incapable of walking at more than a shuffle. It is a horrid nuisance as, if I am away long, I shall probably lose command of the Battalion and also it postpones my leave, probably, as the trouble isn't bad enough to take me home, which would have been best of all! Meanwhile, I am thoroughly bored in a ward with people who groan and cough – cut off from the outside world and having some difficulty in getting my letters – what a life after twenty-six months out here!

On 16th January when the new term started Marjorie went back to teaching.

Charles to Marjorie   No. 10 British Red Cross Hospital
Le Tréport,
18th January, 1918

Two letters from you yesterday just before I left the CCS – in fact I postponed my departure from there till the afternoon because I felt that something would arrive from you and I did want you so badly. By the way, you haven't mixed up our honeymoon with another one, have you?! You speak of our leaving Paddington on 18th <u>January</u> (i.e. today), schoolmistress mine, so your husband is wondering whether you have planned an elopement for today! ... Perhaps this accident will prove a real blessing because sooner or later I am bound to get a longer leave out of it than any I have ever had yet, ... but it will be dreadfully hard waiting till I am discharged from hospital. Oh, if only they will send me home now that I have come so far. ... I only arrived here at six this morning, after travelling all night. ...

I haven't been inspected yet, but I am going to be quite shameless in trying to get home when he does come, and if I don't they will have a very sulky patient. The Sisters all look so surprised when I give my rank as Lt Col! Of course I drop it now, but officially I am a Lt Col for hospital purposes. I will go on with this after the doctor has seen me.

<u>Later</u>: He says <u>probably</u> I shall be sent home. Oh, my darling, I do hope it comes true. It will be about a two months' job, I expect. ...

No. 10 British Red Cross Hospital
Le Tréport
19th January, 1918

No more news yet, except that I am very well and very comfortable, but dreadfully hungry for the sight of my own lady. The various titled people who minister to my needs only make me feel the need of her more badly than ever by being English ladies but not my own private one. I expect you have just about got the news of my original accident when I thought it would only be about a fortnight's job. Until I know definitely what is to happen to me, it doesn't seem any good having my letters forwarded to this place, so that there is one very envious patient when Sister comes in with the letters and he knows there can be none for him.

Yesterday the orderly washed me as I lay in bed. I can't remember having that done to me for twenty-five years! ...

Le Tréport
20th January, 1918
8.50 a.m.

I think you had better begin to write here, as it may be several days before I get shipped across. There are two others in the ward probably coming with me – the one in the bed next to me has been here 3½ months, as he has been too bad to be moved. He had 26 wounds and has had his left leg taken off below the knee and his left arm is still in a splint. Still, he is getting quite all right. He is a fine-looking man and his looks are quite unspoilt. My darling, your husband simply bursts with pride at the comments on your photographs – the only ones visible in the ward. All the Sisters come and ask permission to look at them and all the nice things they say would make you blush; but even then they don't know my Marjorie as she really is and as I know her to be. There is nobody quite so proud in all the world as your husband, dearest, and oh, he will give you a time when he can get about with you again.

RMSP "Essequibo"
Le Havre
21st January, 1918

I hope I shall see you almost as soon as this reaches you, but I can't let a day on which I don't see you go by without writing. I left Le Tréport at nine last night (Sunday) and arrived here at ten this morning. I don't know when we shall sail, nor when we shall arrive. I hope and pray I shall manage to get to London so that there will be no difficulty about your coming to see me as soon and as often as possible. Isn't this one of the very things we foresaw when we decided to get married? I am getting dreadfully impatient for my beloved and am cursing the red tape, or whatever it is, that keeps me waiting about when we are so far on our journey. Never mind, it will be worth it a million times when I hold you in my arms again. It's no good either of us minding kissing in public (if we ever did!) because you shall have to do it for a bit, I expect. My darling, there are such millions of them owing to you. Shall post this as soon as possible after landing.

All my love,
Charles

On 22nd January 1918 Marjorie had a telegram at her school to say that Charles had reached Southampton. The next day she saw him in a hospital in Mount Street, London. His injury had been confirmed as a fractured fibula in his left leg. On 25th Marjorie, with her mother, visited him again to find another caller, Major Stokes from the 1st/19th London Regiment. Charles left hospital on 31st in Marjorie's care and was recommended for six weeks' leave. The couple spent quite a lot of time at Hill House, Stanstead Abbotts, paying visits to Haileybury. Marjorie felt obliged to give up her teaching job on 16th February.

Charles's letter written on the 21st January, 1918 is the last of his war letters in the family archives. He did not return to the Western Front, so there was little incentive for either Marjorie or his father, Robert, to retain any other letters that he might have written in 1918.

Chapter 18

The March Retreat and the Battle of the Lys

(January – June 1918)

By January 1918 the number of young officers introduced into this account of the Great War had been considerably reduced. Three had died – Toby Dodgson, Eric Champion and Reggie Secretan. Although there is no record of Eric and Reggie meeting on the Western Front, they had been contemporaries at a boys' preparatory school in Broadstairs, Kent, and a photograph survives of them together on the school cricket team. Humphrey Secretan and Charles Fair were permanently back in England. Of the remainder, Philip and Guy Dodgson plus Carl and Alan Champion, were still on active service. There was also the step-brother to the Dodgsons, George Fulton, who by 1918 was a Lt Colonel commanding the 9th Cheshires. Philip and Guy were the only two to have left letters of this period, though Carl Champion continued to record events in his diary.

Guy to his mother   16th January, 1918
   I have now transferred my energies to yet another sphere and am attached to HM Flying Corps. I stay here for a week or thereabouts and what I am supposed to do I am not quite sure as

Reggie Secretan and Eric Champion in their preparatory school cricket team

nobody takes much notice of me from an official point of view. I seem to do pretty well what I like. I believe the real idea of it is "to promote good feeling between the two arms of the Service" as they phrase it. We affect exchanges, the Flying Corps sending fellows to us and *vice versa.* We had one with us the last time up the line. Quite a good sort, and luckily he belongs to this Squadron. So I do at least know somebody, which is rather a good thing as there about fifty officers here, all of whom seem to me to look exactly alike. There is a sort of Flying Corps expression which seems to be rather universal! It's really rather a rest and I'm quite enjoying it. The Brigade came out of the line last night. I am afraid they must have had rather a bad time as it simply poured with rain and was a pitch black night.[426] ...

18th January, 1918

I am still with the Flying Corps but have done nothing at all exciting yet, as the weather has been too bad. It has rained or snowed all three days since I have been here and there has been no flying at all, though I hope to be given a short joy-ride before I leave. However, I'm having a very comfortable and quite restful time. In other words, doing nothing at all! As you can imagine, our youthful "lords of the air" manage to lead a fairly happy existence when not actually flying. Their great advantage is, of course, that they are not continually moving about but stay in one place for months at a time. It is worthwhile their taking some trouble to make their places habitable. ...

It is good work, isn't it, raising the infantry officers pay? I believe I get 1/- a day extra to date from 1st October. A 2/Lt gets 3/- a day extra. It's quite time something was done in this direction. The best part of it is the Separation Allowance, though unfortunately this does not affect me as yet.

Well, dear, I am quite contented at the moment and there is a small piano in this Mess which I strum on a good deal.

20th January, 1918

I have flown in an aeroplane! The great deed was done yesterday morning and on the whole I quite enjoyed it. It certainly is a joyous feeling, and one feels such a superior being soaring up above and seeing all the puny little people and things underneath, especially as we went over places that I knew well. In fact we had a look at our last Brigade HQ in the line. We didn't go further than that and then returned for lunch. I can't truthfully say that I wasn't rather glad to see the good solid ground again! Though it really was quite a pleasant experience except at one awful moment when the wretched man driving the machine did rather a sudden sharp turn. It was really a perfectly ordinary manoeuvre but I thought my last hours had come and clung on firmly with both hands, while the earth underneath suddenly seemed to tilt at the most appalling angle. I have never felt so pleased at anything in my life as when that aeroplane flew straight again. Coming down and landing is the most glorious sensation, a kind of magnified Mountain Railway feeling.

....

426   118th Infantry Brigade was relieved on the night of 15th/16th Jan. The war diary records: "Rain fell all day delaying relief until morning of the 16th. The Steenbeek overflowed its banks, and the duckboard tracks were washed away and submerged. A very bad relief ensued, being completed at 4.45 am, 16th Jan. The Brigade moved into [Divisional] Reserve." (TNA WO 95/2589)

I had dinner last night with a neighbouring Squadron and discovered a fellow who was really interested in the piano and more or less decent music. He could play moderately well too in a lazy, artistic sort of way and we had rather a pleasant evening, as I hadn't met anybody like that for ages. ...

[Houtkerque, west of Poperinghe]
22nd January, 1918

... I returned from the RFC this morning and was really quite sorry to leave. They are such a jolly crowd and so refreshingly enthusiastic about their job and the war in general. I am afraid they are about the only people who really are nowadays.

We are safely back now in the land of billets and sheets and are getting ready for our great move, which is really coming off.

* * * * *

In the meantime Guy's brother Philip was still with the 47th Divisional Artillery.

Philip to his mother
[Ribecourt]
C/235 Bty RFA
26th January, 1918

You will notice at the top of this the address of the old Battery. I am back there again as Lieutenant. It's a great disappointment to me to have to go down, but I can't help myself: it's arisen through a Major returning to the Division from England, which necessitates Pilditch reverting to Captain and a Captain going down to Lt. Of course, if I were the junior Captain I could have no complaint, but as it is there are two Captains junior to me who were made Captains while I was in England. They've chosen to put me down as I was the last to be made a Captain. I think this is a great hardship on officers who return after being wounded, and apparently the Staff think the same, but the General has made up his mind so nothing can be done. ...

The worst of this sort of thing is that it takes all the interest out of one's work and I hate to feel that I have not been treated fairly. One of the fellows who is a Captain, though over a year junior to me, I feel particularly annoyed about. He is very young and a so-called "Regular" i.e. he has done a short course at Woolwich and is making the Army his profession. Why a man like this should be promoted over all our heads I fail to see.

I shall only write about this to Evelyn and yourself, and I hope you will both realize that promotion is almost entirely a matter of seniority. I expect everybody will think I have reverted to Lt because I was incapable of doing a Captain's job. If you could persuade them this is not the reason, I shall be much obliged to you. ... Pilditch has had the idea that, as we are both in the same way, it would be a good plan for us each to write a note to each other's family. I think he feels the disappointment more than I. I'm not sorry to leave the Battery: it's not easy to work under a Battery Commander whom you don't respect. ...

26th January, 1918

Dear Mrs. Fulton,

This is just s line to tell you how sorry I am that Philip has had to revert to his last rank.

I can fully sympathise as I am involved in it too, and have had to revert to Captain and lose my majority and Battery on the arrival from England of the old Battery Commander – wounded at Ypres.

I am going to C Battery as Captain, so Philip and I will be together and that is the only consolation in the whole business!

Kindest regards,

Yours sincerely

Philip W. Pilditch

Philip Dodgson to his mother Helen

[Ribecourt]
C/235 Bty RFA
30th January, 1918

I got two letters from you today, also one from Eve. ... Your parcel from the Stewarts has also come, but I'm not opening it for a day or two, so I shall enjoy the anticipation of the contents. The other things have not yet arrived, but it seems to me you are sending a tremendous lot. From all accounts the food shortage is pretty serious in England.[427] It will be a good thing when the winter is over, and I must say I feel that the War will be over before long. ... We are having glorious sunny weather, but the Hun is rather offensive these moonlit nights. We shan't be sorry when the moon disappears. Fortunately for us he pays most of his attention to places further back than we are. The other night we could see one of his planes quite plainly in the moonlight. I see they've had another raid on London, but have not read the particulars. ...

[Ribecourt]
C/235 Bty RFA
19th February, 1918

... I have been playing all the records. You sent a tremendous lot, and I like them all better and better. "Ave Maria" played by M. Elman is beautiful, and I love the Kreisler one too. Have you been playing your gramophone much? I don't know how we should get on without ours here. It's playing as well as ever. It's out on a visit tonight unfortunately: we've sent it on to one of our officers who is living alone. Besides playing it ourselves, we lend it each evening between tea and dinner to the gunners, so it's working pretty hard; which reminds me – could you send me out some more needles?

....

427 The German U-boat blockade of Britain had led to food shortages and by the last weeks of 1917 stocks of a number of important foodstuffs were getting low. "Queues reached ominous proportions." (see Wilson, *The Myriad Faces of War,* p. 513) The government had no choice but to introduce rationing of sugar (Jan. 1918) followed by rationing of meat, bacon and butter and margarine (Apr. 1918).

[Ribecourt]
C/235 Bty RFA
[late February, 1918]

I have just heard that I am to go on a course to Shoebury, leaving France on 2nd [March]. If we get to London early enough, I shall try and get to you for that night. I have to catch a train at 2.45 p.m. on the 3rd from Fenchurch Street. I will call at the RTO's office at Victoria Station in case you want to send one to me. Will you try and get Eve to come in that evening on the chance of my turning up? Isn't it a glorious surprise? My one fear is that something may turn up to stop me going.

Shoeburyness was an important Royal Artillery practice camp and range on the Essex coast east of Southend-on-Sea. Philip was away from France for nearly four weeks and missed the start of a major German offensive on 21st March. Apart from attending the camp, he was best man at the wedding of Philip Pilditch in London on 23rd March. More importantly for himself, he became engaged to Evelyn Fulton, his stepfather Hamilton's niece.

* * * * *

Meanwhile Guy Dodgson with the HQ of 118th Infantry Brigade had moved from Flanders about 80 miles south to the village of Bray which was near the 1916 Somme battlefield.

Guy to his mother   [Bray-sur-Somme]
26th January, 1918

I am so sorry I haven't written to you for a few days but, as I expect you have guessed, we have been on the move, and a move on rather a big scale this time. It has all been very successful and things have gone well and we are getting settled down in our new country, though our wanderings are not quite over yet. ... We are at present living in a somewhat depressing village. It's a place that at one time was quite close to the line and was shelled pretty badly, with the result that the majority of the inhabitants left the place. The houses have never been repaired, though German prisoners are beginning to do so. The inhabitants have never returned; so that you have a village of 1,500 or 1,600 with about 300 people living in it. The whole place has a deserted air. However, we are quite comfortable and are billeted in an old nunnery. ...

Over the next few days the Brigade advanced about 25 miles north-west of Bray and took over positions in the front line at Gouzeaucourt south-west of Cambrai. The 39th Division was now part of VII Corps in General Gough's Fifth Army.

[Gouzeaucourt Wood]
31st January, 1918

We have been in the throes of moving, and staying in different places each night for the last three days and it has been rather impossible to do much in the way of writing. Now we are once again in the line, getting here this afternoon. Personally I am not sorry to have arrived, as continually moving about is very worrying and as usual several things went wrong.

... This is a very different part of the line to where we have come from and, on the whole, far pleasanter. The country is not nearly so knocked about and there are quite a lot of woods and trees left. The only horrible part about it is the villages. When the Hun retired [to the Hindenburg line in the spring of 1917] he absolutely destroyed them and must have literally blown up every house. The result is that there is not a whole building left. It was a disgusting thing to do – pure destruction – and also very annoying for us. If he had left the villages in good condition we should have had quite good billets close behind the line. As it is, we are living in ramshackle old huts. ... I believe I am quite close to Philip and I heard yesterday that his Division was just north of us. I must try and find him; it would be so amusing to see him. ...

[Gouzeaucourt Wood]
2nd February, 1918

We are having quite a pleasant time up here and the weather has been glorious so far, with hard frosts and sun. I had one of my periodical walks with the General this morning and went all over the place. He is always full of energy and walks at a terrific pace with very small steps, I puffing along behind him! This place is altogether entirely different to anything I've ever seen before and it is amazing to walk about on ground which is practically untouched and where there is still grass growing, where correspondingly further north there would be nothing but shell-holes and wooden tracks to walk on.

I have had letters from Marjorie and Mrs Secretan asking me to try and find Reggie's grave and giving me the name of a cemetery where they think he is buried. Unfortunately their letters arrived after we had moved; otherwise I might have found the place. As it was, I did look through the names in several cemeteries I came across but couldn't find his name. I don't really believe anybody knows where he is buried, but I should like to have found out for them. I am living in quite comfortable quarters and sleeping in a deep tunnel quite immune from bombs and shells. What about the strikes in Germany? If only they will go on and spread to the army it ought to be the beginning of the end.[428] ...

[Gouzeaucourt Wood]
9th February, 1918

We are all feeling just a little bit depressed, as the Herts have left the Brigade and gone to another Brigade in the Division.[429] For the present I am staying where I am, though I rather hate it, as I shall hardly ever see the Battalion, but they seem to want me to stay and they have plenty of officers with the Battalion. ...

....

428 The Royal Navy's blockade of the Central Powers had led to food shortages in Germany from as early as the winter of 1916/17. Unlike in Britain, every foodstuff was rationed in Germany and Austria-Hungary with some unobtainable by early 1918. Rising food prices led to increased levels of industrial unrest in Germany as workers went on strike for higher wages.

429 Because of the increasingly acute manpower shortage, the BEF was reorganized from late Jan. 1918 with each infantry brigade being reduced from four battalions to three. The 1/1st Hertfordshires were transferred from 118 Infantry Brigade to 116 Infantry Brigade on 8th Feb. 1918.

[Gouzeaucourt Wood]
10th February, 1918

... How rotten for Philip having to revert: they really have treated him badly. I wish I could get away to see him but it is rather difficult as long as we are in the line. I don't know exactly where he is, though I think I know where his Divisional HQ are. Things are quite uneventful here and moderately quiet. I was very brave yesterday and walked up and had a look at the front line. It seems funny to think it is the first time I have seen anything like a proper trench since I have been out. All my experience has had to do with muddy shell-holes. ...

[Gouzeaucourt Wood]
18th February, 1918

... I was deputed yesterday to take the Army Corps Commander[430] round the line. I was absolutely petrified with fear when they told me, but I really quite enjoyed it. Quite a dear old gentleman, with one hand missing – poor old dear. We went all over the place and he insisted on going up to the front line, though I did my best to dissuade him! He also asked me numerous questions, the answers to which I was rather uncertain of. However, I lied valiantly and I hope I deceived him![431]

I went over the other day to see the Herts. They aren't very far away. I found them quite cheerful and rather bored with their new Brigade. It's gone very cold again, with hard frosts; also the season of the moon has arrived, so we are rather apt to have nightly visitors in the sky – things I hate more than anything! ...

[Gouzeaucourt Wood]
8th March, 1918

I got your letter last night telling me about Philip. How perfectly ripping for him! Almost every gunner in the Army seems to go on that course sometime or other. Does he get leave at the end of it? I still hope I may manage my leave before very long, as I think we are going back in a few days now, and they will probably let me go then. I tried to telephone to Philip the other night. Do tell him, will you? I got as far as his Divisional Artillery quite easily and they were going to put me through to the Battery exchange when somebody cut me off. However, I suppose he'd been some days in England by then. They say the war is nearly over! The Germans, having entirely squashed Russia, are going to offer France and ourselves terms which we shall accept; the only trouble being Alsace Lorraine, which the Hun won't give up and which the French <u>must</u> have.[432] Of course that is quite enough to keep the show going for years. Why we should fight for two provinces which are far more

....

430   Lt Gen Sir Walter Norris Congreve VC CB MVO was GOC VII Corps. As a Captain he was awarded the VC in 1899 after an action at Colenso in South Africa. He commanded 6th Division from May 1915 until he was appointed Lt Gen Commanding XIII Corps. He held that command until he was wounded on 12th June 1917. He lost his left hand and had an iron hook fitted to the stump. In Jan. 1918 he returned to France to command VII Corps. He had a reputation for extraordinary courage and a disregard for his personal safety. (Davies and Maddocks, *Bloody Red Tabs*, p. 128)

431   The war diary for 17th Feb. reports: "The Army Corps Commander visited the Brigade section in the afternoon: he visited Left Bn HQ and the front line of the Right Sub-section." (TNA WO 95/2589)

432   On 3rd Mar. 1918 Russia had signed a peace treaty – the Treaty of Brest-Litovsk – with the Central Powers which ended Russia's participation in the war.

German nowadays than French, it is rather hard to see. I wonder if you have heard any such tales. ... The weather is lovely and quite like spring.

[Gouzeaucourt Wood]
10th March, 1918

... I am afraid I told you about leave rather early. I am so sorry, as it is horrid not knowing for certain. But now I think I can tell you almost definitely. Anyhow, the General has said I can go directly we are out of the line. ... I believe there is a chance of getting a lift in a car some of the way on the 15th. ... I want to get away very much this time. Funnily enough, much more than I did last time. Perhaps it is being in the line rather a long time. I think most people are rather weary and a little bit fed-up; except the General [Bellingham] who is as indefatigable as ever and just as sweet tempered. He never ceases thinking out new schemes where to kill the Boche! ...

Guy did go home on leave during the second half of March and was in England when the Germans launched their offensive on 21st March.

(For 47th Division operations in this period also see Map 7)

On 21st March the Germans launched a massive attack – Operation Michael – on the British front line. They had been hugely reinforced by divisions no longer needed on the Eastern Front, so they outnumbered the British in men and artillery. Their aim was to reach the Channel ports before the Americans had many troops on French soil. The onslaught fell on the British Third and Fifth Armies stretching from near Arras to the junction with the French Army several miles south of St Quentin. The Third Army, under General Byng, had fourteen divisions to defend twenty-eight miles against nineteen German divisions; while in the south, General Gough's Fifth Army had only twelve divisions to cover forty-two miles against forty-three divisions. Most of the British reserve divisions were further north, held there to protect the Channel ports. Lloyd George had been reluctant to let more divisions in the UK move across the Channel. This was the first major defensive battle the British had fought since 1914.

None of the officers whose letters have been quoted in this account was in France at this time. Charles, in England, must have been extremely concerned about what was happening to the 47th Division, which had only just taken over the right flank of the Third Army. He would have been worried about the fate of his old battalion, the 1/19th Londons, of whom he was so proud. Ironically, the Division retreated past High Wood and other places on the Somme that it had captured at such cost in 1916. Between 21st and 28th March it suffered total casualties of 161 officers and 2,230 other ranks of which half were listed as 'missing'.[433] However, the line held by the Division never broke, although it had fallen back some twenty-five miles.

Carl Champion, the Second-in-Command of the 11th South Lancashires (St Helens Pioneers), and his brother Alan were still working as Pioneers with the 30th Division who were with the Fifth Army almost opposite St Quentin. This Division had only recently taken over this section of the line from the French, who had not put in much work to fight a defensive battle. There were no defences equivalent in strength to the Hindenburg Line. The story of Carl and his men at this time can be told through

....

433   Maude, op cit, p. 165

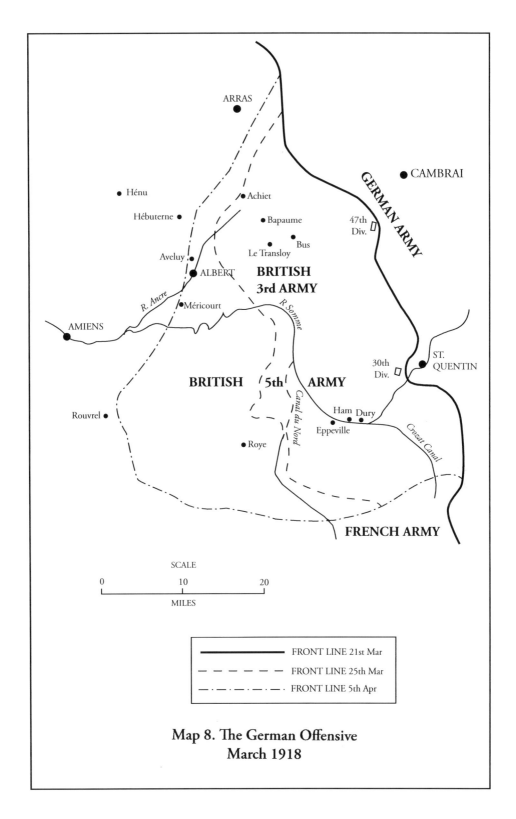

**Map 8. The German Offensive
March 1918**

his personal diary and the Battalion war diary. The theory of defence in this section of the front was to have a "forward zone" where casualties could be inflicted on the enemy before the men retired. Behind that was a zone of "redoubts" (strong points) which were to hold out for forty-eight hours. Further back was a "battle zone" where the attack would be held.

The St Helens Pioneers were spread across the divisional area and were helping to improve the defences. Their headquarters was at Dury near the 30th Division HQ. Some men were on Manchester Hill, one of the redoubts, while others were at another redoubt called "L'Epine de Dallon".

The German attack started with an extremely heavy artillery bombardment of HE and gas shells at 4.40 am. This lasted for five hours. There was fog that morning, helping the attackers more than the defenders. Troops in the forward zone were forced back fairly quickly. The Germans were able to filter between the redoubts, though the defence of Manchester Hill was gallantly led by Lt Col Elstob, DSO, MC. Sadly he lost his life but was awarded a posthumous VC to add to his earlier decorations. Like Carl and Charles, Lt Col Elstob was also a schoolmaster, teaching at Shrewsbury School at the outbreak of war.

In the afternoon the Pioneers were ordered back to Aviation Wood and, more ominously at 7.30 pm, "to be responsible for their own defence". Carl wrote that the Battalion was ordered back through Ham. By the night of the 22nd they were west of the River Somme and the canal near Eppeville. They had hoped to hold the bridges and defend the line of the canal. Carl wrote that the Battalion had manned trenches using a railway embankment but the 30th Division was losing touch with the 36th Division on its right. Carl's diary recorded *"Fought the good fight about 1.00 p.m."* Next morning on the 24th he wrote *"Boche attacked and broke through"*. Their route westward lay across a stream heavily lined with barbed wire. A 22 year old corporal, John Davies, was left there with his Lewis gun to hold off the Germans as long as possible to enable his Company to retreat. His action led to many of the Pioneers escaping, and he was last seen still firing his gun with the enemy almost on top of him. His gallantry led to the award of a posthumous VC. However, he was not killed and his parents had a postcard a few weeks later from a POW camp.[434] The DSO was awarded to Carl Champion, whose citation read:

> "When the troops on the left Bank began to retire, he went forward and took command of two Companies. The only line of withdrawal was through a river staked with barbed wire, and it was largely due to his coolness and organization of covering fire that part of the Companies succeeded in getting back. He then re-formed scattered troops of different units and led them forward, thus enabling a Battery to get its guns away. Later he displayed great courage in a counter-attack."

The Regimental History states that "an indication of the confused nature of this astonishing battle was contained in the adventure of Major C. C. Champion... When the reserve company came up, Major Champion tried to join it, only to find when not

....

434 Cpl John Thomas Davies became a captain in the Home Guard in the Second World War and died on 28th Oct. 1955. He is buried in St Helens Borough Cemetery.

more than a hundred yards away that the troops he was heading for were Germans! Fortunately he escaped."[435]

A fighting retreat followed across the Canal du Nord. For the next three days the 30th Division fought a rearguard action, gaining time for French forces to come to their aid. By the 28th, after a week of fighting, the St Helens Pals were well back at Rouvrel a few miles south-east of Amiens. That city, a vital road and rail link, had been saved and the retreat in that area was over.

The Regimental History records that "in the slowing down and eventual halting of the German advance [the Battalion] had played a very gallant part, and its magnificent fighting qualities are seen to be thrown into even brighter relief when it is remembered that its men had been for so long employed on solely pioneer work." The price was high and in the week's fighting it had suffered 3 officers and 28 other ranks killed, 210 other ranks missing, and 8 officers and 169 other ranks wounded, over half its original effective strength. It had 'indeed earned glory'.[436]

From Rouvrel the Battalion was sent to rest near the coast at Valery-sur-Somme. On 5th April they moved to the Ypres salient, but on the 10th April the Battalion was broken up. The CO, Lt Col Fenn, was appointed to command the 19th Lancashire Fusiliers, taking three hundred men with him. Major Pethick, MC, formed a Battalion

Carl Champion (front) at Royal Free Hospital – May 1918

....

435 *History of the South Lancashire Regiment*, Col B. R. Mullaly, p. 288

436 Mullaly, op cit p. 289

training cadre to instruct US engineers. He was joined by Alan Champion who had been promoted to Major.

Carl recorded in his diary for 9th April that he had the flu. Four days later he was ordered to the Field General Hospital where blood samples were taken. On the 28th he crossed the Channel and arrived at the Royal Free Hospital, Hampstead. By the end of May Carl was Mentioned in Dispatches and the following day he went on leave, but fell ill again in June. By the end of that month the St Helens Pals were reformed in England as part of the 25th Division and Carl rejoined them at Barrow on 22nd July.

* * * * *

Philip Dodgson's Battery C/235 had, by chance, not been near the front line with the 47th Division in the Retreat on 21st March. In that month they had been resting at Bus, a few miles to the west. His Battery, with the rest of the Brigade, fought rearguard actions through Le Transloy, Achiet, Foncquevillers and eventually stabilized their position near Hébuterne. Although the Battery had experienced considerable losses in horses, there was only a small loss in personnel and not a gun was lost.

The crisis of the March Retreat meant that the BEF needed to recall all men on leave at once. Before the end of the month Philip was on his way back to rejoin the 47th Divisional Artillery in France. Guy was also returning from leave at exactly the same moment and looking to rejoin the 1/1st Hertfordshires in the 39th Division.

Philip to his mother Officers' Rest House [Boulogne]
28th March, 1918

Just a line to let you know I've got so far all right. We had no time to wait at Folkestone and directly we landed we were put into lorries and taken up to the Camp. As you can imagine there is a terrible congestion of officers all trying to get back but at present there don't seem to be any trains. About the first person I came across at the Camp was our Guy. Wasn't it lucky meeting him? And, funnily enough, he had already joined up with a fellow from my Brigade, so we are all together. Guy doesn't know how long he's got to wait for his train but I expect we shall both leave here tomorrow. I shan't be sorry as I hate Boulogne. I think there is no doubt that I shall get back to my own Battery. ...

What fun our little stay in London was, and it was splendid being all together right to the last, in spite of the beastly disappointment of having to come back. I can only think how tremendously lucky I am, and I can never be grateful enough to you for everything you've done, and Hamilton too. Guy sends his love.

Guy to his mother [Boulogne]
28th March, 1918

I got across yesterday quite all right but can now get no further. Everything is rather chaotic and nobody seems to know much about anything. ... There are no trains at present to take us on. So here I am stuck in this wretched place. They make us stay in the camp, which is rather uncomfortable and I found my tent decidedly draughty last night. Rather funny – the first person I talked to in this camp last night I find is in the same Brigade as Philip and knows him quite well. ...

Officers' Rest House and Mess
30th March, 1918

I am still here and, as far as I can tell, with very little prospect of getting away. I expect Philip told you in his letter yesterday that we have met, which is rather lucky. He is still here too, so we are going about together. It's so sickening his being recalled in all that hurry and then hanging about for such a long time. ... It has gone rather cold and blustery and the sea is getting rough, and yesterday it rained the whole day. I can't get any news of the Battalion other than what I heard in England. Nobody knows very much, and what they do know they are not inclined to tell you. ...

[Boulogne]
1st April, 1918

We are still here and getting so horribly bored with the place, there being absolutely nothing to do. Luckily the weather is beautiful and we can get out by the sea. Yesterday we sat on the beach in the sun, which was rather lovely. ... The news on the whole is quite good, don't you think? Anyhow, the Boche is not having it quite all his own way. I can still hear very little news of the Regiment, except that I have traced Leslie [Gold].[437] He went to England on 24th with a gunshot wound in the right arm, which doesn't sound too bad. Anyhow, I am glad he is home. Funnily enough I was walking along the quay here the day before yesterday, when I spotted one of our fellows on an ambulance with a bandage round his head and had quite a long talk to him before he sailed. ...

Philip to his mother

Hotel Folkestone
Boulogne
2nd April, 1918

Just a line to let you know that Guy and I are still here, with apparently no prospect of getting away. We're growing more and more bored. It's beastly expensive too as we have to go to restaurants for our meals. We had the excitement of an air raid this morning; a lot of noise, but fortunately they did not come very near to us. ...

[Chateau de la Haye, nr Fonquevillers]
C/235 Bty RFA
5th April, 1918

... You will have already heard from Guy that I had left Boulogne on the 4th. We had a very slow train journey which lasted about ten hours, and it was about 10.30 p.m. and raining hard that we were turned out on an out-of-the-way railway siding. I was with a boy called Colthurst[438] who is in one of the batteries of this Brigade. We fortunately managed to find cover in the office of one of the railway people,

....

437 Capt Leslie Gold (see footnote 341, Chapter 14) had been awarded the MC in Jan. 1918 and would be awarded a bar to his MC in Jan. 1919. (TNA WO 95/2590)

438 Lt Alan St George Colthurst was an Old Haileyburian who had left the school in the summer of 1916 and took a commission in the RFA serving with 47th Divisonal Artillery until the Armistice. He was appointed for service with the West African Frontier Force on 15th Jan. 1919 and served in Nigeria. After his service he read history at Corpus Christi Cambridge and then entered the Church. He became Canon of St Albans Cathedral in 1963 and died in 1983.

but could get nothing to eat, so had to be content with dried figs and biscuits – the remainder of our supplies for the train. These of course made us desperately thirsty, when we found there was no water until one of us had a brainwave to go and try the engine driver, who produced some from somewhere underneath the engine. We then went to bed on the floor and, considering we had no blankets, slept very well. ...

I have not been up to the guns yet, but from what I've heard they've had a pretty hard and thrilling time, but have been very lucky, except that all our kits have been lost – to the last bootlace. So I've just got what I brought back with me, and that's all. The only thing I shall urgently need is a clean vest, pants and shirt. ...

I'm sorry to say the gramophone has gone too. It was an old friend. I only hope the Boche hasn't got it. ...

What you say about Evelyn in your first letter set me thinking, because I hadn't thought much about when we could get married, except that, as I felt pretty sure it couldn't be till after the War was over, I had not mentioned it to Eve herself and so don't really know what she would like. ...

Guy to his mother   British Officers' Club
                                                        5th April, 1918

Philip left me yesterday to go a little nearer the war, but I don't know where he has gone to. He didn't know himself when he went, as nobody seemed able to tell him. He merely got into the train and departed. It's rather dull here without him and I shall be glad to get away myself. I don't think it will be very much longer now as we are beginning to get some idea as to where the Division is. I saw in the paper yesterday that our Divisional Commander has been killed.[439] At first I thought that looked rather bad but I don't really think now that it necessarily does, as he was the most fool-hardy man and always quite thoughtless about his own safety. He was probably killed in some place where he hadn't any business to be, poor man.[440] ... I am staying at this club and, on the whole, finding it very comfortable, though it is absolutely packed, as indeed everywhere is. I shall be glad to get away and find some letters and be able to give you some more interesting news. ...

                                                                    YMCA
                                                        7th April, 1918

This curious paper will tell you that I am more or less wandering and have not yet succeeded in joining the Brigade. I have moved since I last wrote. I got away the day after Philip left me and am now at the place where the Brigade will eventually come in a day or two. I am afraid from all accounts they have had a pretty rough time and there are not many of the officers left. What is so frightfully sad is that

....

439 The GOC 39th Division, Maj Gen Edward Feetham CB CMG, was killed by a shell in Ignaucourt on 29th Mar. 1918. He was educated at Marlborough College, commissioned into the Royal Berkshire Regiment and had served in the Sudan and South Africa. He was on leave when the March Offensive opened, and resumed command on 23rd Mar. Feetham is buried at Picquigny British Cemetery (grave F.10).

440 The General Staff war diary of the Division commented "Scarcely a day passed since he assumed command of the Division without his going to the very foremost positions held by our troops, where, regardless of all dangers, he by his own personal example stimulated his men to maintain their position and defeat the enemy." (TNA WO 95/2567)

our General [Bellingham] is missing[441]. He is believed to be a prisoner, but nobody knows anything about him. I do hope he's all right. Our Colonel is also missing and believed a prisoner.[442] The 2nd-in-command is wounded. All this is only what one has heard, but I am afraid it must be true, as I heard it from one of the Division Staff people I met this morning. I shall be glad when they arrive and one can hear what really happened. At the moment I am staying in this YMCA place where they make you quite comfortable and charge you very little.

Have you heard from Philip yet? He promised he would send me a line, but I don't expect he will have a great deal of time for letters. You needn't feel in the least anxious about me for the present: we are definitely away from the show. ...

The 39th Division began moving northwards on 8th April to the Second Army in the Ypres Salient which at that time was a quiet area of the front. Because of heavy losses in March the Division had been reduced to cadre strength. On the evening of 10th April the Division was ordered to form a strong composite brigade which was to join XXII Corps.[443]

Guy to his mother [St Martin au Laërt, nr St Omer]
10th April, 1918

I found a whole bunch of letters from you yesterday on rejoining the Brigade. Thank you so much for them. I only found the Brigade yesterday, so you can imagine I have had an easy time since leaving you and, as far as I can tell, there is a fairly restful time ahead, although some rather drastic changes are in the air. I think I shall have to go back to the Battalion. They have hardly anybody left at all; hardly an officer per Company.[444] Isn't it too awful? I have also lost all my kit, which is now safely in Boche hands. Somebody I suppose is by now wearing my clothes. I am sending you a long list of things to send out. I am so glad you have heard news of George [Fulton] and that he is all right. How relieved Eleanor must be!

Philip to his mother C/235 Bty RFA
[April, 1918]

... I had rather a disaster last night. Having no blankets I had to get some from the Quartermaster, who only had some belonging to men in hospital. However I had to have blankets and take the risk. I hadn't been between them for long before I knew I wasn't alone, and during the night I caught several. It was only when I took off my vest and pants in the morning that I realised how bad things were. It took me about two hours to clear them off, so I had a good morning's sport, but I'm afraid it's too much to hope I've caught them all, so will you send me some sort of insecticide as

....

441 The 39th Division War Diary for 27th Mar. 1918 records that the Division had been ordered to withdraw, and this movement commenced at 7.00 am. 118th Infantry Brigade covered the withdrawal of 117th Infantry Brigade. Bellingham and his Brigade Major had left Brigade HQ at about 6.30 am to supervise the right flank and rearguard of the Brigade. They were last seen in a trench near the front line where they had taken cover from heavy shelling. (TNA WO 95/2589)

442 Lt Col Eric Charles Malcolm Phillips was taken prisoner on 24th Mar. 1918 and survived the war.

443 Edmonds, Brig Gen Sir James E., *Military Operations, France and Belgium, 1918, Volume 2* p. 246

444 In Mar. 1918 the 1/1st Hertfordshires lost nine officers killed and one officer died of wounds. Lt Col Phillips and four other officers were taken prisoner.

quickly as you can? It's given me rather a shock, because I hadn't realised before what an awful state some of the men must allow themselves to get into. ...

Philip to Hamilton Fulton   [Hénu]
C/235 Bty RFA
16th April, 1918

Thank you so much for your letter which was sent on to me from Boulogne. ... I was so glad to know that you were pleased at what Evelyn told you about herself and myself. I know how fond you have always been of her. As for me, I am of course happier than I have ever been, and it is a tremendous help to have something definite to look forward to. As to getting married before the War is over, I should like to, but owing to the uncertainty of things after the War I have not, up till now, felt that I am altogether in a position to suggest it. But I don't know what Evelyn herself would like, and that after all is what really matters.

I heard yesterday that I am to be a Captain again, and I'm glad to say remaining in this Battery. I'm very pleased as I shall have more interesting work, and I like Major Flynn.

I was so pleased to hear that you had good news of George and I hope that he will now be out of it for a bit. ...

Guy to his mother   [Voormezele]
17th April, 1918

.... Things have moved rather rapidly just lately. We are all quite all right and are not in any show, though there is a certain amount of activity going on not so very far away. However, that doesn't really bother us much. ..... We have moved from the nice quarters where I had a dugout with a fireplace, and have come a bit further back, but the huts are not so comfortable. ..... Our new General [Hubback] is a very good sort and is generally making himself popular, otherwise we are the same as far as Brigade HQ is concerned.[445] The Battalion of course is very different and there seems to be hardly anybody left. ...

[Voormezele]
19th April, 1918

I have written to Mrs Hickley [mother of a fellow subaltern] today and told her what I could.[446] It wasn't much I'm afraid, as nobody knows anything for certain. Apparently he was wounded in the neck and reached a casualty clearing station where he was seen by a man in the Kents who described him exactly and knew he was in the Hertfordshires. This man said he died in the CCS and I'm afraid it looks very much as though this must be true. Anyhow I don't think he can be a prisoner if he got as far back as a CCS. ... We had a wire today about General Bellingham. He

....

445 Brig Gen Arthur Benison Hubback was another rare example of a Territorial Brigadier. He was an architect of some note and had designed many of the principal public buildings in Malaya. In 1913 he was appointed Lt Col commanding the Malay States Volunteer Rifles. On the outbreak of war he came back to England and received a commission as a Maj. in the 19th Battalion, The London Regiment (St Pancras) in Sept. 1914. In Feb. 1915 he became CO of the 1/20th Londons, and then GOC 2nd Infantry Brigade, 1st Division in Mar. 1916. He assumed command of the 118th Infantry Brigade on 3rd Apr. 1918.

446 Lt R. T. N. Hickley of the 1/1st Hertfordshires was killed, aged 20, on 24th Mar. 1918 and is commemorated on the Pozières Memorial to the Missing.

is a prisoner and I think unwounded, which is good news.[447] It's rather an awful day and at the moment it is snowing. What news of Philip? I haven't had a word from him since we were at Boulogne. We are not doing very much just at present, only living under rather rotten conditions, but battles are certainly going on not so far away. ...

[Elzenwalle Château]
21st April, 1918

... We are still in the same place and quite happy. I have managed to secure rather a safer sleeping place than I had at first, and now live in a dugout with quite a lot of earth and bits of house on the top. We had a most beautiful firework display by the Boche last night. He really sent up some quite beautiful lights and, all else being equal, we might well have been at the Crystal Palace. I stood outside for quite a long time and watched them. ...

The German offensive of 21st March had been followed by another major attack – Operation Georgette - on 9th April in the area south of Ypres, around the River Lys. German troops penetrated only ten miles because they were held up by stubborn rearguard fighting and so their objective of the Channel ports was not achieved. The weakened 39th Division had played its part – by the 17th April its strength was only 100 officers and 3,400 other ranks.[448]

Sadly for the Fulton family, Hamilton's son, the CO of the 9th Cheshire Regiment, lost his life. Lt Col George Fulton, DSO, was killed on

Lt Col George Fulton DSO

George Fulton's name on the Tyne Cot Memorial to the Missing

....

447 Brig Gen Edward Henry Charles Patrick Bellingham DSO was repatriated in Dec. 1918 and made a CMG. In 1921 he succeeded his father as the 5th Baronet and was commissioned into the Royal Air Force in the Second World War. He died in May 1956. (Davies and Maddocks, op cit, pp 112-3)

448 This is less than one quarter of its establishment. (Edmonds, Brig Gen Sir James E., *Military Operations, France and Belgium, 1918, Volume 2* p. 353.)

14th April at Crucifix Corner near Neuve Eglise, just inside the Belgian border. He has no known grave but his name is recorded at Tyne Cot on the Memorial to the Missing.

Guy to his mother   [Elzenwalle Château]
                                                             22nd April, 1918

Just a short letter. I have had two from you today, one of them telling me about George. As a matter of fact I saw the notice in "The Times" on the 20th. It is too sad and I can't bear to think what poor Eleanor is going through. Do give her my love. I have written to her and to Hamilton, but it is very difficult to know what to say. Anything that one can say sounds so futile.

My parcels have at last turned up, including one with underclothes for which I am <u>very</u> thankful. Thank you so much for sending me a flea-bag. At present I am getting on all right with Army blankets, but it is much nicer to have something of your own. ...

Philip to his mother   [Hénu]
                                                             C/235 Bty RFA
                                                             25th April, 1918

Your three letters all came together yesterday and, before anything else, I must say how terribly sorry I am to hear about poor George. Somehow, although I had only seen him about twice, I feel almost as if he were my own brother. I suppose it's because Hamilton has been so wonderfully good to me that I have come to feel as if I were really part of his family. I am so thankful you are with him now because I know what a help you must be to him. ... Will you please give Hamilton and Eleanor my love and let them know how much I shall be thinking of them? Poor Eleanor – it is terrible for her. ...

... Things are still fairly quiet round here, except there is a tremendous lot of firing at night, which makes one's sleep rather disturbed. ... However the noise of guns, like thunder, does not do much harm to anybody. I'm finding life much more interesting now that I have the show to look after and be responsible for.

I had the report from the course. The people at Shoebury say "Fit for Battery Commander" and the Salisbury medical report read "Soon will be fit" – so that is satisfactory.

Guy to his mother   [Elzenwalle Château]
                                                             24th April, 1918

... It has been such a lovely spring day today, with sun the whole time and so different to what we've been having lately, and it makes one <u>feel</u> so different, but what a pity to spend it in this stupid country.

Good news about the Colonel [Phillips]: he is a prisoner and not wounded. The Adjutant is also a prisoner, but <u>is</u> wounded. I am awfully glad, but I can't think how the Colonel got through without a scratch as from all accounts he stayed at Battalion HQ to the last possible moment, and until the Boche were practically round the place, even sending his servant back. He's a splendid fellow and a great loss to the Battalion. ...

[Devonshire Camp, Busseboom]
30th April, 1918

They have now taken us out of the line and we are at present living in a funny little farmhouse. The poor people only left the place the day before yesterday and have left all kinds of possessions behind, including most of their furniture. I don't think we shall stay here very long and with any luck should go right back, as our casualties have been fairly bad. But of course one never knows what the authorities will do!

I am so glad Eleanor is getting something to do. It is so much better and life all alone in that little house in Salisbury would have been quite unbearable. You will rather enjoy having Ruth [George and Eleanor's four-year-old daughter] with you – Granny!! Somehow the title doesn't quite seem to fit you.

[Tunnelling Camp, Poperinghe-Watou Road]
3rd May, 1918

At last the joyful news has come through that we are to have a little rest. In consequence everybody is feeling very cheerful and happy. In addition it is the most glorious spring day … . So just at the moment it is rather a pleasant world. … You will have seen a good deal in the papers of the last day or two about the glorious 21st Division, but some of their "glory" was borrowed and by rights belongs to us as we were attached to them at the time.[449] … Thank goodness we are no longer with them and are going back to our old crowd very shortly. …

[Nielles-les-Ardes]
5th May, 1918

I believe we get into a train this evening and I shall be very thankful to get out of this wretched country. Owing to the consequences of the campaign I was forced to ride an Army push-bike the other day for seven miles over the most horrible roads. I arrived back wet to the skin and ached in every joint for the next three days. I always did hate a push-bike. …

* * * * *

Meanwhile, Charles Fair had spent February and March convalescing in England after he had broken his leg in January. At a medical board in late March he was declared fit for light duties. He was posted on 3rd April to the 24th (Tank Corps) Officer Cadet Battalion, which was stationed in a hutted camp on Hazeley Down, some three miles south-east of Winchester. A few of those huts were still standing at the start of the 21st Century. The location could hardly have suited Charles better: he was back in his home county of Hampshire with his father living in retirement at Winchester. Charles and Marjorie had lodgings in the village of Twyford in the Itchen Valley at no great distance from the camp. He commanded "D" company, a job not so dissimilar from that of a housemaster at a Public School as he was responsible for the general welfare of 150 cadets. His experience on the Western Front was invaluable when giving lectures and he was able to help organise various sporting events. One of

....

449 The 39th Division Composite Brigade, which included the remnants of the 1/1st Hertfordshires, had been attached to the 21st Division during the Second Battle of Kemmel (25th/26th Apr.). It successfully held a defensive flank near Voormezeele.

Charles Fair "Don Company" cartoon – 24th Officer Cadet Battalion, Hazeley Down, Winchester, 1918

the highlights of that summer was an inspection of the Battalion by HRH The Duke of Connaught. A medical report in June said Charles was not fit for general service and it would not be until August that he would be declared fully fit again.

* * * * *

By May 1918, the balance of power on the Western Front was shifting. After failing to achieve a breakthrough in the British sector in May, June and early July the Germans shifted the foci of their attacks to the French sector. However, the furious storm of the German offensives blew itself out, with none of the subsequent operations quite reaching the tactical success of the March Offensive. The German gamble for victory in 1918 had failed to defeat the Allies on the Western Front: despite some short term successes, it was a strategic defeat for Germany.

The 47th (London) Divisional History 1914-1919 records that May, June and July were, in fact, very quiet months for the Division. It also states "the summer months were remarkable for two new arrivals". One was the arrival of the American Army; the other was an epidemic of influenza. "The type of fever was fortunately not severe, but it had the effect, especially upon the younger men, of making them unfit for hard work for some weeks after the attack......... Probably the artillery suffered most severely, since they were engaged in strenuous operations."

In June Philip Pilditch wrote, "PUO – THE FLU – has struck. Nearly all 'A' Battery officers have it and also Philip Dodgson rather badly."

Philip Dodgson wrote, "I've been in bed the last few days with an attack of PUO. It is very infectious, so it's fairly fashionable now. I hope to be up in a few days, though after a high temperature I expect I'll feel a bit run down."

Chapter 19

The Advance to Victory and Armistice

July to December 1918

Philip Pilditch struggled hard not to succumb to the flu, but did so on the 4th July. On the way to hospital at Rouen he met Philip Dodgson who was recovering.

There appear to be few surviving letters written during this period from Philip and none from his brother Guy, though it is known that Guy suffered from gas poisoning at this time and was back in England.

On 8th August, described by General von Ludendorff as "the black day of the German army", the Allies launched a joint attack east of Amiens. This was the beginning of a period of uninterrupted allied offensives and advances which came to be known as "the Hundred Days", finishing with the Armistice on 11th November and the Allied victory.

In August Philip did get some leave and had a great time in the Scottish Highlands with his mother and his fiancée Evelyn. By 20th August he was writing from Folkestone on his way back to the Western Front.

Philip to his mother

The Pavilion Hotel
Folkestone
20th August, 1918

We have got a bit of time here so there's time for a short letter. ... I hope when you get back you will find a small rose bowl awaiting you, a small gift from Eve and myself. It's sad to find this leave is over: I've been happy in a way I've never known before. However, I'm starting straight away to look forward to the next. It's been very wonderful being able to see so much of Eve and I know more than ever how extraordinarily lucky I am. ...

The gunners of the 47th Division went into action on the Somme just south of Albert, working with the 18th Division, in support of a new offensive which opened on 22nd August.

Philip to his mother   [in the field near Albert]
B/235 Battery RFA
23rd August, 1918

I suppose by the time you get this you will be safely back at Salisbury and I'm safely back with the Battery again, which doesn't thrill me particularly. In fact I think it's very depressing coming back; specially the feeling of being last on the leave roster, but you can't have your cake and eat it. ... Everybody seems to think leave will be more plentiful before long and already more are going than a short time ago. I'm sorry I didn't write to you from Boulogne. There was very little time as we left there early on Wednesday morning – such a hot train journey and ten-and-a-half hours of it too. We had to stay the night in the village where we got out of the train and came on here yesterday by lorry. I'm back in the same old place and there's plenty doing just at present and things seem to be going well, as you'll be reading in the paper. We seem to be giving the Boche a pretty rotten time all along the line now and, if only we can keep it up, I hope we may see the end of the war some day. ...

[in the field near Albert]
29th August, 1918

Only a line now just to tell you that I've got to go on a course from 3rd September to the 18th on machine guns and my address will then be: c/o GHQ Machine Gun School, BEF.

[in the field near Albert]
30th August, 1918

Poor old Toby; I rode up to see the place where he is buried. I had some difficulty in finding it, as the cross I'd put there has gone and the other one is broken and lying on the ground. I shall try to get another made and put up but, in case I can't do it, I'm writing to the Graves Commission to ask them to put a cross up. ... We have not moved for several days now and are still out of action.[450] We've been very glad of these few days as we've now been able to disentangle the muddle we got into ... All the men were separated from all their belongings which had to be sent for. ... Eve and I did talk a bit on the subject of getting married, but I don't think either of us is quite certain. Of course I think the only thing against it is the uncertainty of what's going to happen to me after the war. I should very much like your advice. ... Eve seems quite keen on going abroad – more so than I am. ... We are getting away from civilization again and we should be very glad indeed of some butter, as the ration never lasts out. I am wondering whether it would be possible to send us out a parcel of groceries periodically as it gets more and more difficult here, and you can't expect a cook to make bricks without straw: such things as custard powder, cornflower, porridge, dried fruits – anything which would be useful to somebody who is <u>not</u> an experienced cook. ... Will you let me know what you think about this? I am running the Mess now and should, of course, send you money to cover the expense. ...

....

450 The war diary for 31st Aug. states "235 Brigade RFA has remained in its wagon lines since 27th inst during which time it has been able to refit, rest and get bathed so that we are perfectly ready to resume work again." (TNA WO 95/2717)

The gunners had crossed the Canal du Nord and were in action on the Nurlu Ridge.

[Bouchesvesnes]
5th September, 1918

Only a line to tell you I'm in the best of health, though have plenty of work. I've not gone on that course after all as there's such heaps to do here. I'll try and write you a proper letter shortly. At present I've been sent as liaison officer to one of the Infantry Brigades and I shall, for the time being, be living with the [Brigadier] General. I'm sorry not to be with the Battery. ...

On the evening of 8th September the 47th Division began moving to the rear for refitting and training. 235th Brigade RFA passed through Lillers, arriving at Amettes on the evening of the next day in Fifth Army area.

[Amettes]
9th September, 1918

... It's been a strenuous time since I got back – continuous moving about, and we've generally not spent more than one night in the same place. However, we've done fairly well and one doesn't mind going through hard times if you feel it's getting on with the war. I think things do look more hopeful now, if only the weather will last. I'm glad to say for the present we are in comfortable billets and I'm writing this in bed with <u>sheets</u> – the height of luxury out here – and electric light too! I had a very good time living with the Infantry Brigade. I liked the General and all the others there. ...

* * * * *

Although the tide of victory was flowing for the Allies in August and September 1918, there was no certainty of an end to the fighting before the year was out. Yet Charles was released from the Army on the 13th September to return to Haileybury College. He had reached the end of his four year Territorial commission, and the Public Schools were desperately short of masters, not least in the OTC – still an important training ground for potential officers.

The Headmaster of Haileybury, F. B. Malim, asked Charles and Marjorie to take over the running of "Trevelyan", one of the few boarding houses with accommodation for a married couple. The vacancy had arisen because the

Charles Fair with ribbons of the DSO and of campaign medals

housemaster, G. T. Waters,[451] a man well over the age for compulsory military service, had volunteered to serve overseas, where he died of wounds in March 1918. Charles and Marjorie had less than two weeks before term began to furnish their large house and make ready for the return of the boys. All went well, however, and they were soon immersed in all aspects of school life.

* * * * *

Carl Champion, Charles's friend and colleague, had rejoined the 11th South Lancashires, which had been reformed in July as part of the 25th Division. On the 30th of that month he wrote, "The CO asked me about a flying course. I hope it's not an omen."

By 3rd August he was on a course at Worthy Down near Winchester. Now back in England he was able to use his camera again. Amongst the photographs he took was one of a crashed aircraft: was this the omen he was thinking of? Another photo of practice trenches dug in the chalk of the area shows just how visible such earthworks were from the air.

Crashed aircraft at Worthy Down near Winchester - 6th Aug. 1918

* * * * *

On the 12th September Philip Dodgson was transferred from B/235 Battery to A/235 Battery RFA.[452]

Philip to his mother [Amettes]
A/235 Battery RFA
14th September, 1918

I received your letter dated 10th telling me about Evelyn. She wrote to me on the 8th telling me she was in bed with flu. ... I feel rather puzzled why, if her

451 Capt George Thorold Waters of the 7th Battalion, The Suffolk Regiment died on 29th Mar. 1918 and is buried in Wimereux Communal Cemetery (grave IV.F.1). He was 44 and had been on the staff at Haileybury since 1900, becoming housemaster of Trevelyan in 1911.
452 TNA WO 95/2717

View when banking – Worthy Down Camp and practice trenches from about 1,500 feet. 9th Aug. 1918

temperature was down, she was sent to the Nursing Home. I'm feeling rather anxious.

I'm now with a different Battery. Pilditch is now my Major … . I'm not sorry to have made the change, as although I didn't actually quarrel with the old Major who came out from England … we didn't quite hit it off. …

Isn't the news of this American push splendid?[453] One really feels more and more hopeful and confident every day that the end of the war may not be far off. …

[Amettes]
17th September, 1918

It is thoughtful of you to tell me all about Eve, as she herself says very little and I have been rather anxious. I still can't quite make out how bad she has been. It seems to me they don't really know what exactly is wrong with her. I do hope when she does get about again everybody will be very firm with her and insist on a good, long convalescence. …

Philip to his step-father, Hamilton Fulton   [La Comte]
22nd September, 1918

… We've had a lot of moving about. This is the third village we've been in in the last few days and all within a few miles of each other. We are now in one of the places we knew about two years ago. Unfortunately, I couldn't get the same billet as I had before. The people remember us quite well, but Pilditch and I are the only two officers who were here before – all the others have become casualties or got jobs elsewhere. …

....

453 On 12th Sept. seven American divisions supported by French troops had successfully attacked the salient at St. Mihiel south of Verdun capturing 460 German artillery pieces and 15,000 prisoners. This was the first significant American-led offensive of the war.

Philip to his mother [La Comte]
22nd September, 1918

... We are still out of action and likely to be, we hope, for some time. ... The duties of liaison officer are not very exacting in ordinary times: simply to keep the Infantry and Artillery commanders informed of each other's wants and intentions; also to advise the Infantry on anything to do with Artillery. ... We're playing lots of bridge; it's rather lucky that everybody in the Mess is keen on it. ... I'm getting on very well with Pilditch and it's good to be with somebody who knows so many people that I do and we've got a lot in common. ...

[La Comte]
25th September, 1918

... I am so sorry to hear Guy has been sent out again, though I dare say he isn't altogether sorry. I hope he'll let me know at once where he is as I should like to see him. ...

We've been playing football today – just one half of the Battery against the other. I thought I should have died – I got so out of breath! The men, of course, love it more than anything. Poor old Pilditch got laid out with a kick on the head. ...

[Amettes]
1st October, 1918

... We are, after a fortnight, back in the same spot once more. After thoroughly rousing your curiosity, it's all off and I shall not be away from the Brigade after all. ... We moved very unexpectedly today – only got word of it at half-past three this morning. ... I am very glad to hear Evelyn is looking so much better. She must have had a very bad time of it. ... No word from Guy yet. I wish he'd let me know where he is, as I don't want to miss an opportunity of seeing him. ... Isn't it splendid news about Bulgaria?[454] We're all looking forward to hearing that Turkey has followed her example. Everything seems to be going splendidly on this front too. ... I wonder what chance there is of the war finishing this winter. I think Evelyn seems to have made up her mind that we are to get married next leave.

... I think today we have really had the satisfaction of scoring off a Frenchman without using any deceit. The only place for our horses was along a road and by the road was a field of potatoes. The horses naturally ate the tops off and the Frenchman claimed 80F for the potatoes. When we argued that only the tops had been eaten, he tried to make us believe all the potatoes were crushed and of no use. We said no more, but quickly went and dug up all the potatoes – two sacks full, and when we left today we offered him fifty instead of eighty francs and he took it without a word. I'm quite sure he thought he'd made 50F for nothing and that he would just have to go and dig the potatoes himself after we'd gone! I should love to see his face when he goes to try!

....

454 The state of Bulgaria was the first of the Central Powers to seek an armistice. This was signed on 30th Sept. 1918.

[Fromelles]
8th October, 1918

... I'm now up with the guns for a few days. Pilditch is also here so, from a Battery point of view, there's not much for me to do. This morning we walked up to have a look at the Boche but, seeing none, we had a shot at where we hoped he might be. This afternoon I've spent working hard, helping the servants make themselves a better place to live in. We are fairly comfortable as we have a Boche concrete pill-box to live in; very cramped and like a prison cell, but fairly secure! ... I had a letter from Guy. He has gone back to where he was before, so there's no chance of our meeting *pro tem*. ...

* * * * *

Carl Champion took over command of the 11th South Lancashires on 17th September. On 7th October the Battalion, largely composed of Class B men with thirty-six officers, landed in France. On the 13th October the Battalion was attached to the 25th Division and went into billets at Prémont, twelve miles south east of Cambrai. From then on the St Helens Pals moved steadily up behind the advancing British troops, clearing roads and repairing bridges. By the 26th October they were at Le Cateau rehearsing for a canal crossing for which pontoon bridges were constructed in readiness.

At 5.45 am on 4th November the First, Third and Fourth Armies opened the BEF's final offensive of the war on a thirty mile front. Under hostile fire, the 11th South Lancashires launched their pontoon bridges across the Sambre-Oise Canal at Landrecies. The Battalion suffered almost fifty casualties.[455] Carl was again Mentioned in Dispatches. By 11th November the Battalion had reached Sars Poterie. Carl's diary just records "Armistice at 11.00". There were few cheers or celebrations. With the fighting over, this Pioneer Battalion still had plenty of work to do – clearing roads, improving billets and salvaging materials. By the end of the war Carl's brother, Alan, was commanding the 2nd Battalion, the West Yorkshire Regiment.

Lt Col Carl Champion (right) with Lt H. L Nash

* * * * *

....
455 The war diary reports that four officers were wounded on 4th Nov. of which one died of wounds. Six other ranks were killed and 34 wounded (of which four later died of wounds). (TNA WO 95/2323)

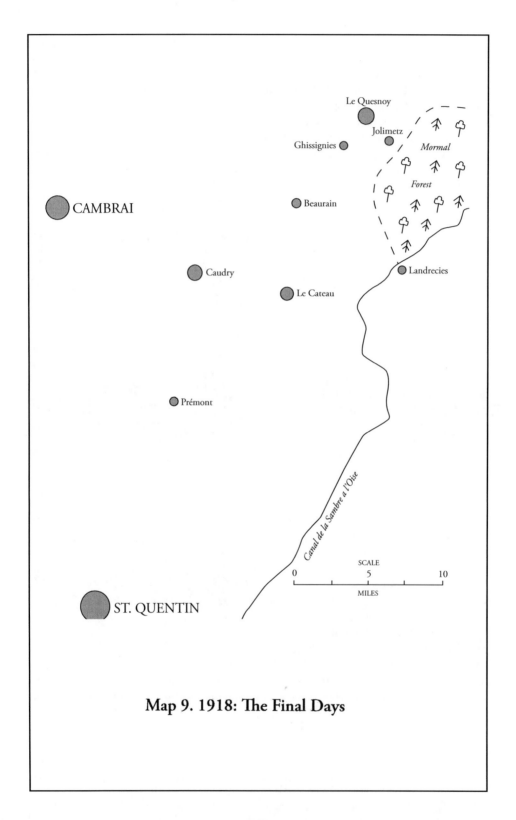

Map 9. 1918: The Final Days

In the meantime Philip Dodgson, with the gunners of 47th (London) Division, had moved back about 15 miles to an area north west of Béthune for training and refitting.

Philip to his mother [Robecq]
22nd October, 1918

... We've been having quite a busy time lately doing a bit of training trying to adapt our methods to suit the new conditions.[456] However, we've now heard that we're to take part in a sort of Lord Mayor's Show, so are hard at work applying the eyewash.[457] The men like the idea and I expect it will be rather interesting. ...

On the 26th October the 47th Division artillery moved forward again to Haubourdin, a village on the western outskirts of Lille. On the 28th they moved through the city.

Philip to his mother [Breucq, east of Lille]
28th October, 1918

... We've had a busy time the last few days and not much chance of writing letters. We were marching all day Saturday for about ten hours and all the way through such devastated country. We eventually emerged the other side, but only after it was dark. We settled down into most comfortable quarters and the French people welcomed us with open arms. It's about the first time we really have been received like that since we came out. Of course, at present they won't accept any money and give us anything we want. They've got so used to the Boche taking everything without asking. I suppose they do like being able to give. Sunday was spent hard at work cleaning up and I must say the men put their hearts into it thoroughly. We were lucky in having all the horses and guns under cover in a factory. Today the great event took place.[458] Thank goodness it was fine as we had to get up horribly early. It really has been rather a wonderful experience. For about two miles the streets were packed with people on either side and it was good to see them all so happy. In addition to the fact that I was at the head of the leading Battery, I was made extra conspicuous by my horse getting thoroughly excited by the crowds of people and the noise they made as they did a certain amount of clapping and cheering, and the more they did the worse she got. Fortunately, at the critical moment in the *Grande Place* she behaved rather better. They made us march at attention the whole way, which made it rather impressive but a bit boring. One rather longed to do something in return when we saw these French people taking off their hats and shouting, *"Vive L'Angleterre!"* and all that sort of thing.

We are in a very good spot now – another factory – and we've got our Mess in the works manager's house. Of course all the machinery has gone, so we've got our men and horses in the works. There are just a few women and two or three men here. They are still so furious with the Boche that I think they'd do anything for us.
....

456 The Germans were now in full scale retreat all along the front. The BEF had to adapt its tactics to this new style of open warfare.

457 On 21st Oct. the war diary reports "Received Warning Order that Division would march through Lille about 29th inst." (TNA WO 95/2717)

458 The 47th Division's Victory Parade through Lille. It marched past a number of dignitaries including the Mayor of Lille, the Fifth Army Commander (General Birdwood) and the Secretary of State for War (Mr Winston Churchill). (For a detailed description see Maude, *op cit*, pp. 203-4.)

I wonder how long it will last. I don't think they'll ever treat us in the same way as the other French people do: four years with Huns will take a lot of forgetting. ...

[Breucq]
31st October, 1918

... We've had a few comfortable days here but have got to move tomorrow and an early start too, so I've got a busy day to look forward to. This is an exceptionally nice Battery to be in. Everything goes so smoothly. It does make the whole thing so much more enjoyable when you haven't got to be driving the men the whole time. We've had congratulatory messages on our procession last Monday from all sorts of high officials and it really was rather a good show, I think. I believe the French people are very surprised at the fine condition of our horses. They've got so used to the scraggy Boche animals! ...

On 1st November 235 Brigade RFA relieved 236 Brigade RFA in the line, crossing the Belgian border east of Lille as it did so. From positions near Cazeau the guns were able to support the continued movement of the 47th Division as it advanced on the Belgian town of Tournai.

[Cazeau]
5th November, 1918

I'm afraid it's a good many days since I wrote but it's been a busy time the last few days as it always is when you get into a new place, and Pilditch being away makes a good bit extra for me. ... The news is splendid about Austria and Turkey[459] and I can't help thinking it won't be long before Germany is in the same state. It will be interesting to see what the Allies' terms for an armistice are. I wish they'd hurry up and decide. If we're going to have one, the sooner the better. Yesterday was a glorious day with lovely sun. I rode down to the wagon line but had to spend all the time among paper. ... In the afternoon I had to write out recommendations for all the men in the Battery I thought required a rest – a most difficult thing to do because honestly I think everybody who had been out in a fighting unit for a long time must feel the strain and yet, if you once start that sort of thing, there's no knowing when it will end. There's not room for a lot of sentiment. It would never do if everybody gave way. ... Everybody is more comfortable than we've ever been and, even in the front line, they are all in good houses. At the moment we're expecting the Boche to go back, so there are probably some busy days in front of us. It's a brute of a day today, so I hope he'll stay where is for the present. We are quite comfortable where we are in a nice little house. It was empty when we arrived and then suddenly an old man and woman with their son arrived, which was rather a shock as we were treating their house as our own and continued to do so. As I don't think they ought to be up here, I got the interpreter to come and tell them to go away again and they've gone. It is extraordinary the way they cling to their homes. Some of them are living right up by the front line. They just sit and do nothing. I suppose they expect the war to move on any day and they will then be left in peace again. In the meantime it's very awkward for us. I was up at the OP the other day and had sent down the order to the guns to shoot on a certain bit of road. Before

....

459 Armistices were signed with Turkey on 30th Oct. and with Austria-Hungary on 3rd Nov.

the guns fired, a Frenchman came and stood on the exact spot where I thought the shell would fall. I could only wait and see, wondering whether I should hit him or not. Fortunately it landed about fifteen yards from him and, to my surprise, he didn't seem to care a bit and walked quite coolly down the road. I wouldn't be a bit surprised if there aren't a good few Boche dressed up as Frenchmen and girls.

I had a line from Guy yesterday – he seems fairly cheerful. It's not such a bad war as it was. ... I wrote and told him he must certainly come home and be my Best Man. I shall be frightfully disappointed if he can't manage it and I don't know who else I can get. ...

However, that autumn Guy was back with the 1/1st Hertfordshire Regiment, who were still involved in fighting. The Germans were resisting strongly and there was heavy fighting across the Cambrai-Le Cateau road. The Battalion, now part of the 37th Division,[460] advanced towards Le Quesnoy in late October, but found this was no easy task. At the end of the month the 1st Hertfordshires were resting at the village of Beaurain. The final battle saw them advance from Ghissignies on 4th November. Guy was wounded at Jolimetz, a little village close to the large Foret de Mormal and taken back for treatment to No. 3 CCS at Caudry, south-east of Cambrai. He sent a postcard to Helen on 6th November:

> I got wounded on the 4th in the right side. Am feeling very comfortable now and shall soon be all right. I think it's a "Blighty" – I hope so. Guy

Underneath this message there is post-script saying it had been written by the Chaplain, E. H. Gallop.

Guy wrote to his mother again on 10th November from the CCS at Caudry:

I know you will have been thinking me an awful beast for not writing you anything better than that horrid little postcard written by the Chaplain. I would have sent you a wire at once, only I haven't yet got far enough down the line to be able to do so. I am still at a Casualty Clearing Station (No. 3 British) and they haven't sent me on yet as they weren't sure whether there was going to be any abdominal trouble. They operated the first day here and found very little wrong and today the surgeon is going to have another look at me and I quite hope to get down to a comfortable base hospital and then across the Channel. I will let you know what base hospital I go to. Don't worry about me. I am getting better quickly and the wound (in the right side between the bottom and the stomach) was never really bad. A devil of a Boche sniper just managed to catch me. My writing is a bit wobbly as I am practically on my back and have had hardly anything to eat except slops since the great event.

....

460 The 1/1st Hertfordshires had been transferred to 112th Infantry Brigade in 37th Division on 11th May 1918.

Philip to his mother [Blandain]
13th November, 1918

... Isn't it wonderful to think we really are at peace once more and it's now only a matter of time before we are home again? Our last few days of the war were really strenuous but now we are back in quite comfortable quarters and expecting to stay here for some time. We've had a thoroughly cheery evening today. We managed to get quite a few bottles of champagne and have drunk everybody's health, including your own – and now it's bedtime. It's just too good to think that dear old England has come out on top after all and the Huns are thoroughly defeated. We are all tremendously pleased with the terms of the Armistice. ...

I've had no letter from Eve now since a letter written on the 4th. I hope there's nothing wrong with her. I feel very anxious with this flu going round but, as she has already had it, I'm hoping she won't get it again.

I wonder how long it will be before we get home. I suppose we shall have to stay out here until the Peace terms are finally settled. ... We are busy now trying to arrange amusements, etc. for the men until we get home. I think if we are kept long it will be a very difficult time, especially as it will be right through the winter when the evenings are so long. There are rumours that we are to go and occupy Germany but I hope they aren't true. I am returning Guy's letters with this. I think he is quite wise to go on with his music, as long as he is prepared to live in a quiet way, which he apparently is. ...

[Blandain]
18th November, 1918

... I got a letter from Eve telling me you had gone off to London to see what you could find out about poor Guy. I am so sorry to hear about his being wounded. Ever since the end of the fighting I'd been waiting to hear news of him and hoping he was all right. In spite of hearing you had gone to Town, I'm still hoping that he's getting on all right and that the telegram was sent on the first report of the wound, because I know they do report all stomach wounds as dangerous. ...

I'm afraid you're having an awfully anxious time, but I know how bravely you will bear it. I only wish we could have been together. I spoke to the Colonel today and I think there will be no difficulty for me to get leave from the base if you *do* come over. I think I shall try and get down to see Guy even if you don't come – as soon as I know where he is. ...

... I've had a very long letter from Pilditch. I don't think he is enjoying the Salisbury hotels very much and was disappointed at not being out here for the Armistice. If he only knew, he's missed nothing and we've had no demonstrations or stirring scenes: nothing except a short note to say hostilities would cease. As there doesn't seem the slightest chance of getting home, nobody is very excited, although of course the stopping of the fighting has lifted a tremendous weight off our shoulders. ...

I can't tell you how I'm hoping for better news of Guy. ...

However, by this time Helen had probably received the following letter from Lt Col H. W. Dakeyne DSO[461] of the 8th Battalion North Staffordshire Regiment:

14th November, 1918

Dear Mrs Fulton,

My excuse in writing to you is that Guy was my dearest friend and I was with him when he died this morning. It is impossible for me to attempt to send you any adequate expression of my sympathy in your loss. Will you please believe me that it is none the less sincere for that? I think I appreciate a little the loss I have suffered today and yours, I know, is a far greater one: he was your son and a more gallant and loveable personality will be impossible to find.

Altho' we were in a different Division and a different Army even, I had managed to keep in touch with him after he came out [to France] this last time, and two days ago I found out that he had been wounded on the 4th; seriously in the thigh and chest, but not dangerously. I sent my groom yesterday to find out how he was and had a note back in the evening from the doctor in charge[462] of No. 3 Casualty Clearing Station at Caudry that, altho' his wounds were progressing favourably, Guy had developed pneumonia and was dangerously ill. I started off early this morning but did not arrive before eleven o'clock and found the poor boy delirious. Everything that was possible was being done for him, including injections and oxygen, and the nurse and the doctor were working incessantly. He apparently had had a very bad night and was barely conscious this morning, altho' he had spoken a few words to the nurse about eight o'clock.

About 11.30, just for a few seconds, he opened his eyes and I hope and think just recognized me, as a smile, the most pitiable ghost of his own charming smile, swept over his face; and his upper lip twitched in the same old characteristic fashion that I knew so well. After that it was obviously only a question of a short time before he died and, I think purposely, everyone else left me alone with him. He died absolutely peacefully and quickly a few minutes after twelve.[463]

If I did wrong I hope you will forgive me, but shortly after he died I kissed him once on the forehead for his Mother and then left him. I took away the Chaplain with me to find his Battalion, which we did luckily not far off, and saw his CO and arranged a proper military funeral for tomorrow at 2.30. I shall go over to it if I possibly can and, if you would care, I will send you an account of it later. The Chaplain whose name is, I think, Gallop, was for many years at Hemel Hempstead, and told me that he and Guy had found many mutual acquaintances.[464] He has promised to write to you and ask the Sister to do the same.

....

461 Harry Dakeyne was a regular officer of the Royal Warwickshire Regiment. He was serving with the 1st Royal Warwicks when he was promoted to Lt on 17th Sept. 1909. He was posted to the West African Regiment on 7th Aug. 1912 and promoted to Captain on 14th Sept.1914. He returned from Africa in the spring of 1916 and appears to have gained some experience on the Western Front with the 10th (S) R Warwicks in the autumn of 1916. He was promoted to Temp Lt Col commanding the 8th N Staffords on 8th Dec.1916. He was awarded the DSO in 1917. (*Army List*)

462 Probably Lt Col M. B. Ray DSO RAMC (TF) who was commanding No. 3 CCS at that time.

463 That day's war diary for No. 3 CCS records "Deaths – Capt G Dodgson, 1st Herts". (TNA WO 95/412)

464 Capt The Reverend Ernest Harold Gallop had been appointed as a 4th Class Chaplain on 7th June 1918 and had only taken up his post at No. 3 CCS on 27th Oct. He was 42, a graduate of Keble College, Oxford, and vicar of St John's Church, Walham Green, SW6. He was an Old Marlburian and his father was Canon of St Albans, so it is not surprising that he and Guy had some mutual acquaintances. (TNA WO 374/26254)

The CO of the Hertfordshire Regiment and the other officers to whom I took the news were all deeply distressed: and I know will do their very best tomorrow to honour the boy they so evidently admired and liked. ... Even the hospital orderlies told me how wonderfully he had behaved since his admission, how cheerful he was and grateful for what they could do for him. He had evidently won all their hearts in that short time.

My writing to you like this may seem rank presumption on my part and a most indelicate interference with your own private grief. My only excuse can be that Guy was to me more than anyone else has ever been and I admired and loved him better than anyone I have ever met in my life. He was such a perfect gentleman. I was also privileged to know your step-son, George Fulton, who commanded the 9th Cheshires in this Brigade.

If there is any single thing I can do, any information I can give you or any question I can answer, will you please write and ask me.

Yours sincerely,

H. W. Dakeyne

Philip to Hamilton Fulton   [Blandain]
19th November, 1918

Thank you so much for your kind and sympathetic letter. The bad news of poor Guy has indeed come as a terrible shock to me and I was, for a time, quite overcome by it. The loss of brothers and friends is one that can never be made good to the end of our lives and nobody can ever replace them. One's heart goes out in gratitude to them and it is a great consolation to know their lives have not been given in vain. Poor Mother: I'm afraid she will be broken-hearted and I hate to think of her having to go through such sorrow. It is a great relief to me to know that you are with her, as I know how well you will be able to comfort her and I only wish I could be with her too. I have been thinking what is the best thing to try and do, and I have decided first of all to go, if possible, to the hospital and find out what I can. I'm also going to try hard to get home. I have been to see the Adjutant and he is going to ask the Colonel to talk it over with the General. If there seems to be no hope I will apply straight away for a month's leave and, if I get that, I might be able to work it at home that I don't come back here. I think it's the right thing to do, as I feel I can no longer have any heart in the work here. ... We are at present situated at Baisieux, about half-way between Lille and Tournai, and expect to stay here for the present. ...

Philip to his mother   [Wannehain]
20th November, 1918

My Darling Mother,

I don't know how to start this letter because it's quite impossible to say how terribly I feel about poor, dear Guy's death. When I first heard of it thank goodness I was alone. I felt perfectly hopeless about everything and just let myself go for a bit. I think it did me good for suddenly I began to think, and I realized how far worse it is for you. I saw that it was up to me to do all I could to help you, so I went on thinking and decided, if possible, first of all to get to the casualty clearing station and after that to get home. ... Everybody has been most sympathetic. The General sent his car round for me this morning and the Adjutant came with me. I have not been altogether successful. We went down to Valenciennes and found out there from Army HQ that the 3rd CCS was at Caudry, about eighteen miles further on. Unfortunately it has been foggy all day and we had to get back by daylight, so that it was impossible to go there in the car. However, I managed to speak very faintly to the 3rd CCS on the telephone. I could just hear that Guy was suffering from a double fracture and that he died of pneumonia, but it was impossible to get any further details. I hope you will have heard more fully from somebody who was with him. I think his wound must have been more serious than anybody or he himself realized. ...

The other thing I've done is to apply for a month's special leave straight away and, as the Colonel told me to do it, I'm hoping it will go through all right and that we may be together sooner than either of us expected. Anyhow, it's something to look forward to .... I've had a very sweet letter from my Eve today and you will understand what a real comfort it is to me to have her to think of. ...

Ever your very loving,

Philip

[Wannehain]

24th November, 1918

Thank you so much for your letter dated 19th enclosing the copy of the Chaplain's letter. I was very glad to see it and it was most comforting to know that Guy was so well liked and cared for, and also that Col Dakeyne was with him to the last. Did Guy ever speak to you of this Col Dakeyne? I wonder how they got to know each other so well.

Well, Mother, there's no more news of my leave at present. I didn't expect to get it for about a week so I'm still living in hopes as I want to get back to you and Evelyn very badly. It is so hateful being here with nobody to talk to. ...

Philip was soon sent home on compassionate grounds. The war diary of 235 Brigade RFA for 30th November records: "A/Capt P. H. Dodgson proceeded on one month's special leave."

Lt Col H. W. Dakeyne wrote to Helen again: 10th December, 1918

It was very kind indeed of you to write to me in answer to my letter and I appreciated it more than I can say, as I am a complete stranger to you. I was afraid Guy's death would come as a very bitter blow to you: more than once he had spoken to me about you and, although he never was very demonstrative, I had realized a little what you meant to him. What he must have meant to you I dare not even guess; except that you must have been an intensely proud mother to have such a son.

I managed to get over to Caudry on the 15th for the funeral. At 2.15 p.m. we were in the square of the town: every officer, who was not on duty, of his Battalion was there; a firing party, buglers, and the whole of his Company. His Colonel, much to his regret, was unable to come as he had to attend a conference at Divisional Headquarters. Guy was brought down from No. 3 CCS on an ambulance and was lifted out and carried from there. His slight figure, wrapped in a blanket and covered by a Union Jack, being carried across the square to where we were drawn up waiting, was I think the most pitiful sight I have ever seen, and one I don't think I

Guy Dodgson's grave at Caudry British Cemetery (grave I.D.32)

shall ever forget. There seemed so little of him and I found myself wondering where he really was, and whether he had carried away with him all the boyish charm and genius that had been his such a short time before.

We fell in behind him, and marched at a slow march to the cemetery, being met a few hundred yards away from it by the Chaplain, who then walked at the head reading the service. It wasn't very long and I don't think anyone was very sorry when it was over, and the firing party had fired their three rounds over the grave. They "Presented Arms" and the buglers sounded The Last Post and all the officers saluted him. It may not have been a very "showy" funeral, but it was a soldier's funeral and I don't know that anyone can ask for a higher honour than that at the end.

A few days later my Battalion moved nearer Cambrai, and I rode over to see the grave and found his CO had put up a cross. I believe if one writes to the Graves Registration Committee, BEF, France, they will take photographs of the grave and send copies. I am not certain about this, but you might care to try. ...

On 12th December Helen Fulton received the following telegram from Buckingham Palace:

> *"The King and Queen are deeply grieved to hear that you have lost yet another son in the service of his country. Their Majesties offer you their heartfelt sympathy in your fresh sorrow."*
> *Keeper of the Privy Purse*

From Lt Col H.W. Dakeyne to Helen: 7th January, 1919

I am sorry I have been unable to answer your letter of 18th December before this and, even now, I fear I can give you little assistance or information. We are a long way north-west of Amiens and no longer near Cambrai or Caudry; and I have no means of finding out if No. 3 CCS is still in existence. ... Doctors and others I have asked can tell me nothing for certain.

I wish I could fill up the gaps for you myself, but while I was there I asked few questions and I only gathered that Guy was brought in on the 5th [Nov]. Although badly hit he was in no great danger. As soon as the operation was over he apparently, for a few days, became his own bright self again. I do not think he can have suffered much pain. The Doctor told me that he very nearly moved him by train on the 9th, I think it was, as his wounds were healing so satisfactorily but ever since his admission he had been a little worried by his cough and, at the last minute, decided not to do so. It was, apparently, not until the 10th that Guy really developed pneumonia which was aggravated, so the Doctor told me, by his previous attack of gas. He gave me to understand that from the 10th onwards he really never had very much hope.

As I told you I believe in my first letter, the Doctor, Sister and two of the orderlies all told me what a wonderful and delightful patient Guy was. He never complained or gave a scrap more trouble than he possibly could. He was always bright and cheerful and had, there was no doubt of it, won all their hearts. As I daresay you know No. 3 was the same CCS and with the same Doctor to which Guy was taken when he was gassed. Some of them remembered him from his first visit.

I really think the Graves Registration Committee are moving now. They have had an enormous job to compete with and are, I believe, rather concentrating their efforts on the many thousands of isolated and unmarked graves that are scattered over the country, before taking in hand those graves that are already in cemeteries and whose crosses are properly marked. I feel sure you will eventually get what you want from them but I can give you no hope that it will take a short time. There are so many, many others in the same way as yourself and so many of them with no chance of ever knowing where the graves are, or even if they exist at all.

...

In mid-December Philip was given leave at very short notice. Back home, he and Evelyn were married in Salisbury Cathedral on 14th December. They travelled around southern England on their honeymoon, eventually joining Helen and Hamilton for Christmas at Budleigh Salterton. Early in January Philip was on his way back to France.

Also with something to celebrate at the end of 1918 were Charles and Marjorie Fair, with the birth in December of their first child – Camilla.

Philip Dodgson and Evelyn Fulton's wedding - 14th Dec. 1918

Chapter 20

The Aftermath

The post-Armistice months were very frustrating for those British soldiers who were keen to return home and be demobilised. The following few letters from Philip Dodgson to his mother illustrate his thoughts on this matter. At least he had the satisfaction of being promoted to the rank of Major before he came home in the late spring.

> Officers' Club, St Pol
> 5th January, 1919

... Evelyn and I caught the 4.30 to Folkestone. We stayed at The Grand – such a nice hotel – but no licence! However, they produced a bottle of 1906 from somewhere, so we were all right. The food there is excellent and we got a fire in our room – a thing London could not produce. On Friday morning we braved the photographer and, just as we were leaving, the porter telephoned the good news that the boats were not running. Wasn't it splendid luck that Evelyn went down with me? ... On Friday morning there was some excitement in Folkestone as the troops waiting to go back to France broke out of the camp and refused to go.[465] ... My boat left at 2.00 p.m. You can imagine what I felt like saying goodbye. ...

> [Marles-les-Mines]
> 6th February, 1919

... Pilditch is going off to England tomorrow [for demobilization] so we've had a busy time checking through the whole equipment of the Battery for me to take it over. We've had an orgy of inspecting Generals around lately – three in the last week. I hope now they'll keep away for a bit. ...

The weather has been very severe lately but yesterday it snowed heavily and for a short time today we had the joy of seeing the sun shining in a cloudless sky on the fresh snow. It made even this depressing place look beautiful. ...

....

465 On the morning of Friday 3rd Jan. 1919 nearly 3,000 men in one of the rest camps had held a meeting at which they had decided not to march down to the leave boats, but to visit the Mayor of Folkestone. By the time they had marched to the town hall their numbers had swelled to over 10,000 men where they were addressed by the Mayor. The demonstration continued on 4th Jan. with pickets at Folkestone Harbour and Folkestone Station. Over these two days only officers and overseas troops embarked for France on leave boats that were 'practically empty'. (*The Soldiers' Strikes of 1919*, Andrew Rothstein, 1985, pp. 37-39)

I think the scheme for the Army of Occupation is quite hopeful for me as far as getting out of the Army is concerned. I believe a great many officers will volunteer for it, so I am feeling fairly confident that I shall not have to go. ...

[Marles-les-Mines]
26th February, 1919

... We had a most interesting day yesterday. They got a lorry to take a party to Ypres and we had a very interesting time going to many of the places we used to frequent when the war was on. We started by going to Zillebeke where we had our guns when I was wounded. We then walked to the top of Hill 60 and had our lunch there; then walked along the old No Man's Land, where we did nearly all our shooting for about eight months before I was wounded, and then made our way home again. It took over three hours each way so it was a good long day. ...

[Marles-les-Mines]
2nd March, 1919

... I haven't any very special news for you. We are still gradually disappearing – bit by bit: only 69 horses left now and about 100 men. We also got rid of half our ammunition yesterday. The rumours are still fairly strong that we are to be home sometime this month. I don't personally see how it can be managed. ... I've had a try for my acting majority today but I'm afraid there's not much hope and, if I press it, there would be the risk of somebody else getting it. ...

[Marles-les-Mines]
21st March, 1919

... Our return home goes on being delayed and so it cannot be before the middle of April or possibly end of May according to the order in which we go. All our horses will be gone by the end of the week, so there's a pretty dull time ahead of us. I suppose we shall get home some day, strikes permitting! I'm rather hoping they'll have a good fight with all those strikers: they want to be taught a good lesson, and now's the time while we've got plenty of troops to do it. ... Bridge and letter-writing take up so much spare time. We are still lucky in having a bridge four in the Mess.

[Marles-les-Mines]
30th March, 1919

... You'll be glad to hear that my efforts to get my promotion have been successful. I haven't heard it officially yet, but have been told it's coming through. ... No more news of our coming home but everybody is leaving us – our Divisional Commander and Brigadier General last week,[466] and the Colonel [Aschwanden] goes on leave tomorrow, preliminary to going to the Army of the Rhine – so we are rapidly becoming very much reduced and, as there are no horses to make work, we have to kill time for the men by taking them for marches and sending them for walks. ...

....

466 The war diary records the departure of the 47th Division CRA, Brig Gen Whitley on 27th Mar. The next day Maj Gen Gorringe "inspected the Brigade and bade us farewell." (TNA WO 95/2717)

[Marles-les-Mines]
11th April, 1919

... As far as I know my promotion is official. There is an order that there are to be no promotions after 1st March, but mine was ante-dated to 7th February. I heard the other day that English people were now being allowed to come to France. I wish you could come before I go home. I think it would be worthwhile your making enquiries from the Passport Office. The worst of trying to make any arrangements is that nobody knows when we are going home and that's what is so very unsatisfactory. If only they would tell us the truth and why we were being kept so long it would be so much easier to put up with it patiently. ...

Philip finally left France with the remaining cadre of the 47th Division and was demobilized at Fovant in Wiltshire on 31st May 1919.

As he hinted in an earlier letter, Philip was determined not to return to working in the City after the war. At one stage he and Evelyn had thoughts of moving abroad, but in the end settled on his becoming a glasshouse nurseryman. This enterprise was located by the village of Hale on the western edge of the New Forest and within easy reach of his mother Helen at Salisbury, some ten miles to the north.

In 1919 Helen Fulton visited France with Philip to pay her respects to her other sons, Toby and Guy. Guy, as already stated, lay buried in the military cemetery at Caudry, but there were problems about finding Toby's grave on the Somme. Helen wrote to Marjorie:

"I was dreadfully harassed over Toby. We went to the spot where we ought to have found his cross. There was nothing, only a large newly dug patch of earth which, at first, we thought was a filled-in shell hole, as I had told the Graves Commission I did not want him moved, as I wanted to buy the little bit of ground if possible, and they had promised not to do it. However they had done so, as we found on making enquiries at the Graves Commission place at Fricourt, and they directed us to the cemetery. There we hunted and could find nothing till at last we saw a heap of little crosses thrown on the ground and amongst them Toby's, the one in which he was described as "BA, Cambridge".

We were horrified, and I felt furious with the GC. We then took the cross, and went to the work depot, who are actually doing the work, and they told us that they had dug and found nothing, and his cross was to be put up in the Cemetery as a memorial with those of others who had not been found. We were so relieved they had found nothing, as Philip and I both knew he was not buried exactly where the cross was, but actually in the shell hole where he fell and, that being full of water when Philip put up the cross, he put it up on the edge.

We said nothing of this to the officer who told us about it, but I went straight to the stonemason at Amiens and ordered a solid granite stone to be put up with his name, etc. on the place where he fell. We found exactly what we wanted at the stonemason. ... This is what is to be on it:

In Memoriam
Francis Dodgson
Captain 8th Yorks Regt
who fell here July 10th, 1916
aged 27
RIP

Toby Dodgson's stone memorial at Contalmaison

... Capt Gregson,[467] who is living at Amiens and has cars to take people to see the battlefields and graves, is seeing to it for me, and will go with the man when he puts it up, and if an owner of the ground should come along he will let me know so that I can pay something for the privilege of putting it up. I don't think the ground there can be cultivated for years, for it is a scene of desolation and shell holes, just like the photograph Humphrey took, only the grass and flowers are growing everywhere.

Philip keeps smiling over the GC, and we both said we could see Toby laughing over having frustrated their little plans, for he knows how I hated the notion of his being moved. I think it is awful what they are doing and so unnecessary. They are trying to do things on much too large a scale... ."

Toby's body was found later and buried in Serre No. 2 Cemetery, which is several miles from Contalmaison. It is one of the largest cemeteries on the Somme and contains the bodies of many men who were gathered in from isolated battlefield locations in the years following the war. Toby's name is also inscribed high up on the Thiepval Memorial to the Missing, though his name does not appear on the register. This is unusual and suggests that he was initially listed as being 'missing'.

By the end of the twentieth century there were only about forty original private British battlefield memorials remaining on the Western Front.[468] In his book *The*

....

467 Capt Gregson founded a motorists' rescue service in 1920 specifically for helping motorists who were visiting the battlefields. This service eventually became the Automobile Association's European Rescue Service.

468 Barrie Thorpe (*Private Memorials of the Great War on the Western Front*, 1999) lists 38 memorials which commemorate 48 individuals. At one time there were more such memorials as several documented examples have disappeared. However, the total number can never have been great as few people in those days would have had the time and money to travel to the Front and erect a memorial. It was therefore a middle class phenomenon: 33 of the memorials commemorate officer casualties. (These men are of course also officially commemorated by the Commonwealth War Graves Commission.)

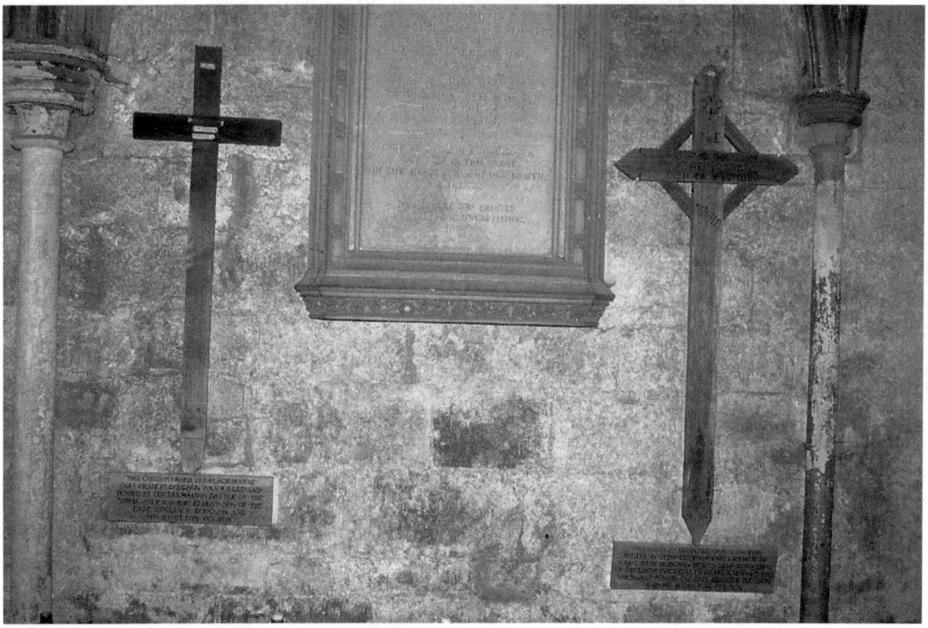

Memorial Crosses for Toby and Guy Dodgson in the cloisters of Salisbury Cathedral

Somme Battlefields Martin Middlebrook describes Toby's stone as "the smallest battlefield memorial I have seen".[469]

The original Graves Registration Unit cross was taken back to England by Helen and can now be seen in the cloister at Salisbury Cathedral. Close by hangs a second cross which originally marked the battlefield grave of her youngest son, Guy.

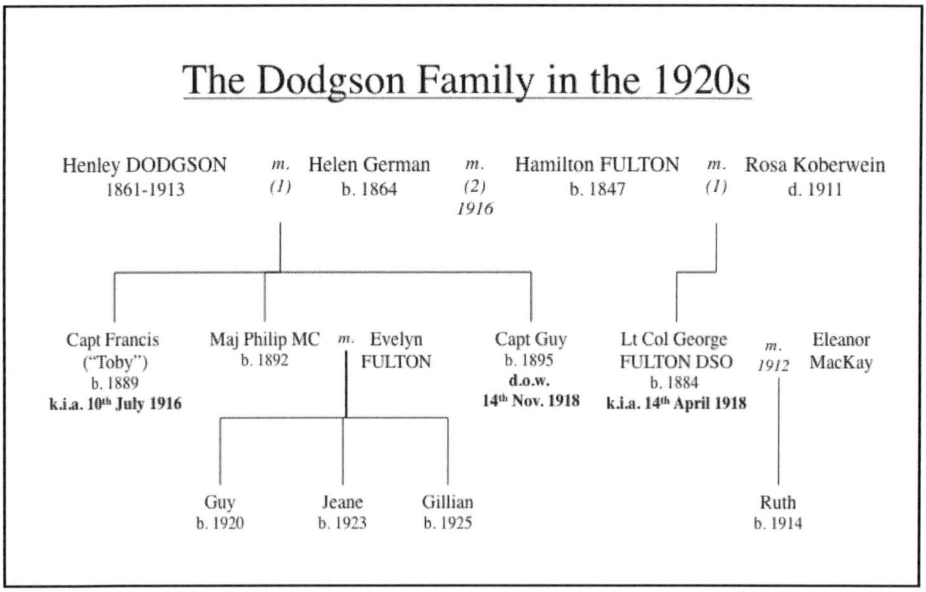
The Dodgson Family in the 1920s
Henley DODGSON 1861-1913
m. (1)
Helen German b. 1864
m. (2) 1916
Hamilton FULTON b. 1847
m. (1)
Rosa Koberwein d. 1911
Capt Francis ("Toby") b. 1889 k.i.a. 10th July 1916
Maj Philip MC b. 1892
m.
Evelyn FULTON
Capt Guy b. 1895 d.o.w. 14th Nov. 1918
Lt Col George FULTON DSO b. 1884 k.i.a. 14th April 1918
m. 1912
Eleanor MacKay
Guy b. 1920
Jeane b. 1923
Gillian b. 1925
Ruth b. 1914

469 Martin and Mary Middlebrook, *The Somme Battlefields*, 1991, p. 126

Helen also erected a brass plaque in Toby's memory in the parish church at Bovingdon, near to the family home he had known. The plaque was unveiled at a memorial service on 10th May, 1917. Following Guy's death in November 1918, a second plaque was added there. Toby is also commemorated in the Memorial Hall at Marlborough College, at Trinity College, Cambridge and on the Stock Exchange war memorial.

* * * * *

In contrast to Philip's gunners, Carl Champion's Pioneer Battalion was kept busily occupied: there was much useful work they could tackle. However, many men of the St Helens Pioneers had been drawn from industries that badly needed their return. As early as December 1918 a hundred and fifteen men were released to return to coal-mining. The months of January and February saw a further three hundred and twenty men demobilized. Carl's diary entries show that he employed his spare time profitably, studying the local flora and fauna of the Cambrai area – as befitted a teacher of biology. Moreover, free from restrictions he was able to resume photography, and a collection survives of his photographs of captured German military equipment, bridges destroyed in the fighting and such major buildings as Cambrai and St Quentin cathedrals. He even took some photos of areas where he had been involved in the fighting.

In March 1919 a hundred and seventy of his men were dispatched to the Army of Occupation in the Rhineland. In June two hundred men were assigned as guards to the POW camp at Étaples. Carl, who was Mentioned in Dispatches for a third time, returned to England with the

Remains of railway bridge at Solesmes - 18th Jan. 1919

British tank that had been captured and used by the Germans – 1st Mar. 1919

77 mm German field gun with blown muzzle

cadre of six officers and thirty-eight men to be disbanded. After a well-earned leave he rejoined the Staff at Haileybury College for the September term.

Early in 1920 the boys at Haileybury were struck by an outbreak of "the flu". Marjorie Fair persuaded her sister, Esmé Secretan, to come with her experienced nursing skills to help combat this epidemic. Also recovering at this time was Carl Champion who had injured a leg in a motorcycle accident. The patient and the nurse met. In due course they became engaged. The following year they were married at St John the Baptist Church, Great Amwell, with the reception being held in Charles and Marjorie's house and garden at Haileybury College.

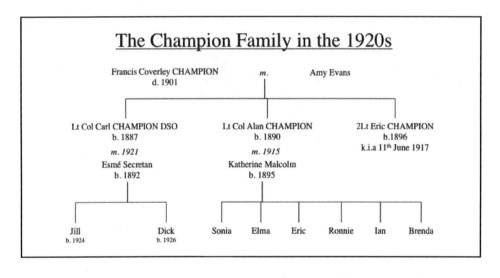

The Champion Family in the 1920s

Francis Coverley CHAMPION d. 1901	*m.*	Amy Evans

| Lt Col Carl CHAMPION DSO b. 1887 *m. 1921* Esmé Secretan b. 1892 | Lt Col Alan CHAMPION b. 1890 *m. 1915* Katherine Malcolm b. 1895 | 2Lt Eric CHAMPION b.1896 k.i.a 11th June 1917 |

| Jill b. 1924 | Dick b. 1926 | Sonia | Elma | Eric | Ronnie | Ian | Brenda |

* * * * *

Humphrey Secretan, Marjorie and Esmé's brother, eventually made a full recovery from his severe wound sustained in October 1917. By 1919 he was officially still in the Army with the 3rd Battalion The Queen's Royal West Surreys but seconded to the Ministry of Shipping, where no doubt his pre-war experience with Lloyds of London was helpful. He was formally discharged from the Special Reserve with the rank of Captain in May 1920 and returned to work at Lloyds, commuting to work from the family home at Leverstock Green in Hertfordshire.

Humphrey kept in touch with his former comrades, in particular those colleagues from the City with whom he had enlisted in the 10th Battalion, The Royal Fusiliers (Stockbrokers) in 1914. On 29th August 1964, the fiftieth anniversary of the swearing in of the Battalion, he attended a drumhead service in the moat of the Tower of London. Among those present were 104 Old Comrades of whom 76 had been present at the first parade. A special guest was Madame Victoria Caudelier who in 1915 kept a well-known *estaminet* at Souastre, a village used for rest when the Battalion was in the line at Fonquevillers.[470]

....
470 Minutes of the Old Comrades Association 10th Royal Fusiliers; *The Royal Fusiliers Chronicle*, 1964.

10th Royal Fusiliers parade in the moat of the Tower of London, 29th Aug. 1964. (Royal Fusiliers Chronicle)

10th Royal Fusiliers Old Comrades with Mme Victoria Caudelier, 29th Aug. 1964. Humphrey Secretan is standing fourth from the right. (Royal Fusiliers Chronicle)

MACINTOSH E.   CLARK

SECOND LIEUT.   COE J
                         COOPE
SECRETAN R. H.   DRAPE

SERJEANT   HALL
                         HUGHE
CALLOW G., M.M.   LINGE
GARROD H. G.   MAYER
GLADDING J. W., D.C.M. RYDER
HAMMOND H. J.   SAUNDE
PAYNE W. J.   SKINNEI
RAND S.   SMITH.
REYNOLDS G. A. M.M.   SOMERV

LANCE SERJEANT   PR

Mary Secretan in Belgium with Mme Monsterleet in 1920

Reggie Secretan's name on the Menin Gate at Ypres

In 1968 Humphrey was interviewed about his wartime experiences by Martin Middlebrook for *The First Day on the Somme*. Humphrey emigrated to South Broom, Natal, South Africa in 1970 and died there in 1974.[471]

Mary Secretan never completely recovered from the death of Reggie, her youngest child. After the war she made a number of visits to France and Belgium. Some of these trips are referred to in the small book "R.H.S.", which Mary put together in 1922. The following is an extract:

> I wrote to Madame Monsterleet [one of the ladies with whom Reggie had been billeted] and had this reply, of course in French —
> "I cried a great deal when Mr Secretan's servant came and told me he was killed—yes, Madame, I embraced your son the last time he stayed fifteen days with me. In spite of my seventy years I used to take up coffee to him and his friend every morning when I called them, and always with his charming smiling face he wished me *"Bonjour!"* What a fine good boy he was. Ah! But he was hard to wake! I used to call him several times. I feared he would be late on parade. I envy the Sergeant who killed the Boche officer: I wish I could have done it!"
> In 1920 we went to see her, she took me into her house and showed me the boy's photograph I had sent her, the tears rolling down her cheeks! She implored us to stay with her, I and my family, as her guests! The following summer I stayed a night with her, after

....

471 Humphrey was not quoted in the book itself. Middlebrook noted that Humphrey "had faith in the overall direction of the war by the Generals. A good opinion of 'Daddy' Plumer. ... Thought at the time and still thinks that the Battle [of the Somme] was a success." Middlebrook observed "typical comment by a man who judged everything by what happened on his own sector." (Middlebrook, M, notes from interview with H.B. Secretan, 1968)

many pressing invitations. I have sent her roses and plants for her garden. She constantly writes to me even now.

On our way to see Madame we spent the night at Hazebrouck, which we found afterwards was much out of our way. When the charming little Madame, who kept the *pension* there where we slept, saw my son's photograph, she was very excited and exclaimed "But I know him, he has slept here!" Seeing my look of surprise she fetched her old father, aged seventy; he had been an officer all through the War. He at once said "He was a motor cyclist!" Now, as the photograph was taken in officer's uniform, this proved the story to be true.

"I was at the station one night in 1915" he said, "and I saw your son sitting there. He looked very unhappy, so I went up to him and I said, 'What is the matter?' and he said 'I have spent all my money; I am tired; I am hungry; I have nowhere to sleep,' so I said, 'You will come to my house. I will give you an omelette and some coffee, a bed and breakfast, and you shall not pay me now, but if you are a gentleman you will return and pay me', and soon after he did come and pay me."

I sent Monsieur the boy's photograph, and on it I wrote his name, etc., and "*I was a stranger and ye took me in.*"

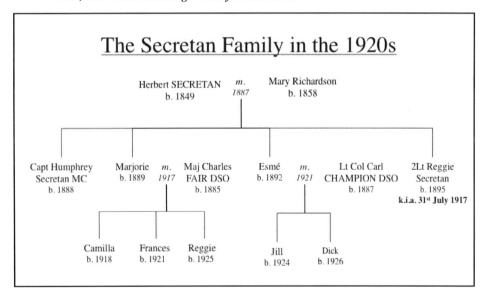

Reggie's body was never identified. If it was found it must lie amongst the many other "unknown soldiers" whose headstones are inscribed "Known unto God". Mary was back at Ypres on 24th July 1927 for the unveiling of the Menin Gate, which is inscribed with nearly 55,000 names of the missing of the Ypres Salient. Reggie Secretan's name is engraved with other soldiers of the Hertfordshire Regiment up the steps on the southern face of the Menin Gate. He is also one of 28 names on the war memorial at Leverstock Green which was unveiled on 5th February 1919. He is commemorated in the Memorial Chapel at Oundle School.

* * * * *

Charles and Marjorie lived in Trevelyan, the boarding house at Haileybury, for twenty-eight years. The private side was an attractive house, with a beautiful well-stocked garden, enjoyed by them and their three children. In Charles and Marjorie's bedroom hung a large photograph of Toby Dodgson: Charles was not the sort of man to resent this. He continued as an officer in the Haileybury OTC until 1927. He had been appointed originally to the staff to teach classics, but after his experiences in France he was able to add French to his teaching skills. One of his former pupils recalled that he provided an "excellent grounding" in French grammar, but "pronounced French exactly as if it were English, much to the mystification of a French theatre company, whom [Charles] looked after when they came to play Molière to us." The pupil recalled being told by Charles "This is an English school and you will talk French like an Englishman. We don't want any of your fancy French accents here."[472]

He remained a member of the 19th London Regt OCA, and even as late as 1938 he was in the chair at their annual dinner and proposed the loyal toast.

Charles Fair (far right in the front row) and Carl Champion (centre of the front row) in the Home Guard in 1944

....

472 In an era in which a large part of the world was in the British Empire, this was a not uncommon approach to foreign languages. (Letter from Col Maurice Willoughby to *The Times*, Jan. 1989 and letter from Col Willoughby to R. H. Fair, 25th January 1989. Willougby's memoir *Echo of a Distant Drum: The Last Generation of Empire* (The Book Guild, Lewes, 2001) contains an excellent description of Haileybury in the late 1920s and 1930s. A description of Charles's teaching of French is on p.162.)

In the school holidays of April 1920 Charles and three companions went on a week's "pilgrimage" to the Western Front to visit again those places where he had served between 1915 and 1918. Photographs were taken of the ruined towns and villages, as well as other localities of particular interest. He gave an account of this tour in *Memories*, the magazine published by the OCA of the 19th London Regiment [see Appendix VI].

Neither Charles nor the other surviving officers in this account talked to their children about their experiences on the Western Front. The next generation all moved into their teens in the 1930s when another World War was becoming a distinct possibility. When war broke out in September 1939 Charles immediately re-joined the Haileybury OTC. The defeat of France in 1940 led to the call for men to join the LDV, later the Home Guard. Charles was quick to enlist, as were Humphrey, Philip, Carl and Alan. In recent years the Home Guard has often been the butt of amusing jokes, but there were many experienced and competent soldiers amongst its number. Charles initially refused to take a Commission, saying he had had enough responsibility in the Great War, but he eventually became a Home Guard officer and was Second-in-Command to Carl Champion of the Company composed of men at Haileybury and the neighbouring village of Hertford Heath.

Lt Col Alan Champion, who lived in Staffordshire, commanded a Home Guard Battalion. Sadly, in 1944 he collapsed at the South Staffs Golf Club, of which he was captain, and died shortly after. He left his widow Catherine and six children. His three sons were all serving in the RAF.

In 1946 Charles retired from Haileybury College and he and Marjorie moved to the village of Hinxworth in North Hertfordshire where they both became involved in village and county life. Two years later Charles's friend and colleague Carl Champion and his wife, Marjorie's sister Esmé, retired to North Curry in Somerset, where Carl found time to continue his interests in cars and golf until his death on 12th June 1963.

On 29th July 1950 Charles died suddenly and quite unexpectedly. The Hinxworth Parish Church of St Nicholas was packed for his funeral service, with his family, friends from Haileybury and some who had served with him in France thirty-five years before. Lt Col Reggie Friend, DSO, wrote, "To me he was not only a very true friend, but also a tower of strength when I suddenly found myself in the old 19th London Regiment, and by his wise advice and help I was able to carry on in a completely strange battalion in rather strenuous days. I always felt that the very fine spirit in the Battalion was largely due to his wise guidance". Another CO of the 1/19th, Lt Col J. G. Stokes, DSO, wrote, "Fair and I spent many happy days together in the old 19th and I highly respected him and looked upon him as a far better man than myself". This was consistent with an earlier appreciation of Charles in *Memories*: "It is probable that nobody ever hated soldiering more than did Major Fair, and so the considerable success he achieved is all the more remarkable. The secret of his success lay in the conscientious way in which he tackled every duty however uncongenial, and a very considerable understanding of human nature."[473]

Marjorie lived on until 1976, enjoying the companionship of her children and grandchildren. When she died the well-known Hitchin rose-grower, Jack Harkness – a friend of Marjorie's, agreed to name a rose after her. The prize-winning shrub

....

473 'Our Portrait Gallery, Major C.H. Fair DSO,' *Memories*, Summer 1926, p. 3

*Toby Dodgson's grave with Marjorie Fair rose,
summer 1993*

rose "Marjorie Fair", with its profuse clusters of carmine red flowers, is now enjoyed by many gardeners.[474] When visiting the Western Front in 1992, Marjorie's son and grandson approached the Commonwealth War Graves Commission in north France to ask if a particular rose could be planted by a certain grave. When they heard the story of Marjorie and Toby they happily agreed, and neither they nor Harkness Roses asked for any payment. So this rose was planted by the grave of Toby, the young man whom she had outlived by sixty years and was seen in bloom in 1993. There is also a pair of these roses by the gateway to the churchyard at Hinxworth, where Charles and Marjorie lie.

....

474 "Marjorie Fair" is a cultivar of the pink "Ballerina" rose and is now sometimes called "Red Ballerina" in the USA. It won first prize in the 1977 international rose trials in Denmark. In 1988 it won first prize in its class in trials held in the Bois de Boulogne by the Parks and Gardens Department of the city of Paris. The Department went on to order 1,450 "Marjorie Fairs" in 1989. (Graham Rose, 'An English Rose's Fame Blooms in France', *The Sunday Times*, 3rd Dec. 1989) Additional information can be found on pp.72-73 of *The Love of Roses: From Myth to Modern Culture* by Graham Rose and Peter King (pub Quiller Press Ltd, 1990).

Appendix I

IN MEMORIAM - S. C. W., VC

**Poem written by the acclaimed war poet, Charles Hamilton Sorley
(19th May 1895 – 13th October 1915),
on hearing of the death of 2/Lt Sidney Woodroffe, VC**

There is no fitter end than this.
No need is now to yearn nor sigh.
We know the glory that is his,
A glory that can never die.

Surely we knew it long before,
Knew all along that he was made
For a swift radiant morning, for
A sacrificing swift night-shade.

Charles Hamilton Sorley
8th September, 1915

This poem was first published in *The Marlburian*, 24th November 1915, and was later included in Sorley's posthumous collection *Marlborough and Other Poems* (first published by Cambridge University Press in January 1916). Sorley had been killed on 13th October 1915 in an attack near Hulluch during the Battle of Loos.

Appendix II

CHRISTMAS 1915

(Written by Charles Fair and first published in "Memories",
the Journal of the OCA 19th London Regt. Dec. 1920 pp. 62-63)

On December 22nd, 1915, I rejoined the 19th Battalion, after a week in hospital with a poisoned arm. They were in Sailly-Labourse district and appeared to be leading an uneventful life. The next day, however, came news that something was afoot. It was proposed to explode a mine at the Hohenzollern Redoubt (a place of evil and blood-stained memory) in front of the line occupied by the London Irish. The 19th were moved up to Lancashire trench, just outside Vermelles, during the night of the 23rd/24th December, in pouring rain, in case they might be required. As it happened our services were not wanted and we spent Christmas Eve in these chilly trenches.

The next morning one heard familiar Christmas hymns and greetings along the trench, in spite of the cold and wet. There were fairly good wooden dugouts, more like narrow sheds than anything else. Our good friends in London had sent out parcels and presents for every man, and things would not have been too bad but for the impending journey to the "Hohenzollern". After dinner (bully beef and a slice of cake, I remember) I set off with A/CSM Simpson[475] to reconnoitre the front line held by a Company of the London Irish. They were commanded by Capt Peter McGinn, who fell afterwards at High Wood, a very gallant officer, worshipped by his men, and a very loyal friend to our Battalion.[476]

Never shall we forget the ensuing twelve hours. Thick mud everywhere and mud so tenacious that even a tall man had difficulty in making his way. We reached the front line just before dark and found the most dismal spot I have ever seen in France. Mine craters everywhere, snipers very active, in and in front of our line many British dead, who had lain there since the bitter fighting of mid-October, and over all the sickly smell of mingled mud and human remains. At least six times that evening I saved myself from falling headlong by clutching what proved to be a dead man's foot projecting from the side of the trench. The rest of the Company were due early in the evening, but hour after hour we waited in an apology for a dugout in just a hole underground into which we slid and then sat upon the mud round a small table lighted by one flickering candle. Eventually the Company began to arrive by degrees under Lt Tipton.[477] The mud in "Bart's Alley" the communication trench, had proved too much for human strength. Many had 'lost' their rations, some their packs, but all had clung to their London sausages, and verily these kept us all alive for the next forty-eight hours. Some men had even come right out of their boots in the effort to extricate themselves. The relief was eventually declared 'complete'; but in Bart's

....

475 668 A/CSM (later CQMS) Ernest Simpson joined the 19th Londons in Feb. 1909. He was one of the original contingent of the 1/19th which arrived in France on 10th Mar. 915 and was still serving on the Western Front with the battalion at the Armistice. He was awarded the MSM (gazetted 18th Jan. 1919).

476 Capt Philip Albert Charles Maginn MC, 18th Battalion the London Regiment (London Irish Rifles), killed in action at High Wood, 15th Sept 1916, buried at Flatiron Copse Cemetery (1.H.37).

477 2/Lt (later Capt) H.T. Tipton was commissioned into the 19th Londons on 7th July 1915. He joined the 1/19th in France on 4th Nov. 1915.

Alley there remained five or six of our men stuck till they were dug out in daylight, with some of the 18th facing them in a similar plight in the same trench!

Such was our Christmas in 1915, but do not think our spirits were as damp as our bodies. There was much that was really humorous and the Londoner's natural spirits pulled him through. In particular do I remember standing round a brazier with Pte Wells,[478] Sgt Few[479] and Cpl Davies[480] at about 2.00 a.m. on the 27th while the last named kept us all in roars of laughter as, in his own inimitable way, he recounted the comic side of a St Albans field-day. Poor gallant Davis! He met his end that same week through impatiently clambering out of a long communication trench, when a sniper's bullet did the rest. His Company Commander and his comrades do not forget. That rare humour and splendid loyalty were a very present help in trouble.

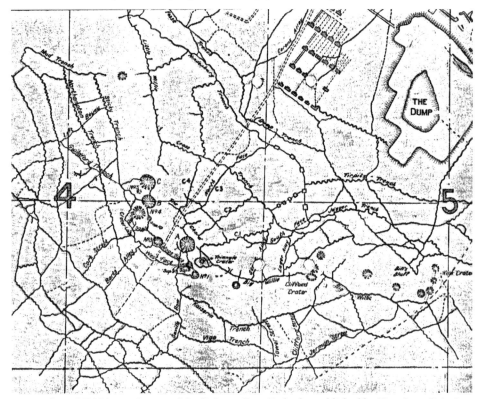

Extract from 1:5,000 trench map of the Hohenzollern Redoubt, published by First Army Printing Section in late 1915 or early 1916. The half moon of craters is the Redoubt, with the British trenches leading to the left and the German trenches leading to the right. The opposing sides occupied opposite rims of Crater A.

....

478 Probably 4353 A/L/Cpl Arthur Wells who enlisted in the 19th Londons on or about 8th May 1915. He arrived in France to join the 1/19th on 10th Oct. 1915 and served until 4th Oct. 1916 when he was either sick, injured or lightly wounded. He served in France with the battalion from 20th Dec. 1916 until 16th Mar. 1918.

479 2201 A/Sgt Benjamin Arthur Few joined the 19th Londons on 7th Aug.1914 and was another of the original contingent of the 1/19th, serving with the battalion until 7th July 1916.

480 2512 Cpl Percy James Davies joined the 19th Londons on 4th Sept. 1914 and was another of the original contingent of the 1/19th. He was killed by a sniper at the Hohenzollern Redoubt on 31st Dec. 1915 and is commemorated on the Loos Memorial to the Missing.

Appendix III

IN MEMORY OF CAPTAIN F. DODGSON

I read his name upon the Roll
I had not heard of him for years -
Strange how a name can wake the soul
Till all the dead past reappears.

In a small classroom years ago
We worked together day by day;
He had not very far to go,
His own was scarce two strides away.

His own, where once he chaffed and laughed,
While kettles made the gas burn dim,
And other fellows laughed and chaffed
And drank their cups of tea like him.

Where are they now, the merry band,
That laughed and chaffed and worked with you?
Scattered they fight on land and sea,
And some lie dead for England too.

Goodbye, old friend, the boy I knew,
It only seems the other day,
The boy who used to work and brew[481]
In classroom scarce two strides away.

John Bain[482]
Assistant Master, Marlborough College
1873-83 and 1886-1913

....

481 Marlborough slang for 'tuck'

482 John Bain filled the pages of *The Marlburian* with elegies to dozens of his former pupils, the majority of which contained analogies of war as sport in the spirit of Henry Newbolt (Play up! play up! and play the game!). Although the sentiments are sincere, according to one critic this is 'vitiated by an egregious banality of imagery and expression. ... The recycling of these stale ... images of sporting soldiers meeting their match is reminiscent of the work of a monumental mason during an epidemic. One cannot help feeling that these young men deserved better.' (See Parker, *The Old Lie*, pp. 216-7) A more charitable critic describes them as 'poetic obituaries of gentle, unsophisticated sorrow'. (see Mangan, *Athleticism in the Victorian and Edwardian Public Schools*, p. 255) It is perhaps a small irony that the war poet Charles Sorley was himself the subject of another of Bain's poems, though Bain was in fact merely repaying a debt. He had been the eponymous subject of Sorley's poem "J. B." which was written in Oct. 1913 and which was included in *Marlborough and Other Poems*. (See p. 16 of the 4th Edition of 1919.)

Appendix IV

EXTRACTS from "R. H. S."

(See Map 6 for places in the 1/1st Hertfordshires area of attack on 31st July 1917)

In 1922 Mary Secretan compiled a small book in commemoration of her son Reggie. It tells of his exploits on the Western Front, and includes the many letters of condolence she received on his death and extracts from published histories and current newspapers. A selection of these follow.

BEF
6th August, 1917

Dear Mrs Secretan,

Your son, I am grieved to say, was killed in action on 31st. He died, being killed instantaneously, while leading his platoon against their final objective, and his men tell me that nothing could have been more gallant than the way in which he led them. He was always so cheerful and ready to do everything that he was a great favourite with everyone, and we all feel his loss very keenly. There was no braver boy in the whole Army.

Yours sincerely,
Eric Phillips, Major
1st Herts Regt

BEF
August, 1917

Dear Mrs. Secretan,

I grieve to have to tell you of the death of your dear son 2/Lt R. H. Secretan.

One of his men tells me he rallied his men to the attack on the final objective, shouting "Come on No. 8!" and was shot by a German officer. His death is a great loss, for he was a gallant boy, full of grit and courage, always cheery, no matter what the work was. We send our sympathy to you all.

Yours sincerely,
Edgar Popham
Chaplain

From the 15th August 1917 edition of "Daily Mail," written by Beach Thomas:
"The highest sacrifice in the third battle of Ypres was perhaps paid by the Hertfordshire Regiment. I have heard no more splendid or moving tale of gallant men going out to death and glory since the War began. About 10 o'clock, after St Julien was captured, the German shelling with 5.9 howitzers grew hotter than many officers had ever seen it...

The men reached the approaches to a trench defended by 400 yards of uncut wire, six yards deep, and running along a contour swept by machine guns from the left, front and flank. Still they did not stop."

Following this extract Mary writes:
This is where R. H. S. fell, about 11 a.m. The Battalion had marched out from a camp outside Poperinghe on Sunday, 29th July. Just before they got to the bivouac camp at Vlamertinghe it began to rain hard. This camp laid among the hop fields. The *Padré* held a service here to which R. H. S. went. One of the hymns was "Lead, Kindly Light". The next morning they marched off and arrived at Juliet Farm that night, where they rested and attacked at dawn, 31st July; it was pouring with rain. No. 2 Company went into the battle about one hundred and twenty strong, and only about eighteen came out.

From Sir Arthur Conan Doyle's "History of the War":
   "The attack was extraordinarily gallant, but was held up by uncut wire and very severely punished ... greater constancy has seldom been seen. The Hertfordshire men were particularly fine. Their Col Page and their Adjutant were both killed, and every combatant officer was on the casualty list, so that it was the Sergeant Major who withdrew the 120 men who had gone forth as a strong Battalion. The doctor was wounded, and only the Chaplain was left, who distinguished himself by being the last man to cross the Steenbeek with a wounded man slung over his shoulder."

Mary continues:
As far as I can understand it, this is what happened. The Brigade had to take the final objective, going through two lines of German trenches which had been taken by other Brigades. They had to cross a small stream, the Steenbeek, take some machine gun posts, advance up a hill, and take the German trenches at the top, the farther side of Springfield Road.

The Springfield Road. No. 2 Company of 1/1st Hertfordshires crossed the road from left to right. Reggie Secretan was killed near the Springfield Pillbox which sat near the edge of the field, about level with the position of the car. (See Point B on Map 6)

The Herts men were in the centre. They soon got to the hill and killed or captured the entire enemy. The weather, which had been very fine, broke on the previous day, so the fearful mud and rain impeded the moving of the big guns.

The Hun aeroplanes were out in numbers, and very few of ours. A tank and three machine guns which were to have protected the Battalion were all knocked out before getting there; so when the Battalion got to the hill they found the wire uncut. I saw the place in 1920: "pill boxes" were dotted about all over the slope of the hill, truly a terrible place to attack. Just beyond Springfield Road, which ran along the commencement of the slope, was a big redoubt full of machine guns, and surrounded by "pill boxes" and wire. It was here that R. H. S. and his platoon stopped for a few minutes, lying down in the shell holes near the road; then he sprang up, shouting "Come on No. 8!" and waving his arms. His Sergeant and several of his men tell me that a German officer with a bandaged head, and some men, ran out from behind the redoubt. They distinctly saw the officer aim at R. H. S.; he fell forward on his hands and knees, and was killed instantaneously, for he never moved again.

Extracts from letters from two brother officers:

BEF
10th August, 1917

I was a very great friend of his, and his death has been a real blow and a great sorrow to me. We got on so well together ever since we met at Gailes, and we have been together ever since. He was one of the most popular officers in our mess, and was beloved by his men, as he was always so keen to join in all their games and listen to their troubles. He was always so cheerful when we were in the trenches, and used to keep our spirits up with his jokes when we were feeling rather down. I have never seen men so really cut up at the death of their officer, and nearly all who have spoken to me about him during the last few days have had tears in their eyes, and I know their sorrow was real. During his lifetime I had often overheard scraps of conversation amongst the men about him, always saying what a good fellow he was. All the officers join with me in sending their sincerest sympathy to you in the loss of a fine officer, and a true gentleman.

* * * * *

I was on a course with him at the back (Volckerinckhove) just before the advance, he had asked to be billeted in the same house as he was in April, when on another course. The old lady (Madame Monsterleet) whose house it was, ran out when she saw him coming, she had the dearest face, a mass of wrinkles, she put both arms round his neck and kissed him, saying *"Mon enfant, mon enfant!"*

He was very good at making people understand, as he could speak French and Flemish so well, we always used to send him shopping, etc., if we wanted anything done. I have often seen him teaching his men the Lewis Gun, they all sat round in a ring, and he in the middle, holding up the parts, and making a joke about each, the men laughing, but he taught them, and they knew their gun. I was on another course with him at Bayenghem, near St Omer, he rigged up a see-saw for the Flemish children in the village, he would sit on one end and they on the other, he made them scream with laughter with his patter and his jokes.

Sgt W., a Dispatch Rider friend, wrote:

He was with us on the eve of the great battle, and was in excellent spirits, and full of confidence that he would achieve the difficult task assigned to him. I shall always treasure the signed photograph he gave me … as long as I live, as sacred to the memory of a true gentleman, a sportsman, and a gallant officer, who made the supreme sacrifice for his country. I was greatly attached to him for his sportsmanlike and manly nature, in spite of his youth. He was loved by all who ever came in contact with him. I can well understand why the men of his platoon loved and respected him as they did, and I greatly envy the Sergeant who had the luck to kill that Hun officer. Dear old "Sec" – the truest comrade I ever had in this land of glory and sadness!

Extracts from letters from men in his Platoon:

Sgt S.:

When that brute of a German officer shot Mr Secretan, I lost my head completely, and went for him, and what was left of the platoon came with me, we had rather a sharp fight, but the men stood by me and I had the pleasure of shooting that German officer (a Colonel) with my own rifle, and when I did it I knew I was avenging an officer and a gentleman, and that he would have done the same for me. Thank you for sending me Mr Secretan's photograph. When I look at it I seem as if I can almost hear him saying, "Are the boys comfortable Sergeant?" as he always did upon our arrival in camp, and if they were not he always did his best to make them so. That is why he was thought so much of by the platoon. … All the boys from the old Regiment will tell you how popular your dear son was, the reason was because he looked after his men before himself, and you may be sure all they say concerning Mr Secretan comes from their hearts. I have been out there with them and him, and I know just how they felt towards him.

L/Cpl P.:

… I was about the last one he spoke to, and I made him laugh just before he was killed, he was laughing and joking all the time. He was the very best officer I had met. When I met Col Page, who was killed just after I left him, I told him about Mr Secretan, and he looked very down-hearted about him, and so did everyone who knew him. His men will tell you how dearly they loved him, and how he loved them. I saw the Hun officer aim at him, Sgt S. killed him. I was next Mr Secretan when he fell, but could not stop.

Pte H.:

I was an officer's runner. I had to take a message from a Captain to the Colonel. When I got there I found he was killed, I went back to the Captain and he was killed too. I was creeping through the shell holes, the machine gun firing being awful, when I suddenly saw Mr Secretan spring up quite close to me, within a few yards, on the edge of Springfield Road. He waved his arms and shouted loudly "Come on No. 8!" he had only dashed forward a few paces towards the big redoubt, when he fell forward on his hands and knees. When he sprang up I thought to myself, well, that's a brave thing to do, for the firing was terrific. I was on duty one night in the trenches and Mr Secretan came along and had a chat with me and asked me if I felt nervous, then he took out his flask and emptied all the whisky in it into my dixie, and said, "Call the other boys and give them a taste." We did feel grateful, because we knew he would not be able to get any more till we all went back together.

Pte H. K.:

I was with him in that raid [between Hooge and Zillebeke Lake],[483] the Huns got through in seven places that night in other Battalions – in every place except where we were under Mr Secretan, he was very excited, and rushed about bringing us ammunition, and fired at them with his revolver. We had Lewis Guns, and had been trained by Mr Secretan. Some of the Huns got right up. Next day there was a notice up from the Brigadier, praising us up. Mr Secretan was very just, he never let the willing ones do more than their share of work. We always liked going to drill with him, he would let us have a smoke in the middle, and then we would all sit round and he would tell us about his adventures when he was a DR. He was a real good chap, seemed like one of us. Sometimes when we got to a fresh billet we would find the last lot had left it in a mess and when we were told to clear it up the men would start grumbling, but he would say "Come on boys and clear up, the Herts have always had the reputation of being a clean lot," and then he would help a bit himself, and we would leave off grumbling and set to work.

Pte S.:

One reason why Mr Secretan was such a good officer was because he had been a Private, and knew how to treat his men. I never saw him out of temper or low spirited, he always had a joke on his lips, even under the most depressing circumstances. The night before the fight we had a long march, and then had to lie in a field [Juliet Farm] until about 5.30. Some slept and some couldn't. I'm sure Mr Secretan did not try to rest: he was always walking round and saying something cheering to a wakeful man. I heard him say, "Seems as if there's a War on!" and you had to laugh. He always went off cheerily to any bit of extra work. It often happened an officer had to take out a fatigue party after a tiring day, but he never grumbled, he might have been resting in bed all night from the way he started off ready for anything. He used always to come and see if we were comfortable after a march, one night he and Mr Penny walked a mile in the pouring rain to see after us. He will be loved and respected always.

Pte S. (terribly wounded on 31st July and killed 1918):

Our platoon always won at games if Mr Secretan and Cpl Bilby played. I was very upset when I heard in hospital that he had been killed. The advance was beautifully planned out, we had been taught by lines at the back. I was with him in No. 8 Platoon. I often used to hear the men discussing the officers, one liked one and one another, but everyone liked him. I never heard a single man say he did not like him. He used to see each had a billet at the end of a march, before he even stopped to take off his pack. He used to exchange packs with "Little Tich" as well as carry his rifle. We thought nothing of Mr Secretan carrying a man's rifle on a march, he was always doing that. I was in the raid too, Mr Secretan was first out of the dugouts
....

483 The raid of 25th/26th Mar. 1917 (see footnote 285, Chapter 13).

when it started, we got very praised up. The night before the attack I had to share a billet with the Sergeants, and heard them discussing the officers, and one Sergeant said, "The officer who will win distinction tomorrow is Lt Secretan, I was with him in that raid," and the other Sergeants agreed. He is always in my thoughts when I am in the line, God grant me strength to avenge his death. He was brave and very daring, when we were in the front line he would come and sit with us for hours.

Appendix V

LETTERS TO THE OFFICIAL HISTORIAN

The following letters were written by Charles Fair to the Official Historian Brigadier General Sir J. E. Edmonds during the drafting of the Official History, Military Operations, France and Belgium, 1916, Volume 2. *(TNA CAB 45/133)*

Haileybury College, Hertford,
15th May, 1935

Dear General Edmonds,

I am much obliged to you for letting me see the enclosed draft concerning the operations in and around 'High Wood' Sept 15th – 16th, 1916. I do not know if I can add very much. I was at the time Second-in-Command to Lt Col A. P. Hamilton (The Queen's) who was commanding the 1/19th London Regt. When he was killed during the morning of 15th I was sent forward to take command by Brig Gen R. McDouall (141st Brigade). The situation was still obscure. I took some Lewis guns through the wood and posted them on the NE side in old German trenches as a precaution against immediate counter attack. Units were hopelessly mixed in the wood and just outside it. We gradually got them disentangled during the next 24 hours.

It has always seemed to me that the confusion and heavy casualties were largely due to the formation laid down for us by which each company of each battalion in each of the two assaulting brigades of the 47th Division were to advance in a series of waves. No local reserves were kept in hand, with the result that after the first check in the wood, every minute brought fresh troops into the front line with no possibility of exploiting success on the flanks, so as to 'pinch out' the wood itself.

In all the period of well over two years which I spent with an infantry battalion in France and Belgium, I never saw such gruesome scenes as in and around High Wood. I went round it with Gen McDouall on the morning of Sept 16th and it seemed that every infantry unit of both armies (German and English) was represented by the dead, some of whom had been lying there since 14th July.

My own Battalion lost eleven officers killed or died of wounds to one wounded. A proportion of deaths [to wounded] which I never heard equalled at any time.

I know that both Lt Col Hamilton and Gen McDouall protested against the formation as ordered, and I have often wondered since if that was the reason why Major General Sir Charles Barter ceased to command the 47th Division a few days later.[484]

....

484 Shortly after the battle Maj Gen Barter was summoned 'at an hour's notice' and was charged with 'wanton waste of men' and sacked. John Bourne writes: "It is now recognised that he was scapegoated by the GOC III Corps, Lt Gen Sir William Pulteney, who had repeatedly refused to listen to Barter's reasoned objections to III Corps' plan of attack. This was based on sending tanks into the wood. Tank commanders were horrified by the idea, arguing that the shattered tree stumps (which were all that remained of the wood) made it impassable to tanks. After making a personal reconnaissance, together with the GOC 141st Infantry Brigade (Brig Gen Robert McDouall), Barter agreed with them. He pressed III Corps to allow him to withdraw his infantry from their forward positions, close to the German front line, so that a proper artillery barrage could proceed the infantry attack, and allow him to send the tanks round the flanks of the wood to pinch it out. III Corps rejected this sensible plan. ...

Barter devoted the rest of his life to an unsuccessful attempt to obtain an enquiry into his dismissal. But his subsequent treatment, including the award of a KCB (1916) and a KCMG (1918) suggest tacit official recognition of his unfair treatment. Surviving members of the division seem not to have laid the blame for the casualties of High Wood at the door of their GOC. Barter was welcomed at post-war divisional reunions and called upon to unveil divisional war memorials. He retired from the Army on 20th Dec. 1918." (http://www.warstudies.bham.ac.uk/firstworldwar/research/donkey/barter.shtml)

I shall be glad if I can give any information about Eaucourt L'Abbaye Oct. 1st – 4th when the time comes.

Yours sincerely,

C. H. Fair.

Haileybury College
Hertford
(*undated - 1935*)

Dear General Edmonds,

I am much obliged to you for letting me see the further draft of the Official History of the War covering the period of operations around Eaucourt L'Abbaye while I was in command of the 19th London Regt. I will make a few comments which may be to the point. I have my notes beside me; consequently dates and facts are accurate.

The 19th London were left in the forward area after the capture of High Wood to provide burial parties – a very doubtful policy in the case of a battalion which had lost very heavily and whose own dead lay thick on the ground they were to clear. Consequently we did not rejoin the rest of 141st Brigade at Bresle until Sept 23rd.

On Sept 24th we received a draft of 250 other ranks, and on 27th we were back at Bazentin le Grand having had only two days to absorb the new men, after losing the Commanding Officer and all four company commanders at High Wood on 15th Sept. The Adjutant had also left us for private reasons.

Consequently it was largely an untried battalion under officers whom they hardly knew which was ordered to make a bombing attack up the two parallel Flers lines on Sept 29th. That this attack was unsuccessful was due to the fact that the German 'egg' bomb outranged the 'Mills', rather than to any lack of courage on the part of the men. On the following day, Sept 30th, when the attack was repeated, we pushed our Lewis Guns into shell-holes with orders to spray the German parapet continuously till our men could get within the range they wanted.

These tactics were completely successful and the line reached its desired jumping-off place for the attack of Oct. 1st.

The main difficulty on this occasion was that the line ran obliquely to the objective. Consequently each wave had to 'get its right shoulder up' as it crossed the open under heavy machine gun fire. That they were mainly successful is a great tribute to the leading of the young officers and NCOs.

Some of the officers who got through Eaucourt L'Abbaye were able to push right on to the Butte de Warlencourt itself and sent back word that the Butte could be had for the asking. I informed Brig Gen MacDouall commanding 141st Brigade, who in turn informed higher authority. But apparently no troops were available for occupying the Butte. Whether this possibility had never been foreseen I do not know; but it has always seemed to me a great pity that a feature which ultimately cost hundreds of lives could not have been occupied there and then. The small parties of the 19th and 20th Londons who had established themselves forward of Eaucourt L'Abbaye were far too few to occupy the Butte and hold it against inevitable counter attacks; but another brigade in readiness for such a possibility might have made all the difference.

I have always been grateful for the willing cooperation of the Otago NZ battalion on our right. It was the only time in my experience when we had colonial troops next [to] us and everything was arranged between myself and their Commanding Officer with the greatest ease and close liaison.[485]

I hope I may have added a few points of interest, and I must apologise for delay in returning the draft owing to the illness of various other people, which has taken up a great deal of my time.

Yours sincerely

C. H. Fair

Major

late acting Lt Col commanding 19th London, 47th Division.

The Butte de Warlencourt. These pictures were taken by Charles Fair during his visit of April 1920 (see Appendix VI). The close up picture shows the 47th Division Memorial Cross, one of a pair which can now be seen at the London Irish Drill Hall in Camberwell.

....

485 According to p. 137 of *The Official History of the Otago Regiment in the Great War* by Lt A. E. Byrne MC, 'On the left of Otago men of the 19th London Regiment connected up at 5.30 pm [on 1st Oct.], but actually they were cut off from their own Division, the 47th, north of Eaucourt L'Abbaye; and arrangements had to be made by the New Zealand Division for the temporary feeding of 80 men.'

Appendix VI

OLD HAUNTS REVISITED

by Major Charles H. Fair DSO 1/19th London Regiment, 47th (London) Division

The following article was first published in two parts in *Memories, The Magazine of the 19th County of London Regiment Old Comrades Association.* (September 1920 pp. 34-35, 37 and 43 and December 1920 p. 74)

On April 13th with three companions I arrived at Amiens on the first stage of a week's trip round the battlefields of northern France and Belgium. The idea was to visit most of the places which had become familiar during the year of 1915-16, the period above all others when our armies were composed of the men who had joined up in the first rush of enthusiasm at the beginning of the war, when conscription and "combing out" were unknown and DORA was yet in her infancy.[486]

We were lucky in being provided with a car driven by an English chauffeur who had himself served in France during most of the war. Directly one landed at Boulogne the flood-tide of memory was let loose and even now it has hardly begun to ebb. At Amiens we saw with regret the damage done in 1918, but were glad to see that the cathedral had been so little hurt. The whole scene brought up at once pictures of those "joy-rides" in August and September 1916 when many of the 1/19th were lucky enough to make a pilgrimage there from Brèsle.

The next day we started off to visit the Somme country. The first village I sighted was Franvillers, where we spent a week of reorganisation in October 1916. After that the familiar sights came thick and fast. The fields over which we practised for High Wood, the hills round Brèsle where we did night attacks behind a creeping barrage of drums, and then Albert itself. A few wooden houses and one new brick house are all the habitations in Albert since 1918. We photographed the ruins of the cathedral and spent some time among the ruins. It was for my companions their first sight of a ruined town and I do not think any of them will forget it. Before going on I insisted on visiting Aveluy where there were some indications of the camp in which the Battalion spent Christmas 1917 and certainly some of the pickets in the horse lines. The village itself is of course in ruins.

We then turned back through Albert and made our way past La Boisselle to Contalmaison of which there is nothing visible at all except three steps of the church. From there we went on through the Bazentins. The machine-gun dugout at the "circus" which served as HQ after High Wood has gone, but a curious shaped tree which I remembered was there. I could not find Col Hamilton's grave, presumably it has been moved. Over what was Brigade HQ on September 15th 1916 some sort of a house has been erected. We then went on through the utter desolation of these grisly fields to High Wood itself. The undergrowth of broom and small shrubs has mercifully covered much of its ugliness but of the original trees only forty bare poles

....

486 The Defence of the Realm Act was passed on 8th Aug. 1914 and gave the government wide ranging pow-ers, for example the power or requisition as well as restrictions on personal freedom. Perhaps the best known restriction was that of pub opening hours which remained in force for decades afterwards.

are still standing. I found without difficulty the 47th Divisional Memorial Cross,[487] and then came upon the remains of the shelter which served as joint HQ for all the Battalions of the Brigade.[488] It was a litter of bomb-boxes and bits of timber, but there is no doubt it was the right place. We wandered about waist-high in the undergrowth gradually finding the trenches, and then I saw some graves outside the wood, and on going over to them I found they were mostly those of officers and men in the regiment.[489] Captains Henderson[490], Gauld[491] and Davis[492]; Lts Pleydell-Bouverie[493], Cooper[494] and Rowson[495]; RSM Ridout[496], CSM Bolton[497], Sgt Deighton[498], Cpl Toole[499],

....

487 This cross is now kept at The London Irish Drill Hall at Flodden Road, Camberwell where it can be seen on one of the outside walls.

488 This HQ was sited on the same spot as the modern farm which is in the southern corner of High Wood.

489 With the exception of CSM Bolton, these men were among the original burials in London Cemetery which is adjacent to High Wood. Their graves can be found just on the left of the entrance in Plot 1A, Row A. According to CWGC records, the cemetery "was begun when 47 men of the 47th Division were buried in a large shell hole on 18th and 21st Sept. 1916. Other burials were added later, mainly of officers and men of the 47th Division who died on 15th Sept.1916, and at the Armistice the cemetery contained 101 graves."

490 Capt David Henderson had enlisted in the Inns of Court OTC on 16th Oct. 1914 and was commissioned into the 8th Battalion the Middlesex Regt on 17th Feb. 1915. He was attached to the 1/19th Londons where he was OC of A Company. He was the son of the influential trade unionist and Labour Party leader Rt. Hon. Arthur Henderson MP. (grave 1A.A.14)

491 Capt Alexander George Gauld was educated at the City of London School and Emmanuel College Cambridge where he served in the OTC. He was commissioned into the 19th Londons on 14th Oct. 1914. He was 23 and the son of Alexander and Isabella Gauld, of 24, Hornsey Lane, Highgate. (grave 1A.A.14) (TNA WO 374/26690)

492 Capt Leigh Jacob Davis had been commissioned into the 19th Londons on 6th Mar. 1911 and was one of the contingent that had arrived in France on 10th Mar.1915. He was one of several officers in the Battalion from north London's Jewish community. He was 24 and the son of Mr and Mrs Arthur Davis of 11 Cleve Rd, West Hampstead. (grave 1A.A.15)

493 Samuel Wilfred Pleydell-Bouverie grew up in South Africa and had served six years in the Natal cadets, leaving school in 1912. He became a civil servant, and had joined the Johannesburg Rifles in May 1914, being discharged on leaving for England in June 1915. He enlisted in the Inns of Court OTC on 26th July 1915 and was commissioned into the 19th Londons on 2nd Nov.1915. He was 20 and related to Jacob-Pleydell-Bouverie, 6th Earl of Radnor and Viscount Folkestone. (grave 1A.A.1) (TNA WO 374/54441)

494 2/Lt Alfred Lynn Cooper was commissioned into the 19th Londons on 25th Aug. 1915. He had started his degree at Clare College, Cambridge in 1913. He was 23 and the son of Mr and Mrs Alfred Cooper of 65 Barkston Gardens, Earls Court. (grave 1A.A.9)

495 After several failed attempts to join the Army because of defective eyesight, Tom Hollingworth Rowson eventually enlisted in the Artists' Rifles on 23rd Aug.1915 and was commissioned into the 19th Londons on 9th Jan. 1916. Originally from Bridport in Dorset, he trained as a schoolmaster and started teaching for London County Council in 1910. He was 27 years old and had got married on 3rd June 1916. According to his obituary he "was killed by a bullet in the head while leading his platoon in the face of murderous machine gun fire." (grave 1A.A.17) (TNA WO 374/59539 and London County Council Roll of Honour Part XLVI)

496 2624 RSM Arthur Frederick Ridout enlisted in the 2/19th Londons on 5th Sept. 1914. Despite having had no previous military experience he had a remarkable record. As a L/Cpl he was one of the original contingent that had arrived in France on 10th Mar. 1915 yet was Acting RSM by the summer of 1916. He was from Dorset, and before the war he had been a supervisor at the Railway Clearing House beside Euston Station. He was married to Ella Ridout of 14 Balham Park Rd, Balham. (grave 1A.A.11)

497 289 CSM George Bolton of B Company had enlisted in the 19th Londons in late June 1908 and had probably previously served in the Volunteers. As a sergeant he was one of the original contingent that had arrived in France on 10th Mar. 1915. He went back to England on 17 June 1915 and returned to France on 11th Nov. 1915. He is buried in Serre Road No. 2 Cemetery (grave V.D.20).

498 5913 L/Sgt Arthur William Deighton was from Stoke Newington and had originally enlisted in the KRRC in 1915 before being transferred to the 19th Londons in early 1916. (grave 1A.D.5)

499 1743 L/Cpl Edward Thomas Toole enlisted in the 19th Londons in Oct. 1913. He was another of the original contingent that had arrived in France on 10th Mar. 1915 and had been wounded at Loos. (grave 1A.D.2)

*Charles Fair at remains of 1/19th London
HQ, High Wood, April 1920*

*Remains of British tank in High Wood, April
1920*

Pts Whybrow[500] and Prewer (the latter my own orderly) were some of the many
names I saw. For me it was I think the most touching moment of the week. The longer
we stayed there the more we became convinced how important a tactical feature
the wood presents. The observation in each direction is wonderful. One of the most
interesting parts of our journey all through, to my mind, was to go into the German
positions and see how completely they dominated ours in almost every place.

On our return journey that day we visited one of the German "Big Berthas" near
Bray.[501] It is believed to have shelled Amiens, Arras, and Béthune, and was captured
eventually by the Australians.

The next day our first objective was Eaucourt L'Abbaye and the Butte de
Warlencourt, certainly the scene of one of the most interesting and thrilling
situations in which the Battalion found itself during the war.[502] I could not find any
graves belonging to the Regiment in the neighbouring cemetery, but here again as at
High Wood we were struck at once with the tactical importance of the 'Butte', though
in itself it is not a place of any size at all. From there we went on through Bapaume
– a terrible sight of ruin and decay – and eventually crossing the Canal du Nord by a

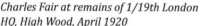

500 2547 Pte Arthur George Whybrow enlisted on 4th Sept. 1914. He had been a keeper of birds at London
Zoo. He was married and 23 years old. (grave 1A.A.10)

501 These guns were 1 km south-west of Chuignies. The IGN 1:25,000 map Bray-sur-Somme (2408 Est) marks
a 'Bois du Grand Canon' where one can find a large, circular and very overgrown hole in the ground. Pictures of
the 15" gun can be found in *Twenty Years After.* (p. 356, Supplementary Vol., pub Newnes c.1939)

502 This was the Le Transloy Ridges phase of the Battle of the Somme in which the Battalion was engaged
between 1st and 4th Oct. 1916.

wooden bridge reached Flesquières after skirting Bertincourt, the scene of a certain dinner on December 10th, 1917. Flesquières had a personal interest as it was the last spot in which I served with the Battalion. The village appeared capable of being rebuilt more than most of the places in the neighbourhood. We could make out the line of the trench which we held in front of the village in January 1918. Then we went on to our furthest objective, Bourlon Wood. Time was pressing and rain was falling so we did not go into the wood, but round the left side of it into the village. In spite of its fearful shelling and the gas, the wood looked more like a wood than the woods of the Somme country or Ypres and will probably recover, but there is something grim and menacing in the way it frowns down on all the country round.

We went back in one stage from Bourlon to Amiens which must be one of the widest strips of devastated country. In almost every village there are a few inhabitants living in anything which can be made to look like a dwelling and endeavour to eke out their existence with vegetables, poultry and a cow or two. But one wonders what joy or happiness can ever come into the lives of these people again. There is no town within reach of many of them. Supply trains are few and far between. There are no schools, churches, or places of entertainment. Education for the children and relaxation for their elders must be non-existent. The feeling in the minds of all our party on this and every day was that those who lived in peace and safety in England could never know what the war had really meant to France, and that nobody can blame her in any demand which she makes for reparation or future security.

The next day we cut through the back areas having lunch at Doullens and picked up the real track of the war again at Arras. There the Hun seems to have deliberately set himself to destroy the more beautiful parts of the town while leaving the meaner quarters comparatively unhurt, though of course suburbs like St Catherine's have suffered badly. Here the work of reconstruction was going on apace, but nothing can replace the noble buildings of ancient Arras. A remarkable sight was a French fair in full swing with its attendant booths and swing-boats for the children, while the workmen went stolidly on mending the roads and houses beside them. Arras would not be a pleasant place to walk about in at night: the square is full of yawning gaps leading to apparently bottomless pits. On leaving Arras we could see Moreuil and its familiar church and *château*. I wondered if any of the elegant handiwork of Sergeant Sewell and the pioneers remained.[503] Then we came in for an appalling storm of hail and rain which however eventually proved a blessing in disguise. For as we reached Cabaret Rouge the sun came out and the view of Notre Dame de Lorette, with Ablain St Nazaire in the foreground, was wonderful. We left the car in Souchez just where Battalion HQ dugout, near the foot of the ridge, used to be in 1916 and then climbed right up to the craters. I managed to identify our old front line near the top of 'Robineau' and then we stood on one of the craters – possibly 'New Cut' – and looked right out into the blue.[504] We could see for miles past Lens and away out towards Douay, and behind us to the Servins and Mont St Eloi. It was a splendid moment to be there and I could have stayed for hours. Some French girls who were

....

503 3139 Sgt Charles Henry Sewell enlisted in the 19th Londons on 16th Sept. 1914, served on the Western Front with the 1/19th from 10th Mar. 1915 until 17th Mar. 1918, and was discharged sick on 16th July 1918.

504 These craters are clearly named on the 1:10,000 trench maps of mid 1916. 'New Cut' crater is shown on the trench maps of the time. These craters were near the northern end of the ridge near a spot called 'The Pimple', a mile or so north of the Canadian memorial. The remains of a memorial to the 44th (Winnipeg) Battalion Canadian Infantry can still be seen there today.

on the crater told us they were natives of Souchez and had been deported in 1914, but repatriated in 1916.

All too soon we had to descend the ridge and make our way through Aix-Noulette, past 'Colonel's House', and the quarry where Battalion HQ was in July 1916. We could see Bully Grenay and Fosse 10 on our right and the slag heaps of Noeux-les-Mines and Ruchel in front of us. Eventually we arrived at Béthune which, like Arras, has suffered more in its better quarters than in the poorer districts. The big square has practically no buildings left except the remains of the belfry. With pathetic and unconscious humour the inhabitants had put up notice-boards to announce that such-and-such a shop had 'removed' elsewhere!

Saturday April 17th was devoted to the Loos district. We started through Philosophe (already busy again) and Vermelles and then skirted the Hohenzollern Redoubt. I did not actually see 'Bart's Alley', but nobody who spent part of Christmas Day 1915 in it is ever likely to forget that health resort. This part of the country struck us as more depressing than almost any other. It could never have been beautiful, and the scars of war take longer to heal in a chalk soil naturally, while in many places the barbed wire was still standing or at best only raked into heaps. We then went on into Loos, of which there is little left. We could get a good idea of the topographical aspect of the battle. It takes more than a war to wipe out Hill 70, the Green Crassier and the Double Crassier. The sight of the latter recalled some chilly days in February 1916. Was there not a wonderful plan for pushing a trolley of explosives along the northern arm of the Crassier? We turned to the left over Hill 70 into Lens itself, a place one had always wondered about and seen perhaps through glasses from the Lorette heights or the Bouvigny Woods. Here was destruction deliberate, naked and unashamed, but at the same time more obvious activity in the work of reparation. In the very centre of the town, on what used to be the principal church, stands a board *'Lens veut renaître'*, a typical motto for the unconquerable spirit of northern France.

From Lens we went over the reverse side of the Vimy Ridge, honeycombed with Bosche dugouts, through Roclincourt where there is part of the Officers' Club still standing and the London Irish transport lines, and then on into Arras for tea. It was strange to find ourselves the only English people in the café and but for the scarred walls and cracked mirrors it might have been a pre-war scene. That evening we came back through Estrée-Cauchie[505], passing the camp where 1/19th and 2/19th were able to exchange greetings in July 1916 and then through Ranchicourt and Houchin back to Béthune.

The last two days were to be spent mainly in the Ypres salient, so we set off on April 18th in the direction of Armentières, passing La Bassée, where the 'leave train' still stands on the rails, and the brick-stacks of Cuinchy. Then on past Neuve Chapelle to Armentières and from there across the frontier near Neuve Eglise. There we made our way to Wytschaete and stood at last on the lip of the Messines ridge and began to realise how every movement on the lower ground must have been visible to German eyes for the greater part of the war. Here, as on the Somme, one could get some idea of the havoc played by modern artillery. No tree showed signs of life and no two bricks anywhere seemed left upon one another. Then we descended into Ypres passing a light railway which carried civilian passengers along the road east of Château Segard and Swan Château! Here the aspect of the country had changed so

....

505 Estrée-Cauchie was generally known by the troops as 'Extra-Cushy'.

much that it was difficult to get one's bearings except by some such spot as "Shrapnel Corner" or "Woodcote House". The remainder of that day we spent in Ypres - the only spot which seemed spoilt by the genuine 'tripper'. Here small boys with picture postcards and girls selling chocolate bombarded us with their attentions. The Belgian authorities are doing their best to leave the Cloth Hall and Cathedral in their ruins as a permanent memorial of British heroism.

We spent two nights at Poperinghe in what used to be the Officers' Club, but is now an hotel most excellently managed by the enterprising ladies who own 'Skindles', which name it bears now. The last day of our tour was spent in such places as Boesinghe, St Julien, Zillebeke, and last but not least The Bluff.[506] Here I found

the old tunnels, fallen in it is true, but still easily recognizable. I could stand at the entrance to Battalion HQ and almost hear the voice of RSM Trezona[507] sending off ration parties. I am sure the Stretcher Bearers will grieve to know that there was some rubbish visible in some of the neighbouring shell holes! Then on up along the 'Wynd' we went, which, at the top, is apparently a natural pond, so no wonder we failed to drain it! At last we stood right on the top of 'A' crater and looked out on all sides at the scarred and battered country beyond. This was certainly one of the most impressive sights of all. The effects of war upon nature are shown here in all their hideousness, and while we stood there, to make a final scene to carry away in one's mind, some Belgian engineers exploded a dump of shells near Ypres with the dull familiar roar, without which the place would not have seemed real.

Charles Fair at site of 1/19th London HQ, The Bluff, April 1920

I began this article meaning it to be quite short, and my pen has run away with me. My only excuse is that this was, I think, the most interesting week I have ever spent. I would like to urge all old comrades to lose no opportunity of taking their friends, and especially the younger generation, to visit some at any rate of these spots. It is only by seeing with their own eyes the devastation of France and Belgium that they can ever realize what they have been spared. Then perhaps they may catch something of the spirit of the men who died for them, for surely that unconquerable spirit amongst all the horrors of trench and mine, of shells and gas, is the greatest legacy that they have left to the race.

....

506 The Battalion was stationed in the Bluff, and was withdrawn the night before Messines. It went into Divisional reserve near Bedford House.

507 617256 RSM Frederick John Trezona MC had been a regular soldier with the Middlesex Regiment with whom he had served in the Boer War. As a Colour Sgt he had arrived in France with the 1/19th Londons on 10th Mar. 1915 and served with the battalion until 29th Mar. 1918. His award of the MC was gazetted on 15th July 1916.

Sources and Bibliography

Primary Sources

Family material and privately held papers
Private letters:
    Dodgson: Toby, Philip and Guy – from the Dodgson and Fair family archives
    Secretan: Humphrey, Reggie, Marjorie and Esmé – from the Fair family archives
    Fair, Charles – from the Fair family archives

Private diaries and notebook:
    Champion, Carl – from the Champion family archives
    Secretan, Marjorie – from the Fair family archives
    Pilditch, Philip – from the Dodgson family archives
    Fair, Charles – notebook from Senior Officers' School, Aldershot 1917 – from the
       Fair family archives

Memorial Booklet:
    Secretan, Mary, "*R.H.S.*" published and printed privately (1922) (A copy exists in
    the Imperial War Museum [accession no. 86/2051 23(=41)/3])

Photographs and papers:
    Glover, Sgt William J, 19th London Battery, 7th London Brigade RFA – held with
    Fair family archives and by Stuart Arrowsmith

The National Archives, Kew (TNA)

Service Records
WO 339 13153 Capt Francis Dodgson
WO 339 14756 Capt Alan T. Champion
WO 339 14844 Capt Humphrey B. Secretan MC
WO 339 15559 2/Lt Eric O. Champion
WO 339 26223 Lt Col George K. Fulton DSO
WO 374 20104 Capt Guy Dodgson
WO 374 20107 Capt Philip Dodgson MC
WO 374 23401 Lt Col Charles H. Fair DSO
WO 374 61195 2/Lt Reginald H. Secretan
Carl Champion's service record has not been released

War Diaries
WO 95 1633   7 Division HQ
WO 95 1667   91 Infantry Brigade HQ
WO 95 1670   2nd Bn, The Queens Royal West Surrey Regiment
WO 95 2077   56 Infantry Brigade HQ
WO 95 2079   9th (Service) Bn, The Cheshire Regiment
WO 95 2183   69 Infantry Brigade HQ

WO 95 2184   8th (Service) Bn, The Yorkshire Regiment (Green Howards)
WO 95 2313   30 Division HQ
WO 95 2323   11th (Service) Bn, The South Lancashire Regiment (St Helens Pals)
WO 95 2532   10th (Service) Bn, The Royal Fusiliers (Stockbrokers)
WO 95 2588   118 Infantry Brigade HQ
WO 95 2590   1/1st Bn, The Hertfordshire Regiment
WO 95 2733-36 141 Infantry Brigade HQ
WO 95 2738   1/19th Bn, The London Regiment (St Pancras)
WO 95 2717   237th (7th London) Brigade RFA, 235th Brigade RFA
WO 95 3031   2/19th Bn, The London Regiment (St Pancras)
WO 256   Diary of Field Marshal Sir Douglas Haig
CAB 45/133   Official History Correspondence - Somme (Authors A-F) - Letters
              from Lt Col Charles H. Fair to Brig Gen Sir James E. Edmonds

Imperial War Museum, Department of Documents (IWM)
80/22/1   Railton MC, Reverend David, transcript of letters

Hertfordshire County Record Office
D/EYO 1/40   Gripper, Lt Col B. J., *Notes for a History of the Hertfordshire
              Regiment*, 1923 (typescript history based on notes in 26821)
26821   Notes for Hertfordshire Regiment history; 1913-23
173   Page, Lt Col Frank, DSO, *1/1st Bn, The Hertfordshire Regiment,
              Operation Order No. 44*, 29 July 1917

The Queen's (Royal West Surrey) Regiment Museum, Clandon Park, Guildford
Secretan H. B. Album of 80 photographs inscribed on the flyleaf: "Some photographs
    of 2 Queens taken from May 1916 to October 1917 in France and Belgium,
    presented by Captain H. B. Secretan." (Accession number 2130)

The Liddle Collection, Brotherton Library, University of Leeds
Martin Middlebrook files – unpublished notes from interview with Humphrey
    Secretan in 1968 for *The First Day on the Somme*

British Red Cross Archive, Wonersh, Surrey
Nursing records of Mary and Esmé Secretan

Other
*Notes for Commanding Officers – Issued to students at the Senior Officers' School,
    Aldershot, 1917 (2ndCourse)*, 1917 (republished by MLRS Books, 2009)
The Army List
The London Gazette
The St Pancras Gazette
The Dump (Trench Journal of the 23rd Division), published annually at Christmas
    1915-1918

Secondary Sources - Published Works
Official Histories
Edmonds, Brig Gen Sir James E., *Military Operations, France and Belgium, 1915, Vol. 2 Aubers Ridge, Festubert and Loos*, Macmillan, 1928

Edmonds, Brig Gen Sir James E., *Military Operations, France and Belgium, 1916*, Macmillan, 1932 (in two volumes)

Edmonds, Brig Gen Sir James E., *Military Operations, France and Belgium, 1917, Vol. 2 Third Ypres*, Macmillan, 1948

Edmonds, Brig Gen Sir James E., *Military Operations, France and Belgium, 1918*, Macmillan, 1935-1938 (in five volumes)

Falls, Cyril, *Military Operations, France and Belgium, 1917, Vol. 1 The Battle of Arras*, Macmillan, 1935

Miles, Wilfred, *Military Operations, France and Belgium, 1917, Vol. 3 The Battle of Cambrai*, Macmillan

Unit Histories and Regimental Journals
Byrne, Lt A. E. MC, *The Official History of the Otago Regiment, New Zealand Expeditionary Force, in the Great War, 1914-1918*, J Wilkie & Co. Ltd, Dunedin, 1921

Dalbiac, Col P. H., *History of the 60th Division (2/2nd London Division)*, Allen & Unwin, 1927

Eames, F. W., *The Second Nineteenth, being the History of the 2/19th London Regiment*, Waterlow & Sons Ltd, 1930

Henriques J. O., *The War History of the 1st Battalion Queen's Westminster Rifles 1914-1918*, The Medici Society Ltd, 1923

Kincaid-Smith, Lt Col M., *The 25th Division in France and Flanders*, Harrison & Sons, 1918

Maude, Alan H. (ed), *The 47th (London) Division 1914-1919*, The Amalgamated Press, 1922

Memories, The Magazine of the 19th County of London Regiment Old Comrades Association, published quarterly from 1920 to 1939

Mullaly, Col. B. R., *History of the South Lancashire Regiment*, White Swan Press, 1955

Pilditch, Capt P. H. and Ullman, Capt R. B., *A Short Summary of the War Services and Actions Fought by the 7th London Brigade RFA and its Component Batteries*, Royal Artillery Institution, Woolwich, no date

Riddell, Brig Gen E. and Clayton, Col M. C., *The Cambridgeshires 1914-1919*, Bowes and Bowes, 1934

Risley, David, and Waring, Richard, *The St. Helens Pals, 11th (Service) Bn. South Lancashire Regiment (St. Helens Pioneers)*, (an early draft consulted – publication scheduled before 2014)

The Royal Fusiliers Chronicle

Sandilands, Brig Gen H. R., *The 23rd Division*, London, Wm Blackwood & Sons 1925

Strachan, Hew, *History of The Cambridge University Officers Training Corps*, Midas Books, 1976

Wylly, Col Howard C., *The Green Howards in the Great War, 1914-1919*, Richmond, Yorks, [printed by Butler & Tanner Ltd., Frome and London] 1926

Wylly, Col Howard C., *History of the Queens Royal Regiment, Vol 7, 1905-1923*, Gale & Polden

Wyrall, Everard, *The Nineteenth Division 1914-1918*, 1932
Young, Michael, *Army Service Corps 1902-1918*, Leo Cooper, 2000

Rolls of Honour from Schools and Universities etc.
Carey, G. V., *The War List of the University of Cambridge 1914-1918*, Cambridge
    University Press, 1921
The Haileyburian and ISC Chronicle
Haileybury and Imperial Service College Register 1862-1994: Volume 1 1862-1911,
    The Haileybury Society, 1995
Wall, A.H. (ed), *Marlborough College Register 1843-1933*, Eighth Edition, Dean & Son
    Ltd, 1936
The Marlburian
Oundle Memorials of the Great War 1914-1919, The Medici Society Ltd, 1920
The Stock Exchange Memorial of Those Who Fell in the Great War, 1914-1919, 1920
Memorials of Rugbeians Who Fell in the Great War, Volume V
Rugby School Register, Annotated 1892-1921
Winchester College Register, 1884-1934
Wykehamists Who Died in the War 1914-1918, Vol. 1
Wykehamist War Service Roll (various issues)

Other works
Armes, Derek, *"Our Boys" Ware Men in the First World War*, The Rockingham Press,
    1998
Bilton, David, *The Home Front in the Great War: Aspects of the Conflict 1914-1918*, Pen
    & Sword, 2004
Brophy, John and Partridge, Eric, *The Long Trail, What the British Soldier Sang and
    Said in 1914-1918*, André Deutsch, 1965
Corrigan, Gordon, *Loos 1915, The Unwanted Battle*, Spellmount, 2006
Castle, Ian, *London 1914-17, The Zeppelin Menace*, Osprey, 2008
Cherry, Niall, *Most Unfavourable Ground: The Battle of Loos 1915*, Helion & Co. Ltd,
    2005
Davies, Frank and Maddocks, Graham, *Bloody Red Tabs, General Officer Casualties of
    the Great War, 1914-1918*, Leo Cooper, 1995
DeGroot, Gerard J., *Blighty: British Society in the Era of the Great War*, Longman, 1996
Gavaghan, Michael, *The Story of the Unknown Warrior – 11 November 1920*, M & L
    Publications, 1995
George, Michael and Christine, *Dover and Folkestone During The Great War*, Pen &
    Sword, 2008
Gliddon, Gerald, *The Battle of the Somme – A Topographical History,* Alan Sutton, 1994
Gliddon, Gerald, *VCs of the First World War – Spring Offensive 1918*, Alan Sutton, 1997
Gregory, Adrian, *The Last Great War: British Society and the First World War*,
    Cambridge University Press, 2008
Griffith, Paddy, *The Great War on the Western Front – A Short History*, Pen & Sword
    Military, 2008
Griffith, Paddy, *Battle Tactics of the Western Front: The British Army's Art of Attack,
    1916-18,* Yale University Press, 1994
Harris, J. P., *Amiens to the Armistice*, Brassey's, 1998

Hart, Peter, 1918 *A Very British Victory,* Weidenfeld & Nicolson, 2008

Hart, Peter, *The Somme,* Weidenfeld & Nicolson, 2005

Jeffery, Keith, *Field Marshal Sir Henry Wilson: A Political Soldier*, Oxford University Press, 1998

Kentish, Basil, *This Foul Thing Called War: The Life of Brigadier-General R. J. Kentish, CMG, DSO (1876-1956)*, The Book Guild Ltd, 1997

King, John, *Grove Park in the Great War*, Grove Park Community Group, 1983

Macdonald, Lyn, *The Last Man – Spring 1918*, Viking, 1998

Macdonald, Lyn, *They Called It Passchendaele - The story of the third battle of Ypres and of the men who fought in it*, Macmillan, 1978

McCarthy, Chris, *The Somme – The Day-by-Day Account,* Arms & Armour Press, 1993

McCarthy, Chris, *Passchendaele – The Day-by-Day Account*, Arms & Armour Press, 1995

McDouall, Brigadier General, Robert A, *To The Subalterns of the Buffs*, 1926 (privately printed memoir)

Mangan, J. W., *Athleticism in the Victorian and Edwardian Public Schools*, Cambridge University Press, 1981

Messenger, Charles, *Call to Arms, The British Army 1914-1918*, Weidenfeld & Nicolson, 2005

Middlebrook, Martin, *The First Day on the Somme - 1st July, 1916,* Allen Lane, 1971

Middlebrook, Martin, *The Kaiser's Battle*, Allen Lane, 1978

Middlebrook, Martin, and Middlebrook, Mary, *The Somme Battlefields – A Comprehensive Guide from Crécy to the Two World Wars,* Viking, 1991

Mitchinson, K. W., *Pioneer battalions in the Great War - Organized and Intelligent Labour*, Leo Cooper, 1997

Moore, William, *A Wood Called Bourlon - The Cover-up After Cambrai*, 1917, Leo Cooper, 1988

Moore, William, *See How They Ran – The British Retreat of 1918*, Leo Cooper, 1970

Mottram, R. H., *Ten Years Ago - Armistice & other memories, forming a pendant to "The Spanish Farm Trilogy".* With a foreword by *W. E. Bates*, Chatto & Windus, 1928

Moynihan, Michael, *God On Our Side - The British Padre in World War I*, Secker & Warburg, 1983

Nicholls, Jonathan, *Cheerful Sacrifice, The Battle of Arras 1917*, Leo Cooper, 1993

Norman, Terry, *The Hell They Called High Wood*, Patrick Stephens Ltd., 1989

Parker, Peter, *The Old Lie, The Great War and the Public School Ethos*, Constable, 1987

Passingham, Ian, *Pillars of Fire: The Battle of Messines Ridge, June 1917*, Sutton Publishing Ltd, 1998

Pidgeon, Trevor, *The Tanks at Flers*, Fairmile Books, 1995

Pidgeon, Trevor, *Tanks on The Somme,* Pen & Sword, 2010

Pope, Stephen and Wheal, Elizabeth-Anne, *The Macmillan Dictionary of the First World War*, Macmillan, 1995

Rawson, Andrew, *British Army Handbook 1914-1918*, Sutton Publishing, 2006

Reed, Paul, *Walking Arras – A Guide to the 1917 Arras Battlefields*, Pen & Sword, 2007

Rothstein, Andrew, *The Soldiers' Strikes of 1919*, Macmillan Press, 1985

Simkins, Peter, *Kitchener's Army: The Raising of the New Armies 1914-1916*, Manchester University Press, 1988

Simkins, Peter, Jukes, Geoffrey and Hickey, Michael, *The First World War: The War to End All Wars*, Osprey Publishing, 2003

Terraine, John, *To Win a War – 1918, The Year of Victory*, Sidgwick and Jackson, 1978

Thorpe, Barrie, *Private Memorials of the Great War on the Western Front*, The Western Front Association, 1999

Walker, Jonathan, *The Blood Tub, General Gough and the Battle of Bullecourt, 1917*, Spellmount, 1998

White, Sir Robert, *Extracts from the diary of Brigadier General The Honourable Robert White*, Dimbleby, Richmond, no date.

Wilson, Trevor, *The Myriad Faces Of War: Britain and the Great War 1914-1918*, Polity Press, 1986

Journal Articles

Fair, Charles, "The Changing Character of the London Territorial Force 1914-18: The case of the 19th (County of London) Battalion, The London Regiment (St. Pancras)," *Mars & Clio, The Newsletter of the British Commission for Military History*, No. 24, Spring 2009, pp. 39-74

"The Other Side of the Hill - No IV, Mametz Wood and Contalmaison", *The Army Quarterly*, Vol 9, 1924-25

Palmer, Peter, "British Tactics During and After the Somme Battle", 18th May 2008, on **http://www.westernfrontassociation.com/great-war-on-land/ battlefields/137-brit-tact-somme.html**, accessed 1 January 2009

Websites

Ancestry - for other ranks' service records and medal index cards: **http://www. ancestry.co.uk**

The Bedfordshire Regiment in the Great War: **http://www.bedfordregiment.org. uk/index.html**

The Centre for First World War Studies, University of Birmingham: **http://www. warstudies.bham.ac.uk/firstworldwar/**

The Commonwealth War Graves Commission: **http://www.cwgc.org/**

The Great War Forum: **http://1914-1918.invisionzone.com/forums/**

The Long, Long Trail: The British Army of 1914-1918: **http://www.1914-1918. net/**

The Western Front Association: **http://www.westernfrontassociation.com/**

The Yorkshire Regiment First World War, Officers Died: **http://www.ww1-yorkshires.org.uk/pdf-files/bob%20coulson/officers-died-ww1.pdf**

Index